Presidential Leadership

Politics and Policy Making

Presidential Leadership

Politics and Policy Making

Ninth Edition

GEORGE C. EDWARDS III
Texas A&M University

STEPHEN J. WAYNE
Georgetown University

CENGAGE
Learning·

Australia • Brazil • Mexico • Singapore • United Kingdom • United States

**Presidential Leadership:
Politics and Policy Making,
Ninth Edition**
George C. Edwards III and
Stephen J. Wayne

Sr. Publisher: Suzanne Jeans

Exec Acquiring Sponsoring
Editor: Carolyn Merrill

Development Editor:
Jean Findley

Assistant Editor: Scott Greenan

Editorial Assistant: Eireann
Aspell

Media Editor: Laura Hildebrand

Brand Manager: Lydia LeStar

Market Development Manager:
Kyle Zimmerman

Sr. Rights Acquisitions
Specialist: Jennifer Meyer Dare

Manufacturing Planner:
Fola Orekoya

Art and Design Direction,
Production Management, and
Composition: PreMediaGlobal

Cover Image: © Mark Makela/
Corbis

Library of Congress Control Number: 2013935539

ISBN-13: 978-0-8400-3012-2

ISBN-10: 0-8400-3012-6

Cengage Learning
200 First Stamford Place, 4th Floor
Stamford, CT 06902
USA

Cengage Learning is a leading provider of customized learning
solutions with office locations around the globe, including
Singapore, the United Kingdom, Australia, Mexico, Brazil, and Japan.
Locate your local office at **international.cengage.com/region.**

Cengage Learning products are represented in Canada by
Nelson Education, Ltd.

For your course and learning solutions, visit
www.cengage.com

Purchase any of our products at your local college store or at our
preferred online store **www.cengagebrain.com**

Instructors: Please visit **login.cengage.com** and log in to access
instructor-specific resources.

Printed in the United States of America
1 2 3 4 5 6 7 17 16 15 14 13

To Carmella and Cheryl

CONTENTS

PREFACE

The presidency is both a much-praised and a much-damned institution. During the early 1960s, many thought presidential power was the key to change and saw the presidency as the major innovative force within the government. People looked to the president to satisfy an increasing number of their demands for public policy.

By the late 1960s and early 1970s, however, many of the same people saw presidential power as a serious problem. Scholars blamed presidents and their excesses for involvement in the war in Southeast Asia and for Watergate and other scandals. Restrain the "imperial" presidency became the cry.

Presidents Gerald Ford and Jimmy Carter responded to this plea by attempting to de-imperialize the office. Ford opened the White House to opposing views; Carter initially reduced the White House staff's size, status, and perquisites. Both were careful not to exceed their constitutional and statutory powers.

Growing institutional conflict between Congress and the presidency and within the executive branch raised questions about the possibility of effective governance. Worsening economic conditions, increasingly scarce resources, and a series of foreign policy crises produced a desire for more assertive leadership. Some observers saw the presidency as imperiled; weakness, not strength, its problem. Disappointment in presidential performance replaced fear of presidential abuses.

The Reagan presidency led scholars once again to reevaluate the workings of the system and the role of the president within it. Ronald Reagan's ability to achieve some of his major policy goals at the beginning of his administration indicated that stalemate need not paralyze the government. However, his leadership style gave rise to fears, particularly after the Iran–Contra affair, of power improperly exercised.

During the George H. W. Bush and Bill Clinton presidencies, the need for change, accompanied by the difficulty of achieving it within a divided government, reemerged. Both presidents were frustrated in their attempts to govern, particularly within the domestic arena, and the public expressed its own disillusionment—first in defeating Bush and then in putting the Republicans in power in both houses of Congress for the first time in forty years. Yet, in the midst of defeat, Clinton rejuvenated himself, his presidency, and his party, winning the 1996 presidential election and reaching agreement with Congress on a balanced budget, proving once again that divided government works during periods of economic prosperity, social tranquility, and world peace—when the government does not face increased demands, and especially when hundreds of billions of dollars of unexpected revenues are predicted for the treasury's coffers.

George W. Bush campaigned on bringing change to Washington. The narrowness of the election outcome in 2000, and the unusual nature of its resolution, denied him any claim to a mandate, but he moved quickly to pass the largest tax cut in a generation, a major change in federal education policy, and in his third year, a substantial increase in Medicare benefits. However, it was the terrorist attacks on September 11, 2001, that transformed his presidency by placing a premium on decisive action and focusing attention on the president's roles as crisis manager, national security director, and commander-in-chief.

Bush interpreted his close but clear reelection victory in 2004 as a public confirmation of his policies and actions during his first term and his proposals for the second, including Social Security, immigration, tax, tort, and bankruptcy reform; a national energy policy; and a continuation of his deregulatory policies within the private sector of the economy. He was much less successful in obtaining congressional support for major policy change in his second term, however, and his public approval ratings declined sharply. His lack of success in achieving his policy initiatives, combined with widespread discontent with the administration's handling of the occupation of Iraq and its response to the devastation of Hurricane Katrina, undermined the public's assessment of the president's competence. Charges of the abuse of executive power and misleading the public about the threat posed by Iraq further diminished the public's confidence in Bush's presidency.

Beset by scandal and inaction, Republicans lost control of Congress in 2006 and the White House in 2008 in an election in which both Democratic and Republican candidates criticized the Bush administration for its heavy-handedness, deficit spending, and failure to anticipate, much less react to, the economic problems that began to surface at the end of 2007. The result was a substantial victory for the Democrats and their presidential candidate, Barack Obama.

President Obama acted quickly to stem further economic deterioration by supporting a stimulus and reinvestment bill of almost $800 billion; strengthening regulation of large investment and banking firms, and increasing accountability for the funds the government provided them; and giving direct relief to people who lost their jobs, were threatened with foreclosure of their homes, and were without adequate health insurance. He also supported reinvestment in America's infrastructure, schools, and policies to promote energy efficiency.

Obama promised policy and political change, but achieving that change within a constitutional system that divides powers, a political system that represents diverse and often competing constituencies, and an increasingly interdependent world in which no country can effectively act alone is an enormous challenge. In addition, the country was, and is, highly polarized. Despite his rhetorical skill, Obama found that he could not move the public to support his policies, nor could he win bipartisan support in Congress. He was, however, able to achieve many of his legislative goals in his first two years as a consequence of Democratic control of Congress. After the Democrats suffered huge losses in the 2010 midterm elections, Obama's legislative initiatives and policy successes dwindled significantly.

The next two years witnessed gridlock on a host of issues, most notably, raising the national debt ceiling and dealing with tax rates. A last-minute compromise on the debt limit and government spending was achieved in the summer of 2011, but the long-term financial issues remained.

The president won reelection in 2012, but divided government persisted. The lame duck session of the 112th Congress enacted a compromise on taxes that resolved the issue in the short run but did not achieve the revenue increases that the president and his party desired. The debt limit, the implementation of previously enacted budget cuts, and long-term spending issues continued to divide the parties and threatened to immobilize the government, problems which the president and the 113th Congress were forced to address.

Facing divided government and partisan polarization with limited resources poses an extraordinary test of leadership for the president, a test that will determine his legacy and the country's future. This book is about the leadership dilemma that presidents face and their institutional, political, and personal capacities to meet it.

We posit two models of presidential leadership: one in which a strong president dominates his environment as a director of change, and one in which the president has a more limited role as facilitator of change. In the director-of-change model, presidents lead the nation by creating opportunities to move in new directions and leading others where they otherwise would not go. In the facilitator model, presidents work, bargaining and pleading, at coalition building, to further the attainment of their goals and the goals of their constituencies. Effective facilitators recognize and exploit opportunities for change already present in their environments. These models provide perspectives that we employ to better understand leadership in the modern presidency and evaluate the performance of individual presidents.

We offer no simple formula for success, but we do assess the costs and consequences of presidential leadership in a pluralistic system in which separate institutions share powers. We believe that effective, responsible presidential leadership can play a vital role in providing the coherence, direction, and support necessary to articulate and achieve national policy and political goals.

The new features to the ninth edition of *Presidential Leadership* include:

- Coverage of the 2012 elections.
- The politics of leadership throughout the Obama presidency.
- Policymaking and the policy agenda in Obama's second term.
- Presidency in Action: Boxes on Obama's major domestic (health care), economic (deficit/debt/taxes), and national security (Bin Laden) decisions.
- The Obama doctrine in foreign affairs.

We thank our friends at Cengage Learning for the help they have provided us in the development, editing, and marketing of the ninth edition of this book and the political scientists whose insightful comments and suggestions helped us improve this volume.

We also want to acknowledge and thank our respective wives, Carmella Edwards and Cheryl Beil, for their patience, encouragement, and help. It is to them that we dedicate this book.

George C. Edwards III
Stephen J. Wayne

ABOUT THE AUTHORS

George C. Edwards III is University Distinguished Professor of Political Science at Texas A&M University and holds the Jordan Chair in Presidential Studies. He has held appointments at Oxford, Sciences Po-Paris, the U.S. Military Academy, Peking University, Hebrew University in Jerusalem, and the University of London. A leading scholar of the presidency, he has written or edited twenty-five books on American politics. He is also the editor of *Presidential Studies Quarterly* and general editor of the *Oxford Handbook of American Politics* series. Among his latest books, *On Deaf Ears: The Limits of the Bully Pulpit* examines the effectiveness of presidential leadership of public opinion; *Why the Electoral College Is Bad for America* evaluates the consequences of the method of electing the president; *The Strategic President* offers a new formulation for understanding presidential leadership; and *Overreach* analyzes leadership in the Obama presidency. Professor Edwards has served as president of the Presidency Research Section of the American Political Science Association, which has named its annual Dissertation Prize in his honor and awarded him its Career Service Award.

A member of Phi Beta Kappa and a Woodrow Wilson Fellow, he has received the Decoration for Distinguished Civilian Service from the U.S. Army and the Pi Sigma Alpha Prize from the Southern Political Science Association. He is also a member of the Council on Foreign Relations. He has spoken to more than 250 universities and other groups in the United States and abroad, keynoted numerous national and international conferences, done hundreds of interviews with the national and international press, and can be heard on National Public Radio. Dr. Edwards also applies his scholarship to practical issues of governing, including advising Brazil on its constitution and the operation of its presidency, Russia on building a democratic national party system, Mexico on elections, and Chinese scholars on democracy. He also authored studies for the 1988 and 2000 U.S. presidential transitions.

Stephen J. Wayne is a well-known author and lecturer on American presidents and the presidency. Professor of Government at Georgetown University since 1989, he teaches course on the American Presidency, U.S. Elections, and Psychology and Politics.

A presidential and a Washington-based "insider" for over forty-five years, Wayne has written or edited twelve books, many in multiple editions, and authored numerous articles, chapters, and reviews that have appeared in professional journals, scholarly compilations, newspapers, and magazines. In addition to *Presidential Leadership*, his best-known works include *The Road to the White House*, now in its ninth edition, and *Is This Any Way to Run a Democratic Election?* His latest book is titled *Personality and Politics: Obama for and Against Himself.*

Professor Wayne, frequently quoted by White House journalists, regularly appears on television and radio news shows and has been interviewed in documentaries on the presidency and political leadership. He lectures widely at home and abroad to international visitors, college students, federal executives, and business leaders. He has testified before Congress on the subject of presidential elections and governance and before the Democratic Party and Republican Party advisory committees on the presidential nomination processes.

1

PRESIDENTIAL LEADERSHIP: AN INTRODUCTION

No official in American government commands the attention, stirs the imagination, and generates the emotions that the president does. The presidency has become the dominant institution in a system designed for balanced government, the prime initiator and coordinator among separate and independent institutions sharing power, the foremost mobilizer among disparate and competing interests, and the principal communications link among a multitude of groups and individuals. It is a many-faceted, dynamic office—with a plethora of responsibilities, a variety of roles, and an impressive range of powers.

Within the presidency, the president is clearly the chief. Executive officials look to the office for direction, coordination, and general guidance in the implementation of policy; members of Congress look to it for establishing priorities, exerting influence, and providing services; the leaders of foreign governments look to it for articulating positions, conducting diplomacy, and flexing muscle; the general public looks to it for enhancing security, solving problems, and exercising symbolic and moral leadership—a big order, to be sure.

Unfortunately for most presidents, these expectations often exceed their abilities to meet them. It is not simply a question of skill or personality, although both contribute to the capacity to do the job well. The challenge is the system, particularly its constitutional, institutional, and political structures. The Constitution divides authority; institutions share power; and parties usually lack cohesion and a sustained policy thrust.

Despite their position and status, presidents find it difficult to overcome these constraints. They cannot easily ignore or diminish expectations. As a consequence, disappointment is frequent, regardless of who occupies the Oval Office.

To some extent this frustration has always been the case, but since the 1970s, the gap between expectations and performance seems to have widened.

Disenchantment in the political system has increased, confidence in the institution of the presidency has declined, and the popularity of each president has plummeted at one time or another during the course of his administration. Exercising effective presidential leadership has thus become more difficult, but no less vital if the American system is to work.

This book addresses these problems and the ability of presidents to surmount them. First and foremost, this is a book about presidential leadership and the capacity of chief executives to fulfill their tasks, exercise their powers, and utilize their organizational structures. It is a book about political leadership—about public opinion, group pressures, media coverage, and presidential salesmanship before, during, and after elections. It is also a book about policy leadership, about institutions and processes, and about priority setting, coalition building, and governmental implementation. Finally, it is a book about personal leadership, incumbents in office and their goals, national needs, and the formal and informal ways of accomplishing presidential objectives.

In order to understand the problems of contemporary presidential leadership, it is necessary to gain perspective on the institution and its development. The first two sections of this chapter provide that perspective. There we present an overview of the creation of the office and its evolution. We place particular emphasis on the growth of presidential policy-making roles, advisory and administrative structures, and the office's political and public dimensions. In the third section, we examine recent changes in the political and policy environment and the impact of those changes on the president's job performance. We assess the sources of the institution's problems and present the dilemmas involved in exercising contemporary leadership. Next, we briefly examine different approaches to studying the presidency, focusing on what each approach helps us understand about the presidency—and what questions each tends to overlook. In the final section, we discuss how we will explore the dilemmas of presidential leadership.

THE ORIGINAL PRESIDENCY

In 1787, the framers of the Constitution faced a challenge in designing the world's first nationally elected chief executive. There were few precedents to guide them, and their experience under a king had made them cautious about centralizing power in one individual.

The Creation of the Institution

Although the Constitution's framers saw the need for an independent executive empowered with its own authority, they did not begin with a consensus on the form this executive should take or the powers it should possess. At the outset of their deliberations, they had to answer two basic questions: (1) Should one person or several individuals hold the office? and (2) What combination of functions, responsibilities, and powers would yield an energetic, yet safe, executive?

The first of these questions was resolved early in the convention after a short, but pointed, discussion. James Wilson, a delegate from Pennsylvania, had proposed that only a single individual could combine the characteristics of "energy, dispatch, and responsibility." Critics immediately charged that such an executive would be dangerous—"the foetus of monarchy," in the words of Edmund Randolph of Virginia.

In denying the allegation that what they really wanted was a king, Wilson and James Madison sought to contrast the powers of their more limited executive with those of a king. As the debate intensified, Madison proposed that the delegates establish the institution's authority before deciding on the number of executives, a proposal that constituted one of the most astute parliamentary moves of the Constitutional Convention. Wilson had previously declared that the prerogatives of the British monarch were not a proper guide for determining the executive's domain, as they were too extensive. The American executive, he argued, should possess only executive authority—the power to execute laws and make those appointments that had not otherwise been provided for. The convention accepted Wilson's delineation, which made it safe to entrust the office to a single individual. Only later did the framers detail executive powers.

Wilson was primarily responsible for this elaboration as well. As a member of the committee charged with taking propositions approved by the convention and shaping them into a constitution, he detailed the executive's powers with language taken from the New York and Massachusetts constitutions. Surprisingly, his enumeration engendered little debate. The powers were not particularly controversial, and couching them in the language of two state constitutions made them even more palatable to the delegates. Thus, the framers quickly and quietly adopted most of these powers.

Achieving agreement on the checks to secure and restrain the executive was a little more difficult. Abuses by past executives—particularly British monarchs and colonial governors—combined with the excesses of contemporary legislatures made the maintenance of an institutional balance essential. The problem was how to preserve the balance without jeopardizing the independence of the separate branches or impeding the lawful exercise of their authority.

In the end, the framers resolved this problem by checking those powers that they believed to be most dangerous (the ones that had been subject to greatest abuse during the colonial era, such as appointments, treaty making, and declarations of war), while protecting the general spheres of authority from encroachment (in the executive's case, by a qualified veto). The provisions for reeligibility and a short term of office also encouraged presidential responsibility. Reappointment was the principal motive to good behavior. For those executives who flagrantly abused their authority, impeachment was the ultimate recourse.

The traditional weapon used to defend executive authority was the veto. Theoretically, it could function to protect those executive prerogatives threatened by the legislature, but in practice, the executive had frequently employed the veto to preclude the enactment of laws it opposed. Herein lay its danger.

The compromise was to give the president the veto but allow two-thirds of both houses to override it.

In summary, the relative ease with which the constitutional delegates empowered the presidency indicates that they had developed a consensus on the bounds and substance of executive authority. Not only did they reject certain traditional prerogatives but also readily accepted others. In deciding which of these powers to give to the new institution, the framers turned to the tenets of balanced government, as articulated by the French theorist Charles de Montesquieu in his often-quoted treatise, *The Spirit of the Laws*, and practiced to some extent in the states of Massachusetts and New York.[1] The founders accepted those powers that conformed to the basic division of authority; they rejected those that, actually or potentially, threatened the institutional balance.

Fears of potential abuse led to differing opinions on how best to constrain the branches without violating the principle of separate spheres of authority. The majority of the delegates opted for sharing powers, particularly in foreign affairs and principally with the Senate. This broad decision, which they reached toward the end of the convention when the pressures to compromise were greatest, exacerbated the fears of those who believed that the Senate would come to dominate the president and control the government.

Many of the opponents of the Constitution saw the sharing of powers as far more dangerous than the general grant of executive authority specified in Article II. Although each of the president's powers engendered some objection during the ratification debate, the most sustained criticism was directed at the president's relationship with the upper chamber. In the end, the proponents of the Constitution prevailed, but the debate over the efficacy of shared powers between the executive and the legislative branches has continued through the years.

The Scope of Article II

In one sense, what the framers did is obvious: It appears in Article II. In another sense, however, their deliberations and decisions have been subject to constant interpretation. Unlike Article I, where the Constitution details the legislative powers given to Congress, Article II describes executive authority in a more general way: "The executive power shall be vested in a President of the United States of America." For years, scholars have debated whether this designation provides presidents with an undefined grant of authority or simply confers on them the title of the office.

Although the answer to this question remains in doubt, the executive portion of the president's responsibilities is relatively clear. The framers charged the executive with the administration of government, the task of faithfully executing the law, and the capacity to do so by overseeing the executive departments. The Constitution does not designate the departments. Rather, Congress establishes them by legislation, and has done so since its first session in 1789. The president, however, has a hand in choosing the people who run them.

The framers also considered it essential to provide the executive with some discretion to respond to emergency or extraordinary situations. They thought the president would be able to respond to events more quickly and decisively than the Congress because the chief executive headed the only institution with continuous tenure—and the only one with a national perspective. Traditionally, this type of emergency power resided in the executive.

In his *Second Treatise of Civil Government*, the British philosopher John Locke had written of the need for such a power, which he termed a prerogative.[2] The framers agreed. Having themselves experienced a legislature unable to respond to emergencies under the Articles of Confederation, they desired to provide such a capacity in their constitutional arrangement, and they gave it to the president.

The debate over the war powers illustrates the framers' dilemma, as well as their solution. Initially, they gave Congress the authority to "make war." However, fearing that the word "make" might preclude the executive from responding to an attack if Congress were not in session, the framers agreed to substitute the word "declare." This change provided the president with flexibility but did not alter the basic intent—to have the Congress decide whether to go to war. Even after making that decision, Congress retains powers regarding personnel and budgets that may affect the conduct of hostilities. These powers, the framers hoped, would limit the president's discretion as commander in chief.

In foreign affairs, the framers similarly limited what the president could do alone without the approval of the Senate or both houses. Although the chief executive exercises the initiative in the treaty-making role, the wording of the Constitution suggests that the Senate was to have a role in the negotiation of treaties as well as in their ratification. Why else would the Senate advise and consent?

Although the framers expected executive powers to expand during emergencies, these powers have never been without limits. The exercise of discretionary powers by the executive is always tied to legislation. Presidents can summon Congress into special session, but they are obligated to report to it on the state of the union; they can recommend necessary and expedient legislation, but it is Congress that has to decide what laws, if any, to enact. Even in the case of the veto, two-thirds of both houses can have the final word.

In short, the relatively general grant of executive authority gives the office broad discretion in exercising its principal responsibility—the execution of the law. Some of its powers are exclusive, but others are shared. Some powers are enumerated, but their enumeration is not exhaustive. Presidents have considerable freedom to oversee subordinates of their own choosing in their administration of government, but their discretion in formulating policy is limited. In the normal course of events, the framers expected Congress, not the executive, to be the center of policymaking.

THE EVOLUTION OF THE PRESIDENCY

The contemporary presidency bears little resemblance to that which the framers of the Constitution had artfully designed in 1787 in Philadelphia. Their executive had less authority, less functional responsibility, and no explicit institutional structure or operating procedures. Of course, their Constitution was designed for different times.

Policy-Making Roles

Although the president's constitutionally designated authority has not been formally amended, law and precedent have expanded the scope of that authority. Over the years, the president's policy-making powers have grown dramatically. Chief executives, starting with George Washington, set the contours of foreign policy. Beginning with Thomas Jefferson, they shaped it to the point of actually defining what the war policy would be. There were other early examples of presidential initiatives in foreign affairs, notably James Monroe's famous doctrine pledging U.S. protection of the independent states on this side of the Atlantic.

Crisis situations expanded the president's powers still further, as Abraham Lincoln's actions during the Civil War demonstrated. Lincoln justified his exercise of power by the gravity of the situation. "Was it possible to lose the nation and yet preserve the Constitution?" he asked. To his own question he replied, "I felt that measures otherwise unconstitutional might become lawful by becoming indispensable to the preservation of the Constitution through the preservation of the nation."[3]

Congress did not check Lincoln's assertion of power during the war, although it did review and then approve it. After the war, however, the legislature reasserted its authority. Throughout the remainder of the nineteenth century, Congress, not the president, dominated the relationship between the branches. In fact, when Woodrow Wilson, then a professor of politics, wrote his perceptive study on the American political system in the mid-1880s, he titled it, *Congressional Government*.

Wilson wrote at the end of an era. By the time he became chief executive, the president's roles in both foreign and domestic affairs had expanded (and Wilson revised his book). Demands for a more activist government had encouraged President William McKinley and, especially, President Theodore Roosevelt to work more closely and harmoniously with Congress in fashioning major policy initiatives.

Assuming an assertive posture in both foreign and domestic affairs, Roosevelt expanded the president's policy-making roles. He sent the navy halfway around the world (and then requested appropriations from Congress to return it home); he announced a corollary to the Monroe Doctrine, further involving the United States in hemispheric activities; he helped instigate a revolution in Colombia; and he quickly recognized the independence of insurgents on the isthmus of Panama and entered into an agreement with them to build a canal. He was the first president to travel outside the United States (to Mexico and Panama) and the first to help settle a war, for which he won the Nobel Peace Prize. Within the domestic sphere, Roosevelt busted trusts, crusaded for conservation, and mediated a major coal strike. He was also instrumental in getting Congress to enact important legislation, including the Pure Food and Drug Act, the Meat Inspection Act, and the Hepburn Act regulating railroads.

Roosevelt's theory of the presidency justified and accommodated his activism. Writing in his autobiography after his political career had ended, Roosevelt stated:"My view was that every executive officer ... was a steward of the people bound actively and affirmatively to do all he could for the people."[4]

In contrast, William Howard Taft, Roosevelt's successor, expressed a much more restrained conception: "The president can exercise no power which cannot be fairly and reasonably traced to some specific grant of power.... . There is no undefined residuum of power which he can exercise because it seems to him to be in the public interest."[5]

But Roosevelt's stewardship theory has prevailed. With the exception of the three Republican presidents of the 1920s, occupants of the Oval Office in the twentieth century have assumed active political and policy-making roles. Woodrow Wilson and Franklin Roosevelt, in particular, expanded Theodore Roosevelt's initiatives in international and domestic matters.

Wilson followed Roosevelt's policy initiatives and proposed a comprehensive legislative program and was the first president to be involved in summitry. He was also the architect of the proposal to establish a League of Nations, although he was unable to persuade the Senate to accept his plan.

Franklin Roosevelt enlarged the president's role in economic affairs. On coming into office in the midst of the Great Depression, he initiated a series of measures to deal with the domestic crisis and succeeded in getting Congress to enact them. He also maintained the posture of an international leader, maneuvering the country's entrance into World War II and participating in summit conferences to win the war and plan the peace. In addition, he made the critical decision to develop the atomic bomb.

Many observers mark the beginning of the modern presidency, characterized by presidential activism in a variety of policy-making roles, in the era of Franklin Roosevelt. His successors have institutionalized many of the practices that Roosevelt initiated or continued, and Congress has required others. America's expanding role in the world and the growth of government services since the New Deal has increased the president's prominence and also created new demands on the office. More recently, the vulnerability of the United States to terrorist attacks has contributed to both the public's psychological dependence on the president and the security responsibilities of the chief executive.

Organizational Structure

The structure of the modern presidency also developed during Franklin Roosevelt's tenure. In 1939, Congress created the Executive Office of the President. Prior to that time, presidents had depended largely on their department heads for administration and advice.

The Constitution did not explicitly provide for an administrative structure. It did, however, contain an oblique reference to one through a provision in Article II stating that the president could demand, in writing, the opinions of subordinate officials. It was up to the first Congress to establish the executive departments as the principal administrative units of government. It created three departments (Foreign Affairs, Treasury, and War) and appointed an attorney general and a postmaster general. Since then, Congress has established twelve more departments and more than 150 executive agencies.

Throughout most of the nineteenth century, it was Congress, not the president, that dominated the administration of government. Statutes specified many organizational details of the departments, including their jurisdiction, staffing levels, and even operating procedures. For the most part, there was little oversight from the president.

The autonomy of the departments contributed to the influence of the secretaries who headed them. Because the department heads were the president's principal advisers, they exercised considerable influence over designing the administration's goals and in mobilizing congressional support. With the exception of the Jefferson, Andrew Jackson, and Lincoln administrations, strong department secretaries and weak presidents characterized executive advisory relationships.

This pattern began to change at the outset of the twentieth century as a consequence of the president's growing influence in Congress. As that influence increased, the potency of the department secretaries, individually and collectively, began to decline. They lost their privileged position between president and Congress, and their support of administration proposals became less critical to the president's legislative success.

The concern that Theodore Roosevelt and, particularly, William Howard Taft evidenced toward the organization of government also contributed eventually to the president's enhanced status and power within the executive branch. Taft appointed a Committee on Economy and Efficiency to recommend improvements. Reporting in 1913, the committee urged the creation of a more hierarchical structure, with the president assuming a larger administrative role.

Initially, Congress was reluctant to comply. However, sizable budget deficits, inflated by U.S. involvement in World War I, provided the legislature with a financial (and political) incentive to do so. Unable to control the deficits, Congress turned to the president for help. In particular, it enacted the Budget and Accounting Act of 1921, which made it a presidential responsibility to estimate the financial needs of the individual departments and agencies on a yearly basis and provided the president with an institutional mechanism to do so: the Bureau of the Budget.

When Franklin Roosevelt took office and expanded the president's domestic policy role, he needed more information, more expertise, and more staff. At first, he depended on personnel provided by the executive departments, but when that did not prove satisfactory, he turned to a small group of experts to advise him on how to make the organizational structure of the executive more responsive to his needs. The group, headed by Louis Brownlow, a noted student of public administration, issued a report that urged the creation of a separate presidential office.[6] In 1939, Congress approved the act that established the Executive Office of the President. Today, the approximately dozen elements of the Executive Office of the President employ a combined staff of about 1,800 and provide the president with personnel directly responsive to his interests.

The president's closest aides are located in the White House Office. Having no constitutional or statutory authority of their own and no political base other than the president's, their influence is dependent on their access to him. Thus, they do his bidding. The White House Office is also flexible, able to accommodate changing needs by adding political and policy advisors, communications aides, and others as demands for their services arise.

Whereas the White House functioned as a personal extension of the president, the Bureau of the Budget (later the Office of Management and Budget) became an institutional extension of the presidency. It coordinates key aspects of policymaking in the departments and agencies, imposing a presidential perspective on the executive branch in the process. More broadly, presidential policy processes have become institutionalized. Officials have developed mechanisms for preparing the budget, formulating a legislative program, building support in Congress, advising the president whether to sign or veto legislation, and evaluating proposed regulations, and succeeding administrations have continued these processes over time.

Public Dimensions

In addition to the development of the presidency as an institution and the growth of its policy-making roles, the public dimension of the office has expanded as well. This, too, has been a relatively recent phenomenon. Franklin Roosevelt was the first to use the mass media (radio) to communicate directly with the American people on a regular basis. His successors have used first television and now also the Internet to the same end.

For most of the nineteenth century, the presidency was not a particularly visible office, although the president received his share of critical commentary. Jefferson was the first to claim a partisan mandate, and Jackson the first to claim a public one.[7]

A variety of factors contributed to the adoption of a more active public posture by presidents toward the beginning of the twentieth century. The growth of newsgathering organizations and newspaper chains made it possible to communicate faster and with more people across the entire nation. The advent of yellow journalism, combined with the increased activism of government, generated more interest in the opinions and behavior of public officials, particularly the president.

Theodore Roosevelt, more than any of his predecessors, took advantage of these developments to focus attention on himself, his policies, and his activities. He was the first president to give reporters a room in the White House and the first to hold regular meetings with the press. Using his position as a "bully pulpit," Roosevelt rallied public support for his positions and proposals.

Roosevelt's presidency prompted Professor Woodrow Wilson to revise his view that Congress dominated the governmental system. The president could have as big a role as he wanted, Wilson asserted in 1908. He could use his position as party and national leader to enhance his political power, and thereby exert influence on Congress:

> His capacity will set the limit; and if Congress be overborne by him, it will be no fault of the makers of the Constitution—it will be from no lack of constitutional powers on its part, but only because the President has the nation behind him, and Congress has not. He has no means of compelling Congress except through public opinion.[8]

Wilson clearly attempted to heed his own words, and we can attribute the enactment of his legislative program in large part to his political leadership and public oratory. His greatest disappointment, however—his inability to persuade the Senate to ratify the Treaty of Versailles, ending World War I—stemmed from his failure to exercise these skills successfully. Wilson, who went on a public-speaking tour to build support for his position, overestimated his ability to lead public opinion and underestimated his opponents' capacity to counter him.

Although Theodore Roosevelt and Woodrow Wilson used the presidency as a podium, neither of them was as skillful at manipulating the press as was Franklin Roosevelt. In his first term, Franklin Roosevelt held more press conferences than any of his predecessors. Meeting frequently with small groups of reporters in the Oval Office, he used these sessions to articulate his views and float trial balloons. He also made extensive and productive use of radio, especially in his famous "fireside chats."

By the end of the Roosevelt era, the news media had permanently altered the presidency. It had become the most visible national office. Coverage of the White House was constant, and the president was always in the news. The intensive media focus on the president permanently added a new role to the president's job, that of communicator in chief, and required that presidents possess skills commensurate with this role if they were to lead effectively.

Media coverage has also linked public approval more closely to the exercise of presidential power. Now most presidents enter the White House convinced that they need to build support outside of government in order to gain support within it. As we will see, presidents find it difficult to succeed in this task, especially when they face an increasingly critical press.

Communications from and to the public are more direct and immediate than in the past. Such communications enable the White House to measure the pulse of public opinion more accurately, but they can also condition responses, shorten the response time, and, ultimately, constrain the president's options.

Media focus on the president has heightened public expectations of presidential performance. Advances in communications have enabled organized groups to promote the desires of their membership more effectively, and the president has become the focal point for many of these increased demands on government. Presidents have not obtained corresponding tools to meet these demands, however. For example, the increasing interdependence of nations limits their ability to manage the economy.

At the same time, events from the late 1960s to the present—U.S. involvement in Vietnam, the Watergate cover-up, the Iran-Contra affair, the Monica Lewinsky scandal, the failure to find weapons of mass destruction in

'Okay, bring in the new guy...'

Iraq, and various departmental and congressional scandals—have impugned the motives and integrity of high officials, including the president. Occupants of the Oval Office no longer enjoy the benefit of the doubt. The media subject presidents' words and behavior to intense scrutiny, making it difficult for them to rally and maintain public support, despite the expectation that they do so.

In addition, the presidential selection process has become more individualized. Parties do not organize campaigns and mediate between candidates and the voters as they did in the past. Performance expectations have increased as a consequence of longer campaigns, more personalized appeals, and many specific promises made to organized groups. However, the electoral coalition required to win election does not provide a reliable basis for governing throughout the administration. The opposition party often controls one or both houses of Congress.

APPROACHES TO STUDYING THE PRESIDENCY

There are many approaches to studying the presidency, ranging from concern with the constitutional authority of the office to dealing with the personality dynamics of a particular president. By *approaches*, we mean orientations that guide researchers to ask certain questions and employ certain concepts in answering them. In this section, we focus on four of the principal approaches employed by political scientists who study the presidency. The categories we use are neither mutually exclusive nor comprehensive.

We present these approaches not to create an ideal typology of scholarship on the presidency but to increase sensitivity to the implications of different approaches for what is studied, how it is studied, and what types of conclusions may be reached. Similarly, our focus is on approaches, rather than the works of individual authors or a comprehensive review of the literature.[9]

Legal

The oldest approach to studying the presidency, what we shall term the legal perspective, concerns the president's formal powers. Legal researchers analyze the Constitution, laws, treaties, and legal precedents to understand the sources, scope, and use of the president's formal powers, including their legal limitations.[10] Because of the significance of the founders' intentions and because these powers have changed over time, the legal approach has a historical orientation.

With its emphasis on the historical development of the office and the checks and balances in the Constitution, the legal perspective also lends itself to discussion of the president's place in our system of government, both as it is and as scholars think it ought to be. Thus, there is often a clear prescriptive or normative element in these studies.

The range of issues involving presidential authority is great. Illustrations from recent decades include the constitutionality of the line-item veto and the right of the president to impound funds appropriated by Congress, to make long-term recess appointments, to issue executive orders and proclamations, to freeze federal hiring, and to use the pocket veto during brief congressional recesses. Other topics include the constitutionality of the legislative veto, the role of the comptroller general in triggering budget reductions, the president's use of signing statements to, in effect, partially veto provisions of statutes he views as unconstitutional, and numerous claims of executive privilege such as those proposed by President Bill Clinton to prevent his senior aides from testifying in the probe of his relations with White House intern Monica Lewinsky, the refusal of President George W. Bush to allow aides to testify about the firings of U.S. attorneys, and the refusal of Barack Obama to release internal Justice Department memos regarding a failed effort to stem the flow of firearms into Mexico.

Foreign policy issues also have important legal dimensions. These have included detention of prisoners and suspected terrorists without recourse to the courts by President George W. Bush; waging the Vietnam War without explicit congressional authorization by President Johnson and President Nixon; using troops in invasions of Grenada by President Ronald Reagan and of Panama by President George H. W. Bush, and to occupy Haiti and bomb Bosnia and Kosovo by President Clinton; terminating a defense treaty with Taiwan by President Jimmy Carter; his settling of Iranian assets and hostage issues; and, more generally, presidents employing executive agreements as substitutes for treaties.

Although the legal perspective has a deservedly honored place among American political scientists—the United States prides itself on the rule of law—it also has its limitations. The Constitution, treaties, laws, and court decisions affect only a small portion of the president's behavior. Most of the president's relationships with the public, the Congress, the White House staff, and the bureaucracy do not easily fall within the purview of the legal perspective. Instead, informal or extraconstitutional powers explain this behavior. Similarly, because the legal perspective is heavily government centered, scholars adopting it largely ignore topics such as press coverage of the presidency, the public's evaluation of the president, and other relationships that involve nongovernmental actors.

It is equally significant that the legal perspective, although it requires rigorous analysis, does not lend itself to explanation of presidential behavior. Studies of the boundaries of appropriate behavior do not explain why actions occur within those boundaries or what their consequences are. Moreover, the heavy reliance on case studies by scholars employing this approach inevitably makes the basis of their generalizations somewhat tenuous.

Thus, although studies that adopt the legal perspective make important contributions to our understanding of American politics, they do not answer many of the questions that entice most people to study the presidency. For answers to these questions, we must turn to alternative approaches.

Institutional

A second basic approach to the study of the presidency focuses on it as an institution in which the president has certain roles and responsibilities and is involved in numerous structures and processes. Thus, the structure, functions, and operation of the presidency become the center of attention. These concerns are broad enough to include agencies such as the Office of Management and Budget (OMB) and units in the White House such as the legislative liaison operation. Scholars following this approach move beyond formal authority and investigate such topics as the formulation, coordination, promotion, and implementation of the president's legislative program; the president's relationships with the media and interest groups; or the president's decision-making processes.[11] Like the legal perspective, the institutional approach often traces the persistence and adaptation of organizations and processes over time. This gives much of its literature a historical perspective and also lends itself to evaluations of the success of institutional arrangements.

The institutional approach plays a crucial role in helping us understand the presidency. Although at one time many institutional studies emphasized formal organizational structure and rules, such as organization charts of the White House or budgetary process procedures, in recent years the behavior of those involved in the operation of the presidency has received more attention. This change in focus has increased the utility of institutional research. It is, after all, necessary to collect empirical data about what political actors are doing before we can discuss the significance of their behavior, much less examine analytical questions of relationships such as those pertaining to influence. By seeking to identify patterns of behavior and studying interactions, such as those between the White House and the Congress, the OMB, or the media, institutional research tells us not only what happens; more significantly, it also helps us to understand why it happens. When scholars examine presidential efforts to influence the media, for example, they are looking at typical, and potentially significant, behavior that may explain patterns of media coverage of the White House.

Historical institutionalism and American political development scholars are also interested in the presidency as an institution but reach beyond the confines of the policy process and presidential agenda success to explore the broader significance of the presidency in American politics. They view the presidency from the standpoint of the political system and focus on modes of governance, the institutionalized authority relations that underpin and legitimate them, and the sources of tension that destabilize them over time and contribute to fundamental political change. Researchers seek to understand the ways in which presidential action facilitates or impedes this change and to document the signature elements of new governing configurations, the factors behind their coalescence, and the location of the presidency within them. One central goal of such scholarship is to understand why successive episodes of political development have, on balance, tended to reinforce and deepen the relative authority of presidents.[12]

The "New Institutionalism" is yet another mode of scholarship that makes useful contributions to the broad institutional approach. It is grounded in rational choice theory and focuses on questions of the origins and effects of institutions, emphasizing challenges for the president such as the transaction costs arising from efforts to get subordinates to act as he wishes (principal-agent issues). It assumes individuals want to maximize benefits for themselves and that outcomes of institutions (including organizational design) have roots in individual behavior. Basic features of the political system provide the opportunities, capabilities, incentives, and interests that drive political actors to behave in predictable ways.[13]

New Institutionalism encourages students of the presidency to think of presidents in impersonal terms, as institutional actors whose institutional locations structure their incentives in particular ways, and who we can thus expect to behave in a characteristic manner—a presidential manner—regardless of who they are.[14] The goal of those applying this approach is to simplify the complexity of presidential studies and focus on one crucial factor influencing presidential behavior.

There are two principal limitations to focusing on the presidency as an institution. Many scholars have emphasized description at the expense of explanation. We know a great deal more about how presidents have organized their White House staffs, for instance, than about how these arrangements have affected the kinds of advice they have received.[15] In other words, we know more about the process than about its consequences. This lack of understanding in turn provides a tenuous basis for the prescriptive aspect of some institutional research. We cannot have confidence in recommendations about presidential advisory systems, for example, until we understand their effects.

The second limitation of some institutional studies is that they may downplay, or even ignore, the significance of political skills, ideology, and personality in their emphasis on organizations and processes. Indeed, the implicit assumption that underlies the often extensive attention scholars devote to structures and processes is that they are very significant. However, this assumption may not always be justified. It may be that the worldview a president brings to the White House or the political environment in which the president operates influences decisions more than the organization of the advisory system or decision-making procedures. Similarly, ideology, party, and constituency views may be more important than the White House legislative liaison operation in influencing congressional votes on the president's program.

Political Power

In the political power approach to the study of the presidency, researchers do not examine institutions but rather the people within them and their relationships with each other.[16] These researchers view power as a function of personal politics rather than formal authority or position. They find the president operating in a pluralistic environment in which there are numerous actors with independent power bases and perspectives and interests different from his. The president must marshal resources to persuade others to do as he wishes; a president cannot rely on expanding the institution's legal authority or adjusting its support mechanisms.

The president's need to exercise influence in several arenas leads those who follow the power perspective to adopt an expansive view of presidential politics that includes both government officials, such as members of the Congress, the bureaucracy, and the White House staff; and those outside of government, such as the public, the press, and interest groups. The dependent variables in studying presidential interactions (what authors are trying to explain) are wide-ranging and may include congressional or public support for the president, presidential decisions, press coverage of the White House, or bureaucratic policy implementation.[17] Because this approach does not assume presidential success or the smooth functioning of the presidency, the influence of bureaucratic politics and other organizational factors in the executive branch is as important to investigate as behavior in more openly adversarial institutions such as Congress.

Power is a concept that involves relationships between people, so this approach forces researchers to try to explain behavior and to seek to develop generalizations about it. However, it also slights certain topics. The emphasis on relationships does not lead naturally to the investigation of presidential accountability, the president's unilateral powers, or the day-to-day operation of the presidency.

Some commentators are bothered by the top-down orientation of the power approach—that is, viewing the presidency from the perspective of the president.[18] They feel that this neglects the question of examining the presidency from the perspective of the American political system and that it carries the implicit assumption that the president should be the principal decision maker in American politics. These critics argue that such premises are too Machiavellian and that analyses of power must include an evaluation of the goals and means of presidents.

Psychological

Perhaps the most fascinating and popular studies of the presidency are those that approach the topic from the perspective of psychological analysis. Some of these take the form of psychobiographies of presidents;[19] others attempt to categorize presidents on the basis of selected personality dimensions.[20] The authors of all these works base their analyses on the premise that personality is a constant and that individuals may displace their personality needs onto political objects and become unconscious motivations for presidential behavior.

We need to take what goes on inside a person's head into account if we are to understand that person's behavior. A psychological perspective forces us to ask why presidents behave as they do and to look beyond external factors, such as advisers, Congress, the media, and interest groups, for answers. If their personalities did not affect individual presidents, presidents would neither be very important nor merit much attention.

Psychological analysis also has a broader application to the study of the presidency. Presidents and their staffs view the world through cognitive processes that affect their perceptions of why people and nations behave as they do; how power is distributed; how the economy functions; and what the appropriate roles of government, presidents, and advisers are. Cognitive processes also screen and organize an enormous volume of information about the complex and uncertain environment in which presidents function. Objective reality, intellectual abilities, and personal interests and experiences merge with psychological needs (such as those to manage inconsistency and maintain self-esteem) to influence the decisions and policies that emerge from the White House. Cognitive processes simplify decision making and lessen stress, especially on complex and controversial policies such as going to war. Group dynamics may also influence decision making, limiting the appraisal of alternatives by group members. Efforts to sort out the impact of these factors are only in their early stages, but there is little question that we cannot claim to understand presidential decision making until those efforts succeed.[21]

Although psychological studies can sensitize us to important personality traits that influence presidential behavior, they are probably the most widely criticized research on the presidency.[22] A fundamental problem is that they often display a strong tendency toward reductionism; that is, they concentrate on personality to the exclusion of most other behavioral influences. As a result, they convey little information about the institution of the presidency or the relationships between psychological and institutional variables. Psychological studies are especially likely to fall prey to a failure to consider alternative explanations for behavior.

A related drawback is that psychological studies tend to stress the pathological aspects of a presidency and do so in a highly subjective fashion.

Scholars, like others, are drawn quite naturally to investigate problems. Their principal interest often becomes the relationship between the personality flaws of presidents and what the authors feel to be some of their most unfortunate actions in office. This reinforces the reductionist tendency, because it is usually not difficult to find plausible parallels between psychological and decisional deficiencies.

The lack of systematic data is also a problem for psychological studies. It is difficult both to discern unconscious motivations or cognitive processes and to differentiate their effect from that of external factors. Often, authors must rely on biographical information of questionable validity about the behavior and environment of presidents, stretching back to their childhoods.

Summary

The legal, institutional, power, and psychological approaches have advantages and disadvantages for the researcher. Each concerns a different aspect of the presidency and concentrates on certain variables at the expense of others. Those thinking of doing research on the presidency should carefully determine what it is they want to investigate before selecting an approach because not all approaches will be relevant to answering their questions. Although the power and psychological approaches are stronger in their concern for explanation, the legal and institutional orientations are better at providing broad perspectives on the presidency. Selecting an approach is not the only decision one must make in building a research strategy, however. Researchers must also choose appropriate methods. We discuss those methods in Appendix A.

ORIENTATION AND ORGANIZATION OF THIS BOOK

Leadership is perhaps the most commonly employed concept in politics. Politicians, pundits, journalists, and scholars critique and analyze public officials, attributing both success and failure to the quality of their leadership. When times are bad, as people often perceive them to be, the reflexive call is for new—and better—leadership.

This book is titled *Presidential Leadership* because it focuses on just that—leadership. The exercise of influence is central to our concept of leadership, as it is for most political scientists. We want to know whether the president can influence the actions and attitudes of others and affect the output of government. It is important to distinguish between attempts to lead and leadership itself. Both concepts are of primary interest in this book, and we devote much of our effort to exploring the relationship between the two.

The American political system is not a fertile field for the exercise of presidential leadership. Most political actors are free to choose whether to follow the chief executive's lead; the president cannot force them to act. At the same time, the sharing of powers established by the Constitution prevents the president from acting unilaterally on most important matters and gives other power holders different perspectives on issues and policy proposals. Thus, the political system compels the president to attempt to lead while inhibiting his ability to do so.

This context presents a challenge to his political leadership. Harry Truman, writing to his sister, made this comment about the president:

> Aside from the impossible administrative burden, he has to take all sorts of abuse from liars and demagogues .... The people can never understand why the President does not use his supposedly great power to make 'em behave. Well, all the President is, is a glorified public relations man who spends his time flattering, kissing and kicking people to get them to do what they are supposed to do anyway.[23]

Thinking about Leadership: Two Perspectives

Although thinking of leadership in terms of influence is useful for the study of the presidency, the concept remains somewhat nebulous. To guide our examination, we find it useful to refine the concept of leadership by contrasting two broad perspectives on the presidency. In the first, the president is the *director* of change, one who creates opportunities to move in new directions and leads others where they otherwise would not go. In this view, the president is out in front, establishing goals and encouraging others inside and outside of government to follow. Accordingly, the president is the moving force of the system and the initiator of change.

A second perspective is less heroic. Here, the president is primarily a *facilitator* of change. Facilitators understand the opportunities for change in their environments and fashion strategies and tactics to exploit them. Rather than create a constituency, they reflect and sometimes clarify, intensify, or channel their constituencies' aspirations, values, and policy views. Instead of persuading others to support them, they skillfully work at the margins of coalition building, perhaps influencing a few critical actors, to obtain support for their initiatives.

It is important not to underrate this role. The facilitator is *not* simply one who seizes opportunities as they present themselves and invites people to do what they already want to do. Change is not inevitable, and facilitators make things happen that otherwise would not. Effective facilitators are skilled leaders who must recognize the opportunities that exist in their environments, choose which opportunities to pursue, when and in what order, and exploit them with skill, energy, perseverance, and will.

The director reshapes the contours of the political landscape to pave the way for change, whereas the facilitator exploits opportunities presented by a favorable configuration of political forces. The director creates a constituency to follow his lead, whereas the facilitator endows his constituency's views with shape and purpose. The range and scope of the director's influence are broad, whereas those of the facilitator are narrower.

The two perspectives are not neat categories; we employ them simply to aid our understanding of leadership by exploring its possibilities. Once we understand the possibilities of leadership, we are in a better position to assess both the performance of presidents and the opportunities for change. Equally important, we will be better positioned to *explain* the success or failure of presidential leadership.

The leadership types also reflect, but do not precisely mirror, different thrusts in the scholarly literature on the presidency. Richard Neustadt's *Presidential Power*, widely considered to be the most influential book on the presidency, focuses on the president as center of government and the one who must lead if leading is to be done.[24]

Other scholars see the presidency differently Charles O. Jones, for example, argued: "The president is not the presidency. The presidency is not the government. Ours is not a presidential system."[25] One of the authors of this book argues that presidential influence is "at the margins" of American politics and emphasizes the importance of the political environment in which the president operates.[26] Stephen Skowronek finds presidents constrained in important ways by the historical context in which they serve, but he also sees them as the major force in causing fundamental political change.[27]

The question is not whether presidents matter. Of course they do. The question is *how* they matter—how do they bring about change? It is not sufficient to conclude, however, that the environment is sometimes receptive to change and at other times not. This viewpoint simply begs the question of whether presidents are able to influence the environment to *create* the opportunity for change.

The Strong President Model

The notion of a dominant president who moves the country and the government by means of strong, effective leadership has deep roots in our political culture. Those chief executives whom Americans revere—from Washington to Franklin D. Roosevelt—have taken on mythical proportions as leaders. Even though both the public and commentators are frequently disillusioned with presidential performance and recognize that stalemate is common in the political system, Americans eagerly accept what appears to be effective presidential leadership as evidence on which to renew their faith in the leadership potential of the presidency. After all, if presidential leadership works some of the time, why not all the time?

Perhaps faith in the potential of presidential leadership persists because such a view simplifies political analysis. Because broader forces that may influence changes in policy are complex, and perhaps even intractable, focusing primarily on the individual as leader eases the burden of explaining policy change. Faith in presidential leadership also simplifies the evaluation of the problems of governing. If it is reasonable to expect the White House to create opportunities for change, then failures of leadership must be personal deficiencies. If problems arise because the leader lacks the proper will, skills, or understanding, then the solution to our need for leadership is straightforward and simple: Elect presidents who are willing and able to lead. Because the system is responsive to appropriate leadership, it will function smoothly with the right leader in the Oval Office. The blame for unsuccessful leadership lies with the leader rather than the opportunities for change in the leader's environment.

The Limited President Model

Conversely, what if presidential leadership is not preeminent in American government? What if presidential leadership has less potential than holders of the conventional wisdom believe, and the president actually operates at the margins in leading the country? What if the national preoccupation with the chief executive is misplaced and belief in the impact of the individual leader is largely a myth—a product of a search for simple solutions in an extremely complex, purposefully inefficient system in which the Founders' handiwork in decentralizing power defeats even the most capable leaders?

If this is the case, the public should expect less of its presidents and be less surprised when they are not successful in leading. To understand better the presidency and the engines of change, we should focus less exclusively on the president and devote more attention to the context in which the president seeks to lead. If there are significant limits on presidential leadership, it follows that major changes in public policy require more than just the "right" person in the job and will not necessarily turn on a president's leadership qualities.

The president's dependency on existing opportunities implies a critical interdependence between leaders and followers, which we miss when we focus only on the pinnacle of power. Moreover, there are many influences on followers and potential followers and many obstacles to influencing them. The president is an important agenda setter,[28] for example, but there are other key influences on the agenda as well.[29] Thus, we need to devote more attention to thinking about politics from the bottom up as well as the top down and to the context in which the president seeks to lead.

It does not follow, of course, that we may never attribute failures of presidential leadership to the White House or that presidents have no control over the outcome of their relations with other political actors. The president may be a vital centralizing force, providing direction and energy for the nation's policy making. However, the limited presidential model does imply that a better understanding of presidential leadership is necessary in order to think sensibly about the role of the chief executive within the nation's political system.

Conceptual Focus

This book explores the president's leadership problems and the attempts by recent chief executives to overcome them. It does so by examining multiple facets of the presidency within the context of its political and policy-making roles. Our orientation is eclectic. Instead of adopting a particular perspective, the book presents several. Instead of imposing a single thesis, it will discuss many of the hypotheses, generalizations, and conclusions that scholars of the presidency have advanced.

The reason for utilizing a variety of approaches and presenting a broad body of research findings is that there is no one generally accepted theory of the presidency or single conceptual framework within which to study the office (other than, perhaps, Richard Neustadt's volume on presidential power)[30] that has commanded the attention and acceptance of most presidency scholars. As we have seen, work within each of a number of approaches to studying the presidency has something to teach us.

Despite an abundance of literature on the presidency, our understanding of how that institution works is not complete. There are fewer testable hypotheses about the presidency than about Congress, less cumulative knowledge than about the Supreme Court and its decisions.

Why is this? What factors have conditioned the methodology, shaped the content, and limited the findings of so much of the presidency literature? Three stand out: (1) the view that each president (and administration) is relatively unique, (2) the difficulty of obtaining firsthand information on the internal operation of the institution at or near the time that operation is occurring, and (3) the absence of a comprehensive theory of presidential behavior. Together these factors have impeded the ability of scholars to do rigorous, analytic, empirical research on the presidency.

The personalities of individual presidents and their staffs, the particular events and circumstances of their times in office, and the specific problems and actions of their administrations have led many scholars to treat each presidency and the times in which it operates as if it were unique. Emphasizing the differences rather than the similarities between presidencies makes the identification of patterns and relations more difficult and, in turn, makes it harder to generalize. Description rather than analysis, and speculation rather than generalization, too often characterizes studies of the presidency.

The relatively closed character of the institution has contributed to the problem. The presidency is not easy to observe from a distance and, up close, the view may be partial and even biased. Public pronouncements and actions tell only part of what happens and why—and usually only the part that the people in power wish to convey. Inside information is difficult to obtain. Decision makers, particularly those at the top of the executive bureaucracy, are not readily accessible. Their busy schedules, combined with their natural reluctance to reveal information that may be embarrassing, sensitive, or in other ways controversial, often make them unwilling, unresponsive, or unreliable sources.

Nor is dependence on journalistic accounts usually satisfactory. Journalists tend to be event oriented and deadline driven. They do not usually employ a time frame or perspective that is sufficiently broad or historical to permit generalizations, particularly on the institutional and behavioral aspects of the office. In addition, time pressures may force journalists to rush to conclusions before they have had an opportunity to collect information from all relevant sources.

The third factor that contributes to the problem is the absence of an overall theory that explains presidential behavior. Unlike other areas in political science—such as individual voting behavior, in which there is a body of theory that explains and predicts who votes and why—the presidency literature has not produced a comprehensive explanation of why presidents do what they do or the consequences of their actions. Nor have we been able to predict what they will do or the consequences of their actions in the future. There are, however, many prescriptions of what presidents should do.

The nature of these problems suggests that when examining the institution and exploring the president's leadership opportunities and problems, we should cast our net as broadly as possible. Thus, we examine a set of critical relationships—the relationships between the president and those whose support he needs to do his job—rather than focus on a single theme, which might exclude important information.

To function effectively, a chief executive must win election; build and maintain popular support; make decisions; and present, promote, and implement policies. Each of these requirements involves reciprocal relationships in which presidents influence, and are influenced by, others. That is why we must examine both sides of these relationships rather than focus exclusively on the president.

Relationships provide a conceptual framework for studying presidential leadership, as they enable us to explain the behavioral causes and consequences of presidential activities. By stressing relationships, however, we do not suggest that legal powers, informal roles, institutional structures, or psychological factors are unimportant. Indeed, we firmly believe that we cannot understand the presidency without an extensive knowledge of these matters. This is the background that we provide here. Our point of departure is a discussion of these matters within the context of presidential relationships, rather than vice versa. We should not view powers, roles, structures, and personality as ends in themselves. Rather, they are important for what they contribute to the president's ability to formulate, establish, and implement policies.

A Preview

This book focuses on four broad areas: (1) politics and public relations, (2) the people in the presidency, (3) the interaction between that institution and the rest of the government, and (4) the policy-making process.

The next four chapters concern the relationship between the president and the public. In Chapters 2 and 3, we discuss nomination politics and the general election. Here, the focus is on the interaction between presidential candidates, the electorate, and the implications of this interaction for governing—what an administration tries to do, when, and to what effect. In Chapter 4, we turn to presidents in office and their relations with the general public, and in Chapter 5, we examine the communications link between the incumbent and the news media. In each of these chapters, we explore leadership problems tied to communication with the public: winning electoral support, gaining job approval, and obtaining favorable media coverage. Presidents engage in a perpetual campaign to woo, win, and maintain the hearts and minds of the body politic. But are they usually successful?

In Chapters 6 and 7, we analyze the relationship between the institution and the people in it—specifically, interactions among the president, senior White House advisers, and others who wish to affect presidential decisions. Here, we direct attention toward decision making at the presidential level: the institutional environment, combined with the incumbent's personal style, conditions, presidential discretion and, ultimately, presidential choices.

In Chapters 8 through 10, we turn to the interactions that the president must have with the executive branch, Congress, and the judiciary, respectively, to achieve policy objectives. Promoting programs in Congress, implementing them in the bureaucracy, and adjudicating them in the courts are necessary if presidential leadership is to be effective.

After scrutinizing presidential relations, we then discuss the formulation of public policy in and by the presidency. Chapters 11, 12, and 13 concern domestic, budgetary and economic, and foreign and defense policy making, respectively. In each chapter, we identify and assess expectations of presidential leadership, the resources available for meeting them, and the policies that presidents have pursued and, to some extent, achieved.

Having explored the critical relationships between the president and the public, the presidency itself, the other branches, and the policy-making process, we end with appendices, one of which discusses another important but different kind of relationship—that of the president and methods of political science. Another appendix provides background on succession, tenure, and removal, including a discussion of the Clinton impeachment. We also list relevant constitutional provisions on the presidency, plus historical data on elections. Thus, we conclude where we began. If the presidency is a multifaceted institution (as we claim it is), then it can best be understood only by adopting a variety of approaches and techniques. That is why our orientation is eclectic, why we have introduced a number of themes, and why we have chosen critical presidential relationships as the conceptual framework for this book.

Selected Readings

Cronin, Thomas E., ed. *Inventing the American Presidency.* Lawrence: University Press of Kansas, 1989.

Edwards, George C., III. *The Strategic President: Persuasion and Opportunity in Presidential Leadership.* Princeton, NJ: Princeton University Press, 2009.

Edwards, George C., III, and William G. Howell. *Oxford Handbook of the American Presidency.* New York: Oxford University Press, 2009.

Edwards, George C., III, John H. Kessel, and Bert A. Rockman, eds. *Researching the Presidency.* Pittsburgh: University of Pittsburgh Press, 1993.

Edwards, George C., III, and Stephen J. Wayne, eds. *Studying the Presidency.* Knoxville: University of Tennessee Press, 1983.

Ellis, Richard, and Aaron Wildavsky. *Dilemmas of Presidential Leadership: From Washington through Lincoln.* New Brunswick, NJ: Transaction Publishers, 1989.

Hamilton, Alexander, James Madison, and John Jay. "Federalist Papers Nos. 67–77." In *The Federalist Papers.* New York: New American Library, 1961.

McDonald, Forrest. *The American Presidency: An Intellectual History.* Lawrence: University Press of Kansas, 1994.

Neustadt, Richard E. *Presidential Power.* New York: Free Press, 1990.

Riccards, Michael P. *A Republic If You Can Keep It.* New York: Greenwood, 1987.

Robinson, Donald L. *To the Best of My Ability.* New York: Norton, 1987.

Skowronek, Stephen. *The Politics Presidents Make.* Cambridge, MA: Harvard University Press, 1993.

Notes

1. Charles de Montesquieu, *The Spirit of the Laws*, vol. 1 (New York: Hafner, 1949).

2. Locke wrote: "Where the legislative and executive power are in distinct hands, as they are in all moderated monarchies and well-framed governments, there the good of the society requires that several things should be left to the discretion of him that has the executive power. For the legislators not being able to foresee and provide by laws for all that may be useful to the community, the executor of the laws, having the power in his hands, has by the common law of Nature a right to make use of it for the good of the society, in many cases where the municipal law has given no direction, till the legislative can conveniently be assembled to provide for it." John Locke, "Second Treatise of Civil Government," in Thomas I. Cook, ed., *Two Treatises of Government* (New York: Hafner, 1956), p. 203.

3. Abraham Lincoln, letter to Albert Hodges, April 8, 1964, Roy P. Basler, *Collected Works of Abraham Lincoln*, vol. 7 (New Brunswick, NJ: Rutgers University Press, 1953), p. 282.

4. Theodore Roosevelt, *The Autobiography of Theodore Roosevelt* (New York: Scribner's, 1913), p. 197.

5. William H. Taft, *Our Chief Magistrate and His Powers* (New York: Columbia University Press, 1916), p. 138.

6. President's Committee on Administrative Management, *Report with Special Studies* (Washington, DC: Government Printing Office, 1937), p. 5.

7. It was during the 1820s that the electorate, rather than state legislatures, began to choose presidential electors directly. This change increased the value of obtaining and maintaining public support for the president. Tradition, however, required that presidents seek public support in a manner befitting the dignity of the office. Public addresses were permissible, but personal campaigning was discouraged. Instead, the expectation was that the party would shoulder the electoral burden for its candidates. Not until William Jennings Bryan's quest for the nation's highest office in 1896 did candidates take to the stump themselves.

8. Woodrow Wilson, *Constitutional Government* (New York: Columbia University Press, 1908), pp. 70–71.

9. For a more extensive discussion of approaches to studying the presidency, see Stephen J. Wayne, "Approaches," in George C. Edwards III and Stephen J. Wayne, eds., *Studying the Presidency* (Knoxville: University of Tennessee Press, 1983), pp. 17–49.

10. The classic work from the legal perspective is Edward S. Corwin's *The President: Office and Powers,* 4th rev. ed. (New York: New York University Press, 1957). More recent examples include Louis Fisher, *Constitutional Conflict between Congress and the President,* 5th ed. (Lawrence: University Press of Kansas, 2007); Michael D. Ramsey, *The Constitution's Text in Foreign Affairs* (Cambridge, MA: Harvard University Press, 2007); Louis Fisher, *Military Tribunals and Presidential Power* (Lawrence: University Press of Kansas, 2006); Louis Fisher, *Presidential War Power,* 2nd ed., rev. (Lawrence: University Press of Kansas, 2004); Mark J. Rozell, *Executive Privilege,* rev. ed. (Lawrence: University Press of Kansas, 2002); Phillip J. Cooper, *By Order of the President* (Lawrence, KS: University Press of Kansas, 2002); Louis Fisher, *Congressional Abdication on War and Spending* (College Station: Texas A&M University Press, 2000); and Michael J. Glennon, *Constitutional Diplomacy* (Princeton, NJ: Princeton University Press, 1990).

11. See, for example, John P. Burke, *Honest Broker?: The National Security Advisor and Presidential Decision Making* (Texas A&M University Press, 2009); Martha Joynt Kumar, *Managing the President's Message: The White House Communications Operation* (Baltimore, MD: Johns Hopkins University Press, 2007); Victoria A. Farrar-Myers, *Scripted for Change* (College Station: Texas A&M University Press, 2007); Charles E. Walcott and Karen M. Hult, *Empowering the White House* (Lawrence: University Press of Kansas, 2004); John P. Burke, *The Institutional Presidency*, 2nd ed. (Baltimore: Johns Hopkins University Press, 2000); Paul C. Light, *The President's Agenda*, 3rd ed. (Baltimore: Johns Hopkins University Press, 1999); Lawrence R. Jacobs and Robert Y. Shapiro, "The Rise of Presidential Polling: The Nixon White House in Historical Perspective," *Public Opinion Quarterly* 59 (Summer 1995): 163–195; Charles E. Walcott and Karen M. Hult, *Governing the White House* (Lawrence: University Press of Kansas, 1995); Thomas J. Weko, *The Politicizing Presidency: The White House Personnel Office, 1948–1994* (Lawrence: University Press of Kansas, 1995); Mark A. Peterson, "The Presidency and Organized Interests: White House Patterns of Interest Group Liaison," *American Political Science Review* 86 (September 1992): 612–625; Joseph Cooper and William W. West, "Presidential Power and Republican Government: The Theory and Practice of OMB Review of Agency Rules," *Journal of Politics* 50 (November 1988): 864–895; and Stephen J. Wayne, *The Legislative Presidency* (New York: Harper and Row, 1978).

12. The leading example of this approach to the presidency is Stephen Skowronek, *The Politics Presidents Make* (Cambridge, MA: Harvard University Press, 1993). See also Scott C. James, "Historical Institutionalism, Political Development, and the Presidency," in George C. Edwards III and William G. Howell, eds., *Oxford Handbook of the American Presidency* (Oxford: Oxford University Press, 2009); and Stephen Skowronek, "The Paradigm of Development in Presidential History," in George C. Edwards III and William G. Howell, eds., *Oxford Handbook of the*

American Presidency (Oxford: Oxford University Press, 2009).

13. See Brandice Canes-Wrone, "Game Theory and the Study of the American Presidency," in George C. Edwards III and William G. Howell, eds., *Oxford Handbook of the American Presidency* (Oxford: Oxford University Press, 2009).

14. See Terry M. Moe, "The Politicized Presidency," in John E. Chubb and Paul E. Peterson, eds., *The New Directions in American Politics* (Washington, DC: Brookings Institution, 1985); Terry Moe, "Presidents, Institutions, and Theory," in George C. Edwards III, Bert A. Rockman, and John H. Kessel, eds., *Researching the Presidency* (Pittsburgh: University of Pittsburgh Press, 1993), pp. 337–386; William G. Howell, *Politics without Persuasion* (Princeton, NJ: Princeton University Press, 2003); Nolan McCarty and Rose Razaghian, "Advice and Consent: Senate Responses to Executive Branch Nominations 1885–1996," *American Journal of Political Science* 43 (October 1999): 1122–1143; Brandice Canes-Wrone, *Who Leads Whom?* (Princeton, NJ: Princeton University Press, 2006); Kenneth R. Mayer, *With the Stroke of a Pen: Executive Orders and Presidential Power* (Princeton, NJ: Princeton University Press, 2001); Charles M. Cameron, *Veto Bargaining: Presidents and the Politics of Negative Power* (New York: Cambridge University Press, 2000).

15. An exception is John P. Burke and Fred I. Greenstein, *How Presidents Test Reality* (New York: Russell Sage Foundation, 1989).

16. The political power approach is most famously represented in Richard E. Neustadt, *Presidential Power and the Modern Presidents* (New York: Free Press, 1990).

17. See, for example, George C. Edwards III, *Overreach: Leadership in the Obama Presidency* (Princeton, NJ: Princeton University Press, 2012); George C. Edwards III, The *Strategic President: Persuasion and Opportunity in Presidential Leadership* (Princeton, NJ: Princeton University Press, 2009); B. Dan Wood, *The Myth of Presidential Representation* (Cambridge University Press, 2009);

David E. Lewis, *The Politics of Presidential Appointments* (Princeton, NJ: Princeton University Press, 2008); William G. Howell and Jon C. Pevehouse, *While Dangers Gather: Congressional Checks on Presidential War Powers* (Princeton, NJ: Princeton University Press, 2007); B. Dan Wood, *The Politics of Economic Leadership* (Princeton, NJ: Princeton University Press, 2007; George C. Edwards III, *On Deaf Ears: The Limits of the Bully Pulpit* (New Haven, CT: Yale University Press, 2003); Jeffrey E. Cohen, *Presidential Responsiveness and Public Policy-Making* (Ann Arbor, MI: University of Michigan Press, 1997); George C. Edwards III, *At the-Margins: Presidential Leadership of Congress* (New Haven, CT: Yale University Press, 1989); and Fred I. Greenstein, *The Hidden-Hand Presidency* (New York: Basic Books, 1982).

18. See Bruce Miroff, "Beyond Washington," *Society* 17 (July/August 1980): 66–72.

19. See, for example, Stephen J. Wayne, Personality and Politics: Obama For and Against Himself (Washington, DC: CQ Press, 2011); Alexander L. George and Juliette L. George, *Woodrow Wilson and Colonel House: A Personality Study* (New York: Dover, 1964); Robert Tucker, "The Georges' Wilson Reexamined: An Essay on Psychobiography," *American Political Science Review* 71 (June 1977): 606–618.

20. The most notable example is James David Barber's *The Presidential Character: Predicting Performance in the White House,* 4th ed. (New York: Longman, 2008). See also Alexander L. George and Juliette L. George, *Presidential Personality and Performance* (Boulder, CO: Westview, 1998), chap. 5.

21. Some relevant studies include Alexander L. George, *Presidential Decisionmaking in Foreign Policy: The Effective Use of Information and Advice* (Boulder, CO: Westview, 1980); Robert Jervis, *Perception and Misperception in International Politics* (Princeton, NJ: Princeton University Press, 1976); John D. Steinbruner, *The Cybernetic Theory of Decision* (Princeton, NJ: Princeton University Press, 1974); Irving L. Janis, *Groupthink: Psychological Studies of Policy Decisions and Fiascoes,* 2nd ed. (Boston, MA: Houghton Mifflin, 1982); Richard E. Neustadt and Ernest R. May, *Thinking in Time* (New York: Free Press, 1986); and Stanley A. Renshon, *In His-Father's Shadow: The Transformations of George W. Bush* (New York: Palgrave Macmillan, 2004).

22. See Alexander L. George and Juliette L. George, *Presidential Personality and Performance* (New York: Westview, 1998), chap. 2.

23. Quoted in David McCullough, *Truman* (New York: Simon and Schuster, 1992), pp. 584–585.

24. Richard E. Neustadt, *Presidential Power and the Modern Presidents* (New York: Free Press, 1990).

25. Charles O. Jones, *The Presidency in a Separated System* (Washington, DC: Brookings Institution, 1994), p. 1.

26. Edwards, *At the Margins*; *On Deaf Ears*; *The Strategic President.* See also Mark A. Peterson, *Legislating Together* (Cambridge, MA: Harvard University Press, 1990); Jon R. Bond and Richard Fleisher, *The President in the Legislative Arena* (Chicago: University of Chicago Press, 1990).

27. Skowronek, *The Politics Presidents Make.* (Cambridge, MA: Harvard University Press, 1993).

28. George C. Edwards III and Andrew Barrett, "Presidential Agenda Setting in Congress," in Jon R. Bond and Richard Fleisher, eds., *Polarized Politics: Congress and the President in a Partisan* (Washington, DC: CQ Press, 2000).

29. George C. Edwards III and B. Dan Wood, "Who Influences Whom? The President, Congress, and the Media," *American Political Science Review* 93 (June 1999): 327–344.

30. Richard E. Neustadt, *Presidential Power and the Modern Presidents* (New York: Free Press, 1990).

2

THE
NOMINATION
PROCESS

E very four years, there are two presidential election processes. The first
is to nominate candidates, and the second is to choose between them.
Both require considerable time, money, and effort.

The nominating system has evolved significantly. Rules governing delegate
selection, laws regulating contributions and expenditures, and communications
(whether controlled or uncontrolled by the candidates) have all changed dramatically since the 1970s. These changes have revolutionized the nomination
process. They have affected the types of candidates who seek their party's nomination, the ways they have done so, the policies they pursue, and the leadership they exert on their party and, as president, on the country.

Today, aspirants for a party's nomination are more on their own. They
articulate their own priorities and shape their own issue agenda, design their
own strategies and tactics with the help of campaign professions, and build
their own political coalitions. In this sense, they are in a good position to
bring new ideas, people, and leadership to the party if they are nominated,
and to the country if they are elected. However, they will also have to appeal
to their party's electoral base, and if successful, to a broader and more diverse
national constituency. And if they win the general election, they then have
to govern within a constitutional system that divides powers, a political system that reflects diverse geographic and interest group constituencies, and a
governmental system composed of elected, appointed, and career officials with
different perspectives, needs, and interests, people who preceded them in office
and may very well be there after they leave. Therein lies a leadership dilemma
to which the nomination process contributes.

The extended quest for the nomination heightens public expectations but
frequently divides the party, accentuating factions within it that the successful

candidate must try to coalesce into a winning electoral coalition. The process encourages personality politics by focusing on the candidates' personal characteristics and qualifications; a theatrical style of campaigning designed to energize as it informs; a barrage of media advertising on television, radio, and the Internet; and a "sound-bite mentality." A more substantive debate of the nation's critical goals and the issues that lie ahead does not usually get the same amount of attention from the candidates, their advertising, and the news media.

The more competition within the nomination process, the greater the likelihood that the candidates will engage in negative campaigning, highlighting the less desirable qualities of their opponents and the most controversial policy positions that these opponents take. This negativism often leaves a residue of cynicism within the party and the electorate, which must be overcome if the winning candidate and party are to govern successfully.

In this chapter, we will discuss the changes in the nominating system and their impact on individuals seeking the presidency. The chapter is organized into four sections. In the first, we present a historical overview of presidential nominations, describing their evolution from congressional caucuses to brokered national conventions, and then to the popular selection of the delegates through primaries and caucuses. In the second part, we examine the environment in which nominations are conducted, focusing on the principal factors that condition delegate selection: party rules, campaign finance, and campaign communications. In emphasizing the changes that have occurred within each of these areas, we describe their impact on the parties, their standardbearers, and the political system. Next, we turn to the strategy and tactics of those seeking the nomination. Here, we discuss the principal strategic components for front-runners and non-front-runners and illustrate our discussion with examples from contemporary nomination campaigns. In the last section of the chapter, we follow this quest from the time a winner emerges during the period in which the primaries and caucuses are competitive until that candidate officially receives the party's nomination at its national convention. We also present a brief characterization of the qualities and attributes that successful candidates possess. In conclusion, we summarize changes in the nomination process and note their implications for mounting successful primary and general election campaigns, and if the candidate is elected, for governing.

THE EVOLUTION OF THE SYSTEM

The nominating system began to evolve after the writing of the Constitution and the holding of the first two presidential elections. The framers had not concerned themselves with nominations because there were no political parties at that time to nominate candidates. Assuming that well-qualified individuals would comprise the pool from which the president and vice president would be selected, the delegates at the Constitutional Convention directed their efforts toward encouraging an independent judgment by the electors. They considered such a judgment to be essential if the two most qualified people were to be chosen as president and vice president.

Once political parties emerged, however, the notion of making an independent decision was constrained by the parties' desire to choose nominees whose views were consistent with their own. Such a choice required a nomination mechanism. In 1796, congressional party leaders gathered informally to agree on their tickets. Four years later, partisan congressional caucuses met for the purposes of recommending candidates. "King Caucus," as it came to be known, became the principal mode of nomination until the 1820s, when factions developed within Thomas Jefferson's Democratic-Republican Party, the only viable national party at the time. These factions eventually led to the demise of the caucus and to the development of a more decentralized mode of nomination, one that was consistent with the increasingly sectional composition of the parties and reflective of the country's federal structure. By the 1830s, national nominating conventions became the principal means for brokering those interests and uniting the parties for a national campaign.

The first convention was held in the year of 1831 by the Anti-Masons, a small but relatively active third party. Having virtually no congressional representation of its own, this party could not use a congressional caucus. Instead, it organized a general meeting in which delegates from its state parties could choose the nominees as well as determine the party's positions on the important issues of the day. The Democratic Party—it had dropped "Republican" from the title—followed suit with a nominating convention of its own in 1832, and thereafter, party conventions became the standard method for selecting nominees and articulating policy positions.

These early conventions were informal and rowdy by contemporary standards. In fact, the delegates themselves decided on the procedures for conducting them. The method for choosing the delegates was left to the state parties and, more specifically, to their leadership. In most cases, public participation was minimal.

Nineteenth-century conventions served a number of purposes. They provided a forum for party bosses and constituted a mechanism by which agreements could be negotiated and support could be mobilized. By brokering interests, they helped unite disparate elements within the party, thereby converting a conglomeration of state party organizations into a national coalition for the purpose of electing a president and a vice president. The nominating system buttressed the position of state party leaders, but it did so at the expense of the rank-and-file partisans. The influence of the leadership depended in large part on its ability to deliver the votes at the nominating convention. To ensure loyalty, the heads of the state parties handpicked their delegations.

Demands for reform began to be heard at the beginning of the twentieth century, when a number of states changed their mode of selection to primaries in order to permit greater public participation. This movement, however, was short-lived. Low voter turnout, the costs of holding elections, and the opposition of party leaders to a process that reduced their clout while increasing that of the partisan electorate persuaded several state legislatures to make their primaries advisory only—or even discontinue them entirely. As a consequence, the number of primaries declined after World War I, as did the percentage of delegates selected in them.

Prior to the middle of the twentieth century, strong candidates avoided the primaries. Running in too many of them was interpreted as a sign of weakness, not strength. It indicated that a candidate lacked national recognition and the support of party leaders. The growth of television, beginning in the 1950s, however, presented new opportunities for candidates who wished to demonstrate their popular appeal. Dwight D. Eisenhower (in 1952), John F. Kennedy (in 1960), and Richard M. Nixon (in 1968) all used this medium and presidential primaries to overcome doubts that a general, a Catholic, or a once-defeated presidential (and later, gubernatorial) candidate, respectively, could be elected president. As a consequence of the success of these primary campaigns, the presidential nomination process became increasingly visible and participatory.

THE ELECTORAL ARENA

Party Rules

State law determines the procedures for delegate selection. Today, these procedures also have to conform to the general guidelines and rules established by the national parties. Prior to the 1970s, they did not. In the tumultuous Democratic convention of 1968, delegates selected Vice President Hubert Humphrey to be the presidential candidate despite the fact that he had not actively competed in the party's primaries.[1] To unify the party and placate supporters of the candidates who did run in the primaries—Eugene McCarthy, Robert Kennedy, and George McGovern—the party established a commission to examine and revise its rules for delegate selection with three principal goals in mind: to encourage greater public participation in party activities, to make conventions more representative of typical Democratic voters, and to give more candidates a realistic opportunity to seek and win the nomination.

The new rules established a calendar during which states could hold their caucuses and primaries, required voting in them to determine the allocation of delegates pledged to candidates at the convention, and forced the candidates to run representative slates of delegates that mirrored a broader cross section of rank-and-file Democrats. Later, the party mandated that half the delegates be women and that party leaders automatically be delegates. They were known as super delegates and initially were not pledged to particular candidates as were most of those that were elected.

The Republicans were affected by these Democratic Party reforms. Although they continued to enforce the rules that their state Republican Parties followed, many state legislatures, under the control of the Democrats in the 1970s and 1980s, changed their election laws to conform to the new Democratic rules, which also had an impact on the Republican presidential nominations in those states. Moreover, the Republicans did want to eliminate discrimination, encourage greater participation, and better represent their electoral base at their nominating conventions, so some state Republican Parties modified their selection processes on their own.

Although the U.S. Constitution gives the states the right to conduct elections for federal officials, the Supreme Court held in the case of *Cousins v. Wigoda*, 419 U.S. 477 (1975), that the national political parties could determine and impose their own rules for delegate selection. In theory, they can refuse to seat state delegations not chosen in accordance with their rules; in practice, however, the need for all state parties to support the presidential ticket in the general election has led the national party to grant exemptions to certain states and penalties to others that do not abide by its rules.

The rules are not neutral. The reforms since the 1970s have led to more primary elections, more candidates running in them, and more appeals to a wider group of voters. But they have also contributed to unequal influence among the states, the candidates, and the participating electorate. They have affected the parties' organization, the influence of their leaders, and the eventual nominees and their campaigns in the general election. These impacts have led both major parties to continue to tinker with their rules for presidential nominations; with the result that three principal changes involving the calendar for caucuses and primaries, Republican allocation of delegates, and Democratic super delegates were instituted for the 2012 delegate selection process.

The Caucus and Primary Calendar

The nomination schedule had become increasingly front-loaded and compressed. In 1996, almost two-thirds of all the convention delegates were selected within a forty-four-day period beginning mid-February and continuing through March 26, 1996. In 2000 and 2004, two-thirds of the delegates had been chosen by mid-March. In 2008, almost 60 percent were selected by the first Tuesday in February and 80 percent by the first Tuesday in March.

A compressed, front-loaded calendar gives an advantage to the states that go first and to the best-known, -financed, and -organized candidates. It encourages them to begin their quest for their party's nomination earlier and earlier in the years prior to the election. It also creates an interval of several

Table 2.1 Cumulative Allocation of Republican Delegates in the 2008 and 2012 Nominations

	Percentage of Convention Delegates Chosen by the First Tuesday of the Month*	
	2008 (%)	2012 (%)
January	1.7	1.2
February	55.2	10.6
March	80.0	35.5
April	82.4	56.2
May	90.8	66.3
June	98.6	95.6

*In 2008, the first Republican contest, the Iowa caucus, was held on Thursday, January 3.

SOURCES: The Green Papers. http://www.thegreenpapers.com/P08/ccad.phtml; http://www.thegreenpapers.com/P12/ccad.phtml.

months between the time that the nominee is effectively determined and the date on which the official selection is made at the national nominating convention. A front-loaded schedule can also result in the selection of a nominee who is not the choice of rank-and-file partisans and may not be the strongest candidate in the general election.

To rectify these problems, both parties moved the beginning of their official period during which any state could hold its nomination contest from the first Tuesday in February to the first Tuesday in March, beginning in 2012. They gave one-month exemptions to the four states that went earlier in previous nominations: Iowa, New Hampshire, Nevada, and South Carolina. They also continued the practice of penalizing states that violated the calendar by reducing the size of their convention delegation and rewarded those that held their contests later by awarding them additional delegates. Although these incentives and disincentives did spread out the 2012 nomination process (see Table 2.1), they did not prevent early contests that violated party rules from occurring. The decision of the Florida legislature to hold its primary in late January motivated Iowa and New Hampshire, whose law requires them to hold the nation's first caucus and primary respectively, to move their contests earlier in January, as did Nevada, South Carolina, and Michigan. The Republican Party, which had the only contested nomination in 2012, penalized these states by reducing their delegations by half.

Vote Allocation

Unlike the Democrats, prior to 2012 the Republicans did not require proportional voting. They allowed states to conduct winner-take-all elections, giving the candidate with the most votes a huge boost in delegates awarded and usually reducing the period of time it took to wrap up the nomination. In 2008, John McCain was the principal beneficiary of winner-take-all voting, getting about twice as many delegates as the percentage of the popular vote he received.[2]

To better reflect the choices of rank-and-file Republican voters and to encourage more people to participate, the Republican Party instituted a proportional voting requirement for all contests held before April 1, 2012. The rule extended the Republican nomination process by keeping the race closer for a longer period. Changes in the finance laws that permitted unlimited contributions to nonparty groups that supported individual candidates also provided the financial resources to campaign for a longer period. Although front-runner Mitt Romney eventually extended his lead, it took him until April to wrap up the Republican nomination, one month later than McCain had in 2008.

Super Delegates

The third rule change, the elimination of unpledged super delegates by the Democrats, had no effect on that party's uncontested nomination, nor have super delegates affected previous Democratic nominations—but they could have in 2008. The fear, expressed by Obama's campaign supporters after he had acquired a delegate lead in the caucuses and primaries, was that Hillary Rodham Clinton, the initial Democratic front-runner who had received the endorsements of a majority of the super delegates, would turn to those "supers" to reverse the results of the elections that had been held in accordance with party rules. They did not do so, however. Most of them backed the candidate that carried their districts and states.

To avoid this potential problem in future nominations, the Democrats decided to add the "supers" to state delegations as pledged delegates, allocated in proportion to the votes candidates received in those states.

Campaign Finance

Although the reforms in party rules have had a profound effect on American electoral politics, they have not been the only major change to affect contemporary nominations. New finance laws, enacted since the mid-1970s, and the Supreme Court's rulings on them have also had a major impact, altering the way in which money is raised and spent and greatly increasing the amount of it available to the candidates, parties, and nonparty groups.

Throughout most of American history, candidates of both parties depended almost exclusively on large contributions from private donors to finance their campaigns. This dependence, combined with spiraling costs, secret and sometimes illegal contributions, and sparse public information about who gave how much to whom (and what they received in return for their donations) raised serious questions about the democratic character of American elections. Can elected officials be responsive to national needs as well as those of their individual and group benefactors? Had the presidency become an office that only those with money or access to it could afford?

Federal Legislation

Public discontent with the financing of elections led Congress in the 1970s to address these issues with legislation designed to limit skyrocketing expenses (especially in the mass media), reduce the influence of large contributors, and reveal contributors' identities. Other legislation established a fund to subsidize the presidential nomination process and support the general election.

The Federal Election Campaign Act (FECA), enacted in 1974, provided for public disclosure, contribution ceilings, campaign spending limits, and federal subsidies for the nomination process. Some of its provisions were highly controversial. Opponents of the legislation challenged the limits on contributions and spending as a violation of the First Amendment right to freedom of speech. In the landmark case of *Buckley v. Valeo* (424 U.S. 1, 1976), the Supreme Court upheld the authority of Congress to regulate contributions to and expenditures of campaign organizations, but not the independent spending of individuals and groups during the campaign.

The Court's decision forced Congress to revise the law so as not to violate the First Amendment. New legislation enacted in 1976, subsequently amended in 1979, provided for public disclosure of all contributions and expenditures over a certain amount (now $200), set limits on individual and group contributions to candidates, and made federal subsidies available for the nomination process and outright grants for the general election.

Federal funds were intended to reduce the burden of fund-raising for the candidates, even the playing field, and give candidates who were less well known a chance to demonstrate their qualifications. They were also intended to reduce the influence of the wealthy on the election process. For a limited time and to a limited extent, the funds achieved these objectives but did not reduce the advantage that money provided.

Over time, federal funds created two classes of candidates, those who relied solely on private funds, their own and the contributions they received from others, and candidates who accepted public funds and, by doing so, were forced to abide by the overall and individual state spending limits that the acceptance of those funds required. Naturally, such limits—in 2012, the overall limit was about $44 million and the state limits, based on the voting-aged population of the state, ranged from $885,000 in the smallest states to $19.7 million in California—put them at a competitive disadvantage if their opponents did not abide by them and had sufficient funds to raise and spend more. As a consequence, none of the major candidates for the 2012 Republican presidential nomination accepted matching grants.[3]

In 1979, the FECA was amended. To encourage voting and party-building activities, the new law permitted an unlimited amount of money to be raised and spent on voluntary efforts by state and local parties to build their electoral coalitions and get people out to vote. This money, referred to as "soft money," opened a large loophole in the law, one that both parties exploited between 1980 and 2002 by soliciting sizable donations for these types of activities. In exchange for their generosity, large contributors were offered VIP treatment, including invitations to private briefings and social events as well as access to party leaders and elected officials.[4] These benefits raised questions of equity in a democratic electoral process.

In his 2000 campaign for the Republican presidential nomination, John McCain brought attention to this issue and subsequently introduced legislation along with Senators Russ Feingold and Ernest Hollings to prohibit the national parties from soliciting and spending soft money. To compensate the parties for their loss of revenue, the legislation raised the individual contribution limits from $1,000 to $2,000 and adjusted that amount to the rate of inflation. In 2012, the contribution limit was $2,500 per candidate, per election. Individual contributions to political parties were also increased.

Doubling the amount individuals could donate to federal candidates greatly increased the amount of money that candidates could raise from private donors. In the first presidential election held after the 2002 legislation went into effect, George W. Bush raised $269.5 million, of which $258.9 million was contributed from individual donors, for his uncontested primary campaign. In 2008, Barack Obama raised $414.2 million through August 31, 2008; in the 2012 contest, he raised $432.5 million, running unopposed for the Democratic nomination. Mitt Romney raised $97.6 million in contributions through April 2012 and an overall total of $274 million through August 31, 2012.[5]

The 2002 law, known as the Bipartisan Campaign Reform Act, also placed limits on nonparty group advertising that had been used to supplement candidate advertising and in that way circumvent the spending limits placed on candidates who accepted federal funds. The legislation prohibited groups from mentioning the names of candidates in their ads thirty days or less before a primary and sixty days or less before the general election. Although the Supreme Court initially upheld most of the provisions of the new law in the case of *McConnell v. FEC* (540 U.S. 93 2003), it subsequently decided that the blanket prohibition on mentioning the names of candidates violated a group's freedom of speech. See *Wisconsin Right to Life, Inc. v. FEC* (551 U.S. 2007).

But the controversy continued, with the focus changing to the regulations that the Federal Election Commission (FEC) issued to enforce the legislation. In 2008, the Commission prohibited a documentary film attacking Hillary Clinton from being distributed to cable television on the grounds that it was produced by a corporation, which violated a long-time ban on corporate giving and spending in federal elections. The Supreme Court, however, reversed the FEC's judgment. In the case of *Citizens United v. Federal Election Commission* (558 U.S. 08-205 2010), the Court held that corporations have free speech rights that are protected by the First Amendment to the Constitution.

Following the Court's decision, a unanimous Court of Appeals ruled that the *Citizens United* judgment also applied to other nonparty groups, including those created by individuals for the purpose of supporting or opposing particular candidates.[6] This Court of Appeals decision enabled the candidates, or more precisely their aides, friends, and financial backers, to establish their own, candidate-oriented Super PACs. As a consequence, money poured into the 2012 campaign. Table 2.2 indicates the amounts the principal Republican candidates and their Super PACs raised and spent through April 30, 2012, the contested portion of the contest.

Table 2.2 Revenues and Expenditures of Republican Candidates and Their Super PACs through April 30, 2012 (in millions)

	Revenue ($)	Expenditure ($)
Gingrich Campaign	23.1	22.6
Super PAC	24.2	18.2
Paul Campaign	38.7	36.6
Super PAC	5.3	3.9
Perry Campaign	19.7	20.1
Super PAC	5.5	4.8
Romney Campaign	97.5	91.0
Super PAC	52.3	41.2
Santorum Campaign	21.8	21.0
Super PAC	8.5	7.7
Huntsman Campaign	7.8	7.8
Super PAC	3.2	3.2

SOURCES: Data for candidate revenue and disbursements come from "Presidential Pre-Nomination Campaign Receipts through April 30, 2012," Federal Election Commission, May 2012, www.fec.gov/press/bkgnd /pres_cf_odd_dpoc/presreceiptsm52012.pdf, and from "Presidential Pre-Nomination Campaign Disbursements through April 30, 2012," Federal Election Commission, May 2012 (both accessed October 5, 2012), www.fec.gov /press/bkgnd/pres_cr_odd/dpoc/presdisbursm52012.pdf. Data on candidate Super PAC revenue and expenditures come from "Obama's and Romney's Reports Each Point Up Vulnerabilities as the Campaigns Turn toward the General Election," Campaign Finance Institute, May 23, 2012, http://cfinst.org/Press/PReleases/12-05-23 /Obama%E2%80%99s_and_Romney%E2%80%99s_Reports_Each_Point_Up_Vulnerabilities_as_the_Campaigns_ Turn_Toward_the_General_Election.aspx.

During this same period (through April 30, 2012), President Obama, running unopposed for the Democratic nomination, raised approximately $217 million and spent $109 million, and his Super PAC raised $10.6 million and spent $2.2 million.[7] Table 2.3 lists the total preconvention revenues and expenditures of the Romney and Obama campaigns and those of their candidate-oriented Super PACs for the entire nomination period.

The Importance of Money

Money buys recognition for those who need it. H. Ross Perot bought that recognition in the 1992 general election, as did Steve Forbes in 1996 and Mitt Romney in 2008 during their quests for the Republican nomination. Each spent millions of dollars of his own funds. Howard Dean and Barack Obama gained the recognition in 2004 and 2008 when they ran for the Democratic nomination by raising millions in private funds, using the Internet as a principal means of solicitation.

Early money is also important because it is viewed by the press, politicians, and partisan donors as a sign of viability, that a candidate has the broad-based support necessary to win the nomination. In addition, large war chests provide candidates with greater flexibility in deciding where and how to campaign. But there are drawbacks as well to spending campaign funds too quickly and too early. If the race persists, candidates may find themselves at a disadvantage. Hillary Clinton faced this problem in 2008. She raised and spent as much as Obama in

Table 2.3 Preconvention Fundraising and Expenditures of the Obama and Romney Campaigns and Their Super PACs (in millions)

	Revenue ($)	Expenditure ($)
Barack Obama Campaign	432.2	354.4
Super Pac (Priorities USA Action)	35.6	30.8
Total	467.8	385.2
Mitt Romney Campaign	274.0	233.1
Super PAC (Restore Our Future, Inc.)	96.7	90.3
Total	370.7	323.4

SOURCES: "Presidential Pre-Nomination Campaign Receipts through August 31, 2012," Federal Election Commission, September 20, 2012, www.fec.gov/press/bkgnd/pres_cf_odd_dpoc/presreceiptsM92012.pdf (accessed October 5, 2012); "Presidential Pre-Nomination Campaign Disbursements through August 31, 2012," Federal Election Commission, September 20, 2012, www.fec.gov/press/bkgnd/pres_cf_odd_dpoc/presdisbursM92012.pdf (accessed October 5, 2012); and "2012 Individual PAC Details," Federal Election Commission, www.fec.gov/disclosure /PACCommitteeDetail (accessed October 5, 2012).

the year before the caucuses and primaries began, but she did not have as large a fund-raising base as he did. As a consequence, she was forced to lend her campaign $13.2 million of her own money just to stay competitive in the large states.

Campaign Communications

Another major development in the nomination process has been the expansion of its public dimension, particularly the use of new communication technologies to reach, energize, and mobilize partisans. Until the mid-twentieth century, the quest for the nomination was an internal party affair; today, it is not. Campaigns require hundreds of staff and volunteers at their headquarters and thousands in the field. Most of the senior campaign advisers are professional consultants—pollsters, media gurus, grassroots organizers, direct mailers, accountants, attorneys, and, now, computer specialists and Internet experts—all of whom specialize in electoral politics.

Even the demands on today's candidates are different. They must be willing to campaign continuously in the public eye through the mass media for up to two years. They need to be well versed on a range of issues (which should be detailed on their websites); they need to have relatively well-defined messages targeted to specific groups within their party's electoral coalition and avoid alienating others whose support they may need down the road. They need to control their own narrative, not have the news media do so.

Public Opinion

The first step for most campaigns is to determine how much the public knows about the candidate and the extent to which this information is evident across the electorate. A second step is to expand this knowledge base and shape it to the benefit of the candidate. Both steps require accurate public opinion polling. John F. Kennedy was the first presidential candidate to engage a pollster in his quest for the nomination. Surveys conducted for his campaign indicated that his principal rival, Senator Hubert Humphrey, was vulnerable in a few key states to which Kennedy wisely devoted his time and resources.

Since 1960, polls have become standard fare. To hone their messages and target them successfully, candidates also rely on focus groups, a collection of individuals who are brought together and asked to discuss and react to a variety of real and hypothetical campaign appeals and situations involving candidates, issues, and ideology.

Polls also shape news media coverage. During the nomination process, when the outcome is in doubt, the candidates' standings in the polls influence the amount of coverage they receive and often the spin on that coverage. In general, those who are deemed most electable get the most coverage, which, in turn, increases their ability to raise money, gain volunteers, and extend their appeal. The absence of media attention, particularly critical in the early stages of the nomination process when less is known about the candidates, can be fatal.

News Coverage

For the last sixty years, television has been the vehicle by which candidates communicated campaign appeals and leadership imagery to voters. Radio and, more recently, the Internet have also become major communication channels. With multistate primaries concentrated toward the beginning of the nomination process, candidates have little choice but to depend on electronic media to reach voters through news media coverage, television advertising, and personal contact.

The early contests receive the most attention. Naturally, candidates who do surprisingly well in them have benefited enormously from this news coverage. Barack Obama's surprising win over John Edwards and Hillary Clinton in Iowa in 2008, a state in which African Americans constituted only 4 percent of the voters, elevated him to Democratic front-runner overnight. Similarly, Rick Santorum's virtual tie with front-runner Mitt Romney in Iowa in 2012 gave his candidacy a legitimacy (and press coverage) that it lacked prior to that time. In New Hampshire, surprise winners—Eugene McCarthy in 1968, George McGovern in 1972, Jimmy Carter in 1976, Gary Hart in 1984, George H. W. Bush in 1988, Pat Buchanan in 1996, John McCain in 2000 and 2008, and Hillary Clinton in 2008—all gained visibility and credibility, which in turn opened the checkbooks of many contributors and generated media coverage even though none of these candidates won a majority of their party's vote in that primary.

Doing more poorly than expected has the opposite effect, as Democrats Howard Dean and Richard Gephardt found following their poor showings in the 2004 Iowa caucus, as did fellow partisans Joseph Biden and Chris Dodd in 2008 and Republicans Michele Bachmann, John Huntsman, and Rick Perry in 2012. Recovery is possible, but only if a candidate has sufficient resources and organizational support to overcome the disappointing showings. George H. W. Bush (1992) and George W. Bush (2004) came back to win the Republican nomination after their losses in the New Hampshire primary, as did

Barack Obama in 2008, in part because he was able to sandwich his New Hampshire defeat (which was only by 3 percent) between his victory in Iowa and in South Carolina ten days later.

The news media interpret caucus and primary results. The winners and losers are not necessarily the candidates with the most or least votes, but those that do better or worse than expected. Hillary Clinton's loss in Iowa in 2008 and Obama's in New Hampshire in that same year garnered the headlines, not John Edwards's second-place finish in Iowa ahead of Clinton. On the Republican side, Romney's loss in South Carolina to Gingrich in 2012 had a similar effect. Knowing the press will evaluate the contest from the perspective of expectations, candidates tend to "low-ball" their prediction of how they will do so as to be able to claim victory almost regardless of the outcome.

Not only is the outcome of the vote subject to interpretation, so also is the importance attached to particular contests. Generally speaking, the news media give more attention to primaries than caucuses, big states than small ones, and early contests than later ones. Of course, close elections receive more emphasis than one-sided ones, and statewide contests get better coverage than do district elections. The bottom line is that the greater the competition and the number of delegates at stake, the more coverage the election gets.[8]

The press concentrates on the competitive aspects of campaign strategies, fund-raising activities, and policy stands in that order. During 2011–2012, the news media gave a lot of attention to the twenty Republican debates. Why the extensive news coverage of repetitive debates? The answer is that they were live on television and fit into the horse race story of the campaign.

According to an analysis by the Center for Media and Public Affairs, the broadcast evening news shows gave four times more television emphasis to the race than to the candidates' positions on the issues and twice as much as to the candidates' backgrounds and their qualifications.[9] A study by the Pew Research Center's for Excellence in Journalism reported similar findings in its computer-based content analysis of 11,000 news outlets; almost two-thirds of the election stories they sampled concerned aspects of the "momentum, strategy, horse race polls, advertising and fundraising."[10]

As long as the nomination remains competitive, policy issues tend to receive less attention. Although the positions of the candidates are noted, the details of their proposals are not. There are several reasons for this. Part of it has to do with the news media's perception that viewers are more interested in who is ahead and who is going to win than in the specifics of the candidates' policy proposals. Another factor concerns the relatively small differences in the policy positions of candidates of the same party. The policy differences between the major parties' nominees in the general election tend to be larger and get more attention. When candidates depart from the dominant view of their party, such as McCain in 2008 and Perry and Gingrich in 2012 on immigration policy, their stands get highlighted, and they become the focus of their opponents' criticism. Ron Paul's opposition to the war in Iraq (in 2008) and to U.S. military involvement around the world (in 2012) received similar attention suffered a similar fate.

The emphasis on the horse race affects the tone of coverage as well. With a journalistic intent to keep the race going to maintain audience interest, the press is harsher on the front-runner than on challengers. Hillary Clinton received more negative coverage than Barack Obama, and Mitt Romney received more than his Republican opponents through February of their respective nomination campaigns in 2008 and 2012. After Mrs. Clinton complained about the imbalance, the news media became more critical of Obama and less critical of her.

In general, candidates tend to receive more negative than positive coverage until the nomination is effectively decided. Barack Obama and Mike Huckabee were exceptions in 2008, but there were none in the 2012 Republican nominations until Romney solidified his position as front-runner and built an increasing delegate lead. At that point in March, the tone of his coverage improved. The press had concluded that the Republican race was about over and the next, the general election, was about to begin.[11]

The "spin" on the news coverage of the 2012 preconvention period was more negative than in previous campaigns. The Pew Center for Excellence in Journalism reported that the major narratives about the character and records of both candidates were over 70 percent negative, comparable only to the 2004 presidential campaign. For Obama the negativity focused on his economic record and his beliefs in free enterprise and individual initiative in a capitalistic economic system; for Romney the negatives pertained to whether his experience as a wealthy venture capitalist provided him with sufficient understanding and sympathy for the economic difficulties average Americans face.[12]

Naturally, candidates try to affect the coverage they receive. They do so by orchestrating events for the news media, releasing information, and sometimes making themselves available for interviews. In 2012, campaigns by candidates and the groups associated with them were responsible for about one-third of the information that the news media included in their campaign coverage.[13] Campaigns respond immediately to any attack against them. McCain was particularly good at interacting with the reporters; Obama and Clinton in 2008 and Romney and Obama in 2012 were less accessible. Candidates also stick to the scripts that their advisers prepare for them. Even debate performances are usually rehearsed to avoid controversial statements, mistakes, and faux pas that the press will spotlight, such as Michele Bachmann's incorrect historical references, Rick Perry's inability to recall one of the three government agencies he had said he would eliminate, and Newt Gingrich's intent to spend billions for moon exploration despite his and his party's desire to cut government spending.

Campaign Advertising

Advertising on radio, television, and the Internet is another way to shape and, if need be, change public perceptions. Although political ads have their limits—they are blatantly partisan—they do serve to provide information, create an image, and highlight issue positions. The ads, as with speeches, are tested before they are aired to make sure that they achieve their desired effect on their targeted audience. About half the funds in a campaign budget are usually spent on advertising.

In the 2008 nomination contests, hundreds of thousands of ads were run. Barack Obama spent the most on advertising, about $75 million through May. Romney was the leading advertiser for the GOP, spending $31.7 until he dropped out in early February.[14] In 2012, it was more of the same. According to the *Washington Post*, nearly $110.4 million was spent on television commercials in the competitive phase of the Republican nomination through April 15, 2012.[15] Romney's fund-raising advantage allowed him and the Super PAC supporting him to spend more than his opponents and their Super PACs combined during this period.

Much of the advertising is negative. In 2012, Romney and his Super PAC aired the most negative commercials of the Republican candidates, targeting Perry first, then Gingrich, and finally Santorum. According to the *Washington Post*, the Republican ads became nastier as the nomination campaign progressed. Whereas only 6 percent of the 2008 Republican nomination ads were negative, over 70 percent of those aired during the competitive part of the 2012 nomination contest were negative.[16]

In addition to the advertising run by the candidates and their Super PACs, groups representing business, labor, and other special interests air commercials. During the early period, most of the nonparty group advertising was anti-Obama. One hundred percent of the advertising by Republican Super PACs was negative; 69 percent of the anti-Romney ads sponsored by Obama's campaign committee and 100 percent of the advertising by the Democratic National Committee and Super PACs supporting Obama were negative.[17] In contrast, during the 2008 nomination campaign, only 21 percent of Obama's ads were negative.[18]

Personal Contact

Personal contact is necessary in nomination campaigns, particularly at the beginning of the process. Candidates open offices and often spend considerable time in the states that hold their first caucuses and primaries. Republicans made 243 visits and stayed 507 days prior to the Iowa caucus, compared to 283 visits and 551 days four years earlier. In New Hampshire, Republican activity was greater during the previous nomination cycle.[19] By the end of 2011, the Obama campaign had set up offices in Iowa, New Hampshire, and the other early states, held 57 training sessions for precinct leaders around the country, and scheduled thousands of events prior to the caucuses and primaries.[20]

Unless a campaign is able to attract and train a large number of volunteers early, it will have to depend on paid staff and outside groups to establish phone banks, go door-to-door, check registration lists, and organize and run a get-out-the-vote drive on election day. Candidates use their website, rallies, and smaller meetings to acquire a list of people to whom they can turn for help.

Once that list, complete with e-mail addresses and cell phone numbers, begins to grow, candidates can use the Internet to get money and volunteers as Democrat Howard Dean did in 2004.

Although Dean did not win the nomination, he did demonstrate the potential of the Internet, a potential that the Obama campaign maximized in 2008 and 2012. Using social networking—blogs on its own website and YouTube, Facebook, and other popular sites—the campaign extended its electoral base, solicited donations, and involved millions of Internet users in its campaign at relatively little financial cost.

The Pew Research Center's Project for Excellence in Journalism studied online postings during a two-week period in June 2012 and found that the Obama campaign put up almost four times as much content on Internet sites as did the Romney campaign and was active on nearly twice as many platforms as Romney's.[21] With the exception of Romney, none of the other candidates for the 2012 Republican nomination began the campaign with a significant database and Internet operation. As a result, they had to stick to the airways, using the debates and advertisements to spread the word and mobilize their supporters.

THE QUEST FOR THE NOMINATION: A STRATEGIC GAME PLAN

Greater public involvement in the nomination process has changed the strategy and tactics of the candidates. Campaigns begin much earlier than in the past. They require more money up front, an in-place organization, and a strategic approach that builds a winning coalition from the ground up. Nomination strategies are based on certain fundamental assumptions:

1. Sufficient time and energy must be devoted to personal campaigning in the preprimary and early preconvention periods. Even incumbents cannot take renomination for granted, although by raising large sums of money, they can usually block a quality challenger.

2. A strong field organization must be in place for the initial caucuses and primaries. Television advertising is also an important component of multi-state campaigns if the primaries are front-loaded and concentrated. Finally, the Internet has also proven to be an effective instrument to solicit money, energize and involve potential supporters, mobilize people for rallies and other campaign events, and get out the vote on election day if candidates are able to develop a large database of potential supporters. But that takes time and requires an interactive website and a team of technology experts. It gives advantage to candidates who have begun this process in their previous campaigns for elective office.

3. A firm financial foundation must be created. In the light of the 2012 campaign experience, candidate-oriented Super PACs must be established at the outset and wealthy donors tapped for funds early and often. Spending strategies must also be devised. Not all caucuses and primaries are equally important; the first ones, which receive the most attention, require the allocation of greater resources. However, allocating too many resources to a few early states can also be dangerous if it depletes a campaign's treasury and the candidate does not do as well as expected. It can force an end to a campaign before it even gets off the ground.

4. The order of caucuses and primaries and their rules and procedures must be understood and, if possible, manipulated to the candidate's advantage well before the year of the election. The type of state contest, the date on which it is scheduled, and the allocation of delegate votes can give advantage to certain candidates, such as the winner-take-all primaries did for McCain in 2008.

5. Groups within the party must be targeted and appeals must be made to them. Once the nomination has been won, however, these appeals must be broadened, and often moderated, without necessarily contradicting previously taken stands or negating earlier promises. If the overall constituency is too narrow, it will be difficult to gain the nomination, much less win the general election.

Non-Front-Runners

The actual strategy that candidates adopt depends on their status at the beginning of the campaign. If they are not front-runners and well known, then their initial goal must be to establish their credentials as viable contenders. At the outset, the key is recognition, whereas over the long haul it is the acquisition of delegates, not necessarily the popular vote a candidate receives. What counts is the perception of electability and the number of pledged delegates.

Recognition may be gained from the news media if non-front-running candidates raise more money, gain more endorsements, or do better than expected in the early primaries and caucuses. Momentum can be achieved by winning a series of prenomination victories and doing well in the early public opinion polls; the size of the popular vote may be less important than the number of delegates acquired. That is why the underdogs concentrate their time, efforts, and resources on the first few contests. They have no choice. Winning will provide them with opportunities later on, whereas losing will confirm their secondary status.

Jimmy Carter's 1976 quest for the Democratic nomination and Barack Obama's in 2008 are good examples of successful non-front-runner strategies. Carter began his campaign as a relatively unknown southern governor with limited financial resources and organizational support. He concentrated his efforts in Iowa and New Hampshire. By attracting the attention of the press, he hoped to establish his credibility as a viable candidate. Early success, he anticipated, would facilitate fund-raising, organization building, and continued media coverage—and he was right. For Obama, the task was to demonstrate that he could defeat Democratic front-runner Hillary Rodham Clinton. By matching her campaign's fund-raising; developing large, sophisticated Internet and on-the-ground operations that enlarged the Democratic base; and winning the Iowa caucus, Obama showed that his movement was real, he was electable, and Clinton was not the inevitable nominee. The Carter and Obama strategies have become the models for most non-front-runners in both parties.

Pulpit Candidates

Jesse Jackson's campaigns in 1984 and 1988, and to a lesser extent Pat Robertson's run in 1988, Pat Buchanan's in 1992 and 1996, and Ron Paul's in 2008 and 2012, do not fit the typical non-front-runner's strategic model. Lacking a large financial base, Jackson, Robertson, and Buchanan tried to mobilize armies of volunteers in grassroots efforts in states in which their supporters constituted a significant portion of the electorate. They also attracted considerable press coverage by virtue of their extreme policy positions, their passionate supporters and detractors, their effectiveness as speakers and campaigners, and the perennial desire of the news media to add color and excitement to the race. Paul achieved attention by raising relatively large amounts of money; by gaining a core of strong supporters that created a buzz for him on Twitter, blogs, and other social networking sites;[22] and for his consistent and confidence articulation of his libertarian views, particularly during the Republican debates.

In each of these four cases, these nontraditional candidates used the campaign as a "bully pulpit" to articulate their political philosophy, demonstrate that others within the party's electorate shared their views, and give themselves greater influence within the party and among their supporters.

Front-Runners

For the front-runners, the task is different. They have to maintain credibility, not establish it. At the outset, they have a little more flexibility, which derives from having greater name recognition, a larger resource base, more political endorsements, and usually an established organization led by experienced campaign professionals. Status and position make it easier to raise money and build an organization that not only enhances their potential but also creates expectations that may be difficult to meet and easier for the press to deflate. A front-runner can overcome a single defeat but will find it more difficult to survive a string of setbacks. Once a front-runner establishes momentum and a growing delegate lead, it is difficult to overtake that candidate, particularly if most of the delegates are allocated in proportion to the popular vote.

Box 2.1 A Non-Front-Runner's Strategy: The Rise and Fall of Howard Dean in the 2004 Democratic Nomination

For political pundits, campaign operatives, and the news media, the big news of the 2003–2004 Democratic nomination process was the rise and fall of Howard Dean. When Dean announced his presidential ambitions in the fall of 2001, few people had ever heard of him[23] and few politicians and political pundits took him seriously.

Dean did not fit the mode of successful Democratic nominees. He did not come from a southern state as Carter and Clinton did. He was not associated with the moderate wing of his party. In fact, his support of a bill to grant civil unions to same-sex couples was seen as a major liability for a candidate in the general election. He did not have a lot of wealthy backers, a national political organization, or even much public recognition.

Dean's rise to prominence was a result of his innovative campaign appeal and a successful strategy to build a base of core supporters on the Internet, a strategy that other candidates now emulate. He was the first candidate to make effective use of the Internet to raise money, involve his supporters in the activities of his campaign, and provide them with information to convince others to join his cause. By the end of 2003, the names of 500,000 subscribers were in the campaign's database, ready to be mobilized for the caucus and primary elections that lay ahead.

The only Democratic candidate, other than Congressman Dennis Kucinich, who opposed the Iraq war from the beginning, Dean used his opposition to project strong convictions and toughness. Dean's campaign drew the attention of news reporters who evaluate the candidates in the year before the election on the basis of the money they raise, the recognition they gain, their standing in the polls, the endorsements they get, and the seriousness with which they are viewed by their opponents. He scored well in all these categories. That he exceeded initial expectations was newsworthy. He became the front-runner in the fall of 2003, but he did not fare well under the microscope of media attention and opposition attacks. His words and actions as Vermont governor and later as presidential candidate were used against him and raised questions about his readiness for the presidency.[24] Dean finished a disappointing third in the Iowa caucus despite all the money he spent and publicity he generated.

In an effort to rally his faithful backers after his disappointing third-place finish in Iowa, Dean gave a rousing speech to those who had gathered at his campaign headquarters on the night of the caucus vote. His reddening face and primal yell at the end of his pep talk, captured by television cameras, presented an emotional candidate, seemingly out of control. The speech played over and over on the news in the days following the Iowa caucus and mocked by late-night comics raised questions about Dean's emotional balance, maturity, and self-control, three attributes that candidates for the presidency must demonstrate. Unable to resurrect his campaign, he finished well behind Kerry in New Hampshire, lost in Wisconsin, and subsequently dropped out of the race.

Box 2.2   Front-Runner Campaigns: The Failure of Hillary Rodham Clinton and the Success of Barack Obama in 2008 and Mitt Romney in 2012

Hillary Clinton (2008)

Hillary Clinton began her quest for the 2008 Democratic nomination as the best-known candidate and odds-on favorite. A former First Lady and New York senator, she had access to a large base of party leaders and financial supporters who had backed the Clintons in their previous election campaigns. She also had a $10 million surplus from her last successful Senate race that she transferred to her presidential campaign. Gaining endorsements from well-known Democrats, Clinton led Obama by about 25 percent in the public opinion polls throughout most 2007 and seemed well on her way to the nomination.

Clinton's strategy was to use her financial resources to score an early knockout. Victories in the initial contests would reinforce the "inevitability" theme of her campaign. She directed her appeal to voters who had supported her husband, women, minorities, and labor. As the Obama campaign picked up steam, however, Clinton lost the support of African Americans and increasingly men and women under the age of thirty. Her high negatives from her activities as First Lady hurt her among the independent voters who participated in the Democratic primaries.

The Clinton game plan was to play it safe, make no mistakes, and take centrist positions on the issues. She refused to apologize for her 2002 Senate vote to give President Bush authority to use force in Iraq although she was critical of the administration's policy in Iraq. She supported a resolution in the Senate that categorized the Iranian Revolutionary Guard as a terrorist organization. Her opponents hammered her on these votes while the news media focused on her negative evaluations by independents and Republicans in public opinion polls, raising the question of whether she could win a general election.

Obama's prodigious fund-raising, John Edwards's populist appeal, and the news media's penchant for subjecting the front-runner to more critical scrutiny than her opponents countered her campaign's narrative that she would be the inevitable nominee. Obama's win in Iowa and Edwards's second-place finish in that state not only indicated that the nomination was indeed competitive but also woke up the Clinton campaign.

After Iowa, Clinton became more aggressive; women's groups mobilized voters on her behalf. An incident in New Hampshire in which she showed emotion from the pressures of the campaign revealed a human dimension that had been absent in her carefully scripted candidacy. Women responded by shifting support to her in the days preceding the New Hampshire primary. Her victory over Obama, who had led her in New Hampshire public opinion polls following his win in Iowa, gave her campaign a much-needed boost and helped to renew her spirits.

The Democratic nomination campaign then moved into Nevada, a caucus state in which Clinton won more popular votes but fewer pledged delegates, revealing a fundamental flaw in her campaign's strategy: emphasizing the popular vote over the delegate count. There were other strategic problems. By relying on large contributions from an established Democratic donor base, she was unable to expand her fundraising to keep pace with Obama's. Her campaign also failed to develop as large a field operation, particularly in the caucus states that require staff and volunteers to turn out voters. Lack of money and on-the-ground organization forced Clinton to concentrate her efforts in the larger states of California and New York plus Massachusetts, New Jersey, and Missouri, all of which she won. But again her popular vote total exceeded the proportion of the delegates she received, in large part because her campaign failed to focus its resources on delegate-rich districts in these states, many of which had concentrations of African American voters.

Clinton also did not compete with Obama in most of the caucus states that held the first round of their nomination process on Super Tuesday. Of the eight caucuses held on that day, she lost all but one. When the Super Tuesday results were tallied, Clinton trailed Obama by about fifty pledged delegates.

February proved to be Clinton's worst month. After Super Tuesday, February 2, 2008, she lost the five caucuses and five primaries held in that month, swelling Obama's pledged delegate lead to around 150. She also fell further behind in the money race, forcing her to lend her campaign more money just to stay competitive. Her organization began to unravel. She fired her campaign manager. Dissent within the staff erupted.[25] Her advisers voiced mutual recriminations against each other that were leaked to the news media. And her options became more limited. She had to win the remaining large states (Texas, Ohio, Indiana, and Pennsylvania) by a sizable percentage just to catch up, but had much less money to advertise than did Obama. Although Clinton received more popular votes in most of these states, she was unable to substantially reduce Obama's delegate lead.

Behind in pledged delegates, her campaign turned to the super delegates; Obama followed suit and gradually decreased her advantage among party leaders and elected officials.

The front-runner had been overtaken by a more skillful challenger with a popular message and a more energetic base of supporters. The Obama campaign had outorganized, outfunded, and outlasted Clinton's. Obama's strategists used the rules to their benefit. They mastered and advanced the new communications technology. They had defeated the "inevitable" Democratic nominee.

Barack Obama (2008)

Preliminary planning for Obama's presidential campaign began in 2006, right after the midterm elections, when David Axelrod and David Plouffe, the political consultants who had managed Obama's 2004 Senate campaign, met with him to explore the possibilities of a presidential run. Once he decided to do so in January 2007, his campaign advisers set up a small and highly focused campaign concentrating on his critical needs: personnel, money, communications, and scheduling.

Winning the Iowa caucus was the campaign's initial strategic goal. Iowa was important for three reasons: to demonstrate that Obama, an African American, could win in a predominantly white state; to show that Hillary Clinton's nomination was not inevitable; and to prove that an army of volunteers could be identified, organized, and mobilized, using the Internet as a primary vehicle of communications. Obama had to enlarge the Democratic electorate by attracting new voters.

With the caucus a year away, the campaign literally set up shop in Iowa. Obama visited the state forty-four times and stayed there a total of eighty-nine days.[26] During his visits he held up to six events a day. His campaign flooded Iowa with volunteers that went to every high school,

(continued)

(continued)

college, and university to inform students about Obama, recruit in-state volunteers, and generate excitement about his candidacy. The campaign set up three- to four-day training sessions at which volunteers, many of whom had never worked in a political campaign, were given instruction on how to identify potential supporters, mobilize them, and interact with voters. The payoff was evident at caucus night when almost twice as many Democrats turned out than in the party's previous presidential caucus. Obama won 37.6 percent of the vote compared Edwards's 29.7 percent and Clinton's 29.5 percent.

Before Iowa, Obama had not commanded national attention. Thus his victory in the first caucus surprised many of those who had not been following the campaign that closely. In the first nationwide poll following Iowa, Obama surged ahead of Clinton after trailing her by about 25 percent throughout 2007. Obama had ended 2007 even with Clinton in fund-raising but with several advantages going into election year. He had a larger donor base but had received smaller average contributions, so he could go back to that base for more money. A larger proportion of Clinton's contributors had given the maximum amount.

With his victory in Iowa, revenues shot up. In January and February of 2008, Obama took in revenues almost equal to the amount he received in all of the previous year and almost double the money Clinton received during the same period. His campaign was also more frugal in spending than Clinton's.

The victory in Iowa raised expectations for Obama, but the New Hampshire primary, scheduled five days later, presented additional problems for the grassroots component of his campaign.[27] It is harder to enlarge the electorate as much in a primary as in a caucus, particularly in a state that traditionally has a high rate of voting. Clinton had a stronger base in New Hampshire. Obama was also competing against McCain for the votes of independents.

Clinton beat Obama by 3 percent of the popular vote in New Hampshire, but they divided the delegates evenly. Following New Hampshire, the Democratic contest turned to the Nevada caucus, in which Clinton won the popular vote by 6 percent, but the delegates were again divided with Obama eventually getting a majority.

South Carolina, the last primary before Super Tuesday, was critical for Obama. With Clinton expected to do well in the large states, Obama needed a victory in South Carolina to regain momentum after New Hampshire and Nevada. His campaign had been active in the state, visiting barber shops, beauty salons, and college and university campuses. Its goal, to maximize the votes of African Americans and whites under 40, was hugely successful, receiving 55 percent of the popular vote and twenty-five of the state's forty-five delegates.

Going into Super Tuesday, Obama had momentum although Clinton remained popular among the Democratic rank and file. To counter her advantage, Obama used his large and growing war chest to advertise extensively in the large, populous states and compete on the ground in *all* the caucuses. In contrast, Clinton contested only one caucus state, Colorado. The results—Clinton won the large states and Obama the small states—gave Obama a total of fifteen more delegates than Clinton. Not only had he survived Super Tuesday, but his campaign was in a position to extend his delegate lead in February against a Clinton campaign that was becoming increasingly disorganized and underfinanced. By the first Tuesday in March,

Obama held a lead of 150 pledged delegates.

At this point the press's campaign narrative began to change from its emphasis on popular vote to one that emphasized pledged delegates. David Plouffe, Obama's campaign manager, helped this narrative along by convincing the *New York Times* to count delegates in caucus states on the basis of the vote in the first stage of the caucus process even though the actual delegates would not be chosen until state conventions later in the spring.[28]

Although Clinton won the Ohio, Texas, and Rhode Island primaries on March 4, the date on which 85 percent of the Democratic delegates had been selected, she had reduced the Obama delegate lead by only six. Her only hope was to gain the support of most of the 852 unpledged super delegates, a group that constituted 19 percent of the convention. However, as Obama built a lead among the pledged delegates, his campaign launched a public relations effort to convince the "supers" not to reverse the judgment of the people who had already voted, and they did not. Instead, they jumped on his bandwagon.

Although the Democratic campaign continued until all the primaries and caucuses were completed, Obama never relinquished his delegate lead. His campaign had designed and executed a successful strategy. The use of the Internet as a communications tool to identify volunteers, solicit contributions, and mobilize supporters contributed substantially to that success. Although there were unexpected bumps along the way—Clinton's New Hampshire victory, the incendiary remarks of Obama's minister the Rev. Jeremiah Wright, and a few careless ad lib comments by Obama—they did not matter in the end. He won the most delegates and with them, the Democratic Party's presidential nomination.

Mitt Romney (2012)

Mitt Romney began the campaign in May of 2011 as the Republican front-runner. He purposely maintained a low profile, fearing that he would raise expectations that he could not meet, the experience he had in the 2008 campaign. As a consequence, he did less campaigning in 2011, raised less money, and held fewer events during the 2011 phase of the 2012 nomination. He made only 11 visits to Iowa and stayed only 20 days prior to its 2012 caucus; four years earlier, he had made 43 visits and stayed 77 days.[29] He did pick up the pace prior to the New Hampshire primary, however.[30]

Because he was the poll leader and perceived his challengers as weak, Romney focused on the economic issues and pointed to his successful business experience as evidence that he could deal with the country's economic problems. He directed most of his criticism toward President Obama, not initially toward his GOP opponents. Only when polls revealed that he was running into difficulty in the early states did he turn his attention to challengers who seemed to be moving up in popularity. Similarly, the few ads he aired in 2011 were positive and focused on his qualifications for president, although he did run some negative ads directed at Obama's performance in office.

To maintain low visibility he desired when he began his campaign, Romney limited his access to the news media. When he did meet with the press, he preferred structured situations in which he could respond to media questions. He was cautious in his words and activities.

Romney had to share his front-running status with Rick Perry after Perry entered the race in July 2011. A popular governor from a large state, Perry was well known and well liked among Republicans, had solid conservative credentials, and had

(continued)

(continued)

the potential to raise a lot of money. Within a month of his declaration of candidacy, he led Romney among Republicans in the early polls. But Perry faded quickly after committing a number of faux pas in the Republican debates, including his famous "oops" moment in which he could not remember one of the three federal agencies he had promised to eliminate.

After Romney's virtual tie with Santorum in Iowa and his loss to Gingrich in South Carolina, the Republican front-runner adopted a more adversarial strategy in January, using negative advertising to drive home his criticism of his Republican opponents. By going on the attack, he took some of the heat off his own personal and policy vulnerabilities—his support for Massachusetts health care and his decisions as a venture capitalist to streamline newly purchased companies by eliminating hundreds of jobs.

Aside from these vulnerabilities, Romney also had to deal with an image problem. He did not convey warmth or authenticity. After making several careless remarks in the early months of his campaign to which the press drew attention, he stuck closely to script; relied on speeches and responses his staff had written, tested, and placed on a teleprompter; hired a debate coach to improve his verbal and nonverbal responses; and kept the news media at a distance. The campaign realized that Romney's image and his lack of charisma was a problem, one which they had to address during the general election campaign.

Romney's superior financial support and on-the-ground organization enabled him to run in all states, whereas his opponents had to pick and choose where best to concentrate their limited resources. Thus, Romney gained delegates even in the states he did not win. By the end of February, he had built a sizeable lead; by the beginning of April, the race was effectively over. Rick Santorum, the last of his major opponents, dropped out on April 10.

From WAYNE, The Quest for the 2004 Nomination and Beyond, 1E. © 2005 Cengage Learning.

THE NONCOMPETITIVE PHASE OF THE NOMINATION PROCESS

Until the 2012 Republican nomination, the front-loading and compression of the primaries and caucuses had ended the competitive phase of the nomination process earlier and earlier. Conversely, it had lengthened the period during which the victorious candidates need to maintain media attention, improve their presidential image, broaden their issue appeals, and set the stage for launching their "official" campaign at their party's nominating convention. During this noncompetitive period, which could extend to five months, the challenges of staying in the spotlight may be considerable.

Continuing to raise money is also necessary for both major-party candidates, not only for the period prior to the convention but for following it as well since public funding is no longer viewed as a viable option. The expansion of Super PAC activities has become increasingly important, particularly for nominees challenging an unopposed incumbent. Romney had to spend large amounts of money to win the nomination and thus was dependent on Super PACs support-ing him and the Republican National Committee (RNC) to mount a campaign in the period after he won the nomination and before the GOP convention.

If candidates have to contend with an unpopular incumbent of their party, as John McCain did in 2008, they also have to differentiate their style of lead-ership and policy positions from that president. John McCain made much of the fact that he was an independent thinker, a Republican maverick, an image that helped with people who were disillusioned with the Bush administration—independents, moderate Republicans, and some Democrats—but not necessarily with his conservative Republican base.

If they are challenging an incumbent, candidates have to make the case for change. In Kerry's case in 2004, he used the increasingly unpopular war in Iraq to rally Democrats and raise concerns about the president's policy judgments. In 2012, it was the tepid economy, particularly the high levels of unemploy-ment, that Romney highlighted in his criticism of Obama's policies.

For incumbents, the principal task is to reenergize their electoral coalition, which probably frayed during their term in office when the expectations of certain groups and individuals are not realized. They also have to defend their policy record within the context of the country's economic, social, and politi-cal environment. If conditions are unsatisfactory, they will have to explain why they need more time to fix them, even though they may have limited power to do so.

Obama campaigned actively during the interregnum period in 2012. His goals were to raise money, reinvigorate and expand his electoral base, and de-fine Romney to the American people before his Republican opponent had a chance to define himself. He also wanted to attack Republican policy and Republican politicians as responsible for the country's economic woes.

Obama spent much of late 2011 and 2012 raising money; he went to hundreds of private fund-raising events after he declared his candidacy for ree-lection, more than twice the number that George W. Bush had attended when he was running for reelection.[31] The Obama campaign spent $400 million, much of it after Romney had wrapped up the Republican nomination.[32] Of this amount, $114 million was spent on advertising, with the Democratic National Committee and Democratic Super PACs spending an additional $13 million.[33] In contrast, the Romney campaign spent only $61 million on ads and the RNC and Republican Super PACs spent $100 million.[34]

In his campaign rhetoric and advertising, Obama painted his Republican opponent as a heartless business executive and investment capitalist who elimi-nated rather than created jobs, a rich Republican whose policies benefited the wealthy at the expense of the middle class. Obama ran a huge number of television and Internet ads during this period, most of them negative, anti-Romney ads in key battleground states.

A substantial portion of Obama's expenditures were directed toward building an extensive ground and computer-based operation. The campaign established numerous offices in key battleground states, set up training pro-grams for staff and volunteers, and developed a highly sophisticated Internet operation with a website, known as "Dashboard," on which Obama supporters could place personal information, join neighborhood canvassing groups, and learn about campaign activities. Obama targeted eighteen constituency groups in which people could join and receive directed messages designed to increase their enthusiasm for Obama and incentivize them to volunteer to help the campaign. Romney's campaign targeted fewer groups and provided more generalized voter appeals.[35] The emphasis Obama placed on field and Internet activities was premised on the belief that personal contact, initiated early, is critical to turning out votes, more so than media advertising.

Obama's spending prior to the Democratic convention partially offset the financial advantage he had enjoyed during most of the nomination stage. Although his campaign's fund-raising exceeded Romney's by \$38.8 million in the four months leading up to the nominating conventions,[36] Super PACs supporting Republican candidates including Romney were amassing considerably more money than their Democratic counterparts. The Romney campaign hoped that this nonparty group support would provide it with a strategic advertising advantage in the months preceding the general election. It did not, however.

Nonetheless, the gains that Obama was making in public opinion polls contributed to pressure on Romney to reenergize his campaign. His choice of Representative Paul Ryan as his running mate was intended to achieve this goal. Conservatives liked Ryan, who had proposed an alternative budget to Obama's, but he also gave Democrats an opportunity to turn the election debate to a controversial proposal that Ryan had made to convert the Medicare system into a voucher program.

The Medicare issue, combined with information that Romney's taxes constituted less than 14 percent of his total income 2010, reinforced the economic inequity issue that the president—the rich versus everyone else. It also set the stage for the parties to widen the ideological divide. Partisan polarization once again framed the campaign debate.

Launching the Presidential Campaign: The National Conventions

Since the 1990s, national nominating conventions have been highly scripted affairs, designed to show unity and generate enthusiasm. They are public relations spectaculars, made-for-television productions, less newsworthy than entertainment, although they do provide the candidate and party with a launch pad for the general election campaign.

Conventions used to be different. Prior to the movement to primaries and caucuses, conventions determined the party's nominees, formulated the platform, decided the rules, and approved the credentials of the delegates, all in addition to having a gala event for the loyal workers and big contributors. Today, those decisions are made before the convention meets. With a paucity of news, press coverage. As a consequence, news coverage of nominating conventions by the major broadcast networks has declined markedly, as has the number of viewers.

Today, a majority of Americans do not watch much of the conventions. Of those who do, most are inadvertent viewers, surfing the channels and coming to view part of them by accident. Most viewers do not stay tuned for long.[37] Those people who do are partisans; the convention reinforces and energizes their beliefs. It does not usually convert the undecided.

The absence of real news puts the burden on party leaders, convention planners, and the communications team of the winning candidate to design and produce an entertaining show, one that will hold the attention of the delegates, viewers, and listeners. Professionals are hired for the task. They use a variety of entertainment formats: short speeches, film clips that highlight the leaders of the party and their policies, and video biographies of the soon-to-be-nominated presidential and vice presidential candidates. Another component is the pageantry, the banners, the cheers, and the demonstrations on behalf of the candidates who get nominated.

Events are scheduled and sequenced to occur during prime time. The first night is usually reserved for past or current presidents who are completing their second term in office. The plan is to recognize their achievements but not dwell on them. The convention needs to address the issues of the day, the candidates about to be nominated for president and vice president, and the speeches they will make to launch their campaigns.

Most conventions have a keynote address designed to rally the delegates, critique the opposition party and its nominees, and highlight the achievements and objectives of the party as it begins the general election campaign. In 2004, there were two noteworthy keynotes. Senator Zell Miller, a Democrat, addressed the Republican convention, lambasted the Democrats, and praised George W. Bush's response to the terrorist attacks of 2001. Barack Obama, a candidate for the U.S. Senate from Illinois, spoke to the Democrats. His speech articulated the themes he was to stress in his 2008 presidential campaign: unity, hope, empowerment, and policy change. The speech and the reaction of Democratic delegates and the general public to it catapulted Obama into the national spotlight.

The principal address with the largest audience is the nominee's acceptance speech. In the past, some of these speeches have been occasions for great oratory. Harry Truman's address to the 1948 Democratic convention is often cited as one that fired up the party for its fall campaign. Chiding the Republicans for obstructing and ultimately rejecting many of his proposals, Truman challenged them to do so in a special session of Congress. When the Republican-controlled legislature failed to enact legislation, Truman labeled it a "do-nothing" Congress, campaigned against it, and won.

Most modern acceptance speeches reiterate the themes and emphasize the priorities the candidates have espoused in their nomination campaigns. In 2000, Bush stressed inclusiveness, compassion, and morality, stating that he wanted to maximize opportunities for all Americans; in 2004, he lauded the achievements of his administration, beginning with the successful response to the terrorist attacks of 2001, the revitalization of the American military and the improvement in homeland security, and the economic recovery, which he attributed in part to the tax cuts he proposed.

In 2000, Gore differentiated himself from Bill Clinton with the words, "I stand here tonight as my own man." He urged people to vote for him for his policies, not Clinton's. Four years later, Democratic candidate John Kerry, a Vietnam veteran, saluted Democrats and said he was ready for duty. Kerry wanted to demonstrate his credentials for fighting the terrorist threat at home or abroad.

The 2008 nominating conventions contrasted markedly with one another. The Democrats, who held their convention first that year, were brimming with enthusiasm for Obama and confidence that he would win. The Republican convention was more low-key, with vice presidential nominee Sarah Palin getting a more enthusiastic reception than the party's standardbearer, John McCain.

In 2012, the Democrats also seemed to get more of a boost from their convention than did the Republicans. An address by former President Bill Clinton excoriated Republican policies, defended Obama's, and revved up the delegates and the party's rank and file. Democratic enthusiasm following the convention was reflected in polls that indicated increased support for the president and his policies.[38]

Conventions help to inform and educate the electorate. Surveys taken by the Shorenstein Center at Harvard University and the Annenberg Center for Public Policy at the University of Pennsylvania have found that public interest and knowledge increases during the period in which the conventions are held.[39] Conventions also serve to enhance candidate images and clarify policy positions.

For partisans, conventions tend to deepen their positive feelings toward their own nominees, energizing them for the campaign and reinforcing their voting decisions. For independents, their effect, though less intense, still helps color perceptions and judgments of the candidates and their issue orientations, thereby framing the campaign for the general election. Candidates use this frame for projecting their personal images and issue positions.

Characteristics of the Nominees

The nomination of small-state governors by the Democrats in 1976, 1988, and 1992, and a senator with only three years' experience in national politics in 2008, a former movie actor and big-state governor by the Republicans in 1980, and a Mormon in 2012 indicate that changes in the preconvention process have affected the kinds of people chosen by the parties. In theory, many are qualified, but in practice, a number of informal qualifications have limited the pool of potential nominees. Successful candidates have usually been well known prior to the delegate selection process. Most have had promising political careers and held high government positions. Of all the positions from which to seek the presidential nomination, the presidency is clearly the best. Few incumbent presidents fail in their quest for reelection.

Other informal criteria have less to do with qualifications for office than with public prejudices and prescriptions of the most desirable presidential traits. Until 2008, only white males had ever been nominated for president by the two major parties. No woman has received a major-party presidential nomination, although Hillary Clinton came close in 2008. Two women have been nominated as vice presidential candidates.

Personal matters such as health, age, finances, and family life can also be factors. After George Wallace was crippled by a would-be assassin's bullet in 1972, people, including his own supporters, began to question his ability to withstand the rigors of the office. Even the stamina of healthy but seventy-three-year-old Robert Dole and seventy-two-year-old John McCain raised questions in the minds of voters of whether they were still up to the arduous job of the presidency. Today, presidential candidates are expected to release medical reports and financial statements and to respond to potentially damaging personal allegations. That Mitt Romney initially refused to release his income tax returns became an issue in 2012.

Family ties have affected nominations and elections. Obviously, George W. Bush was helped by the Bush name and the affection that Republicans felt for his father. The only other father–son combination to be elected to the presidency was John Adams and his son, John Quincy Adams. Benjamin Harrison was the grandson of William Henry Harrison. Hillary Clinton would have been the first presidential spouse to be nominated had she won the Democratic nomination. Mitt Romney's father, a governor of Michigan, ran unsuccessfully for the Republican presidential nomination in 1968.

Lacking a familiar name and family connection, nominees still benefit from having a happy family life. Only two bachelors have been elected president: James Buchanan and Grover Cleveland. During the 1884 campaign, Cleveland was accused of fathering an illegitimate child for whom he admitted responsibility—even though he was not certain the child was his. Although the dissolution of Nelson Rockefeller's marriage and his subsequent remarriage in 1964, Senator Edward Kennedy's marital problems and an accident in which he drove off a bridge in Chappaquiddick and a young woman traveling with him drowned, and Gary Hart's alleged affair in 1984 seriously damaged the presidential aspirations of these three candidates, Bill Clinton has shown that those types of personal allegations need not be career ending. Similarly, George W. Bush's youthful drinking problem, even his arrest for driving while intoxicated, did not prevent him from becoming president; neither did Barack Obama's use of drugs as a teenager. In recent years, three divorced candidates, Ronald Reagan, Robert Dole, and John McCain, were nominated by their party.

Most of the characteristics of the presidential nominee apply to the vice presidential candidate as well. However, Walter Mondale's and John McCain's choices of women and Gore's choice of an observant Jew indicate that gender and religion may no longer be a barrier to the nation's highest offices.

CONCLUSION

The nominating process has evolved significantly over the years. Although it was developed initially to enable the parties to influence electoral selection, it now permits the partisan electorate, particularly those that are politically active, to affect that selection. Moreover, with broader rank-and-file participation have come expanded appeals and activities by candidates and expanded coverage by the news media. These appeals, and that coverage, affect delegate selection, but they also have an impact on the presidential election and can affect the agenda and operation of government.

When the presidency was created, the nomination of presidential candidates was not considered apart from the election of the president. The development of political parties at the beginning of the nineteenth century led to an informal modification of the electoral system. At first, congressional caucuses performed the nominating function, but as the parties acquired a broader, more decentralized base, the caucus system broke down and was replaced by national nominating conventions. These conventions have continued to operate, although within these meetings, power shifted from national and state party leaders to partisan activists and others who participate in caucuses and primaries. The growth of primaries; the increasing impact of the news media; and eventually changes in party rules, finance laws, and campaign technology, particularly the Internet; have accelerated the movement toward a more participatory nominating process.

On balance, these changes have made the presidential nominations more democratic. To some extent, they have also factionalized the parties. States continue to exercise considerable influence over scheduling, election type, and eligibility rules. One consequence of this influence has been the front-loading of the nominations since the 1970s. Parties have tried to counter this trend with some success by imposing rules for allocating delegates in accordance with the popular vote and by providing scheduling rewards or penalties that affect the size of a state's convention delegation.

For the candidates, the nomination process has become more arduous. They have to spend years preparing and running. They have to raise huge sums of money that takes considerable time and effort and creates the appearance of obligations to large contributors. The also have to hire a large and professional campaign staff and design a technologically sophisticated outreach operation if they are to be successful.

The name of the game is to win a majority of the delegates. Obama's 2008 victory over Clinton reiterated the importance of focusing on the acquisition of delegates rather than amassing a large popular vote. Candidates design strategies based on their reputation, resources, and political connections. Non-front-runners have little choice but to concentrate on the early caucuses and primaries. A win helps demonstrate their viability; a loss reinforces their secondary status. Doing better than expected in the nomination contests gains candidates media attention and dollars, volunteers, and press coverage. But it also subjects them to greater scrutiny from the news media and their political opponents.

Front-runners have more flexibility. They can survive some losses if their organization and resources remain strong. Over time, however, disappointing performances, even with the acquisition of delegates, weaken candidates and raise doubts about their electability. Nonetheless, the system favors front-runners, and in recent years, most of them have won their party's nomination.

Once a candidate nears a majority of convention delegates, the focus shifts to the general election, but the campaign continues right up to the national nominating conventions. In that interim period, the prospective nominees must raise more money, repair any image that was damaged during the caucuses and primaries, work to unify the party, gain the backing of partisans who supported other candidates, and plan for the convention. Nonincumbents also have to designate their vice presidential choice, which is usually done in the days before the nominating convention opens. If they are not incumbents, nominees have to define themselves. If they are, then they have to defend their record. Both potential nominees have to articulate positive themes, criticize their partisan opponent, and project a strong leadership image.

Conventions are well-orchestrated, designed for television and watched primarily by partisan supporters and others who view them, sometimes inadvertently, for shorter periods of time. From the party's perspective, conventions should reinforce partisan loyalties, generate excitement for the nominees, give them an opportunity to address the country, and launch the general election campaign. For the press, conventions provide interviews with well-known politicians and government officials, endless commentary about the candidates, and speculation about the presidential campaign, but very little news. Partisan divisions are magnified.

Discussion Questions

1. Critically assess the strategies of the candidates for the Republican presidential nomination in 2012. What were the principal factors that contributed to Romney's victory? Does the 2012 Republican nomination offer any lessons for future GOP contests?

2. Assess the Obama campaign from the time he declared his candidacy for reelection in April 2011 through the 2012 Democratic convention. Did he run a smart campaign? Did he make good use of his resources? Did his preconvention campaign help, hurt, or not affect his chances in the general election? Describe his principal preconvention themes.

3. Contrast the Democratic and Republican platforms on the major, most salient issues in 2012. Did they differ more than the candidates did on these issues? To what extent did each candidate highlight or de-emphasize his party's platform?

4. Why is the vice presidency considered a stepping stone to the presidential nomination? What advantages do contemporary vice presidents have in their quest for their party's presidential nomination? Do vice presidents have any disadvantages?

Web Exercises

1. Access the website of the Republican National Committee and the Democratic National Committee at http://www.gop.com and http://www.democrats.org. Download and compare their 2012 platforms. Indicate the principal issues on which the parties took different positions, and then explain which of these positions has become public policy. From your analysis, address the question: Do party platforms really matter?

2. Compare the levels of funding for the various candidates who sought their party's nomination in 2012 by accessing the Federal Election Commission's website at http://www.fec.gov or the Campaign Finance Institute at http://www.cfinst.org. Note the amounts the candidates have received and spent. At what points in the nomination process did money seem to matter the most, and at what points did it matter less or make no apparent difference?

3. Now look at the spending by Super PACs by going to the website of the Center for Responsive Politics: http://www.opensecrets.org. How did this spending affect the nomination?

4. Look at the sources for campaign contributions and group expenditures during the last presidential nomination cycle at the website of the Campaign Finance Institute (www.cfinst.org). Which candidates were most dependent on large donations and which ones on smaller donations? Does the pattern of giving support or undercut a democratic nomination process?

Selected Readings

Bartels, Larry M. *Presidential Primaries and the Dynamics of Public Choice.* Princeton, NJ: Princeton University Press, 1988.

Burden, Barry. "The Nominations: Rules, Strategies, and Uncertainty." In *The Elections of 2008,* Michael Nelson, ed. Washington, DC: CQ Press, 2010. pp. 22–44.

Chadwick, Andrew. *Internet Politics: States, Citizens, and New Communications.* Oxford: Oxford University Press, 2006.

Corrado, Anthony, Michael J. Malbin, Thomas E. Mann, and Norman J.

Ornstein, *Reform in an Age of Networked Campaigns.* Washington, DC: Campaign Finance Institute, Brookings Institution, and American Enterprise Institute, 2010. cfinst. org/Press/PReleases/10-01-14 /Reform_in_an_Age_of_Networked_ Campaigns.aspx.

Green, Joshua. "The Front-Runner's Fall." *The Atlantic* (September, 2008). http:// www.theatlantic.com/doc/200809 /hillary-clinton-campaign.

Hershey, Marjorie Randon. "The Media: Coloring the News." In *The Elections of 2008,* Michael Nelson, ed. Washington, DC: CQ Press, 2010. pp. 122–144.

Kamarck, Elaine C. *Primary Politics: How Presidential Candidates Have Shaped the Modern Nomination System.* Washington DC: Brookings Institution, 2009.

Maisel, L. Sandy. "The Platform-Writing Process." *Political Science Quarterly* 108 (Winter 1993–1994): 671–698.

Malbin, Michael J., ed. *The Election after Reform: Money, Politics and the Bipartisan Campaign Reform Act.* Lanham, MD: Rowman and Littlefield, 2006.

Mayer, William G., ed. *The Making of the Presidential Candidates 2012.* Lanham, MD: Rowman and Littlefield, 2012.

Norrander, Barbara. *The Imperfect Primary.* New York: Routledge, 2010.

Panagopoulos, Costas, ed. *Rewriting Politics: Presidential Nominating Conventions in the Media Age.* Baton Rouge, LA: Louisiana State University Press, 2007.

Plouffe, David. *The Audacity to Win.* New York: Viking, 2009.

Shafer, Byron E. *Bifurcated Politics: Evolution and Reform in the National Party Convention.* Cambridge, MA: Harvard University Press, 1988.

Tolbert, Caroline, and Peverill Squire, eds. "Reforming the Presidential Nomination Process." *PS: Political Science and Politics* 42 (January 2009): 27–79.

Wayne, Stephen. *The Road to the White House 2012.* Belmont, CA: Wadsworth/Cengage, 2013.

Notes

1. Humphrey, however, was listed on the ballot in the District of Columbia and won that primary.

2. McCain received 38 percent of the Republican vote in states holding winner-take-all primaries on or before February 5, 2008, but won 81 percent of the delegates from those states, giving him a seemingly insurmountable lead over his primary opponents.

3. Former governors Charles E. "Buddy" Roemer and Gary Earl Johnson did; Roemer received a total of $351,961 and Johnson $308,235 through August 2012. "Federal Election Commission Certifies Federal Matching Funds for Johnson," Federal Election Commission, November 15, 2012. www.fec.gov /press/press2012/20121115_Johnson_ MatchFund.shtml.

4. President Clinton went to great lengths to extend White House hospitality to Democratic donors. Major contributors were invited to sleep in the Lincoln bedroom, drink coffee with the president, and even ride on Air Force One. The Republicans, not to be outdone, also invited large donors to meals with President George W. Bush and Vice President Dick Cheney, gave them

access to Cabinet members and the congressional leadership, and provided VIP treatment at the Republican National Convention.

5. "Presidential Pre-Nomination Campaign Receipts through August 31, 2012," Federal Election Commission, September 20, 2012. www.fec.gov/press/bkgnd /pres_cf_odd_dpoc/presreceiptsM92012. pdf (accessed October 5, 2012).

6. *SpeechNow v. Federal Election Commission,* United States Court of Appeals for the District of Columbia circuit, No. 08-5223, decided on March 26, 2010. http://www .fec.gov/law/litigation/speechnow_ac_ opinion.pdf.

7. "Obama's and Romney's Reports Each Point Up Vulnerabilities as the Campaigns Turn Toward the General Election," Campaign Finance Institute, May 23, 2012. http://cfinst.org/Press/ PReleases/12-05-23/Obama%E2% 80%99s_and_Romney%E2%80%99s_ Reports_Each_Point_Up_Vulnerabilities_ as_the_Campaigns_Turn_Toward_the_ General_Election.aspx.

8. There was 33 percent less news coverage during the competitive stage of the 2012 nominations than there was four years earlier because there were two

contests in 2008 and one lasted until June of that year. The Republican nomination in 2012 was over by early April. Monica Anderson, "This Time Around Less News, from the Campaign," Pew Research Center's Project for Excellence in Journalism, May 17, 2012. http://www.journalism.org/numbers_report/time_around_less_news_campaign_front.

9. "Study: TV News Coverage Helped Sink Santorum Romney Rebounded in Race for Good Press," Center for Media and Public Affairs, April 10, 2012. http://cmpa.com/media_room_press_4_10_12.html.

10. Tom Rosenstiel, Mark Jurkowitz, and Tricia Sartor, "How the Media Covered the 2012 Primary Campaign," Pew Research Center's Project for Excellence in Journalism, April 23, 2012. http://www.journalism.org/analysis_report/romney_report.

11. "Campaign 2012 in the Media: Romney's Press Narrative Gets Better and Better," Pew Research Center's Project for Excellence in Journalism, March 19, 2012. http://www.journalism.org/commentary_backgrounder/pejs_election_report.

12. "The Master Character Narratives in Campaign 2012: Press Coverage of the Character of the Candidates Is Highly Negative and Neither Obama Nor Romney Has an Edge," Pew Research Center's Project for Excellence in Journalism, August 23, 2012. http://www.journalism.org/analysis_report/2012_campaign_character_narratives.

13. Ibid.

14. "Nearly $200 Million Spent on Presidential Campaign TV Ads to Date, "Wisconsin Advertising Project, June 2, 2008. http://swiscadproject.wisc.edu/wiscads_pressreleeases_060d208.pdf.

15. "Campaign 2012: Mad Money: Campaign Ads," *Washington Post* (CMAG/Kantar Media), http://www.washingtonpost.com/wp-srv/special/politics/track-presidential-campaign-ads-2012/?tid=rr_mod (accessed April 24, 2012); "Weekly Ad Spending," *Washington Post* (accessed August 27, 2012).

16. T. W. Farnam, "Study: Negative Campaign Ads Much More Frequent, Vicious than in Primaries Past," *Washington Post*, February 20, 2012. http://www.washingtonpost.com/politics/study-negative-campaign-ads-much-more-frequent-vicious-than-in-primaries-past/2012/02/14/gIQAR7ifPR_story.html.

17. "Spending on Ads; Who's Going Negative?" *Washington Post* (accessed August 27, 2012). http://www.washingtonpost.com/wp-srv/special/politics/track-presidential-campaign-ads-2012/?tid=rr_mod.

18. Hillary Clinton aired more negative commercials but overall still had more positive than negative ones. "Nearly $200 Million Spent on Presidential Campaign TV Ads to Date," *Wisconsin Advertising Project*, June 2, 2008. http://swiscadproject.wisc.edu/wiscads_pressrelease_060d208.pdf.

19. "P2012 Race to the White House," Democracy in Action. http://www.p2012.org.

20. Andrew Romano, "Team Obama Has Quietly Built a Juggernaut Reelection Machine in Chicago. Andrew Romano Goes Inside." *The Daily Beast*, January 1, 2012. http://www.thedailybeast.com/newsweek/2012/01/01/inside-president-obama-s-reelection-machine.html; Amanda Michel, "Obama Campaign to Break Ground with Tech Volunteer Office in San Francisco," *The Guardian,* March 22, 2012. http://www.guardian.co.uk/world/2012/mar/22/obama-campaign-san-francisco-office.

21. "How the Presidential Candidates Use the Web and Social Media," Pew Research Center's Project for Excellence in Journalism. http://www.journalism.org/print/30477 (accessed August 20, 2012.).

22. "Campaign 2012 in the Media: Tone on Twitter," Pew Research Center's Project for Excellence in Journalism. http://features.journalism.org/campaign-2012-in-the-media/tone-on-twitter.

23. Brian Faler, "Dean Leaves Legacy of Online Campaign," *Washington Post*, February 20, 2004, p. A12; and Brian Faler,

"Add 'Blog' to the Campaign Lexicon," *Washington Post*, November 15, 2003, p. A4.

24. As governor, he had called Medicare "a bureaucratic disaster" and cautioned against creating a national health system modeled on it; as candidate, he had advocated strengthening and expanding the benefits of the Medicare program. As governor, he had disparaged the Iowa caucus, saying that it was "controlled by special interests"; as candidate, he appealed to Iowans for their support. When Dean left the governorship, he ordered many of his files closed for ten years; as candidate, he railed against the secrecy of the Bush White House and the president's failure to disclose the records of his service in the National Guard. After the capture of Saddam Hussein, Dean asserted that America was no safer than before he was apprehended, a view that was not shared by most U.S. citizens at that time. As a presidential candidate, he said, "I still want to be the candidate of guys with Confederate flags in their pick-up trucks," a comment that was viewed as prejudicial.

25. Joshua Green, "The Front-Runner's Fall," *The Atlantic.com*, September 2008, http://www.theatlantic.com/doc/200809/hillary-clinton-campaign.

26. "Democracy in Action: Race for the White House, 2008," http://www.gwu.edu/~action/2008/ia08/iavisits08d.html.

27. Although Obama had visited New Hampshire often, his grassroots operation was smaller than in Iowa. http://www.gwu.edu/~action/2008/nh08/nhvisits08d.html.

28. David Plouffe, *The Audacity to Win* (New York: Viking, 2009), pp. 183–184.

29. "P2012 Race to the White House," Democracy in Action. http://www.p2012.org.

30. Ibid. Romney made the same number of visits to New Hampshire in the 2011–2012 election cycle as he had done in 2007–2008.

31. Mark Landler, "Obama Parries Criticism as Fund-Raising Eats into His Schedule," *New York Times*, March 17, 2012, http://www.nytimes.com/2012/03/17/us/politics/obama-faces-criticism-over-time-spent-fund-raising.html?_r=1.

32. Much of the money he had to spend because it was donated for the preconvention period, not the general election.

33. "Election 2012: Ad Advantage," *New York Times*, August 26, 2012 p. 15.

34. Ibid *New York Times*, August 26, 2012, p. 15.

35. T.W. Farnam and Dan Eggen, "Obama's Campaign Strategy Emphasizes Feet on Ground," *Washington Post*, August 24, 2012, p. A4.

36. "Presidential Campaign Finance Summaries," Federal Election Commission, May–August 2012. http://www.fec.gov/press/bkgnd/pres_cf/pres_cf_Odd.shtml.

37. According to the Shorenstein Center for the Press, Politics and Public Policy, most of these people watch only for a few minutes. "GOP Convention Struggles for Audience," *Vanishing Voter*, August 11, 2000, http://www.vanishingvoter.org/releases/8-25-00conv.

38. Jeffrey M. Jones, "Obama Gets Three-Point Convention Bounce," Gallup Poll, September 11, 2012, http://www.gallup.com/poll/157406/obama-gets-three-point-convention-bounce.aspx.

39. Kathleen Hall Jamison, et al. "The Public Learned about Bush and Gore from Conventions; Half Ready to Make an Informed Choice," Annenberg Public Policy Center, August 25, 2000, p. 2, http://www.appcpenn.org/reports/2000/082500_5; "Despite Limited Convention Coverage, Public Learned about Campaign from Democrats," Annenberg Public Policy Center, August 29, 2004, www.naes04.org (accessed September 7, 2004); "Americans Say National Party Conventions Still Important," Vanishing Voter, August 5, 2004, www.vanishingvoter.org/Releases/release080504 (accessed September 7, 2004).

3

THE PRESIDENTIAL ELECTION

Winning the nomination is only half the battle: Winning the election is the real prize. For most candidates, the general election campaign is at least as arduous as the nomination struggle. Directed toward a larger and more heterogeneous electorate, it requires more extensive organization skills but different strategic plans and public appeals to build a majority coalition. For the party, the quest for the presidency is only one election among many, although usually the most important. Like the other elections, the campaign is subject to the party's influence, but not its control. For the voter, the effective choice is usually narrower than in the nomination process, but the criteria for judgment are more extensive. Personal evaluation is not the only factor and may not be the primary one that affects the decision of whether to vote and, if so, for whom. For outside groups, the election provides a public arena in which to affect the outcome; pursue their economic, social, or political interests; and mobilize supporters and convince others of the merits of their cause and candidates.

For the presidency, the campaign has significant implications. Not only does it designate which team and party will direct activities for the next four years, but it also highlights the key policy issues at the beginning of a president's term and the priorities attached to them. It provides the contours of the administration's agenda and comprises its initial governing coalition. Moreover, it indicates the kind of leadership that the public expects, wants, and has been promised. In this sense, the campaign defines the president's leadership tasks and opportunities, whether they be to direct change or simply facilitate it by pointing the machinery of government in the right direction and keeping it running as smoothly as possible.

In this chapter, we will explore these factors and their implications for the U.S. electoral and governing systems. We will do so by examining the strategic environment in which presidential elections occur, the critical factors that must be considered when planning and conducting campaigns, and the meaning of elections for the voters and new administration.

The chapter is organized into three sections. In the first, we focus on the strategic environment and its impact on the election: the constitutional features, notably the Electoral College; the political climate, particularly the partisanship of the electorate; and financial matters and press coverage. In the second, we then turn to the strategy and tactics of the campaign itself. Here, we discuss how organizations are constructed; how appeals are designed, projected, and targeted; and how coalitions are built. In the third section, we evaluate the election outcome from two perspectives: what it suggests about the moods, opinions, and attitudes of the electorate at the time of the vote; and what it portends for the president and the capacity of the new administration to govern.

THE STRATEGIC ENVIRONMENT

Every election occurs within an environment that shapes its activity and affects its outcome. For the presidency, the Electoral College provides the legal framework, while public attitudes and group loyalties condition the political climate. Money and media constitute the principal resources and instruments by which campaign objectives may be achieved. Each of these factors must be considered in the design and conduct of a presidential campaign.

The Electoral College

Of all the elements that affect presidential campaigns, only the Electoral College is truly unique. It was designed by the framers of the Constitution to solve one of their most difficult problems: how to protect the president's independence and, at the same time, have a technically sound, politically efficacious electoral system that would be consistent with a republican form of government. Most of the delegates at the Philadelphia convention were sympathetic to a government based on consent, but not to direct democracy. They wanted an electoral mechanism that would choose the most qualified person, not necessarily the most popular, and one that would not be subject to cabal and fraud—and they had no precise model to follow.

Creation

Two methods of choosing the president had been initially proposed at the Constitutional Convention: selection by the legislature and election by the voters. Each, however, had its drawbacks. Legislative selection posed a potential threat to the independence of the office. How could the executive's independence be preserved if election and reelection hinged on the president's popularity with Congress?[1] However, popular election was seen as undesirable and impractical. Not only did most of the delegates lack faith in the public's ability to make an enlightened judgment by choosing the best-qualified candidate, but they also feared that the size of the country and its communication and transportation systems at the time would preclude holding and effectively monitoring a national election. Sectional distrust and rivalry aggravated this problem because the states were obligated to oversee the conduct of the election. A third alternative, consisting of some type of indirect election, was proposed a number of times but not seriously considered until near the end of the convention after the delegates deadlocked over the voting procedures for legislative selection.[2]

According to the terms of the Electoral College compromise, presidential electors were to be chosen by the states in a manner designated by their legislatures. In order to ensure their independence, the electors could not simultaneously hold a federal government position. The number of electors equaled the number of senators and representatives from each state (see Appendix C).

The electors had two votes each but could not cast them both for inhabitants of their own state.[3] At a designated time, the electors would meet, vote, and send the results to Congress, where they were to be announced to a joint session by the president of the Senate, the incumbent vice president. The person who received a majority of votes cast by the Electoral College would be president, and the one with the second highest total would be vice president. In the event that no one received a majority, the House of Representatives would choose from among the five candidates with the most electoral votes, with each state delegation casting one vote. The Senate was to determine the vice president should there be a tie for second place.

The new mode of selection was defended on two grounds. First, it allowed state legislatures to establish the procedures for choosing electors, but if there were no Electoral College majority, it permitted a national institution, the House of Representatives, voting by state delegations, to decide the outcome. Second, it gave the larger states an advantage in the initial voting for president (in accordance with the principle of representation based on population) but provided the smaller states with an equal voice if the electoral vote was not decisive (in accordance with the principle of equal representation for each of the states). These compromises placated sufficient interests to get the proposal adopted and subsequently ratified as part of the Constitution.

Evolution

Only in the first two elections, when Washington was the unanimous choice, did the electors exercise a nonpartisan and presumably independent judgment. Within ten years from the time the federal government began to operate, a party system had developed, and the electors became its political captives. Nominated by their party, they were expected to vote for its candidates, which almost all of them did. In 1800, all the Democratic-Republican electors voted for Thomas Jefferson and Aaron Burr. Because the procedure for casting ballots did not permit electors to distinguish between their presidential and vice presidential choices, the election ended in a tie, which the House of Representatives, controlled by the Federalist Party at the time, resolved by choosing Jefferson. To avoid such a problem in the future, the Constitution was amended in 1804 to provide for separate votes for president and vice president.

The next nondecisive presidential election occurred in 1824, when four candidates received votes for president: Andrew Jackson (99 votes), John Q. Adams (84), William Crawford (41), and Henry Clay (37). The new amendment, the twelfth, required the House of Representatives to choose from among the three candidates with the most electoral votes, not the top five as the Constitution had originally prescribed. Eliminated from the competition was Henry Clay, the most powerful member of the House and its speaker. Clay then threw his support to Adams, who won. It was alleged that Clay did so in exchange for an appointment as secretary of state, a charge that Adams vigorously denied. After he became president, however, Adams nominated Clay to be the secretary of state, a position that in those days was considered a stepping stone to the presidency.

Jackson, the winner of the popular vote in 1824, was outraged at the turn of events and urged the abolition of the Electoral College. Although his claim of a popular mandate is open to question,[4] opposition to the state legislatures choosing the electors mounted, and a gradual democratization of the election process occurred. An increasing number of states began to elect their electors directly, and by 1832, only South Carolina retained the practice of having its legislature choose them.

There was also a trend toward the election of the entire slate of electors. In the past, some states had chosen them within legislative districts. Choosing the entire slate of electors on an at-large basis produced a bloc of votes. Whichever candidate received the most popular votes in a state got all of its electoral votes. This winner-take-all method of voting had two principal effects: It maximized the state's voting power, but it also created the possibility of a disparity between the popular and the electoral votes in the nation as a whole. Thus, it became possible for the candidate with the most popular votes to lose in the Electoral College.

The next nonplurality winner was elected in 1876. In the presidential election of that year, Democrat Samuel J. Tilden received 250,000 more popular votes and nineteen more electoral votes than his Republican rival, Rutherford B. Hayes. However, Tilden was one short of a majority in the Electoral College. Moreover, twenty electoral votes were in dispute as dual returns had been filed from three southern states. Allegations of fraud and voting irregularities were made.

Three days before the Electoral College vote was to be officially counted, Congress established a commission to resolve the dilemma. Consisting of eight Republicans and seven Democrats, the commission, voting strictly along partisan lines, validated all the Republican claims, thereby giving Hayes a one-vote victory. Tilden could have challenged the results in federal court but chose not to do so.

The next election in which the popular vote winner was beaten in the Electoral College occurred in 1888, when Democrat Grover Cleveland won a plurality of 95,096 popular votes but only 168 electoral votes, compared with

233 for the Republican candidate, Benjamin Harrison. No major disputes, however, marred this election. Cleveland defeated Harrison four years later.

In the twentieth century, all of the popular vote leaders won a majority of electoral votes. However, in 1948, 1960, and 1976, shifts of just a few thousand popular votes in a few states could have altered the results.[5] Additionally, in 1948, 1960, 1968, and 1992, there was a further possibility that the Electoral College vote might not have been decisive because of the existence of strong third-party candidates that threatened to secure enough votes to prevent either of the major candidates from obtaining a majority.[6] The combination of close competition between the major-party candidates and a strong third-party or independent candidacy presents the greatest potential for a nondecisive Electoral College vote.

The first election in the twenty-first century, however, posed an additional problem—voting irregularities in the state of Florida, which put the results of that state in doubt. Without Florida, neither candidate had a majority of the total electoral vote. With Florida, both did. Thus, the Florida vote was critical to the election outcome.

Several issues marred the Florida vote: the machine tabulation of punch card ballots, the validity of some absentee ballots, and allegations of voter intimidation and fraud. These problems, as well as confusing ballots, inaccurate vote counts, and absentee ballots with late postmarks or none at all, were not unique to Florida. They have occurred in almost every national election. In most states, however, the number of disputed votes would not have changed the outcome. In Florida, they could have; the election was that close.

The nub of the controversy centered on the voting instrument itself and its machine tabulation. The issue was whether the ballots and their tabulation truly reflected the intent of the Florida electorate. The most populous counties of the state used a method of voting in which voters were instructed to punch through a perforated spot on the ballot, or "chad." In one county, Palm Beach, the chads were not ordered in the same way on the ballot as were the names of the candidates. The mixed ordering confused some voters who either punched two chads, thereby automatically voiding their vote, or the chad of another candidate. In other counties, the problem pertained to the accuracy of the machine count. Only chads that were completely pushed through would automatically be tabulated. If a chad was left hanging or was simply dimpled, it might not be counted. Democrats contended that the uncounted ballots at the presidential level occurred disproportionately in Democratic precincts, thus adversely affecting their candidates' vote total in the state. They went to court to force a hand count of these disputed ballots. Democrats also tried to invalidate absentee ballots with improper postmarks from counties that had a heavy concentration of military personnel, fearing those ballots would disproportionately favor Republican George W. Bush.

Much legal maneuvering followed as representatives of both sides fought in state and federal courts, as well as in the court of American public opinion. In the end, the U.S. Supreme Court decided that a hand count could not be undertaken without statewide standards to ensure that the rights of all Florida citizens were equally protected. Nor did a majority of the Court believe that there was sufficient time to establish such uniform standards in light of the deadline that the Florida legislature had set for certifying the state's electors. Thus, the tabulated vote in which Bush led Gore by 537 votes out of almost 6 million cast was upheld, thereby giving the state's 25 electoral votes and the presidential election to Bush. A subsequent recount of all the disputed votes by a consortium of news media confirmed Bush's victory; however, had all uncounted ballots from all Florida counties been included, Gore might have won.[7] In the light of the Florida controversy, the possibility of changing the system to a direct election received considerable media attention and public support but no serious congressional consideration.

There were vote challenges in subsequent elections as well, but not of the magnitude of those in Florida in 2000. Moreover, with the possible exception of the Ohio vote in 2004, a state that Bush won by approximately 119,000 votes, the controversies would not have changed the outcome of the presidential election.

Bias

It is quite clear that the Electoral College is not neutral: No system of election can be. In general, it works to the benefit of the largest states (those with more than fourteen electoral votes) and the smallest (those with less than four). It helps the largest states, not only because they have the most electoral votes but also because those votes are cast in a bloc. The smallest states are aided because they are over-represented in the Electoral College. States have a minimum of three electoral votes regardless of size, thereby giving people in sparsely populated states, such as Alaska and Wyoming, more influence than they would otherwise have in a direct popular vote.

In the Electoral College, the states that receive the most attention are those that are most competitive. In most contemporary elections, the campaigns of both major-party candidates focus their attention at the beginning of the race on only about one-third of the states, conceding or claiming the others. As the campaign progresses, their focus becomes even narrower. The battleground states are frequently reduced to a handful of states, which receive the bulk of the advertising, candidate visits, and grassroots operations in the closing days of the election. As a consequence, turnout in these states is usually higher than the rest of the country. In 2008 and 2012, turnout averaged 68.2 and 66.2 percent of eligible voters in the battleground states compared with 61.7 and 59.4 in the nation as a whole.[8]

The winner-take-all system also gives some advantage to groups within the larger states: Latinos in California, Jews in New York, African Americans in the urban industrial areas of the Northeast and Midwest, Hispanics in the Southwest, and Christian fundamentalists in the rural South and Midwest. Part of the opposition to changing the system has been the reluctance of these and other pivotal groups to give up what they perceive as their competitive edge.

The Electoral College works to the detriment of third parties and independent candidates. The winner-take-all system within all but two of the states, combined with the need for a majority within the College, makes it difficult for third parties or independent candidates to accumulate enough electoral votes to win. To gain such votes, their support must be geographically concentrated, such as Strom Thurmond and George Wallace's was in 1948 and 1968 respectively, rather than evenly distributed across the country, such as John Anderson's in 1980, Ross Perot's in 1992 and 1996, and Ralph Nader's in 2000. However, third-party and independent candidates can affect the results by siphoning off votes that would have otherwise gone to one of the major-party candidates. Had Nader not been on the Florida ballot in 2000, Gore would have probably won that state.[9]

Periodically, proposals to alter or abolish the Electoral College have been advanced. Most of these plans would eliminate the office of elector but retain the College in some form. One would allocate a state's electoral vote in proportion to its popular vote; another would determine the state's electoral vote on the basis of separate district and statewide elections. Neither proposal, had either been in effect at the time, would have changed the outcome of recent presidential elections. A third proposal, the direct election of the president, would abolish the Electoral College entirely in favor of the national popular vote.[10]

Each of these proposals would require a constitutional amendment. Although the public favors a direct vote, states and groups that perceive they benefit from the current system oppose changing it.[11] A group, the Center for Voting and Democracy (www.fairvote.org), has proposed an interstate compact in which states agree to force their electors to support the national popular vote winner, regardless of how their state votes. The compact would go into effect when states comprising a majority of the Electoral College agreed to it; by 2012, only nine states, including the District of Columbia, with 132 electoral votes have enacted legislation to do so.

The Polity

As the constitutional framework structures presidential elections, so do partisan attitudes and group loyalties affect the conduct of campaigns and the outcome of the election. Voters do not come to the election with completely open minds but rather with preexisting views. They do not see and hear the campaign in isolation; they observe it within the framework of their attitudes and associations. This is why it is important for students of presidential elections to examine the electorate's political attitudes and patterns of social interaction.

Research conducted on these topics suggests that people develop political attitudes early in life.[12] Over time, these attitudes tend to become more intense, more resistant to change, and therefore an increasingly important influence on voting behavior. Attitudes affect perceptions of the campaign and evaluations of the parties, the candidates, and the issues as well as assessments of those in office.

Partisanship

Of all the factors that contribute to the development of a political attitude, identification with a political party has been the most important. For most people, party identification operates as a conceptual filter, providing cues for interpreting the issues, judging the candidates, and deciding if, and how, to vote. The stronger this identification, the more compelling the cues are likely to be.

The amount of information that is known about the candidates also affects the influence of partisanship on voting behavior. In general, the less people know about the candidates and the issues, the more likely they are to follow their partisan inclinations when voting. Since presidential campaigns normally convey more information than do other elections, the influence of party is apt to be weaker in these higher-visibility contests than in congressional and state elections, but it is still present. In fact, partisanship has highly correlated with the presidential vote in the last seven presidential elections. (For data on some of these elections, see Table 3.3.)

When identification with a party is weak or nonexistent, other factors, such as the personalities of the candidates and their issue positions, will be correspondingly more important. In contrast to party identification, which is a long-term, stabilizing factor, candidate and issue orientations are shorter-term, variable influences that change from election to election. Of the two, the image of the candidate has been more significant in recent presidential elections, due in part to the emphasis placed on image by news coverage and the campaign themselves.

Candidate Orientation and Issue Positions

Candidate images turn on personality and policy dimensions. People tend to form general impressions about candidates on the basis of what is known about their leadership potential, decision-making capabilities, and personal traits. For an incumbent seeking reelection, accomplishments in office provide many of the criteria for anticipating future performance. People make a retrospective judgment when deciding whether to vote for an incumbent seeking reelection. It is a "thumbs-up or thumbs-down" vote. In such a judgment, the past is prologue to the future.

For the challenger, the criteria are slightly different. Experience, knowledge, confidence, and assertiveness substitute for performance and provide a basis for anticipating how well the candidate might do if elected. For both, character issues such as trustworthiness, integrity, empathy, and candor also shape people's perceptions, which in turn can affect voting. Any traits that the current president lacks should be correspondingly more important criteria for voters in the subsequent election. George W. Bush made much of his personal integrity in 2000, promising to model the qualities and behaviors that people believe the president should exemplify in office; in 2004, John Kerry criticized Bush's decision making in his rush to war in Iraq and his failure to anticipate future postwar problems in that country. In 2008, Barack Obama differentiated his character and style with those of his opponent, John McCain. In 2012, he compared his modest upbringing to Mitt Romney's more affluent background.

The policy stands of the incumbent and challenger are obviously important too. Knowing the candidates' positions on the issues permits voters to make a judgment on what the consequences of electing them will be. However, the complexity of many issues, the low level of information and awareness of the electorate, and the fact that a candidate's policy stands may not be clear or may change over the course of the campaign or after it reduces the salience of issues for many people.

Ironically, that portion of the electorate that can be more easily persuaded—weak partisans and independents—tends to have the least information. Conversely, the most committed voters are usually the most informed. They use their information to support their partisanship. Thus, the partisan disposition of the electorate is important because it has a direct and indirect influence on who votes and how they vote.

Turnout

For a country whose foreign policy goals include the promotion of democratic values and human rights, the turnout of voters, particularly in the second half of the twentieth century, has been viewed as a problem by many adherents of a democratic electoral process. Reaching a high point in 1960, turnout declined until 1992; it has rebounded since then (see Table 3.1).

A variety of factors accounts for the gap between eligible and actual voters. Registration requirements are one of them. The more restrictive the requirements, the lower turnout tends to be. Congress has tried to rectify this problem by enacting laws to limit the residence requirement for federal elections to thirty days and to make it easier for people to register to vote. The Motor-Voter bill (1993) permits registration by mail and requires states to make registration forms available at many statewide offices, including the Department of Motor Vehicles. The legislation has helped increased registration, but getting all registered voters to vote is another problem.

Table 3.1 Suffrage and Turnout, 1980–2012

Year	Voting Age Population (VAP)	Voter Eligible Population (VEP)	Presidential Vote	VAP %	VEP %
1980	164,445,475	159,635,102	86,515,221	52.6	54.2
1984	173,994,610	167,701,904	92,652,680	53.3	55.2
1988	181,955,484	173,579,281	91,594,691	50.3	52.8
1992	190,777,923	179,655,523	104,405,155	54.7	58.1
1996	200,015,917	186,347,044	96,262,935	48.1	51.7
2000	210,721,837	194,331,436	105,375,486	50.0	54.2
2004	220,803,686	203,483,455	122,294,978	55.4	60.1
2008	231,229,580	213,005,467	131,237,136	56.8	61.6
2012	240,926,957	219,296,589	129,058,169	53.6	58.4

SOURCE: Michael McDonald, "Voter Turnout: 1980–2012," February 9, 2003. http://elections.gmu.edu/Turnout_2012G.html. (Accessed March 3, 2013.) Reprinted with permission.

The requirement that some states have established for the presentation of government-issued photo IDs prior to voting initiated a new partisan controversy on election laws. Proponents of the legislation argue that it is necessary to prevent fraudulent voting. Opponents charge that it discriminates against social and economic minorities that are less likely to have the requisite identification. These minorities are more likely to vote Democratic than Republican. A related issue has been the shortening of the period during which people can vote in certain states. Shortened hours save money for the states, but they also reduce turnout, particularly for people with job or family obligations that limit the time in which they can get to the polls or obtain absentee ballots.

Longer-term trends, such as citizen satisfaction with, and trust in, government; feelings of political efficacy (the belief of citizens that they can make a difference and their vote really matters); and partisan identification are additional factors that affect turnout. Interest in the election, concern over the outcome, and feelings of civic responsibility affect the proportion of the population voting. Naturally, people who feel strongly about the election and its consequences are more likely to vote than those who do not care or do not feel that voting makes a difference.

In addition to attitudes, demographic characteristics relate to turnout. People that are older, more educated, farther up the socioeconomic ladder, and in higher-status jobs are more likely to vote than people who are younger, less educated, and have lower incomes and job skills. Of these variables, education is the most important.[13]

Turnout has partisan implications as well. In general, Republicans tend to vote with greater regularity than Democrats, given that party's higher age, education, and income levels. Stronger turnout has helped the Republicans counter the Democrats' advantage in the number of registered voters.

Beginning with the 2000 election, both parties and their nominees have mounted extensive registration and get-out-the-vote drives, turning out millions of new voters. In 2004 in the key battleground states, Republican turnout exceeded that of the Democrats; in 2008 and 2012, it did not. The Obama turnout operation expanded the Democratic base, particularly among minority groups.

Electoral Coalitions

It was during the Depression that the Democrats became the majority party. They built their coalition primarily along economic lines, with the bulk of their supporters coming from people in the lower socioeconomic strata. In addition, the party maintained the backing of white southerners, who had voted Democratic since the end of the Civil War.

Today, the Democrats no longer constitute a national majority. The major parties are at rough parity with one another. According to the exit poll in the 2012 presidential election, 38 percent of the voters identified themselves as Democrats, 32 percent as Republicans, and 29 percent as independent (see Table 3.3 for these and other demographic and attitudinal data).

Groups within each party's electoral coalition have also shifted since the 1930s. White southern support for the Democrats has eroded as a consequence of the civil rights movement and the laws enacted to end racial discrimination; organized labor's contribution to that party's electorate has also declined. Similarly, nonHispanics Catholics are not as loyal to the Democratic Party as they once were.

Conversely, Democrats have benefited from continuing support from African American, Hispanic, and Jewish voters. In recent years, the Democrats have also attracted a larger vote from women, particularly those who are unmarried and working, and younger voters aged thirty and under. Democratic support remains concentrated in the cities of the large industrial states in the Northeast, the mid-Atlantic, and the Pacific Coast, although in the last two presidential elections, the Democrats made inroads in the South.

The Republicans were the majority party before the 1930s. During the Depression, however, the GOP lost much of its working-class support and was unable to attract new immigrant groups to its electoral coalition. Business and professional people, however, did maintain their Republican affiliation, as did non-southern white Protestants. Today, the Republican Party receives much of its backing from white-collar workers, small business owners, and the upper income groups. The party has maintained its white support in the Sunbelt and the Rocky Mountain states, but growing Hispanic populations in some of those areas, such as the Southwest, have made previously safe Republican states more competitive. Republicans have also continued to receive the backing of mainline Protestant groups and have gained support from fundamentalist and evangelical Christians. The more regularly people participate in religious activities, the more likely they are to vote Republican. In addition, since 1980, white male voters have given GOP candidates greater support than have white female voters.

Financial Considerations

A third factor that affects the strategic environment of presidential campaigns is money. The high costs of campaigning, which began to escalate in the 1960s with the advent of television advertising, dependence on large donors, and inequities in the amounts of money candidates received and could spend, prompted a Democratically controlled Congress to enact legislation in the 1970s that addressed some of these issues. The Federal Election Campaign Act (FECA), enacted in 1971, set ceilings on the amount of money presidential and vice presidential candidates and their families could contribute to their own campaigns. It allowed unions and corporations, which had been prohibited from contributing, to form political action committees (PACs), consisting of their members, employees, and stockholders, to solicit voluntary contributions to be given to candidates or parties or to fund the group's election activities. The law also established procedures for public disclosure of contributions over a certain amount.

A second statute, the Revenue Act of 1971, created tax credits and deductions to encourage private contributions. It also provided for public funding by creating a presidential election campaign fund. Financed by an income tax checkoff provision, the fund initially allowed taxpayers to designate a small amount of their federal income taxes to a special presidential election account.

These laws began a period of federal government regulation of national elections that has continued into the twenty-first century. The history of that regulation is a history of good intentions built on political compromise but marred by unintended consequences of the legislation and its implementation as candidates, parties, and nonparty groups have circumvented the letter and spirit of the law to gain electoral advantage.

After the Supreme Court held part of the FECA unconstitutional, Congress enacted new legislation in 1976 that set contribution ceilings for individuals and groups and spending limits for the campaigns that accepted federal funds. The law created a six-person commission, the Federal Election Commission (FEC), to implement and enforce the legislation.

With limited amounts of money available, the candidates opted to spend most of it on television advertising. Gone were the buttons, bumper stickers, and other election paraphernalia that had characterized previous campaigns. Fewer resources were directed toward grassroots organizing. Turnout fell.

In 1979, additional amendments to the FECA were enacted to rectify these problems. To encourage voluntary activities and higher voter turnout, the amendments allowed party committees at the national, state, and local levels to raise and spend unlimited amounts of money for party-building activities such as registration and getting out the vote. Known as the *soft money provision*, this amendment, as interpreted by the FEC, created a gigantic loophole in the law, encouraging the major parties to solicit large contributions and distribute the money to their state and local affiliates as they saw fit. They did so in part by granting access and influence to large donors.

It was not until 2002 that Congress tried to stop these activities by banning the national parties from raising and spending soft money. To compensate the parties for the decline in this revenue, the new law, the Bipartisan Campaign Reform Act, raised the individual contribution limits and adjusted the new figure to inflation. The "dotcom" boom coincided with this reform, enabling candidates to raise substantial contributions by expanding their fund-raising base on the Internet. Democrat Howard Dean was the first to do so in 2004. The ability to solicit private funds from millions of donors combined with the spending limits attached to accepting government funds eliminated the public funds option for most candidates, who could raise and spend more on their own. In 2008, Barack Obama raised $745.7 million ($408.7 million for the nomination and $337 million for the general election) compared to the $84.1 million that John McCain received in public support for the general election;[14] in 2012, Obama had revenues of $782 million compared to Romney's $494 million. However, when the money raised by joint committees and the national party committees is included, campaign revenues were nearly equal ($1.1 billion for Obama and $1 billion for Romney).[15]

The second major development in campaign finance has been the Supreme Court's decision in the case of *Citizens United v. Federal Election Commission* (130S.Ct.876 2010) and the emergence of Super PACs in 2012. The Court held that corporations (and by implication, labor unions) have free speech rights that are protected by the First Amendment. They can spend unlimited amounts in federal elections so long as they do so independently. A subsequent Court of Appeals decision held that nonparty groups could also raise and spend unlimited amounts. This decision enabled individuals—friends, aides, and financial advisers to candidates—to establish their own Super PACs. According to the Center for Responsive Politics, approximately $1.3 billion was spent by nonparty groups in the 2012 federal elections, with Super PACs raising and spending about half that amount.[16]

Many troublesome issues follow from the solicitation and expenditure of such large amounts. Some have to do with the burdens of constant fundraising; others concern equity between the parties and the candidates; a third problem pertains to the influence that big donors and spenders have on the election outcome and on elected public officials. The perception that public officials are unduly influenced by the individuals and groups that helped them get elected has contributed to the public's distrust of government and cynicism toward politicians.

News Coverage

News coverage is another factor that shapes the strategic environment. The press reports the drama and excitement of the campaign by emphasizing the horse race. Who is ahead? How are the candidates doing? Is the leader gaining or slipping in the polls?

The need to stress the contest affects which issues are covered. Most news stories tend to focus on those issues that provide clear-cut differences between the candidates, provoke controversy, and can be presented in a simple, straightforward manner. These are not necessarily the issues that the candidates wish to stress during their campaigns or the ones that will confront government following the election. In general, substantive policy questions of what the government should do receive less coverage than events surrounding the campaign itself and the strategies, controversies, and activities of the candidates.

Moreover, much of the "spin" is negative. Sometimes good news is hard to find. According to the Center for Media and Public Affairs' analysis of the evening news on the three major television networks from 1988 to 2004, the Republican presidential candidate averaged 35 percent favorable coverage compared with 46 percent for the Democrat.[17] In 2008, the coverage was even more favorable for Democrats, with Obama receiving 68 percent positive coverage compared with McCain's 33 percent.[18] Obama received more critical coverage in 2012. Pew Research Center's Project for Excellence in Journalism found that "20 percent of stories during the fall period about Obama were favorable compared with 29 percent that were unfavorable (a gap of 9 points). For Romney, 15 percent of stories during this full period were favorable while 37 percent were unfavorable, a gap more than twice as large as Obama's."[19]

Why is the press generally more negative than positive in its election coverage? The answer relates in large part to the definition of what is newsworthy. Bad news tends to merit more attention than good news; unexpected events are more newsworthy than those that are anticipated. The horse race is also newsworthy. Reporting the candidate ahead in the polls is favorable news for that candidate and unfavorable for the person who is behind.

Since candidates give similar versions of their stump speech to different audiences, the speech itself loses its newsworthiness, but deviations from the theme, mistakes, and verbal slips do not. Past private behavior, which may have little relevance to contemporary issues and job performance, also gains considerable attention. The penchant of the press to report offhand comments as news discourages candidates from being spontaneous or even candid. In effect, it forces them to rehearse their words and orchestrate their actions during the campaign to limit the negative fallout.

To make matters worse from the perspective of the candidates, they are usually not given the opportunity to tell their own story in their own words, at least not on the major networks' newscasts. The average length of a quotation from the candidates on national news in 1968 was 42.3 seconds. Now it is less than 8.0 seconds. Television anchors, correspondents, and commentators tell the story of the election, not the candidates themselves.

In addition to the presumption about the nature of news and the format in which it is presented, there is a framework into which news is fitted. According to Thomas E. Patterson, a dominant story line emerges, and much of the campaign is explained in terms of it.[20] The story line in 2000 focused on the competitive nature of the race; in 2004, the focus was more on issues such as Iraq and the war on terrorism; in 2008 and 2012, the economy received the most attention, followed by candidate strategies and the horse race.[21]

Candidates try to affect the campaign narrative by staging events; including sound bites and applause lines in their speeches; and providing film clips, fact sheets, and press releases to the news media. They twitter, use YouTube, and set up blogs. They design ads, including some that never air, to generate favorable news stories, direct press attention to an opponent's weakness, or even confuse other campaigns.

Given the ability of the news media to control the campaign narrative, fit events into a story line, and assess the qualities of the candidates, their impact on the election is considerable; however, the media's influence also varies with the strength of the voters' partisan identity. The news media tend to reinforce the feelings and loyalties of the party faithful for whom the campaign is too short to change their beliefs or attitudes but long enough to affect their perceptions of the candidates and issues and thus influence their vote. The effects on independents are different. For this group of voters, the media can excite interest, arouse concern, improve knowledge, and, in the end, affect their judgment of whether to vote and, if so, for whom.

THE PRESIDENTIAL CAMPAIGN

Presidential candidates did not always run in a political campaign. For much of American history, personal solicitation by the party nominees was viewed as demeaning and unbecoming to the dignity and status of the presidency. It was not until 1840 that this tradition of nonparticipation by the candidates was broken; that year, candidate General William Henry Harrison made twenty-three speeches in his home state of Ohio.[22] His precedent was not quickly followed, however. It was twenty years before another presidential candidate, Senator Stephen A. Douglas of Illinois, spoke out on the slavery issue as the Democratic nominee, but in so doing, he denied that his motive was to be elected president.

Major-party standard bearers remained on the sidelines until the 1880s, when Republican James Garfield broke tradition by receiving visitors at his Ohio home. Four years later, Republican James Blaine made hundreds of campaign speeches in an unsuccessful effort to offset public accusations that he had profited from a fraudulent railroad deal. Benjamin Harrison, the Republican candidate in 1888, resumed the practice of front-porch campaigning. William McKinley saw even more visitors than did Harrison, but his front-porch campaign paled in comparison to William Jennings Bryan's traveling road show in 1896. Bryan, who gained the Democratic nomination after making his famous "cross of gold" speech at his party's national convention, traveled more than 18,000 miles, made more than 600 speeches, and (according to press estimates) spoke to almost 5 million people.[23] In 1900, Republican vice presidential candidate Theodore Roosevelt challenged Bryan, "making 673 speeches, visiting 567 towns in 24 states, and traveling 21,209 miles."[24] Campaigning across the country was fast becoming the rule; the last of the front-porch campaigns was staged in 1920 by Warren G. Harding.

Herbert Hoover was the first incumbent to campaign actively for reelection. He did so to counter his opponent, Franklin Roosevelt, who crisscrossed the country by railroad, making it possible for thousands of people to see him and thereby undermining a whispering campaign that he had been disabled by polio.[25] Roosevelt's skillful use of radio magnified the impact that a personal appeal can have for winning the election and leading the country.

Television accelerated personal campaigning. However, this medium also created new obstacles for the nominees and their parties. For one thing, the physical appearance of the candidates became more important as attention was directed to their public images. New game plans had to be designed to contain broad campaign appeals that were candidate oriented, projected by sophisticated marketing techniques, and carefully targeted to specific groups within the electorate via cable, the Internet, and various mobile apps. Candidates use their website to announce policy positions, personnel selections, and major campaign events. They solicit funds, communicate with their supporters, air ads, and provide other information about themselves as well as criticism of their opponents.

Creating an Organization

A large, specialized political organization is essential to coordinate the myriad activities that must be performed in any presidential campaign. These include advance work, scheduling, press arrangements, issue and candidate research, speech writing, polling, advertising, grassroots events, Internet communications, accounting, budgeting, legal activities, and liaison with state and local party committees and other "friendly" groups.

For many years, the Democrats had stronger state parties and a weaker national base, with the consequence that their presidential candidates tended to rely mostly on state party organizations. The national party structure has been strengthened in recent years, and the Democratic candidates, like their Republican counterparts, now have established separate organizations to run their presidential campaigns. Nonetheless, both also rely on the state parties to help them turn out the vote.

The George W. Bush campaigns in 2000 and 2004 were models of well-run and well-coordinated efforts, as were Clinton's campaigns of 1992 and 1996 and the Obama campaigns in 2008 and 2012. Tightly controlled operations, each of these campaigns had carefully designed strategic plans and were highly centralized, dependent on pollsters, engaged in targeted television advertising, and capable of rapidly responding to criticisms. In contrast, their opponents' efforts were not nearly as well orchestrated. The losers' campaigns were plagued by mixed messages, shifting targets and resources, and staff turmoil and turnover during periods in which they seemed to be losing ground to their opponents. Tension among campaign personnel—the natural consequence of ambitious people working long hours under constant pressure—is nothing new, but it does tend to be accelerated when the candidate appears to be losing, and candidates, their handlers, and the press search for scapegoats.

Campaign organizations are important, not only for winning the election but also for making the transition to government and providing a preview of the new administration, its personnel selections, and its management style. Ronald Reagan and George W. Bush's reliance on their campaign organizations and their reluctance to second-guess their advisers augured their style in the White House. In contrast, Clinton's penchant for details, his involvement in campaign strategic and tactical decisions, and his constant desire to assess the public mood were also reflected in the way he operated as president. Obama falls somewhere in between. Although he left much of the campaign planning, organization, and day-to-day activities to his principal campaign strategists and operational managers, he was involved in strategic decisions, message development including the drafting of major speeches, and some tactical decision making.

Campaign personnel are frequently recruited for key administration positions, particularly for those in the White House. Many of the senior aides in recent White Houses served in the inner circles of presidential campaigns, as did many of their assistants. However, the success with which these campaign personnel have made the adjustment to White House staff has been mixed at best. Carter and Clinton's aides experienced the most difficult and error-prone transitions, while those of the Reagan, George W. Bush, and Obama campaigns were the smoothest and most professional during their first year in office.

Designing an Image

To become president, a candidate must act presidential by displaying the traits that people desire in their president. Strength, boldness, decisiveness, and conviction are intrinsic to the public's image of the office. During times of crisis or periods of social anxiety, these leadership characteristics are considered absolutely essential. The strength that Franklin Roosevelt was able to convey by virtue of his successful bout with polio, that Eisenhower imparted by his military command in World War II, that George W. Bush showed by his response to the terrorist attacks of September 2001, and that Obama exhibited in his response to the economic crisis contrasted sharply with the perceptions of Adlai Stevenson (in 1956), George McGovern (in 1972), and Jimmy Carter (in 1980) as weak, indecisive, and vacillating. John Kerry and Mitt Romney's images also suffered, in part because of the success their opponents had in defining them negatively: Kerry as a flip-flopper and Romney as a profit-oriented investment capitalist, out of touch with mainstream Americans.

Honesty, integrity, and trustworthiness are also essential attributes for the presidency. Clinton's lack of candor about his personal life, his draft status, and his campaign finance activities, as well as his equivocation on controversial issues, were factors in both the 1992 and 1996 elections that plagued him throughout his presidency. George W. Bush gained stature by virtue of his not-so-subtle contrast with his predecessor on the moral and ethical dimensions of leadership in 2000 and as a strong, no-nonsense, clear-headed decision maker in 2004. Barack Obama also profited from comparison with his predecessor's speaking abilities, intellectual prowess, and openness to alternative perspectives.

Incumbency contributes to a perception of leadership. George W. Bush did not have to prove that he had the requisite knowledge, skills, and experience in 2004 as he did in 2000. But incumbency can also be a two-edged sword if there are national problems that the government is unable to address successfully. The candidate of the party that controls the White House is usually blamed for problems regardless of whether the president could have affected adverse events and conditions; Hoover in 1932, Carter in 1980, and G. H. W. Bush in 1992 are examples. Romney tried unsuccessfully to make that case against Obama in 2012.

Presidents also tend to receive more credit for good times than they deserve. In their campaigns for reelection, incumbents emphasize that they have done well but that there is more to do, and that their steady hand and experience are required. They play on the public's fear of the unknown and scare the electorate about what their opponents might do if elected.

Challengers usually face the more difficult task. Not only must they make a case against the incumbent, but they also must appear presidential when doing so, even without a presidential podium. This is why campaign debates are usually more important to challengers than incumbents. By appearing on the same stage as their more experienced opponents, they can seem to be their equals.

Projecting a Partisan Appeal

Presidential images are usually set within a partisan context. Since the 1930s, Democratic candidates have traditionally clothed themselves in the garb of their party by stressing the "bread and butter" economic issues—jobs, wages, and benefits—that lay at the core of their New Deal electoral coalition. As long as the Republicans were the smaller of the two major parties, their candidates for the presidency did not emphasize partisanship, preferring instead to stress their own personal qualifications and foreign policy and national security issues. Since 1980, however, Republican candidates have not shied away from their partisan affiliation, although in 2008 McCain and his running mate, Sarah Palin, tried to distance themselves from the policies and actions of the unpopular Bush administration.

Republican candidates also have emphasized traditional "family values," code words for conservative social positions such as prayer in schools and opposition to abortion and same-sex marriages. In 1992 and 1996, the Clinton campaign effectively countered this Republican imagery by taking policy positions that promoted family and community values, personal safety, and a less intrusive role for government. George W. Bush adopted the same strategic approach as Clinton in 2000, emphasizing his "compassionate conservatism" to counter the Democrats' emphasis on issues such as education, health care, and Social Security. In 2004, Bush reverted to more traditional Republican stands, stressing moral values, support for faith-based groups performing community service, and his own religious beliefs in appealing to his Christian fundamentalist base. In 2008 and 2012, social issues were not as salient as economic ones.

Naturally, candidates can be expected to raise questions about their opponents. These questions assume particular importance if the public's initial impression of a candidate is fuzzy, as it tends to be with challengers as compared to incumbents. When Republican polls revealed Governor Michael Dukakis's imprecise image in 1988, Vice President Bush, the GOP candidate, was advised to take advantage of this situation by defining Dukakis in ways that would discredit him. George W. Bush and his Republican backers adopted a similar successful strategy toward John Kerry in 2004, as did Barack Obama toward Mitt Romney in 2012.

Emphasizing the negative is a strategy based on the premise that the higher the negative perceptions of a candidate, the less likely that candidate will be to win. Lee Atwater, architect of this strategy, put it this way: "When I first got into politics, I just stumbled across the fact that candidates who went into an election with negatives higher than 30 or 40 points just inevitably lost."[26]

Clinton put a new twist on this strategy in 1996. Rather than putting a negative spin on Bob Dole's personal traits, which might bring attention to the president's own character weaknesses, he stressed Dole's positions on issues, painting his Republican opponent as "Mr. No," a senator who opposed practically every popular program including Medicare, family leave, and education. Dole countered, but with character ads that raised questions about Clinton's personal integrity and behavior. Clinton's issue-oriented ads seemed informative, whereas Dole's personal attacks were perceived by voters as more negative. This perception worked to reinforce Clinton's depiction of Dole as mean-spirited.

Negative campaigning has increased in recent presidential elections. (See pages 83–84 for a discussion of negative advertising.)

Building a Winning Coalition

In addition to creating a presidential image, designing a basic appeal, and criticizing the opponents and their party, candidates need to pull together a winning coalition. They need to target appeals and messages to potentially receptive voters. In the process, they must consider their political bases of support as well as the geographic foundations of the Electoral College. The goal is to build a coalition that wins a majority of the electoral votes, not necessarily a huge popular victory. For both parties, this goal translates into three operational strategies: rekindle partisan loyalty, generate an appeal to independents, and turn out a sizable base. Early and absentee voting is used to secure that vote whenever possible.

During the nomination process, candidates aim their message at party activists; during the general election, they usually moderate that appeal to reach out to other voters. In 2004, Bush adopted a different strategy. He directed his appeal to his partisan coalition to maximize Republican turnout. Although neither presidential candidate in 2008 stressed partisanship, those themes reemerged in 2012, with the Democrats stressing policies designed to help the middle class while Republicans emphasized the free enterprise system as an antidote to the nation's economic travails. The focus on partisanship in contemporary campaigns reflects the country's deep political divide and the increasing influence of strong partisan loyalties on turnout and voting.

In addition to group appeals, campaigns have a geographic thrust, which must be consistent with building an Electoral College majority. In the last three decades, both major-party candidates have focused on the most competitive states. The key is winning at least 270 electoral votes rather than a large popular vote victory.

Media Tactics

Campaign organizations work very hard to influence the news coverage they receive. Speeches are scripted and events staged with television in mind. Satellite broadcasting has made it possible for campaign press secretaries to give local newspaper reporters, radio, and television stations more direct access to the candidates. Interviews conducted by the local press and entertainment/ talk-show hosts are apt to be less hostile than those conducted by the national reporters covering the campaign.

Campaigns are designed for maximum public impact. Symbols are used to convey images; themes are presented on a weekly or biweekly basis. Press releases, advertisements, and speeches are carefully synchronized to reinforce a candidate's appeal. Even seemingly off-the-cuff remarks are usually prepared and timed to contribute to the overall thematic effect. Leaks are intended to alert the news media to unfavorable information about one's opponent.

Successful presidential campaigns try to control their own narrative. In 1992, Clinton constantly talked about the economy and the need for change; in 1996, he reiterated his priorities: the economy, education, health, and the environment. In 2000, Bush stressed moral issues and his compassionate conservative policies. In 2004, he redefined himself as a war president and harped on the terrorist threat. Obama ran on a theme of change in 2008 that was so powerful that his opponent had to stress his change orientation as well; in 2012, Obama promised to stay the course while his opponent emphasized the need for change.

Presidential candidates may face difficulties in controlling the pace and tone of the campaign, however.

1. Unexpected actions and events frequently take center stage, preempting their planned activities and themes. The economic meltdown in September 2008 is a case in point. There was little that McCain could do about the salience of these conditions, although he tried to turn attention from the economy to Obama's judgment and lack of experience.

2. They may have trouble getting their message across. Remarks may be edited for the sake of the story. Moreover, candidates can be interrupted, their comments interpreted, their policies evaluated, and any mistakes or gaffes highlighted. The national press corps is usually confrontational, which is why candidates like to avoid tough interviews and press conferences in favor of folksy talk shows and local reporters. But sometimes limiting press access backfires when reporters question a campaign's commentary and choreography or reject reporting them entirely in favor of less flattering incidents.

3. Candidates even have trouble controlling the message of advertising that is aired on their behalf. By law, they cannot coordinate their campaigns with nonparty groups. The amount of money raised and spent by these groups, especially Super PACs in 2012, increased the proportion of advertising, not subject to the candidate's control.

Debates

A format that has become part of the American political tradition is the presidential debate. More than any other single campaign event, presidential debates gain public attention. It is estimated that more than half the adult population in the United States watched all of the 1960 Kennedy–Nixon debates, which were the first between presidential candidates, and almost 90 percent of the electorate saw one of them. Even though less attention has been riveted on any single debate since then, the debates still attract millions of television viewers.[27] An average of 57.4 million people saw one or more of the presidential debates in 2008, and 69.9 million saw all or part of the vice presidential one; in 2012, the average viewership during the presidential debates was 64 million while 51.4 million saw the vice presidential one.[28]

Meticulous planning goes into each debate. Campaign representatives study the locations, try to anticipate questions, and brief and rehearse the candidates. Mock studios are built and the debate environment simulated. In 1980, this elaborate preparation took a bizarre twist when the staff readying Ronald Reagan for his debate with President Jimmy Carter obtained briefing material prepared for Carter by his aides. Knowing the questions that Carter anticipated and the answers he had been advised to give helped Reagan counter his opponent's comments and responses.[29]

Candidates have viewed presidential debates as vehicles for improving their images and damaging those of their opponents. They seek to establish their leadership credentials and critique those of their rivals. Strategic goals of most candidates during debates are to overcome any negative perceptions that have developed about them and, at the same time, to magnify their positive attributes. For challengers the task is to demonstrate presidential qualities: knowledge of the issues, clarity and confidence in the policies they propose, and empathy for the problems people feel. They need to present a demeanor that makes Americans feel comfortable with them.

For incumbents, the goals are different: to raise doubts about their opponent's skills, judgment, and experience; defend their policies and actions; and trumpet their achievements. Unless there is a high level of public dissatisfaction, being incumbent is an advantage. People generally are more comfortable with known than unknown qualities.

Once the debate ends, the news media are preoccupied with evaluating it. They use the winner/loser format when doing so, fitting the debate results into the dominant horse race story. Knowing that they will do this, the campaigns try to affect their press evaluation through the use of "spin doctors," luminaries who speak to the media following the debate.

Few voters admit that the debates actually changed their vote. More often than not, debates reinforce the views and perceptions that those in the viewing and listening audience bring to the debate. People inclined toward a particular party tend to see that party's nominees in a more favorable light than their opponents. Even a weak performance, such as Ronald Reagan's in his first debate with Walter Mondale in 1984, George W. Bush's in his first debate with John Kerry, or Barack Obama's in his first with Mitt Romney, did not seem to change the voting decisions of their partisan supporters.

Debates tend to be decisive only in very close elections in which influencing a relatively small proportion of voters can make a difference. In 1960, 1976, and again in 2000, the debates may have affected who won and who lost. In 1980, the single presidential debate probably contributed to Reagan's margin of victory. In 1992, they may have elevated Perot's vote; in 2000, they helped

Bush; and in 2008, Obama was able to allay the concerns that he lacked experience, was more style than substance, and had the requisite leadership skills; in 2012, the first debate helped solidify Romney's Republican vote and gave him a slight boost among independents, one that he was unable to extend.

Political Commercials

Presidential campaigns have used television advertising since 1952. To be effective, ads must seem truthful, convey relevant information, and engage viewers. Ads reinforce political beliefs, particularly for partisans. For those with weaker partisan ties or none at all, ads can shape perceptions about candidates, their parties, and the merits of their issue positions. However, since the absence of strong partisan ties is usually associated with less interest in politics and elections, ads need to be repetitive to make the point stick in most people's minds.

Positive ads describe the merits of a particular candidate and/or policy position. They tend to be aired at the beginning of campaigns when the public is less knowledgeable about the candidates and the issues. Designed to highlight a candidate's strongest attributes, they also try to convey warm feelings, patriotic emotions, and optimism, and frequently project a larger-than-life image of the person running for office.

Candidates work as hard to destroy their opponent's image as they do to build their own. They do this through contrast advertising, which provides them with favorable comparisons. Contrast ads are usually drawn sharply so that the judgment of who is the better candidate or what is the stronger policy position is obvious. Negative ads raise the attention level. They often contain both evocative arguments as well as emotional appeals: outrage, exaggeration, even anger are used.

One of the most famous negative ads, "Daisy Girl," pictured a cute little girl standing in a meadow and plucking petals from a daisy. Counting softly to herself, she reached eleven, her voice faded, and a stern-sounding announcer began counting down from nine. At zero, there was an explosion, the little girl disappeared, and a mushroom-shaped cloud covered the screen. President Lyndon Johnson was then heard saying: "These are the stakes, to make a world in which all of God's children can live or go into the dark. The stakes are too high for you to stay at home." The ad ended with a plea to vote for Lyndon Johnson on Election Day.[30]

In 1988, negative ads themselves became a campaign issue when a PAC supporting George H. B. Bush showed a picture of Willie Horton, a convicted murderer who stabbed a man and raped his female companion while on a furlough from a Massachusetts prison. Amid gruesome commentary about Horton's criminal acts, the ad contrasted the positions of Dukakis and Bush on crime, much to Dukakis's disadvantage. This ad was particularly controversial because it had racial overtones. Horton, an African American, had attacked victims who were white. Dukakis countered Bush's negative advertising with ads about Bush's negative advertising.[31]

The majority of recent advertising in presidential campaigns has been of the confrontational variety. According to the Washington Post/Katar Media analysis of the advertising in 2012, close to 90 percent of the ads run by the

presidential campaigns were negative, 85 percent for Obama and 91 percent for Romney.[32] Party, Super PAC, and other nonparty group advertising were even more negative, approaching 100 percent.[33] Campaigns usually become increasingly negative, especially in the closing days.

People tell pollsters that they dislike negative advertising, but campaign media consultants believe that such ads "work": They raise questions of character and policy; they create doubts about untested leadership qualities; and they reinforce bad news. Moreover, they turn on and turn out partisan supporters.[34]

THE MEANING OF THE ELECTION

From the candidate's perspective, the name of the game is to win. From the voter's perspective, it is to decide who will govern for the next four years. Naturally, throughout the campaign there is considerable interest in what the probable results will be.

Forecasting Models

Prior to the election, political scientists look at the basic fundamentals that affect voting in the United States. They quantify such factors as the health of the economy, the popularity of the president, the length of time one party has controlled the White House, and the satisfaction of the people and place these data in models, constructed on the basis of past elections, to predict the likely outcome of the current contest. They assume that these fundamentals will affect how voters process the campaign and how they will vote. They cannot predict idiosyncrasies, an international crisis, natural disaster, or even which campaigns will be more effectively run.[35]

In 2000, all of these models forecast a Gore victory with anywhere from 52.8 to 60.3 percent of the two-party vote. He won the popular vote with 50.2 percent of the two-party vote, but lost in the Electoral College.[36] In 2004, all the forecasters predicted a Bush victory, but most of them thought it would be larger than the vote he actually received. The average prediction was 53.8 percent of the two-party vote; he actually got 51.2 percent of that vote. The outcome of the 2008 election was not in doubt given the strong disapproval of President Bush and his policies, the economic recession, and especially the financial crisis that began in September 2008. Most of the political science models predicted an Obama victory with 52 percent of the two-party vote. He received 53.7 percent. The models were close.[37]

Anticipating the results of the 2012 election months in advance was much harder, with a tepid economy, political polarization, and mixed evaluations of President Obama's performance. The forecasters were divided over who the winner would be, and most anticipated that it would be a close election. The median forecast predicted Obama with 50.6 percent of the two-party vote. He actually received 50.6 of the total vote and 51.4 percent of the two-party vote.[38]

Of course, presidential elections in the United States are not decided by a direct popular vote; they are determined by the electoral vote, which is related to the popular vote winner within the states.[39] A few modelers used state-based data in their analyses; most, however, rely on national economic and political indicators.

Public Opinion Polls

There are literally hundreds of election polls. News organizations use them to inform the public. They also lend an aura of objectivity to the reporting as well as fit nicely into the horse race orientation of campaign coverage. Campaign organizations conduct their own polls to determine where and how they will allocate their resources and which of their appeals are working and which are not.

Election polling has occurred since 1916. The early polls, however, were not nearly as accurate as today's. The most notable gaffes in presidential election polling were in 1936 and 1948, when major surveys predicted that Alfred M. Landon and Thomas E. Dewey, respectively, would win. The principal errors in these surveys were that the selection of people to be interviewed in the 1936 poll was not random, and the polling in 1948 was concluded too soon before the election.

These problems have subsequently been corrected. Although public opinion surveys have become much accurate, they only measure opinion at the time they are taken. Thus, the nearer to the election they are conducted, the more likely they are to reflect the final vote. Table 3.2 lists the final Gallup polls in presidential elections since 1960 and the difference between these polls and the actual results.

Table 3.2 Gallup Poll Accuracy, 1960–2012

Year	Candidates	Final Gallup Survey %	Election Result %	Gallup Deviation %
2012	Obama	49	51	2.0
	Romney	50	47	3.0
2008	Obama	55.0	53.0	2.0
	McCain	44.0	46.0	2.0
2004	Bush	49.0	50.7	1.7
	Kerry	49.0	48.3	.7
2000	Bush	48.0	47.9	.1
	Gore	46.0	48.4	2.4
	Nader	4.0	2.7	1.3
1996	Clinton	52.0	49.2	2.8
	Dole	41.0	40.7	.3
	Perot	7.0	8.4	1.4
1992	Clinton	49.0	43.3	5.7
	Bush	37.0	37.7	.7
	Perot	14.0	19.0	5.0
1988	Bush	56.0	53.0	3.0
	Dukakis	44.0	46.1	2.1
1984	Reagan	59.0	59.2	.2
	Mondale	41.0	40.8	.2
1980	Reagan	47.0	50.8	3.8
	Carter	44.0	41.0	3.0
	Anderson	8.0	6.6	1.4
	Other	1.0	1.6	0.6
1976	Carter	48.0	50.1	2.1
	Ford	49.0	48.1	.9
	McCarthy	2.0	0.9	1.1
	Other	1.0	0.9	.1
1972	Nixon	62.0	61.8	.2
	McGovern	38.0	38.2	.2
1968	Nixon	43.0	43.5	.5
	Humphrey	42.0	42.9	.9
	Wallace	15.0	13.6	1.4
1964	Johnson	64.0	61.3	2.7
	Goldwater	36.0	38.7	2.7
1960	Kennedy	50.5	50.1	.4
	Nixon	49.5	49.9	.4

SOURCE: Gallup Poll, "Election Polls—Accuracy Record in Presidential Elections." [updated Gallup source after election http://www.gallup.com/poll/9442/Election-Polls-Accuracy-Record-Presidential-Elections.aspx. © 2009, The Gallup Organization

In addition to preelection polling, political scientists rely on a national exit poll for their instant analysis of the vote. This poll surveys thousands of voters as they leave voting booths across the country. In 2012, 26,565 people leaving 350 voting places throughout the United States on election day were polled. In addition, the exit poll included 4,408 telephone interviews of early and absentee voters.[40] Another source of information about election attitudes and behavior is the National Election Survey (NES), conducted by the Center for Political Studies at the University of Michigan and Stanford University.

The principal advantage of the exit poll is that it provides an accurate snapshot of the electorate at the time of the vote. The large size permits considerable analysis of how various demographic groups voted, what their opinions were on a range of issues, and how these opinions affected their vote. The NES, in contrast, while smaller in number, provides a longitudinal perspective because its sample includes many of the same respondents, who are questioned before and after the election.

The availability of data from the exit poll, which is conducted throughout the day, has been the subject of occasional controversy. In 1980, for example, President Carter conceded defeat on the basis of election day polls his campaign conducted. He did so at 9:30 P.M. Eastern Standard Time, 6:30 P.M. Pacific Standard Time. West Coast Democratic candidates complained that Carter's early concession, reinforced by the broadcasting of exit polling results, cost them their election. Another controversy arose in 2000 when television networks predicted early in the evening that Gore would carry Florida, even though voting was still taking place in the western part of the state that was in the central time zone.[41]

Although the evidence is not conclusive, studies by political scientists suggest that early predictions may depress later turnout but do not appreciably affect the direction of the vote.[42] Nonetheless, these early predictions have been an object of public criticism, a topic of congressional inquiry, and a source of concern. Responding to criticism they received after the 2000 election, the networks no longer report the results of state exit polls before all polling places in the state have closed.

Analyzing the Results

What does the election mean? Obviously, it indicates who wins and who loses—who will control the White House and Congress. With the help of the exit poll and other surveys, it also provides a demographic snapshot of the electorate on election day: Which people voted for which candidates? More than this information, however, in-depth surveys can indicate public expectations for the new president. Is the president expected to change policy, as Reagan was expected to do in 1980, Clinton in 1992, and Obama in 2008, or to continue the policy, as George H. W. Bush was in 1988, Clinton in 1996, and Obama in 2012? The exit polls also reveal public perceptions of the candidates at the time of the vote. In this way, they explain the election outcome.

Take Carter's election in 1976, for example. According to analyses of the exit poll data, Carter won because he was unconnected to the Watergate scandals, whereas Ford, by virtue of his party and his pardon of predecessor

Richard Nixon, was connected to it. That Carter was the candidate of the majority party, came from the South, and was viewed as a highly religious and moral man certainly helped, given the atmosphere that Watergate fostered. However, none of these reasons for winning provided much direction for his new administration.

Lacking an electoral blueprint, Carter pursued policy that divided his Democratic supporters. Adverse economic conditions, embarrassments in U.S. foreign policy (particularly the Iranian hostage crisis), and the president's inability to provide strong leadership doomed his presidency. In the 1980 election, voters looked back at Carter's record and found it wanting.

Reagan won in 1980 for the same reason Carter had four years earlier: The voters did not believe that the incumbent president deserved another four years in office. Reagan was not elected because of his conservative ideology, policy positions, or personal appeal, but in spite of them. Nonetheless, he was seen as having a greater potential for leadership than President Carter had displayed.

Four years later, it was another story. The voters rewarded Reagan for a job well done. The 1984 election was a referendum on Reagan's performance in office. The electorate voted for him then just as they had voted against Carter in 1980. The American people approved of Reagan's leadership and wanted him to continue in office.

The 1988 election constituted still another referendum on the Reagan presidency, although not directly on President Reagan. Vice President Bush benefited from the public's perception of good times and greater national security. Bush had promised to pursue the policies of the still-popular Reagan administration but to do so in a "kinder and gentler" way. Most of those who had cast ballots for Reagan in 1984 voted for Bush in 1988: Republicans and conservatives did so overwhelmingly, while independents gave him a solid 12 percent lead; Democrats and liberals stayed with Dukakis.

Four years later, the electorate made a retrospective judgment; voters rejected George H. W. Bush. In the light of the economic recession, he was found wanting. The principal beneficiary of this anti-incumbency vote was Bill Clinton. Aided by Ross Perot, who siphoned votes from Bush by appealing to independents and, to a lesser extent, Republicans, Clinton won 69 percent of the Electoral College vote but only 43 percent of the popular vote, a very thin "mandate" for the magnitude of the policy changes he had promised. When combined with the slow and unsteady start of his administration, this fragile mandate proved to be insufficient for achieving many of his major policy objectives.

By 1996, with the economy stronger, a lower crime rate, and no major national security threat, Clinton won reelection easily. The electorate evaluated conditions at the end of first term favorably. They also saw him as more capable of understanding and handling the challenges of the 1990s and, in his own words, "building a bridge to the twenty-first century" than either of his opponents, Senator Robert Dole or Reform Party candidate H. Ross Perot.

Although the 2000 election could have been a referendum on the Clinton presidency, it was not, in large part because of Vice President Gore's decision to run as his own man, not on the basis of his contributions and experience as

Clinton's vice president. Gore emphasized his policy and personal differences with Governor George W. Bush. This emphasis turned out to be a poor strategic decision. The exit poll in 2000 showed that Clinton's job approval and the strong economy would have been more helpful to Gore than were his own liberal policy views.

In 2000, the electorate was evenly divided. The major parties remained at parity with one another. Partisans overwhelmingly supported their party's ticket, whereas independents split almost evenly between Bush and Gore. Core groups within each party's traditional electoral coalition also voted in record proportions and along party lines. With a few minor exceptions, the same divisions in the electorate were evident in 2004 as was the geographic breakdown in the Electoral College. The only states to reverse their vote in 2004 were New Hampshire, New Mexico, and Iowa.

The election of 2008, however, provided a very different story. Barack Obama was the first Democratic candidate in 32 years to receive a majority of the popular vote. He also redrew the Electoral College map, winning states in the South, Southwest, and Midwest that had previously voted Republican at the presidential level. His effective grassroots operation also turned out record numbers of Democratic voters. Obama won traditional Democratic groups by large margins: African Americans (91 percent), Hispanics (67 percent), and labor union households. He increased the gender and age gaps to the Democrats' advantage.

Similar voter patterns reemerged in 2012, although Obama's overall support declined. A deep partisan divide remained within the American polity, with over 90 percent of party identifiers voting for their party's presidential and vice presidential candidates. Gender, racial, and ethnic differences continued, with women and minorities supporting Obama and men and whites backing Romney. Age, income, and religious trends also persisted. People in the older and higher income groups gave proportionately more support to Romney, as did voters who were more active within their religious communities. However, the proportion of the religious cohort within the electorate declined slightly while the percentage of individuals identifying themselves as secular or nonregular churchgoers increased.

Obama also received more support than Romney from the groups that were least educated (no high school diploma) and most educated (postgraduate degrees). The voting behavior of those with less education was probably influenced by their lower socioeconomic position, while the most educated may have had a more sophisticated understanding of the complexity of the country's economic problems and the limitations on the president's ability to improve them quickly. In the end, Obama's vote reflected his job approval rating, which was 53 percent, the same percent that approved George W. Bush's performance as president when he was reelected in 2004.

The bottom line in 2012 was that the changing demographics of the U.S. population, the increasing multiethnicity in the electorate favored the Democrats; moreover, the Obama campaign was able to turn out young and minority voters as a slightly higher level than in the past (see Table 3.3).

Table 3.3 Portrait of the American Electorate, 2000–2012

Year	2000		2004		2008		2012	
Candidates	Bush	Gore	Bush	Kerry	Obama	McCain	Obama	Romney
Total Vote^	48	48	50	49	53	46	51	48
47 Men	53	42	54	45	49	48	45	52
53 Women	43	54	47	52	56	43	55	44
72 White	54	42	57	42	43	55	39	59
13 Black	9	90	11	89	95	4	93	6
10 Hispanic	35	62	42	55	67	32	71	27
3 Asian	41	55	41	59	62	35	73	26
60 Married	53	44	56	43	47	52	42	56
41 Unmarried	38	57	40	59	65	33	62	35
19 18–29	46	48	44	54	66	32	60	36
27 30–44	49	48	51	47	52	46	52	45
38 45–64	49	48	50	49	50	49	47	52
16 65 & Older	47	51	53	46	45	53	44	56
3 Not High School	38	59	49	50	63	35	64	35
21 High School Grad.	49	48	51	48	52	46	51	48
29 Some College	51	45	53	46	51	47	49	48
29 College Grad.	51	45	51	47	50	48	47	51
18 Postgraduate	44	52	43	55	58	40	55	42
53 Protestant/Other Christian	56	42	58	41	45	54	42	57
25 Catholic	47	50	51	48	54	45	50	48
2 Jewish	19	79	24	76	78	21	69	30
26 Born Again/Fundamentalists	80	18	77	22	24	74	21	78
18 Union Household	37	59	39	60	59	39	58	40

Under $15,000	37	57	36	63	73	25	35	63
20 $15,000–$29,999*	41	54	41	58	60	37	42	56
21 $30,000–$49,999	48	49	48	51	55	43		
$50,000–$74,999	51	46	55	44	48	49	52	46
31 $75,000–$99,999*	52	45	53	46	51	48		
$100,000–$149,999	54	43	56	43	48	51		
21 $150,000–$199,999*					48	50	54	44
7 $200,000 (& over)*					52	46	54	44
25 Better Today	36	61	79	20	37	60	15	84
41 Same Today	60	35	48	50	45	53	40	58
33 Worse Today	63	33	19	80	71	28	80	18
32 Republican	91	8	93	7	9	90	93	6
29 Independent	47	45	47	50	52	44	45	45
38 Democrat	11	86	10	89	89	10	7	92
25 Liberal	13	80	13	86	89	10	11	86
41 Moderate	44	52	44	55	60	39	41	56
35 Conservative	81	17	83	16	20	78	82	17
60 Work Fulltime+	48	49	52	46	55	44	49	49
40 Do Not Work Fulltime	48	47	49	50	50	48	45	53
53 Approve Incumbent's Performance	20	77	90	9	10	89	9	89

^ Remaining percentage for other candidates

*Income breakdown in 2012 was as follows: Under $30,000; $30,000–$49,999; $50,000–$99,000; $100,000–$199,999; $200,000–$249,999; $250,000 and over.

+Question in 2008 was: Do you work fulltime for pay?

SOURCE: 2012 Exit Poll, Edison Media Research for the National Election Pool as reported in New York Times, November 11, 2012, p. SR 7. http://www.nytimes.com/interactive/2012/11/10/opinion/20101104_POLL-MARSH.html?ref=sunday-review and Fox News http://www.foxnews.com/politics/elections/2012-exit-poll (accessed November 8, 2012). Data for 2012 were collected by Edison Research for the National Election Pool; in 2008 and 2004, the exit poll was conducted by Edison/Mitofsky.

Assessing the Mandate[43]

Even when the vote has been very close and the judgment of the electorate mixed, the campaign still provides the agenda for governing. Kennedy pledged to get the country moving again in 1960; Johnson fashioned much of his Great Society and civil rights legislation from his 1964 campaign; Nixon promised to bring a divided nation together in 1968 and keep it together in 1972; and Carter, in the aftermath of Watergate, said that his would be an honest, open, and responsive presidency in contrast to the imperial and seemingly corrupt style of his predecessor. In 1980, Reagan urged Americans to return to their traditional values of economic individualism and political freedom; in 1984, he promised to continue his strong leadership at home and abroad. His vice president, George H. W. Bush, said he would continue Republican policies of less government, lower taxes, and a strong military. Clinton pledged to stimulate the economy, reduce the deficit, cut middle-class taxes, reform health care, and change welfare "as we know it" in 1992. Four years later, he promised to balance the budget without hurting education, the environment, or the Medicare and Social Security systems.

In 2000, George W. Bush said he would reform education, revitalize the military, cut taxes, and pursue a foreign policy based on U.S. national security interests and democratic values. In 2004, he emphasized the continuing war against terrorism plus domestic priorities that had to be shelved after the 2001 attacks: partial privatization of Social Security, tort reform, tax simplification, and a national energy policy.

In 2008, Obama called for change in policy and politics. He advocated that government serve as a positive force, providing opportunities for those who needed them the most. He also railed against the strident, ideological partisanship that had divided the country since the 1980s. Four years later, he promised to continue the progress he had made, protect the middle class, and reduce the budget deficit by increasing tax revenue and keeping the lid on government spending.

Converting the Electoral Coalition for Governance

Not only does the selection process inflate performance expectations and create a set of diverse policy goals, but it also may lessen the president's power to achieve them. The transition from a winning electoral coalition to a successful governing coalition has become much more arduous. The growing power of congressional party leaders, particularly in the House of Representatives; autonomous state and congressional electoral systems; and the personalization of the election process have left presidents with fewer dependable allies, particularly when government is divided.

In the aftermath of Watergate, Jimmy Carter made much of the fact that he did not owe his nomination to the power brokers within his party, or his election to them or to members of Congress. But the same can be said for members of Congress elected with him, and for that matter, governors and state legislators, thereby decreasing their incentives to follow the president's lead.

Bill Clinton found this out the hard way. He ran away from fellow Democrats in Congress during the 1992 election, not wanting to be tainted by the anti-incumbent, anti-Congress, anti-Washington attitude of voters at that time. But he soon found that he needed the support of Democratic members of Congress to obtain his legislative objectives. Nor could he easily or effectively go over their heads to the voters. His inability to obtain congressional support for health care and his other legislative priorities led to the Democratic debacle of 1994, when that party lost control of Congress to the Republicans.

Similarly, George W. Bush claimed that he had acquired political capital following his reelection and the GOP's pick-up of seats in Congress in the 2004 elections. However, on his first legislative test of that capital, the creation of a national director of intelligence, he ran into difficulty when leaders of his own party in the House refused to bring the legislation to a vote because a majority of Republicans opposed it. Embarrassed, the White House had to initiate a full-court, behind-the-scenes press led by the vice president to get House Republicans to support the legislation. The president learned that he could not assume that Congress would follow his lead; he had to cajole and bargain with members to get them to do so.

The economic crisis in 2008 gave Obama more political influence than he might otherwise have had at the beginning of his administration. Along with his large partisan majority, he achieved much of his economic and social legislative policy agenda, but he delegated significant discretion to the Democratic leadership in Congress to draft the legislation. When the Republicans won control of the House of Representatives in the 2010 midterm elections, the environment for presidential–congressional cooperation decreased. Partisan confrontation led to a policy stalemate. Although a last minute deal on the budget and debt in the summer of 2011 prevented a governmental crisis and possible debt default, the political climate stifled new domestic policy initiatives and set the stage for the 2012 presidential election.

In his successful campaign for reelection, Obama was careful not to create great expectations as he had done four years earlier. With a divided government, a polarized political climate, and major financial issues to resolve, he emphasized the need for compromise, as did the Republican Speaker of the House. But deep partisan divisions remained.

Lacking a crisis or strong partisan advantage in Congress, presidents find it difficult to achieve their campaign promises even though those promises are expected to become the agenda for the winning administration as well as the criteria by which that administration will initially be judged. What candidates promise matters even though they may not be able to deliver on all or most of those promises.

To be successful, presidents must take advantage of their opportunities, particularly in the period following the election. They must construct their own policy alliances; they must mobilize their own supporters. They must also reach beyond partisanship to the country as a whole. Those who fail to do so, who do not articulate their goals clearly and effectively to the general and specialized publics, and who do not build political capital, will have more difficulty creating and maintaining the coalitions they need to govern effectively.

CONCLUSION

The system of election designed by the framers of the Constitution has been substantially modified over the years. Theoretically, the electors, designated by states, select the president. In practice, it is the popular vote, aggregated by states, that decides the outcome.

During much of America's electoral history, political parties were the principal link between candidates and voters. They chose the nominees, organized their campaigns, mobilized their support, and stood to gain if they were elected while partisan attitudes conditioned the perceptions and voting behavior of much of the electorate.

Times have changed. Although political parties remain the principal organizing body, nonparty groups have become more active. There are also more campaign professionals and more communications consultants today than in the past. Pollsters, grassroots organizers, high-tech communication consultants, political advertising firms, and computer experts and Internet specialists now plan and run the general election campaigns. These handlers discern attitudes, design and project appeals, target voters, directly and indirectly communicate with them, and mobilize what they hope will be a winning electoral coalition. They utilize techniques of market research to do so, particularly the microtargeting of voters through radio and television, direct mail, phone banks, and the Internet.

Presidential campaigns have also become more candidate-oriented. Candidates now create their own organizations, raise their own money, design and implement their own strategies, and mount highly personalized appeals. Moreover, the electorate's evaluation of the candidates, as seen through the prism of a partisan lens, plays an increasingly important role in its voting decisions. Personalities matter, although they usually do not dictate the results.

The personalization of the presidential selection process has serious implications for the exercise of presidential leadership. It tends to inflate public expectations yet may reduce the capacity to achieve them. Presidents may be more on their own. Their electoral coalitions are not easily converted into governing coalitions, and even when they are, coalitions fray over time, forcing presidents to devote more time, energy, and resources to mobilizing and maintaining public support, controlling the focus of the national news media, and worrying about reelection and their place in history. In short, presidential candidates campaign as if they are going to be directors of change, but when they get into office, they usually find that the best they can do, barring a crisis or an overwhelming partisan majority, is to facilitate the operation of government in accordance with public sentiment.

Discussion Questions

1. Explain some of the ways in which advances in communications technology have changed the conduct of presidential elections, the campaigns of candidates and political parties, and the relationship between elections and government.

2. For many years, political scientists have debated the merits and liabilities of the Electoral College, in particular whether the College should be reformed and, if so, how. In light of recent presidential elections, do you think that the Electoral College has outlived its usefulness? Does the College facilitate or impede the principle of one person–one vote? Should it be changed? If so, how? If not, why not?

3. Design a campaign strategy for the Republican and Democratic nominees for the next presidential election. In your strategy, discuss the substance and targets of the candidates' basic appeals (based on today's most salient issues), how they should project these appeals in paid and unpaid media, and the geographic/Electoral College emphases they should employ. Which of these strategies do you think will be most successful and why?

Web Exercises

1. Contrast the style and content of the major party candidates' campaign advertising in 2012 with that of Democratic and Republican candidates in earlier campaigns. You can find many of the campaign ads from 1952 to the present on the website livingroomcandidate.org (www.livingroomcandidate .org). A more complete inventory from 2000 to the present exists at the Political Communication Lab at Stanford University (http://pcl.stanford .edu/campaigns). Do you think the ads are more or less effective today than in the past? Which type of ads do you think give voters the most information on which to make an enlightened judgment? Are any of the ads harmful to the free flow of ideas in a democratic election process?

2. Try to ascertain how effective the candidates were in 2012 by analyzing the exit poll data available on the websites of major news organizations and also summarized in Table 3.3. Look at the appeals of the candidates in 2012. Which groups were targeted, and how effective do you think those appeals were in influencing turnout and shaping voting behavior?

Selected Readings

Abramson, Paul R., John H. Aldrich, and David W. Rhode. *Change and Continuity in the 2008 and 2010 Elections.* Washington, DC: Congressional Quarterly, 2011.

Campbell, Angus, Philip E. Converse, Warren E. Miller, and Donald E. Stokes. *The American Voter.* New York: Wiley, 1960.

Conley, Patricia H. *Presidential Mandates: How Elections Shape the National Agenda.* Chicago: University of Chicago Press, 2001.

Corrado, Anthony, Michael J. Malbin, Thomas E. Mann, and Norman J. Ornstein. *Reform in an Age of Networked Campaigns.* Washington DC: Campaign Finance Institute, Brookings Institution, and the American Enterprise Institute, 2010. www.cfinst .org/Press/PReleases/10-01-14 /Reorm_in_an_Age_of_Networked_ Campaigns.aspx.

Dahl, Robert A. "Myth of the Presidential Mandate." *Political Science Quarterly* 105 (Fall 1990): 355–372.

Edwards, George C. III. *Why the Electoral College Is Bad for America.* 2nd ed. New Haven, Conn.: Yale University Press, 2011.

Green, Donald P., Bradley Palmquist, and Eric Schickler. *Partisan Hearts and Minds: Political Parties and the Social Identities of Voters.* New Haven, Conn.: Yale University Press, 2002.

Jamieson, Kathleen Hall. *Everything You Think You Know about Politics and Why You're Wrong.* New York: Basic Books, 2000.

Kenski, Kate, Bruce W. Hardy, and Kathleen Hall Jamieson. *The Obama Victory: How Media, Money, and Message Shaped the 2008 Election.* Oxford, UK: Oxford University Press, 2010.

Nelson, Michael, ed. *The Elections of 2012.* Washington, DC: Congressional Quarterly, 2013.

Plouffe, David. *The Audacity to Win.* New York: Viking, 2009.

Popkin, Samuel L. *The Candidate.* New York: Oxford University Press, 2012.

Troy, Gil. *See How They Ran: The Changing Role of the Presidential Candidate.* New York: Free Press, 1991.

Wayne, Stephen J. *The Road to the White House, 2012.* Wadsworth/Cengage Learning, 2013.

West, Darrell M. *Air Wars: Television Advertising in Election Campaigns, 1952–2008.* 5th ed. Washington, DC: Congressional Quarterly, 2009.

White, Theodore. *The Making of the President: 1960.* New York: Atheneum, 1988.

Notes

1. The initial solution to this problem was to lengthen the president's term in office but also make the incumbent ineligible for reelection. Such a plan created additional dilemmas, however: It provided little incentive for the president to perform well and denied the country the possibility of reelecting an experienced and successful incumbent. Reflecting on these concerns, delegate Gouverneur Morris urged the removal of the ineligibility clause on the grounds that it "intended to destroy the great motive to good behavior, the hope of being rewarded by a re-appointment." Gouverneur Morris, *Records of the Federal Convention*, ed. Max Farrand (New Haven, CT: Yale University Press, 1921), pp. 2, 33.

2. The large states favored a joint vote of the combined legislature, House and Senate, to select the president; the small states, fearing that the larger ones would dominate such a vote, wanted separate ballots for each house. After the delegates decided in favor of a joint ballot, the small states proposed that the vote of individual legislators be aggregated by state, each having an equal vote. The delegates rejected this proposal but then postponed further deliberation and subsequently sent the issue, along with other unfinished matters, to a Committee on Unfinished Parts to resolve. Composed of representatives of each of the states, the committee devised the Electoral College compromise, which met with general approval of the delegates.

3. So great was the sectional rivalry, so parochial the country, and so limited the number of people with national reputations that it was feared that electors would vote primarily for people they knew from their own states. To prevent the largest states from exercising undue influence in the selection of the president and vice president, this restriction was included, and it remains in effect today.

4. The most populous state at the time, New York, did not permit its electorate to participate in the selection of electors. Moreover, in three of the states in which Jackson won the electoral vote but lost in the House of Representatives, he had fewer popular votes than Adams. He captured the majority of electoral votes in two of these states because the electors were chosen on a district, rather than a statewide, basis.

5. Thomas E. Dewey could have denied Harry S. Truman a majority in the Electoral College in 1948 with 12,487 more California votes; and in 1960, a change of fewer than 9,000 votes in Illinois and Missouri would have meant that John F. Kennedy lacked an Electoral College majority. In 1968, a shift of only 55,000 votes from Richard M. Nixon to

Hubert H. Humphrey in three states (New Jersey, Missouri, and New Hampshire) would have thrown the election into a Democratic House of Representatives; in 1976, a shift of only 3,687 votes in Hawaii and 5,559 in Ohio would have cost Jimmy Carter the election; and in Ohio in 2004, a shift of about 60,000 votes would have given Kerry an Electoral College victory but not a popular vote plurality.

6. In 1948, Henry Wallace (Progressive Party) and Strom Thurmond (States' Rights Party) received almost 5 percent of the total popular vote, and Thurmond won 39 electoral votes. In 1960, 14 unpledged electors were chosen in Alabama and Mississippi. In 1968, Governor George Wallace of Alabama, running on the American Independent Party ticket, received almost 10 million popular votes (13.5 percent of the total) and 46 electoral votes. In 1992, H. Ross Perot received 19.7 million votes (19 percent of the total) but no electoral votes. In 1996, he received about 8 million (8.5 percent of the total) but still no electoral votes.

7. Dan Keating and Dan Balz, "Florida Recounts Would Have Favored Bush," *Washington Post*, November 12, 2001, pp. A1, A10.

8. Michael McDonald, "2008 General Election Turnout Rates," December 13, 2008, http://www.elections.gmu.edu /Turnout_2008G.html (accessed December 27, 2008); Michael McDonald, "2012 General Election Turnout Rates", December 31, 2012; http:llelections.gmy .edu?Turnout_2012G.html. (accessed January 7, 2013).

9. The exit poll in 2000 found that 69 percent of Nader voters said that they would have voted had he not run. They favored Gore by a 2 to 1 margin. Thus if the national exit poll reflected the judgment of voters in Florida and New Hampshire, Gore would have probably won both states if Nader had not been on the ballot.

10. In a direct election, some plans require that the winning candidate receive at least 40 percent of the total vote. Otherwise, a runoff would be held or the House of Representatives would determine the winner. The only American president not to receive 40 percent of the popular vote was Lincoln in 1860. He received 39.8 percent.

11. American public opinion strongly favors a direct popular vote according to Gallup polls taken over the last three decades. Darren K. Carlson, "Public Funks Electoral College System," Gallup Poll, November 2, 2004, http://www.gallup .com/poll/releases/pr001116.asp (accessed May 2, 2005).

12. Much of this research has been conducted by the Center for Political Studies at the University of Michigan. Starting in 1952, that center began conducting national surveys, known as American National Election studies, during the presidential elections. The object of these surveys has been to identify the major influences on voting behavior by interviewing a random sample of the electorate before and after the election. Data from these surveys are made available to political scientists and others who analyze American voting behavior following each presidential election.

There has also been some preliminary research on the genetic component of attitude formation. See J. R. Alford, C. L. Funk, and J. R. Hibbing, "Are Political Orientation Genetically Transmitted?" *American Political Science Review* 99 (2005): 153–167.

13. Raymond E. Wolfinger and Steven J. Rosenstone, *Who Votes?* (New Haven, CT: Yale University Press, 1980), pp. 13, 226.

14. The Republican National Committee supplemented the McCain campaign with $150 million in coordinated and independent expenditures.

15. "Money vs. Money-Plus: Post-Election Reports Reveal Two Different Campaign Strategies," Campaign Finance Institute, January 11, 2013. http://cfinst.org/Press /PReleases/13-01-11/Money_vs_Money-Plus_Post-Election_Reports_Reveal_ Two_Different_Campaign_Strategies.aspx

16. "Outside Spending," Center for Responsive Politics. http://www .opensecrets.org/outsidespending/index .php. (Accessed January 7, 2013).

17. "Campaign 2004 Final: How TV News Covered the General Election Campaign," *Media Monitor,* November/ December 2004.

18. "Campaign 2008 Final," *Media Monitor,* November/December 2008.

19. "The Final Days of the Media Campaign 2012," Pew Research Center's Project for Excellence in Journalism, November 19, 2012, http://www .journalism.org/analysis_report /final_days_media_campaign_2012.

20. Thomas E. Patterson, *Out of Order* (New York: Knopf, 1993), pp. 106–121.

21. "Campaign 2008 Final," *Media Monitor November/December 2008.*

22. Keith Melder, *Hail to the Candidate: Presidential Campaigns from Banners to Broadcasts* (Washington, DC: Smithsonian Institution Press, 1992), pp. 70–74.

23. William J. Bryan, *The First Battle* (Port Washington, NY: Kennikat Press, 1971), p. 618.

24. Keith Melder, *Hail to the Candidate: Presidential Campaigns from Banners to Broadcasts* (Washington, DC: Smithsonian Institution Press, 1992), p. 129.

25. To demonstrate that he was not confined to a wheelchair, Roosevelt appeared standing while he addressed groups from the rear platform of his train. Because he could not get up or sit down without aid, Roosevelt's staff would assist him but do so out of public view before and after the train entered and left the station.

26. Lee Atwater as quoted in Thomas B. Edsall, "Why Bush Accentuates the Negative," *Washington Post*, October 2, 1988, p. C4.

27. The presidential debates are sponsored by a bipartisan Commission on Presidential Debates. The commission decides their location, the dates and times at which they will be held, format and moderators, and the rules of engagement. The candidates have some say in camera angle, audience participation, and content. The Commission also makes videos and transcripts of the debates available online and maintains an archive of past debates. Its website is www.debates.org.

28. "Nielsenwire," The Nielsen Company, October 23, 2012, http://blog.nielsen .com/nielsenwire/politics/final-presidential-debate-draws-59-2-million-viewers.

29. The same thing almost happened in 2000 when a Gore adviser received a Bush briefing book in the mail. However, he immediately gave the package to the FBI, which investigated the matter and subsequently arrested an employee of a Texas media firm hired by the Bush campaign on charges of mail fraud and perjury (lying to a grand jury). In a plea bargain with the government, the employee was sentenced to a year in prison, a $3,000 fine, and three years on probation.

30. The commercial was run only once. Goldwater supporters were outraged and protested vigorously. Their protest kept the issue alive. In fact, the ad itself became news, and parts of it were shown on television newscasts, thereby reinforcing the impression the Democrats wished to leave in the voters' minds.

31. The most contentious attack ads in 2004 were designed and aired by outside groups, not the presidential campaigns. Swift Boat Veterans for Truth, a Texas-based, pro-Bush group composed of Vietnam veterans, sharply criticized Kerry's war record and his postwar activities against the war.

32. "Mad Money: TV Ads in the 2012 Presidential Campaign," *Washington Post*, http://www.washingtonpost.com /wp-srv/special/politics/track-presidential-campaign-ads-2012/.

33. "Outside Spending," Center for Responsive Politics, http://www.opensecrets. org/outsidespending/index.php (accessed November 20, 2012).

34. Paul Freedman and Ken Goldstein, "Measuring Media Exposure and the Effects of Negative Campaign Ads," *American Journal of Political Science* 43 (September 1999): 1189–1208; Kim Fridkin Kahn and Patrick Kenny, "Do Negative Campaigns Mobilize or Suppress Turnout? Clarifying the Relationship between Negativity and Participation," *American Political Science Review* 93 (December 1999): 877–890; Martin Wattenberg and Craig Brians, "Negative Campaign Advertising: Demobilizer or Mobilizer?" *American Political Science Review* 93 (December 1999): 891–900.

35. For an excellent discussion of forecasting models, what they can and cannot predict, see James E. Campbell, ed. "Forecasting the 2012 American National Elections," *PS: Political Science and Politics* 45 (October 2012): 610–613. See also James E. Campbell, ed. "Recap: Forecasting the

2012 Election," *PS: Political Science and Politics* 46 (January 2013): 37–48.

36. Thomas M. Holbrook, "Forecasting with Mixed Economic Signals: A Cautionary Tale," *PS: Political Science and Politics* 34 (March 2001): 39, 44.

37. James E. Campbell, et al., "Forecasting the 2004 Presidential Election," *PS: Political Science and Politics* 37 (October 2004): 733–767; James E. Campbell, "Forecasting the 2008 National Elections," *PS: Political Science and Politics* 51 (October 2008): 679–732.

38. James E. Campbell, "Forecasting the 2012 American National Elections," *PS: Political Science and Politics* 45 (October 2012).

39. Two states, Maine and Nebraska, use a district system of voting in which only two of their electors are determined by the statewide vote, the rest in legislative districts.

40. Marjorie Connelly and Bill Marsh, "The Building Blocks of Re-election," *New York Times*, November 13, 2012, SR 7, http://www.nytimes.com/interactive /2012/11/10/opinion/20101104_ POLL-MARSH.html?ref=sunday-review.

41. The Florida forecast was also controversial because the networks had to withdraw it after CNN discovered a difference between the actual and predicted vote in the precincts in which the exit polls were conducted. At 2:16 A.M., the Fox News Channel declared Bush the winner on the basis of the tabulated results. (The person who did so happened to be a cousin of Bush's.) Other networks quickly followed suit.

42. See, for example, Raymond Wolfinger and Peter Linquiti, "Tuning In and Turning Out," *Public Opinion* 4 (February/March 1981): 57–59.

43. Sometimes, the closeness of the vote, however, makes a mandate difficult to discern. For a mandate to exist, political scientists suggest that the party's candidates must take discernible and compatible policy positions, and the electorate must vote for them because of those positions. Moreover, the results of the national election must be consistent. If one party wins the White House and another the Congress, it is difficult for the president to claim a partisan mandate. See Robert A. Dahl, "Myth of the Presidential Mandate," *Political Science Quarterly* 105 (Fall 1990): 355–372. For another perspective, see Patricia Heidotting Conley, *Presidential Mandates: How Elections Shape the National Agenda* (Chicago: University of Chicago Press, 2001).

4

THE PRESIDENT AND THE PUBLIC

"Public sentiment is everything. With public sentiment nothing can fail, without it nothing can succeed."[1] These words, spoken by Abraham Lincoln, pose what is perhaps the greatest challenge to any president: to obtain and maintain public support. Presidents usually make substantial efforts to lead the public. Sometimes their goals have been to gain long-term personal support, while at other times they have been more interested in obtaining support for a specific program. Often, of course, both goals are present.

In this chapter, we explore presidential attempts to understand public opinion and the public's expectations and evaluations of the chief executive. We are interested in identifying and explaining the public's attitudes to deepen our understanding of expectations and evaluations and also of the obstacles the White House faces in measuring public opinion.

We also examine presidential efforts to influence public opinion. We do not assume that presidents are successful in influencing the public, and thus we are also concerned with the effectiveness of the various techniques of opinion leadership that presidents use. Ultimately, we want to know whether presidents can direct change by imposing their priorities on the national agenda and creating and mobilizing a constituency to follow their lead or whether they are more likely to facilitate change by reflecting, and perhaps intensifying, widely held views that may guide their policy making. Their challenge is to convert these views into political capital to achieve their programmatic goals.

UNDERSTANDING PUBLIC OPINION

Presidents need public support, and understanding public opinion can be a considerable advantage to them in gaining and maintaining it. At the very least, presidents want to avoid needlessly antagonizing the public. Thus, they need reliable estimates of public reactions to the actions they are contemplating. They also need to know what actions and policies, either symbolic or substantive, the public wants. By knowing what the public desires, presidents may use their discretion to gain public favor whenever they feel the relevant actions or policies are justified.

In addition, presidents often want to lead public opinion to increase support for themselves and their policies. To do so, they need to know the views of various segments of the public, whom they need to influence and on what issues, and how far people can be moved. Presidents usually want to avoid expending their limited resources on hopeless ventures. Nor do they want to be too far ahead of the public, lest they risk losing their followers and alienating segments of the population. These motivations encourage contemporary presidents to poll the public on a regular basis as well as to have their aides organize groups to test some of their ideas and the rhetoric they use to explain them.

Americans' Opinions

Before a president can understand what opinions the public holds, individual citizens must form opinions. Although Americans are usually willing to express opinions on a wide variety of issues, these responses cannot be interpreted as reflecting crystallized and coherent views. Opinions are often rife with contradictions because the public often fails to give views much thought or consider the implications of policy stands for other issues.[2] For example, national polls show consistently that the American people place a very high priority on controlling government spending. At the same time, however, majorities favor maintaining or increasing expenditures on many domestic programs.[3]

Policy making is a complex enterprise, and most voters do not have the time, expertise, or inclination to think extensively about most issues (especially those distant from their everyday experiences; for example, federal regulations, nuclear weapons, and bureaucratic organization). The public can miss the point of even the most colorful rhetoric. In his 2010 State of the Union address, President Obama declared that as part of their economic recovery, his administration had passed twenty-five different tax cuts. "Now, let me repeat: We cut taxes," he said. "We cut taxes for 95 percent of working families. We cut taxes for small businesses. We cut taxes for first-time homebuyers. We cut taxes for parents trying to care for their children. We cut taxes for 8 million Americans paying for college." In his Super Bowl Sunday interview with Katie Couric, he touted the tax cuts in the stimulus package: "we put $300 billion worth of tax cuts into people's pockets so that there was demand and businesses had customers." (The only tax increases passed in 2009 were on tobacco.)

Shortly afterward, a major polling organization asked, "In general, do you think the Obama Administration has increased taxes for most Americans, decreased taxes for most Americans or have they kept taxes the same for most Americans?" Twenty-four percent of the public responded that the administration had *increased* taxes, and 53 percent said it kept taxes the same. Only 12 percent said taxes were decreased.[4] In July, that figure dwindled to 7 percent of the public.[5] Misperceptions only grew as the midterm elections approached. In September, 33 percent of the public thought that Obama had raised taxes for most Americans.[6] By the end of October, 52 percent of likely voters thought taxes had gone up for the middle class.[7]

Before the war with Iraq in 2003, two-thirds of the public expressed the belief that Iraq played an important role in the 9/11 terrorist attacks. After the war, substantial percentages of the public believed that the United States had found clear evidence that Saddam Hussein was working closely with al-Qaeda, that the United States had found weapons of mass destruction in Iraq, and that world opinion favored the United States going to war in Iraq.[8] All of these beliefs were inaccurate, as even the White House admitted.

Conversely, collective public opinion has properties quite different from those of individual citizens. There is evidence that the general public holds real, stable, and sensible opinions about public policy, which develop and change in a reasonable fashion in response to changing circumstances and new information. Changes that occur are usually at the margins and represent different trade-offs among constant values.[9]

In short, as the White House attempts to understand American public opinion, it is handicapped by the fact that many people have no opinion on issues of significance to the president and, moreover, that many of the opinions the public does express are neither crystallized, coherent, nor informed. In contrast, it is possible to grasp the essential contours of public opinion, especially where opinions on policies that touch the public directly—for example, on issues such as economic conditions and civil rights—are widely held. Moreover, the president desires to know the distribution of whatever opinions do exist. Under these circumstances, what means can the White House rely on to measure public opinion?

Public Opinion Polls

A common tool for measuring public attitudes is public opinion polling. Whether commissioned on behalf of the White House or by various components of the mass media, polls help the president to learn how a cross section of the population feels about a specific policy, general living conditions, or the administration's performance.

In an attempt to understand public opinion on matters of special concern to them, modern presidents have commissioned their own polls. Franklin D. Roosevelt was the first to pay close attention to polls, which were just becoming scientific during his tenure in office. All presidents since John F. Kennedy have retained private polling firms to provide them with soundings of American public opinion, and in the last six administrations, pollsters have also played a significant role as high-level political advisers.[10]

Despite their widespread use in the contemporary White House, public opinion polls are not completely dependable instruments for measuring public opinion. An important limitation of polls is that the questions they contain usually do not attempt to measure the intensity with which opinions are held. In reality, however, people with intense views will probably be more likely to act on those views to reward or punish politicians than people whose preference for the issue is a matter of indifference.

A related problem with polls is that the questions asked of the public seldom mesh with the decisions that presidents face. In fact, the executive rarely considers issues in the "yes/no" terms presented by most polls. Moreover, evidence of widespread support for a program does not indicate how the public stands on most of the specific provisions under consideration, much less how it balances certain programs with others. Such details do not lend themselves to mass polling because they require specialized knowledge of the issues, which few Americans possess.

Another problem is that responses may reflect the particular wording of the choices that are presented, which is a problem especially for people who lack crystallized opinions on issues. Moreover, if questions are of the "agree/ disagree" variety, there may be a bias toward the "agree" alternative. On policies that are very controversial, it may be impossible to ascertain public attitudes without some contamination caused by the use of "loaded" symbols in the questions. For example, in one poll, when people were asked to evaluate the amount government spends on "welfare," only 13 percent replied that it was "too little." When asked about expenditures for "assistance to the poor," however, 57 percent replied that government did not spend enough.[11]

Some questions inevitably arise when discussing presidents and polls: How should presidents use public opinion data? Does the use of these data constrain presidents rather than indicate where their persuasive efforts should be focused? By using polls, do presidents, in effect, substitute "followership" for leadership?

Presidents ritually deny that their decisions are influenced by polls. According to President Carter's chief media adviser, Gerald Rafshoon, "If we ever went into the president's office and said, 'We think you ought to do this or that to increase your standing in the polls,' he'd throw us out."[12] Polls do indeed influence White House political strategy, however.

More than any previous administration, the Reagan White House used polling in its decision-making process. Reagan's pollster, Richard Wirthlin, took polls for the president every three or four weeks (more often during a crisis) and met regularly with Reagan and his top aides. Wirthlin's goal was to determine when the nation's mood was amenable to the president's proposals and gauge public reactions to the president's actions. The White House wanted the timing of the president's proposals to be compatible with the political climate so as to maximize the probabilities of achieving its objectives; thus, polls were used to help set the presidential agenda.[13]

Presidents George H. W. Bush and Bill Clinton used their pollsters to perform similar functions, although Bush commissioned only a small number of polls (however, he did use focus groups regularly).[14] President Clinton, in contrast, was very attentive to polls, and his administration had the most comprehensive White House polling operation in history. Within a week of taking office, Clinton directed his aides to begin regular polling on issues, and pollsters were thoroughly integrated into the Clinton White House planning and strategy sessions on legislation. They assessed public support for various policy options (such as how to fund health care or providing drug addicts clean needles) and tested market phrases for describing proposals ("anticrime" was found to be preferable to "gun control" and helping "working families" was more popular than helping "poor children," for example). In 1998, the White House regularly polled regarding the Lewinsky scandal. Whenever the president gave a speech, pollsters gathered groups of people to watch and register their reactions on a handheld device called a "dial-a-meter."[15]

Despite its claims of disdain for polls and focus groups, the George W. Bush White House had extensive involvement in polling. The White House Office of Strategic Initiatives monitored and analyzed the results of numerous national polls, and it commissioned millions of dollars for its own polls and focus groups. Polls conducted by Republican pollsters at the state level also informed its analyses.[16]

Barack Obama has commissioned millions of dollars of polls through the Democratic National Committee. His pollsters and other top advisers meet regularly to discuss their latest polling and how to use the results to advance the president's agenda.[17] At the beginning of his second term, he made David Simas, who coordinated his reelection campaign's extensive focus group and polling operation, Assistant to the President and Deputy Senior Advisor for Communications and Strategy.

Much of the White House's effort to poll the public is designed to frame the president's message most effectively in order to win public support for his policies, such as when he attempted to frame the debate over health care reform as a campaign against irresponsible insurance companies (polling found that people dislike insurance companies).[18] At other times, the White House may be trying to identify possible pitfalls in its path or to clarify the administration's policies. When polls have revealed that the public was ignorant about an issue such as President Reagan's education policy or President Clinton's cooperation with the Whitewater investigation, the White House has gone to great lengths to talk about it.

Presidential Election Results

Although presidents cannot always rely on polls to inform them about public opinion, they can, theoretically, gain valuable insights through the interpretation of their own electoral support in the period following the election. In other words, they may be able to learn what voters are thinking when they cast their ballots for president. For such an approach to be useful for a president seeking to understand public opinion, the following conditions must be met:

1. Voters must have opinions about policies.
2. Voters must know candidates' stands on the issues.

3. Candidates must offer voters the alternatives the voters desire.
4. There must be a large voter turnout so that the electorate represents the population.
5. Voters must vote on the basis of issues.
6. It must be possible to correlate voter support with voters' policy views.

As we saw in Chapter 3, these conditions rarely, if ever, occur, making presidential election results a tenuous basis for interpreting public opinion.

In addition, voters may be concerned with several issues in an election, but they have only one vote with which to express their views. Citizens may support one candidate's position on some issues yet vote for another candidate because of concern for other issues or general evaluations of performance. When they cast their ballots, voters signal only their choice of candidate, not their choice of the candidates' policies. As Ken Mehlman, George W. Bush's 2004 campaign manager, put it, "This election is a choice—not a referendum."[19] The White House must be cautious in inferring support for specific policies from the results of this process, for the vote is a rather blunt instrument for expressing policy views.

Even landslide elections are difficult to interpret. For example, political scientist Stanley Kelley found that in Lyndon Johnson's victory in 1964, issues gave the president his base of support, and concerns over the relative competence of the candidates won the swing vote for him. In 1972, however, the question of competence dominated the election. Although traditional domestic issues associated with the New Deal were salient, they actually favored George McGovern, not the landslide winner, Richard Nixon.[20] In 1984, voters preferred Walter Mondale to Ronald Reagan on the issues of defense spending, aid to the contras, environmental protection, protection of civil rights, and helping the poor and disadvantaged, but most voted for Reagan for president.[21]

Mail from the Public

The mail, including both letters and e-mail, is another potential means for the president to learn about public opinion. Although estimates vary and record keeping is inconsistent,[22] there can be no doubt that the White House receives several million communications from the public each year, including more than 25,000 letters, phone calls, and electronic mail messages daily. (The president's e-mail address is president@whitehouse.gov.) The White House staff screen the mail and keep a log summarizing opinion on critical issues. Correspondence that requires a response is forwarded to the relevant agencies.

The president usually reads only a few items from a day's mail, primarily communications from personal friends, prominent and influential citizens, and interest-group leaders. President Obama also reads a small sampling of the week's mail. Although the president may answer a few letters from ordinary citizens, primarily as a public relations ploy, top White House aides usually answer mail from important individuals and organizations. Lower-level officials and volunteers using computer-designated responses answer the rest.

Even if the president could read more mail, this effort would not necessarily provide a useful guide to what the public is thinking about policy issues, considering that little of the mail focuses on the issues with which the president must deal, particularly at the depth with which the president evaluates options. In addition, those who communicate with the White House are not a cross section of the American people. Instead, they overrepresent the middle and upper classes and people who agree with the president.

Acting Contrary to Public Opinion

Presidents often find it difficult to understand public opinion, and there is no lack of examples of the White House being surprised by public reaction to events and presidential actions. These range from President Nixon's decision to invade Cambodia in 1970 and Ronald Reagan's efforts to halt increases in Social Security benefits in 1981 to President Clinton's proposal to lift the ban against homosexuals in the military in 1993.[23]

Even if presidents believe (or, at least, claim to believe) that they understand public opinion on a particular issue, they do not necessarily follow it.[24] Throughout most of Ronald Reagan's tenure in office, polls showed that the public wanted him to lower the federal deficit but not to cut social programs. Moreover, people were willing to decrease planned military spending to accomplish these goals. However, the president refused to act accordingly. President Obama persisted in advocating health care reform in the face of substantial public opposition.

Presidents offer several rationales for not following public opinion. President Nixon claimed that he was not really acting contrary to public opinion at all but instead represented the "silent majority," which did not express its opinion in activist politics. Similarly, presidents may argue that their actions are carried out on behalf of underrepresented groups, such as the poor or an ethnic minority, or of a future generation. Advocates employ this kind of rationale today on behalf of efforts designed to decrease the burden of debt for future generations by paying down the national debt and environmental protection policies designed to preserve a healthy and rich natural environment for others to share.

Presidents have also wrapped themselves in the mantle of the courageous statesman following his principles and fighting the tides of public opinion. For example, President Bush told his staff that if the United States had to fight Iraqi leader Saddam Hussein to liberate Kuwait, "it's not going to matter to me if there isn't one congressman who supports this, or what happens to public opinion. If it's right, it's gotta be done."[25] His son articulated the same sentiment regarding the invasion of Iraq. After a year in office, President Obama declared in a televised interview that he would not sacrifice his ambitious goals simply to win a second term in the White House: "I'd rather be a really good one-term president than a mediocre two-term president." He added that

"I don't want to look back on my time here and say to myself all I was interested in was nurturing my own popularity."[26]

Presidents often feel (and with good reason) that they know more about policy than most members of the public and that they sometimes must lead public opinion instead of merely follow it. In the words of Gerald Ford:

> I do not think a President should run the country on the basis of the polls. The public in so many cases does not have a full comprehension of a problem. A President ought to listen to the people, but he cannot make hard decisions just by reading the polls once a week. It just does not work, and what the President ought to do is make the hard decisions and then go out and educate the people on why a decision that was necessarily unpopular was made.[27]

PUBLIC EXPECTATIONS OF THE PRESIDENT

When new presidents assume the responsibilities of their office, they enter into a set of relationships, the contours of which are largely beyond their control. The nations with which they will negotiate, the Congress they must persuade, and the bureaucracy they are to manage, for example, have well-established routines and boundaries within which they function and which set the context of the president's relationships with them.

Public evaluations of the president also occur within an established environment: that of public expectations. The president is in the limelight of American politics. Although this prominence provides the potential for presidential leadership of the public, it is purchased at a high cost. The public has demanding expectations of what presidents should be, how they should act, and what their policies should accomplish. The burden falls on chief executives to live up to these expectations.

Although some presidents may, over time, succeed in educating the public to alter its expectations, views change slowly, and the changes that do take place usually create more hurdles for the president to overcome. In addition, the static nature of the president's personal characteristics and leadership style, and the American political system's inherent constraints on executive power in terms of choosing the most effective policies, limit the executive's ability to meet the public's expectations. Frustration, on the part of both the president and the public, is inevitable in such a situation.

High Expectations

The public's expectations of the president in the area of policy are substantial and include the assurance of peace, security, and prosperity. Table 4.1 shows the results of a poll taken in January 2009 just before the inauguration of President Obama. Performance expectations of the new president were quite high and

Table 4.1 Early Expectations of President Obama

	% Confident That the President Can
Work effectively with Congress to get things done	89
Manage the executive branch wisely	84
Fulfill the proper role of the United States in world affairs	80
Defend U.S. interests abroad	75
Prevent major scandals in his administration	74
Handle an international crisis	73
Use military force wisely	71

SOURCE: Gallup Poll, January 9–11, 2009. © 2009, The Gallup Organization. All rights reserved. Reprinted with permission.

covered a broad range of activities.[28] Clearly, Americans expect the president to do well at the core activities of the presidency.

Interestingly, there is a substantial gap between the public's expectations of what presidents should accomplish (and for which it will hold them accountable) and the degree of success it expects presidents to have in meeting such expectations. For example, we have seen that most people were optimistic about the Obama presidency at the time of his first inauguration (as they were for all recent presidents).[29] At the same time, however, bare majorities expected the president could remove all the U.S. troops from Iraq in sixteen months and cut taxes for most Americans, two of his signature campaign issues (see Table 4.2). The fact that such a juxtaposition of views might be unfair to the president seems irrelevant to many of his constituents.

Later in this book, we will emphasize how the president's influence on public policy and its consequences is often limited. Nevertheless, the public

Table 4.2 Expectations of Policy Accomplishments for President Obama

Issue	% Yes, Will Accomplish
Enact major spending program on infrastructure	80
Increase military strength in Afghanistan	68
Ensure all children have health insurance	62
Lift restrictions on government funding of embryonic stem cell research	61
Double production of alternative energy	59
Close Guantanamo prison	59
Make it easier for unions to organize	59
Reduce health care costs for families	56
Withdraw most troops from Iraq within sixteen months	54
Cut taxes for 95% of working families	53

SOURCE: Gallup Poll, January 9–11, 2009. © 2009, The Gallup Organization. All rights reserved. Reprinted with permission.

holds the president responsible. To quote President Carter: "When things go bad you [the president] get entirely too much blame. And I have to admit that when things go good, you get entirely too much credit."[30] Because the press tends to emphasize bad conditions more than good, the attention presidents receive is usually more negative than positive.

In addition to expecting successful policies from the White House, Americans expect their presidents to be extraordinary individuals.[31] (This, of course, buttresses the public's policy expectations.) The public desires the president to be honest, intelligent, cool in a crisis, compassionate, strong and decisive, inspiring, and a competent manager and politician. People also expect the president to exercise sound judgment and to possess both a vision for the country and a sense of humor. Substantial percentages also want the nation's leader to have imagination and charisma. Obviously, it is not easy to meet these diverse and somewhat unrealistic expectations.

The public not only has high expectations for the president's official performance but also lofty expectations for their leader's private behavior.[32] Substantial percentages of the population strongly object if a president engages in bad behaviors that are nonetheless very common in American society. For example, when the Watergate tapes revealed that President Nixon frequently used profane and obscene language in his private conversations, many Americans were outraged. Similarly, revelations regarding President Clinton's extramarital affairs and his failure to tell the truth about them, as well as the favorable treatment he accorded political donors, substantially diminished the public's regard for him as a person.

Sources of High Expectations

The tenacity with which Americans maintain high expectations of the president may be due in large part to the encouragement they receive from presidential candidates to do so. As noted in Chapter 3, the lengthy process by which Americans select their presidents lends itself to political hyperbole. For at least one year out of every four, the public is encouraged to expect more from the president than it is currently receiving. Evidently, people take this rhetoric to heart and hold presidents to high standards of performance, independent of the reasonableness of these expectations.

Political socialization also supports high expectations of presidents; for example, schoolchildren often learn American history organized by presidential eras. Implicit in much of this teaching is the view that great presidents were largely responsible for the freedom and prosperity that Americans enjoy. From such lessons, it is a short step to presuming that contemporary presidents can be wise and effective leaders and, therefore, that the public should expect them to be so. Furthermore, commentators may compare contemporary presidents to an ideal president—a composite created out of the strongest attributes (but none of the liabilities) of their predecessors.

Another factor encouraging high expectations is the prominence of the president. As the nation's spokesperson and the personification of the nation, the chief executive is the closest thing Americans have to a royal sovereign.

Especially at election time, presidents and their families—even their pets—dominate the news in America. Presidents' great visibility naturally induces people to focus attention, and thus demands and expectations, on them.

Related to the president's prominence is the tendency to personalize. Issues of public policy are often extremely complex. To simplify them, Americans tend to think of issues in terms of personalities, especially the president's. It is easier to blame a specific person for personal and societal problems than it is to analyze and comprehend the complicated mix of factors that really forms the cause. Similarly, it is easier to project frustrations onto a single individual than it is to deal with the contradictions and selfishness in people's own policy demands. At the midpoint of his term in office, President Carter reflected: "I can see why it is difficult for a President to serve two terms. You are the personification of problems and when you address a problem even successfully you become identified with it."[33]

Part of the explanation for the public's high expectations of the president probably lies in its lack of understanding of the context in which the president functions. We shall see in later chapters that the president's basic power situation in the nation's constitutional system is one of weakness rather than strength. However, this fact is widely misperceived by the public, most of whom do not feel that the president has too little power.[34]

Consequences of High Expectations

Do high expectations of our presidents affect the public's evaluations of their performance? Although we lack sufficient data to reach a definitive conclusion, there is reason to believe that the wider the gap between expectations and performance, the lower the approval of the president.[35]

Sometimes the negative impact of high expectations in the public's support for the president is of the chief executive's own making. George H. W. Bush promised, in dramatic fashion, not to raise taxes and to create millions of jobs. When he agreed to a tax increase as part of a deficit reduction agreement with Congress and the jobs failed to materialize, his opponents, and even his friends, wasted no time in criticizing him. Bill Clinton began his administration on a sour note when he announced that he would not be able to provide a tax cut for the middle class as he had promised during the campaign. During his campaign for the presidency in 2000, George W. Bush said the U.S. military should not be involved in peacekeeping operations, but after he became president he ordered its involvement in peacekeeping in Afghanistan and Iraq. Barack Obama promised hope and change in the 2008 election, but once in office, Republican opposition prevented him from delivering on many of his pledges.

We have, of course, no way to calculate precisely the influence of such unkept promises on the president's standing with the public, and many of them may be of little significance in isolation. However, their collective impact, particularly during periods of some domestic distress, undoubtedly depresses the president's approval ratings. They help to undermine the aura of statesmanship and competence that attracted support in the election campaign. According to Richard Wirthlin, President Reagan's pollster, expectations are the ultimate source of public frustration.[36] Perhaps presidents should lower expectations, especially at the beginning of their terms, so they will not have to mortgage their reputations and prestige to nuances of governing that they have yet to learn.

Contradictory Expectations

The contradictions in the public's expectations present an additional obstacle to presidents in their efforts to gain public support. As the focus of contradictory expectations, it is very difficult for them to escape criticism and loss of approval—no matter what they do. Contradictory expectations of presidents deal with either the content of policy or their style of performance. The public's expectations of policy are confused and seemingly unlimited. We want low taxes and efficient government, yet we do not want a decrease in most public services. We expect plentiful gasoline, but not at a higher price. We want economic inflation to be controlled, but not at the expense of higher unemployment or interest rates. We want a clean environment, yet we support industrial development and energy production.

It is true, of course, that the public is not entirely to blame for holding these contradictory expectations. Presidential candidates often enthusiastically encourage voters to believe that they will produce the proverbial situation in which the people can have their cake and eat it too. In the 1980 presidential campaign, Ronald Reagan promised, among other things, to slash government expenditures, substantially reduce taxes, increase military spending, balance the budget, and maintain government services. Similarly, in 1992 Bill Clinton promised to increase social services while lowering taxes on most Americans— a feat he was not able to accomplish. George W. Bush promised a large tax cut, debt reduction, and substantial expenditure increases for defense and Medicare. The deficit, in fact, ballooned during his presidency.

Our expectations of presidential leadership style are also crucial in our evaluation of the president. The public wants a president who embodies a variety of traits, some of which are contradictory:

1. We expect the president to be a leader—an independent figure who speaks out and takes stands on the issues, even if the views are unpopular. We also expect the president to preempt problems by anticipating them before they arise. Similarly, we count on the president to provide novel solutions to the country's problems. To meet these expectations, the president must stay ahead of public opinion, acting on problems that may be obscure to the general populace and contributing ideas that are different from those currently in vogue in policy discussions.

   In sharp contrast to our expectations for presidential leadership are our expectations that chief executives be responsive to public opinion and that they be constrained by majority rule, as represented in Congress. The public overwhelmingly wants Congress to have final authority in policy disagreements with the president, and it does not want the president to be able to act against majority opinion.[37]

These contradictory expectations of leadership versus responsiveness place presidents in a no-win situation. If they attempt to lead, they may be criticized for losing contact with their constituents, being unrepresentative, and, at worst, acting like demagogues. Conversely, if they try to reflect the views of the populace, they may be reproached for failing to lead, following the polls, and settling for the easiest, rather than the optimal, solution to a problem.

2. We expect our presidents to be open-minded politicians in the American tradition and thus exhibit flexibility and willingness to compromise on policy differences. At the same time, we expect presidents to be decisive and to take firm and consistent stands on the issues. These expectations are also incompatible, and presidents can therefore expect to be criticized for being rigid and inflexible when they are standing firm on an issue. Critics will disparage presidents for being weak and indecisive when they do compromise or change their policy proposals.

3. We want the president to be a statesman—to place the country's interests ahead of politics—yet we also want a skilled politician who exercises loyalty to his political party. A president who acts in a statesmanlike manner may be criticized for being an ineffective idealist who is too far above the political fray and insufficiently solicitous of party supporters. Jimmy Carter began his term on such a note when he attempted to cut back on "pork barrel" water projects. A president who emphasizes a party program, however, may be criticized for being a crass politician who lacks concern for the broader national interest; this happened to Bill Clinton when he proposed an economic stimulus plan in his first year in office that contained billions of dollars for projects designed to please Democratic constituents around the country.

4. We like our presidents to run open administrations. We expect a free flow of ideas within the governing circles in Washington, and we want the workings of government to be visible, not sheltered behind closed doors. At the same time, we want to feel that the president is in control of things and is providing a rudder for government. If presidents allow internal dissent among their aides and this becomes visible to the public, critics will complain that the White House is in disarray. However, if presidents should attempt either to stifle dissent or to conceal it from the public, critics will accuse them of being isolated, undemocratic, unable to accept criticism, and desirous of muzzling opposition.

5. Finally, we want our presidents to be able to relate to the average person in order to inspire confidence in the White House and promote compassion and concern for the typical citizen. However, we also expect the president to be above the crowd—to possess characteristics far different from our own and to act in ways that are beyond the capabilities of most of us. To confuse the matter further, we also expect the president to act with a special dignity, befitting the leader of the country (and the free world) and to live and entertain royally, with much pomp and circumstance. In other words, presidents are not supposed to resemble the average person at all.

On the one hand, if presidents seem too common, opponents may disparage them for being just that. One only has to think of the many political cartoons of Harry Truman, Gerald Ford, and George W. Bush that implied they were really not up to the job of president. On the other hand, if presidents seem too different, appear too cerebral, or engage in too much pomp, they will likely be denounced as snobbish and isolated from the people and as too regal for Americans' tastes. The Nixon White House evoked such criticisms about the president and his aides because of its seeming isolation and formality, while Barack Obama is often criticized for being too dispassionate and analytical.

PUBLIC APPROVAL OF THE PRESIDENT

The most visible and significant aspect of presidents' relations with the public is their level of approval. Presidents' efforts to understand and lead public opinion and their efforts to influence the media's portrayal of them are aimed at achieving public support. This support is related to their success in dealing with others, especially the Congress. A high level of public approval increases the chances of the president receiving support in Congress for his programs.[38]

Whether they base their judgments on perceptions encouraged by the White House, the media, or other political actors or on detached and careful study, people constantly form and reform opinions about presidents and their policies. The impact of foreign and domestic policies also affects opinions, sometimes quite directly. In this section, we examine issues, the president's personality and personal characteristics, and dramatic international events as possible influences on presidential approval. In addition, there are certain less dynamic factors in the form of predispositions that citizens hold, such as political party identification and the positivity bias, that may strongly influence their evaluations of the president. Political party identification, in particular, not only directly affects opinions of the president but also mediates the impact of other influences.

Levels of Approval

Presidents cannot depend on the public's approval. Presidents Nixon, Ford, Carter, George W. Bush, and Obama did not receive approval from 50 percent of the public on the average (see Figure 4.1). Even Ronald Reagan, often considered the most popular of recent presidents, averaged only 52 percent approval—a bare majority. George H. W. Bush achieved a high average approval, 60 percent. Yet when he needed the public's support the most, during his campaign for reelection, the public abandoned him. He received only 38 percent of the popular vote in the 1992 presidential election. The fact that Bill Clinton enjoyed strong public support during his impeachment trial, helping him obtain an average approval level of 55 percent, should not mask the fact that he struggled to obtain even 50 percent approval during his first term and did not exceed such an average for a year until his fourth year in office.

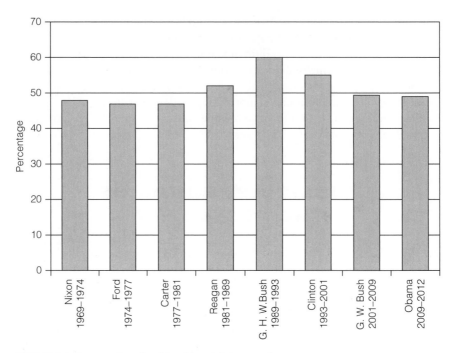

FIGURE 4.1 Average Levels of Presidential Approval

Source: George C. Edwards III with Alec M. Gallup, *Presidential Approval* (Baltimore, MD: Johns Hopkins University Press, 1990); updated by the author/Cengage Learning

Party Identification

Evaluations of the president's performance reflect the underlying partisan loyalties of the public. Members of the president's party are predisposed to approve of his performance, whereas members of the opposition party are predisposed to be less approving.[39] Independents (those without explicit partisan attachments) fall between the Democrats and Republicans in their levels of approval. The average difference in support between Democrats and Republicans over the past forty years has been about 40 percentage points, a very substantial figure. Independents fall in between, averaging a difference of about 20 percentage points from both the Democrats and the Republicans.

The public has been especially polarized along party lines in recent decades. During the tenures of Ronald Reagan and Bill Clinton, the gap between Democrats and Republicans widened to more than 50 percentage points. Polarization increased even more in George W. Bush's presidency, with a partisan gap often exceeding 70 percentage points in his second term.[40]

The fact that the public had been polarized under his predecessor was of little comfort to Barack Obama. It merely showed the stability of the partisan divide and indicated the difficulty of reaching those identifying with the opposition party. After a month in office, Obama averaged 89 percent approval from Democrats but only 28 percent approval from Republicans.[41] There was an average gap of 65 percentage points between Democrats' and Republicans' evaluations of the president in his first year, and a 68-percentage point gap in his second year, setting records in each case.[42] Since that time, the gap has grown to over 70 percentage points.

Positivity Bias

Another predisposing factor is the "positivity bias," which one authority defined as the tendency "to show evaluation of public figures and institutions in a generally positive direction."[43] Americans have a general disposition to prefer, to learn, and to expect positive relationships more than negative ones and to perceive stimuli as positive rather than negative. Thus, they tend to have favorable opinions of people.

Although the positivity bias should encourage presidential approval throughout a president's tenure, it is likely to be especially important at the beginning, when no record exists. As presidents perform their duties, citizens obtain more information and thus a more comprehensive basis for judging them. Moreover, as time passes, people may begin to perceive greater implications of presidential policies for their own lives. If the public views these implications unfavorably, it may be more open to, and pay more attention to, negative information about the president.

A related factor may affect public approval early in a president's term. As people have little basis on which to evaluate the president, they may turn elsewhere for cues. A new chief executive is generally treated favorably in the press. Moreover, there is excitement and symbolism inherent in the peaceful transfer of power, the inaugural festivities, and the prevalent sense of "new beginnings." All this creates a positive environment in which initial evaluations of elected presidents take place, buttressing any tendency toward the positivity bias.

The Persistence of Approval

We have seen that presidents typically begin their initial terms with the benefit of substantial support from the public, but how long does this honeymoon last? Conventional wisdom indicates that it does not last long. The thrust of the argument is that the president will soon have to begin making hard choices, which will inevitably alienate segments of the population. Additional support for this view comes from a revealing response by President Carter in 1979 to a reporter's question concerning whether it was reasonable to expect the president to rate very highly with the American people. The president answered:

> In this present political environment, it is almost impossible. There are times of euphoria that sweep the Nation immediately after an election or after an inauguration day or maybe after a notable success, like the Camp David Accords, when there is a surge of popularity for a President. But most of the decisions that have to be made by a President are inherently not popular ones. They are contentious.[44]

Despite the reasonableness of these expectations, presidential honeymoons are not always short-lived. Examining shifts in presidents' approval ratings reveals that although declines certainly do take place, they are neither inevitable nor swift. Eisenhower maintained his standing in the public very well for two complete terms. Kennedy and Nixon held their public support for two years, as did Ford (after a sharp initial decline). Johnson's and Carter's approval losses were steeper, although Johnson's initial ratings were inflated by the unique emotional climate at the time he assumed office. (The same was true, of course, for Ford.) Reagan's approval ratings were volatile, but he stood at 64 percent approval at the time of his second inauguration, 13 percentage points higher than when he began. Bush maintained very high levels of public support until about the last year of his tenure. Clinton sank in the polls soon after taking office but enjoyed higher average levels of approval in his fourth through eighth years than for any of his first three years. George W. Bush rose to extraordinary heights in the polls after the 9/11 terrorist attacks and enjoyed strong support for the next two years before his approval plummeted.

Thus, honeymoons are not necessarily fleeting times during which the new occupant of the White House receives a breathing period from the public. Instead, the president's constituents seem to be willing to give a new chief executive the benefit of the doubt for some time. It is up to each president to exploit this goodwill and build solid support for his administration in the public. This is why the first few months are often critical for setting the tone of the administration, shaping the president's reputation, and establishing a popular base. In particular, President Clinton's rocky early months in office made it more difficult for him to obtain the public's support. Similarly, the controversy attending Barack Obama's early proposals to deal with the economic crisis, stimulate the economy, and reform health care kept his approval ratings low throughout his first term in office.

Long-Term Decline

In addition to examining approval levels within presidential terms, we need to look for trends in public support across presidents. As shown in Figure 4.2, from 1953 through 1965, with the single exception of 1958, at least 60 percent of the public, on average, approved of the president. At that time, support from two out of three Americans was not unusual. Starting in 1966, however, approval levels changed dramatically. Since that time, presidents have obtained support from even a bare majority of the public less than half the time.

Personality or Policy?

One factor commonly associated with approval of a president is personality. In common usage, the term *personality* refers to personal characteristics, such as warmth, charm, and humor, that may influence responses to an individual on a personal level. It is not unusual for observers to conclude that the public evaluates presidents based more on style than substance, especially in an era in which the media and sophisticated public relations campaigns play such a

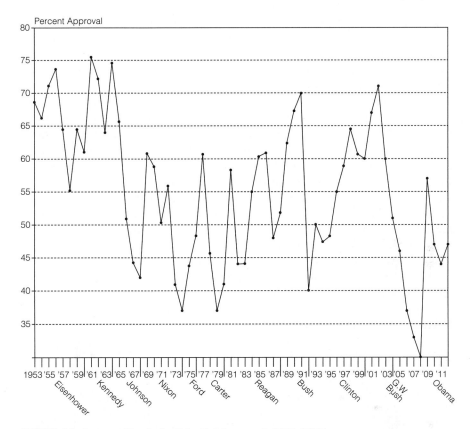

FIGURE 4.2 Average Yearly Presidential Approval, 1953–2012

Source: George C. Edwards III with Alec M. Gallup, *Presidential Approval* (Baltimore, MD: Johns Hopkins University Press, 1990); updated by the author.

prominent role in presidential politics. The fact that Americans pay relatively little detailed attention to politics and policy adds further support to the view that the president's personality plays a large role in the public's approval or disapproval. In other words, some argue that members of the public evaluate the president by how much they like him as a person.

Personality may buttress presidential approval, but it is not a dynamic factor. In other words, it cannot explain shifts in the president's standing with the public. Sharp changes in approval have occurred for presidents whose public manners have remained unaltered. Although the impressions the public holds of the president's personality form early and change slowly, factors such as what the public feels ought to be and the way people evaluate what they see can change more rapidly. "Cleverness" can also be viewed as "deceit," "reaching down for details" as "a penchant for the trivial," "evaluating all the alternatives" as "indecisiveness," "charm" as "manipulative" or simply "acting common" (or, even worse, "vulgar"), and "staying above politics" as "naiveté." The contradictory expectations that people hold about the president help to set the scene for these changing interpretations of presidential behavior, allowing the public to switch emphasis in what it looks for in a president and how it evaluates what it sees.

In addition, Americans appear to compartmentalize their attitudes toward the president and seem to have little difficulty in separating the person from the performance. Dwight Eisenhower was unique among modern presidents in that his public standing preceded, and was independent of, his involvement in partisan politics. He was a likable war hero who had recently been a principal leader in the highly consensual policy of defeating Germany in World War II. His image following the war was so apolitical that both parties approached him about running for president. Nevertheless, the public evaluated Eisenhower as a partisan figure. Thus, the public may "like" a president but still disapprove of the way he is handling his job. The public typically liked Jimmy Carter but disapproved of his performance as president.[45] In Bill Clinton's case, compartmentalization also occurred—but in reverse. Most Americans believed that he engaged in behavior of which they disapproved, yet a clear majority approved of the president's performance in office throughout his second term.[46]

Personal Characteristics

Much of the commentary on presidents in the press and other forums focuses on their personal characteristics, especially integrity, intelligence, and leadership abilities. When the public is asked about such job-related characteristics, its responses are clearly related to its evaluations of the president.[47] Assessments of characteristics such as the president's integrity, reliability, and leadership ability may change as new problems arise or in relation to the president's past performance. Certain characteristics may become more salient in response to changing conditions. For example, when the Iran-Contra affair became news, President Reagan's decision-making style became a prominent issue. Many people came to evaluate his focus on the "big picture" and detachment from the details of governing in a less positive light. Similarly, George W. Bush's decisiveness became less attractive as his decisions regarding the war in Iraq lost favor with the public.

Issues

Ultimately, the public cares about presidents because of issues of public policy. For an issue to have a significant influence on presidential evaluation, it must be salient to people; the people must hold the president responsible for it, and they must make their evaluation in terms of the president's performance regarding the issue. Obviously, perceptions of reality, sometimes influenced by interest groups,[48] mediate each of these components of assessment.

Salience of Issues
For most of his first term in office, George W. Bush stood high in the polls despite the public's low rating of his performance on a wide variety of issues,

ranging from abortion to the economy. How could the public approve of a president who was considered to be doing a poor job on so many issues? The answer is that it evaluated the president primarily in terms of other issues, especially foreign policy, on which it approved of his performance.

If a matter is not salient to people, it will be unlikely to play a major role in their evaluations of the president. Understanding presidential approval, then, requires identifying what is on the minds of Americans. One cannot assume that people always judge the president by the same benchmarks. In fact, people generally have only a few issues that are particularly important to them and to which they pay attention.[49] The importance of specific issues to the public varies over time and is closely tied to objective conditions such as unemployment, inflation, international tensions, racial conflict, and fatalities during war.[50] Increasing fatalities and other issues are likely to be salient to different groups in the population at any given time. For example, some groups may be concerned about inflation, others about unemployment, and yet others about a particular aspect of foreign policy or race relations.[51]

The relative weights of values and issues in evaluations of the president also vary over time. Valence or style issues are values—such as patriotism, morality, or a strong national defense—on which there is a broad consensus in the public and that are more basic than a position on a specific policy. The president's articulation of valence issues, directly and in the symbols the White House employs in speech and actions, can affirm the values and beliefs that define citizens' political identities. Valence issues can be powerful instruments for obtaining public support because presidents often prefer to be judged on the basis of consensual criteria with which they can associate themselves.

Research has found that values are relatively constant over time and that policy debates are rarely single-valued. Some values become more salient and some less so in making such trade-offs.[52] For example, antigovernment and antiwelfare attitudes give way to concerns for health and compassion if it is discovered that children are going hungry. Similarly, in the debate over abortion, the salience of values represented by "life" and "choice" varies substantially among citizens.

Finally, within an issue area, the bad news may outweigh the good in capturing the public's attention. People weigh negative information more heavily than positive—that is, bad news is more salient to them.[53] If the economy slumps, for example, this may be more salient to the public than if it continues to grow at a moderate rate. Thus, it is possible that presidents may be punished in the polls if the economy is not doing well yet not be comparably rewarded for prosperity.[54] It may be that an issue comes to the public's attention only when it reaches a certain threshold level, which usually means that there is a problem.[55] This, in turn, may provide the basis for more vocal, and thus more salient, opposition to the president.

Responsibility

Even if a matter such as the economy is salient to the public, it is not likely to affect people's evaluations of the president unless they hold him responsible for it.[56] Furthermore, the more the public attributes responsibility for an issue to the president, the more the issue is likely to affect evaluations of his performance.[57]

Despite the prominence of the chief executive, there are several reasons why people may not hold the president responsible for all the problems they face personally or for some problems that they perceive to be confronting the country. Most people do not politicize their personal problems, and most of those who are concerned about personal economic problems, such as credit card debt, do not believe the government should come to their assistance.[58] There is also evidence that people do not necessarily exaggerate the importance of the president or ignore contextual and institutional factors beyond his control.[59] In addition, some people may feel that those who preceded the president or who share power with him are to blame for important problems. Few people blamed Barack Obama for the economic downturn in 2009.

Presidential Performance

For an issue that is salient to the public and for which it holds the president accountable, the quality of the president's performance on that issue should become a factor in presidential approval. Many observers assume that, for example, if unemployment is rising, the public will evaluate the president negatively. Perhaps this is true, but perceptions may not follow directly from objective indicators of the economy's performance.

The unemployment level was virtually the same in summer 1984 as it was in summer 1992, yet the public evaluated the economic performance of President Reagan and President Bush (respectively) quite differently. Reagan was rewarded for bringing the level down, whereas Bush suffered the consequences of economic stagnation.

The public may be less harsh in its evaluations of presidents who are struggling with difficult situations, even if they are not meeting with short-term success. Franklin D. Roosevelt may have enjoyed the public's tolerance in 1933 and 1934 not only because he could not be held responsible for the Great Depression but also because he was seen as doing the best that could be done under trying circumstances. Jimmy Carter's standing in the public benefited for several months from favorable public perceptions of his handling of the Iranian hostage crisis, despite the fact the hostages were not freed during this period.

In addition, a substantial body of evidence supports the argument that the political attitudes of Americans are more influenced by what they see as important national issues than by their personal experience. Focusing on the most often-discussed issue area, the economy, will clarify the point.

The conventional view is that people's evaluations of the president are affected strongly by their personal economic circumstances. That is, they are more likely to approve of the president if they feel they are prospering personally. In recent years, an impressive number of studies have found that when people evaluate government performance or individual candidates, personal economic circumstances are typically subordinated to other, broader considerations.[60] More specifically, it appears that citizens evaluate the president on the basis of broader views of the economy rather than simply their narrow self-interests. In other words, rather than asking what the president has done for them lately, citizens ask what the president has done for the nation.[61]

Furthermore, people typically differentiate their own circumstances from those of the country as a whole. For example, polls regularly report that people are much more satisfied with their personal lives than with the way things are going in the nation.

Rally Events

To this point, we have examined factors that may affect presidential approval systematically over time, yet sometimes public opinion takes sudden jumps, as in the case of the 18-percentage point increase George H. W. Bush received in the polls after the Persian Gulf War began in January 1991. Even more dramatically, George W. Bush went from 51 percent in the Gallup Poll on September 10, 2001, to 90 percent on September 22. The cause for this change, of course, was the great national outpouring of patriotism in response to the terrorist attacks on September 11, much of which focused on the commander in chief.

One popular explanation for these surges of support involves "rally events." John Mueller, in his seminal definition, explained the concept as an event that is international; directly involves the United States (and particularly the president); and is specific, dramatic, and sharply focused. Such events confront the nation as a whole, are salient to the public, and gain public attention and interest.[62]

The theory behind attributing significance to rally events is that the public will increase its support of presidents in times of crisis or during major international events, at least in the short run, because at such times they are the symbol of the country and the primary focus of attention. Moreover, people do not want to hurt the country's chances of success by opposing the president. The president, meanwhile, has an opportunity to look masterful and evoke patriotic, consensus-building reactions among the people.

Conversely, there is also reason to expect the potential for the public rallying around the flag to be limited. Studies of American public opinion regarding national security have found little inherent deference to the president as an individual.[63] More than patriotic fervor is involved in rallies, as those who rally are the most disposed to support the president in the first place,[64] and those most politically aware are less likely to make a sudden switch in their judgments regarding the president.[65]

Individual citizens seem to respond to criticism from members of both parties, especially from the president's party, and praise from members of their own party in evaluating incursions. Interestingly, press commentary by members of Congress following the typical incursion tends to be critical of the president, making a rally less likely. Conflicts involving substantial incursions of ground forces such as the U.S. invasions of Grenada, Panama, Afghanistan, and Iraq in both 1991 and 2003 may be partial exceptions because in the short run they tend to evoke less credible criticism and more credible praise relative to less extensive uses of force.[66]

The preponderance of evidence indicates that the rally phenomenon rarely appears and that the events that generate it are highly idiosyncratic and do not seem to differ significantly from other events that were not followed by surges in presidential approval. Moreover, the events that cause sudden increases in public support are not restricted to international affairs, and most international events that would seem to be potential rally events fail to generate much additional approval of the president. Rather than being a distinctive phenomenon, a rally event seems to be simply an additional force that pushes potential supporters over the threshold of approval. For a rally to sustain support for the president, it requires the event that produced the rally to remain as the most salient issue for the public and for the president's response to receive widespread support. When people turn their attention to more divisive issues, the president's standing in the polls inevitably declines.

LEADING THE PUBLIC

If public support can be a useful leadership resource for presidents, are they in a position to call on it when needed? Commentators on the presidency often assume that the White House can persuade or even mobilize the public, provided the president is a skilled enough communicator. Various presidents have agreed. In the words of Franklin Roosevelt, "All our great Presidents were leaders of thought at times when certain historic ideas in the life of the nation had to be clarified." His cousin, Theodore Roosevelt, had earlier observed:

"People used to say of me that I . . . divined what the people were going to think. I did not 'divine.' I simply made up my mind what they ought to think, and then did my best to get them to think it."[67] Just how useful is the "bully pulpit"?

Direct Opinion Leadership

The most visible and obvious technique employed by presidents to lead public opinion is to seek the public's support directly. Presidents frequently attempt to do so with speeches and public statements. In a typical year, for example, Bill Clinton spoke in public 550 times,[68] and he traveled around the country every fourth day.[69] President George W. Bush continued these practices,[70] and shortly after his inauguration President Obama ordered his staff to schedule him to speak outside of Washington, D.C., at least once a week. Nevertheless, there are a number of important constraints on the White House's ability to move the public.

Presentation Skills

All presidents since Truman have sought media advice from experts on lighting, makeup, stage settings, camera angles, clothing, pacing of delivery, and other facets of speech making. Despite this aid and the experience that politicians inevitably gain in public speaking, presidential speeches aimed at leading public opinion directly have typically been less than impressive. Not all presidents are effective speakers, and not all look good under the glare of hot lights and the unflattering gaze of television cameras. Only Kennedy, Reagan, Clinton, and Obama mastered the art of speaking to the camera.

Presidents not only have to contend with the medium but also must concern themselves with their messages. It is not clear what approach works best. Many of the most effective speeches seem to be those whose goals are gaining general support and image building rather than gaining specific support. They focus on simple themes rather than complex details. Calvin Coolidge used this method successfully in his radio speeches, as did Franklin Roosevelt in his famous "fireside chats."[71] The limitation of such an approach, of course, is that general support cannot always be translated into public backing for specific policies.

There is no magic associated with certain leaders, and the "charisma" and personality of leaders are not the keys to successfully leading the public. Even George Washington, who was better positioned than any of his successors to dominate American politics because of the widespread view of his possessing exceptional personal qualities, did not find the public particularly deferential.[72]

Public's Predispositions

No matter how effective presidents may be as speakers or how charming their personality, they still must contend with the predispositions of their audience. Most people ignore or reject arguments contrary to their predispositions. Thus, the White House wants to influence opinion before it has developed because aides know they are unlikely to change it.[73]

Those who pay close attention to politics and policy are likely to have well-developed views and thus be less susceptible to persuasion. In the typical situation of competing views offered by political elites, reinforcement and polarization of views are more likely than conversion among attentive citizens. Those with less interest and knowledge lack the information to resist arguments, but they are also less likely to be aware of the president's messages, limiting the president's influence.[74] To the extent that they do receive the messages, they will also hear from the opposition how the president's views are inconsistent with their predispositions. They may also lack the understanding to make the connection between the president's arguments and their own underlying values, and the more abstract the link between message and value, the fewer people who will make the connection.[75]

In addition, people are frequently *misinformed* (as opposed to uninformed) about policy, and the less they know, the more confidence they have in their beliefs. Thus, they resist correct factual information. Even when presented with factual information, they resist changing their opinions.[76] Thus, it is not surprising that more than a year after President Obama's health care reform bill passed Congress, most Americans were unaware that the health care reform law would close the Medicare "doughnut hole" on prescription drugs, while 31 percent of the public incorrectly believed the law allowed a government panel to make decisions about end-of-life care for people on Medicare—and another 20 percent were unsure.[77]

A related matter of perception is the credibility of the source. Perceived source credibility is a prerequisite for successful opinion leadership.[78] The president is likely to be more credible to some people (those predisposed to support him) than to others. Many people are unlikely to find him a credible source on most issues, especially those on which opinion is divided and on which he is the leader of one side of the debate.

Loss Aversion

A special type of predisposition is the preference for avoiding loss,[79] which encourages people to place more emphasis on avoiding potential losses than on obtaining potential gains. In their decision making, people place more weight on information that has negative, as opposed to positive, implications for their interests. Similarly, when individuals form impressions of situations or other people, they weigh negative information more heavily than positive. Impressions formed on the basis of negative information, moreover, tend to be more lasting and more resistant to change.[80]

Risk and loss aversion and distrust of government make people wary of policy initiatives, especially when they are complex and their consequences are uncertain. Because uncertainty accompanies virtually every proposal for a major shift in public policy, it is not surprising that people are naturally inclined against change.[81] Further encouraging this predisposition is the media's focus on political conflict and strategy, which elevates the prominence of political wheeling-dealing in individuals' evaluations of political leaders and policy proposals. The resulting increase in public cynicism highlights the risk of altering the status quo.

The predisposition for loss aversion is an obstacle for presidential leadership of the public. Most presidents want to leave some substantial change at the core of their legacies. Yet those proposing new directions in policy encounter a more formidable task than advocates of the status quo. Those opposing change have a more modest task of emphasizing the negative to increase the public's uncertainty and anxiety to avoid risk.[82] In addition, fear and anger, which negative arguments presumably evoke, are among the strongest emotions and serve as readily available shortcuts for decision making when people evaluate an impending policy initiative.[83]

Public Attentiveness

If the president is going to lead the public successfully, the public must receive and understand his messages. Yet the president cannot depend on an attentive audience. Most people are not very interested in politics. It seems reasonable to assume that because the president is so visible and speaks on such important matters, he will always attract a large audience for his speeches. Wide viewership was certainly common during the early decades of television. Presidential speeches routinely attracted more than 80 percent of those watching television, an audience no one network could command.[84]

Things have changed, however. Audiences for presidential speeches and press conferences have declined steadily since the Nixon administration in the early 1970s.[85] Only 40 million viewers saw at least part of George W. Bush's first nationally televised address on February 27, 2001, compared with 67 million viewers for Bill Clinton's first nationally televised address in 1993.[86] Barack Obama attracted more than 52 million viewers to his nationally televised first address in February 2009, which occurred during a severe economic crisis (see Table 4.3). The size of his audience dropped off substantially, however. When he spoke on behalf of his health care reform proposal the following September, he drew only 32 million viewers.

The root cause of this drop in viewership is access to alternatives to watching the president provided by cable, the Internet, and television.[87] Almost all households receive cable service and also own a VCR[88] (providing yet additional opportunities to avoid watching the president). New networks such as WB and UPN, which have no news departments and thus run entertainment programming during important speeches, provide yet additional distractions from the president.

Television is a medium in which visual interest, action, and conflict are most effective. Unfortunately, presidential speeches are unlikely to contain these characteristics. Only a few addresses to the nation—such as President George W. Bush's address to a joint session of Congress on September 20, 2001—occur at moments of high drama.

The public's general lack of interest in politics constrains the president's leadership of public opinion in the long run, as well as on any given day. Although they have unparalleled access to the American people, presidents

Table 4.3 Subjects and Audiences for Barack Obama's Nationally Televised Speeches

Date	Venue	Topic	Audience Size
February 24, 2009	Joint session of Congress	Overview of administration	52.4 million
September 9, 2009	Joint session of Congress	Health care reform	32.1 million
December 1, 2009	USMA, West Point	Afghanistan	40.8 million
January 27, 2010	Joint session of Congress	State of the Union message	48 million
June 15, 2010	Oval Office	Gulf of Mexico oil spill	32.1 million
August 31, 2010	Oval Office	End of Iraq war	29.2 million
January 12, 2011	Tucson, Arizona	Memorial for shooting victims	30.8 million
January 25, 2011	Joint session of Congress	State of the Union message	42.8 million
March 28, 2011	National Defense University	Libya	25.6 million
May 1, 2011	White House	Death of Osama bin Laden	56.7 million
June 22, 2011*	White House	Troops cuts in Afghanistan	million
July 25, 2011	White House	Debt limit	30.3 million
September 8, 2011	Joint session of Congress	Jobs proposals	31.4 million
January 24, 2012	Joint session of Congress	State of the Union message	37.8 million
May 1, 2012**	Afghanistan	War in Afghanistan	NA
February 12, 2013	Joint session of Congress	State of the Union	33.5 million

*Univision did not carry the speech.
**Not delivered in prime time; no audience ratings.

SOURCE: Nielsen Company

cannot make much use of it. If they do, their speeches will become common-place and lose their drama and interest. That is one reason why presidents do not make formal speeches to the public on television very often—only four or five times a year, on average.[89] Recent presidents, beginning with Richard Nixon, have turned to radio and midday addresses to supplement their prime-time televised addresses,[90] although media coverage of these addresses has diminished over the years.[91] To increase the visibility of his radio addresses, Barack Obama recorded them for digital video and audio downloads from venues such as YouTube and iTunes. As a result, people can access them whenever and wherever they want. Weekly video addresses are also available at http://www.whitehouse.gov.

In addition to the challenge of attracting an audience for the president's television appearances, the White House faces the obstacle of obtaining television coverage in the first place. Traditionally, presidents could rely on full network coverage of any statement they wished to make directly to the American people or any press conference they wished to be televised. The networks began to rebel against providing airtime in the 1970s and 1980s when one or more of them occasionally refused to carry an address or a prime-time press conference held by Presidents Ford, Carter, Reagan, or Bush. Bill Clinton encountered so much resistance from the networks to covering his speeches and press conferences that he held only four evening press conferences in his eight years in office (only one of which all the networks covered live) and made only six addresses on domestic policy, all of them in his first term.

In the two months following the terrorist attacks on the United States on September 11, 2001, George W. Bush received plenty of prime-time coverage for his speeches and a press conference. By November 8, however, most networks viewed the president's speech on the U.S. response to terrorism as an event rather than news and did not carry it. Nearly a year later, on October 7, 2002, Bush made his most comprehensive address regarding the likely need to use force against Saddam Hussein's regime in Iraq. Nevertheless, ABC, CBS, NBC, and PBS chose not to carry the president's speech, arguing that it contained little that was new.

In addition, for the president to lead opinion, people must perceive accurately the view offered by the White House. Yet different people perceive the same message differently.[92] With all his personal, ideological, and partisan[93] baggage, no president can assume that all citizens hear the same thing when he speaks.

Focusing Attention

"From the perspective of White House staff, the key to successful advocacy is controlling the public agenda."[94] Thus, the president wants to focus the public's attention on his priorities, and he has to do this for a sustained period of time. As a former White House public relations counselor put it, "History teaches that almost nothing a leader says is heard if spoken only once."[95] Yet the president communicates with the public in a congested communications environment clogged with competing messages from a wide variety of sources, through a wide range of media, and on a staggering array of subjects.[96]

The Reagan White House was successful in maintaining a focus on its top-priority economic policies in 1981. It molded its communication strategy around its legislative priorities and focused the administration's agenda and statements on economic policy to ensure that discussing a wide range of topics did not diffuse the president's message.[97] In contrast, the Clinton administration blurred its focus by raising a wide range of issues in its first two years in office. The president later lamented that in the beginning of his tenure,

> I gave almost no thought to how to keep the public's focus on my most important priorities, rather than on competing stories that, at the least, would divert public attention from the big issues and, at worst, could make it appear that I was neglecting those priorities.[98]

Sustaining such a focus is very difficult, however, as there are many competing demands on the president to act and speak which divert attention from his priorities. After 1981, President Reagan had to deal with a wide range of noneconomic policies. As Barack Obama's communications director, Daniel Pfeiffer, put it: "In the White House, you have the myriad of challenges on any given day and are generally being forced to communicate a number of complex subjects at the same time."[99] Thus, according to the president's senior advisor, David Axelrod, the sheer volume of crises overwhelmed the message.[100]

At the beginning of May 2010, the president's top advisors thought they had a public relations plan for the week: a focus on jobs and the White House's efforts to boost the economic recovery.[101] That agenda lost focus, however, when three unanticipated events with which Obama had to deal dominated the news. First, the BP oil spill and possible environmental crisis in the Gulf of Mexico required a presidential visit to the area and regular commentary from the White House. Then a terrorist's bomb found in New York's Times Square provided yet another distraction. There was no way the president could not comment on such an event, and there was no way it would not dominate the news. Finally, Arizona passed a controversial immigration law, focusing attention on yet another issue.

Presidents only rarely consistently and repeatedly go public regarding even their most significant legislative proposals.[102] Commentary cascades from the White House, of course. One official estimated that the White House produces as many as 5 million words a year in the president's name in outlets such as speeches, written statements, and proclamations.[103] The number of presidential statements regarding a prominent policy can exceed 200 in a year.

Wide audiences hear only a small proportion of the president's comments, however. Comments about policy proposals at news conferences and question-and-answer sessions and in most interviews are also usually brief and made in the context of a simultaneous discussion of many other policies. Remarks to individual groups and written statements may be focused, but the audience for these communications is modest. In addition, according to David Gergen, nearly all of the president's statements "wash over the public. They are dull, gray prose, eminently forgettable."[104]

The largest audiences, of course, are for the president's nationally televised addresses, but most of the comments in these addresses are made in the context of remarks about many other policies. There is little opportunity to focus on one issue area, especially in domestic policy. Bill Clinton made twenty-eight nationally televised addresses. Ten of these addresses were of a general nature, including his inaugural and State of the Union messages. Another nine announced U.S. military interventions, and three dealt with his impeachment problems. The president made only six national addresses on legislation before Congress, four of them in 1993 and the last one in June 1995. In the remaining five-and-a-half years of his presidency, he never again made a nationally televised address on legislation, except for his obligatory State of the Union addresses!

George W. Bush delivered thirty-three nationally televised addresses but used them even less than his predecessors to speak to the country about his initiatives. Almost all of his nationally televised addresses either were general addresses or related to the war on terrorism. Regarding other initiatives, he made one address on his decision regarding stem cell research in 2001, one on his nomination of John Roberts to the Supreme Court in 2005, and one on immigration reform in 2006.

In his first term, Barack Obama delivered fifteen nationally televised addresses, all but one in prime time. Four were general addresses, and six focused on foreign policy. He made another speech at a memorial service for shooting victims in Arizona. Only four of his speeches dealt with domestic policy issues, and these were on four different matters—health care, an oil spill, the debt limit, and jobs.

The hurdles that the White House faces in presenting its case, including overcoming the public's predispositions, attracting an audience, obtaining airtime, and sustaining a communications focus, encourage presidents to rely on more subtle methods of opinion leadership.

Framing Issues

The president is interested in not only what the public thinks about a policy but also *how* they are thinking about it. As a result, the White House attempts to influence the public's understanding of what issues are about and the questions it asks about them as it evaluates the president's positions. Structuring the choices about policy issues in ways that favor the president's programs may set the terms of the debate on his proposals and thus the premises on which the public evaluates them. As one leading adviser to Reagan put it, "I've always believed that 80 percent of any legislative or political matter is how you frame the debate."[105]

Policy issues are usually complex and subject to alternative interpretations. Issues within the direct experience of citizens, such as poverty, health care, and racial inequality, as well as those more remote from everyday life, such as arms control and international trade, are susceptible to widely different understandings. The sheer complexity of most issues combined with the competing values that are relevant to evaluating them create substantial cognitive burdens for people. They cope by acting as cognitive misers and employing shortcuts to simplify the decisional process.[106]

Thus, when people evaluate an issue or a public official, they do not search their memories for all the considerations that might be relevant; they do not incorporate all the dimensions of a policy proposal into the formulation of their preferences. The intellectual burdens would be too great and their interest in politics too limited for such an arduous task. Instead of undertaking an exhaustive search, citizens minimize their cognitive burdens by selecting the dimensions they deem to be most important for their evaluations. In this decisional process, people are likely to weigh most heavily the information and values that are most easily accessible. Recent activation is one factor that determines their accessibility.[107]

The cognitive challenges of citizens are both an opportunity and a challenge for the White House. Because individuals typically have at least two, and often more, relevant values for evaluating issue positions and because they are unlikely to canvass all their values in their evaluations, the president cannot leave to chance the identification of which values are most relevant to the issues he raises. Instead, the White House seeks to influence the values citizens employ in their evaluations.

In most instances, the president does not have much impact on the values that people hold. Citizens develop these values over many years, starting in early childhood. By the time people focus on the president, their values are for the most part well established. So the president is not in a position to, say, convince people that they ought to be more generous to the poor or more concerned with the distribution of wealth in the country.

However, people use cues from elites as to the ideological or partisan implications of messages[108] (the source of a message is itself an important cue).[109] By articulating widely held values and pointing out their applicability to policy issues, events, or his own performance, the president may increase the salience (and thus the accessibility) of those values to the public's evaluations of them. In the process, the president attempts to show the public that his position is consistent with their individual values. Thus, if the president opposes an expansion of the federal workforce to perform a service, he will probably articulate his opposition in terms of concern for big government, an attitude already held by many in the public.

Instead of trying to persuade the public directly on the merits of a proposal, then, the White House often uses public statements and the press coverage they generate to articulate relatively simple themes. Public opinion research may have identified these themes as favoring the president's positions. For example, on the eve of the vote in the House on the climate change bill, President Obama shifted his argument for the bill to emphasize its potential economic benefits. "Make no mistake," he declared, "this is a jobs bill."[110]

Through framing, the president attempts to define what a public policy issue is about. A *frame* is a central organizing idea for making sense of an issue or conflict and suggests what the controversy is about and what is at stake.[111] Thus, a leader might frame health care for those with low incomes as an appropriate program necessary to compensate for the difficult circumstances in which the less fortunate find themselves, or as a giveaway to undeserving slackers committed to living on the dole.

By defining and simplifying a complex issue through framing, the president hopes to activate and make more salient particular considerations that citizens will use for formulating their political preferences. It is not clear whether an issue frame interacts with an individual's memory so as to *prime* certain considerations, making some more accessible than others and therefore more likely to be used in formulating a political preference, or whether framing works by encouraging individuals to think deliberately about the importance of considerations suggested by a frame.[112] In either case, the frame raises the priority and weight that individuals assign to particular attitudes already stored in their memories.[113] The president's goal is to influence the attitudes and information people incorporate into their judgments of his policies and performance.[114]

For example, if the president favors increasing the minimum wage, he may focus his arguments on *equity*: It is important to pay those making the lowest wages at least enough to support a minimally acceptable lifestyle. If he opposes an increase, however, he may focus on *efficiency*: Raising the cost of labor puts businesses that employ low-wage earners at a disadvantage in the marketplace and may cause some employers to terminate workers in order to reduce their costs. In both cases, the president is emphasizing different values in the debate in an attempt to frame the issue to his advantage.

Presidential Framing

Framing and priming have a number of advantages for the president, not the least of which is that they demand less of the public than directly persuading citizens on the merits of a policy proposal. The president does not have to persuade people to change their basic values and preferences. He does not have to convince citizens to develop expertise and acquire and process extensive information about the details of a policy proposal. In addition, framing and priming—because they are relatively simple—are less susceptible to distortion by journalists and opponents than direct persuasion on the merits of a policy proposal.[115]

Portraying policies in terms of criteria on which there is a consensus and playing down divisive issues are often at the core of efforts to structure choices for both the public and Congress. The Reagan administration framed the 1986 tax reform act as revenue-neutral, presenting the choice on the policy as one of serving special interests or helping average taxpayers. Few people would choose the former option. Federal aid to education had been a divisive issue for years before President Johnson proposed the Elementary and Secondary Education Act in 1965. To blunt opposition, he successfully changed the focus of debate from teachers' salaries and classroom shortages to fighting poverty, and from the separation of church and state to aiding children. This frame changed the premises of congressional decision making and eased the path for the bill.[116]

Dwight Eisenhower employed the noncontroversial symbol of national defense during the Cold War, even when it came to naming legislation, to obtain support for aiding education (the National Defense Education Act) and building highways (the Interstate and Defense Highway Act). Franklin D. Roosevelt's adoption of the "New Deal" to characterize his administration and Richard Nixon's description of the January 1973 peace agreement ending the involvement of American troops in Vietnam as "peace with honor" are other examples of using consensual positive symbols to frame administrations or policies in a positive light.

At other times, the president must try to frame choices in an atmosphere inflamed by partisanship. Independent Counsel Kenneth Starr accused

President Clinton of eleven counts of impeachable offenses, perjury, obstruction of justice, witness tampering, and abuse of power. The White House fought back, accusing Starr of engaging in an *intrusive* investigation motivated by a *political vendetta* against the president. The basic White House defense was that the president made a mistake (*personal failing*) in his *private* behavior, apologized for it, and was ready to move on to continue to do the people's business of governing the nation. Impeachment, the president's defenders said, was grossly *disproportionate* to the president's offense. The public found the White House argument compelling and strongly opposed the president's impeachment.

The White House can use symbols to label opponents as well as policies. For example, President Clinton referred to conservative talk-show hosts as "purveyors of hatred and division" following the 1995 Oklahoma City bombing.

Sometimes presidents add new attributes to a policy[117] to increase the public's support for it.[118] To obtain support for using the budget surplus to pay down the national debt rather for funding a tax cut, Bill Clinton urged Congress to "save Social Security first." Framing the issue of paying down the national debt as being for or against this popular policy increased the salience of the issue to the public and made it difficult for Republicans to argue that Congress should use the surplus to fund a tax cut.

Similarly, in 1984 Ronald Reagan failed to win congressional support for additional MX missiles when the debate focused on the utility of the missiles as strategic weapons. He was more successful the next year, however, after the terms of the debate changed to focus on the impact of building the missiles on the arms control negotiations with the Soviet Union that had recently begun in Geneva. Senators and representatives who lacked confidence in the contribution of the MX to national security were still reluctant to go to the public and explain why they were denying American negotiators the bargaining chips they said they required.

Reagan also understood instinctually that his popular support was linked to his ability to embody the values of an idealized America. He continually invoked symbols of his vision of America and its past—an optimistic view that did not closely correspond to reality but did sustain public support. He projected a simple, coherent vision for his presidency that served him well in attracting adherents and countering criticism when the inevitable contradictions in policy arose. For example, he maintained his identification with balanced budgets even though he never submitted a budget that was even close to balanced and his administration was responsible for more deficit spending than all previous administrations combined. More broadly, Reagan employed the symbols of an idealized polity to frame his policies as consistent with core American values.[119]

Presidents try to frame themselves as chiefs of state, nonpartisan statesmen personifying both the government and the nation's heritage. They frequently appear on television welcoming heads of state or other dignitaries to the White House, dedicating federal projects, speaking before national groups, or performing ceremonial functions, such as laying a wreath at the Tomb of the Unknowns in Arlington National Cemetery or lighting the national Christmas tree. Foreign travels provide additional opportunities for presidents to present themselves as statesmen, dealing with the leaders of other nations on matters of international importance.

While engaging in these and other functions, presidents often make appeals to patriotism, traditions, and U.S. history (and its greatness) to move the public to support them, thus reminding people of their common interests. They also frequently invoke the names of revered leaders of the past who made difficult decisions on the basis of high principles, such as Abraham Lincoln or Harry Truman, and then relate themselves or their decisions to these paragons.

Presidents also make gestures to show that they are really "one of the people." President Carter made considerable use of this technique in his desire to be seen as a people's president. At his inauguration, he chose to walk (instead of ride) down Pennsylvania Avenue from the Capitol to the White House after taking the oath of office. He conducted a "fireside chat" over national television, seated before a blazing fire and dressed casually in a sweater instead of a suit. He also staged the first press conference in which private individuals could call in from around the country and directly ask him questions, and he held many town meetings where he could be questioned directly by local citizens. Most subsequent presidents have adopted the town meetings format and other means for meeting with average citizens.

Limits to Framing

Despite its potential advantages, framing issues successfully is a challenge for the White House. The president faces committed, well-organized, and well-funded opponents who provide competing frames. When there is elite

President Obama reviews an international honor guard in his role as head of state.

consensus, and thus only one set of cues offered to the public, the potential for opinion leadership may be substantial. However, when elite discourse is divided, generating conflicting messages, people respond to the issue according to their predispositions, especially their core partisan and ideological views.[120]

Occasions in which elite commentary is one-sided are rare. Most issues that generate consensual elite discourse arise from external events. A surprise attack on the United States, such as the terrorist assaults on 9/11, or its allies, such as the invasion of Kuwait in 1990, would be examples of galvanizing incidents. Consensual issues also tend to be new, with few people having committed themselves to a view about them. In his examination of public opinion regarding the Gulf War, John Zaller argues that the president's greatest chance of influencing public opinion is in a crisis (which attracts the public's attention) in which elites articulate a unified message. At other times, most people are too inattentive or too committed to views to be strongly influenced by elite efforts at persuasion.[121]

The Obama administration was unable to frame its economic program in terms of economic growth and opportunity. Instead, the Republicans succeeded in defining it in terms of wasteful pork-barrel expenditures that added massively to the deficit. Similarly, opponents characterized the president's health care reform plan as expensive, experimental, providing lower quality and rationed care, and job killing. Opponents emphasized "big government" to prompt people to put conservative attitudes toward government in the forefront of their minds and use them to evaluate health reform.

Public Relations

In its efforts to mold public opinion, the White House employs public relations techniques modeled after those of commercial advertising firms. One indicator of the importance of public relations to contemporary presidents is the presence of advertising specialists and those with television backgrounds in the White House. More broadly, the White House invests a substantial amount of staff, time, and energy into focusing the public's attention on the issues it wishes to promote and encouraging the public to see its proposals for dealing with those issues in a positive light. A count of the second term of the George W. Bush presidency found that the number of White House communications staff outnumbered the economic and domestic policy staff. If one includes all those who worked on the presentation of the president and development of his communications, a conservative estimate is that there were 350 people on the president's staff working on communications.[122]

A focus on public relations may influence the substance, presentation, and especially the timing of policy. Being human, all presidents are subject to the temptation to do the most popular thing.[123] The potential for subordinating substance to style is clearly present. Reagan aide and public relations specialist Michael Deaver freely admitted that he had little interest in matters of public policy and argued that "image is sometimes as useful as substance."[124]

A focus on public relations also encourages running the White House like an advertising agency. A close observer of the Reagan administration found that a single focus permeated staff meetings of top White House officials: how the topic under discussion would play in the media.[125] Advertising stresses a uniform image, and attempts to achieve this orientation can be a centralizing force in an administration. However, an emphasis on "team play" may discourage dissent because it might cloud the president's image. The Nixon and George W. Bush White Houses were especially concerned with message discipline, and critics charged each with being unduly closed to alternative views. Both administrations also found it difficult to maintain message discipline, however.[126]

Spreading the Word

The primary goal of White House public relations efforts is to build support for the president and his policies. Part of this job is "getting the word out" about the president, his views, and his accomplishments. The president, of course, carries much of this burden and appears in many venues. Bill Clinton even appeared on MTV within six weeks of taking office in an attempt to reach a more youthful audience, and Barack Obama has appeared on the Jay Leno and David Letterman shows as well as ESPN. The White House also places representatives of the administration (the vice president, cabinet members, and senior White House staff) on television programs such as the Sunday interview shows and weekday morning news shows. Similarly, the White House provides or clears speeches for officials to give at university commencement ceremonies and in other visible settings.

Although technological change has made it more difficult for the president to attract an audience on television, other changes may have increased the White House's prospects of reaching the public. Teddy Roosevelt gave prominence to the bully pulpit by exploiting the hunger of modern newspapers for national news. Franklin D. Roosevelt broadened the reach and immediacy of presidential communications with his use of radio. More recently, John F. Kennedy and Ronald Reagan mastered the use of television to speak directly to the American people. Now Barack Obama has positioned himself as the first Internet president.

The Obama White House created a private organization, Organizing for America, to communicate over the Internet with those on its list of 13 million e-mail addresses that was developed during the 2008 election. The ultimate goal is to mobilize these core supporters behind the president's legislative program. The White House Office of New Media spreads Obama's perspective wherever it can on the Web, providing a counterweight to the often virulent anti-Obama chatter there. White House officials follow the president's message with more personal responses to thousands of questions submitted by everyone from casual observers to seasoned experts.

The president has answered questions submitted over the Internet and held interviews with YouTube, Twitter, and Facebook users. The White House produces and distributes much more video than any past administration, which can be found on whitehouse.gov, Obama's YouTube channel, and other video

AP Photo/Pablo Martinez Monsivais

President Barack Obama types the answer to a question during his live-tweet as Twitter Executive Chairman Jack Dorsey looks on during the first ever Twitter Town Hall.

depots. The administration also holds regular question-and-answer Webcasts with policy officials on whitehouse.gov. In addition, the administration introduced *West Wing Week*, a video blog consisting of six- to seven-minute compilations that appear each week on the White House's website and on such video-sharing sites as YouTube.

Of course, widespread access to the Internet has created the potential for people to communicate easily with each other as well as to receive communications from leaders. White House opponents can exploit this technology to reinforce their opposition to an administration. Even the president's ideological supporters can harness the new technologies to oppose a president's pragmatism and tendencies toward moderation.

The White House regularly disperses information to editors, commentators, and reporters. In addition, it reaches out to ethnic, religious, geographic, professional, and other types of groups interested in particular policies. As Clinton press secretary Mike McCurry put it, "most presidential communications are not aimed at the entire country; they're aimed at different segments of the total population."[127]

The president's aides may also try to stimulate favorable articles on the First Family and is happy to provide photographs portraying the president as family oriented, a pet owner, or the like. For example, Reagan White House aides ghostwrote, under the president's name, a story on keeping physically fit and had it published in a popular Sunday newspaper magazine supplement. The idea was to make the point subtly that Ronald Reagan was not too old for the job. Likewise, the White House paid close attention to the president's image, trying to portray him as busy and engaged in important decision making rather than remote and passive, as critics charged.

Reaching the television audience for news is especially important to the White House, and the president's staff builds his schedule around efforts to do so. As one press aide put it: "Whenever possible, everything was done to take into account the need for coverage. After all, most of the events are done for coverage. Why else are you doing them?"[128]

Presidents and their aides tailor the messages they wish to transmit to the public to the needs of the press. The Reagan White House was especially skilled at providing vivid pictures and effective sound bites for the television news. Similarly, the president and his aides time announcements so that reporters can meet their papers' deadlines. Those made too late in the evening will not appear in the next morning's newspapers.

If the White House wants to decrease the coverage of an event, it can wait until after the evening news programs or weekends to announce it. Then it might be buried among the next day's occurrences. (In the age of twenty-four-hour news channels, however, a cable channel is likely to pick it up.) The White House can also order administration officials to avoid appearing on interview programs or holding press conferences. The White House can make an announcement right before a press deadline, decreasing the opportunity for reporters to obtain unfavorable reactions. Finally, the president can discourage coverage of a divisive issue by acting away from reporters and cameras, such as when President Obama quietly signed an order allowing federal funds to be used for international groups that promote abortion.

Alternately, the president might take another newsworthy action at the same time. President Clinton timed his firing of Federal Bureau of Investigation (FBI) director William Sessions so that it would cut into the news coverage of a speech on his policy on homosexuals in the military, and he vetoed a ban on late-term abortions on a heavy news day dominated by the funeral of Commerce Secretary Ron Brown. George W. Bush announced his proposal for a Department of Homeland Security just as the Senate Judiciary Committee began hearings on failures of the FBI regarding preventing terrorist attacks.

The White House tries to avoid associating the president with bad news. When the United States pulled the marines out of Lebanon, it was announced after President Reagan flew to his California ranch for a vacation and was not available for questions.[129] It was preferable to let a subordinate serve as the lightning rod.[130] Similarly, when a U.S. plane collided with a Chinese aircraft in April 2001, the White House was determined to keep George W. Bush away from the issue so he would not appear to be emotionally involved or to be the negotiator with the Chinese. Secretary of State Colin Powell took the lead—but the White House did not want Powell on television to take the credit when he succeeded in winning the crew's release.[131] The general rule of thumb is that the president delivers good news, but bad news comes from his staff or other administration officials.

Presidents may also try to avoid being caught up in controversies. Presidents Reagan and both Bushes addressed the annual Washington antiabortion rally by phone, even though it was held only a short distance from the White House. They wanted to avoid being seen with the leaders of the movement on the evening news. Similarly, President Clinton left a recorded message for those participating in a 1993 gay rights rally in the capital.

Conversely, the White House loves good news, which it tries to distribute over time so that each incident receives full coverage. The president does not want bad news to drive out the good, yet this does happen. The first major piece of legislation that President Clinton signed was the popular Family Leave Act. Coverage of the signing ceremony was diluted, however, by media attention focused on Kimba Wood's withdrawal from consideration as attorney general.

Media Events

In addition to general efforts to publicize the president, the White House often stages "media events" in the hope of obtaining additional public support. No administration was more attentive to the potential of media events than Ronald Reagan's. His press secretary, Larry Speakes, kept a sign on his desk that read, "You don't tell us how to stage the news, and we don't tell you how to cover it." Michael Deaver carefully scripted every second of the president's public appearances, right down to placing tape on the floor to show Reagan where to stand for the best camera angles.[132] Deaver was clear about the importance of appealing to television: "You get only 40 to 80 seconds on a given night on the network news, and unless you can find a visual that explains your message you can't make it stick."[133]

The George W. Bush White House was also skilled at using the powers of television and technology to promote the president. "We pay particular attention to not only what the president says but what the American people see," said Office of Communications Director Dan Bartlett. Thus, the White House hired experts in lighting, camera angles, and backdrops from network television to showcase the president in dramatic and perfectly lighted settings. In May 2003, at a speech promoting his economic plan in Indianapolis, White House aides went so far as to ask people in the crowd behind Bush to take off their ties so they would look more like the ordinary people the president said would benefit from his tax cut. For a speech that the president delivered in the summer of 2002 at Mount Rushmore, the White House positioned the platform for television crews off to one side so that the cameras caught Mr. Bush in profile, his face perfectly aligned with the four presidents chiseled in stone.[134]

Perhaps the most elaborate White House event was Bush's speech aboard the *Abraham Lincoln* announcing the end of major combat in Iraq. The Office of Communications choreographed every aspect of the event, including positioning the aircraft carrier so the shoreline could not be seen by the camera when the president landed; arraying members of the crew in coordinated shirt colors over Bush's right shoulder; and placing a banner reading "Mission Accomplished" to capture the president and the celebratory two words perfectly in a single camera shot. It also specifically timed the speech so the sun would cast a golden glow on Bush. One of the president's aides proclaimed, "If you looked at the TV picture, you saw there was flattering light on his left cheek and slight shadowing on his right. It looked great."[135]

At times, media events can be used quite cynically. When President Reagan was under fire for not supporting civil rights, he paid a visit to a black family who had had a cross burned in their front yard. However, the White House did not mention that the cross burning had occurred five years earlier. When the president's pollster found that the public overwhelmingly disapproved of the administration's reductions in aid to education, Michael Deaver arranged for Reagan to make a series of speeches emphasizing quality education. As Deaver later gloated, public approval of the president regarding education "flip-flopped" without any change in policy at all.[136]

Some of the emphasis on media events is the White House's response to the nature of the media (which we will examine in Chapter 5). According to Larry Speakes, the White House press spokesman during most of Ronald Reagan's tenure in the White House:

> We knew that television had to have pictures to present its story. . . . So when Reagan was pushing education, the visual was of him sitting at a little desk and talking to a group of students, or with the football team and some cheerleaders, or in a science lab. Then we would have an educators' forum where the president would make a noteworthy statement. We learned very quickly that the rule was no picture, no television piece, no matter how important our news was.[137]

Operating on similar premises of the value of combining pictures with words, President Obama announced his timeline for withdrawing troops from Iraq before thousands of U.S. marines at Camp Lejeune, North Carolina. When he ordered 30,000 additional troops to Afghanistan, he did so in a prime-time speech to the cadets at West Point. The president also traveled to Tucson, Arizona, in 2011 to speak at a memorial service for those killed in a shooting. Pictures of the president as First Mourner made the story, and his speech was nationally televised.

Information Control

George W. Bush's press secretary described the Bush White House as "engaging in spin, stonewalling, hedging, evasion, denial, noncommunication, and deceit by omission."[138] There are less direct ways, then, for influencing public opinion than appealing to the public directly. Many of these less savory techniques fall under the category of information control. The goal is to influence public opinion by controlling the information on which the public bases its evaluations of chief executives and their policies and which it analyzes to determine if there is cause for concern. If the public is unaware of a situation or has a distorted view of it, then presidents may have more flexibility in achieving what they desire—which often is public passivity as much as public support.

Withholding Information
Classifying information under the rubric of "national security" is frequently used to withhold information. Most people support secrecy in handling

national security affairs, especially in such matters as defense plans and strategy, weapons technology, troop movements, the details of current diplomatic negotiations, the methods and sources of covert intelligence gathering, and similar information about other nations. However, there has been controversy over the amount of information classified and whether the president and other high officials have used classification strategies to influence public opinion. An official might withhold crucial information from the public in order to avoid embarrassment. Yet this may hinder the public's ability to evaluate an official's performance and ask fully informed questions of public policy. In an attempt to increase or maintain support, an official may provide a distorted view of reality. The Bush White House ordered the CIA not to release the reservations and nonconforming evidence in the full National Intelligence Estimate of October 2002 before the U.S. invasion of Iraq,[139] and it kept classified the evidence of how badly things were going in Iraq in the years immediately after the invasion.[140]

There are other means of withholding information besides classification. One of the highest priorities of the George W. Bush administration in 2004 was to pass a prescription drug bill under Medicare. Many members of Congress were concerned about the program's cost, especially at a time of record budget deficits. Medicare's chief actuary, a nonpartisan official, concluded that the bill would cost considerably more than the administration projected. Thomas Scully, the presidentially appointed administrator of the agency overseeing Medicare, ordered him not to provide to Congress the most recent estimates of the cost of the bill while Congress considered it. Similarly, the administration was notable for placing political constraints on scientific findings, ranging from public health reports of the U.S. surgeon general to studies on climate change by the Environmental Protection Agency (EPA) and NASA. The White House even refused to open an e-mail message from the EPA so there would be no official record of the agency's official conclusion that greenhouse gases are pollutants that must be controlled.

Withholding information may not always advance an administration's priorities. During the Tet holiday in the spring of 1968, the North Vietnamese launched a massive attack against U.S. and South Vietnamese forces. U.S. intelligence and military officials, including the president, anticipated this attack, prepared for it militarily, and rapidly defeated it. Yet Tet was the turning point in support for the war, as the nation was shocked by the scale of the attack. President Johnson had led the nation to believe that we had been so successful that such an attack would not be possible. Moreover, he failed to explain what had happened, what the administration knew and what it was doing beforehand, and how Tet affected long-term U.S. goals. Media reports focusing on the spectacular reinforced the public's shock and gave the appearance of a major setback and proof that U.S. policies had failed.[141]

Timing of the Release of Information

Sometimes the White House provides information but uses the timing of its release to try to influence public opinion. For example, on November 2, 1970, the White House announced the most recent casualty figures from Vietnam. They were at a five-year low, and their announcement was made on Monday instead of the usual Thursday, presumably because the 1970 congressional elections were being held the next day. Similarly, the Carter administration revealed that the Pentagon had developed a new technology that made aircraft virtually invisible to enemy detection devices. This disclosure coincided with an administration effort during the 1980 presidential election campaign to show that it was working to strengthen national defense. Taking the opposite tack, the Ford administration announced that the country was in a recession one week after the 1974 congressional elections. The Reagan administration knew that its economic forecasts had been too optimistic, but it did not change them until after the crucial vote on the president's tax cut proposal in 1981.

Obfuscation

Presidents and their aides may also attempt to obscure or distort the truth in order to confuse or mislead the public. President Eisenhower regularly gave purposefully ambiguous answers at his press conferences.[142] When George Bush agreed to accept "tax revenue increases" as part of the 1990 budget agreement with Congress, his announcement was so confusing that it took officials in Washington several days to determine whether he meant increases resulting from increased economic growth, a cut in capital gains taxes, or an increase in tax rates—and his press secretary refused to define the president's terms, in large part because of Bush's campaign promise not to raise taxes. Bill Clinton carried semantic hairsplitting to new heights with his arguments regarding smoking marijuana (he claimed he did not inhale), dodging the draft, raising campaign funds within the White House, and, of course, the nature of his relationship with White House intern Monica Lewinsky.[143]

Distortion

Distortion comes in many forms. One of the most common is to provide impressive statistics without going into the details of how they were compiled. For example, Reagan's budget director, David Stockman, admitted "rigging the [budget] numbers to the point that even we couldn't understand them."[144]

In the selling of the 2003 tax cut, the catch phrase used by the George W. Bush administration was that "92 million Americans will receive an average tax cut of $1,083." That sounded, and was intended to sound, as if every American family would get about $1,083. Although it was true that those who received tax cuts averaged about $1,100, the administration omitted the fact that 50 million citizens would receive no tax cut at all, and about half of those American families who would receive a tax cut would get less than $100. The $1,083 number was inflated by the very big tax cuts received by a few wealthy people.[145]

It is not only what goes into compiling a "fact" that is important for public evaluation but also the context of events in which the so-called fact occurs. For example, in 1964 Lyndon Johnson went before Congress to ask for a resolution supporting retaliation against North Vietnam for two "unprovoked" attacks on U.S. ships in the Gulf of Tonkin. The Gulf of Tonkin Resolution was subsequently passed, marking a watershed in the nation's military actions in Vietnam. The public might have been less enthusiastic in its backing of military reprisals, however, if it had known that the United States had been supporting covert South Vietnamese operations against North Vietnam for several years and that, moreover, there was considerable reason to doubt that the second attack had ever occurred! As President Johnson later said privately, "For all I know, our Navy was shooting whales out there."[146]

Attempts to distort information are not always successful. For example, by 1967 two-thirds of the American people felt that the Johnson administration was not telling them the whole truth about the Vietnam War, and in 1971, a similar percentage felt the same way about the Nixon administration.[147] Out of such attitudes emerged a credibility gap and low levels of popular standing for these presidents.

Prevarication

The most extreme form of information control is lying. The range of subjects about which presidents have lied is great, ranging from U–2 spy plane flights over the Soviet Union and the nation's attempts to prevent the election of Marxist Salvador Allende as president of Chile, to the U.S. military situation in Vietnam and the Watergate cover-up.[148] Bill Clinton lied about his relationship with Monica Lewinsky (which he later admitted in a plea bargain with the Special Prosecutor). White House press secretaries have often misled the press regarding imminent U.S. military actions.[149]

The war with Iraq presented a number of opportunities to lie to the public. The administration repeatedly implied that there was a link between al-Qaeda, the 9/11 attacks, and Iraq. It was not until September 18, 2003—months after the war started—that President Bush conceded the United States had no evidence of any Iraqi involvement in the attacks. President Bush also continually claimed that Saddam Hussein had reconstituted his nuclear weapons program and was potentially "less than a year" away from possessing nuclear weapons, placing the United States in immediate peril. This allegation was a powerful argument that deposing Saddam Hussein was important for U.S. national security. However, the evidence on which it was based was wrong. Even at the time the president made the claims, the evidence was questionable, including the assertion that Iraq had purchased uranium oxide, "yellowcake," from Niger, and that aluminum tubes shipped to Iraq were intended to be used as centrifuges to create the fissile material necessary for a nuclear bomb. One of the keys to broad public support for an invasion of Iraq was the fear that the U.S. mainland could be attacked. Thus, the possibility of Iraq using unmanned, drone airplanes to deliver chemical or biological weapons—a possibility raised by President Bush in his important October 7, 2002, speech—provoked serious concern. However, the U.S. Air Force had discounted this possibility in its assessments of Iraq's capabilities.[150]

The president and other administration officials, most notably Vice President Cheney, often made statements that in hindsight were wrong.[151] The president may well have believed his statements, although he did not reveal the tenuous basis for his inferences about the threat that Iraq posed to the United States. Nor did he clarify the lack of evidence of any role of Iraq in the 9/11 attacks.

One thing is clear: The American people resent being lied to. Most feel it is unacceptable for the government to lie—even to achieve foreign policy goals (although it is acceptable to confuse an enemy).[152] When an administration is seen as being untruthful, it loses credibility—a precious resource in White House efforts to lead the public.[153]

Information Control and National Security

Information control is most common in the national security area because it is difficult for the public to challenge official statements about events in other countries, especially military activities, which often are shrouded in secrecy. It is much easier to be skeptical about domestic activities that American reporters can scrutinize and to which they can provide alternative views. In addition, people can relate many domestic policies to their own experiences more easily than they can relate to most foreign and military policies. When official statements fail to correspond to people's experiences, the stage is set for skepticism.

Officials deny information not only to a foreign adversary but also to the American public. In virtually all the examples involving national security policy, from the U-2 flight over the Soviet Union to the secret bombing of Cambodia, the "foreign adversary" knew the truth. Only the American public was left in the dark.

Success of Opinion Leadership

We have seen that presidents invest a great deal of effort and employ a wide range of techniques to lead the public. How successful are they in using the "bully pulpit" to move the public to support their policies?[154]

Ronald Reagan offers a best-test case for presidential leadership of the public. He displayed formidable rhetorical skills and went to unprecedented lengths to influence public opinion. Both his supporters and detractors frequently commented on his unusual rapport with the public and often termed him the "The Great Communicator." Was he able to function as a director of public opinion?

Reagan knew better. In his memoirs, he reflected on his efforts to ignite concern among the American people regarding the threat of communism in Central America and to mobilize them behind his program of support for the Contras.

> For eight years the press called me the "Great Communicator." Well, one of my greatest frustrations during those eight years was my inability to communicate to the American people and to Congress the seriousness of the threat we faced in Central America.
>
> . . . Time and again, I would speak on television, to a joint session of Congress, or to other audiences about the problems in Central America, and I would hope that the outcome would be an outpouring of support from Americans . . . .

But the polls usually found that large numbers of Americans cared little or not at all about what happened in Central America—in fact, a surprisingly large proportion didn't even know where Nicaragua and El Salvador were located—and, among those who did care, too few cared enough about a Communist penetration of the Americas to apply the kind of pressure I needed on Congress.[155]

Numerous national surveys of public opinion have found that support for regulatory programs and spending on domestic policy increased, rather than decreased, during Reagan's tenure. Conversely, support for increased defense expenditures was decidedly lower at the end of his administration than when he took office. In each case, the public was moving in the opposite direction to that of the president.[156] Indeed, there was a movement away from conservative views almost as soon as he took office. According to one scholar, "Whatever Ronald Reagan's skills as a communicator, one ability he clearly did not possess was the capacity to induce lasting changes in American policy preferences."[157] As press secretary Marlin Fitzwater put it, "Reagan would go out on the stump, draw huge throngs and convert no one at all."[158]

Bill Clinton was an articulate, knowledgeable, energetic, and experienced communicator who came to office with an explicit theory of governing by going to the public. Nevertheless, he was repeatedly disappointed in the results of his efforts at public leadership. Health care reform was to be the centerpiece of the Clinton administration. In September 1993, the president delivered a well-received national address on the need for reform. Yet the president was not able to sustain the support of the public for his bill. The White House held out against compromise with the Republicans and conservative Democrats, hoping for a groundswell of public support for reform. It never came. In the meantime, opponents of the president's proposal launched an aggressive counterattack, including running negative television advertisements. As the figures in Table 4.4 show, by mid-July 1994, only 40 percent of the public favored the president's health care reform proposals, and 56 percent opposed them. The bill did not come to a vote in either chamber of Congress.

No issue was more important to George W. Bush's presidency than the war with Iraq. In the late summer of 2002, the White House decided to remove Saddam Hussein from power and aggressively sought the public's backing. The context in which Bush sought this support was certainly favorable. In surveys stretching back to the end of the Gulf War in 1991, majorities of the public had generally supported U.S. military action on behalf of regime change in Iraq. Most Americans felt that Iraq had developed or was developing weapons of mass destruction; many concluded that if left alone, Iraq would use those weapons against the United States within five years; and most believed that Saddam Hussein sponsored terrorism that affected the United States. A little more than half of the public took the additional inferential leap and concluded that he was directly involved in the September 11, 2001, terrorist attacks.[159]

Figure 4.3 shows public support for the invasion of Iraq did not change in response to the administration's blitzkrieg. Instead, it stayed within a narrow

Table 4.4 Public Support for Clinton's Health Care Reform

Date	Favor (%)	Oppose (%)	Don't Know (%)
September 24–26, 1993	59	33	8
October 28–30, 1993	45	45	10
November 2–4, 1993	52	40	8
November 19–21, 1993	52	41	7
January 15–17, 1994	56	39	6
January 28–30, 1994	57	38	5
February 26–28, 1994	46	48	5
March 28–30, 1994	44	47	9
May 20–22, 1994	46	49	5
June 11–12, 1994	42	50	8
June 25–28, 1994	44	49	8
July 15–17, 1994	40	56	5

SOURCE: Gallup Poll question, "From everything you've heard or read about the plan so far . . . do you favor or oppose President Clinton's plan to reform health care?" © 1994, The Gallup Organization. All rights reserved. Reprinted with permission.

range throughout the fall and winter until early February 2003. At that point, it increased 5 percentage points in response to Secretary of State Colin Powell's presentation of evidence against Iraq to the UN. In the month following Powell's speech, support for an invasion drifted downward until the middle of March, when the president issued the final ultimatum to Saddam Hussein that marked the beginning of a rally in support of war.

Barack Obama entered the presidency with an impressive record of political success, at the center of which were his rhetorical skills. In college, he concluded that words had the power to transform: "with the right words everything could change—South Africa, the lives of ghetto kids just a few miles away, my own tenuous place in the world."[160] Nevertheless, the president was constantly frustrated in his efforts to obtain support for his major initiatives if they were not already popular with the public.

The biggest legislative battle of the Obama administration was health care reform. Substantially changing any policy that dealt with 17 percent of the nation's GDP was going to be difficult. Doing so in a context of highly polarized partisan politics, enormous budget deficits, and broad skepticism about government activism only made matters worse for the White House. Nevertheless, the president forged ahead. Yet despite the president's efforts to address the public's misgivings in speeches, news conferences, town-hall-style meetings, and interviews, the public did not respond. Instead, the public displayed a lack of support for Obama and what it perceived as his health care plan (Table 4.5). Despite all his and his administration's efforts, the president never obtained majority—or even plurality—support for health care reform. He could not create an opportunity for change.

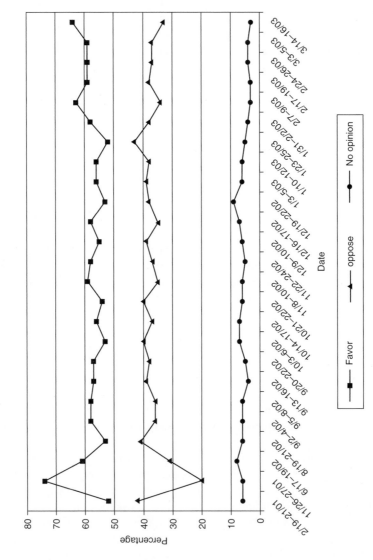

FIGURE 4.3 Public Support for Invasion of Iraq

Source: Gallup Poll question: "Would you favor or oppose sending American ground troops to the Persian Gulf in an attempt to remove Saddam Hussein from power in Iraq?" © The Gallup Organization. All rights reserved. Reprinted with permission.

Table 4.5 Support for Obama's Health Care Plan

Date of Poll	% Favor	% Oppose	% Don't Know
July 22–26, 2009	38	44	18
August 20–27, 2009	39	46	15
September 10–15, 2009	42	44	14
September 30–October 4, 2009	34	47	19
October 28–November 8, 2009	38	47	15
November 12–15, 2009	42	39	19
December 9–13, 2009	35	48	17
January 6–10, 2010	39	48	13
February 3–9, 2010	38	50	12
March 10–14, 2010	38	48	13
April 1–5, 2010	40	44	16
July 8–11, 2010	35	47	17
September 9–12, 2010	38	45	17

SOURCE: Pew Research Center for the People and the Press poll question: "As of right now, do you generally favor or generally oppose the health care proposals being discussed in congress?"

The difficulty presidents have in moving public opinion poses a direct challenge to the faith that many have in the broad premise of the potential of presidential leadership of the public. Yet it is consistent with important and wide-ranging works on public opinion, including studies by James Stimson,[161] Benjamin Page and Robert Shapiro,[162] and Benjamin Page and Marshall Bouton.[163] They find that the public's collective policy preferences generally are stable and change by large margins only in response to world events. Even on foreign policy, Page and Bouton find that there are often large gaps between public opinion and the views of leaders, and the two are not converging. Thus, there is little evidence of opinion leadership.

CONCLUSION

A president's relations with the public are complex. All chief executives need the support of the people in order to play an effective leadership role, yet they have a difficult time obtaining it. Expectations are high and contradictory, and the public's desires are frequently difficult to ascertain. Although the public appears to award or withhold its support of the chief executive based largely on job performance, its perceptions of issues and the president's actions may be hazy. Just how the public reaches its conclusions about the president's performance is not well understood. In theory, however, there is ample opportunity for the president, directly and through the press, to influence public perceptions.

Given this environment, presidents are not content to follow public opinion. In their search for public support, they invest substantial time, energy, ingenuity, and personnel in techniques that include directly appealing to the

public, framing issues and using symbols, employing public relations techniques, and exercising information control. Some of this activity is quite legitimate. Some is not, instead following Richard Nixon's view that "[i]t's not *what*
Presidents do but how they do it that matters."[164]

There is no guarantee of success in these efforts, however, and presidents
often fail to achieve their desired effects. Even those who are considered "great
communicators" are not able to move the public much on their own; they cannot reshape the contours of the political landscape to pave the way for change.
Instead, they are facilitators who depend on the public moving at its own pace
to provide opportunities to accomplish their goals. The White House is also
dependent on the press to deliver its message.

Discussion Questions

1. Private public opinion polls, commissioned by the White House, have
    become common. Should presidents take so many polls? How should
    they use the results?

2. Do presidents suffer politically from public expectations that are contra-
    dictory and unreasonably high? If so, how would you advise a president
    to deal with this problem? Illustrate your answer with examples from the
    presidency of Barack Obama. What were the public's expectations when
    he was elected, and how successful was he in meeting them?

3. Leading the public is difficult to do, and presidents employ many tech-
    niques to influence public opinion. What are the most useful approaches
    to obtaining the public's support? How successful has President Obama
    been in moving public opinion?

Web Exercises

1. Listen to the president's weekly radio address and read the text along with
    the president. Why is the address so short? Go to http://www.whitehouse.
    gov/news/radio/. Then read the Sunday newspapers, watch the Saturday
    evening news, or visit a media website to see whether the radio address
    was mentioned. What did the address accomplish for the president?

2. Check the president's public approval since he took office at http://www.
    gallup.com/poll/124922/Presidential-Approval-Center.aspx or at http://
    www.pollingreport.com/obama.htm. Given our discussion in this chapter,
    why does the president have this level of public support? How do you
    explain the fluctuations during his presidency?

Selected Readings

Baum, Matthew A., and Samuel Kernell.
"Has Cable Ended the Golden Age
of Presidential Television?" *American*
Political Science Review 93 (March
1999): 99–114.

Canes-Wrone, Brandice. *Who Leads*
Whom? Princeton, NJ: Princeton
University Press, 2006.

Druckman, James N., and Lawrence R. Jacobs. "Presidential Responsiveness to Public Opinion." In *Oxford Handbook of the American Presidency,* edited by George C. Edwards III and William G. Howell. Oxford: Oxford University Press, 2009.

Edwards, George C., III. *Governing by Campaigning,* 2nd ed. New York: Pearson Longman, 2007.

Edwards, George C., III. *On Deaf Ears: The Limits of the Bully Pulpit.* New Haven, CT: Yale University Press, 2003.

Edwards, George C., III. *Overreach: Leadership in the Obama Presidency.* Princeton, NJ: Princeton University Press, 2012.

Edwards, George C., III. *The Strategic President: Persuasion and Opportunity in Presidential Leadership.* Princeton, NJ: Princeton University Press, 2009.

Farnsworth, Stephen J. *Spinner-in-Chief: How Presidents Sell Themselves and Their Policies.* Boulder, CO: Paradigm, 2008.

Gronke, Paul, and Brian Newman. "Public Evaluations of Presidents." In *Oxford Handbook of the American Presidency,* edited by George C. Edwards III and William G. Howell. Oxford: Oxford University Press, 2009.

Jacobs, Lawrence R., and Robert Y. Shapiro. *Politicians Don't Pander.* Chicago: University of Chicago Press, 2000.

Jacobson, Gary C. *A Divider, Not a Uniter: George W. Bush and the American People.* 2nd ed. New York: Pearson Longman, 2007.

Kernell, Samuel. *Going Public.* 4th ed. Washington, DC: CQ Press, 2007.

Simon, Dennis M. "Public Expectations of the President." In *Oxford Handbook of the American Presidency,* edited by George C. Edwards III and William G. Howell. Oxford: Oxford University Press, 2009.

Tulis, Jeffrey K. *The Rhetorical Presidency.* Princeton, NJ: Princeton University Press, 1987.

Wood, B. Dan. *The Myth of Presidential Representation.* Cambridge University Press, 2009.

Notes

1. "First Debate with Stephen A. Douglas, August 21, 1858," in Roy P. Asler, ed., *The Collected Works of Abraham Lincoln* (New Brunswick, NJ: Rutgers University Press, 1953), p. 27.

2. See Stanley Feldman and John Zaller, "The Political Culture of Ambivalence: Ideological Responses to the Welfare State," *American Journal of Political Science* 36 (February 1992): 268–307.

3. See, for example, *Gallup Poll,* January 14–16, 2011.

4. CBS News/*New York Times* poll, February 5–10, 2010.

5. Bloomberg Poll conducted by Selzer & Co., July 9–12, 2010.

6. CBS News/*New York Times* poll, September 10–14, 2010.

7. Bloomberg News National Poll, October 24–26, 2010.

8. Steven Kull, Clay Ramsay, and Evan Lewis, "Misperceptions, the Media, and the Iraq War," *Political Science Quarterly* 118 (Winter 2003–2004): 569–598.

9. Benjamin I. Page and Robert Y. Shapiro, *The Rational Public* (Chicago: University of Chicago Press, 1992); James A. Stimson, *Public Opinion in America: Moods, Cycles, and Swings* (Boulder, CO: Westview, 1991).

10. On the development of White House polling, see Kathryn Dunn Tenpas and James A. McCann, "Testing the Permanence of the Permanent Campaign: An Analysis of Presidential Polling Expenditures, 1977–2002," *Public Opinion Quarterly* 71 (Fall 2007): 349–366; Diane J. Heith, *Polling to Govern: Public Opinion and Presidential Leadership* (Palo Alto, CA: Stanford University Press, 2004); Robert M. Eisinger, *The Evolution of Presidential Polling* (Cambridge, UK: Cambridge University Press, 2003); Shoon Kathleen Murray and Peter Howard, "Variations in White

House Polling Operations," *Public Opinion Quarterly* 66 (Winter 2002): 527–558; Lawrence R. Jacobs and Robert Y. Shapiro, "The Rise of Presidential Polling: The Nixon White House in Historical Perspective," *Public Opinion Quarterly* 59 (Summer 1995): 163–195; Lawrence R. Jacobs and Robert Y. Shapiro, "Issues, Candidate Image, and Priming: The Use of Private Polls in Kennedy's 1960 Presidential Campaign," *American Political Science Review* 88 (September 1994): 527–540; and Bruce Altschuler, *LBJ and the Public Polls* (Gainesville: University of Florida Press, 1990).

11. R. Kent Weaver, Robert Y. Shapiro, and Lawrence R. Jacobs, "The Polls—Trends: Welfare," *Public Opinion Quarterly* 59 (Winter 1995): 607, 618, 619.

12. Quoted in Dom Bonafede, "Carter and the Polls—If You Live by Them, You May Die by Them," *National Journal*, August 19, 1978, pp. 1312–1313.

13. Interview with Richard Wirthlin, West Point, NY, April 19, 1988; John-Anthony Maltese, *Spin Control* (Chapel Hill: University of North Carolina Press, 1992), p. 185.

14. Diane Heith, "One for All: Using Focus Groups and Opinion Polls in the George H. W. Bush White House," *Congress and the Presidency* 30 (Spring 2003): 81–94.

15. Dick Morris, *Behind the Oval Office* (New York: Random House, 1997), pp. 10–11, 83, 338; James A. Barnes, "The Endless Campaign," *National Journal*, February 20, 1993, p. 461; James A. Barnes, "Polls Apart," *National Journal*, July 10, 1993, pp. 1750–1752; Richard L. Berke, "Clinton Adviser Says Polls Had a Role in Health Plan," *New York Times*, December 2, 1993, p. A17; James Carney, "Playing by the Numbers," *Time*, April 11, 1994, p. 40; James M. Perry, "Clinton Relies Heavily on White House Pollster to Take Words Right Out of the Public's Mouth," *Wall Street Journal*, March 23, 1994, p. A16; David Gergen, *Eyewitness to Power: The Essence of Leadership* (New York: Simon and Schuster 2000), p. 331; Kathryn Dunn Tenpas, "Words vs. Deeds: President George W. Bush and Polling," *Brookings Review* (Summer 2003): 33–35; John F. Harris, *The Survivor: Bill Clinton in the White House* (New York: Random House, 2005), p. 331.

16. Tenpas, "Words vs. Deeds."

17. Sam Stein, "Obama Mocks Polls But Spends More on Them ($4.4M) Than Bush Did," *Huffington Post*, July 29, 2010; Michael D. Shear, "Poll Results Drive Rhetoric of Obama's Health-Care Message," *Washington Post*, July 30, 2009.

18. Shear, "Poll Results Drive Rhetoric of Obama's Health-Care Message."

19. Quoted in Robert Draper, *Dead Certain: The Presidency of George W. Bush* (New York: Free Press, 2007), p. 234.

20. Stanley Kelley, Jr., *Interpreting Elections* (Princeton, NJ: Princeton University Press, 1983), pp. 72–125.

21. Martin P. Wattenberg, *The Rise of Candidate-Centered Politics: Presidential Elections of the 1980s* (Cambridge, MA: Harvard University Press, 1991), chaps. 5–6.

22. Brandon Rottinghaus, "Following the 'Mail Hawks': Alternative Measures of Public Opinion on Vietnam in the Johnson White House," *Public Opinion Quarterly* 71 (Fall 2007): 367–391.

23. See, for example, Saul Pett, "Interview Draws Rare Portrait of Carter," *New Orleans Times-Picayune*, October 23, 1977, sect. 1, p. 13; Richard M. Nixon, *RN: The Memoirs of Richard Nixon* (New York: Grosset and Dunlap, 1978), pp. 935, 945; and Herbert G. Klein, *Making It Perfectly Clear* (Garden City, NY: Doubleday, 1980), p. 341.

24. B. Dan Wood, *The Myth of Presidential Representation* (Cambridge University Press, 2009; Jeffrey E. Cohen, *Presidential Responsiveness and Public Policy-Making* (Ann Arbor: University of Michigan Press, 1997).

25. Quoted in Tom Matthews, "The Road to War," *Newsweek*, January 28, 1991, p. 65.

26. Quoted in Peter Baker, "Obama Says He'd Rather Be a 'Really Good One-Term President,'" *New York Times*, January 25, 2010.

27. Gerald R. Ford, "Imperiled, Not Imperial," *Time*, November 10, 1980, p. 31.

28. Similar results were found for presidents Carter, Reagan, and George W. Bush. See "Early Expectations: Comparing Chief Executives," *Public Opinion*, February/March 1981, p. 39; *Gallup Poll*, January 15–16, 2001.

29. See *The Polling Report* 5 (January 30, 1989): 2–4; *Gallup Poll*, November 10–11, 1992; *Gallup Poll*, January 15–16, 2001.

30. President Carter, quoted in Godfrey Hodgson, *All Things to All Men: The False Promise of the Modern American Presidency* (New York: Simon and Schuster, 1980), p. 25.

31. George C. Edwards III, *The Public Presidency* (New York: St. Martin's, 1983), pp. 189–190; Times Mirror Center for the People and the Press, public opinion survey, October 25–30, 1995; Frank Newport, "Public Values Vision, Leadership and Economic Stewardship in President," *The Gallup Poll Monthly,* November 1999, pp. 4–6; Pew Research Center for the People and the Press, *Retro-Politics,* November 1999, p. 45.

32. Edwards, *The Public Presidency,* pp. 189–191; Newport, "Public Values Vision, Leadership and Economic Stewardship in President."

33. "Carter Interview," *Congressional Quarterly Weekly Report,* November 25, 1978, p. 3354.

34. See, for example, Gallup Poll, *Attitudes toward the Presidency,* January 1980, p. 21.

35. Edwards, *The Public Presidency,* pp. 193–195; Richard C. Waterman, Hank C. Jenkins-Smith, and Carol L. Silva, "The Expectations Gap Thesis: Public Attitudes toward an Incumbent President," *Journal of Politics* 61 (November 1999): 944–966; Hank C. Jenkins-Smith, Carol L. Silva, and Richard W. Waterman, "Micro- and Macrolevel Models of the Presidential Expectations Gap," *Journal of Politics* 67 (August 2005): 69–715.

36. Wirthlin interview.

37. See, for example, *The Gallup Poll Monthly,* May 1993, p. 13; *The Gallup Poll Monthly,* September 1994, pp. 17, 39, 44; George Gallup, Jr., and Frank Newport, "Wary Americans Favor Wait and See Posture in Persian Gulf," *The Gallup Monthly Report,* November 1990, p. 14; Jack Dennis, "Dimensions of Public Support for the Presidency" (paper presented at the Annual Meeting of the Midwest Political Science Association, Chicago, April 1975), Tables 4, 8; Hazel Erskine, "The Polls: Presidential Power,"

Public Opinion Quarterly 37 (Fall 1973): 492, 495.

38. George C. Edwards III, "Presidential Approval and Congressional Support," in George C. Edwards III and William H. Howell, eds., *Oxford Handbook of the American Presidency* (Oxford, UK: Oxford University Press, 2009); George C. Edwards III, *At the Margins: Presidential Leadership of Congress* (New Haven, CT: Yale University Press, 1989), chap. 6.

39. See, for example, Matthew J. Lebo and Daniel Cassino, "The Aggregated Consequences of Motivated Reasoning and the Dynamics of Partisan Presidential Approval," *Political Psychology* 28, no. 6 (2007): 719–746.

40. Gary C. Jacobson, *A Divider, Not a Uniter: George W. Bush and the American People,* 2nd ed. (New York: Pearson Longman, 2007).

41. *Gallup Poll* at www.gallup.com /poll/116479/Barack-Obama-Presidential-Job-Approval.aspx.

42. Jeffrey M. Jones, "Obama's Approval Most Polarized for First-Year President," Gallup Poll, January 25, 2010; Jeffrey M. Jones, "Obama's Approval Ratings More Polarized in Year 2 Than Year 1," Gallup Poll, February 4, 2011.

43. David O. Sears, "Political Socialization," in Fred I. Greenstein and Nelson Polsby, eds., *Micropolitical Theory,* Vol. 2 of *Handbook of Political Science* (Reading, MA: Addison-Wesley, 1975), p. 177.

44. "Remarks of the President at a Meeting with Non-Washington Editors and Broadcasters," White House Transcript, September 21, 1979, pp. 11–12.

45. See, for example, *Gallup Opinion Index,* November 1978, pp. 8–9.

46. See, for example, *The Pew Research Center for the People and the Press* survey of January 30–February 2, 1998. See also Gallup Poll of March 20–22, 1998.

47. Brian Newman, "Integrity and Presidential Approval, 1980–2000," *Public Opinion Quarterly* 67 (Fall 2003): 335–367; Brian Newman, "Presidential Traits and Job Approval: Some Aggregate-Level Evidence," *Presidential Studies Quarterly* 34 (June 2004): 437–448.

48. Jeffrey E. Cohen, *Presidential Studies Quarterly* 42 (September 2012): 431–454.

49. Philip E. Converse, "The Nature of Belief Systems in Mass Publics," in David Apter, ed., *Ideology and Discontent* (New York: Free Press, 1964), pp. 206–261.

50. Scott Sigmund Gartner, "The Multiple Effects of Casualties on Public Support for War: An Experimental Approach," *American Political Science Review* 102 (March 2008): 95–105.

51. Charles W. Ostrom, Jr., and Dennis M. Simon, "The President's Public," *American Journal of Political Science* 32 (November 1988): 1096–1119.

52. Stimson, *Public Opinion in America*, pp. 24–25.

53. David J. Lanoue, *From Camelot to the Teflon President* (New York: Greenwood Press, 1988); Howard S. Bloom and H. Douglas Price, "Voter Response to Short-Run Economic Conditions: The Asymmetric Effect of Prosperity and Recession," *American Political Science Review* 69 (December 1975): 1240–1254; Samuel Kernell, "Presidential Popularity and Negative Voting: An Alternative Explanation of the Midterm Congressional Decline of the President's Party," *American Political Science Review* 71 (March 1977): 44–66; Richard R. Lau, "Two Explanations for Negativity Effect in Political Behavior," *American Journal of Political Science* 29 (February 1985): 119–138; Clyde Wilcox and Dee Allsop, "Economic and Foreign Policy as Sources of Reagan Support," *Western Political Quarterly* 44 (December 1991): 941–958. However, compare Morris P. Fiorina and Kenneth A. Shepsle, "Is Negative Voting an Artifact?" *American Journal of Political Science* 33 (May 1989): 423–439.

54. Lanoue, *From Camelot to the Teflon President*; George C. Edwards III, "Comparing Chief Executives," *Public Opinion*, June/July 1985, p. 54. However, compare Michael S. Lewis-Beck, *Economics and Elections* (Ann Arbor: University of Michigan Press, 1988).

55. Ostrom and Simon, "The President's Public."

56. See, for example, Jon Hurwitz and Mark Peffley, "The Means and Ends of Foreign Policy as Determinants of Presidential Support," *American Journal of Political Science* 31 (May 1987): 236–258.

57. Thomas J. Rudolph, "Who's Responsible for the Economy? The Formation and Consequences of Responsibility Attributions," *American Journal of Political Science* 47 (October 2003): 698–713; Stephen P. Nicholson, Gary M. Segura, and Nathan D. Woods, "Presidential Approval and the Mixed Blessing of Divided Government," *Journal of Politics* 64 (August 2002): 701–720; Shanto Iyengar, *Is Anyone Responsible?* (Chicago: University of Chicago Press, 1992), chap. 8; Shanto Iyengar, "Television News and Citizens' Explanations of National Affairs," *American Political Science Review* 81 (September 1987): 815–831.

58. Richard A. Brody and Paul Sniderman, "From Life Space to Polling Place," *British Journal of Political Science* 7 (July 1977): 337–360; Paul Sniderman and Richard A. Brody, "Coping: The Ethic of Self-Reliance," *American Journal of Political Science* 21 (August 1977): 501–522. See also Stanley Feldman, "Economic Self-Interest and Political Behavior," *American Journal of Political Science* 26 (August 1982): 449–452; and Kay L. Schlozman and Sidney Verba, *Injury to Insult: Unemployment, Class, and Political Response* (Cambridge, MA: Harvard University Press, 1979).

59. K. Jill Kiecolt, "Group Consciousness and the Attribution of Blame for National Economic Problems," *American Politics Quarterly* 15 (April 1987): 203–222; Iyengar, *Is Anyone Responsible?* p. 80; Neil Malhotra and Alexander G. Kuo, "Attributing Blame: The Public's Response to Hurricane Katrina," *Journal of Politics* 70 (January 2008): 120–135.

60. See Edwards, *The Public Presidency*, chap. 6; George C. Edwards III, *Presidential Approval* (Baltimore, MD: Johns Hopkins University Press, 1990), and sources cited therein; Martha Joynt Kumar, *Managing the President's Message: The White House Communications Operation* (Baltimore, MD: Johns Hopkins University Press, 2007), p. 8.

61. See, for example, Michael B. MacKuen, Robert S. Erikson, and James A. Stimson, "Peasants or Bankers? The American

Electorate and the U.S. Economy," *American Political Science Review* 86 (September 1992): 597–611; Donald R. Kinder, "Presidents, Prosperity, and Public Opinion," *Public Opinion Quarterly* 45 (Spring 1981): 1–21; Richard Lau and David O. Sears, "Cognitive Links between Economic Grievances and Political Responses," *Political Behavior* 3, no. 4 (1981): 279–302; Diana C. Mutz, "Mass Media and Depoliticization of Personal Experience," *American Journal of Political Science* 36 (May 1992): 495–496.

62. John E. Mueller, *War, Presidents, and Public Opinion* (New York: Wiley, 1970), pp. 208–213.

63. See, for example, Market Opinion Research, *Americans Talk Security,* no. 12 (January 1989): 31–32, 106.

64. George C. Edwards III and Tami Swenson, "Who Rallies? The Anatomy of a Rally Event," *Journal of Politics* 59 (February 1997): 200–212; Matthew A. Baum, "The Constituent Foundations of the Rally-Round-the-Flag Phenomenon," *International Studies Quarterly* 46 (2002): 263–298.

65. Jonathan McDonald Ladd, "Predispositions and Public Support for the President during the War on Terrorism," *Public Opinion Quarterly* 71 (Winter 2007): 511–538.

66. Tim Groeling and Matthew A. Baum, "Crossing the Water's Edge: Elite Rhetoric, Media Coverage, and the Rally-Round-the-Flag Phenomenon," *Journal of Politics* 70 (October 2008): 1065–1085.

67. Franklin Roosevelt and Theodore Roosevelt, quoted in Emmett John Hughes, "Presidency vs. Jimmy Carter," *Fortune,* December 4, 1978, pp. 62, 64; italics added for emphasis.

68. Michael Waldman, *POTUS Speaks* (New York: Simon and Schuster, 2000), p. 16. See also Marc Lacey, "Guarding the President's Words and, Maybe, His Legacy," *New York Times,* January 24, 2000, p. A12.

69. Samuel Kernell, *Going Public.* 4th ed. (Washington, DC: CQ Press, 2007), p. 129.

70. Martha Joynt Kumar, *Managing the President's Message: The White House Communications Operation* (Baltimore, MD: Johns Hopkins University Press, 2007), p. 8.

71. One scholar counted only four times when Roosevelt used a fireside chat to discuss legislation under consideration in Congress. See Elmer E. Cornwell, Jr., *Presidential Leadership of Public Opinion* (Bloomington: Indiana University Press, 1965), p. 263.

72. George C. Edwards III, *On Deaf Ears: The Limits of the Bully Pulpit* (New Haven, CT: Yale University Press, 2003), chaps. 4–5.

73. Kumar, *Managing the President's Message,* p. 7.

74. John R. Zaller, *The Nature and Origins of Mass Opinion* (New York: Cambridge University Press, 1992), pp. 102–113; John R. Zaller, "Elite Leadership of Mass Opinion: New Evidence from the Gulf War." In W. Lance Bennett and David L. Paletz, eds., *Taken by Storm: The Media, Public Opinion, and U.S. Foreign Policy in the Gulf War* (Chicago: University of Chicago Press, 1994).

75. Converse, "The Nature of Belief Systems in Mass Publics"; William G. Jacoby, "The Sources of Liberal-Conservative Thinking: Education and Conceptualization," *Political Behavior* 10 (1988): 316–332; Robert C. Luskin, "Measuring Political Sophistication," *American Journal of Political Science* 31 (November 1987): 856–899; Neuman, *The Paradox of Mass Politics*; Edward G. Carmines and James A. Stimson, "The Two Faces of Issue Voting," *American Political Science Review* 74 (March 1980): 78–91; Zaller, *The Nature and Origins of Mass Opinion,* p. 48.

76. James H. Kuklinski, Paul J. Quirk, Jennifer Jerit, David Schwieder, and Robert F. Rich, "Misinformation and the Currency of Democratic Citizenship," *Journal of Politics* 62 (August 2000): 790–816.

77. Kaiser Health Tracking Poll, June 9–14, 2011.

78. James N. Druckman, "On the Limits of Framing Effects: Who Can Frame?" *Journal of Politics* 63 (November 2001): 1041–1066. See also Joanne M. Miller and Jon A. Krosnick, "News Media Impact on the Ingredients of Presidential Evaluations: Politically Knowledgeable Citizens Are Guided by a Trusted Source," *American*

Journal of Political Science 44 (April 2000): 301–315; and James N. Druckman, "Using Credible Advice to Overcome Framing Effects," *Journal of Law, Economics, and Organization* 17, no. 1 (2001): 62–82.

79. David Kahneman and Amos Tversky, "Prospect Theory: An Analysis of Decision under Risk," *Econometrica* 47 (March 1979): 263–292; David Kahneman and Amos Tversky, "Choices, Values, and Frames," *American Psychologist* 39 (April 1984): 341–350.

80. David L. Hamilton and Mark P. Zanna, "Differential Weighting of Favorable and Unfavorable Attributes in Impressions of Personality," *Journal of Experimental Research in Personality* 6, nos. 2–3 (1972): 204–212; Susan T. Fiske, "Attention and Weight in Person Perception: The Impact of Negative and Extreme Behavior," *Journal of Personality and Social Psychology* 38, no. 6 (1980): 889–906.

81. Richard Lau, "Two Explanations for Negativity Effects in Political Behavior," *American Journal of Political Science* 29 (February 1985): 119–138.

82. Michael D. Cobb and James H. Kuklinski, "Changing Minds: Political Arguments and Political Persuasion," *American Journal of Political Science* 41 (January 1997): 88–121.

83. George E. Marcus, W. Russell Neuman, and Michael MacKuen, *Affective Intelligence and Political Judgment* (Chicago, IL: University of Chicago Press, 2000); Joanne M. Miller, "Examining the Mediators of Agenda Setting: A New Experimental Paradigm Reveals the Role of Emotions," *Political Psychology* 28 (December 2007): 689–717.

84. Joe S. Foote, "Ratings Decline of Presidential Television," *Journal of Broadcasting and Electronic Media* 32 (Spring 1988): 225.

85. Matthew A. Baum and Samuel Kernell, "Has Cable Ended the Golden Age of Presidential Television?" *American Political Science Review* 93 (March 1999): 99–114; Jeffrey E. Cohen, *The Presidency in the Era of 24-Hour News* (Princeton, NJ: Princeton University Press, 2008).

86. *Washington Post,* March 1, 2001, p. C1.

87. Matthew A. Baum and Samuel Kernell, "Has Cable Ended the Golden Age of Presidential Television?" *American Political Science Review* 93 (March 1999): 99–114; Markus Prior, "News vs. Entertainment: How Increasing Media Choice Widens Gaps in Political Knowledge and Turnout," *American Journal of Political Science* 49 (July 2005): 577–592.

88. Nielsen Media Research.

89. Paul Brace and Barbara Hinckley, "Presidential Activities from Truman through Reagan: Timing and Impact," *Journal of Politics* 55 (May 1993): 387.

90. See Lori Cox Han, "New Strategies for an Old Medium: The Weekly Radio Addresses of Reagan and Clinton," *Congress & the Presidency* 33 (Spring 2006): 25–45.

91. Beverly Horvit, Adam J. Schiffer, and Mark Wright, "The Limits of Presidential Coverage of the Weekly Radio Address," *Press/Politics* 13, no. 1 (2008): 8–28.

92. See, for example, James H. Kuklinski and Norman L. Hurley, "On Hearing and Interpreting Political Messages: A Cautionary Tale of Citizen Cue-Taking," *Journal of Politics* 56 (August 1994): 729–751.

93. See Edwards, *On Deaf Ears,* chap. 9; Larry Bartels, "Beyond the Running Tally: Partisan Bias in Political Perceptions," *Political Behavior* 24 (2): 117–150; and Brian J. Gaines, James H. Kuklinski, Paul J. Quirk, Buddy Peyton, and Jay Verkuilen, "Same Facts, Different Interpretations: Partisan Motivation and Opinion on Iraq," *Journal of Politics* 69 (November 2007): 957–974, on how partisanship biases processing perceptions, interpretations, and response to the political world.

94. Kumar, *Managing the President's Message,* p. 9.

95. David Gergen, *Eyewitness to Power: The Essence of Leadership* (New York: Simon & Schuster 2000), pp. 54, 186. Also see Martha Joynt Kumar, *Managing the President's Message: The White House Communications Operation* (Baltimore, MD: Johns Hopkins University Press, 2007), chaps. 2–3.

96. See George C. Edwards III, *The Strategic President: Persuasion and Opportunity in Presidential Leadership* (Princeton, NJ:

Princeton University Press, 2009), pp. 96–104.

97. Mark Hertsgaard, *On Bended Knee: The Press and the Reagan Presidency* (New York: Farrar, Straus, and Giroux, 1988), pp. 107–108; Larry Speakes, *Speaking Out* (New York: Scribner's, 1988), p. 301; James A. Baker III, *"Work Hard, Study . . . and Keep Out of Politics!"* (New York: G. P. Putnam's Sons, 2006), pp. 132–133, 136–137, 148, 171; Lou Cannon, *President Reagan: The Role of a Lifetime* (New York: Simon & Schuster, 1991), pp. 163, 344.

98. Bill Clinton, *My Life* (London: Hutchison, 2004), p. 467.

99. Quoted in Dan Balz, "For Obama, a Tough Year to Get the Message Out," *Washington Post*, January 10, 2010.

100. George Packer, "Obama's Lost Year," *New Yorker*, March 15, 2010, p. 46.

101. Michael D. Shear, "Times Square Bomb, Oil Spill Complicate White House Agenda," *Washington Post*, May 3, 2010.

102. See, for example, Matthew Eshbaugh-Soha and Jeffrey S. Peake, *Breaking Through the Noise* (Stanford, CA: Stanford University Press, 2011); Matthew Eshbaugh-Soha and Thomas Miles, *Congress & the Presidency* 38, no. 3 (2011): 301–321.

103. Gergen, *Eyewitness to Power*, p. 54.

104. Ibid., p. 54.

105. Quoted in Gerald M. Boyd, "'General Contractor' of the White House Staff," *New York Times*, March 4, 1986, sec. A, p. 22.

106. See, for example, Daniel Kahneman, Paul Slovic, and Amos Tversky, *Judgment under Uncertainty: Heuristics and Biases* (New York: Cambridge University Press, 1982); Arthur Lupia, "Shortcuts versus Encyclopedias: Information and Voting Behavior in California Insurance Reform Elections," *American Political Science Review* 88 (March 1994): 63–76; Herbert A. Simon, "A Behavioral Model of Rational Choice," *Quarterly Journal of Economics* 69 (February 1955): 99–118; Samuel L. Popkin, *The Reasoning Voter* (Chicago: University of Chicago Press, 1991); Paul M. Sniderman, Richard Brody, and Philp E. Tetlock, *Reasoning and Choice* (New York: Cambridge University Press, 1991).

107. E. Tory Higgins and Gary A. King, "Accessibility of Social Constructs: Information-Processing Consequences of Individual and Contextual Variation," in N. Cantor and J. F. Kihlstrom, eds., *Personality, Cognition, and Social Interaction* (Hillsdale, NJ: Erlbaum, 1981); Robert S. Wyer, Jr., and Jon Hartwick, "The Recall and Use of Belief Statements as Bases for Judgments," *Journal of Experimental Social Psychology* 20 (January 1984): 65–85; Thomas K. Srull and Robert S. Wyer, Jr., *Memory and Cognition in Their Social-Context* (Hillsdale, NJ: Erlbaum, 1989); Thomas K. Srull and Robert S. Wyer, Jr., "The Role of Category Accessibility in the Interpretation of Information about Persons: Some Determinants and Implications," *Journal of Personality and Social Psychology* 37, no. 10 (1979): 1660–1672; Thomas K. Srull and Robert S. Wyer, Jr., "Category Accessibility and Social Perception: Some Implications for the Study of Person Memory and Interpersonal Judgments," *Journal of Personality and Social Psychology* 38, no. 6 (1980): 841–856; Richard R. Lau, "Construct Accessibility and Electoral Choice," *Political Behavior* 11 (March 1989): 5–32.

108. Converse, "The Nature of Belief Systems in Mass Publics."

109. Zaller, *The Nature and Origins of Mass Opinion,* pp. 42–48; James H. Kuklinski and Norman Hurley, "On Hearing and Interpreting Messages: A Cautionary Tale of Citizen Cue-Taking," *Journal of Politics* 56 (August 1994): 729–751; Jeffrey Mondak, "Source Cues and Policy Approval: The Cognitive Dynamics of Public Support for the Reagan Agenda," *American Journal of Political Science* 37 (February 1993): 186–212.

110. "Remarks by the President on the Importance of Passing a Historic Energy Bill," White House Transcript, June 25, 2009.

111. See, for example, William A. Gamson and Andre Modigliani, "The Changing Culture of Affirmative Action," in Richard D. Braungart, ed., *Research in Political Sociology,* vol. 3 (Greenwich, CT: JAI Press, 1987), p. 143; William A. Gamson and Andre Modigliani, "Media Discourse and Public Opinion on Nuclear Power: A Constructionist Approach," *American*

Journal of Sociology 95 (July 1989): 1–37; William A. Gamson, *Talking Politics* (Cambridge, UK: Cambridge University Press, 1992); Donald R. Kinder and Lynn M. Sanders, *Divided by Color: Racial Politics and Democratic Ideals* (Chicago: University of Chicago Press, 1996); and Zhongdang Pan and Gerald M. Kosicki, "Framing Analysis: An Approach to News Discourse," *Political Communication* 10, 1 (1993): 55–75.

112. For the latter view that framing does not work by altering the accessibility to different considerations, see Druckman, "On the Limits of Framing Effects." See also Thomas E. Nelson, Rosalee A. Clawson, and Zoe M. Oxley, "Media Framing of a Civil Liberties Conflict and Its Effect on Tolerance," *American Political Science Review* 91 (September 1997): 567–584; and Miller and Krosnick, "News Media Impact on the Ingredients of Presidential Evaluations."

113. See George C. Edwards III, *The Strategic President: Persuasion and Opportunity in Presidential Leadership* (Princeton, NJ: Princeton University Press, 2009), chap. 3, for a discussion of literature showing the effects of framing.

114. There is some evidence that the president's rhetoric can prime the criteria on which the public evaluates him. See James N. Druckman and Justin W. Holmes, "Does Presidential Rhetoric Matter? Priming and Presidential Approval," *Presidential Studies Quarterly* 34 (December 2004): 755–778.

115. See Lawrence R. Jacobs and Robert Y. Shapiro, *Politicians Don't Pander* (Chicago: University of Chicago Press, 2000), pp. 49–52.

116. See, for example, Carl Albert, interview by Dorothy Pierce McSweeny, April 13, 1969, interview 3, transcript, pp. 8–9, Lyndon Johnson Library, Austin, Texas.

117. See Bryan D. Jones and Frank R. Baumgartner, *The Politics of Attention: How Government Prioritizes Problems* (Chicago: University of Chicago Press, 2005), chap. 3; Bryan D. Jones, *Reconceiving Decision-Making in Democratic Politics* (Chicago: University of Chicago Press, 1994), chap. 4.

118. See E. E. Schattschneider, *The Semisovereign People: A Realist's View of* *Democracy in America* (New York: Holt, Rinehart and Winston, 1960).

119. Gergen, *Eyewitness to Power,* p. 348.

120. Zaller, The Nature and Origins of Mass Opinion, p. 99, chapter 9; Paul M. Sniderman, "Taking Sides: A Fixed Choice Theory of Political Reasoning," in Arthur Lupia, Mathew D. McCubbins, and Samuel L. Popkin, eds., *Elements of Reason: Understanding and Expanding the Limits of Political Rationality* (New York: Cambridge University Press, 2000); Paul M. Sniderman and Sean M. Theriault, "The Structure of Political Argument and the Logic of Issue Framing," in Willem E. Saris and Paul M. Sniderman, eds., *Studies in Public Opinion: Attitudes, Nonattitudes, Measurement Error and Change* (Princeton, NJ: Princeton University Press, 2004); James N. Druckman and Kjersten R. Nelson, "Framing and Deliberation: How Citizens' Conversations Limit Elite Influence," *American Journal of Political Science* 47 (October 2003): 729–745. But see Dennis Chong and James N. Druckman, "Framing Public Opinion in Competitive Democracies," *American Political Science Review* 101 (November 2007): 637–655.

121. Zaller, "Elite Leadership of Mass Opinion," pp. 186–209.

122. A key source on these activities is Kumar, *Managing the President's Message.* See especially pp. 4–5.

123. An analysis of President Johnson's public statements on Vietnam shows that he varied their content—that is, their "hawkishness"—depending on the audience he was addressing. Lawrence C. Miller and Lee Sigelman, "Is the Audience the Message? A Note on LBJ's Vietnam Statements," *Public Opinion Quarterly* 42 (Spring 1978): 71–80. See also Malcolm Goggin, "The Ideological Content of Presidential Communications," *American Politics Quarterly* 12 (July 1984): 361–384.

124. Michael K. *Deaver, Behind the Scenes* (New York: William Morrow, 1987), p. 73; see also pp. 126–127, 135.

125. Laurence I. Barrett, *Gambling with History* (New York: Penguin, 1983), p. 442.

126. See, for example, Karen Hughes, *Ten Minutes from Normal* (New York: Viking, 2004), pp. 85–86, 219–220.

127. Quoted in Kumar, *Managing the President's Message*, p. 40.

128. Quoted in Michael Baruch Grossman and Martha Joynt Kumar, *Portraying the President: The White House and the News Media* (Baltimore, MD: Johns Hopkins University Press, 1981), p. 29.

129. Cannon, *President Reagan*, p. 453.

130. See Richard Ellis, *Presidential Lightning Rods: The Politics of Blame Avoidance* (Lawrence: University Press of Kansas, 1994); Fred I. Greenstein, *The Hidden-Hand Presidency: Eisenhower as Leader* (New York: Basic Books, 1982), pp. 90–92.

131. Bob Woodward, *Bush at War* (New York: Simon and Schuster, 2002), p. 13.

132. See Donald T. Regan, *For the Record* (San Diego: Harcourt Brace Jovanovich, 1988), pp. 247–249.

133. Deaver, *Behind the Scenes,* p. 141.

134. Elisabeth Bumiller, "Keepers of Bush Image Lift Stagecraft to New Heights," *New York Times,* May 16, 2003, pp. A1, A8.

135. Bumiller, "Keepers of Bush Image Lift Stagecraft to New Heights."

136. Quoted in Rich Jaroslovsky, "Manipulating the Media Is a Specialty for the White House's Michael Deaver," *Wall Street Journal,* January 5, 1984, p. 44.

137. *Speakes, Speaking Out,* p. 220.

138. Scott McClellan, *What Happened: Inside the Bush White House and Washington's Culture of Deception* (New York: Public Affairs, 2008), p. 229.

139. Spencer Ackerman and John B. Judis, "The First Casualty," *The New Republic,* June 30, 2003, pp. 17–18.

140. Bob Woodward, *State of Denial* (New York: Simon and Schuster, 2006), pp. 337, 471, 480, 491.

141. See, for example, James S. Robbins, *This Time We Win: Revisiting the Tet Offensive* (New York: Encounter Books, 2010).

142. Fred I. Greenstein, "Eisenhower as an Activist President: A Look at New Evidence," *Political Science Quarterly* 94 (Winter 1979–1980): 588–590.

143. See, for example, Howard Kurtz, *Spin Cycle* (New York: Free Press, 1998), pp. 300–301.

144. David Stockman, *The Triumph of Politics* (New York: Harper and Row, 1986), p. 173; see also pp. 132, 353.

145. For other budgetary distortions, see Tim Muris, "Budget Manipulations," *The American Enterprise*, May/June 1993, pp. 24–28.

146. Quoted in Joseph C. Goulden, *Truth Is the First Casualty* (Chicago: Rand McNally, 1969), p. 160. See also See Edwin E. Moise, *Tonkin Gulf and the Escalation of the Vietnam War* (Chapel Hill: University of North Carolina Press, 1996).

147. Mueller, *War, Presidents, and Public Opinion,* pp. 112–113.

148. For a more complete discussion, see Edwards, *The Public Presidency,* pp. 60–64; and James P. Pfiffner, *The Character Factor* (College Station, TX: Texas A&M University Press, 2004). See also *Speakes, Speaking Out,* pp. 141, 160–162, 172.

149. Kurtz, *Spin Cycle*, pp. xxi–xxii.

150. James P. Pfiffner, "Did President Bush Mislead the Country in His Arguments for War with Iraq?" *Presidential Studies Quarterly* 34 (March 2004): 25–46.

151. See, for example, Barton Gellman, *Angler: The Cheney Vice Presidency* (New York: Penguin Press, 2008), pp. 149, 217–222.

152. See, for example, CBS News/*The New York Times Poll,* October 30, 1986, Table 29.

153. See, for example, William Schneider, "Opinion Outlook," *National Journal,* November 29, 1986, pp. 2908–2909; George C. Edwards III, *Governing by Campaigning: The Politics of the Bush Presidency,* 2nd ed. (New York: Longman, 2007), chap. 4.

154. On presidents' success in leading the public, see Edwards, *On Deaf Ears;* George C., III. *The Strategic President: Persuasion and Opportunity in Presidential Leadership*. Princeton, NJ: Princeton University Press, 2009; George C. Edwards III, *Overreach: Leadership in the Obama Presidency* (Princeton, NJ: Princeton University Press, 20012); and Edwards, *Governing by Campaigning*.

155. Ronald Reagan, *An American Life* (New York: Simon and Schuster, 1990), pp. 459, 471.

156. This discussion is based on Edwards, *On Deaf Ears*, chap. 3.

157. William G. Mayer, *The Changing American Mind* (Ann Arbor: University of Michigan Press, 1992), p. 127.

158. Quoted in R. W. Apple, "Bush Sure-Footed on Trail of Money," *New York Times*, September 29, 1990, p. 8.

159. Frank Newport, "Public Wants Congressional and U.N. Approval before Iraq Action," *Gallup Poll*, News Release, September 6, 2002.

160. Barack Obama, *Dreams from My Father* (New York: Crown Publishers, 1995), p. 106.

161. Stimson, *Public Opinion in America: Moods, Cycles, and Swings.*

162. Page and Shapiro, *The Rational Public.*

163. Benjamin I. Page with Marshall M. Bouton, *The Foreign Policy Disconnect: What Americans Want from Our Leaders but Don't Get* (Chicago: University of Chicago Press, 2006).

164. Quoted in John Ehrlichman, *Witness to Power: The Nixon Years* (New York: Simon and Schuster, 1982), p. 267.

5

THE PRESIDENT
AND THE MEDIA

Despite all their efforts to lead public opinion, presidents do not directly reach the American people on a day-to-day basis. It is the news media, or press, that provide people with most of what they know about chief executives, their policies, and their policies' consequences. The media also interpret and analyze presidential activities, including even the president's direct appeals to the public.

The media act as the principal intermediary between the president and the public, and relations with the press are an important aspect of the president's efforts to lead public opinion. Presidents whom the media portray in a favorable light will face fewer obstacles in obtaining public support than those who are treated harshly by the media.

Bill Clinton took office with an antagonistic attitude toward the national media, which he planned to bypass rather than use as part of his political strategy. As he told an audience of journalists shortly after taking office: "You know why I can stiff you on press conferences? Because [talk-show host] Larry King liberated me by giving me to the American people directly." After this rocky start in his press relations, Clinton's orientation changed. He found that he could not avoid the national press, which remains the primary source of news about the federal government. "I did not realize the importance of communications," he confessed, "and the overriding importance of what is on the evening television news. If I am not on there with a message, someone else is, with their message."[1] Clinton even hired David Gergen, who had been a communications adviser in Republican administrations, as a top aide.

In this chapter, we examine the nature and structure of presidential relationships with the press, emphasizing both the context of these relationships and the White House's attempts to obtain favorable coverage through holding press conferences and providing services for the press. We also focus on the substance of the news media's coverage of the president, discussing the controversial issues of leaks to the press and of superficiality and bias in the news. Finally, we consider the evidence regarding the important, but generally overlooked, question of the effects of press coverage of the White House on public opinion.

Presidents fitting the director model would tend to receive favorable press coverage of their administration and reliably use the press to advance their interests. In contrast, facilitators will tend to experience a more adversarial relationship, which will be characterized by more negative coverage and a constant struggle by the White House to obtain both space and sympathetic treatment in the media.

THE EVOLUTION OF MEDIA COVERAGE

Today, we are accustomed to turning to our newspapers, television sets, or even the Internet to learn almost immediately about what the president has said or done. Things have not always been this way: Before the Civil War, newspapers were generally small, heavily partisan, and limited in circulation. Between 1860 and 1920, however, a number of changes occurred that permanently altered the relationship between the president and the press.

Several technological innovations—from the electric printing press, the telegraph, the typewriter, and the telephone to linotype and wood pulp paper—made it both possible and economical to produce mass-circulation newspapers carrying recent national news. Aside from the sales efforts of the newspapers themselves, the increasing literacy of the population helped to create a market for these papers.

The growing interest in national affairs as a result of the Civil War and the new importance of the national government also fostered the newspapers. The government began to regulate the economy with the Interstate Commerce Commission and its antitrust efforts. Moreover, it expanded its role in world affairs during the Spanish-American War and World War I. These events kindled support for, and great interest in, the activities of the government in Washington. The renewed prominence of the presidency following an era of congressional ascendancy also increased interest in national affairs.[2]

Reporters first obtained space in the White House in 1896,[2] but it was Theodore Roosevelt who made the greatest strides in exploiting the new opportunities to reach the public provided by the mass-circulation press. He took an activist view of the presidency and used the White House to dramatize himself and the issues in which he was interested. He sought and gained extensive access to the press in order to forge a more personal relationship with the American people. Establishing a casual and candid relationship with journalists, he floated trial balloons, leaked stories, and held informal press conferences (some while he was receiving his daily shave). For the next century, news about the president played an increasingly prominent role in the printed and electronic press, both in absolute terms and relative to coverage of Congress or the national government as a whole.[3]

Presidents have found that they need the press because it is their primary link to the people. The press, in turn, finds coverage of the president indispensable in satisfying its audience and reporting on the most significant political events. The advent of radio and television has only heightened these mutual needs.

Unlimited goodwill has not characterized the history of relations between the president and the press. President George Washington complained that the "calumnies" against his administration were "outrages of common decency" motivated by the desire to destroy confidence in the new government.[4] John Adams was so upset at criticism in the press that he supported the Sedition Act and jailed some opposition journalists under its authority.

Thomas Jefferson, certainly one of America's greatest defenders of freedom, became so exasperated with the press as president that he argued, "even the least informed of the people have learned that nothing in a newspaper is to be believed." He also felt that "newspapers, for the most part, present only the caricature of disaffected minds. Indeed, the abuses of freedom of the press have been carried to a length never before known or borne by any civilized nation." These observations, we should note, come from the man who earlier had written, "[W]ere it left to me to decide whether we should have a government without newspapers or newspapers without a government, I should not hesitate to prefer the latter."[5]

Almost two centuries later, things have changed very little. Although all presidents have supported the abstract right of the press to criticize them freely, while in office, most have found this criticism uncomfortable. They have viewed some of the press as misrepresenting (perhaps maliciously) their views and actions, failing to perceive the correctness of their policies, and being dedicated to impeding their goals. For example, as the Iran-Contra scandal unfolded, Ronald Reagan complained of the press circling the White House like "sharks." A quarter-century earlier, John F. Kennedy, a favorite of the press, exulted in the potential of television for going directly to the people when he told journalist Ben Bradlee that "when we don't have to go through you bastards, we can really get our story to the American people."[6] President Clinton, who expressed a desire to punch columnist William Safire in the nose for calling Hillary Clinton a "congenital liar," complained that "you get no credit around here for fighting and bleeding. And that's why the know-nothings and the do-nothings and the negative people and the right-wingers always win. Because of the way people like you [the press] put questions to people like me."[7]

No matter who is in the White House or who does the reporting, presidents and the press always struggle for dominance. Presidents are inherently policy advocates and want to be able to define a situation and receive favorable coverage. They will naturally assess the press in terms of how it aids or hinders their goals. The press, conversely, has the responsibility for presenting and assessing what is really going on. Although the press may fail in its efforts, it will assess itself on those criteria. Presidents want to control the amount and timing of information about their administrations, while the press wants all the information that exists without delay. As long as their goals are different, presidents and the press are likely to be adversaries.

RELATIONS BETWEEN THE PRESIDENT AND THE PRESS

To understand presidential relations with the press, we must understand the journalists with whom the White House deals and the ways in which the president's staff tries to influence them. Because of the importance of the press to the president, the White House goes to great lengths to encourage the media to project a positive image of the president and the administration's policies. These efforts include coordinating the news, holding press conferences, and providing a range of services such as formal briefings, interviews, photo opportunities, background sessions, travel accommodations, and daily handouts.

The White House Press Corps

Who are the reporters who regularly cover the White House? This elite contingent represents diverse media constituencies, including daily newspapers like the *Washington Post* and *New York Times*; weekly newsmagazines like *Time* and the *National Journal*; wire services like the Associated Press (AP), Reuters, and Bloomberg; newspaper chains like McClatchy, Gannett, Media General, Scripps, Newhouse, and MediaNews Group; the television and radio networks; the foreign press; and "opinion" magazines like the *New Republic* and the *National Review*.

In addition, photographers, columnists, television commentators, and magazine writers are regularly involved in White House–press interactions. About 800 journalists have White House press credentials. Fortunately, not everyone shows up at once (there are only 49 seats in the White House briefing room). Fewer than 70 reporters and 15 photographers regularly cover the White House, although the total increases to more than 100 when an important announcement is expected. Attendance at presidential press conferences varies from about 150 for a prime time evening event in the East Room of the White House to about 75 in one held in the briefing room.

The great majority of daily newspapers in America have no Washington correspondents, much less someone assigned to cover the White House. The same is true for almost all of the country's individual television and radio stations. These papers and stations rely heavily on a national news service such as the Associated Press or, if part of a network or newspaper chain, their chain's Washington bureau for news about the president.

The Presidential Press Operation

White House relations with the media occupy a substantial portion of the time of a large number of aides. About one-third of the high-level White House staff is directly involved in media relations and policy of one type or another, and most staff members are involved at some time in influencing the media's portrayal of the president.[8]

Press Secretary

The president's press secretary is the person in the White House who daily deals directly with the press, making announcements regarding policies, responding to the actions and criticisms of others, and commenting on breaking news. According to Marlin Fitzwater, press secretary to President Reagan and President Bush, "The press secretary stands between the opposing forces, explaining, cajoling, begging, sometimes pushing both sides toward a better understanding of each other."[9]

The central function of press secretaries is to serve as conduits of information from the White House to the press. They must be sure that clear statements of administration policies have been prepared on important policy matters. The press secretaries usually conduct the daily press briefings, giving prepared announcements and answering questions. In forming their answers, they do not always have specific instructions on what to say or not say. Instead, they must be able to think on their feet to ensure that they accurately reflect the president's views. Sometimes these views may be unclear, however, or there may be views that the president may not wish to articulate. Therefore, press secretaries may seem to be evasive or unimaginative in public settings. They also hold private meetings with individual reporters, where the information they provide may be more candid and speculative.

To be effective in the conduit role, the press secretary must maintain credibility with reporters. Credibility rests on at least two important pillars: (1) truth and (2) access to (and respect of) the president and senior White House officials. Press secretaries viewed as not telling the truth or (like President Clinton's first press secretary, Dee Dee Myers) as being too distant from the top decision makers (and therefore not well informed) will not be effective presidential spokespeople because the press will give less credence to what they say. Credibility problems have arisen for several press secretaries as a result of these perceived deficiencies. Barack Obama's press secretaries have been close to the president.

Press secretaries also serve as conduits from the press, sometimes explaining the needs of the press to the president. For example, all of Lyndon Johnson's press secretaries tried to persuade the president to issue the press advance information on his travel plans. When he refused, they provided the information anyway (and then had it expunged from the briefing transcript so the president would not see it). Press secretaries also try to inform the White House staff of the press's needs and the rules of the game, and they help reporters gain access to staff members.

Press secretaries typically are not involved in substantive decisions, but they do give the president advice—usually on what information the White House should release, by whom, in what form, and to what audience. They also advise the president on rehearsals for press conferences and on how to project the proper image and use it to political advantage.

Coordinating the News

Since the time of William McKinley and Theodore Roosevelt, the White House has attempted to coordinate executive branch news. Presidents have assigned aides to clear the appointments of departmental public affairs officials, to keep in touch with the officials to learn what news is forthcoming from the departments, and to meet with them to explain the president's policy views and try to prevent conflicting statements from emanating from the White House and other units of the executive branch. Specialists have had responsibility for coordinating national security news. Of course, such tactics do not always work. President Ford wanted to announce from the White House the results of the successful effort to rescue seamen from the *Mayaguez*, but he found, to his disappointment, that the Pentagon had already done so, making any presidential announcement anticlimactic.

Coordinating the news from the White House itself has also been a presidential goal. Presidents have sometimes monitored and attempted to limit the press contacts of White House aides, who have annoyed their bosses by using the media for their own purposes. President Reagan, for example, instituted a policy midway through his administration that required his assistant for communications to approve any interview with any White House official requested by a member of the media. Aides monitored all requests and entered them on a computer, so the White House could keep tabs on whom reporters wanted to see. Because members of the White House press cannot wander through the East Wing or West Wing on their own, the only way to speak to aides without administration approval was to call them at home, a practice discouraged by presidential assistants and generally avoided by reporters. Recent presidents have also made substantial efforts to control which administration officials appear on major news programs, including the weekday and Sunday morning news shows. To influence both the topics and the responses provided in interviews, the White House only allows officials who receive its permission to appear on these shows.

Recent administrations have made an effort to coordinate publicity functions within the White House and to attempt to present the news in the most favorable light, such as preventing two major stories from breaking on the same day, smothering bad news with more positive news, and timing announcements for maximum or minimum effect (discussed in Chapter 4).

Attending to the News

All recent presidents have read several newspapers each day, especially the *New York Times*, the *Wall Street Journal*, and the *Washington Post*, and most have also been very attentive to television news programs. Barack Obama also reads *USA Today* and his hometown Chicago newspapers. He rarely watches television news.[10] Johnson had a television cabinet with three screens in order to watch all three commercial networks at once. However, even this was not enough to satisfy his thirst for news. He also had Teletypes installed in the Oval Office that carried the latest reports from the wire services, which he monitored regularly.

President Nixon rarely watched television news and did not peruse large numbers of newspapers or magazines, but he was extremely interested in the press coverage of his administration. He had his staff prepare a daily news summary of newspapers, magazines, television news, and the news wires.

Often, this summary triggered ideas for the president, who gave orders to aides to follow up on something he read.[11] The news summary also went to White House assistants. Subsequent presidents have continued the news summary, altering it to meet their individual needs, and have circulated it to top officials in their administrations. The Carter White House instituted a separate magazine survey and even began producing a weekly summary of Jewish publications after it became concerned about a possible backlash within the American Jewish community against the administration's Middle East policy.

The Presidential Press Conference

The best-known direct interaction between the president and the press is the formal press conference. The large number of reporters covering these press conferences and the setting in which they take place (such as the East Room in the White House) have inevitably made them more formal than in the days when Franklin D. Roosevelt held forth from his desk in the Oval Office. Transcripts of the press conferences were first made during Dwight Eisenhower's tenure, and the conferences were televised live beginning in the Kennedy administration. Presidents since Harry Truman frequently have begun their press conferences with carefully prepared opening statements that give them an opportunity to reach the public on their own terms.

Presidents have taken other steps that contributed to the formalization of press conferences. Beginning with Truman, they have undergone formal briefings and dry runs in preparation for questions reporters might ask, in which aides are asked to submit possible questions and suggested answers. In 1982, President Reagan began holding full-scale mock news conferences. Anticipating the media's questions is not too difficult. There are obvious areas of concern, and questions raised at White House and departmental briefings and other meetings with reporters provide useful cues. The president can also anticipate the interests of individual reporters and can exercise some discretion over whom to recognize.

From the press's perspective, the change in the nature of presidential press conferences from semiprivate to public events diminished their utility in transmitting information from the president to the press. Since every word they say is transmitted verbatim to millions of people, modern-day presidents cannot speak as candidly as, say, Franklin D. Roosevelt could. Nor can they speculate freely about their potential actions or evaluations of people, events, or circumstances. Instead, they must choose their words carefully, and, as a result, their responses to questions are often not very enlightening. In addition, the increased number of reporters attending press conferences has meant a wider range of questions and thus less likelihood of covering any one subject in depth.

The White House saw the presidential press conferences differently, however. As President Kennedy's press secretary, Pierre Salinger, put it: "The idea of going to television . . . was to jump over the press and go directly to the people."[12] Thus, the White House viewed the press as a prop with which to speak to the public. Presidents have usually been firmly in control of their press conferences. They may declare that they will not entertain questions on certain topics, and they may also evade questions with clever rhetoric or a simple "no comment." Alternately, they can use a question as a vehicle to say something that they had planned ahead of time. If necessary, they can reverse the attack and focus on the questioner, or, conversely, they can call on a friendly reporter for a "soft" question.

The artificial nature and increasingly low ratings of press conferences has discouraged the networks from broadcasting them. Until the end of George H. W. Bush's tenure, the networks would preempt programs for a live presidential press conference almost without question. In June 1992, however, all three major networks refused to run one of President Bush's press conferences on the grounds that it was mostly a campaign event. Since that time, the major television networks have been less than eager to give up their regular entertainment programming to cover presidential press conferences.

The trend is clearly in the direction of holding fewer formal press conferences: Franklin Roosevelt held about seven a month, whereas Ronald Reagan held only about one press conference every two months. In a break with precedent, President George H. W. Bush virtually abandoned formal, prime time press conferences in favor of frequent, brief, informal morning sessions with reporters, which he often called on short notice. He held more press conferences in a year than Ronald Reagan did in eight years and met frequently with reporters in informal ways as well. It was difficult for the commercial networks to provide live broadcasts without costly interruptions of scheduled programs, and many reporters were absent. Oddly, in an age of television, Bush's format was aimed at the newspapers. He used press conferences to respond to journalists' inquiries rather than as part of an effort to advance his own policies. In other words, he talked to the press, not over it.

Despite his extraordinary mastery of government and public policy, Bill Clinton felt that the price of making a mistake in a press conference was too high in the age of television. To reduce his vulnerability and to save the five hours or so that it takes to prepare for a full-blown press conference, he turned to remarks in controlled settings such as events at the White House, especially sessions with visiting foreign leaders. There, he would occasionally answer a few questions from the press—but many fewer than he would have answered at a traditional press conference. Three-fourths of George W. Bush's press conferences were of this variety.

President Clinton held just four evening press conferences in his eight years in office, only one of which received live coverage on all the networks (CNN and C-SPAN did provide coverage for all, however), all in his first term. George W. Bush also held only four during his tenure. Barack Obama has held only four, all in his first year.[13]

Presidents Clinton, George W. Bush, and Obama found that they could get on television without suffering the disadvantages of the press conference. Their frequent travel around the country brought them substantial local coverage.[14] The payoff was even greater because people are more likely to trust local television stations as a news source than any other major media outlet.

Alexis C. Glenn/UPI/Newscom

Presidents devote a substantial amount of time dealing with the media. Here President Obama holds a press conference.

Indeed, Clinton ran ads in twenty key states from the summer of 1995 until the Democratic convention a year later to reach the public through these stations.[15]

In addition, the White House has adopted a "rolling" announcement format in which it alerts the press that it will be making an announcement (such as a legislative initiative) in coming days, sparking stories on the upcoming news. Then it makes the announcement, generating yet additional stories. Finally, the president travels around the country repeating the announcement he just made, obtaining both local and network coverage of his media events.

Barack Obama combined all these techniques early in his tenure. When he faced resistance to his high-priority economic stimulus bill, he made his case for the bill in his first prime time press conference. Earlier in the day, he traveled to one of the most economically distressed corners of the nation, Elkhart, Indiana. The next day, he continued advocating passage of the bill in visits to Ft. Myers, Florida, and East Peoria, Illinois.

Services for the Press

In order to get their messages across to the American people and to influence the tone and content of press presentation of those messages, presidents have provided services for the press.

Briefings
The White House provides briefings each weekday, usually in the morning, for the press, and at other times as the situation requires. In these daily briefings, reporters receive information about appointments and resignations, decisions

of the president to sign or not to sign routine bills and explanations for these actions, and the president's schedule (appointments, meetings, future travel plans, and availability to the press). More significant from the standpoint of the press, the briefings provide presidential reactions to events, the White House "line" on issues and whether it has changed, and a reading of the president's moods and ideas. Reporters obtain this information through prepared statements or answers to their queries. (Responses to the latter are often prepared ahead of time by the White House staff.) The daily briefings, of course, also provide the press with an opportunity to have the president's views placed on the public record, which eases the burdens of reporting.

Usually, the president's press secretary or the press secretary's deputy presides over these briefings, although sometimes the president participates. White House staff members and executive branch officials with substantial expertise in specific policy areas, such as the budget or foreign affairs, sometimes brief the press and answer questions at the daily briefing or at special briefings, especially if the White House is launching a major publicity campaign. Transcripts of the briefings are available on the White House website at www.whitehouse.gov.

There are also more private briefings. After the protracted decision-making process that climaxed with President Obama's December 1, 2009, announcement of sending an additional 30,000 U.S. troops to Afghanistan, the White House briefed the *New York Times*, the *Washington Post*, and the *Los Angeles Times* on the policy discussions. In early December, each newspaper carried behind-the-scenes stories on the process, all reflecting Obama as a deliberative and tough-minded manager.[16]

Backgrounders

One of the most important services for the press is the *backgrounder*. The president's comments to reporters may be "on the record" (remarks may be attributed to the speaker); "on background" (a specific source cannot be identified but the source's position and status can, such as a "White House source"); "deep background" (no attribution); or "off the record" (the information reporters receive may not be used in a story). For purposes of convenience, we shall term all sessions between White House officials (including the president) and the press that are not on the record as "backgrounders." All recent presidents, especially Lyndon Johnson and Gerald Ford, have engaged in background discussion with reporters, although President Nixon's involvement was rare. Some presidents, especially Dwight Eisenhower and Richard Nixon, have relied heavily on their principal foreign policy advisers to brief reporters on foreign affairs.

The most common type of White House discussion with reporters on a background basis is a briefing. In a typical background briefing, a senior presidential aide, such as the director of the Office of Management and Budget or the president's national security assistant, explains a policy's development and what it is expected to accomplish. Interestingly, the White House does not appear to stress the substance of policy and seldom makes "hard" news statements in background briefings because this would irritate absent members of the press. The briefings do play an important role in preparing the news media for legislative and administrative initiatives, presidential trips, and important speeches, however. Some administrations have held special background sessions for the weekly newsmagazines at the end of the week. The George W. Bush administration targeted many backgrounders for specific reporters—for example, the *New York Times* for a story on foreign policy.

Backgrounders have a number of advantages for the White House. Avoiding direct quotation allows officials to speak on sensitive foreign policy and domestic policy matters candidly and in depth, something domestic politics and international diplomacy would not tolerate if speakers were held directly accountable for their words. The White House hopes such discussions will help it communicate its point of view more clearly and serve to educate journalists and make them more sympathetic to the president's position in their reporting. Moreover, they can use background sessions to scotch rumors and limit undesirable speculation about presidential plans and internal White House affairs. An impressive performance in a background session can also display the administration's competence and perhaps elicit the benefit of the doubt in future stories.

The White House may aim backgrounders at the public (in the form of trial balloons which it can disclaim if they meet with disapproval) or at policy makers in Washington. They may also be directed at other countries. For example, to discourage the Soviet Union's support of India in its war with Pakistan, Henry Kissinger told reporters in a backgrounder that the Soviet policy might lead to the cancellation of President Nixon's trip to Moscow. Because the statement was not officially attributed to Kissinger, it constituted less of a public threat to the Soviet Union, while it simultaneously communicated the president's message.[17]

Reporters have generally been happy to go along with protecting the identities of "spokespeople" and "sources" (although an experienced observer can identify most of them) because the system provides them more information than they would have without it. This increase of information available to reporters adds to the information available to the public and probably helps advance journalistic careers as well.

In addition to official backgrounders, White House aides may provide reporters information "on background." Reporters tend to view middle-level aides as the best sources of such information because they have in-depth knowledge about the substance of programs and are generally free from the constraints of high visibility. Most interviews with White House staff are made on this basis because presidents are generally intolerant of staff members who seek publicity for themselves. Sometimes an aide will say more than his or her superiors would like in order to prod the president in a particular policy direction or cast doubt on a rival in the administration. Self-serving propaganda is a common feature of these sessions.

Interviews
Modern presidents give hundreds of interviews during their tenures. Barack Obama particularly favored televised interviews as a means of reaching the

public in an unmediated form. Interviews with the president and top White House staff members are a valuable commodity to the press, and sometimes the White House uses them for its own purposes. For example, President Nixon traded an exclusive interview with *Time* for a cover story on him. Similarly, in order to obtain an interview with President Ford, even the venerable Walter Cronkite agreed to use only questions the president could handle easily. At other times, the White House may give exclusives to a paper like the *New York Times* in return for getting a story in which it is interested located in a prominent place in the paper.[18]

In 2012, President Obama held his "first completely virtual interview" as part of an event hosted by Google+. He joined a "hangout" and took questions through YouTube on everything from unemployment to streamlining the federal government. He has also held town hall meetings on Facebook, Twitter, and LinkedIn. These virtual interviews were part of a larger effort by the White House to connect directly to Americans without going through the traditional news media.

Cultivation

Recent presidents, with the exceptions of Richard Nixon, Jimmy Carter, and George W. Bush, have regularly cultivated elite reporters and columnists, the editors and publishers of leading newspapers, and network news producers and executives with small favors, social flattery, and small background dinners at the White House. (Nixon turned these chores over to top aides; Carter was neither interested in, nor skilled at, cultivation; the George W. Bush White House cultivated reporters with information but not frequent social occasions.)[19] President Clinton invited the television network anchors to lunch at the White House before delivering his first prime time address to the nation. The first phone call ABC network anchor Peter Jennings received after landing his job was from Ronald Reagan.[20] Barack Obama has hosted lunches and dinners for TV anchors and columnists, had dinner with conservative columnists at George Will's house shortly before he took office, and has held off-the-record sessions with liberal columnists and historians.[21] He also holds meetings with niche online outlets.

Since the 1960s, the White House has had, first, a designated person, and then an office for media liaison to deal directly with the representatives of news organizations, such as editors, publishers, and producers, in addition to the press office that deals with reporters' routine needs.

Servicing the Local and Specialty Press

Once the Washington press reports an issue, it tends to drop it and move on to the next one; however, repetition is necessary to convey the president's views to the generally inattentive public. Moreover, the Washington press tends to place more emphasis on the support of, or opposition to, a program than on its substance, although the White House wants to communicate the latter. The Washington- and New York–based national media also have substantial resources to challenge White House versions of events and policies and to investigate areas of government not covered by briefings or press releases. As a result, the White House provides services for the local as well as the national media.

The White House invites local editors, reporters, and news executives to Washington for exclusive interviews and briefings by the president and senior administration officials. Recent presidents have also arranged to be interviewed from the White House by television and radio stations through satellite hookups, and the White House provides briefings for the local press using the same technology. It also sends administration briefing teams around the country to discuss the president's policies with local media representatives and provides press releases, speeches, other documents, and audio clips for local media. Recent presidents have met frequently with journalists representing local media during their trips around the country. These efforts enabled the White House to tailor unedited messages for specific groups and reach directly into the constituencies of members of Congress while reinforcing its policy message. Naturally, presidents hope to create goodwill and to receive a sympathetic hearing from journalists who are grateful for contact with the White House and, perhaps, susceptible to presidential charm.

The Obama White House has made a concerted effort to tap into alternatives to the mainstream national media, including Spanish-language magazines, newspapers, and television and radio stations and those oriented to African Americans. The White House is also oriented toward blogs, Internet videos, Facebook, and Twitter. Obama's Twitter feed, with nearly 27 million followers, reaches more people than all of the nightly news broadcasts combined and more than the total circulation of the 75 largest daily papers. The press pool that takes turns covering the president up close now includes Web-only publications like *Talking Points Memo*, the *Huffington Post*, and the *Daily Caller*.

Additional Services
There are many additional services that the White House provides for the press. It gives reporters transcripts of briefings and presidential speeches and daily handouts containing a variety of information about the president and his policies, including advance notice of travel plans and upcoming stories. (These items are also available to the general public at the White House's Internet site.) It oftentimes makes major announcements to accommodate the deadlines of newspapers, magazines, and television networks.

Photographers covering the president are highly dependent on the White House press office, which provides facilities for photographers on presidential trips and arranges photo opportunities to make sure they will produce the most flattering shots of the president (for Johnson, his left profile). President Reagan even prohibited impromptu questions from reporters at photographing sessions. Moreover, the official White House photographers provide many of the photographs of the president that the media use. Naturally, these are screened favorably to feature the president's "warm," "human," or "family" side. These photos please editors and the public alike.

When the president goes on trips, whether at home or abroad, the White House travel and press offices make extensive preparations for the press (perhaps explaining why the press was so critical of Bill Clinton when he summarily fired travel office employees in 1993). These preparations include arranging transportation and lodging for the press, installing equipment for radio and television broadcasting, obtaining telephones for reporters, erecting platforms for photographers, preparing a detailed account of where and with whom the president will be at particular times, providing elaborate information about the countries the president is visiting, forming pools of press members to cover the president closely (as in a motorcade), and scheduling the press plane to arrive early so the press can cover the president's arrival.

As many of these services suggest, the press is especially dependent on the White House staff in covering presidential trips, particularly abroad. There are usually fewer sources of information on such trips, and access of the press to the principal figures it wishes to cover is limited. Thus, the president's aides are in a good position to manage press coverage to their advantage. Coverage of foreign trips is generally favorable, although less so than in the past now that reporters with expertise in foreign affairs have started to accompany the president. The press will point out the relationship of the trip and its goals and accomplishments to the president's domestic political problems. (It is interesting that foreign travel does not seem to increase a president's approval ratings.)[22]

Even in Washington, however, reporters are very much in a controlled environment. Reagan aides went so far as to have the motor of the president's helicopter revved to prevent him from hearing questions shouted by the press as he left for a weekend at Camp David. Similarly, when presidents wish to avoid the press during their reelection campaigns, they can simply hold no formal press conferences at all.

Managing the News

Reporters may not freely roam the halls of the White House, interviewing whomever they please. In one of its first acts, the Clinton White House even barred reporters from the area behind the press room, where the offices of the press secretary and communications director are located (it changed this policy after a few months). Reporters are highly dependent on the press office for access to officials, and about half of their interviews are with the press secretary and his or her staff. Much of their time is spent waiting for something to happen or watching the president at formal or ceremonial events. Because most news stories about such occurrences show the president in a favorable light, the press office does everything possible to help reporters record these activities.

The White House can use briefings, press releases, and the like to divert the media's attention from embarrassing matters. Reagan's aides adopted a strategy of blitzing the media with information to divert its attention after the press raised questions about the president's sleeping through Libyan attacks on U.S. forces off the coast of Africa.[23] To avoid publicity about illegal transfers of arms to Nicaragua, the Reagan White House spearheaded a drive for an "Economic Bill of Rights."[24]

More frequently, the White House, by adopting an active approach to the press, gains an opportunity to shape the media's agenda for the day. Through announcements and press releases, it attempts to focus attention on what will reflect positively on the president. Such information frequently generates questions from reporters and subsequent news stories. Representatives of the smaller papers, who have few resources, are more heavily dependent on White House–provided news than are the larger news bureaus, including the major networks. Thus, the former are the most likely to follow the White House's agenda. Moreover, since White House reporters, especially the wire services, are under pressure to file daily "hard news" reports, the White House is in a strong position to help by providing information— much of it trivial, some of it personal, and all of it designed to reflect positively on the president. As a Ford official put it: "You can predict what the press is going to do with a story. It is almost by formula. Because of this they are usable."[25]

The White House has a special advantage in managing the news on national security issues. In the case of Iraq and weapons of mass destruction, the media amplified the administration's voice through straightforward transmissions of White House, Pentagon, and official administration statements, validating the administration's messages in the process. The conventions of breaking stories tied journalists to leading with the "news," which meant reporting the president's assertions about the threat that Iraq posed because it had such weapons. There were few critical voices, and the press only rarely covered them.

Many observers, including journalists, feel that, especially early in a president's term, the press tends to parrot the White House line, conveniently provided at a briefing or in a press release. The pressure among journalists to be first with a story increases the potential for White House manipulation inherent in this deferential approach, as concerns for accuracy give way to career interests.

Presidents have undoubtedly hoped that the handouts, briefings, and other services they and their staffs provide for reporters will gain them some goodwill. They may also hope that these services will keep the White House press from digging too deeply into presidential affairs. In addition, they want to keep reporters interested in the president's agenda because bored journalists are more negative in their reporting and may base their stories on trivial, embarrassing incidents like the president stumbling while getting off a plane or getting a $200 haircut while on one.

In addition, the White House controls a commodity of considerable value to the press: information on the president's personal life. Most reporters are under pressure to provide stories on the minutiae of presidents' lives, no matter what they do. Some White House aides have found that the provision of such information can co-opt journalists or sidetrack them from producing critical stories. Some reporters will exploit the opportunity to please their editors instead of digging into more significant subjects; others reciprocate their favorable treatment by the White House with positive stories about the president.

The Obama administration has been less successful when wielding the stick. It soon grew weary of Fox News's unrelenting and often vitriolic criticism and limited the appearances of top officials on some Fox News shows. More visibly, it excluded "Fox News Sunday with Chris Wallace"—which it had previously treated as distinct from the network—from a round of presidential interviews with Sunday morning news programs in mid-September 2009. In late October, the White House tried to exclude Fox from a round of interviews with the executive-pay czar Kenneth R. Feinberg. When Fox's television news competitors refused to go along, the White House relented.[26] Fox's access soon returned to normal.[27]

PRESS COVERAGE OF THE PRESIDENT

In addition to the chief executive's efforts to influence the media, there is another side of this relationship we must examine: the content of the news. Ultimately, it is the written and spoken word that concerns the president. Leaks of confidential information and what the White House sees as superficial or biased reporting exacerbate the tensions inherent in relations between the president and the press. Presidents commonly view the press as a major obstacle to their obtaining and maintaining public support. Most administrations criticize the media for its trivial coverage, for its distortions, and for violating confidences. The White House feels that this type of reporting hinders its efforts to develop public appreciation for the president and his policies.

Leaks

After some time in office, Bill Clinton made it a rule not to say anything sensitive in a room with more than one aide. If he did, he felt, he might as well speak directly to the Associated Press.[28] Barack Obama hated leaks[29] and his Department of Justice formally investigated a substantial number of them.

Leaks bedevil most presidents. Sometimes, they are potentially quite serious, as when leakers disclosed the U.S. negotiating strategy for nuclear disarmament talks during the Nixon administration. When the *Pentagon Papers* (on decision making on the war in Vietnam) were leaked to the public, President Nixon felt that there was a danger that other countries would lose confidence in our ability to keep secrets and that information on the delicate negotiations then in progress with China might also be leaked, endangering the possibility of rapprochement.[30] At other times, leaks are just embarrassing—for example, when they reveal internal dissent in the administration to the public. President Johnson feared that leaks would signal what he was thinking and he would lose his freedom of action as a result.

Who leaks information? The best answer is "everybody." Presidents themselves do so, sometimes inadvertently. As Lyndon Johnson once put it: "I have enough trouble with myself. I ought not to have to put up with everybody else too."[31] Once John F. Kennedy ordered Secretary of State Dean Rusk to find out who had leaked a story on foreign policy only to discover that the culprit was the president himself.[32]

Top presidential aides may also reveal more than they intend. When a leak regarding President Reagan's willingness to compromise on his 1981 tax bill appeared in the *New York Times*, White House aides tracked down the source of the story and found it to be budget director David Stockman.[33] A year earlier, a leak revealing secret Central Intelligence Agency arms shipments to Afghan rebels was attributed to the office of the president's chief national security adviser.[34]

Most leaks, however, are deliberately planted. As one close presidential aide put it, "99 percent of all significant secrets are spilled by the principals or at their direction."[35] Presidents are included in those who purposefully leak. For example, *Newsweek* used to hold space open for the items John Kennedy would phone to his friend Benjamin Bradlee right before the magazine's deadline.[36]

There are many reasons for leaks. The White House often uses them as trial balloons to test public or congressional reaction to ideas and proposals or to stimulate public concern about an issue. Both the Ford and Carter White Houses used this technique to test reaction to a tax surcharge on gasoline. When the reaction to these proposals turned out to be negative, both administrations denied ever contemplating such a policy. President Clinton's task force on health care reform engaged in a series of leaks regarding a wide range of health policy options.

At other times, aides leak information to reporters who will use it to write favorable articles on a policy. Alternately, as the Clinton White House often did, the administration may leak an exclusive story on relatively modest proposals, such as plans to renovate schools or to crack down on truants, to one news organization. This technique encourages that organization to give it added coverage as an exclusive story and forces the competition to play catch-up and give the president two days of favorable publicity instead of only one.[37]

Diplomacy is an area in which delicate communications play an important role. Officials often use leaks to send other nations nuanced signals of friendship, anger, or willingness to compromise. While sending messages to other nations, leaks provide the president with the opportunity to disavow publicly or to reinterpret what some might view as, for example, an overly "tough" stance or an unexpected change in policy. This makes it easier for these countries to respond to U.S. wishes. For example, during negotiations with the Japanese regarding restricting imports, the Reagan administration leaked a story that the talks were going badly so as to pressure Japan into moderating its position. President Clinton's national security assistant regularly leaked stories to CNN for diplomatic purposes, including using a leak to warn Iraqi leader Saddam Hussein to move his troops away from the Kuwaiti border in 1994.[38] Diplomatic leaks also have the advantage of speed. When President Bush wanted to send a message of U.S. support for Soviet President Mikhail Gorbachev during the attempted coup to remove him, he wanted to use the fastest source available for getting a message to Moscow, so he chose to leak the message to CNN.[39]

People may also use leaks to influence personnel matters. The release of information letting a stubborn official know that the official's superiors wish him or her to leave may force a resignation and thus save the problem of firing the official. Conversely, a leak may make the official's position a public issue, increasing the costs of such a firing. Similarly, the release of information on an appointment before it is made places presidents in an awkward position and can help ensure that they follow through on it or else prematurely deny they have such plans.

Some leaks are designed to force the president's hand on policy decisions. Officials in the Clinton administration who were hostile to welfare reform regularly leaked stories critical of the plan the administration was formulating. They also tried to tie the president's hands by leaking false stories that the president had made a decision, thus hoping to encourage him actually to make that decision to avoid being viewed as flip-flopping.[40] During the Indian–Pakistani War, President Nixon maintained a publicly neutral stance but really favored Pakistan. When this fact was leaked, there was inevitable pressure to be neutral in action as well as in rhetoric.[41] Conversely, a leak about what Lyndon Johnson was thinking about a decision would generally ensure that he would take no such action.

Leaks may serve a number of other functions. They may make some individuals feel important or help them gain favor with reporters. Officials may also use leaks to criticize and intimidate personal or political adversaries in the White House itself or to protect and enhance reputations. In the Ford administration, White House counsel Robert Hartmann and Chief of Staff Richard Cheney often attacked each other anonymously in the press. Several members of the White House staff attacked Press Secretary Ron Nessen in an effort to persuade the president to replace him. When negotiations with North Vietnam broke down in late 1972, White House aides employed leaks to dissociate the president from Henry Kissinger, his national security assistant.

Presidents sometimes leak information for their own political purposes. By leaking findings about lax security measures regarding the deaths of 241 marines in Beirut in 1983, Reagan White House aides focused press attention on security lapses rather than the criticism of the ill-defined nature of the marines' mission in Lebanon, a mission given to them by the president.[42] George W. Bush, through Vice President Dick Cheney, secretly declassified an intelligence estimate and authorized Cheney's aide, I. Lewis Libby Jr., to leak it to fight back against critics of the Iraq war.

In all these cases, government officials were using the press for their purposes, not vice versa. Although reporters may well be aware of being used, the competitive pressure of the news business makes it difficult for them to pass up an exclusive story. Nevertheless, most good reporting, even investigative reporting, does not rely heavily on leaks. Instead, reporters put together stories by bits and pieces.

It is generally fruitless to try to discover the source of a leak. The Reagan administration tried everything from lie detector tests to logging every journalist's interviews on a computer, but nothing stopped the leaking. According to White House Chief of Staff Donald Regan: "In the Reagan Administration the leak was raised to the status of an art form. Everything, or nearly everything, the President and his close associates did or knew appeared in the newspapers and on the networks with the least possible delay."[43]

The Clinton White House made some progress in discouraging leaks when Chief of Staff Leon Panetta began trying to identify who had leaked and then retaliating by leaking a critical story to a major news outlet about the suspect.[44] Nevertheless, leaks remain common in press coverage of the president, and the incentives to leak remain as strong as ever.

Superficiality

A common complaint in the White House is that the press is interested in the superficial layer of politics rather than the meat and potatoes of governing. Woodrow Wilson, one of the first presidents to serve in the era of a mass media with a national focus, complained that most reporters were "interested in the personal and trivial rather than in principles of policies."[45] More recently, Jimmy Carter complained to reporters, "I would really like for you all as people who relay Washington events to the world to take a look at the substantive questions I have to face as a president and quit dealing almost exclusively with personalities."[46] Barack Obama has criticized the media's preoccupation with conflict and complained that too often press coverage focuses on political winners and losers rather than substance, thereby reflecting a "false balance" in which two opposing sides are given equal weight regardless of the facts.[47]

Brevity and simplicity characterize media coverage of national news in mainline media such as most newspapers and broadcast networks. Editors do not want to bore or confuse their viewers, listeners, or readers. Stories must be few in number and short in length. The amount of information transmitted under such conditions is inevitably limited and insufficient for the president to educate the public about his policies. Moreover, the amount of coverage of the president seems to be decreasing,[48] and this lower profile is unlikely to be an asset in advancing the president's agenda.

The substance as well as the amount of media coverage hinders the president's efforts to persuade the public. Rather than focusing on policy issues, the news is becoming more personality-centered, less time-bound, more practical, and more incident-based. About 50 percent of all news stories have no clear connection to policy issues.[49] News organizations demand information that is new and different, personal and intimate, or revealing and unexpected. Most reporting is about events, actions taken, or words spoken by public figures, especially if the events are dramatic and colorful, such as ceremonies and parades. According to ABC correspondent Sam Donaldson, "A clip of a convalescent Reagan waving from his window at some circus elephants is going to push an analytical piece about tax cuts off the air every time."[50] In such a news environment, there is little time or space for reflection, analysis, or comprehensive coverage.

Human interest stories, especially those about presidents and their families, are always in high demand. Socks, the Clintons' cat, and Buddy, their dog, became overnight celebrities. Such stories are novel, and the public can relate to the subjects more easily than to complex matters of public policy such as a presidential tax proposal.

Related to human interest stories is what George W. Bush's first two press secretaries, Ari Fleischer and Scott McClellan, concluded was the press's primary bias—toward conflict.[51] Conflicts between clearly identifiable antagonists (President Obama versus Speaker of the House John Boehner) are highly prized, particularly if there is something tangible at stake such as the passage of a bill or impeachment of the president. As one prominent White House correspondent put it,

> Most reporters I know are not passionately political, left or right. Our real ideology is a love of conflict, meaning that we have a bias for stories about, yes, personality feuds, but also about disputes over policy.[52]

In the process of covering such controversies, the press may repeat distortions, half-truths, and even untruths about the president and his opponents and reduce complex matters to black-and-white terms, thus obscuring the real issues that underlie the conflict. The same thing occurs when the media increasingly devote extensive attention to negative ads in presidential campaigns.[53]

President Obama's health care reform proposal evoked an eruption of anger at town hall meetings, which became the story the media presented rather than the substance of the plan. After the president convened a low-key town hall in New Hampshire, Fox broke away from the meeting and anchor Trace Gallagher told her audience, "Any contentious questions, anybody yelling, we'll bring it to you."[54]

Scandals involving the president or those close to him receive high-priority coverage in the media, often driving out coverage of news on the president's policies. For example, on April 22, 1994, President Clinton held a press conference on imminent air strikes in Bosnia, which only CNN carried live. On the same day, First Lady Hillary Rodham Clinton held a press conference on the Whitewater investigation, which all the networks carried. When Paula Jones charged President Clinton with sexual harassment (while he was governor of Arkansas), the media devoted extensive coverage to the case, yet even this attention paled in comparison to the frenzy of coverage devoted to the president's sexual relationship with a White House intern, Monica Lewinsky. No policy issue received as much attention, especially on television, until the Senate acquitted the president more than a year later. Indeed, one-seventh of the network news in 1998 focused on the scandal.[55]

Most of the White House press activity comes under the heading of the "body watch." In other words, reporters focus on the most visible layer of the president's personal and official activities and provide the public with a step-by-step account. They are interested in what the president will do, how his actions will affect others, how he views policies and individuals, how he presents himself, and whose stars are rising and falling, rather than in the substance of policies or the fundamental operations of the executive branch. Coverage of the consideration of both President Obama and President Clinton's massive health care proposals in 1993–1994 and 2009–2010 focused much more on strategy and legislative battles than on the issues of health care.[56]

Editors expect this type of coverage (which they believe will please their readers), and reporters do not want to risk missing a story. As the Washington bureau chief of *Newsweek* said: "The worst thing in the world that could happen to you is for the President of the United States to choke on a piece of meat, and for you not to be there."[57] When President Bush vomited at a state dinner in Japan, television networks had a field day and ran the tape again and again of the president being taken ill.

Major news organizations spend a great deal of money covering the presidents, including following them around the globe on official business and vacations. Because of this investment and the public's interest in the president, reporters must come up with something each day. Newsworthy happenings do not necessarily occur every day, however, so reporters either emphasize the trivial or blow events out of proportion. While covering a meeting of Western leaders on the island of Guadeloupe, Sam Donaldson faced the prospect of having nothing to report on a slow news day. Undaunted, he reported on the roasting of the pig that the leaders would be eating that evening, including "an exclusive look at the oven in which the pig would be roasted."[58]

Similarly, the White House press often focuses on the exact wording of an announcement in an effort to detect a change in policy, frequently finding significance where none really exists. It often blows presidential slips of the tongue or gaffes out of all proportion.

In its constant search for "news," the press, especially the electronic media, is reluctant to devote repeated attention to an issue even though this might be necessary to explain it adequately to the public. As a deputy press secretary in the Carter administration said: "We have to keep sending out our message if we expect people to understand. The Washington press corps will explain a policy once and then it will feature the politics of the issue."[59] This is one incentive for the president to meet with the non-Washington press and to address the nation directly on television or radio.

To delve more deeply into the presidency and policy requires not only substantial expertise but also certain technical skills. Washington reporters in general, and White House reporters in particular, do little documentary research. They are trained to conduct interviews and transmit handouts from press secretaries and public information officials rather than to conduct research. Moreover, in-depth research demands a slower pace and advance planning, and journalists tend to be comfortable with neither requirement.

Sometimes, several factors influence coverage of the presidency at the same time. Despite the glamour attached to investigative reporting since the

Watergate scandal, not much of it actually takes place. Most news organizations are unwilling or unable to devote the time and resources necessary for investigative work or the coordination required with other reporters and news bureau staff to cover all leads successfully. The maxim of journalism is to go it alone, and the incentives are generally to get the news out fast—and first. Similarly, the slowness of the process of using the Freedom of Information Act to force the release of documents inhibits its use.

The speed of the modern news cycle also promotes superficiality. Instead of seeking context or disputing a claim, reporters often simply get two opposing quotes and file a he-said/she-said story. As Peter Baker of the *New York Times* put it, a decade ago, a reporter could write for the next day's newspaper. He or she had time to call people, access information, and provide context. Today, you have to file for the Web, radio, and perhaps appear on television and a blog. "Even with a well-staffed news organization, we are hostages to the non-stop, never-ending file-it-now, get-on-the-Web, get-on-the-radio, get-on-TV media environment."[60]

Not only does the press provide superficial coverage of the stories it reports, but it also misses many important stories about the presidency altogether because of its emphasis. The implementation of policy, which is the predominant activity of the executive branch, is very poorly covered because it is not fast-breaking news; it takes place mostly in the field, away from the reporters' natural territory; and it requires documentary analysis and interaction with civil servants who are neither famous nor experts at public relations. Similarly, the White House press misses most of the flow of information and options made available to the president from the rest of the executive branch unless a scandal is involved.

In sum, although the president is dependent on the media to disseminate his views, the superficiality of the news is often an obstacle to obtaining public support. The press transmits only limited information to the public and the nature of this information ill-equips people to deal with the ambiguities and uncertainties of most complex events and issues. Moreover, the news provides little in the way of the background and contextual information that is essential for understanding political events. Although the electronic media, especially television, are the most typical source of news for Americans, they do a relatively poor job of providing information to the public. According to CBS network anchor Dan Rather, "You simply cannot be a well-informed citizen by just watching the news on television."[61] Yet television is the principal source of news for most people.

Bias

Bias is the most politically charged issue in press relations with the president. It is also an elusive concept with many dimensions. Although we typically envision bias as news coverage favoring identifiable people, parties, or points of view, there are more subtle and more pervasive forms of bias that are not motivated by the goal of furthering careers or policies.

Many studies covering topics such as presidential election campaigns, the Vietnam War, and local news conclude that the news media are not biased systematically toward a particular person, party, or ideology, as measured in the amount or favorability of coverage.[62] In the same vein, after six years as President Reagan's press secretary, Larry Speakes concluded that the news media had generally given the administration "a fair shake" and that "they probably gave us a longer honeymoon than we deserved."[63] Lanny Davis, a prominent defender of Bill Clinton during his impeachment and trial, found reporters wrote fair stories if the White House gave them full information.[64] Scott McClellan, a George W. Bush press secretary, concluded that media bias was not a problem and that any liberal bias had minimal impact on the way the public was informed. The "Bush administration had no difficulty in getting our messages across to the American people," he declared.[65]

This discussion of the general neutrality of news coverage in the mass media pertains most directly to traditional television news shows and newspaper and radio reporting. Columnists, commentators, and editorial writers usually cannot even pretend to be neutral. Typical newspaper endorsements for presidential candidates overwhelmingly favor Republicans (1992 and 2004 were exceptions).[66] Newsmagazines are generally less neutral than newspapers or television because they often adopt a point of view in their stories. Hosts of many cable television and radio shows, such as those on Fox and MSNBC, have an explicitly ideological edge.[67]

Restraints on Bias

A number of factors help to explain why most mass media news coverage is not biased systematically toward a particular person, party, or ideology. Reporters tend not to be partisan or strong ideologues, nor are they politically aligned or holders of strong political beliefs. Journalists are typically not intellectuals or deeply concerned with public policy. Moreover, they share journalism's professional norm of objectivity. The organizational processes of story selection and editing also provide opportunities for softening reporters' judgments. The rotation of assignments and rewards for objective newsgathering are further protections against bias. Local television station owners and newspaper publishers are in a position to apply pressure regarding the presentation of the news, and, although they rarely do so, their potential to act may restrain reporters.

Self-interest also plays a role in constraining bias. Individual reporters, as opposed to media commentators, may earn a poor reputation if others view them as biased. The television networks, newspaper news services, newsmagazines, and wire services, which provide most of the Washington news for newspapers, have a direct financial stake in attracting viewers and subscribers and do not want to lose their audience by appearing biased, especially when multiple versions of the same story are available to major news outlets. Slander and libel laws and the "political attack" rule, providing those personally criticized on the electronic media with an opportunity to respond, are formal limitations on bias.

There is a tendency of the press to defer to the best-packaged officially advanced stories, according an advantage to officials with the greatest perceived power to affect the issues at hand, the greatest capacity to use the levers of office to advance their news narratives on a regular basis, and the best communications operations to spin their preferred narratives well. Of the 414 stories on the buildup to and the rationale for the Iraq war presented by ABC, CBS, and NBC from September 2002 through February 2003, only 34 originated outside the White House.[68]

News organizations do not want to be seen as crusaders. Thus, it is difficult for journalists to report and sustain stories opposing the president unless they have credible sources with power in government articulating opposition. Even strong newspapers like the *Washington Post* and the *New York Times* relied heavily on the Bush administration's assertions about the existence of weapons of mass destruction in Iraq and downplayed stories questioning them. Without some government mechanism such as congressional hearing or a serious election challenge from Democrats, there was nothing to sustain an opposing story or Iraq.[69]

Distortion

To conclude that the news contains little explicit partisan or ideological bias is not to argue that it does not distort reality in its coverage. Even under the best of conditions, some distortion is inevitable as a result of simple error or such factors as lack of careful checking of facts, the efforts of news sources to deceive, and short deadlines.

We have already seen that the news is fundamentally superficial and oversimplified and is often overblown, all of which provides the public with a distorted view of, among other things, presidential activities, statements, policies, and options. The emphasis on action and the deviant (and therefore "newsworthy" items) rather than on patterns of behavior, and the implication that most stories represent more general themes of national significance, contribute further to this distortion. Personalizing the news downplays structural and other impersonal factors, which may be far more important in understanding the economy, for example, than individual political actors.

Themes

The press prefers to frame the news in themes and story lines, which both simplify complex issues and events and provide continuity of people, institutions, and issues. As we noted in Chapter 3, once these themes and story lines have been established, the press tends to maintain them in subsequent coverage. Stories that dovetail with the theme are more likely to be in the news. By necessity, framing the news in this fashion emphasizes some information at the expense of other data, often determining what information is most relevant to news coverage and the context in which it is presented.

George Bush's privileged background gave rise to a greatly distorting media theme of isolation from the realities of everyday life in the United States. Thus, a story that he expressed amazement at scanners commonly used at supermarket checkout lines was widely reported as further evidence of his isolation—even though the story was incorrect. Similarly, once the theme of Bill Clinton's weak political and ethical moorings had been established, even the most outrageous tabloid claims of his past misbehavior received media attention, while stories about his policy stances frequently focused on whether or not he was displaying backbone.

Once the press typecasts a president, news coverage and late-night comedians repeatedly reinforce his image, and a negative image is difficult to overcome. For example, after a stereotype of President Ford as a "bumbler" had been established, his every stumble was magnified as the press emphasized behavior that fit the mold. Ford was repeatedly forced to defend his intelligence, and many of his acts and statements were reported as efforts to "act" presidential.[70] There was a similar theme to the coverage of Vice President Dan Quayle, and as a result, after he misspelled "potato" during the 1992 presidential campaign, it became a widely reported story.

In 1992, the press's predominant theme regarding the presidency was that President Bush was in trouble, so it focused on information that would illustrate the theme. Bush received overwhelmingly negative coverage during the year. Indeed, the television networks' portrayal of the economy became more negative even as the economy actually improved! Similar themes were established for President Carter in 1980 and President Ford in 1976.[71]

Media Activism

Some people may equate objectivity with passivity and feel that the press should do no more than report what others present to it. This simple conveyance of news is what occurs much of the time, and it is a fundamental reason for the superficiality of news coverage. If the press is passive, however, it can be more easily manipulated and even made to represent fiction as fact. Reporters increasingly feel the necessity of setting the story in a meaningful context. The construction of such a context may entail reporting what was not said as well as what was said; what had occurred before; and what political implications may be involved in a statement, policy, or event. More than in the past, reporters today actively and aggressively interpret stories for viewers and readers. They no longer depend on those whom they interview to set the tone of their stories, and they now regularly pass sweeping (and frequently negative) judgments about what politicians are saying and doing.[72]

Negativity

Increasingly, the public receives news about the president in a negative context.[73] To meet their needs for a story containing conflict, it is routine for reporters to turn to opponents of the president when he makes a statement or takes an action.[74] President Clinton received mostly negative coverage during his tenure in office, with a ratio of negative to positive comments on network television of about two to one.[75] The trend continued in the George W. Bush presidency.[76] Although Barack Obama enjoyed a brief honeymoon with the press,[77] the news soon turned negative for him as well. Coverage of his economic stimulus proposal and his health care reform plan was more negative than positive,[78] as was coverage of the 2012 presidential campaign.[79]

Journalists typically present negative stories in a seemingly neutral manner. Such "objective" reporting can be misleading, however, as the following excerpt from Jimmy Carter's diary regarding a visit to Panama in 1978 illustrates:

> I told the Army troops that I was in the Navy for eleven years, and they booed. I told them that we depended on the Army to keep the Canal open, and they cheered. Later, the news reports said that there were boos and cheers during my speech.[80]

Similarly, an emphasis on scandals in an administration, even if the press presents the stories in an even-handed manner, rarely helps the White House. The coverage of the Monica Lewinsky story seems to be an exception, as President Clinton benefited, at least for most of 1998, from a backlash against media intrusiveness into his private life. Nevertheless, President Clinton received mostly negative coverage during his tenure in office.[81]

Some observers feel that the press is biased against whoever holds office at the moment and that reporters want to expose them in the media. Reporters, they argue, hold disparaging views of most politicians and public officials, whom they find self-serving, dishonest, incompetent, hypocritical, and preoccupied with reelection. Thus, it is not surprising that, as part of the "watchdog" function of the press, journalists see a need to expose and debunk them. This orientation to analytical coverage may be characterized as neither liberal nor conservative, but reformist.[82]

White House reporters are always looking to expose conflicts of interest and other shady behavior of public officials. Moreover, many of their inquiries revolve around the question of whether the official is up to the job. Reporters who are confined in the White House all day may attempt to make up for their lack of investigative reporting with sarcastic and accusatory questioning. Moreover, the desire to keep the public interested and the need for continuous coverage may create in the press a subconscious bias against the presidency that leads to critical stories. In the end, some observers agree with George W. Bush's chief political strategist, Karl Rove, that the press is "less liberal than it is oppositional."[83]

Conversely, one could argue that the press is biased toward the White House. Reporters' general respect for the presidency may be transferred to individual presidents. Framed at a respectful distance by the television camera, the president is typically portrayed with an aura of dignity and as working in a context of rationality and coherence on activities benefiting the public. The press's word selection often reflects this orientation as well. It has only been in recent years that journalists stopped following conventions that protected politicians and public officials from revelations of private misconduct.

The White House enjoys a great deal of positive coverage in newspapers, magazines, and network news. The most favorable coverage comes in the first year of a president's term, before there is a record to criticize or critics for reporters to interview. Coverage focuses on human interest stories of the president and on his appointees and their personalities, goals, and plans. The president is pictured in a positive light as a policy maker dealing with problems. Controversies over solutions typically arise later.[84] President Clinton was not as fortunate in his first year because of especially active congressional critics; his own partisans, who clamored for policies they had been denied during twelve years of Republican presidencies; an inability of the White House to keep its internal dissensions to itself; and the poor performance of the White House public relations staff.

Ultimately, the issue of bias may hang on questions of nuance. As public affairs analyst and former presidential press secretary Bill Moyers put it, "Depending on who is looking and writing, the White House is brisk or brusque, assured or arrogant, casual or sloppy, frank or brutal, warm or corny, cautious or timid, compassionate or condescending, reserved or callous."[85] Given the limitations of language and the lack of agreement on the exact nature of reality, it is almost impossible for the media to please everyone.

MEDIA EFFECTS

The most significant question about the substance of media coverage, of course, is about the impact it has on public opinion. Most studies on media effects have focused on attitude changes, especially in voting for presidential candidates, and have typically found little or no evidence of influence. Reinforcement of existing attitudes and opinions was said to be the strongest effect of the media.[86] In the words of one expert: "Most media stories are promptly forgotten. Stories that become part of an individual's fund of knowledge tend to reinforce existing beliefs and feelings. Acquisition of new knowledge or changes in attitude are the exception rather than the rule."[87] There are other ways to analyze media effects, however.

Setting the Public's Agenda

The public's familiarity with political matters is closely related to the attention they receive in the mass media,[88] especially in foreign affairs. The media also have a strong influence on the issues the public views as important.[89] "Many people readily adopt the media's agenda of importance, often without being aware of it."[90] Moreover, when the media cover events, politicians comment on them and take action, reinforcing the perceived importance of these events and ensuring more public attention to them.

During the 1979–1980 Iranian hostage crisis, in which several dozen Americans were held hostage, ABC originated a nightly program entitled *America Held Hostage*. On CBS television, Walter Cronkite provided a "countdown" of the number of days of the crisis at the end of each evening's news. Countless feature stories on the hostages and their families were reported in all the media, and the press gave complete coverage to "demonstrations" held in front of the U.S. embassy in Tehran (often artificially created by demonstrators for consumption by Americans). This crisis dominated American politics for more than a year and gave President Carter's approval rating a tremendous, albeit short-term, boost. In the longer term, however, the coverage destroyed his leadership image. Conversely, when North Korea captured the American ship *Pueblo* in 1968, there were many more American captives and they were held for almost as long as the hostages in Tehran, but there were also no television cameras and few reporters to cover the situation. Thus, the incident played a much smaller role in American politics.

Media Framing and Priming

At any one time, there are many potential criteria for evaluating the president, ranging from personal characteristics such as integrity to performance on the economy or foreign affairs. In Chapter 4, we learned that the concept of priming is premised on the fact that most of the time the cognitive burdens are too great for people to reach judgments or decisions based on comprehensive, integrated information and the consideration of a large number of criteria. Instead, the public takes shortcuts or uses cues. One source of cues is the White House, but another is the mass media.

Media coverage of issues and events may prime the criteria most people select for evaluating the president. In the words of a leading authority on the impact of television news on public opinion: "The themes and issues that are repeated in television news coverage become the priorities of viewers. Issues and events highlighted by television news become especially influential as criteria for evaluating public officials."[91]

The media are more likely to influence perceptions than attitudes. The press can influence the perceptions of what public figures stand for and what their personalities are like, what issues are important, and what is at stake. If the media raise certain issues or personal characteristics to prominence, the significance of attitudes that people already hold may change and thus alter their evaluations of, say, presidential performance, without their attitudes themselves changing. In other words, the media can influence the criteria by which the public judges the president.

If the media were simply following the White House's lead in priming criteria for evaluating the president, the media's impact would not pose an obstacle to presidential priming. Instead, it would reinforce the White House's efforts. The media, however, typically follow their own course.

When the media began covering the Iran-Contra affair, Ronald Reagan's public approval took an immediate and severe dip as the public applied new criteria of evaluation.[92] The role of George Bush's economic performance in overall evaluations of him decreased substantially after the Gulf War began, and it is reasonable to conclude that media priming effects caused a shift of attention to his performance on war-related criteria.[93] Although the president wanted the public to continue to weigh heavily his foreign policy stewardship in its evaluations of his performance after the war, the public did not comply. Instead, both the media and the public turned their focus to the economy.[94]

Coverage of the Camp David peace accords boosted the impact of President Carter's performance in dealing with foreign countries on overall evaluations of the president.[95] Similarly, experiments found that network news affected his overall reputation and, to a lesser extent, views of his apparent competency. The standards people used in evaluating the president, what they felt was important in his job performance, seemed to be influenced by the news they watched on television.[96]

When the press gave substantial coverage to President Ford's misstatement about Soviet domination of Eastern Europe, this coverage had an impact on the public. Polls show that most people did not realize the president had made an error until the press told them so. Afterward, pro-Ford evaluations of the debate declined noticeably as voters' concerns for competence in foreign policy making became salient.[97] A somewhat similar switch occurred after the first debate between Walter Mondale and Ronald Reagan in 1984.[98]

Although the public's information on and criteria for evaluating presidential candidates parallel what the media presents,[99] the press probably has the greatest effect on public perceptions of individuals and issues between election campaigns, when people are less likely to activate their partisan defenses.

The extraordinary attention that the press devotes to presidents magnifies their flaws and makes them more salient to the public. The prominent coverage of Gerald Ford's alleged physical clumsiness naturally translated into suggestions of mental ineptitude and became a prominent criterion for evaluating the president. In the president's own words, "Every time I stumbled or bumped my head or fell in the snow, reporters zeroed in on that to the exclusion of almost everything else."[100]

Even completely unsubstantiated charges against presidents may make the news because of their prominence. Familiarity may not breed contempt, but it certainly may diminish the aura of grandeur around the chief executive. In the past, criticism of presidents was restrained by the reluctance of many editors to publish analyses sharply divergent from the president's position without direct confirmation from an authoritative source who would be willing to go on the record in opposition to the president. During the famous investigation of the Watergate scandal, the *Washington Post* verified all information attributed to an unnamed source with at least one other independent source. It also did not print information from other media outlets unless its reporters could independently verify that information.[101] Things have changed, however.

When the story broke about charges that President Clinton had sexual relations with a young White House intern named Monica Lewinsky, virtually all elements of the mass media went into a feeding frenzy,[102] relying as much on analysis, opinion, and speculation as on confirmed facts. Even the most prominent news outlets carried unsubstantiated reports about charges that had not received independent verification by those carrying the story. If another news outlet carried a charge, most of the rest soon picked it up because they did not want to be scooped. For example, the media widely reported unsubstantiated charges that members of the Secret Service had found the president and Ms. Lewinsky in a compromising position. Such reporting helped sensationalize the story, keeping it alive and undermining the president's efforts to focus the public's attention on matters of public policy.

Similarly, the press gave immediate attention to a story on the CBS television program *60 Minutes* that revealed documents regarding President George W. Bush's service in the National Guard. The documents purported to show dissatisfaction with the president's performance—or nonperformance. Upon closer scrutiny, however, it turned out that the documents were forgeries.

In addition to framing evaluations of the president in terms of some criteria rather than others, the media also frame individual issues in certain terms.[103] Once again, the media is not an agent of the White House. For example, the media framed the issue in the debate over President Obama's health care reform proposal in 2009–2010 as one of strategy and conflict between the president and his opponents rather than emphasizing the consequences of the issue for the nation. Thus, the media did not mirror the president's attempts to frame the issue.[104] In addition, public support for rebuilding the health care system varied in tandem with changes in media.[105] In general, the media's focus on political conflict and strategy elevates the prominence of political wheeling and dealing in individuals' evaluations of political candidates and policy proposals.[106]

Public Knowledge

Because people receive most of their information on public affairs from the media, it is likely that the media will have a significant influence on the public's knowledge about public policies. Research has found that people are frequently *misinformed* (as opposed to uninformed) about policy, and the less they know, the more confidence they have in their beliefs. Thus, they resist correct factual information. Even when presented with factual information, they resist changing their opinions, including those that were the objects of elite framing.[107]

In recent years, there has been an explosion of media outlets that offer news in a variety of formats and with a variety of viewpoints. One important question is whether different news sources provide different levels of information. There is some evidence that the media can have a significant influence on what people know.[108] There is also evidence that political talk radio, which is overwhelmingly conservative, misinforms listeners and influences their attitudes.[109] Regular viewers of the Fox News Channel were far more likely than viewers of other cable news channels to believe the false claim that President Obama's health care reform contained "death panels."[110]

Similarly, how did so many people hold such mistaken notions about major issues like the presence of weapons of mass destruction in Iraq? There were substantial differences in the misperceptions held by people who relied on different sources for their news. Those who relied on Fox had the most misperceptions, followed by those relying on CBS. Listeners and viewers of National Public Radio and PBS had the fewest misperceptions. These relationships between news sources and misperceptions held true even after taking into consideration ("controlling for") a person's education, age, partisanship, and presidential vote intention.[111]

Interestingly, the two networks least likely to present critical commentary in their prime time news programs were Fox and CBS, the same two networks whose viewers were most likely to hold misperceptions. Although no network interviewed many commentators who opposed the war, Fox had the highest percentage of prowar commentators (81 percent) on its prime time evening broadcast, and CBS was next (77 percent).[112] In addition, the more attention viewers reported giving to Fox News, the higher their levels of misperception.

Perhaps viewers only watched the news of local affiliates instead of the networks' national news programs. Perhaps there is some other characteristic of viewers that explains the differences in misperceptions. Or perhaps the content of the news affects what people learn about important issues of the day.

Recently, there has been increased attention to the "soft news" found in network newsmagazines, entertainment newsmagazines, tabloid newsmagazines, and talk shows. For audiences relatively uninterested in politics and who tune in primarily for entertainment, soft news increases their attentiveness to, and to a smaller degree their knowledge about, some high-profile political issues, including foreign policy crises, that involve scandal, violence, heroism, and other forms of sensational human drama that are amenable to framing as dramatic human interest stories. One study found that those who consume soft news are more likely to oppose proactive or interventionist foreign policies. It also found that watching soft news affected vote choices in the 2000 presidential election.[113]

Limiting the President's Options

If the media affect mass attitudes about the importance of issues and the president's handling of them, the president has a strong incentive to address those issues—to put them on his agenda. Analysts have found that even in foreign policy, the media more often influence the president's agenda rather than the other way around.[114] (There are, of course, important exceptions, such as health care in 1993–1994.)[115] Former Secretary of State James Baker argued that media coverage of issues creates powerful new imperatives for prompt action, making it more difficult for the president to engage in world affairs selectively.[116] This pressure may force presidents to state policies or send troops when they would prefer to let situations develop or encourage other nations to deal with a problem. Bill Clinton complained that television coverage of Bosnia was "trying to force me to get America into a war."[117] In fact, the president did respond to images of atrocities in Haiti, Bosnia, and Kosovo.[118]

Colin Powell recalled, "The world had a dozen other running sores that fall [1992], but television hovered over Somalia and wrenched our hearts, night after night, with images of people starving to death before our eyes." Scenes of children starving in Somalia pressured the United States to send in armed forces to maintain peace and deliver food to the hungry. Things changed after eighteen soldiers were killed in Somalia, however. When scenes of an American soldier being dragged through the streets of Mogadishu were shown on television, Powell reflected, "We had been drawn into this place by television images, now we were being repelled by them." Television coverage now forced President Clinton to begin a troop withdrawal.[119]

Television coverage may limit the president's options even during a crisis. Pictures of Iraqi troops retreating from Kuwait on the "Highway of Death" created an impression of a bloodbath and thus influenced President Bush's decision to end the Gulf War. Bush himself described the "undesirable public and political baggage [that came from] all those scenes of carnage" appearing on television.[120] Similarly, during the 1990 invasion of Panama, the press noticed that a radio tower was standing near the center of Panama City. Reports of the tower led policy makers to order its destruction, although it had no value to the enemy.[121]

Undermining the President

Presidents need public understanding of the difficulty of their job and the nature of the problems they face. The role of the press here can be critical. Watching television news seems to do little to inform viewers about public affairs; reading the printed media is more useful. This may be because reading requires more active cognitive processing of information than watching television and because more information is presented in the newspapers.

We have seen that press coverage of the president is often superficial, oversimplified, and overblown, thus providing the public with a distorted picture of White House activities. This trivialization of the news drowns out the coverage of more important matters, often leaving the public ill-informed about matters with which the president must deal (ranging from the negotiations over international trade to funding Social Security benefits). The underlying problems that the president must confront may be largely ignored. The preoccupation of the press with personality, drama, and the results of policies does little to help the public appreciate the complexity of presidential decision making, the trade-offs involved in policy choices, and the broad trends outside the president's control. Instead, illustrations of international conflict—scenes of combat or demonstrations, for example—may become the essence of the issue in the public's mind.

In Chapter 4, we saw that the president's access to the media is at least a potential advantage in influencing public opinion. However, the president has to compete with other media priorities while attempting to lead the public. The television networks created distractions during President Clinton's 1997 State of the Union message when they delivered the news of the verdict in the civil suit against O. J. Simpson *during his speech*, and the front page of the *Washington Post* the next day led with the story on Simpson, not the story on the president.

Press focus on the president has disadvantages as well. It inevitably leaves the impression that the president *is* the federal government and is crucial to our prosperity and happiness. This naturally encourages the public to focus its expectations on the White House. Another problem arises from the national frame of reference provided by a truly mass media and the media's penchant for linking coverage of even small matters with responses from the president or presidential spokespersons.

Commentary following presidential speeches and press conferences may influence what viewers remember and may affect their opinions.[122] Although the impact of commentary on presidential addresses and press conferences is unclear, it is probably safe to argue that it is a constraint on the president's ability to lead public opinion. In the words of observers David L. Paletz and Robert M. Entman:

> Critical instant analysis undermines presidential authority by transforming him from presenter to protagonist. . . . Credible, familiar, apparently disinterested newsmen and—women—experts too . . . , comment on the self-interested performance of a politician. Usually the president's rhetoric is deflated, the mood he has striven to create dissipated.[123]

The increasing negativism of news coverage of presidents parallels the increasingly low opinions voters have of them. The media impugn the motives of presidents and presidential candidates and portray them as playing a "game" in which strategy and maneuvers, rather than the substance of public policy, are the crucial elements. This coverage fosters public cynicism and encourages citizens to view presidents and other political leaders in negative terms.[124] If politics is a game played by deceptive politicians, it is less attractive for a person to be influenced by the president's arguments.

The framing of issues in terms of strategy and wheeling and dealing may also undermine efforts to change the status quo by highlighting the risk of deferring to people who engage in such maneuvering. In general, the media's focus on political conflict and strategy elevates the prominence of political wheeling and dealing in individuals' evaluations of policy proposals.[125]

Limits on Media Effects

While reviewing evidence of the impact of the media on public opinion concerning the president, it is important to keep in mind the significant limitations on this influence. Characteristics of readers and viewers—including short attention spans, lack of reading ability, selective perception (especially for those who have well-developed political views), general lack of interest in politics, lack of attentiveness to the media when exposed to them, and forgetfulness—limit the impact of the media. Another limitation is the ability of people to reject or ignore evaluations (implicit or explicit) in stories, particularly evaluations that conflict with their own.[126] In addition, viewers have many options other than watching the news.

The nature of the news message also affects the impact of the media, and the factors constraining their influence are many: the great volume of information available in the news; the limited time available in which to absorb it (especially for television viewers); the superficial coverage of people, events, and policies; the presentation of the news on television and in most newspapers in disconnected snippets; and the lack of guidance through the complexities of politics. As a result, people often do not understand the news and actually learn little in the way of specifics from it. The lack of credibility of news sources among some readers and viewers further limits the impact of the media.[127]

Visuals may also distract from verbal messages. For example, Leslie Stahl of CBS News did a long report on Ronald Reagan during the 1984 presidential campaign in which she criticized him for deceiving the American people with public relations tactics. Instead of the complaints she expected from the White House, however, she received thanks. Reagan's press aides appreciated the pictures of the president campaigning and were not concerned with the journalist's scathing remarks.[128]

CONCLUSION

The mass media play a prominent role in the public presidency, providing the public with most of its information about the White House and mediating the president's communications with constituents. Presidents need the press in order to reach the public, and relations with the press are an important complement to the chief executive's efforts at leading public opinion. Through attempts to coordinate news, press conferences, and the provision of a wide range of services for the press, the White House tries to influence its portrayal in the news.

The president's press relations pose many obstacles to efforts to obtain and maintain public support. Although it is probably not true that press coverage of the White House is biased along partisan or ideological lines or toward or against a particular president, it frequently presents a distorted picture to the public and fails to impart an appropriate perspective from which to view and evaluate complex events. Moreover, presidents are continuously harassed by leaks to the press and are faced with superficial, oversimplified coverage that devotes little attention to substantive discussions of policies and often focuses on trivial matters. This type of reporting undoubtedly affects public perceptions of the president, usually in a negative way. It is no wonder that chief executives generally see the press as a hindrance to their efforts to develop appreciation for their performance and policies in the public.

It is clear that in relation to the press, presidents are facilitators rather than directors. They engage in a constant struggle with the press and cannot depend on it to stress what they feel is most important about their administration or provide favorable coverage in the stories it produces. Presidents vary in their success in using the media to promote their goals, but all are limited in doing so by the nature and independence of this "fourth branch of government."

Before ending this chapter, we feel it is important to put the subject in perspective. Americans benefit greatly from a free press, a fact that should not be forgotten as we examine the media's flaws. The same press that provides superficial coverage of the presidency also alerts people to abuses of authority and efforts to mislead public opinion. Furthermore, it is much less biased than the heavily partisan newspapers that were typical early in the nation's history. Clearly, the press is an essential pillar in the structure of a free society.

Moreover, perhaps the fundamental reason that press coverage is much less than its critics would like it to be is that it must appeal to the general public.

If the public, or a sizable segment thereof, demands more substance from the mass media, it undoubtedly will receive it. In short, although mass media coverage of the presidency is often poor, it could be much worse, and it is probably more or less what the public desires. Thus, the media reflect, as well as influence, American society.

Discussion Questions

1. It is common to criticize the media for providing the American people with superficial coverage of presidents and their policies. What should the balance be between "hard news" on public policy and human interest stories such as scandals and personal conflicts? Can the media educate a public that prefers superficial coverage?

2. How can we identify bias when we see it? Was the media biased in covering the various charges of misdeed levied against President Clinton or the opposition to the invasion of Iraq?

3. Journalists have become more active in interpreting stories for their viewers and readers rather than depending on those they interview to set the tone for their stories. Is the public better served by this approach to journalism?

Web Exercises

1. Read some White House press releases and the press secretary's briefing for reporters. Notice the give and take between the press secretary and the journalists. You can also subscribe and have the White House send you these releases and briefings every day. Go to http://www.whitehouse.gov/news/briefings/.

2. The Pew Center for the People and the Press regularly surveys people about which news events they follow most closely. Examine the list of stories since the mid-1980s. Which type of stories do people follow most closely? How much interest do people have in the typical issue with which the president deals? Go to http://people-press.org/reports/.

Selected Readings

Althaus, Scott L., and Young Mie Kim. "Priming Effects in Complex Information Environments: Reassessing the Impact of News Discourse on Presidential Approval." *Journal of Politics* 68 (November 2006): 960–976.

Baum, Mathew A. *Soft News: Public Opinion and American Foreign Policy in the New Media Age.* Princeton, NJ: Princeton University Press, 2003.

Cohen, Jeffrey E. *The Presidency in the Era of 24-Hour News.* Princeton, NJ: Princeton University Press, 2008.

Cohen, Jeffrey E. "Presidency and the Mass Media." In *The Oxford Handbook of the American Presidency,* edited by George C. Edwards III and William G. Howell. Oxford: Oxford University Press, 2009.

Edwards, George C., III, and B. Dan Wood. "Who Influences Whom? The

President, Congress, and the Media." *American Political Science Review* (June 1999): 327–344.

Groeling, Tim, and Samuel Kernell. "Is Network News Coverage of the President Biased?" *Journal of Politics* 60 (November 1998): 1063–1087.

Hallin, Daniel C. *The "Uncensored War": The Media and Vietnam.* New York: Oxford University Press, 1986.

Krosnick, Jon A., and Donald R. Kinder. "Altering the Foundations of Support for the President through Priming." *American Political Science Review* 84 (June 1990): 497–512.

Krosnick, Jon A., and Laura A. Brannon. "The Impact of the Gulf War on the Ingredients of Presidential Evaluations: Multidimensional Effects of Political

Involvement." *American Political Science Review* 87 (December 1993): 963–975.

Kull, Steven, Clay Ramsay, and Evan Lewis. "Misperceptions, the Media, and the Iraq War." *Political Science Quarterly* 118 (Winter 2003–2004): 569–598.

Kumar, Martha Joynt. *Managing the President's Message: The White House Communications Operation.* Baltimore, MD: Johns Hopkins University Press, 2007.

Kurtz, Howard. *Spin Cycle.* New York: Free Press, 1998.

Prior, Markus. "News vs. Entertainment: How Increasing Media Choice Widens Gaps in Political Knowledge and Turnout." *American Journal of Political Science* 49 (July 2005): 577–592.

Notes

1. Quoted in Bob Woodward, *The Agenda: Inside the Clinton White House* (New York: Simon and Schuster, 1994), p. 313.

2. Martha Joynt Kumar, "The White House Beat at the Century Mark," *Press/Politics* 2 (Summer 1997): 10–30.

3. Doris A. Graber, *Mass Media and American Politics,* 7th ed. (Washington, DC: CQ Press, 2006), pp. 271–275; Elmer E. Cornwell, Jr., "Presidential News: The Expanding Public Image," *Journalism Quarterly* 36 (Summer 1959): 275–283; Alan P. Balutis, "The Presidency and the Press: The Expanding Presidential Image," *Presidential Studies Quarterly* 7 (Fall 1977): 244–251; *Media Monitor,* July/August 1994, pp. 1–2; *Media Monitor,* September/October 1994, pp. 1–2; *Media Monitor,* May/June 1995, pp. 1–2.

4. Richard Harris, "The Presidency and the Press," *New Yorker,* October 1, 1973, p. 122; Dom Bonafede, "Powell and the Press: A New Mood in the White House," *National Journal,* June 25, 1977, p. 981.

5. Quoted in Harris, "The Presidency and the Press," p. 122; and Peter Forbath and Carey Winfrey, *The Adversaries: The President and the Press* (Cleveland: Regal Books, 1974), p. 5.

6. Quoted in Joseph P. Berry, Jr., *John F. Kennedy and the Media: The First Television*

President (Lanham, MD: Rowman and Littlefield, 1987), p. 66.

7. See Jann S. Wenner and William Greider, "President Clinton," *Rolling Stone,* December 9, 1993, p. 81.

8. A key source on these activities is Martha Joynt Kumar, *Managing the President's Message: The White House Communications Operation* (Baltimore, MD: Johns Hopkins University Press, 2007).

9. Marlin Fitzwater, *Call the Briefing* (New York: Times Books, 1995), p. 4.

10. Jonathan Alter, *The Promise: President Obama, Year One* (New York: Simon and Schuster, 2010), p. 213; Amy Chozick, "Obama Is an Avid Reader, and Critic, of the News," *New York Times,* August 7, 2012.

11. There is some question as to whether the summary was an accurate representation of the news. See Christopher F. Karpowitz, "What Can a President Learn from the News Media? The Instructive Case of Richard Nixon," *British Journal of Political Science* 39 (October 2009): 755–780.

12. Quoted in "Press Secretaries Explore White House News Strategies," *APIP Report* 1 (January 1991):2.

13. On the number and type of press conferences, see Kumar, *Managing the*

President's Message, chap. 7. Professor Kumar has updated this data.

14. Andrew W. Barrett and Jeffrey S. Peake, "When the President Comes to Town: Examining Local Newspaper Coverage of Domestic Presidential Travel," *American Politics Research* 35 (January 2007): 3–31; Jeffrey S. Peake and Matthew Eshbaugh-Soha, "The Presidency and Local Media: Local Newspaper Coverage of President George W. Bush," *Presidential Studies Quarterly* 38 (December 2008): 609–630.

15. Kumar, *Managing the President's Message*, p. 42.

16. Auletta, "Non-Stop News," p. 41.

17. Doris A. Graber, *Mass Media and American Politics,* 6th ed. (Washington, DC: CQ Press, 2002), p. 291.

18. Michael Baruch Grossman and Martha Joynt Kumar, *Portraying the President: The White House and the News Media* (Baltimore, MD: Johns Hopkins University Press, 1981), pp. 59–60, 63–64, 280–281.

19. Mark J. Rozell, "Presidential Image-Makers on the Limits of Spin Control," *Presidential Studies Quarterly* 25 (Winter 1995): 77.

20. Interview by author with Peter Jennings, New York, October 18, 1987.

21. Ken Auletta, "Non-Stop News," *New Yorker,* January 25, 2010, p. 42.

22. Paul Brace and Barbara Hinckley, *Follow the Leader: Opinion Polls and the Modern Presidents* (New York: Basic Books, 1992), chap. 3.

23. Dom Bonafede, "The Washington Press: It Magnifies the President's Flaws and Blemishes," *National Journal*, May 1, 1982, pp. 267–271.

24. Graber, *Mass Media and American Politics*, 6th ed., p. 285.

25. Quoted in David L. Paletz and Robert M. Entman, *Media–Power–Politics* (New York: Free Press, 1981), pp. 55–56.

26. Brian Stelter, "Fox's Volley with Obama Intensifying," *New York Times*, October 12, 2009; Jim Rutenberg, "Behind the War between White House and Fox," *New York Times*, October 23, 2009.

27. Auletta, "Non-Stop News," p. 47.

28. Howard Kurtz, *Spin Cycle* (New York: Free Press, 1998), p. 134.

29. Alter, *The Promise*, pp. 154–156, 386.

30. William Safire, *Before the Fall: An Inside View of the Pre-Watergate White House* (New York: Doubleday, 1975), p. 373; Henry Kissinger, *Years of Upheaval* (Boston: Little, Brown, 1981), p. 116.

31. Lyndon Johnson quoted in George Christian, *The President Steps Down: A Personal Memoir of the Transfer of Power* (New York: Macmillan, 1970), p. 203.

32. Gerald S. Strober and Deborah H. Strober, *"Let Us Begin Anew"* (New York: HarperCollins, 1993), p. 156.

33. "The U.S. vs. William Colby," *Newsweek,* September 28, 1981, p. 30.

34. "The Tattletale White House," *Newsweek,* February 25, 1980, p. 21.

35. Robert T. Hartmann, *Palace Politics: An Inside Account of the Ford Years* (New York: McGraw-Hill, 1980), p. 38.

36. William J. Lanouette, "The Washington Press Corps: Is It All That Powerful?" *National Journal*, June 2, 1979, p. 898.

37. Kurtz, *Spin Cycle,* p. 92.

38. "Power Couple," *Newsweek*, October 31, 1994, p. 6.

39. James A. Baker III, *The Politics of Diplomacy* (New York: Putnam, 1995), p. 520; see also pp. 34, 154.

40. Dick Morris, *Behind the Oval Office* (New York: Random House, 1997), pp. 101–102.

41. Henry Kissinger, *Years of Renewal* (New York: Simon and Schuster, 1999), pp. 79, 83.

42. Lou Cannon, *President Reagan: The Role of a Lifetime* (New York: Simon and Schuster, 1991), p. 452.

43. Donald T. Regan, *For the Record: From Wall Street to Washington* (San Diego, CA: Harcourt Brace Jovanovich, 1988), p. xiv.

44. Morris, *Behind the Oval Office*, p. 122.

45. Woodrow Wilson quoted in William Small, *To Kill a Messenger: Television News and the Real World* (New York: Hastings, 1970), p. 221.

46. President Carter, quoted in Michael Baruch Grossman and Martha Joynt

Kumar, "Carter, Reagan, and the Media: Have the Rules Really Changed or the Poles of the Spectrum of Success?" Paper presented at the Annual Meeting of the American Political Science Association, New York, September 3–6, 1981, p. 8.

47. Chozick, "Obama Is an Avid Reader, and Critic, of the News"; Auletta, "Non-Stop News," p. 47.

48. The Project for Excellence in Journalism, *The First 100 Days: How Bush versus Clinton Fared in the Press* (2001). http://www.journalism.org/publ_ research/100days1.html. See also Jeffrey E. Cohen, *The Presidency in the Era of 24-Hour News* (Princeton, NJ: Princeton University Press, 2008), chap. 4.

49. Thomas E. Patterson, *Doing Well and Doing Good* (Cambridge, MA: Shorenstein Center, 2000), pp. 2–5.

50. Sam Donaldson, quoted in "Washington Press Corps," *Newsweek*, May 25, 1981, p. 90.

51. Ari Fleischer, *Take Heat* (New York: William Morrow, 2005), pp. 43, 76, 86, 276; Scott McClellan, *What Happened: Inside the Bush White House and Washington's Culture of Deception* (New York: Public Affairs, 2008), pp. 124, 125, 158.

52. Elisabeth Bumiller, "The White House without a Filter," *New York Times*, June 4, 2006.

53. John G. Geer, "The News Media and the Rise of Negativity in Presidential Campaigns," *PS: Political Science & Politics* 45 (July 2012): 422–427.

54. Howard Kurtz, "Journalists, Left Out of the Debate: Few Americans Seem to Hear Health Care Facts," *Washington Post*, August 24, 2009.

55. See "1998 Year in Review," *Media Monitor* 13 (January/February 1999).

56. Project for Excellence in Journalism, "How the Press Covered Health Care Reform," June 21, 2010; Kathleen Hall Jamieson and Joseph N. Capella, "The Role of the Press in the Health Care Reform Debate of 1993–1994," in Doris Graber, Denis McQuail, and Pippa Norris, eds., *The Politics of News: The News of Politics* (Washington, DC: CQ Press, 1998), pp. 118–119; Lawrence R. Jacobs and

Robert Y. Shapiro, *Politicians Don't Pander* (Chicago: University of Chicago Press, 2000), chaps. 5–6.

57. Quoted in Grossman and Kumar, *Portraying the President*, p. 43.

58. Sam Donaldson, *Hold On, Mr. President* (New York: Random House, 1987), pp. 196–197.

59. Ibid., p. 26.

60. Quoted in Auletta, "Non-Stop News," p. 42.

61. Dan Rather, quoted in Hoyt Purvis, ed., *The Presidency and the Press* (Austin, TX: Lyndon B. Johnson School of Public Affairs, 1976), p. 56.

62. See David D'Allessio and Mike Allen, "Media Bias in Presidential Elections: A Meta-Analysis," *Journal of Communication* 50 (2000): 133–156; Maria Elizabeth Grabe and Erik Page Bucy, *Image Bite Politics: News and the Visual Framing of Elections* (New York: Oxford University Press, 2009); and Edwards, *The Public Presidency*, p. 156, and sources cited therein.

63. Larry Speakes, quoted in Eleanor Randolph, "Speakes Aims Final Salvos at White House Practices," *Washington Post*, January 31, 1987, p. A3.

64. Lanny J. Davis, *Truth to Tell* (New York: Free Press, 1999), p. 252.

65. McClellan, *What Happened*, pp. 156–158.

66. John P. Robinson, "The Press as King-Maker: What Surveys from Last Five Campaigns Show," *Journalism Quarterly* 51 (Winter 1974): 587–594, 606.

67. Kathleen Hall Jamieson and Joseph N. Cappella, *Echo Chamber: Rush Limbaugh and the Conservative Media Establishment* (Oxford: Oxford University Press, 2008).

68. Brent Cunningham, "Re-thinking Objectivity," *Columbia Journalism Review* 4 (July–August 2003).

69. W. Lance Bennett, Regina G. Lawrence, and Steven Livingston, *When the Press Fails* (Chicago, IL: University of Chicago Press, 2007), chaps. 1–2. See also Daniel C. Hallin, *The "Uncensored War": The Media and Vietnam* (New York: Oxford University Press, 1986); Jonathan Mermin, *Debating War and Peace: Media Coverage*

of U.S. Intervention in the Post-Vietnam Era (Princeton, NJ: Princeton University Press, 1999); John Zaller and Dennis Chiu, "Government's Little Helper: U.S. Press Coverage of Foreign Policy Crises, 1945–1991," *Political Communication* 13, no. 4 (1996): 385–405.

70. See Mark J. Rozell, *The Press and the Ford Presidency* (Ann Arbor: University of Michigan Press, 1992).

71. Thomas E. Patterson, *Out of Order* (New York: Knopf, 1993), chap. 3; Matthew Robert Kerbel, *Edited for Television* (Boulder, CO: Westview, 1994), pp. 60–64, 88; S. Robert Lichter and Richard E. Noyes, *Good Intentions Make Bad News*, 2nd ed. (Lanham, MD: Rowman and Littlefield, 1996), chaps. 6–7.

72. Patterson, *Out of Order*, pp. 16–21, 113–115; Kerbel, *Edited for Television*, pp. 111–112; Kevin G. Barnhurst and Catherine A. Steele, "Image-Bite News: The Visual Coverage of Elections on U.S. Television, 1968–1992," *Press/Politics* 2, no. 1 (1997): 40–58; Lichter and Noyes, *Good Intentions Make Bad News*, pp. 116–126; Richard Nadeau, Richard G. Niemi, David P. Fah, and Timothy Amato, "Elite Economic Forecasts, Economic News, Mass Economic Judgments, and Presidential Approval," *Journal of Politics* 61 (February 1999): 109–135; "Campaign 2000 Final: How TV News Covered the General Election Campaign," *Media Monitor* 14 (November/December 2000).

73. Patterson, *Doing Well and Doing Good*, pp. 10, 12; Patterson, *Out of Order,* pp. 3–27; "Clinton's the One," *Media Monitor* 6 (November 1992): 3–5; Lichter and Noyes, *Good Intentions Make Bad News*, chaps. 6–7, esp. pp. 288–299; and "Campaign 2000 Final: How TV News Covered the General Election Campaign," *Media Monitor* 14 (November/December 2000). See also Stuart N. Soroka, "The Gatekeeping Function: Distributions of Information in Media and the Real World," *Journal of Politics* 74 (April 2012): 514–528.

74. Tim Groeling and Matthew A. Baum, "Crossing the Water's Edge: Elite Rhetoric, Media Coverage, and the Rally-Round-the-Flag Phenomenon," *Journal of Politics* 70 (October 2008): 1074.

75. *Media Monitor*, May/June 1995, pp. 2–5; Thomas E. Patterson, "Legitimate Beef: The Presidency and a Carnivorous Press," *Media Studies Journal* 8 (Spring 1994): 21–26. However, compare Andras Szanto, "In Our Opinion . . . : Editorial Page Views of Clinton's First Year," *Media Studies Journal* 8 (Spring 1994): 97–105; Lichter and Noyes, *Good Intentions Make Bad News*, p. 214.

76. Stephen J. Farnsworth and S. Robert Lichter, *The Mediated Presidency: Television News and Presidential Governance* (Lanham, MD: Rowman and Littlefield, 2006), pp. 40–45, chap. 4; Stephen J. Farnsworth and S. Robert Lichter, *The Nightly News Nightmare: Television's Coverage of U.S. Presidential Elections, 1988–2004*, 2nd ed. (Lanham, MD: Rowman and Littlefield, 2007), chap. 4. See also Cohen, *The Presidency in the Era of 24-Hour News*, chaps. 5–6.

77. Stephen J. Farnsworth and S. Robert Lichter, "The Return of the Honeymoon: Television News Coverage of New Presidents, 1981–2009," *Presidential Studies Quarterly* 41 (September 2011): 590–603.

78. Pew Research Center's Project for Excellence in Journalism, "How the Press Covered Health Care Reform," June 21, 2010; Pew Research Center's Project for Excellence in Journalism, "Stimulus News Seen as More Negative than Positive," February 11, 2009.

79. Pew Research Center's Project for Excellence in Journalism, *Winning the Media Campaign 2012*, November 2, 2012.

80. Jimmy Carter, *Keeping Faith: Memoirs of a President* (New York: Bantam, 1982), pp. 179–180.

81. "The Invisible Man: TV News Coverage of President Bill Clinton, 1993–1995," *Media Monitor* 12 (May/June 1995); Patterson, "Legitimate Beef"; "Sex, Lies, and TV News," *Media Monitor* 12 (September/October 1998); "TV News Coverage of the 1998 Midterm Elections," *Media Monitor* 12 (November/December 1998). However, compare Andras Szanto, "In Our Opinion . . . : Editorial Page Views of Clinton's First Year," *Media Studies Journal* 8 (Spring 1994): 97–105; Lichter and Noyes, *Good Intentions Make Bad News*, p. 214. See also Tim Groeling and Samuel Kernell, "Is Network News Coverage of

the President Biased?" *Journal of Politics* 60 (November 1998): 1063–1087.

82. See Edward Jay Epstein, *News from Nowhere: Television and the News* (New York: Vintage, 1973), pp. 215–220; Herbert J. Gans, *Deciding What's News* (New York: Vintage, 1979), pp. 68–69, 187; Stephen Hess, *The Washington Reporters* (Washington, DC: Brookings Institution, 1981), p. 88; Patterson, *Out of Order*, chap. 2; and Kerbel, *Edited for Television*, p. 116.

83. Quoted in Dana Milbank, "Rove's Reading: Not So Liberal as Leery," *Washington Post*, April 20, 2005, p. A4.

84. Grossman and Kumar, *Portraying the President*, pp. 255–259, 270–271, 274–279; Grossman and Kumar, "Carter, Reagan, and the Media," p. 13; Hess, *The Washington Reporters*, p. 98.

85. Bill D. Moyers, "The Press and Government: Who's Telling the Truth?" in Warren K. Agee, ed., *Mass Media in a Free Society* (Lawrence: University Press of Kansas, 1969), p. 19.

86. For an overview, see Cliff Zukin, "Mass Communication and Public Opinion," in Dan D. Nimmo and Keith R. Sanders, eds., *Handbook of Political Communication* (Beverly Hills, CA: Sage, 1981), pp. 359–390. See also Diana C. Mutz and Joe Soss, "Reading Public Opinion: The Influence of News Coverage on Perceptions of Public Sentiment," *Public Opinion Quarterly* 61 (Fall 1997): 431–451. However, compare Russell J. Dalton, Paul A. Beck, and Robert Huckfeldt, "Partisan Cues and the Media: Information Flows in the 1992 Presidential Election," *American Political Science Review* 92 (March 1980): 111–126; and Paul M. Kellstedt, *The Mass Media and the Dynamics of American Racial Attitudes* (Cambridge, UK: Cambridge University Press, 2003).

87. Graber, *Mass Media and American Politics*, 7th ed., p. 189.

88. Benjamin I. Page and Robert Y. Shapiro, *The Rational Public* (Chicago: University of Chicago Press, 1992), pp. 12–13.

89. Shanto Iyengar, Mark D. Peters, and Donald R. Kinder, "Experimental Demonstrations of the 'Not-So-Minimal'

Consequences of Television News Programs," *American Political Science Review* 76 (December 1982): 848–858; James P. Winter and Chaim H. Eyal, "Agenda-Setting for the Civil Rights Issue," *Public Opinion Quarterly* 45 (Fall 1981): 376–383; Michael Bruce MacKuen and Steven Lane Coombs, *More Than News* (Beverly Hills, CA: Sage 1981), chaps. 3–4; Fay Lomax Cook, Tom R. Tyler, and Edward G. Goetz, "Media and Agenda-Setting: Effects on the Public, Interest Group Leaders, Policy Makers, and Policy," *Public Opinion Quarterly* 47 (Spring 1983): 16–35; David L. Portess and Maxwell McCombs, eds., *Agenda Setting: Readings on Media, Public Opinion, and Policymaking* (Hillsdale, NY: Lawrence Erlbaum Associates, 1991); Doris A. Graber, "Agenda-Setting: Are There Women's Perspectives?" in Laurily Epstein, ed., *Women and the News* (New York: Hastings House, 1978), pp. 15–37; James W. Dearing and Everett M. Rogers, *Agenda Setting* (Thousand Oaks, CA: Sage, 1996); William Gonzenbach, *The Media, the President, and Public Opinion: A Longitudinal Analysis of the Drug Issue, 1984–1991* (Mahwah, NJ: Lawrence Erlbaum Associates, 1996); Maxwell McCombs and George Estrada, "The News Media and the Pictures in Our Heads," in Shanto Iyengar and Richard Reeves, eds., *Do the Media Govern? Politicians, Voters, and Reporters in America* (Thousand Oaks, CA: Sage, 1997); Maxwell McCombs and Donald Shaw, "The Evolution of Agenda Setting Research: Twenty-five Years in the Marketplace of Ideas," *Journal of Communication* 43, no. 2 (1993): 58–67; Stuart N. Soroka, "Media, Public Opinion, and Foreign Policy," *Press/Politics* 8 (Winter 2003): 27–48; Jeffrey S. Peake, "Presidential Agenda Setting in Foreign Policy," *Political Research Quarterly* 54 (March 2001): 69–86.

90. Graber, *Mass Media and American Politics*, 7th ed., p. 194.

91. Shanto Iyengar, *Is Anyone Responsible?* (Chicago: University of Chicago Press, 1991), p. 2. See also Scott L. Althaus and Young Mie Kim, "Priming Effects in Complex Information Environments: Reassessing the Impact of News Discourse on Presidential Approval," *Journal of*

Politics 68 (November 2006): 960–976; Iyengar, Peters, and Kinder, "Experimental Demonstrations of the 'Not-So-Minimal' Consequences of Television News Programs"; Larry M. Bartels, "Messages Received: The Political Impact of Media Exposure," *American Political Science Review* 87 (June 1993): 267–285; and Dhavan V. Shah, Mark D. Watts, David Domke, David P. Fan, and Michael Fibison, "News Coverage, Economic Cues, and the Public's Presidential Preferences, 1984–1996," *Journal of Politics* 61 (November 1999): 914–943. But see Neil Malhorta and Jon A. Krosnick, "Retrospective and Prospective Performance Assessments during the 2004 Election Campaign: Tests of Mediation and News Media Priming," *Political Behavior* 29 (June 2007): 249–278. There is also evidence that presidential approval is influenced by elite opinion, as brought to the public's attention in the mass media. See Richard A. Brody, *Assessing the President* (Stanford, CA: Stanford University Press, 1991).

92. Jon A. Krosnick and Donald R. Kinder, "Altering the Foundations of Support for the President through Priming," *American Political Science Review* 84 (June 1990): 497–512; Iyengar, *Is Anyone Responsible?* chap. 8.

93. Jon A. Krosnick and Laura A. Brannon, "The Impact of the Gulf War on the Ingredients of Presidential Evaluations: Multidimensional Effects of Political Involvement," *American Political Science Review* 87 (December 1993): 963–975. See also Shanto Iyengar and Adam Simon, "News Coverage of the Gulf Crisis and Public Opinion," in W. Lance Bennett and David L. Paletz, eds., *Taken by Storm* (Chicago: University of Chicago Press, 1994).

94. George C. Edwards III, Andrew Barrett, and Reed Welch, "Explaining Presidential Approval: The Significance of Issue Salience," *American Journal of Political Science* 39 (February 1995): 108–134.

95. Shanto Iyengar and Donald R. Kinder, *News That Matters* (Chicago: University of Chicago Press, 1987).

96. Iyengar, Peters, and Kinder, "Experimental Demonstrations of the 'Not-So-Minimal' Consequences of Television News Programs." See also Larry M. Bartels,

"Messages Received: The Political Impact of Media Exposure," *American Political Science Review* 87 (June 1993): 267–285.

97. Frederick T. Steeper, "Public Response to Gerald Ford's Statements on Eastern Europe in the Second Debate," in George F. Bishop, Robert G. Meadow, and Marilyn Jackson-Beeck, eds., *The Presidential Debates: Media, Electoral, and Public Perspectives* (New York: Praeger, 1978), pp. 81–101.

98. Michael J. Robinson, "News Media Myths and Realities," in Kay Lehman Schlozman, ed., *Elections in America* (Boston: Allen and Unwin, 1987), p. 149.

99. Thomas E. Patterson, *The Mass Media Election: How Americans Choose Their President* (New York: Praeger, 1980), pp. 84–86, 98–100, 105, chap. 2; Doris A. Graber, "Personal Qualities in Presidential Images: The Contribution of the Press," *Midwest Journal of Political Science* 16 (February 1972): 295; Graber, *Mass Media and American Politics*, pp. 240–243; Barry C. Burden and Anthony Mughan, "The International Economy and Presidential Approval," *Public Opinion Quarterly* 67 (Winter 2003): 555–578.

100. Gerald R. Ford, *A Time to Heal: The Autobiography of Gerald R. Ford* (New York: Harper and Row, 1979), p. 289; see also pp. 343–344.

101. Katherine Graham, *Personal History* (New York: Vintage, 1998).

102. See, for example, *Media Monitor,* June/July 1998.

103. Adam J. Berinsky and Donald R. Kinder, "Making Sense of Issues through Media Frames: Understanding the Kosovo Crisis," *Journal of Politics* 68 (August 2006): 640–656.

104. Pew Research Center's Project for Excellence in Journalism, "How the Press Covered Health Care Reform," June 21, 2010. See also Jacobs and Shapiro, *Politicians Don't Pander,* pp. 176–182, 214–215; Jamieson and Cappella, "The Role of the Press in the Health Care Reform Debate of 1993–1994" on Bill Clinton's health care proposal in 1993–1994.

105. Jacobs and Shapiro, *Politicians Don't Pander,* pp. 232–255.

106. Joseph M. Capella and Kathleen Hall Jamieson, *Spiral of Cynicism: The Press and the Public Good* (New York: Oxford University Press, 1997). Apparently, people, especially those with higher levels of political engagement, are drawn to stories on the horse race and strategy. See Shanto Iyengar, Helmut Norpoth, and Kyu S. Hahn, "Consumer Demand for Election News: The Horserace Sells," *Journal of Politics* 66 (February 2004): 157–175.

107. See James H. Kuklinski, Paul J. Quirk, Jennifer Jerit, David Schwieder, and Robert F. Rich, "Misinformation and the Currency of Democratic Citizenship," *Journal of Politics* 62 (August 2000): 790–816.

108. Jennifer Jerit, "Understanding the Knowledge Gap: The Role of Experts and Journalists," *Journal of Politics* 71 (April 2009): 442–456; Jason Barabas and Jennifer Jerit, "Estimating the Causal Effects of Media Coverage on Policy-Specific Knowledge," *American Journal of Political Science* 53 (January 2009): 73–89.

109. David C. Barker, *Rushed to Judgment: Talk Radio, Persuasion, and American Political Behavior* (New York: Columbia University Press, 2002). But see Diana Owen, "Talk Radio and Evaluations of President Clinton," *Political Communication* 14, no. 3 (1997): 333–353.

110. Pew Research Center for the People & the Press poll, August 14–17, 2009. See also NBC News poll, August 15–17, 2009.

111. Steven Kull, Clay Ramsay, and Evan Lewis, "Misperceptions, the Media, and the Iraq War," *Political Science Quarterly* 118 (Winter 2003–2004): 569–598.

112. Steve Rendell and Tara Broughel, "Amplifying Officials, Squelching Dissent," *Extra!* (May/June 2003), Fairness and Accuracy in Reporting, http://www.fair.org /extra/0305/warstudy.html.

113. Mathew A. Baum, Soft News Goes to War: Public Opinion and American Foreign Policy in the New Media Age (Princeton, NJ: Princeton University Press, 2003).

114. George C. Edwards III and B. Dan Wood, "Who Influences Whom? The President, Congress, and the Media," *American Political Science Review* (June 1999): 327–344. See also B. Dan Wood and Jeffrey S. Peake, "The Dynamics of Foreign Policy Agenda Setting," *American Political Science Review* 92 (March 1998): 173–184; Matthew Eshbaugh-Soha and Jeffrey S. Peake, "Presidents and the Economic Agenda," *Political Research Quarterly* 58 (March 2005): 127–138.

115. Jacobs and Shapiro, *Politicians Don't Pander,* chaps. 5–6; Edwards and Wood, "Who Influences Whom?"

116. Baker, *Politics of Diplomacy,* p. 103. See also Eytan Gilboa, "Television News and U.S. Foreign Policy," *Press/Politics* 8 (Fall 2003): 97–113.

117. Quoted in Morris, *Behind the Oval Office,* pp. 197, 245.

118. Carl M. Cannon, "From Bosnia to Kosovo," *National Journal,* April 3, 1999, p. 881.

119. Colin Powell, *My American Journey* (New York: Ballantine, 1995), pp. 550, 573.

120. Quoted in Powell, *My American Journey,* p. 507. See also Richard N. Haass, *War of Necessity, War of Choice: A Memoir of Two Iraq Wars* (New York: Simon and Schuster, 2009), pp. 129, 143.

121. Ibid., p. 418.

122. Kim L. Fridkin, Patrick J. Kenney, and Sarah Allen Gershon, "Spinning Debates: The Impact of the News Media's Coverage of the Final 2004 Presidential Debate," *Press/Politics* 13, no. 1 (2008): 29–51; Dwight F. Davis, Lynda Lee Kaid, and Donald L. Singleton, "Information Effects of Political Commentary," *Experimental Study of Politics* 6 (June 1977): 45–68; Lynda Lee Kaid, Donald L. Singleton, and Dwight F. Davis, "Instant Analysis of Televised Political Addresses: The Speaker versus the Commentator," in Brent D. Ruben, ed., *Communication Yearbook I* (New Brunswick, NJ: Transaction Books, 1977), pp. 453–464.

123. Paletz and Entman, *Media–Power–Politics,* p. 70.

124. Patterson, *Out of Order,* p. 22, chap. 2.

125. Cappella and Jamieson, *Spiral of Cynicism*.

126. Doris A. Graber, *Processing the News*, 2nd ed. (New York: Longman), pp. 90–93.

127. See, for example, Pew Research Center for the People & the Press poll, September 6–9, 2012.

128. Interview by author with Leslie Stahl, West Point, NY, 1986. See also James N. Druckman, "The Power of Televised Images: The First Kennedy-Nixon Debate Revisited," *Journal of Politics* 65 (May 2003): 559–571.

6

PRESIDENTS
AND THEIR
ADVISERS

I t matters who is president. It also matters whom presidents choose as their principal advisers, how they organize those advisers, and the ways they interact with them. Professional and personal relationships with other elected and appointed officials and family and friends are also important and potentially affect what presidents say and do.

This chapter discusses presidents as individuals and those who interact with them, primarily their cabinet heads and senior officials in their Executive Office. Part I focuses on the components of personal leadership. It examines formal and informal qualifications for office as well as personality and how it shapes a president's thought process, decision making, and public and private communications. The emphasis here is on character and operating style. Part II turns to the president's advisory system: the evolution of the cabinet, the creation of an Executive Office, and within that office, the institutionalization of the White House staff. The final section of the chapter deals with the vice presidency and the president's spouse and how their roles and responsibilities have evolved over the years.

COMPONENTS OF PERSONAL LEADERSHIP

The framers of the Constitution were naturally aware that personal factors could and would affect presidential performance. Although they hoped that presidents would have altruistic motives and set laudatory examples in their public and private behavior, they could not predicate the powers and responsibilities of the office on that assumption. Rather, they had to take precautions

The third component, *worldview*, is the politically relevant beliefs that condition perceptions, thinking, and judgment, beliefs about the world, explanations about its history, and convictions about how individuals and groups can affect the environment in which they live and work.[7] Personal experience frames the mindset in which information is digested and understood. It contributes to the belief systems (ideology) that people adopt. These systems provide cognitive guides for decision making and for actions that follow from those decisions. (We discuss these beliefs and the ways in which they affect decision making in the next chapter.) The interesting aspect of worldview is that Barber believed it to be psychologically based, that there is a link between thoughts and personality.

These three psychological dimensions contribute to a person's beliefs and behavior. Once developed, character, style, and worldview tend to produce patterns of beliefs and behavior that persist over time. As a result, Barber argues that they are better predictor of how candidates will perform in office than what candidates says during the electoral campaign.[8]

In evaluating character, Barber designed a typology based on two observable behavioral dimensions: activity and affect. *Activity* is the level of energy that is devoted to the job, and *affect* is the satisfaction that is obtained from it.[9] Thus, there are four possible combinations of character-oriented tendencies, which are summarized in Box 6.1.

Box 6.1 Presidential Character Types

Active–Positive

This type is characteristic of an energetic person who enjoys work, is productive, and adjusts well to new situations. Such a person generally feels confident and makes rational decisions based on the information available but may also be highly competitive and not sufficiently attuned to the irrational responses of others.

Passive–Positive

This type describes a relatively receptive, laid-back individual who wants to gain agreement and mute dissent at all costs. Such a person is apt to feel pessimistic and unloved and compensates for these feelings by being overly optimistic and by continually trying to elicit agreement and support from others.

Active–Negative

Active–negative types work hard but do not gain much pleasure from their work. In fact, they tend to be intense, compulsive, and aggressive. They often feel insecure and crave power to overcome feelings of inadequacy, even impotency.

Passive–Negative

Inactivity and withdrawal characterize passive–negative types. They often suffer from low self-esteem and a sense of uselessness, take refuge in generalized principles and standard procedures, and abhor politics. Fortunately, people with negative character dimensions do not usually become president.

SOURCE: Adapted from James David Barber, *The Presidential Character*, 4th ed. (Englewood Cliffs, NJ: Prentice-Hall, 1992), pp. 8–11.

Of these types, the active–positive is clearly the one Barber believed to be best suited for the presidency. Being active contributes to the energy needed to do the job; being positive eases the inevitable interpersonal conflicts that result from competing perspectives, interests, policy goals, and ambitions. It increases tolerance. However, each of the character types, including the active–positive, has built-in weaknesses that could impede presidential performance—thereby adversely affecting vision, judgment, or actions.

Political scientists have pointed out several methodological problems with Barber's analysis. One relates to his typology, its simplicity, ambiguity, and even its relevancy for evaluating performance in office. Another problem relates to the absence of specific criteria for placing a president in a particular box. Was Eisenhower a passive–negative type, as Barber claims, or active–positive, as scholar Fred Greenstein concludes?[10] A third difficulty relates to the circularity of Barber's argument. He categorizes behavior on the basis of personality traits and then explains actions and inactions on the basis of those same traits. And finally, even if there were agreement on the character categorization, it has not always followed that one type, active–positive presidents, have turned out to be better and other types to be less effective and more dangerous.[11] Compare Presidents Gerald Ford and Jimmy Carter, both of whom are categorized by Barber as active–positive, with Woodrow Wilson and Abraham Lincoln, both of whom had active–negative tendencies.

In an attempt to overcome the shortcomings of Barber's model, Stanley Renshon, a political scientist and psychoanalyst, provides a more detailed theoretical framework for understanding political behavior from a psychological perspective in his book, *The Psychological Assessment of Presidential Candidates.*[12] Renshon focuses on three character dimensions: ambition, integrity, and relatedness.

Ambition encourages goal achievement. It is a drive to pursue and accomplish one's objectives and values. That drive consists of a set of skills that can be used to initiate, act, and achieve. Without ambition, the motive for being involved in the political world would be lacking. Too much of it, however, can be dysfunctional because it warps perceptions, obscures reality, interferes with judgment, and tends toward rationalizing decisions rather than reaching them rationally. Overly ambitious people are said to stop at nothing to succeed.[13] The absence of constraints makes them dangerous in powerful positions. Nixon and Clinton are two of the contemporary presidents who are often cited as examples of uncontrolled ambition that marred their professional judgments and allowed their private needs to intrude adversely on their public performance.

A second component is *integrity*. It is the capacity to remain true to one's ideals and beliefs. Integrity provides an ethical framework that makes it possible for people to see and understand themselves within greater society. The absence of integrity removes a critical barrier that controls thinking and acting in a blatantly self-interested manner. Integrity extends peoples' focus from themselves to those around them.

For politicians, Renshon states that ambition in the pursuit of ideals contributes to a strong sense of self, but ambition in the pursuit of self-interest does not; rather, it compensates for self-perceived inadequacies and needs.[14]

Relatedness—how a person interacts with others—is a third aspect of character. Interpersonal relations can be friendly or hostile, intimate or distant, spontaneous or contrived. Obviously, elective politicians need to interact with the public. Some do so more easily and effectively than others. Bill Clinton was particularly skilled at public relations. He mastered the art of identifying and empathizing with his audience. George W. Bush also did well in small public settings when he interacted with people of similar interests and views; in larger settings he was less sure of himself. In contrast, Obama, though an effective campaigner, is perceived by much of the general public as more distant and less emotive than Clinton and Bush. (See Box 6.2.)

Box 6.2 Presidential Character Profiles: Bill Clinton, George W. Bush, and Barack Obama

Bill Clinton

Bill Clinton's persona dominated his presidency. He was constantly front and center, constantly in the media spotlight. He needed to be noticed. He craved public attention, attribution, and adulation. What distinguished Clinton from many of those who preceded him in office were his personal excesses, emotional immaturity, imposing manner, political resiliency, inordinate drive, and desire to make his presence felt.

Ambition
Bill Clinton has always been goal oriented; he has tried to achieve his goals through political activity. Clinton has had a nonstop political career: band major in high school, president of his freshmen and sophomore classes in college, Rhodes Scholar, Yale law school graduate, Arkansas attorney general at age thirty-two, six terms as state governor, and two as president of the United States. He explained his frantic activity and drive to achieve as a reaction to the death of his biological father before he was born and the precariousness of life as he saw it:

> For a long time I thought I would have to live for both of us in some ways . . . I think that's one reason

I was in such a hurry when I was younger. I used to be criticized by people who said, "Well, he's too ambitious," but to me, because I grew up sort of subconsciously on his timetable, I never knew how much time I would have . . . It gave me an urgent sense to do everything I could in life as quickly as I could.[15]

Clinton's political career was not without its setbacks. But he managed to survive all of them and rebound, much like Richard Nixon did, until he was forced from office. Clinton's ability to persevere despite adversity has distinguished his political life.

Integrity
Political and personal needs have masked and undercut Clinton's integrity. A student leader, Vietnam War protestor, and liberal to moderate Democrat, Clinton regularly compromised beliefs. During his presidency, the public came to question Clinton's integrity, honesty, and moral character while approving of his job performance and acknowledging his considerable political skills.

Relatedness
Interpersonal skills, the ability to empathize and relate to others, have been key to Clinton's political success.

(continued)

(continued)

Throughout his life, getting along for Bill Clinton has meant trying to please as many people as possible. Clinton's backers saw his people-oriented manner as natural and desirable. His critics saw it as manipulative, hence the appellation "Slick Willie."[16]

George W. Bush

In many respects, George W. Bush's early life was a mirror image of Clinton's. Easygoing, almost rebellious in his youth, Bush was gregarious and popular in school but not an outstanding student, not particularly ambitious, and not initially oriented toward a career in politics. He remembered little of the Vietnam War protests that were occurring during his college years, but he did follow his father's political career closely. George H. W. Bush was a man whom the younger Bush admired greatly but felt he could not possibly emulate.[17] His father had excelled in school, distinguished himself as a young naval aviator during World War II, made a fortune in the Texas oil industry in the 1950s, and then pursued a successful career in politics. The younger Bush was a mediocre student, avoided the war in Vietnam by serving in the Texas Air National Guard, did not do well in the oil business in Texas, ran for Congress and lost, and by his own admission, drank and caroused too much. His first business success occurred while his father was vice president. The younger Bush put together a group of wealthy friends to buy the Texas Rangers baseball team for $34 million and then sold it for $250 million a few years later.

Ambition

As a young man, George W. Bush did not achieve much personal success or notoriety. It was almost as if his father's business and political career extenuated his own failures. It was not until the age of forty that he was able to turn his life around.

He stopped drinking and smoking, had his first business success with the Rangers, and participated in his father's victorious campaigns. He became more content and self-confident, feelings that he attributed to his newly found inner strength, a consequence of a deepening faith in God and in himself. That faith provided him with direction, conviction, and a sense of purpose.

His father's electoral defeat in 1992 provided the younger Bush with the motive and opportunity to get involved in politics. Furious at Texas Governor Ann Richards's mocking his dad at the Democratic National Convention (she said that he was "born with a silver foot in his mouth"), the younger Bush was determined to run against her for office, which he did and won. After four years of general prosperity in Texas, he was overwhelmingly reelected, and with the help of political strategist Karl Rove began his successful quest for the presidency.

Integrity

George W. Bush's political beliefs conform to classic conservative economic and national security views. Much more ideological in his thinking than his father, the younger Bush used his belief system as a shortcut for thinking and a guide for decision making and action. When the terrorist attacks of September 11, 2001, turned his focus from economic to national security affairs, Bush redefined the goal of his presidency as a war against terrorism and his principal job as protecting the nation's security. He used military force to pursue terrorists abroad and greatly expanded executive powers at home. He saw his cause as just—to rid the world of evildoers—and his actions as necessary to protect and promote "God-given" human rights and democratic values.

Bush maintained his resolve and his high moral ground throughout his presidency, despite growing criticism of his foreign and domestic policies and the assumptions on which they were based. The president's adamant stand in the face of growing opposition to the war in Iraq and his inability to reverse worsening economic conditions at home contributed to his unpopularity. In the end, Bush was forced to change course within the economic arena and support a massive government bailout of U.S. investment banks and a large insurance company and accept a timetable for the withdrawal of American forces from Iraq.

Relatedness
Bush was more people oriented than idea oriented. Leery of advisers who engaged in abstract thinking, added complexity to policy deliberations, and were not sufficiently attuned to his way of thinking, Bush surrounded himself with aides who believed in the same neoconservative ideology, echoed and articulated similar policy beliefs, and were personally and politically loyal to him. As president, Bush tended to make decisions quickly, almost instinctively, and did not agonize over them.

Not a great communicator, Bush tended to be most effective in small groups, particularly those outside of the public view, in which he did not have to worry about mispronounced words, inappropriate phrases, or repetition of his ideas. In the public arena, he stayed highly scripted while his handlers shielded him from political opponents at home and tried to fashion situations abroad that did not diminish his presidential stature. His was an increasingly protected and isolated presidency, much like Nixon's abortive second term.

Barack Obama

Barack Obama, the son of an African father and an American mother, believes his dual ancestry has given him the credentials and experience to bridge the racial divide in ways that most Americans, black or white, cannot. An extremely intelligent and confident person, he sees his political success as evidence that the American Dream is possible for every American. That conviction fuels and justifies his political ambitions. He sees himself as a role model for minorities in America.

Ambition
Barack Obama describes his ambition as "relentless"[18] and justifies it in socially accepted terms. "I got into politics to have some influence on the public debate, because I thought I had something to say about the direction we need to go as a country."[19] Acutely aware that self-interest drives his desire for power, Obama periodically warns himself of its dangers in his books and speeches. Nonetheless, politics has provided a salve for his ego, a direction for his restlessness, and a channel through which he can achieve desirable social goals, such as health care reform.

Integrity
In 2008, Obama saw his mission as unifying America, renewing its spirit, and achieving the common good. He considers himself a progressive pragmatist. He has little patience with "true believers," claiming that "it's precisely the pursuit of ideological purity, the rigid orthodoxy, and the sheer predictability of our current debate that keeps us from finding new ways to meet the challenges we face as a country. It's what keeps us locked in 'either/or' thinking."[20] Similarly, he is critical of religious zealots who would impose their faith on those who do not share it.[21]

Obama is a compromiser. His desire to find common ground and his aversion to fighting for his personal policy preferences has encouraged

(continued)

(continued)

him to delegate the details of domestic and economic policy making to Congress and policy oversight to his presidential aides and department heads. His preference is to be a visionary, a philosopher, rather than an in-your-face power broker. His tendency to allow others to do the bargaining occasionally has made him look weak and passive and subjected him to both partisan and nonpartisan criticism. Yet he is assertive as a candidate and resolute in the pursuit of his policy goals as president. He sees government as an instrument to help those who need help the most, a vehicle for promoting greater economic and social equality.

Relatedness
Obama is self-assured and can be self-contained. He along well with people, but he maintains his distance from them, leading to the accusation that he is elitist—a charge reinforced by his Ivy League education and by the degrees and accomplishments of those with whom he has chosen to surround himself. He can be a charismatic speaker and a skilled listener, but also can be impatient and argumentative. In making decisions, he thinks like a lawyer and emphasizes rationality over emotion. He has a stoic temperament, noting about himself, "I don't get too high when I'm high and I don't get too low when I am low."[22] He does not anger easily.

Operating Style

Presidents set the tone for their White Houses. How they approach their job and interact with their aides, what they demand from their subordinates, and how much supervision they exercise has a lot to do with how their presidency functions.

Some presidents work constantly. Carter, George H. W. Bush, Clinton, and Obama regularly put in twelve- to fourteen-hour days. Eisenhower, Reagan, and George W. Bush had more leisurely schedules. Reagan worked from 9 a.m. to 5 p.m., Monday through Thursday, and he would usually leave early Friday afternoon for the presidential retreat at Camp David in Maryland. Before the 9/11 terrorist attacks, Bush began his day around 7:20 a.m., took an exercise and lunch break midday, and left the office regularly at 6:30 p.m. Following the attacks his workday lengthened and he was forced to work on weekends.[23]

Some presidents feel the need to dominate relationships. Lyndon Johnson monopolized discussions and was unable to accept criticism. Others, such as Kennedy and Ford, treated their senior staff almost as equals.

Some presidents need to operate in a very protective environment. Nixon saw only a few trusted aides and wanted all recommendations and advice written and presented as option papers. Carter and Clinton, although much more open than Nixon, also operated primarily off paper. Eisenhower, Reagan, and George W. Bush preferred oral briefings to written memoranda. Ford is said to have maintained a "revolving door" into and out of the Oval Office, as did Clinton at the beginning of his administration. Both Bush and Obama have been highly disciplined in their personal and public behavior. They have stressed staff loyalty, railed against internal leaks, and have tended to promote from within as their term progressed.

Some presidents need to be involved in almost everything. Johnson, Carter, and Clinton maintained a hands-on approach; Eisenhower, Reagan, and George W. Bush waited for major policy and personnel decisions to reach them. Nixon, Ford, and Obama fall somewhere in between these two extremes.

Presidents create the mood and condition the way their White House operates. During the Nixon years, the mood was competitive, the style "macho," and the operation closed to public view. Aides had to prove how tough they were, how long they worked, and how many sacrifices they were making for the job. In contrast, Presidents Ford and Carter permitted a looser operation. They were more tolerant, more open, and less imposing.[24] The early Clinton White House also illustrated a fluid staff system, described by *New York Times* reporter Richard L. Berke as "controlled pandemonium."[25] The Clinton White House became more disciplined over time.

The George W. Bush staff system resembled Eisenhower and Reagan's in its hierarchical structures and businesslike mode of operation. Designed to contrast with the looser, less formal Clinton model, the Bush White House was a structured, top-down operation in which a strong chief of staff and a small cadre of loyal advisers regulated the flow of information, made recommendations to the president, and carried out his decisions. The White House erected a high and at times impenetrable wall to keep its critics at bay. Bush felt comfortable within the White House bubble.

When Obama entered office, he feared being encased in that bubble, arguing that he needed his Blackberry to maintain contact with the outside world. But as president, he too followed the script his advisers prepared. His presidency, along with those of Reagan and George W. Bush, has been highly choreographed and tightly run.

In studying the style and qualities that contribute to a successful presidency, Professor Fred I. Greenstein identifies six components of presidential leadership in his book, *The Presidential Difference*.[26] These include public communication, organizational capacity, political skill, vision, cognitive style, and emotional intelligence. Assessing contemporary presidents on the basis of these components, Greenstein notes which stylistic traits contributed to or detracted from their ability to exercise leadership in the presidency.

Being an effective *public communicator* is a requirement of the modern presidency. Until the twentieth century, presidents were not expected to communicate to the general public. In fact, personal campaigning for the presidency was the exception, not the rule. Today, that communication is essential; the bully pulpit is seen as a critical component of presidential leadership.

Presidents Roosevelt and Reagan used their communication skills effectively to build support for their policy goals and to enhance the public evaluation of their job performance. John F. Kennedy, Bill Clinton, and Barack Obama also tried to do so with varying degrees of success. In contrast, Lyndon Johnson, Gerald Ford, and George H. W. Bush were less effective spokesmen for their respective administrations. When the public turned against their efforts (Johnson's war in Vietnam; Ford's pardon of Nixon; Bush's absence of an economic plan during the 1991–1992 recession), these presidents were unable to reverse the public mood by successful communications campaigns. Similarly, when opposition mounted to George W. Bush's policy in Iraq and Barack Obama's health care reform, neither president was able to use his bully pulpit to reverse public opinion although both were reelected by a majority of voters.

Organizational capacity is the ability to utilize subordinates to inform decisions, extend influence, and design, explain, and implement policy. It consists of structuring and staffing the White House and other Executive Office units, developing processes that coordinate the actions and advocacy of the departments and agencies, and creating an information and advisory system in which presidential aides report the facts as they see them, even if they constitute bad news for the president, and the advice that they deem most appropriate, rather than tell presidents what they want to hear.

According to Greenstein, Eisenhower's advisory councils and mechanisms were designed to facilitate such an effort in foreign and domestic policy, whereas Johnson's, and to a lesser extent Carter's and Clinton's, were not.[27] Reagan and George W. Bush also set up centrally managed and strategically run policy and public relations staffs, but they chose to delegate much of the hands-on work to others. In both cases, some of this delegation was not adequately supervised, resulting in bad judgments that embarrassed the president and reduced public support for his administration.

Political skill is what presidents need to exercise to get others to follow their lead. In a constitutional system of internal checks and shared powers, such skills are essential. They counter institutional rivalries, external group pressures, and partisan opposition, helping to overcome the inertia that a division of powers often produces.

Franklin Roosevelt, Lyndon Johnson, and Bill Clinton were three of the most skillful political operatives in the White House and with the Congress. Roosevelt, responding to the depressed economy he inherited, designed political initiatives and gained congressional support for them. Johnson was also a successful legislative president, breaking a logjam on civil rights and committing the government's finances and expertise to social welfare. Clinton's political skills were used primarily in a defensive manner to prevent the Republican Congress from enacting many of the proposals in their "Contract with America" and to prevent himself from being removed from office via impeachment. George W. Bush and Barack Obama used the crises precipitated by the terrorist attacks of 9/11 and the economic meltdown of 2008–2009 to advance relevant parts of their agendas and gain congressional support for their policy proposals to deal with these crises.

There is a downside to being too political, however. It undercuts a president's broad-based national constituency; it makes bipartisan support less likely; and it can damage an image of leadership by making the president look overtly partisan. Both Clinton and George W. Bush suffered from allegations that their every move was dictated by political self-interest. Barack Obama tried to adopt a more bipartisan approach to governing but found it difficult to do so within the highly partisan political environment in which he was forced to operate; as the 2012 presidential campaign got underway, he adopted a more overtly partisan perspective.

Vision constitutes broad policy goals and the ways to achieve them. Ronald Reagan had a vision of a strong and vibrant America in which individual initiative in the private sector contributes to greater economic prosperity and national security for the country as a whole. His budget reallocation from domestic to defense spending and tax relief proposals incorporated the policy components of this vision and put them into a legislative format. George W. Bush's belief in the free enterprise system, the value of religion, and a world of good and evil led him to propose tax cuts, faith-based initiatives, and the use of force to defend democratic values. George H. W. Bush, Bill Clinton, and Barack Obama have been more pragmatic in their policy orientation. They were not guided by a compelling worldview that dictated certain decisions and actions.

Cognitive style relates to how a president thinks about a problem. Carter, trained as an engineer, focused on the components of complex issues whereas Reagan saw the problem and solution in terms of the big picture. Nixon had an analytical mind that was particularly adept at dissecting, analyzing, and evaluating foreign policy dilemmas. Clinton had a deep and detailed understanding of domestic policy issues and their political implications. George W. Bush took a more commonsense, down-to-earth approach but frequently showed impatience with what he perceived to be information overload or abstract thinking. Trained as a lawyer, Barack Obama emphasized cogent argument, deliberation, and rational, nonemotive decision making. He did not rush his policy judgments or political decisions but defended them 'tenaciously'.

Emotional intelligence represents the extent to which public officials such as the president can separate their own feelings from their public policies. To the extent that they personalize political and policy judgments, they run the risk of becoming overly rigid and defensive, protecting themselves against information that raises questions about the merits of their decisions or actions.

Emotional intelligence and cognitive style are not synonymous. Two of our most intellectually gifted presidents, Nixon and Clinton, suffered from emotional immaturity, more specifically, a failure to control their own feelings and ambitions. Nixon acted as if he were always in a hostile environment; Clinton saw conspiracies. Both demonized their political opponents, thereby deflecting criticism from themselves to others. Lyndon Johnson also had mood swings that affected his behavior. He was never able to accept criticism. Bush and Obama evidenced more self control. Obama, in particular, rarely showed his emotions.

For Greenstein, the absence of emotional intelligence can be the most debilitating and destructive of all stylistic attributes. It can undercut other qualities that augment political leadership.[28]

In the end, people come to the presidency with stylistic strengths and weaknesses. Those who gear their role as president and their actions in the office to their strengths; those whose staffing systems control and counter their own dysfunctional emotions; those who are able to impose discipline on themselves; and those who can distinguish their public actions from their private feelings are apt to be most successful.

THE PRESIDENT'S ADVISERS

The many and varied tasks expected of contemporary presidents are too complex for any one person to perform. Presidents need help in making, promoting, and implementing their decisions. They also need help in public relations and in discerning and responding to public moods, opinions, and expectations as well as meeting the symbolic and ceremonial functions of their office. Initially, the heads of the executive departments and agencies were intended to provide such help, and they did.

The Evolution of the Cabinet

The Constitution did not create a separate advisory council for the president. The framers had discussed the idea but rejected it largely out of the fear that presidents might try to sidestep responsibility for their decisions and actions by using their council as a foil. In order to avoid the legal fiction, popular in England at the time, that the king could do no wrong, that any mistake or harmful action the monarch committed was always the result of poor or even pernicious advice from his counselors, the Constitution specifically authorized presidents to demand written opinions of their subordinates. Having these in writing, it was hoped, would pinpoint responsibility. Today, the written and electronic correspondence to and from the president is part of the public record, as is most official government communication.[29]

Although presidents had been expected to use their department secretaries in both administrative and advisory capacities, there was no expectation that the secretaries would function as the principal body of advisers. However, in 1791, as George Washington prepared to leave the capital city, he advised his vice president, secretary of state, secretary of the treasury, secretary of war, and the chief justice of the Supreme Court to consult with each other on governmental matters during his absence. The following year, Washington began to meet more regularly with the heads of the executive departments. During the undeclared naval war with France, these meetings became even more frequent. James Madison referred to this group as the president's cabinet, and the name stuck. Jefferson's resignation as secretary of state in 1794 in protest over the administration's economic policies fixed the partisan nature of the group. In addition to giving policy advice, cabinet members were expected to provide political support to the president.

For the next 140 years, the cabinet functioned as the president's major advisory body for both foreign and domestic affairs. Administrative positions on controversial proposals were thrashed out at cabinet meetings. Presidents also used their cabinets to exercise influence on Capitol Hill. The personal relationships among the individual secretaries and members of Congress frequently put the cabinet officials in a better position than the president to achieve the administration's legislative goals. Strong cabinets and weak presidents characterized executive advisory relationships during most of the nineteenth century.

The president's influence began to increase in the twentieth century. The ability to shape public opinion and mobilize partisan support, evident during the administrations of Theodore Roosevelt and Woodrow Wilson, strengthened the chief executive's hand in dealing with Congress and with department heads. Beginning in 1921, the power to affect executive-branch decision making through the budget process also contributed to a stronger presidency.

As a consequence of these developments, cabinet meetings became more of a forum for discussion than a mechanism for formulating administration policy positions and proposals. Franklin Roosevelt even trivialized the forum. His practice was to go around the table asking each participant what was on his or her mind. Frequently after the session, some secretaries remained to discuss their important business alone with the president without others in attendance. Truman continued Roosevelt's emphasis on one-to-one relationships with his department heads rather than calling on them collectively for advice.

The cabinet enjoyed a resurrection under President Dwight Eisenhower, meeting 230 times during his eight years in office. As president, Eisenhower personally presided over many of these meetings and used his presence to help forge a consensus on major administration policies and programs. After Eisenhower's presidency, the cabinet functioned less and less as a policy-making or advisory body. Presidents continued to meet with their cabinets in part because they were expected to do so, but the meetings decreased in frequency.

The cabinet's decline has been caused by the increasingly complex and technical nature of policy making, which makes it difficult for secretaries to be sufficiently versed in the intricacies of issues outside their substantive policy areas. At best, the need for specialized knowledge has limited participation at cabinet meetings to the few individuals who were informed and competent; at worst, it reduced the level of the discussion to the lowest common denominator and extended the time of debate. Increasing pressure from outside groups has also forced secretaries to assume more of an advocacy role for their respective departments (referred to as "going native"), particularly when they have to go on the record.[30] Their need to advocate departmental interests and attend to their administrative responsibilities makes it more difficult for them to see problems from the president's perspective and recommend solutions that accord with the president's priorities rather than their own department's.

Despite the decline in the importance of the cabinet as a collectivity, it is necessary for the president to maintain ongoing channels of communication to and from the heads of the executive departments. An office of cabinet affairs within the White House facilitates this flow of information as well as coordinates the involvement of cabinet secretaries in promoting administration policies in Congress. Table 6.1 lists the departmental components of the contemporary cabinet and their proposed funding levels for the 2014 fiscal year.

Table 6.1 The President's Cabinet

Department	Year Created	President	Current Service Budget Outlays FY 2014 (in Billions [$])
State	1789	Washington	48.1
Treasury	1789	Washington	12.9
Interior	1849	Polk	11.7
Agriculture	1862	Lincoln	21.5
Justice	1870	Grant	16.3
Commerce (formerly part of Department of Commerce and Labor, 1903)	1913	Wilson	9.6
Labor (formerly part of Department of Commerce and Labor, 1903)	1913	Wilson	12.1
Defense (consolidated Department of War, 1789, and Department of Navy, 1798)*	1947	Truman	526.6
Housing and Urban Development	1965	Johnson	31.1
Transportation	1966	Johnson	16.3
Energy	1977	Carter	28.4
Health and Human Services (formerly part of Department of Health, Education, and Welfare, 1953)	1980	Carter	78.3
Education (formerly part of Department of Health, Education, and Welfare, 1953)	1980	Carter	71.2
Veterans Affairs	1988	Reagan	63.5
Homeland Security	2002	Bush	39.0

*Combined civilian and military budgets for DOD.

SOURCE: U.S. Budget, FY 2014, "Table S-11. "Funding Levels for Appropriated (Discretionary) Programs by Agency." http://www.whitehouse.gov/sites/default/Fy2014/assets/tables.pdf

The Executive Office of the President

The growth of the executive branch, the need for coordination within it, and the orientation of the departments toward their clientele have given presidents little choice but to create their own office within their branch of government. That office, the Executive Office of the President (EOP), was created in 1939. The title is a misnomer, however. Its functions are not exclusively executive, nor is it a single office, but its staffers do work for a single client—the president.

The principal objective of the EOP has always been to help presidents perform central, nondelegable tasks, including those involved in their expanded policy-making and policy implementation roles. The various offices in the EOP have not taken over the administrative responsibilities of the departments and agencies, although they do coordinate interagency projects and impose a presidential perspective on policy making and public relations.

The first Executive Office was composed of five separate units, including the Bureau of the Budget and the White House. Over the years, a variety of different boards, councils, and offices have been placed within its purview. Today the Executive Office has a budget of almost $400 million and a staff size of about 1,800 people. (See Table 6.2.)

In addition to the Executive Office, other departments and agencies contribute to the everyday needs of presidents, vice presidents, their spouses, their official residences, and their duties and activities. These include the Department of Defense—the White House Communications Agency (secure communications), the U.S. Air Force (air transportation), the U.S. Army (explosive detection and ground transportation), and the U.S. Navy (helicopter transportation, marine guards, food, medical facilities, and Camp David, the presidential retreat in Maryland)—the General Services Administration (buildings and grounds), National Park Service (visitors and the fine arts collection), National Archives (custody of official documents), Secret Service in the Department of Homeland Security (protection of the president, vice president, and their families as well as those of former presidents), Commission on White House Fellowships, U.S. Postal Service, and State Department (official visits and receptions for foreign dignitaries).[31]

Table 6.2 Executive Office of the President, 2014

	Budget (in Millions)	Full-Time Employees
Council of Economic Advisers	$ 4	26
Council on Environmental Quality	3	24
Executive Residence	18	96
National Security Council	13	77
Office of Administration	113	230
Office of Management and Budget	93	506
Office of National Drug Control Policy	23	96
Office of Science and Technology Policy	6	32
Office of the United States Trade Representative	56	254
Office of the Vice President	5	24
White House Office	60	450
Misc.	15	5
Total	$409	1,820

SOURCE: United States Budget for Fiscal Year 2014.
www.whitehouse.gov/sites/default/files/omb/budget/fy2014/assts/eop/pdf

Political and Structural Changes

Since the Executive Office has served the president, its composition has changed with the needs and goals of different administrations. Its most extensive reorganization occurred in 1970 when Richard Nixon centralized power within it. Nixon also added more appointive positions in the executive branch. He did not trust career executives who worked in government during the previous Democratic administrations to follow his lead and implement his more conservative policy agenda.

The centralization and politicization of power within the executive branch is designed to ensure that the president's policy goals and political interests will be carried out. To do so, presidents want their own team of political appointees, who demonstrate their loyalty and work ethic during the winning election campaign, to be in charge.

Proponents of this shift of power see it as necessary to keep a large and complex executive branch responsive to the president. They argue that in a democratic political process, government should reflect the will of the people as expressed in the last election.[32] Opponents, however, point to the dangers of an overly political executive branch: instability in organization, irregularity in operations, and inexperience and turnover in personnel. They contend that these problems, most severe during transitions from one party to the other, impede the effectiveness of government and hinder the president's ability to achieve and manage policy goals.[33] Delays in the appointment process have contributed to these problems.

The appointment process has become increasingly complex, political, and arduous.[34] Presidential nominees have to provide detailed personal and professional information to White House aides charged with vetting their nomination. FBI field checks have to be conducted for most senior executive branch positions. Committees in the Senate hold hearings, and their staff conducts their own investigations. Senate rules allow individual Senators to place indefinite holds on nominees; they allow committee chairs to effectively kill nominations by delaying consideration of them. The rule on unlimited debate also applies. That rule requires a minimum of 60 senators to impose cloture and bring a nomination being filibustered to a vote.

There is greater external scrutiny by the press, outside groups, and the opposition party. Ideological politics has added a dimension to an already partisan process. The result has been slower and slower confirmations. The average amount of time from designation by the president to confirmation by the Senate has grown from 2.4 months during the first year of the Kennedy administration to more than 8 months today. Of the approximately 3,000 appointments a new president has to make, over one thousand require Senate confirmation.

There are other problems. The lack of experience of some new appointees can adversely affect a new administration's ability to follow through on the president's policy agenda.[35] If new appointees harbor distrust of the career civil servants who know the issues and are familiar with government operations, that distrust magnifies the problem. Partisan and personal differences between the outgoing and incoming administrations can also be an issue, as it was following the disputed presidential election of 2000. Under the best of times, presidential transitions are short (about 75 days), and planning for them is often delayed until after the election because candidates do not want to give the impression that they take victory for granted.

Transition problems have been magnified in recent years by events that have forced presidents to address major, complex national and international issues at the beginning of their administration. For example, only 30 percent of the national security positions had been filled by September 11, 2001, the date of the terrorist attacks in New York and Washington. For the first two months of the Obama administration, treasury secretary Timothy Geithner was the only appointed official in the department that had responsibility for accounting for the expenditure of the rescue, recovery, and reinvestment funds, approximately $1.5 trillion; establishing new rules and procedures for the banking and investment communities; and making sure that the government funds were spent properly.

Internal Rivalries and Power Relationships
The shift of power to the presidency has also generated tension among the new appointees themselves. Cabinet secretaries and their principal assistants, who thought they would be advising the president in their areas of expertise, have complained about being left out of the loop or being required by junior White House aides to perform what they consider relatively unimportant and time-consuming functions. Take the incident that Robert Reich embellishes in his diary of his years as secretary of labor during the Clinton administration.

Reich's Aide: "The White House wants you to go to Cleveland."

Reich: "Why?"

Aide: "Because we're hitting the first hundred days of the Clinton administration and the President along with his entire cabinet are fanning out across America to celebrate, because Ohio is important, because there are a lot of blue-collar voters out there, and because you haven't been to Ohio yet. . . ."

Reich: "Who wants me to go . . . ?"

Aide: "The White House. They called this morning."

Reich: "Houses don't make phone calls. Who called?"

Aide: "I don't know. Somebody from Cabinet Affairs. Steve somebody."

Reich: "How old is Steve? . . . I bet he's under thirty."

Aide: "He is probably under thirty. A large portion of the American population is under thirty? So what?"

Reich: "Don't you see? Here I am, a member of the president's cabinet, confirmed by the Senate, the head of an entire government department with eighteen thousand employees, responsible for implementing a huge number of laws and rules, charged with helping people get better jobs, and who is telling me what to do? . . . Some twerp in the White House who has no clue what I'm doing in this job. Screw him. I won't go. . . ."

Aide: "You'll go to Cleveland. The President is going to New Orleans, other cabinet members are going to other major cities. You're in Cleveland."

Reich: "I'll go this time. . . . But I'll be damned if I'm going to let them run my life." (Reich resigned at the end of Clinton's first term.)[36]

Reich's attitude is not unique. Not only do senior departmental officials resent relatively junior aides telling them what to do, they also resent being "corrected" by the White House after they have made a decision, issued a press release, or appeared on a news program. After EPA administrator Christy Todd Whitman announced a new emission standard early in the administration of George W. Bush, one that had been cleared in advance by the White House, she was overruled by the president after representatives of the energy industry made the case to him that the new standard was too restrictive and would contribute to higher energy prices.[37] Similarly, Obama's treasury secretary, Timothy Geithner, told the president that bonuses given out by the giant insurer AIG, a company bailed out by the government in 2008, could not be prevented because it would violate the company's contracts with its executive employees, a position that he and Obama's chief economic adviser, Lawrence Summers, explained on the Sunday morning interview shows. Several days later, responding to negative public opinion, however, the president expressed his anger and reputedly told Geithner to do what he could to prevent the bonuses or to recoup the money for the taxpayers.

Not only can cabinet officials be locked in their departments and out of White House decision making, but they can also be kept in the dark about what the administration plans to do. Richard Nixon did not tell his secretary of state, William Rogers, that he was going to China until 30 minutes before he told the nation on a national television address. George W. Bush informed his secretary of state, Colin Powell, about his decision to use military force against Iraq only after he informed other key national security officials as well as the Saudi Arabian ambassador to the United States.[38]

Although the establishment and expansion of the Executive Office has increased the president's ability to meet the multiple demands of the office, it has also helped continue those demands. Bureaucracies—even presidential bureaucracies—have a self-perpetuating character. By performing functions and meeting expectations, these structures encourage those expectations and the operations that support them to continue. In short, the layering of the presidency has increased the burdens on an activist president and the dangers for a passive one. It has required presidents to depend increasingly on their White House staffs to exercise the power of their office.

Trends in White House Staffing

Although presidents have always had personal aides, they did not have an official White House office until the twentieth century. For the first seventy years, Congress did not even provide the president with secretarial support. Early presidents were expected to write their own speeches and answer their own correspondence. Most employed a few aides and paid them out of their own salary. These assistants tended to be young and undistinguished. Frequently, they were related to the president. They were paid low wages and generally performed clerkship tasks.

In 1857, Congress enacted a separate appropriation for a personal secretary for the president, but the position did not assume great importance or even much potential at the time. If anything, the quality of the secretaries actually employed by presidents declined. Andrew Johnson's aide, his son Robert, was an alcoholic; Ulysses S. Grant's secretary, General Orville E. Babcock, was indicted for fraud; Rutherford B. Hayes's assistant, William Rogers, was generally regarded as incompetent.[39]

The presidential secretary's role began to expand with the administration of Chester Arthur (1881–1885). Theodore Roosevelt's principal aide, William Loeb Jr., began to deal with the press on a regular basis. Wilson's secretary, Joseph Tumulty, controlled access to the Oval Office and functioned as an appointments scheduler, political adviser, administrative manager, and public relations aide, much like latter-day chiefs of staff.

The number of presidential assistants also began to increase during the early part of the twentieth century. Whereas Benjamin Harrison could place his entire staff on the second floor of the White House, near his own living quarters, during William McKinley's administration a separate group of offices had to be constructed outside the mansion for the president's staff. When the West Wing was completed in 1909, the president's aides came to occupy an even larger space near the president's new Oval Office.

Herbert Hoover doubled the number of his administrative aides from two to four. However, it was Franklin Roosevelt who established a separate White House Office, placed it in the Executive Office of the President, and appointed six key aides that performed tasks dictated by the president's needs and activities. Roosevelt supervised the staff himself, giving out assignments, receiving reports, and generally coordinating activities. His assistants were expected to work behind the scenes, not in full public view. Roosevelt purposely blurred the lines of authority and overlapped assignments to encourage competition among his aides in order to maximize his information and extend his influence. According to presidential scholar and former presidential aide, Richard E. Neustadt, Roosevelt enjoyed "bruised egos.[40]

The informal organization and operation of Roosevelt's White House was a prescription for exercising personal control; it was a model that Truman basically followed. Eisenhower, a career military officer, however, was used to having a chief of staff to relieve him of routine decisions and give him more time and greater flexibility. He believed that the president should set overall policy and then work behind the scenes to get that policy adopted.[41] As a consequence, he set up a more hierarchical White House staff, run by a chief of staff with the title "assistant to the president."

Changes began to occur in the White House in the 1960s as presidential policy staffs were added. Presidential aides also became better known, exercised more power, and tended to monopolize the president's attention and time. Kennedy consciously attempted to emulate Franklin Roosevelt's model but without the internal competition Roosevelt had generated. Johnson, who inherited Kennedy's staff and mode of operation after the assassination, eventually replaced them with his own trusted aides and set up a system more consistent with his style of operating. Nixon preferred a centralized management approach run by a strong chief of staff. His White House had clear lines of authority and vertical patterns of decision making, but it also shielded the president from others in the government and outside of it. Primary access to the president was limited to just a few senior White House aides. After his reelection in 1972, Nixon sought to expand his influence by transferring trusted White House assistants and their deputies to the departments and agencies, but the events of Watergate aborted the plan. The Watergate scandal and other secret White House operations raised doubts about the wisdom of having such a large, powerful staff operate outside of public view.

Ford and Carter both reacted to the Nixon experience by organizing their White Houses initially like the spokes of a wheel, with themselves at the hub and the senior staff reporting directly to them. Ford stated:

> I started out with the concept that any cabinet member or top executive in the administration could have direct access to me. In effect, that undercut the role of the chief of staff. I shortly found out that was impractical. A president doesn't have that much time every day to meet with the various cabinet officers and other top people. You've got to have the chief of staff as a sort of filtering spot. I changed the policy . . . within two months.[42]

Internal turf battles and mixed messages from presidential aides added to the difficulties in the Ford and Carter White Houses and eventually required both presidents to designate a chief of staff to coordinate activities and look out for their political interests. Carter added offices to reach out to interest and community groups and state and local governments.

Reagan also depended on the strong chief-of-staff model in organizing and operating his White House staff. Like Eisenhower, he wanted his aides to handle decisions that did not require a presidential judgment. Reagan's critics derided his "hand-off" management style, pointing to the Iran–Contra example to illustrate the dangers of over-delegation; his backers pointed to Reagan's political and policy successes and his personal popularity as evidence that his White House facilitated his exercise of power. Reagan also expanded the political and public relations staffs in the White House.

Although the style and priorities of Reagan's successors have differed, the structure and functions of their White Houses have remained relatively constant, with individual presidents adding their own personal touch, usually at the beginnings of their terms in office. For example, the priority that Barack Obama gave to new policy initiatives led him to set up a relatively large number of policy-making offices at the start of his presidency. In addition to the traditional staffs for domestic, economic, and national security policy, Obama created offices for energy and climate change, social innovation, urban affairs, health care reform, homeland security and counterterrorism, community and faith-based initiatives, and a council on women and girls. The job of these policy units was to coordinate interagency input, brief the president, and interact with congressional committee members on issues within their spheres of expertise. Obama continued the outreach activities of the White House to the general public, special interest groups, and state and local governments.

There is now a standard organizational model for the White House that consists of policy-making and public relations staffs as well as those that orchestrate the president's day and support his activities.[43] The location of these offices has also become institutionalized. Figure 6.1 lists the units of the contemporary White House; Figure 6.2 maps their location in the West Wing.

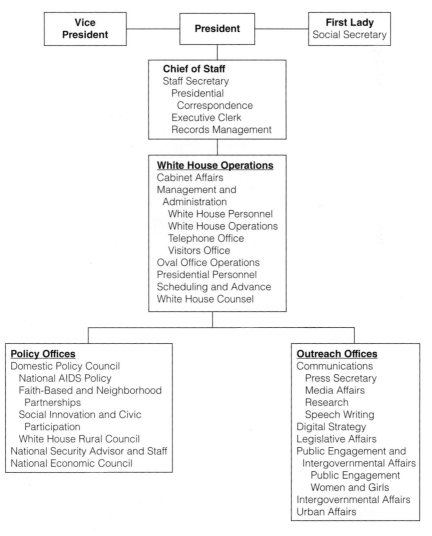

FIGURE 6.1 The White House Office

Source: White House www.whiterhouse.gov/administration/eop

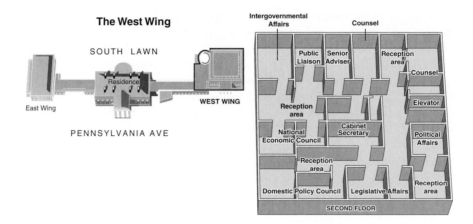

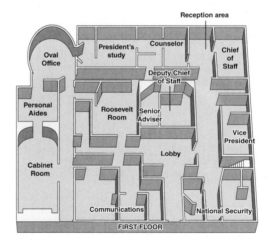

FIGURE 6.2 SOURCE: The West Wing

Adapted from "Inside the West Wing," Washington Post, March 7, 2013.

Which staff structure is best for managing the White House depends on the operating style of individual presidents and the priorities they establish over the course of their administrations.[44] In general, those presidents who wish to maximize their involvement and influence will benefit from a more fluid staffing arrangement. In contrast, those who prefer to leave the burden of soliciting, collecting, and coordinating advice and implementing presidential decisions to others are better served by a more formal, hierarchal structure. Kennedy, Johnson, Carter, and Clinton fall into the first category; Eisenhower,

Nixon, Reagan, and George W. Bush fall into the second; and the rest, including Obama, lie somewhere in between.

Presidents who wish to depart from existing policy, particularly policy based on strong outside interests, will tend to gain most from the flexible advisory arrangement. The less formal the structure, the more quickly it can respond to crises and changing conditions and the more easily it can produce innovative policy. Kennedy is an example of a president who desired new and creative policy, and Johnson is another. Nixon and Carter, in contrast, were less interested in innovation and more interested in obtaining the careful analysis that a well-staffed White House policy operation could produce.

Most presidents strive for consensus. A staffing structure based on multiple advocacy in which White House and departmental personnel present their differing perspectives and positions on policy issues provides the presidents with a wide range of information and options but also demands more time at meetings when these issues are discussed; can create more internal conflict, which may be leaked to the press; and makes policy agreement more difficult to achieve. A hierarchical system allows presidents to get involved in the latter stages of decision making, but their options may also be more limited at this stage of policy development. In a top-down system, consensus can be created or imposed by choosing appointees that have similar ideological orientations and political perspectives. George H. W. Bush, Bill Clinton, and Barack Obama purposely utilized the multiple advocacy approach in the early years of their administration[45] whereas Eisenhower, Reagan, and George W. Bush from the outset preferred a staffing system that did not involve them in a lot of the details of policy formulation, including early discussion.

THE VICE PRESIDENCY AND THE PRESIDENT'S SPOUSE

Presidential support has been supplemented in recent years by the activities and influence of the vice president and by the public relations role of the president's spouse. The staffs of both offices have increased in size and specialization as well. The personal and professional roles and public visibility of the vice president and presidential spouse differ significantly from what they were for most of the country's history.

The Vice Presidency

For years, the vice presidency was regarded as a position of little importance; in fact, it was the butt of jokes and laments. The nation's first vice president, John Adams, complained, "My country has in its wisdom contrived for me the most insignificant office that ever the invention of man contrived or his imagination conceived."[46] Thomas Jefferson, the second person to hold the office, was not quite as critical. Describing his job as "honorable and easy," he added, "I am unable to decide whether I would rather have it or not have it."[47]

Throughout most of the nineteenth century, the vice president performed very few official functions. Other than succeeding to the presidency, the holder of this position had only one designated constitutional job—to preside over the Senate and vote in case of a tie. Nor did eighteenth- and nineteenth-century presidents enhance that job very much. Vice presidents played only a peripheral role within their respective administrations, so much so that when Professor Woodrow Wilson published his classic treatise on American government in the 1880s, he devoted only one paragraph to the vice president, writing: "The chief embarrassment in . . . explaining how little there is to be said about it is that one has evidently said all there is to say."[48] John Nance Garner, Franklin Roosevelt's first vice president, offered perhaps the most earthy description in his much-quoted refrain that the office was "hardly worth a pitcher of spit."[49]

Were Adams, Jefferson, and Garner alive today, they would have to reevaluate their comments.[50] The position of vice president has increased enormously in importance and visibility. Roosevelt's sudden death, Eisenhower's illness, and Kennedy's assassination focused attention on the vice president and generated a debate that resulted in a constitutional amendment on presidential disability and vice presidential selection should the position become vacant (see Appendix B). Public awareness and concern about the state of health of presidents encouraged them to do more to prepare their vice president for the presidency should that be necessary due to permanent or temporary disability of the president.

Eisenhower was the first of the modern presidents to upgrade the vice president's role. He invited Richard Nixon, his vice president, to attend cabinet, National Security Council, and legislative strategy meetings, and during Eisenhower's illness, Nixon presided over these sessions.[51] In addition, as vice president, Nixon was sent on a number of well-publicized trips for the administration.

Lyndon Johnson was also involved in a variety of activities as John Kennedy's vice president. He helped coordinate administration efforts to eliminate racial discrimination and promote exploration of outer space; participated in legislative lobbying efforts, joining Kennedy at the White House breakfasts for congressional leaders; and also traveled abroad on behalf of the administration. Still, however, Johnson was not enamored with his job, telling biographer Doris Kearns:

> Every time I came into John Kennedy's presence, I felt like a goddamn raven hovering over his shoulder. Away from the Oval Office, it was even worse. The Vice Presidency is filled with trips around the world, chauffeurs, men saluting, people clapping, chairmanships of councils, but in the end, it is nothing. I detested every minute of it.[52]

Despite their own experiences as vice presidents, neither Johnson nor Nixon added new responsibilities to that office during their presidencies, although they did have their vice presidents perform a variety of ceremonial, diplomatic, and political roles.[53]

Nelson Rockefeller, Gerald Ford's vice president, was given an important policy-making assignment—to shape the Ford administration's domestic policy goals and prepare the president's agenda for his 1976 campaign. Rockefeller's proposals, however, clashed with those of other Republicans within the administration and Congress. Coming under increasing criticism from fellow partisans, including senior White House staffers, the vice president, who had been nominated by the president and confirmed by a majority vote in both Houses of Congress, announced his intention not to seek the vice presidency in 1976 and subsequently removed himself from an active advisory role.

Whereas Rockefeller failed to realize the potential of the office, Walter Mondale did. The first vice president to have an office in the West Wing of the White House, Mondale saw President Carter on a regular basis. He had *carte blanche* to attend any conference, see any paper, and participate in any study in which the president was involved.[54] Carter also provided opportunities for Mondale to shape policy and facilitate congressional relations. Mondale headed a presidential priority-setting group, lobbied on key bills, and helped establish a public liaison operation in the White House. His staff was integrated with Carter's. Although Mondale became an important policy adviser, he was careful not to intrude on the president's decision-making authority.[55]

When President Reagan wished to demonstrate his concern with crisis management, drug enforcement, and government relations, he appointed his vice president, George H. W. Bush, to head committees studying these issues. Bush also served as a personal envoy of the president by visiting North Atlantic Treaty Organization (NATO) countries, making a fact-finding trip to Lebanon, and attending the funerals of several foreign policy leaders. However, Bush was not considered an influential Reagan adviser, nor was he outspoken at the policy meetings he attended.

Dan Quayle played a similar role for the Bush administration. Although Quayle attracted more public attention than did George H. W. Bush as vice president, he did not become a major adviser to Bush. The president even considered dropping him from the ticket in 1992 but chose not to do so out of fear of alienating the conservative Republicans to whom Quayle appealed. Bush also did not want to admit that he erred in choosing Quayle in the first place. As vice president, Quayle was sent on a number of foreign trips for the administration, chaired the committee overseeing space exploration (as Lyndon Johnson had done during the Kennedy administration), and served as a liaison to the party, outside groups, and members of Congress.

Vice President Al Gore had considerably more policy and personal influence in the Clinton administration, participating in the selection of cabinet and subcabinet secretaries, reviewing the drafts of presidential speeches, and, in his most important responsibility, directing the National Performance Review project, the administration's effort to "reinvent government" by making it more efficient and less costly. As a key Clinton adviser, Gore lunched regularly with the president, attended political strategy sessions, and had regular input into most major policy decisions, especially in the areas of the environment, high technology, and matters of science. A principal link to organized labor, Senate Democrats, and the Democratic Party, Gore also played a prominent role in foreign affairs as a personal representative of the president. Clinton usually did not make a major policy decision without consulting Gore, although he did not always follow Gore's advice.

Dick Cheney exercised more power in this position than any other vice president before him. He presided over the Bush transition, led a task force on energy policy, and another to coordinate the administration's response to future terrorist attacks. With the president out of town on the day of the terrorist attacks, Cheney directed White House operations. For much of the Bush presidency, he functioned as the president's principal adviser and policy enforcer.

Bush delegated considerable operational authority to Cheney, whose experience as Ford's chief of staff, member of the Republican leadership in Congress, and secretary of defense during the senior Bush's administration gave him knowledge and experience that few, if any, in the administration could match. He had a staff of approximately ninety people working out of three offices (in the West Wing, the Eisenhower Executive Office Building, and the Senate).[56] He also served as a spokesman for the administration on the Sunday talk shows, a liaison to business, political, and veteran groups and Republican Party leaders, as well as a frequent diplomatic representative for the country.

Cheney involved himself in a range of policy matters, frequently behind closed doors. He was particularly active in forging a policy for combating terrorism at home and abroad. His office drafted the orders that extended CIA and military discretion on methods for obtaining information from those suspected of aiding and abetting terrorist activities. He was also a forceful advocate of using military force in Afghanistan and Iraq.[57]

Cheney's vice presidency was controversial, however. He came into criticism for the secretive manner in which he and his aides operated, the way in which they were able to circumvent normal channels of government decision making, and the power they exercised.

Partially in reaction to these criticisms, Joseph Biden said that he would model his office on that of Mondale, not Cheney. An influential negotiator and adviser, Biden played a key role in negotiations with congressional party leaders during the budget debate of 2010, the deficit and debt limit discussions of 2011, and the resolution of fiscal cliff crisis at the end of 2012. His recommendation of fighting terrorism abroad with special forces, drones and other advanced technologies, and enhanced on-the-ground intelligence became U.S. policy during the first term of the Obama administration. The president asked him to play a key role in designing new gun legislation after the school shootings in Newtown, Connecticut. He also has been active as an administration spokesperson, party advocate, and personal representative of the president with foreign governments and domestic groups.

The President's Spouse

The president's spouse has the potential to become an important component or point of controversy in the contemporary presidency. Although the Constitution does not acknowledge a spousal responsibility, presidential spouses have performed social and ceremonial functions from the time the government first began to operate. Initially and throughout the nineteenth century, spouses avoided involvement in policy matters and, to a slightly lesser extent, in politics. Even though they were expected to stay out of the limelight, some presidential wives became controversial, Rachel Jackson and Mary Todd Lincoln in particular.

At the beginning of the twentieth century, and with the development of a White House press corps, spouses became more visible but not necessarily more influential. The exception was Edith Wilson after her husband suffered a major stroke in the fall of 1919. She made decisions in his name; shielded him from Washington politicians, the press, and the public; and may have even forged his signature to legal documents including legislation.[58]

Eleanor Roosevelt established an important communications link between her husband, who had been physically disabled by polio and moved with great difficulty, and the American people during his twelve years in office. Mrs. Roosevelt traveled across the country, monitored public opinion, and reported the country's mood to the president. She was an advocate for the poor and an early supporter of civil rights. She also wrote a column, entitled "My Day," which appeared in newspapers around the country.[59]

Jacqueline Bouvier Kennedy and "Lady Bird" Johnson supplemented the policy interests of their husbands with their concerns about American history, culture, and landscaping. Mrs. Kennedy was instrumental in the restoration of the Lafayette Park area across from the White House and the preservation and restoration of the White House interior. Mrs. Johnson cared deeply about the environment and worked to enhance the beautification of Washington in parks and along public highways.

Betty Ford and Rosalyn Carter spoke out on health care issues and other family-related concerns. Mrs. Carter was the first spouse to attend a cabinet meeting.[60] Nancy Reagan played the role of a spokesperson, spearheading the administration's antidrug policy with her "Just Say No" campaign. In addition, Mrs. Reagan was involved in internal personal and personnel matters, particularly as they pertained to the staffing and travel of her husband. She was instrumental in the removal of several key aides who, she believed, were serving the president poorly. Barbara Bush and Laura Bush served as advocates for literacy; Hillary Rodham Clinton, for universal health care, human rights, and family values; and Michele Obama for health and physical fitness issues.

Mrs. Clinton's involvement in the development and marketing of the administration's health reform proposal, however, went well beyond advocacy. She had an office on the policy floor of the West Wing in addition to the suite of offices in the East Wing that is normally reserved for the First Lady. As chief architect and lobbyist for the administration's health care reform proposal, she testified before Congress and attended negotiating sessions with congressional leaders. Her policy advocacy embroiled her in partisan politics. Her alleged involvement in the firing of personnel in the White House Travel Office, combined with the disappearance of some of her legal records (Mrs. Clinton was the first presidential spouse to be subpoenaed to testify about her activities before a federal grand jury.), added to her image as a partisan and raised questions about the proper role for a presidential spouse.[61]

People who admired the Eleanor Roosevelt—Hillary Rodham Clinton model saw the presidential spouse as a valuable partner who could help the administration in a variety of ways, from performing ceremonial duties to meeting with government leaders, workers, or the general public, to making policy and even exercising political leadership. A spouse may be in a unique position to say what the president does not want to hear—and what other advisers might be fearful of saying.

Others, however, point with some trepidation to the unique relationship that the president's spouse enjoys with the president. The fact that spouses cannot be fired makes them less vulnerable to the usual constraints on and criticism of presidential advisers. Moreover, it places them in a position to impose their own views on others and be more persuasive with the president, given the intimacy and time spent together. These dangers, however, may be partially offset by the visibility of the spouse and the desire not to be a source of negative press attention and commentary.

CONCLUSION

In the Constitutional Convention, the framers briefly debated whether to entrust the presidency to one person or several individuals. The decision to have a single president, intended to promote "energy, dispatch, and responsibility,"[62] enhanced the influence of the person holding that office, but it did not eliminate the need for information and advice from others, hence the provision that the president could demand that advice in writing.

Presidents' personalities are evident in the decisions they make, the advisers they choose, and the ways in which they interact with others. Thinking, doing, and communicating are three critical activities in which personality can affect performance. It is not the only factor that does so; external conditions, institutional structures, law, precedent and current practices, even timeframes may impact decisions and actions, but personality is always present and potentially relevant.

The key personality traits on which political scientists have focused are character, style, and worldview. These traits, developed from personal experience and perhaps genetics, help shape perceptions, instincts, and judgments. Character is a core component; style is a way of doing things; and worldview a body of beliefs about the environment in which people live.

James David Barber and Stanley Renshon, two students of political psychology, argue that certain personal attributes contribute to or detract from presidential leadership. Thus, they should be considered when assessing qualifications for office, explaining a particular decision or action, and even anticipating responses to possible events or situations in the future. Presidential leadership skills, according to Fred Greenstein, include effective public communication, a capacity to organize and think clearly, political savvy, vision, and emotional maturity.

Not only do leaders need to demonstrate these skills, but they also need a climate in which those skills can be effectively exercised, particularly in a constitutional system designed to constrain the exercise of personal and institutional power. From a presidential perspective, the sad fact is that presidents can exercise only limited influence over people, conditions, and events despite the campaign promises they may have made, leadership images they projected, and public expectations they created.

Leadership is not only a result of personal attributes and skills that presidents bring to their office, but also a consequence of the personnel they select and the ways in which they interact with them. The tasks of contemporary presidents are far too numerous, require far too much knowledge, and may be fraught with far too many obstacles to be undertaken alone. Presidents need information and advice from others; they need to build and maintain political alliances; and they need to increase the credit and reduce the blame for their actions. These needs are serviced primarily by political appointees in the executive branch, and especially the Executive Office, the vice president, and to a lesser extent, the president's spouse.

The White House has become more powerful, specialized, and politicized, with greater emphasis placed on policy making and public relations. It has developed an independent capacity to advise and inform the president, to formulate and prioritize policy, to orchestrate and oversee department and agency input, and to build public and congressional support.

Senior presidential aides have become more important, prestigious, and visible; they are also subject to more press scrutiny and criticism. In contrast, the department secretaries have lost some of their notoriety and status, access to the president, and influence over policy development.

The creation and maintenance of a presidential office has occurred not only at the expense of the departments' and agencies' access to and influence with the president but also at some cost to presidents themselves. Although the reach of the presidency has been expanded and its capacity to affect policy enhanced, the president's personal ability to oversee staff on an ongoing basis has decreased.

The evolution of the presidency confronts contemporary presidents with a dilemma: They need a large, functionally differentiated staff to exercise leadership, yet their leadership ability is frequently at the mercy of that staff, especially for those presidents who tend to delegate a lot. Thus, the expansion of the presidency has been a mixed blessing. Although created to meet increased expectations, the presidential office has generated new ones. Designed to coordinate and facilitate executive-branch decision making, it has produced tensions within the executive branch. Tailored to systematize advice to the president, it has also proliferated that advice, sometimes has worked to isolate presents from their advisers and from the public, and occasionally to produce a groupthink mentality.

However, the White House expansion has obviously been necessary. It has been both a cause and consequence of the growth of government, the executive branch, and the president's leadership responsibilities.

Discussion Questions

1. Character, cognition, and decisional style can affect presidential judgments and contribute to the ability of a president to make sound policy judgments. Discuss the impact of these variables, singularly or together, on a major presidential policy decision, such as George W. Bush's decision to use military force against Iraq in 2003 or Barack Obama's to pursue health care reform.

2. Has the institutionalization of the presidency contributed to or detracted from the president's personal power and accountability? Explain the impact of institutionalization and give examples from recent presidencies.

3. Assume that you are an expert on the presidency and have been asked by a presidential candidate to prepare a memo on staffing the White House. Write a memo in which you indicate the units you would set up in the White House, the type of people you would appoint to top positions, and the kinds of problems that they might encounter in their first year. Which contemporary White Houses would you cite as the most and least effective during their first one hundred days and then their first year in office?

 ## Web Exercises

1. Go to the White House website at http://www.whitehouse.gov and examine the transcript of a recent presidential news conference. Do you discern any patterns in the president's words that might suggest a character tendency, mindset, or style of decision making that may have affected the explanation or rationalization for a decision the president made?

2. Go to the White House website and look at how the institutional structure of the Executive Office of the President and the White House staff are described. How does this description reflect the administration's current priorities in policy and public relations? What is missing?

Selected Readings

Barber, James David. *The Presidential Character.* 4th ed. New York: Pearson, Longman, 2009.

Burke, John P. *The Institutional Presidency: Organizing and Managing the White House from FDR to Clinton.* Baltimore: The Johns Hopkins University Press, 2000.

Bush, George W. *Decision Points.* New York: Crown, 2010.

Clinton, Bill. *My Life.* New York: Knopf, 2004.

George, Alexander L. "Assessing Presidential Character." In Aaron Wildavsky, ed., *Perspectives on the*

Presidency. Boston: Little, Brown, 1975, pp. 91–134.

George, Alexander L., and Juliette L. George. *Woodrow Wilson and Colonel House: A Personality Study.* New York: Dover Publications, 1956.

Greenstein, Fred I. *The Presidential Difference.* New York: Free Press, 2000.

Kumar, Martha Joynt, and Terry Sullivan, eds. *The White House World.* College Station, TX: Texas A&M University Press, 2003.

Kumar, Martha Joynt, and Terry Sullivan, eds. *The White House Transition Project: Institutional Memory Series.* 2008. http:// www.whitehousetransitionproject. org/#WHOseries.

Lewis, David E. *The Politics of Presidential Appointments: Political Control and Bureaucratic Performance.* Princeton, NJ: Princeton University Press, 2008.

Martin, Janet M. *The Presidency and Women.* College Station, TX: Texas A&M University Press, 2003.

Moe, Terry M. "The Politicized Presidency." In *The New Direction in American Politics,* edited by John E. Chubb and Paul E. Petersen. Washington, DC: Brookings Institution, 1985, pp. 235–271.

Obama, Barack. *The Audacity of Hope.* New York: Crown, 2006.

Patterson, Bradley H., Jr. *To Serve the President: Continuity and Innovation in the White House Staff.* Washington, DC: Brookings Institution, 2008.

Ponder, Daniel E. *Good Advice: Information and Policy Making in the White House.* College Station, TX: Texas A&M Press, 2000.

Reich, Robert. *Locked in the Cabinet.* New York: Alfred A. Knopf, 1997.

Renshon, Stanley A. *The Psychological Assessment of Presidential Candidates.* New York: New York University Press, 1996.

Sullivan, Terry, ed. *The Nerve Center: Lessons in Governing from the White House Chiefs of Staff.* College Station: Texas A&M University Press, 2004.

Walcott, Charles, and Karen M. Hult. "White House Structure and Decision Making: Elaborating the Standard Model." *Presidential Studies Quarterly* 35 (June 2005): 303–318.

Watson, Robert P. *The President's Wives: Reassessing the Office of First Lady.* Boulder, CO: Lynne Rienner, 2000.

Wayne, Stephen J. *Personality and Politics: Obama For and Against Himself.* Washington, DC: CQ Press, 2012.

Notes

1. Ten have come from five families: John Adams and John Quincy Adams (father and son) and George H. W. Bush and George W. Bush (father and son); William Henry Harrison and Benjamin Harrison (grandfather and grandson); Theodore Roosevelt and Franklin Roosevelt (first cousins); and James Madison and Zachary Taylor (who had common grandparents).

2. Although social and political position have given certain individuals an advantage in winning the presidency, it is much less clear whether that position contributes to success in office.

3. Political scientists are just beginning to examine the relationship between people's genetic structure and their political attitudes and activities. Much of this research examines identical twins that were separated and grew up in different environments. See John Alford, Caroline Funk, and John Hibbing, "Are Political Orientations Genetically Transmitted?" *American Political Science Review* 99 (November 2005): 153–169.

4. James David Barber, *The Presidential Character,* 4th ed. (New York: Pearson/ Longman, 2009).

5. Ibid. p. 5.

6. Ibid.

7. Ibid.

8. The study of personality is important, not only for those who wish to understand the "whys" of presidential behavior but also to those who must decide which

candidates have the temperament, style, and vision that is most likely to succeed in office. Helping the American electorate in its voting decisions was an important objective of Barber's work.

9. Barber, *The Presidential Character*, pp. 8–11.

10. Ibid, pp. 192–193. For a discussion of Eisenhower's activism, see Fred I. Greenstein, *The Hidden-Hand Presidency* (New York: Basic Books, 1982).

11. Alexander L. George, "Assessing Presidential Character," *World Politics* 26 (1974); this essay also appears in Aaron Wildavsky, ed., *Perspectives on the Presidency* (Boston: Little, Brown, 1975), pp. 91–134.

12. Stanley A. Renshon, *The Psychological Assessment of Presidential Candidates* (New York: Routledge, 1998).

13. Ibid., pp. 186–188.

14. Ibid., pp. 188–190.

15. William J. Clinton, quoted in David Maraniss, "Clinton's Life Shaped by Early Turmoil," *Washington Post*, January 26, 1992, pp. A1, A17.

16. John Brummett, "As Governor, Clinton Remade Arkansas in His Own Image," *New York Times*, March 31, 1992, p. A16.

17. George W. Bush, "In His Own Words," *Washington Post*, July 27, 1999, p. A11.

18. Barack Obama, *The Audacity of Hope*. New York: Crown, 2006, pp. 3, 205–206.

19. Ibid, p. 359.

20. Ibid, p. 40.

21. Ibid, p. 220.

22. Jann S. Wenner, "A Conversation with Barack Obama," *Rolling Stone*, July 10, 2008, http://www.rollingstone.com/news/coverstory/21472234.

23. Richard L. Berke, "Bush Is Providing Corporate Model for White House," *New York Times*, March 11, 2001, p. 18.

24. Stephen J. Wayne, "Working in the White House: Psychological Dimensions of the Job," paper presented at the annual meeting of the Southern Political Science Association, New Orleans, November 1977.

25. Richard L. Berke, "Inside the White House: Long Days, Late Nights," *New York Times*, March 21, 1993, p. 1.

26. Fred I. Greenstein, *The Presidential Difference* (New York, Free Press, 2000).

27. Ibid., pp. 55–66, 87–88, 132, 186.

28. Ibid., p. 195.

29. It may also be regarded by the president as privileged information, communication that presidents wish to protect. If Congress requests such information and presidents refuse to provide it, the federal judiciary may have to resolve the matter. Such a confrontation occurred in 2012 when President Obama ordered Attorney General Eric Holder not to provide a congressional committee with internal Justice Department memos on the investigation of an operation, known as "fast and furious," in which firearms were used to trace Mexican drug cartel activities. The House of Representatives, which had subpoenaed these documents, subsequently voted to hold the attorney general in contempt of Congress, thereby setting the stage for a legal battle with the White House.

30. The secretaries of certain department heads, the so-called inner cabinet—state, defense, justice, and the treasury—have tended to have closer and more collaborative relationships with the president than the secretaries of the other departments. Thomas E. Cronin, *The State of the Presidency* (Boston: Little, Brown, 1980), p. 283.

31. Bradley H. Patterson Jr., *To Serve the President: Continuity and Innovation in the White House Staff* (Washington, DC: Brookings Institution, 2008).

32. For a justification of the centralization and politicization of power in the presidency see, Terry M. Moe, "The Politicized Presidency," in J. E. Chubb and Paul E. Petersen eds., *New Directions in American Politics* (Washington, D.C.: Brookings Institution, 1985), pp. 235–271.

33. Hugh Heclo, *A Government of Strangers* (Washington, DC: Brookings, 1977); Francis Rourke, "Responsiveness and Neutral Competency in American Bureaucracy," *Public Administration Review* 52 (November/December 1992): 539–546.

34. Terry M. Sullivan, "Rescuing the Presidential Appointments Process,"

White House Transition Project. http:// whitehousetransitionproject.org /resources/briefing/WHIP-2009-01b.

35. David E. Lewis, *The Politics of Presidential Appointments: Political Control and Bureaucratic Performance* (Princeton, NJ: Princeton University Press, 2008).

36. Robert B. Reich, *Locked in the Cabinet* (New York: Knopf, 1997), pp. 108–109.

37. Richard L. Berke, "Bush Is Providing Corporate Model for White House," *New York Times*, March 11, 2001, p. A18.

38. Bob Woodward, *Plan of Attack* (New York: Simon and Schuster, 2004), pp. 266–270.

39. William C. Spragens, "White House Staffs, 1789–1974," in Bradley D. Nash et al., eds., *Organizing and Staffing the Presidency* (New York: Center for the Study of the Presidency, 1980), pp. 20–21.

40. Richard E. Neustadt, "Approaches to Staffing the Presidency," *American Political Science Review* 54 (December 1963): 857.

41. Fred I. Greenstein, *The Hidden Hand President* (New York: Basic Books, 1982).

42. President Gerald Ford interview with Martha Kumar, "Presidency Research Group's 2000 Transition Project," October 10, 2000, http:// www.whitehousetransitionproject.org.

43. Charles E. Walcott and Karen M. Hult, "Organizing the White House: Structure, Environment, and Organizational Governance," *American Journal of Political Science* 3 (February 1987): 109–125; Charles E. Walcott and Karen M. Hult, "White House Structure and Decision Making: Elaborating the Standard Model," *Presidential Studies Quarterly* 35 (June 2005): 303–318.

44. Richard Tanner Johnson, *Managing the White House: An Intimate Study of the Presidency* (New York: Harper and Row, 1974); Daniel E. Ponder, *Good Advice: Information and Policy Making in the White House* (College Station, TX: Texas A&M Press, 2000); and John P. Burke, "Organizational Structure and Presidential Decision Making," in George C. Edwards III and William G. Howell, eds., *The Oxford Handbook of the American Presidency* (Oxford: Oxford University Press, 2009): 501–527.

45. Alexander George, *Presidential Decisionmaking in Foreign Policy: The Effective Use of Information and Advice* (Boulder, CO: Westview Press, 1998); Roger Porter, "Economic Advice to the President: From Eisenhower to Reagan," *Political Science Quarterly* 98 (August 1983): 403–426; David Mitchell, "Does Context Matter? Advisory Systems and the Management of Foreign Policy Decision-Making Process," *Presidential Studies Quarterly* 40 (December 2010): 631–659.

46. John Adams, *The Works of John Adams*, vol. 1, ed. C. F. Adams (Boston: Little, Brown, 1850), p. 289.

47. Thomas Jefferson, *The Writings of Thomas Jefferson*, vol. 1, ed. P. L. Ford (New York: Putnam, 1896), pp. 98–99.

48. Woodrow Wilson, *Congressional Government* (New York: Meridian Books, 1956; originally printed in 1885), p. 162.

49. Whether Garner actually used the word "spit" or an even more objectionable word (a colloquial expression for urine) is subject to some controversy.

50. For a brief legal history of the evolution of the vice president's office, see Harold C. Relyea, "The Law: The Executive Office of the Vice President," *Presidential Studies Quarterly* 40 (June 2010): 327–341.

51. Bradley H. Patterson, Jr., *The Ring of Power* (New York: Basic Books, 1988), p. 287.

52. Doris Kearns, *Lyndon Johnson and the American Dream* (New York: Harper and Row, 1976), p. 164.

53. Spiro Agnew, Nixon's vice president, found his access to the president increasingly limited. Aides joked that Nixon kept the vice president under "house arrest" in the Executive Office Building even before Agnew was forced to resign for allegedly accepting kickbacks from Maryland contractors and failing to pay taxes on his illegal supplementary income. Neither Humphrey nor Agnew exercised major influence on the formulation of policy initiatives within their respective administrations.

54. Carter wrote in his memoirs that Mondale "received the same security

briefings I got, was automatically invited to participate in all my official meetings, and helped to plan strategy for domestic programs, diplomacy, and defense." Jimmy Carter, *Keeping Faith* (New York: Bantam Books, 1982), p. 39.

55. Joel K. Goldstein, "The Rising Power of the Modern Vice Presidency," *Presidential Studies Quarterly* 38 (September 2008): 371.

56. Patterson, *To Serve the President*, pp. 238–239.

57. Joel K. Goldstein, "The Contemporary Presidency: Cheney, Power, and the War on Terror," *Presidential Studies Quarterly* 40 (March 2010): 102–139.

58. Gene Smith, *When the Cheering Stopped: The Last Years of Woodrow Wilson* (New York: William Morrow, 1964).

59. Doris Kerns Goodwin, *No Ordinary Time: Franklin and Eleanor Roosevelt: The Home Front in World War II* (New York: Simon & Schuster, 1994).

60. Hillary Clinton attended cabinet meetings as well. Robert P. Watson, *The President's Wives: Reassessing the Office of First Lady* (Boulder, CO: Lynne Rienner, 2000), p. 56.

61. By law, no member of the president's immediate family may hold an appointive position within the federal government.

62. James Wilson as quoted in Madison's journal that appears in Max Farrand, ed., *Records of the Federal Convention*, vol. I (New Haven, CT: Yale University Press, 1921), p. 66.

7

PRESIDENTIAL DECISION MAKING

T he essence of the president's job is making decisions—about foreign affairs, economic policy, and literally hundreds of other important matters. The task is a difficult one, and there are many obstacles to making rational decisions. Leadership in the area of decision making is of a different nature than in the other arenas of presidential activity. Presidents need to ensure that they have before them a full range of options and the appropriate information necessary for evaluating them.

The president's leadership in decision making requires the establishment of a working relationship with subordinates and an organization in the White House that serves presidential decision-making needs. Often, presidents have to persuade their own appointees in the White House and the bureaucracy to provide the options and information that they require. However, these appointees have many incentives not to do so. Lack of time to consider decisions and previous commitments of the government may constrain a president's decision making, as may the president's own personal experiences and personality.

Presidents fitting the director model would have a full range of options and information at their disposal and be relatively unencumbered by environmental constraints on their range of choices. Presidents in the facilitating mode, conversely, would be more subject to the influence of contextual factors, more dependent on their environment for options and information, and thus more constrained in their decision making.

Figure 7.1 is a graphical representation of the influences on presidential decision making. In the outer circles are the broad contexts in which decisions take place; in the inner circles are the more immediate influences.

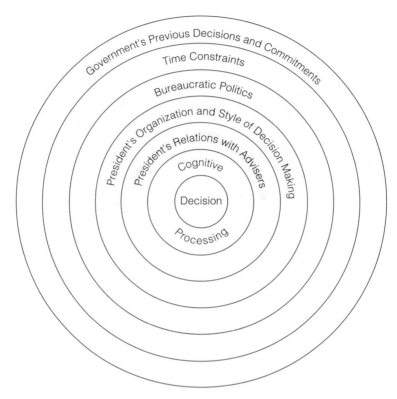

FIGURE 7.1 Influences on Presidential Decision Making

PREVIOUS COMMITMENTS

The first step in understanding presidential decision making is to recognize that presidents operate under severe constraints in their decision making, no matter what their approaches to making decisions are. As John Kennedy aide Theodore Sorensen observed:

> Presidents rarely, if ever make decisions . . . in the sense of writing their conclusions largely on a clean slate. They make choices. They select options. They exercise judgments. But the basic decisions, which confine their choices, have all too often been previously made by past events or circumstances, by other nations, by pressures or predecessors or even subordinates.[1]

Thus, the president's decisions usually fall within parameters set by prior commitments of the government that obligate it to spend money, defend allies, maintain services, or protect rights.[2] Thus, when Barack Obama took office in January 2009, he was not able to start from scratch and consider how best to allocate federal expenditures. Almost the entire federal budget was already committed before Obama took the oath of office. He could not choose, for example, to end health care for the indigent or eliminate the Navy. These public services were embodied in law.

The president is also constrained by the institutional capabilities of the executive branch, which are also products of past decisions. For example, the option of airlifting aid to a country experiencing famine is a viable one because the Air Force has a well-established airlift capability. However, rapidly allocating federal police officers to a city experiencing a crime wave is not feasible because the national government does not have a large police force. Similarly, in 2010 President Obama was not able to provide federal assistance when a BP oil well spilled millions of gallons of crude into the Gulf of Mexico because the government has no capability for doing this.

TIME CONSTRAINTS

The diverse obligations of the president and his top aides impose severe constraints on the amount of time they can devote to generating and evaluating options and information. According to a Jimmy Carter aide, "When the President asks to see all the potential alternatives, it is an impossible request [because] . . . it involves too much time."[3]

Overloaded advisers may rely on others, who may be equally overloaded, to bring crucial information to the attention of the president. Several of President Harry Truman's advisers believed there would be a serious danger of Chinese intervention in the Korean War if the president attempted to reunite all of Korea under a noncommunist government. However, no one went to him to argue that he should reverse his decision allowing General Douglas MacArthur to invade communist North Korea. Each person thought that someone else would do it.[4]

The president and his advisers rarely have the luxury of anticipating new issues. According to Jim Baker, secretary of state for President George H. W. Bush, due to the demise of the Soviet empire, the unification of Germany, the 1989 massacre in Tiananmen Square in Beijing, the Middle East peace process, and the civil wars in Central America, the administration paid little attention to Iraq prior to the invasion of Kuwait.[5] As former White House aide Jim Cicconi put it, "I can recall many instances when a White House [tried] long-term planning. In no instance that I can recall did it ever work. The White House is inexorably tugged toward the here and now, the immediate. It is the nature of the place."[6]

Fighting terrorism was not the highest priority for the George W. Bush administration in 2001. A cabinet-level meeting did not approve an antiterrorism plan until a week before the 9/11 attacks, and there was no further discussion among the president and his top advisers about al-Qaeda before the attacks. The president's chief adviser on terrorism never briefed him on the plan. The secretary of defense was focused on placing personnel in the Department of

White house is here and now [handwritten marginal note]

Defense and reviewing defense policy, and the Treasury Department was more concerned with high-level international fraud and the laundering of drug money than with terrorist financing.[7] Similarly, CIA Director George Tenet declared that the CIA was too busy with fighting al-Qaeda in 2002 to devote time to producing a high-quality national intelligence estimate on Iraq's possession of weapons of mass destruction (WMDs) before the United States invaded in March 2003.[8] Thus, the president did not make the organizational reforms necessary to combat terrorism before the 9/11 attacks.[9]

Sometimes deadlines make it necessary for the president and his aides to cease the consideration of information and options and make a decision. In the words of President Ronald Reagan's budget director David Stockman:

> I just wish that there were more hours in the day or that we didn't have to do this so fast. I have these stacks of briefing books and I've got to make decisions about specific options. . . . I don't have time, trying to put this whole package together in three weeks, so you just start making snap judgments.[10]

Because of such time limits, the less controversial parts of elaborate policies often receive inadequate attention.

ORGANIZATION AND STYLE OF DECISION MAKING

Each president is unique and has broad discretion in structuring the decision-making process in the White House. There are many ways to do this, and each has consequences for the effectiveness of the advisory system. In this section, we explore the ways in which the organization and style of the presidential advisory process can affect the president's consideration of options and information.

White House Organization

There is no ideal organization for the White House that is appropriate for every president. Political scientist Alexander George came to this conclusion: "There appears to be no single structural formula by which the chief executive and his staff can convert the functional expertise and diversity of viewpoints of the many offices concerned with international affairs into consistently effective policies and decisions."[11] We may confidently add that this is also true for domestic policy decisions.

The organization of the White House will inevitably reflect the personality and work habits of the incumbent. (For a discussion of the impact of personal style on presidential performance, see Chapter 6.) Moreover, the chief executive's personal style will dominate any organizational scheme, no matter what the organizational charts may say. If presidents have a penchant for acting without adequate study, they will defeat any advisory system they may have established in the White House. According to an experienced presidential aide, "The nature of the man is absolutely crucial and decisive, altogether overriding the issue of organization."[12] Henry Kissinger added that the influence of a presidential assistant "derives almost exclusively from the confidence of the President, not from administrative arrangements."[13]

Presidents may simultaneously use several approaches to organizing their decision making, depending on their level of interest in a policy area, their policy priorities, and the strengths and limitations of their principal advisers in each policy area. For example, President Gerald Ford employed a hierarchical model of centralized management for foreign policy, whereby he concentrated responsibility in Henry Kissinger's hands. In economic policy, he employed a managed multiple-advocacy system in which collegial discussions among a wider range of advisers occurred. In the area of domestic policy, where he did not want to undertake policy initiatives, he delegated responsibility to Vice President Nelson Rockefeller and dealt with issues on an ad hoc basis.[14] George H. W. Bush employed much the same structure in each of these policy areas.

Thus, it is possible to overemphasize the formal aspects of White House organization. As Kennedy aide Theodore Sorensen commented, "to ascribe to . . . form and structure a capacity to end bad decisions—is too often to overlook the more dynamic and fluid forces on which presidential decisions are based."[15] Nevertheless, organization does indeed make a difference.

The two most common White House organizational schemes are the hierarchical and the "spokes of the wheel." Even presidents like Ford, Carter, and Bill Clinton, who began their tenures trying to employ the latter approach, had to alter their organizational schemes to establish more hierarchical systems headed by a chief of staff to coordinate the flow of White House business. Someone has to be responsible for scheduling appointments, coordinating the paper flow, following up on decisions, and giving status reports on projects and policy development.[16]

hierarchical system is a must!

Presidents need their staff to give them time to focus on priorities and reflect on questions of basic strategy. The president's staff also needs to screen issues so that only those requiring the president's direct involvement will arrive on his desk. If he attempts to solve all the problems that come to the White House, the president will spread his attention and that of his advisers too thinly, wasting time and scarce resources. In addition, the more the president does, the more problems will arise for which others will hold him accountable. Presidents Ford, Carter, and Clinton all tended to become involved in relatively minor matters and were criticized, in some cases even by their own aides, for lacking the appropriate breadth of vision and understanding that are necessary to shape and guide the government.

Most presidents prefer for their principal advisers to reach agreement on recommendations on routine matters. This saves time and the cost of overruling senior officials. On major issues, however, presidents typically like to have alternatives.

Problem w/
→ honesty-guy]
broker

Hierarchical staff organizations save the president's time and promote thorough evaluation of the options, yet many observers of the presidency are concerned that a centrally managed system may aggravate the proclivity toward isolation that White Houses usually evidence over time. A hierarchy that screens information may distort it and insulate the president and those around him from both public and private criticism. Important decisions may also be made before they even reach the president. This occurred during Reagan's second term, when Chief of Staff Donald Regan unduly restricted the flow of people and paper into the Oval Office and isolated the president. The risk is that sufficient weight will not be given to countervailing views, and bad policy decisions and poor political judgments can result.

We should not assume that presidential aides can easily "capture" the president, however. Even in the Richard Nixon administration, which boasted a "palace guard" around the president, whatever isolation occurred in the Oval Office had the full concurrence and encouragement of the president. The president used his staff to serve his own needs and to keep out those individuals he did not want to see. As long-time presidential adviser Clark Clifford put it, "In the end, every President gets the advice—and the advisers—that, in his heart, he really wants."[17] Moreover, we lack systematic evidence that Nixon's chiefs of staff provided the president with a distorted view of the issues with which he dealt.

The Form of Advice

Different presidents prefer to receive advice in different forms. Presidents Nixon and Carter preferred to reach their decisions on the basis of written memoranda discussing the pros and cons of various options. In contrast, most recent presidents have used memos to focus the discussion but frequently explored the issues with advisers in relatively open settings. President Reagan had a more detached style, reading less than other recent presidents and instead talking directly to a small number of aides. Barack Obama likes to have a range of opinions argued before him.

There are advantages and disadvantages to both the verbal and paper approaches. The latter requires that options that go to the president be thoroughly "staffed out"—that is, that relevant officials comment on them following a careful analysis. This analysis decreases the chances that verbal fluency will overwhelm cool analysis and that a fleeting and superficial consensus will leave crucial assumptions unexamined. It also makes it more likely that recommendations will be translated into specific operational terms and that advisers will rigorously evaluate the consequences of the options they present to decision makers.[18]

Reviewing advice on paper saves the president time and protects the confidentiality of communications. It may also provide an outlet for those who find it difficult to express themselves directly to the president in order to articulate their views. It is not unusual for the most vociferous critic out of the president's presence to become the meekest lamb when meeting the president personally. People's oral skills often desert them when in the Oval Office. As Henson Moore, deputy chief of staff during the George H. W. Bush administration, put it, "It's just something about the Oval Office; there's something about the aura of the power of a president that people just won't say what really needs to be said to a president."[19]

However, face-to-face discussions with advisers may provide the president with information that is not reflected in the written word. Direct confrontation between advocates of diverse positions allows the participants to pinpoint their critiques of each other's positions and raise relevant follow-up points. Oral discussions also provide opportunities for advisers to highlight the most important points and crucial nuances in arguments and for presidents to learn the intensity of officials' views and the confidence with which they hold them. This may alert the chief executive to the level of support he may expect from officials who oppose his ultimate decision. In addition, some ideas, especially those that are highly sensitive, can be best, or perhaps only, advanced personally and informally in the give-and-take of conversation.

For reliance on oral communication to be effective, the president must not dominate the discussion. If he does, he may not devote sufficient attention to the advice he receives and may influence that advice by his comments. According to Hamilton Jordan, Carter's White House chief of staff:

> I had learned . . . that if I wanted to change his mind or challenge him on something that was important or complicated, it was best to do it in writing. If I went into his office to argue with him, armed with five reasons to do something, I would rarely get beyond point one before he was aggressively countering it. I seldom got to the second or third point.[20]

When personally confronted, President Carter may have gone on the defensive; written differences of opinion were perhaps easier for him to accept.

Multiple Advocacy

→ *against one source of information*

Closely related to the form in which presidents receive advice is the range of options they receive and the effectiveness with which those options are presented. The president needs to hear a wide range of options, vetted by neutral parties who have no personal stake in them. He should not be dependent on a single channel of information, as occurred, for example, when the president and other high officials, including the Joint Chiefs of Staff, relied on the CIA's estimates of the success of the 1961 invasion of Cuba at the Bay of Pigs. Moreover, only the CIA evaluated the Bay of Pigs plan, with disastrous consequences.

Quality decision making requires more than simply presenting the president with a diversity of views. It is also necessary that an effective advocate represent each point of view. This is not always the case, however, because differences exist among advisers in persuasive skills, intellectual ability, policy expertise, power, status, standing with the president, and analytical staff support. These disparities may distort the decision-making process by giving some viewpoints an undue advantage. As Theodore Sorensen observed, "The most formidable debater is not necessarily the most informed, and the most reticent may sometimes be the wisest."[21]

Presidents need advice that gives them a manageable amount of useful information that relates to real-world options. Multiple advocacy forces a large number of issues to the top—that is, to the president. Debate and give-and-take on issues require a substantial commitment of time on the part of both the president and his staff, and time is a scarce commodity in the White House. According to a Ford assistant: "We don't have time to make sure all the advisors have access to the President."[22]

A multiple-advocacy system also requires that the president want to hear the effective presentation of a wide range of views. The president may not be interested in hearing much about some issues. Some presidents may simply not want to hear the effective presentation of a wide range of views. Bill Clinton and Barack Obama are notable for typically examining issues from every angle, although this sometimes led to policy drift. Obama is careful to include representatives of an array of opinions and often seeks information from expert advisers to senior officials. He also insists on being offered more than one viable option.[23]

In order for debate among advisers and the chief executive to be useful, the president must be able to accommodate the interpersonal tensions inherent in an advisory system of close give-and-take. However, not all presidents possess this tolerance. Ronald Reagan hated conflict, as did Richard Nixon, whose personality was not amenable to dealing with oral confrontations. Thus, Nixon conducted as much business as possible by memos. In fact, his aversion to open disagreement both affected the quality of his decision-making process and led him to alter policy decisions to achieve consensus. According to national security assistant Henry Kissinger:

> So much time, effort, and ingenuity were spent in trying to organize a consensus of the senior advisers that there was too little left to consider the weaknesses in the plan or to impose discipline on the rest of the government.[24]

Multiple advocacy also runs a considerable risk of increasing staff conflict. Presidents must engage in the delicate balancing act of being in firm control of the process of decision making while encouraging free and open discussion. This is difficult enough to accomplish while they are considering options. It is even more of a challenge after they decide on a course of action because it is not uncommon for both winners and losers among presidential advisers to be less than gracious and turn to backstabbing and leaking information to the press.

Some political scientists have suggested that the president needs a process manager to balance the resources of his advisers and strengthen the weaker advocates, ensure that all options are articulated and have effective advocates, set up additional channels of information, arrange for independent evaluations of decisional premises and options when necessary, and generally monitor the decision-making process and identify and correct any malfunctions. This delicate role can easily be undermined if the custodian is also a policy adviser, presidential spokesperson, enforcer of decisions, administrative operator, or watchdog for the president's power stakes. He or she must remain an "honest broker" who is concerned with the process of advising the president. This adviser must also keep his or her own staff small so that it will not become specialized and circumvent established channels of advice.[25]

In some decision-making situations, an adviser may adopt the role of "devil's advocate" in order to provide a challenge to the dominant point of view. The devil's advocate may relieve some of the stress of decision making because officials feel they have considered all sides of an issue, and there may be some public relations benefits for publicizing the fact that the president considered a full range of views. Decision makers may also benefit from listening to and rebutting challenges to their course of action, and those who are least enthusiastic about a decision may be more willing to join in a consensus view if there was prior debate.

Nevertheless, the devil's advocate does not necessarily improve the quality of White House decision making. Because the devil's advocate is playing a role and is not a true dissenter, he or she is unlikely to persist in opposition or try to form coalitions or employ all resources to persuade others. Such an advocate is not really engaged in a truly competitive struggle. Moreover, officials may discount ahead of time the comments of someone who persistently plays the devil's advocate role. Nonetheless, if devil's advocacy is not routinized, there is no assurance that it will operate when needed to provide balance to an argument.

Presidential Involvement

In his classic study of presidential power, Richard Neustadt alerted future presidents that they would need information, including tangible details, to construct a necessary frame of reference for decision making.[26] Presidents cannot assume that any person or advisory system will provide them with the options and information they require, and thus they must be actively involved in the decision-making process, setting the tone for other participants, maintaining the integrity of the advisory system, and reaching out widely for options and information. When presidents fail to follow these principles, the consequences may be profound.

Maintaining the Process
Despite their different styles, every president needs a systematic process for decision making, and it is up to the president to maintain that process. Failure to do so may lead to the haphazard consideration of options and information. Early in his tenure, Barack Obama was insensitive to organizational issues, and the White House advisory and policy development process suffered from disorganization and distortion in the personnel and options included in important discussions.[27]

In general, the George W. Bush White House lacked a process to ensure that the right questions—such as the consequences of actions—were asked and answered or that alternatives were considered.[28] Even many of the leading policy makers and advisers complained that the policy process was dysfunctional.[29] Secretary of Defense Donald Rumsfeld felt that the president did not always receive, and may not have insisted on, a timely consideration of his options before he made a decision. Rumsfeld also found National Security Council meetings often to be disorganized, decisions to be poorly summarized, and discussion papers late in arriving to the participants.[30]

diverting information

Vice President Cheney's office sometimes diverted information from the president[31] or took information directly to Bush without the normal interagency review.[32] Some officials injected raw, unvetted intelligence directly into discussions regarding the war in Iraq.[33] Senior officials also sometimes used back channels and informal meetings for real decisions, short circuiting debate and interagency reviews.[34]

In meetings of top officials, the secretaries of state and defense generally did not comment on each other's statements or views,[35] so Bush missed the benefit of serious, substantive discussion between his principal advisers. Moreover, the president did not force a discussion or support his national security assistant in efforts to intervene to compel the secretary of defense to answer critical questions about the war in Iraq. Nor did the president press for resolution of differences or contradictions in evaluations and recommendations among his advisers.[36] We will see later that the president also did not push his top officials to focus on the basic premises of U.S. policy.

Probing Questions

Barack Obama has a reputation for asking probing questions that challenge assumptions.[37] In contrast, in 1986 President Ronald Reagan approved a proposal to sell arms to Iran in hopes of obtaining the release of American hostages held in the Middle East without insisting on thorough staff work on the initiative. In the end, the policy was a failure and undermined the nation's strongly asserted position of refusing to trade arms—or anything else—for hostages. In addition, the president's standing fell substantially in the polls, diminishing his political clout. The situation became even worse when the diversion of funds to the Contras came to light, and Reagan had to endure a year of congressional hearings and a critical investigation by a special commission examining his handling of the matter.

A series of books written by top officials in the Reagan administration reveal that the president was a peculiarly detached decision maker. He had strong views on the basic goals of public policy but left it to others to implement his broad vision. Aides prepared detailed scripts on index cards for his use in meetings. Reagan's detachment and lack of mastery of policy details hindered his evaluation of policy options, a process he left to others. As he explained in his memoirs, "Because I was so concerned about getting the hostages home, I may not have asked enough questions about how the Iranian initiative was being conducted."[38]

Two of the most important events of the past generation have been the September 11, 2001, terrorist attacks on the United States and the U.S.

invasion of Iraq in 2003. The terrorist attacks caught the country by surprise. The United States invaded Iraq on the premise that it possessed substantial stocks of WMDs. In both cases, there were serious problems with the information the president received. The George W. Bush White House portrayed the president and his top advisers as consumers of imprecise intelligence, making the best decisions they could in a murky world of secret plots and illicit programs.

There is another view, however. President Bush often described himself as an instinctual decision maker,[39] a view shared by other close observers.[40] A drawback to relying on instinct is acting impulsively rather than delving deeply into a range of possible options. Gut reactions also discourage investing time in soliciting and cultivating the views of others and asking probing questions of advisers.

In addition, Bush seemed to be intellectually passive, lacking inquisitiveness and resisting reflection, which also discouraged tough questioning and thorough analysis.[41] Rather than complicated, rigorous analysis of what policies should be, his intellectual curiosity focused on reaching the bottom line of a solution and knowing what he needed to do to sell and implement his policies.[42] Such an approach may not do justice to issues such as terrorism that are laced with subtlety and nuance.

When the CIA briefed the president on August 6, 2001, about the threat from al-Qaeda, he did not follow up with questions, instructions, or discussions with his top advisers.[43] When the president expressed dismay at the CIA's information regarding Iraq's possession of WMDs following a briefing on December 21, 2002, CIA Director George Tenet replied that the case was a "slam dunk." Instead of pushing the CIA to reexamine its data or to obtain better information, Bush relied on Tenet's reassurance.[44] Bush later concluded, "In retrospect, of course, we all should have pushed harder on the intelligence and revisited our assumptions. But at the time, the evidence and the logic pointed in the other direction."[45] It is at such times that reassessments may be most crucial.

Actually, the White House never requested an intelligence estimate on Iraq before the invasion; Democrats on the Senate Intelligence Committee requested a National Intelligence Estimate. When the CIA produced the estimate, the White House did not engage in a thorough assessment of the evidence.[46] Indeed, Bush often failed to ask experts and relevant officials probing questions, including what they thought about an issue.[47] For example, after the president met with David Kay, the chief U.S. weapons inspector, who reported on the lack of evidence of WMDs, Bush seemed disengaged. "I'm not sure I've spoken to anyone at that level who seemed less inquisitive," Kay recalled.[48] Even when it came to going to war, he decided early to go to war without systematic, rigorous internal debate of the pros and cons of doing so.[49] He also did not ask the opinion of many of his chief advisers.[50] As a result, although both Secretary of State Colin Powell and CIA Director George Tenet opposed going to war, neither ever told Bush.[51] Thinking you already know where your advisers stand, as Bush did,[52] is not the same as having them debate an issue in front of you.

Similarly, well-placed officials in the administration were skeptical about the intelligence on WMDs in Iraq, but an effective expression of these views apparently did not reach Bush,[53] at least partly because he did not encourage dissent. In fact, the president's emphasis on expressing certainty and optimism[54] rather than engaging in substantive policy debate regarding Iraq discouraged officials from reconsidering policy, even when it was clear that it was failing.[55] Nuanced analysis is incompatible with certainty.

Bush's lack of inquisitiveness, failure to ask probing questions, and disinterest in rigorous policy analysis discouraged coherent discussions about policy and led to carelessness in evaluating options. Top officials never systematically discussed disbanding the Iraqi army, de-Baathification of the Iraqi public service,[56] or the controversial questions regarding detainees and electronic surveillance.[57] In retrospect, the president concluded he should have insisted on more debate on such decisions.[58]

The president's approach also delayed reaction to realities such as the insurgency in Iraq and deterred advice that ran counter to his instincts.[59] Thus, in the president's words, it "took four painful, costly years" to change U.S. military policy in post-invasion Iraq.[60] At that point, Bush authorized a thorough review of U.S. policy in Iraq. "I wanted to challenge every assumption behind our strategy and generate new options," he reported. After gathering facts and options from inside and outside the administration, he challenged assumptions and weighed all the options carefully.[61] Ultimately, he decided to support the "surge" option, which proved to be successful.

Reaching Out

Bill Clinton was blindsided by the negative congressional and public response to his proposal to lift the ban on homosexuals in the military. He saw the issue as one of discrimination, but many others saw it in other terms—as an issue of morality, of military readiness, or both. By not seeking other perspectives, the president subjected himself to a firestorm of criticism and had to backtrack on his policy. Similarly, at the end of his administration Clinton issued a large number of pardons, bypassing the normal vetting process for pardons. He was widely criticized for pardoning people who had used family and political connections to get their cases to the Oval Office.

One reason the George W. Bush White House was so slow to recognize the disaster occurring in New Orleans in the wake of Hurricane Katrina is that it was primarily dependent on one line of communication about conditions in the flooded city. It took the president some days to realize that the levees had been breached and the terrible conditions of people trapped at the convention center—or even that there were people there at all.[62] Much of the rest of America knew these facts, however, and never forgave the president for his reaction to the worst natural disaster in a century. Bush also did not consult with people outside the White House on Iraq and relied heavily on his national security assistant to drive the reevaluation of U.S. strategy in Iraq.[63] Once again, the president suffered the loss of the public's confidence.

RELATIONSHIPS WITH ADVISERS

Presidents require the services of personal aides to carry out their duties. Because they must rely heavily on their aides and work closely with them, they naturally choose people of similar attitudes and compatible personalities. Moreover, strong personalities—and most presidents have them—create environments to their liking and weed out irritations.

Disagreeing with the President

Many—perhaps most—people have found it difficult to stand up to a president and disagree with him. For example, several of President Reagan's top aides had doubts about his economic policies even in 1981 but did not relay them to the president until after the program was enacted. At times, advisers may be strong advocates of a position before a meeting with the president yet will completely switch their arguments during the meeting if they learn the president has accepted the opposite view. It was because of this phenomenon that President Kennedy often absented himself from meetings of his advisers during the Cuban missile crisis—he wanted the participants to feel free to speak their minds.

Cartoon. "All those in favor say 'Aye.'"

© The New Yorker Collection 1979 Henry Martin from cartoonbank.com. All Rights Reserved.

Sometimes advisers find it difficult to disagree with the president due to his strong, dynamic, or magnetic personality. These traits are certainly not unusual in successful politicians, especially presidents. For example, former White House assistant Chester Cooper wrote that President Lyndon Johnson often polled his foreign policy advisers one at a time to hear their views on the Vietnam War. Each dutifully would respond, "I agree," even though Cooper, and undoubtedly others, did not. Cooper even dreamed of answering no, but he never did.[64] Other Johnson administration officials reported a similar tendency for those around the president to tell him what they thought he wanted to hear about the war rather than what they really thought.

One reason for the reluctance of presidential aides to challenge the president is that they are completely dependent on him for their jobs, their advancement, and the gratification of their egos through his favor. Cabinet members are nearly as dependent, although they may also have support in Congress or from interest groups. Because aides usually desire to perpetuate their positions, they may refrain from giving the president "unpleasant" information or from fighting losing battles on behalf of their principles. Even Nixon's White House chief of staff, H. R. Haldeman, felt that in order to survive in his own job, he could not fight sufficiently to counter the dark side of the president's character.

Thus, presidents often find it difficult to evoke critical responses from staff members. Gerald Ford made this observation:

> Few people, with the possible exception of his wife, will ever tell a President that he is a fool. There's a majesty to the office that inhibits even your closest friends from saying what is really on their minds. They won't tell you that you just made a lousy speech or bungled a chance to get your point across. . . . You can tell them you want the blunt truth; you can leave instructions on every bulletin board, but the guarded response you get never varies.
>
> And yet the president—any president—needs to hear straight talk. He needs to be needled once in a while, if only to be brought down from the false pedestal that the office provides. He needs to be told that he is, after all, only another human being with the same virtues and weaknesses as anyone else. And he needs to be reminded of this constantly if he's going to keep his perspective.[65]

Discouraging Advice

An executive who "punishes" those aides who present options or information he dislikes may reinforce the reluctance of advisers to disagree with the president. Lyndon Johnson was such a person. He forced top aides and officials who dissented on Vietnam to leave his administration, and he went so far as to reduce contact with such key people as Secretaries of Defense Robert McNamara and Clark Clifford and Vice President Hubert Humphrey. In response to a cautionary memo from Humphrey about Vietnam, Johnson said "we don't need all these memos" and excluded him from his inner circle.[66]

Johnson's press secretary, George Reedy, observed that the Johnson White House had an inner political life of its own. Consequently, the staff carefully studied the president's state of mind to gain and maintain access to him. They wanted to be around when there was good news to report and discreetly absent when the news was bad in hopes that someone else would receive the blame.[67] Naturally, this gamesmanship served to distort Johnson's view of reality.

Richard Nixon had little interest in hearing critiques of his weak points, and those who attempted to criticize him did not maintain their influence for long. Even as secure and personable a president as Franklin Roosevelt is reported to have permitted only staffers who would not challenge him. Bill Clinton was generally open to a range of views, but he had a hot temper, which he frequently unleashed at aides.

The dampening effect of behavior like that of Johnson, Nixon, or Clinton on discussions even outside the Oval Office can be substantial. Aides may be fearful of presidential punishment or tirades and therefore remain silent lest they provoke the president to anger. Johnson's Office of Congressional Relations chief Lawrence O'Brien and Vice President Hubert Humphrey were in constant contact for months before they became aware of each other's views on Vietnam. Because President Johnson equated criticism with disloyalty, even the highest officials in the White House kept their dissent to themselves.

There was a similar phenomenon in the George W. Bush White House, which put a premium on loyalty and team play. As a result, at least some officials did not deliver bad news to the president or sugarcoated it in order to remain in the president's good graces.[68] When the administration publicly rebuked and undermined Army Chief of Staff General Eric K. Shinseki after he testified to Congress that it would take several hundred thousand troops to stabilize Iraq after the invasion, it sent a chilling message through the military and discouraged other generals from requesting troops.[69]

The Bush administration also employed more subtle tactics to influence the information intelligence agencies presented to it. Officials, especially Vice President Richard Cheney and his chief of staff, Scooter Libby, persistently asked the CIA questions regarding Saddam Hussein's ties to terrorists. Some analysts chafed at this constant drumbeat of repetitive questions. More importantly, despite no obvious pressure to change answers, officials' questions and visits to CIA headquarters created an environment that subtly but unmistakably influenced the agency's work. As the president's commission on intelligence failures regarding Iraq concluded, "it is hard to deny that intelligence analysts worked in an environment that did not encourage skepticism about the conventional wisdom." There are many opportunities for bias when the evidence is fragmentary and uncertain, which can be expressed in caveat, nuance, and word choice. Moreover, reeling from its failure to predict the 9/11 attacks, the CIA could not assess intelligence free of the administration's assumptions and the obvious context that the United States was going to war. The vice president's statements of uncertain and ambiguous intelligence as facts skewed the balance of considerations the analysts were weighing. Some skeptical CIA officials were shunted aside while more hawkish officials found it easy to get their reports to the attention of the CIA leadership and other high officials, who did not want to hear skepticism. There was widespread acceptance of weak intelligence. A Department of Energy edict to scientists not to talk to the media about aluminum tubes suspected (wrongly) of being part of a nuclear weapons program prevented them from challenging the CIA's analysis and sent fear throughout the department's nuclear labs.[70]

Presidents with heightened fears of security leaks may place loyalty above competence, independence, or openness among their advisers. They may also control the information flow tightly and keep everyone, even insiders, in the dark. One of the reasons why President Johnson relied so heavily on a group of five or six high officials (called the "Tuesday lunch group") to advise him on the Vietnam War was that he felt the larger National Security Council leaked too much information. According to Secretary of State Dean Rusk, "The Tuesday luncheons were where the really important issues regarding Vietnam were discussed in great detail. This was where the real decisions were made. And everyone there knew how to keep his mouth shut."[71]

Ironically, one inhibition on freedom of dissension in the White House and the upper levels of the bureaucracy is public opinion. If the president allows an open discussion of policy views, there will inevitably be disagreement, which the press may present as evidence that the president is not in control and the White House lacks a sense of direction—or even that it is in disarray. Thus, by being open, the president may lose some public support, but by being closed to options and information, he may make poor decisions.

Not all presidents discourage dissent, however. George H. W. Bush was a secure decision maker who was well informed, knowledgeable, experienced, and involved in decision making. He wanted to hear a wide range of options, and he worked at maintaining civility and openness in discussion. Similarly, Dwight Eisenhower established an environment in which his advisers felt free to challenge his views. Barack Obama appears to be following the same pattern.

Groupthink

Psychologist Irving Janis argued that another factor discouraging disagreement among presidential advisers is a psychological phenomenon he termed *groupthink*. Groupthink refers to the conformist thinking that may result when people are intensely involved in small, cohesive decision-making groups, such as are formed during crisis situations. According to Janis, the stress of a crisis generates a desire for unity among policy advisers that, in turn, reduces their uncertainty over the proper course of action and helps to preserve their emotional well-being. The advisers' desire for unanimity overrides their motivations to appraise situations and policy alternatives realistically. They suspend critical opinions and produce a consensus.[72] The groupthink effect may have influenced a number of high-level administration decisions.

The ill-fated decision by almost all of President Kennedy's advisers to support an invasion of the Bay of Pigs in Cuba in 1961 is one illustration that Janis used to support his thesis. Other examples of conformist—and incorrect—decision making include the failure to anticipate the Japanese attack on Pearl Harbor, the North Korean attacks on South Korea that began the Korean War, and the initial thinking on Vietnam at the beginning of the Johnson administration.

Staff Rivalries

Feuding and infighting for power and access to the president among ambitious aides are also obstacles to rational decision making. This rivalry takes several forms. One of the most common techniques is to attack rivals through leaking to the press that they are out of favor with the president or not competent to carry out their duties. Sometimes the leaks place competitors for power in a context that is favorable but will displease the president, who may prefer having credit and publicity for himself rather than his aides.

In recent years, the Nixon, Ford, and Reagan administrations stand out for the extent of their internal feuding and infighting. One high-level Reagan aide disclosed how he and other White House officials tried to undercut Secretary of State Alexander Haig: "In a classic case of Washington infighting, we threw virtually every booby trap in his way that we could, planted every story, egged the press on to get down on him."[73]

This widespread feuding encourages self-interested behavior by presidential advisers, which may distort their vision and cause them to overextend their arguments and present unbalanced discussions of options and their consequences to the president. There is also a tendency for competing advisers to seek to aggrandize influence and monopolize the counsel on which presidents base decisions, thereby providing insufficient information, analysis, and deliberation for decisions. Staff rivalry also detracts from the efficiency of White House operations, as it wastes time and lowers morale. Moreover, feuding in the White House can embarrass the president if it is covered in the press (which it inevitably is).

High officials in Washington know that their ability to interact effectively with the bureaucracy depends on being known for their effectiveness with the president. Former Secretary of State Dean Rusk argued that "the real organization of government at higher echelons is . . . how confidence flows down from the President."[74] To maintain their reputations for effectiveness with the president, officials may not strongly advocate positions that they consider sound if they feel the president is unlikely to adopt their proposals. An official does not usually want to be known as someone whose advice the president rejected.

Loss of Perspective

An additional potential hindrance to sound advice for the president is the loss of perspective by White House aides. Because working in the White House is a unique experience, a narrowing of viewpoints can easily occur. Especially for top aides, the environment is luxurious, secure, and heady; the exercise of power is an everyday experience. The potential for isolation is real, and therefore the chief executive must fight these insulating tendencies. President Johnson was very sensitive about the risk that his aides might lose perspective, so he closely controlled the use of White House perks and stripped his staff of pretensions with a "merciless persistency."[75]

Role Conceptions

Advisers' conceptions of their jobs influence their delivery of information and options. President Eisenhower's secretaries of defense, Charles Wilson and Neil McElroy, considered themselves managers of the department and did not become heavily involved in disputes over foreign policy or strategic doctrine. By contrast, Secretary of Defense Robert McNamara adopted an aggressive stance as an adviser; yet McNamara's colleague, Secretary of State Dean Rusk, did not consider it his job to participate in policy disputes with his colleagues or the president. In fact, many observers thought that Rusk failed to present effectively State Department views on important foreign policy issues.

Similarly, Secretary of State Condoleezza Rice did not see it as her role to criticize prominent officials with whom she disagreed such as Vice President Cheney or Secretary of Defense Donald Rumsfeld.[76] Her predecessor as George W. Bush's secretary of state, Colin Powell, met privately with the president to express concerns about war in Iraq rather than speaking frankly in front of other senior advisers who were pressing forward with battle plans. Powell and Secretary of Defense Donald Rumsfeld frequently disagreed but did not confront each other face to face.[77]

Box 7.1   The Impact of the Decision-Making Process

Presidents Eisenhower and Johnson both faced the decision of military intervention in Vietnam (in 1954 and 1964–1965, respectively). Eisenhower chose not to intervene, whereas Johnson eventually sent more than a half million American troops. How did the two presidents' decision-making processes affect their decisions?

Eisenhower, who had headed organizations of enormous size and complexity as a military commander, was sensitive about the impact of the structure of advisory systems on the process of analyzing policies and making decisions. His system produced spirited, open debate; his aides would challenge the president, often tenaciously, even though he openly expressed his own opinions. He was exposed to diverse views (rather than "loaded" presentations of options), sharply focused alternatives, and advice separated from parochial interests. In addition, he supplemented his formal advisory system with an informal, fluid process of consultation that interacted with, and reinforced, the formal system.

Eisenhower was clearly in charge and kept his options open. He reasoned explicitly about the means and ends, the trade-offs, and the consequences of options, and he thought strategically, viewing issues as parts of more comprehensive patterns. In this way, he set the tone for decision making in his administration.

Johnson, in contrast, was insensitive to the impact of advisory structures.

His advisory system was organizationally chaotic, marked by an absence of regular meetings and routinized procedures, shifts in the membership of advisory and decision-making groups, a reliance on out-of-channel advocacy, weak staff work, and other impediments to rigorous policy analysis.

Johnson's heavy reliance on informal advising by a few people and a lack of systematized staff work left many policy disagreements unresolved and unexamined. Frequently, options were neither coherently assembled nor carefully considered, and there was a lack of broad strategic debate in which the underlying assumptions of policy could be questioned. Policy differences at all levels were typically not sharply stated or directly analyzed, and there was a lack of forums in which contradictory views could be clarified, studied, and debated. The views of most dissenters were not rejected after discussion; instead, they were simply not discussed. The lack of systematic policy analysis and the reliance on a few advisers left the upper and lower levels of the foreign policy community separated, and the impact of advice became more a function of skill and resources in bureaucratic politics than the logic of the argument.

In many ways, the president was his own worst enemy. He immersed himself in detail rather than focusing on broad policy questions, and he was insulated from confrontation with his advisers' views. Johnson failed to press for additional alternatives or question incisively the options presented to him. Continuing the pattern of his years in the Senate, he remained preoccupied with searching for consensus within, and probing for areas of agreement rather than disagreement. His personal interactions with his advisers encouraged a narrowing rather than a broadening of options, and his intolerance of disagreement had a chilling effect on the range of advice he received.

In sum, Eisenhower was a planner and conceptualizer, whereas Johnson was an individualistic political operator. Eisenhower was preoccupied with analyzing policy; Johnson, with the politics of making it. Each constructed an advisory system to meet his needs. At least in the case of Vietnam, these advisory systems, as well as the people who composed them and the presidents themselves, made a difference in the options the president chose.[78]

COGNITIVE PROCESSING

Presidents and their advisers, no matter how accomplished, are human beings, subject to the same tendencies and limitations as less prominent people. They have views about the nature of the problems the country faces and appropriate policies to deal with them. They also have cognitive needs that condition their processing of information, evaluating considering options, and making decisions.

Impact of Worldviews

Presidents and their aides bring to office sets of beliefs about politics, policy, human nature, and social causality—in other words, beliefs about how and why the world works as it does. These beliefs provide a frame of reference for evaluating policy options, for filtering information and giving it meaning, and for establishing potential boundaries of action. Beliefs also help busy officials cope with complex decisions to which they can devote limited time, and they predispose people to act in certain directions. Although sets of beliefs are inevitable and help to simplify the world, they can be dysfunctional as well.

There is a psychological bias toward continuity that results from the physiology of human cognitive processes that are reinforced from thinking a certain way and are difficult to reorganize. As a result, there is an unconscious tendency to see what we expect to see, which distorts our analytical handling of evidence and produces what is called a confirmation bias.

Worldviews may distort the identification of a problem that requires attention. Surprise attacks by one country on another—unfortunately, not a rare occurrence—perhaps most dramatically illustrate this phenomenon.[79] The George H. W. Bush White House was surprised when Iraq invaded Kuwait in 1990, even though it had obtained substantial evidence of a massive military buildup on the Kuwaiti border. As Secretary of State Jim Baker put it, no one believed that Saddam Hussein would attack because an attack made no sense from the perspective of those who calculated his interests.[80]

It is natural to assume foreign leaders are rational as Americans understand rationality, so we frequently misread the intentions of other countries. The United States did not anticipate the Soviet Union's invasion of Afghanistan because we knew it would be a mistake. We could not believe Mikhail Gorbachev was serious about reforms because we knew they would undermine the stability of the USSR and thus his position. It did not occur to us in 1941 that Japan thought we would be willing to fight and lose a limited war, and we could not believe Nikita Khrushchev would place Soviet missiles in Cuba.[81] We were surprised by the Indian nuclear weapons test in 1998 because it did not seem in India's best interests.[82]

The Bush administration operated on several basic premises regarding the aftermath of the war in Iraq, such as that Iraqis would greet Americans as liberators, that the Iraqi infrastructure would be in serviceable condition, that the army would remain in whole units capable of being used for reconstruction, that the Iraqi police were trustworthy and professional and thus capable of securing the country, and that there would be a smooth transition to creating a democratic nation. Each of these premises was faulty, but the administration made no systematic evaluation of them before the war and was slow to challenge them, even in the wake of widespread violence.[83]

At other times, worldviews may encourage policy makers to *assume* problems rather than subject their premises to rigorous analysis. Because after 9/11 the Bush White House was highly risk adverse[84] and because it was certain that Saddam Hussein possessed WMDs and was a threat to the United States, the administration never organized a systematic internal debate within the administration on the fundamental questions of whether Iraq actually possessed WMDs, whether the Iraqi threat was imminent, whether it was necessary to overthrow Saddam, and, if so, the likely consequences of such an action. Instead, it focused on the question of how to invade successfully.[85] As the national intelligence officer for the Middle East put it, the Bush administration "went to war without requesting . . . any strategic-level intelligence assessments on any aspect of Iraq."[86] Moreover, it does not appear that either the president or his national security assistant studied closely the National Intelligence Estimate done before the war at Congress's request or followed up on the dissents and caveats in the assessment.[87]

It is not surprising, then, that the weakness of the data on Iraq never called into question the quality of basic assumptions. Officials did not interpret the absence of evidence of WMDs as evidence of their absence. Instead, U.S. officials viewed Saddam Hussein's efforts to remove any residue from his old programs to develop WMDs as efforts to *hide* the weapons rather than destroy them.[88] Moreover, it seemed implausible that Saddam would risk destruction of his regime if he had actually met international demands regarding WMDs.[89] We did not account for Saddam's own view that he could not be too open about his compliance for fear of showing weakness in a dangerous part of the world.[90] In addition, officials remembered that the United States had underestimated Iraq's progress in developing nuclear weapons in the late 1980s and early 1990s and inferred that Iraq had WMD because it had such a complex organization dedicated to concealing them.[91] In other words, they saw what they expected to see.

The consensus of top officials that a Vietnam free of communism was important to the security and credibility of the United States, that the war-torn country was a critical testing ground for the ability of the United States to counter communist support for wars of national liberation, that communism was a world conspiracy, that South Vietnam would fall to North Vietnam without American aid, and that if South Vietnam did fall to the communists, the rest of Southeast Asia would follow molded the decisions about U.S. participation in the Vietnam War. This doctrinal consensus made it difficult to challenge U.S. policy and foreclosed policy options such as not escalating the fighting. As a result, "no comprehensive and systematic examination of Vietnam's importance to the United States was ever undertaken within the executive branch. Debates revolved around how to do things better and whether they could be done, not whether they were worth doing."[92]

The worldviews of top decision makers also affect the options they raise to deal with issues and the choices they make. President Reagan believed that the Soviet Union would only enter into serious negotiations with the United States if it were facing an overwhelmingly powerful military force. Consequently, Reagan believed he had no choice but to increase military spending substantially, which he did.

In a crisis, a president's view of a problem and the need to respond to it decisively may foreclose alternatives that do not put a premium on rapid and decisive action. For example, in the period directly preceding the actual fighting in the Persian Gulf War, General Colin Powell, then chairman of the Joint Chiefs of Staff, wanted to consider the option of continuing economic sanctions against Iraq. President George H. W. Bush, however, told him there was not time to try such a strategy.[93]

Managing Inconsistency

The environment in which the president operates is complex and uncertain, characteristics with which the human mind is not comfortable. People prefer stable views to a continuous consideration of options. About a month before the commencement of hostilities in the Gulf War, George H. W. Bush told an interviewer: "I've got it boiled down very clearly to good and evil. And it helps if you can be that clear in your own mind."[94]

Presidents have to find a level of consistency with which they are comfortable and that is compatible with their intellectual capacities and psychological needs. This may be a difficult task. Decision makers often experience stress as they try to cope with the complexity of decisions, especially in times of crisis. Warren Harding, Ronald Reagan, and sometimes George W. Bush had difficulty analyzing complex policy issues.[95] They dealt with these difficulties by delegating to others much of the responsibility for sorting out the issues and presenting viable options. They also depended on developing clear-cut (some would say "simplistic") cognitive frameworks for making decisions. These frameworks helped them simplify reality and gave their decisions the appearance of consistency. Once Reagan came to an "understanding" of an event, he did not want to deal with facts that challenged his understanding. As Secretary of State George Schultz put it, "no fact, no argument, no plea for reconsideration would change his mind."[96] Richard Clarke, a former anti-terrorism top adviser to George W. Bush, said that the president "looked for the simple solution, the bumper sticker description of the problem."[97] Former treasury secretary Paul O'Neill was even more critical, declaring that he never heard George W. Bush "analyze a complex issue, parse opposing positions, and settle on a judicious path."[98]

Bill Clinton enjoyed grappling with tough policy problems and synthesizing large amounts of data. His elaborate study of an issue could have a political downside, however. It took him longer than promised to design his legislative proposals, the proposals themselves were subject to continuing shifts in emphasis and content, and they were difficult to explain to the American people, which was necessary to build support for them in Washington. Moreover, throughout the process the president appeared indecisive and inconsistent.

There is widespread agreement about the importance of identifying and examining the major assumptions underlying policy options and evaluating alternatives in light of these assumptions.[99] Yet we have seen that it is difficult to do this, especially when the truth is implausible and the actions of other leaders are unexpected and self-defeating. Moreover, it is not possible to examine all assumptions, and some of policymakers' assumptions are likely to be correct. However, decision makers can ask what it would take to disprove their premises and what evidence should be present if their views are correct. They can also focus on the key assumptions of a policy choice, carefully scrutinize the information they use to support those assumptions, and force themselves to consider alternative explanations for behavior. Reflecting on the war in Iraq, George W. Bush's national security assistant Condoleezza Rice lamented, "we had not—I had not—done a good enough job of thinking the unthinkable."[100]

Inference Mechanisms

function of the human mind

People often simplify reality to deal with the world's complexities and resolve uncertainty by ignoring or deemphasizing information that contradicts their existing beliefs. To do this, they employ inference mechanisms that operate unconsciously and that may have as great an influence on a person's judgments as objective evidence. Consequently, most policy makers remain unreceptive to any major revision of their beliefs in response to new information, especially if they have had success in the past with applying their general beliefs to specific decisions or have held their beliefs for a long time. Moreover, they are unlikely to search for information that challenges their views or options contrary to those they advocate. Instead, they tend to incorporate new information in ways that render it comprehensible within their existing frames of reference. In other words, they rationalize it to support their previously held beliefs.

This rationalization process, combined with the stake presidents have in their previous decisions, explains why it is so difficult for them to change those decisions or even to reconsider them unless circumstances force them to do so. A good example of this phenomenon is the Clinton administration's failure to consider the changing role of the American military in Somalia in 1993. It took a tragic confrontation between U.S. troops and Somalis backing a local warlord to force the administration to confront the issue and ultimately to terminate the mission. Unless presidents make it clear that they really want to hear criticism within their administration, they may not become aware of it until they see it on the news. Advisers find it extremely difficult to tell presidents what they do not wish to hear.

There are various devices that presidents use to manage inconsistency. One is to attach very negative consequences to alternatives such as showing weakness. President Johnson and his top aides did not contemplate the option of disengaging from the war in Vietnam because they considered such a move would weaken the United States' position within the international community. Similarly, Ronald Reagan would never consider the option of negotiating about his Strategic Defense Initiative ("Star Wars") because he saw it as an instrument to protect the United States against enemy attack. George W. Bush feared that unless America took action against terrorists and those states that harbored them, it would encourage further attacks by its inaction. In an address on October 7, 2002, he stated, "Failure to act would embolden other tyrants, allow terrorists access to new weapons, new resources, and make blackmail a permanent feature of world events."[101]

Officials may also employ selective information to infer that a particular situation could not possibly occur. If policy makers accept this inference of impossibility, there is no need for them to consider information pointing to the opposite conclusion. Most officials believed that the Japanese could not attack Pearl Harbor. Because they were not expecting an attack, American officials did not notice the signs pointing toward it. Instead, they paid attention to signals supporting their current expectations of enemy behavior. Similar behavior inhibited policy makers from anticipating the North Korean attacks on South

Korea in 1950 that precipitated the Korean War, the massive Tet invasion of South Vietnam by the North in 1968, and the Iraqi attack on Kuwait in 1991.

Another means of reducing inconsistency and thereby decreasing the pressure to consider alternatives is similar to what we commonly term "wishful thinking." Secretary of State George Shultz has described his boss, Ronald Reagan, as engaging in wishful thinking regarding issues and events, sometimes rearranging facts and allowing himself to be deceived—for example, when he insisted that he had not traded arms for hostages in the Iran-Contra affair.[102] Wishful thinking also played a prominent role in decision making about the ill-fated invasion of Cuba at the Bay of Pigs at the beginning of the Kennedy administration and the lack of adequate planning for the U.S. peacekeeping operation in Iraq in 2003 following the war.

A form of wishful thinking occurs when information inconsistent with ongoing policy is deemphasized and policy makers conclude that undesirable conditions are only temporary and will ameliorate in response to current policy. Officials used this type of reasoning to garner support for the continued escalation of the Vietnam War. All that was needed to force the enemy to succumb, they argued, was to keep up the pressure. Thus, they resisted rigorous evaluation of their military strategy.[103]

Reasoning by analogy is yet another means of resolving uncertainty and simplifying decision making. The conclusions supported by this type of reasoning seem to have strength independent of the available evidence, probably because the analogies simplify and provide a coherent framework for ambiguous and inconsistent information.

Metaphors and similes simplify a complex and ambiguous reality by relating it to a relatively simple and well-understood concept. If policy makers then use one as the basis of an analogy, the possibilities for error are considerable. For example, "domino theory"—which held that the United States must prevent countries from falling to the communists because a chain reaction would occur and the countries would fall one after another, like falling dominoes—was part of the theoretical underpinning for the Vietnam War. The simplistic nature of the simile indicates how much room exists for differences between that view and reality.[104] MacGeorge Bundy, President Johnson's national security assistant, later concluded that the simile of the domino was inadequate and a "preventer of discourse," but it was powerful enough during the war that it led him to disregard analyses that challenged the theory.[105]

Discrediting the source of information and options is another means of reducing the complexity and resolving the contradictions with which policy makers must deal. At first, President Johnson handled the critics of his Vietnam policy quite well, inviting them to his office and talking to them for hours. However, as opposition increased and polls indicated a dip in his popularity, he responded to criticism by discrediting its source. He maintained that Senator William Fulbright (the chairman of the Senate Foreign Relations Committee) was upset at not being named secretary of state; the liberals in Congress were angry at him because he had not gone to Harvard, because the Great Society was more successful than Kennedy's New Frontier, and because he had

LBJ invited dissent AT FIRST

blocked Robert Kennedy from the presidency; columnists were said to oppose him so as to make a bigger splash; and young people were hostile because they were ignorant.

At other times, presidents may simply avoid information they fear will force them to face disagreeable decisions that complicate their lives and produce additional stress. Richard Nixon is a classic example. In his memoirs, he wrote of putting off a confrontation with his own attorney general, John Mitchell, because of Mitchell's hypersensitivity and his own desire to remain ignorant about Mitchell's involvement in Watergate in case it would prove harmful for him to know about it. Referring to Nixon's ability to engage in self-delusion and avoid unpleasant facts, White House Chief of Staff H. R. Haldeman argued that the "failure to face the irrefutable facts, even when it was absolutely clear that they were irrefutable, was one of our fatal flaws in handling Watergate at every step."[106]

Each of the cognitive processes that reduce uncertainty and complexity can be a reasonable response to a situation. The point is that people have a tendency to rely on them not only by conscious choice but also because of their need for certainty and simplicity. In each of the examples cited, the president and his advisers made use of an inference mechanism that diverted their attention from vital information and led them to ignore appropriate options. Potential actions that policy makers considered disastrous would have been far less so than those that they took, situations they thought to be impossible actually occurred, results they hoped for from policies never materialized, their inferences were based on inappropriate analogies, and they rejected worthwhile criticism. Thus, the inference mechanisms that top decision makers employ to manage inconsistency may jeopardize sound policy judgments.

At the same time, it is important to recognize the interplay between motivation and cognition. Many people can tolerate at least some inconsistency, and there are other motives aside from consistency that drive behavior, including accuracy, fairness, efficiency, accountability, ideological biases, and time pressure. Consequently, presidents and their advisers have a variety of cognitive strategies available to them and may choose to face the facts rather than simplify them if they have sufficient motivation and intellectual curiosity. Understanding which motivations are operative in a given situation remains one of the most intriguing questions of presidential politics.

BUREAUCRATIC POLITICS AND DECISION MAKING

A primary source of options and information for the president is the bureaucracy. It is not always a neutral instrument, however. Individuals and the agencies they represent have interests of their own to advance and protect and may not necessarily view issues from the president's perspective. Moreover, the structure of the flow of information and the development of options in the White House may also hinder decision making.

Organizational Parochialism

Government agencies have a tendency toward homogeneous attitudes. People who are attracted to work for government agencies are likely to support the policies carried out by those agencies, whether they are in the fields of medical research, agriculture, or national defense. Naturally, agencies prefer hiring like-minded people. Within each agency, the distribution of rewards creates further pressure to view things from the perspective of the status quo. Personnel who do not support established organizational goals and approaches to meeting them are unlikely to be promoted to important positions. Moreover, all but a few high-level policy makers spend their careers within a single agency or department. Even with the introduction of the Senior Executive Service (SES) in 1978, very few career SES officials have moved across agency lines.[107] Because people want to believe in what they do for a living, this long association strongly influences the attitudes of bureaucrats.

An additional factor encouraging homogeneous views is the relatively narrow range of each agency's responsibilities. Officials in the Department of Education, for example, do not deal with the budget for the entire national government but only with the part that pertains to their programs. It is up to others to recommend to the president what is best allocated to education and what should go to national defense, health, or housing. With each bureaucratic unit focusing on its own programs, there are few people to view these programs from a wider, national perspective.

Influences from outside an agency also encourage parochial views among bureaucrats. When interest groups and congressional committees support an agency, they expect continued bureaucratic support in return. Because these outsiders generally favor the policies the bureaucracy has been carrying out all along (and which they probably helped initiate), what they really want usually is to perpetuate the status quo.

The combination of these factors results in a relatively uniform environment for policy making. Intra-organizational communications pass mainly among people who share similar frames of reference and reinforce bureaucratic parochialism by their continued association.

The influence of parochialism is strong enough that even some presidential appointees, who are in office for only short periods of time, are "captured" and adopt the narrow views of their bureaucratic units. As President Nixon observed, "it is inevitable when an individual has been in a Cabinet position or, for that matter, holds any position in Government, [that] after a certain length of time he becomes an advocate of the status quo; rather than running the bureaucracy, the bureaucracy runs him."[108] The dependence of such officials on their subordinates for information and advice, the need to maintain organizational morale by supporting established viewpoints, and the pressure from their agencies' clienteles combine to discourage high-ranking officials from maintaining broad views of the public interest. Thus, parochialism can lead officials to see different faces on the same issue.

In May 1990, President George H. W. Bush faced a judgment about cutting off agriculture credit guarantees to Iraq. To the deputy national security adviser, this action provided an opportunity to show displeasure with Iraq's clandestine weapons program and threats toward Israel; to the Department of Agriculture, it was a decision about the fate of a controversial program that helped agribusiness; and to the State Department, cutting off credit guarantees represented a turn away from a strategy of constructive engagement that could influence Iraqi behavior toward the Arab-Israeli peace process. To the Treasury Department, the judgment was a threat to Iraq's readiness to continue paying its debts; to the Defense Department, it was an occasion to reevaluate the posture of its central command; and to the president's congressional adviser, it was an opportunity to remove an irritant in relations with Capitol Hill.[109] In other words, policy makers in different bureaucratic units with different responsibilities saw the same policy in a different light and reacted differently to it.

A president can benefit from a diversity of views among the organizational units, but the White House must recognize that each view is likely to be articulated from a biased perspective.

Maintaining the Organization

As a result of parochialism in the bureaucracy, career officials come to believe that the health of their organization and its programs is vital to the national interest. In their eyes, this well-being depends, in turn, on the ability of the organization to fulfill its missions, secure the necessary resources (personnel, money, and authority), and maintain its influence. Organizational personnel can pursue their personal quests for power and prestige, the goals of their organization, and the national interest simultaneously without perceiving any role conflicts. Moreover, policy makers in different organizational units are prone to see different faces on the same issues due to their different organizational needs.

The single-mindedness of policy makers who are attached to various agencies causes them to raise options and gather information that support the interests of their organization and avoid or oppose those that may challenge those interests. In this way, the goals of maintaining an organization may actually displace the goals of solving the problems for which the organization was created. As one former high White House official wrote, "For many cabinet officers, the important question was whether their department would have the principal responsibility for the new program—not the hard choices that lay hidden within it."[110]

Within most organizations, there is a dominant view of the essence of the organization's mission and of the attitudes, skills, and experience that employees should have to carry it out. Organizations usually propose options that they believe will build up and reinforce the essential aspects of their organizations. For example, during the Vietnam War, the Air Force lobbied for strategic bombing and deep interdiction, even though its bombing campaigns had not enjoyed unqualified success in previous wars. One way to promote this goal was to argue for bombing as a central feature of U.S. policy in order to show its utility. The lack of success only reinforced the Air Force's efforts to step up the bombing even further; its commanders never admitted that it was not accomplishing its objectives.

Organizations will also vigorously resist the efforts of others to take away, decrease, or share their essence and the resources deemed necessary to realize it. In 2008, Secretary of Defense Robert Gates complained about the resistance to a shift from piloted aircraft to less expensive, and less glamorous, surveillance vehicles in the wars in Iraq and Afghanistan. The Air Force allowed only those officially rated as pilots to sit at the remote controls of its unmanned reconnaissance vehicles, a policy that Gates said limited how many of these aircraft it could deploy. (The Army allows enlisted personnel and noncommissioned officers to apply for those jobs.) Throughout the George W. Bush administration, the Air Force also was not eager to use pilots in low-tech fixes such as inexpensive aircraft fitted with surveillance gear.[111]

Gates also criticized the Pentagon bureaucracy for a narrow commitment to buying new generations of conventional weapons, which kept it from rapidly developing equipment that would save lives in Iraq and Afghanistan. He had to force the bureaucracy to accept systems to detect improvised bombs and heavily armored transports to protect troops.[112]

In their struggles over roles and missions, bureaucrats may distort the information and options they provide to senior officials. For example, during the Vietnam War, the Air Force and Navy were each concerned that the other might encroach on its bombing missions; the Navy was also concerned about justifying the high cost of its aircraft carriers. Thus, the two branches competed in their efforts at air warfare. The aspect of this interservice competition that was most damaging to the accuracy of the perceptions of high-level decision makers concerning the degree of American success in the war was the battle over the relative effectiveness of each service's air warfare. Each service was concerned about future budgets and missions and felt it could not let the other get the upper hand. Thus, each branch exaggerated its own performance and expected the other to do likewise.

Although the FBI recognized terrorism as a major threat in the 1990s, it was not able to make the cultural change from a police agency to an intelligence agency. It did not reallocate resources to counterterrorism; downplayed the role of analysis, especially strategic analysis; did not ensure its analysts access to information; did not build an effective intelligence collection effort; and maintained "woefully inadequate" information systems.[113] Thus, the agency was not in a position to provide the president with the information he needed on terrorists in the United States. Even after the 9/11 terrorist attacks, the bureau's resistance to change forced the director to issue a warning that he would not tolerate bureaucratic intransigence.

Budgets are another vital component of the strategies necessary to maintain an organization. This is true for grant-awarding agencies as well as for agencies with large operational capabilities like the military services and the Department of Agriculture. Because the staff within governmental organizations generally believe that their work is vital to the national interest, and because conventional wisdom stipulates that a larger budget enables an organization to perform its functions more effectively, units will normally request an increase in funding and fight any decreases. The size of a group's budget not only determines the resources available for its services but also serves as a sign of the importance that others attach to the organization's functions.

Agency personnel also examine any substantive proposal to ascertain its impact on the budget and will rarely suggest adding a new function to their responsibilities if it must be financed from monies already allocated for ongoing activities. Moreover, components of large organizations, like units in the military or the Department of Health and Human Services, are concerned about maintaining or increasing their percentage of the larger unit's budget.

An organization's staff members are likely to raise and support options that give them autonomy. In their view, they know best how to perform their essential mission. Consequently, they tend to resist options that would place control in the hands of higher officials or require close coordination with other organizations. This desire for autonomy helps explain why several agencies independently gather and evaluate national security intelligence from their own perspective. As Richard Nixon complained after being disappointed by the intelligence reports he received, "Those guys spend all their time fighting each other."[114]

Because organizations seek to create and maintain autonomous jurisdictions, they rarely oppose each other's projects. This self-imposed restraint reduces the conflict between organizations and correspondingly reduces the options and information available to the president. In dealing with their superiors, the leaders of an organization often guard their autonomy by presenting only one option for a new program. The rationale is that if higher officials are not permitted to choose among options, they also cannot interfere with the organization's preference. Once an agency of government has responsibility for a program, however, it has a tendency to evaluate it positively.

Organizational and Personal Influence

To achieve the policies they desire, organizations and individuals seek influence. In pursuing power, officials often further distort the processes of generating options and gathering information for the president. One way for organizations to increase their influence is to defer to one another's expertise. The operations of all large-scale organizations, including governments, require a considerable degree of specialization and expertise. Those who possess this expertise, whether within executive agencies or on congressional committees, naturally believe that they know best about a subject in their field and therefore desire primary influence over the resolution of issues in their subject area. Because each set of experts has a stake in deference to expertise (each receives benefits from it), reciprocal deference to expertise becomes an important theme in policy making. One result of this reciprocity is that fewer challenges to expert views are aired than might otherwise be the case.

In the prelude to the Bay of Pigs invasion, the Joint Chiefs of Staff were bureaucratically cautious about dissecting the CIA's most cherished enterprise.[115] For several decades, there was an implicit agreement between the Departments of State and Defense that each would stay out of the other's affairs. Thus, during the Vietnam War, the State Department often took no part in shaping war policies and refrained from airing many of its views. Contributing to this restraint was Secretary of Defense Robert McNamara's adamant belief that the State Department should not challenge the military's appraisal of the actual progress of the war. He thus deliberately blocked the flow of information on the war. As a result, policy makers had to defer to Defense Department assessments, which were often inaccurate and biased toward military rather than political solutions. During the Iraq war and its aftermath, Secretary of Defense Donald Rumsfeld resisted other members of the National Security Council reviewing military plans.[116]

Although deference to expertise is not always a satisfactory way of resolving conflicts in policy making, it is often the only possible course of action. Governmental agencies are the sole source of data and analysis on many issues. As their work becomes increasingly specialized, it becomes harder to check their information and evaluations. This problem is exacerbated by a need for secrecy on most national security policies, which makes it necessary to limit even further the number of participants in the policy-making process.

To take full advantage of deference to expertise and increase their influence further, organizations seek to prevent their own experts from disseminating conflicting information and options. Contrary information and evaluations are believed to undercut the credibility of a unit's position. Moreover, by presenting several real options, a unit increases the range of possible policy decisions and commensurately decreases the probability that the option favored by the unit's leaders will be selected. Thus, the Joint Chiefs of Staff rarely disagree in their recommendations. Similarly, the relevant departments never presented President Carter with real options on welfare reform, in part because they were afraid he would select an alternative they opposed. No one would insist to the president that reform would be costly because they feared he would then reject their reform efforts.[117]

If disagreements exist among the experts in an organizational unit, efforts to produce an appearance of unanimity can reduce the experts' recommendations to broad generalizations. A record of agreement on the least disputed common denominators usually fails to mention many controversial points, which may be crucial to the ultimate success of the policy at issue. When compromise positions reach the president in a form that suggests a unified consensual judgment, they can give him a false sense of security because he may lack an awareness of the potential problems buried within the recommendations.

The imperative of consensus can also stifle innovative thinking. For example, the George H. W. Bush administration launched a strategic review of foreign policy early in its first year. Bureaucratic units that had vested interests in established policy produced the papers. As Secretary of State Jim Baker put it, "In the end what we received was mush," with potentially controversial and interesting ideas omitted in the name of bureaucratic consensus.[118] To avoid a similar situation in designing a military strategy for the twenty-first century, Secretary of Defense Donald Rumsfeld in the George W. Bush presidency excluded uniformed military and most civil servants in the Defense Department from the group that devised the strategy.

For bureaucrats interested in their own careers, the prospect of a deferred promotion, or even dismissal, makes them reluctant to report information that undercuts the official stands of their organizations.[119] The example of the Foreign Service officers who frankly (and accurately) reported on the strength of the communists in China during the late 1940s was not quickly forgotten in the bureaucracy. They were driven from the Foreign Service for allegedly holding procommunist sympathies. More than forty years later, in 1992, then CIA Director Robert Gates announced that many within the CIA felt that intelligence reports were still being tailored to please superiors.

Experts can create an illusion of competition when they agree to compare their preferred action to unfeasible alternatives. Lyndon Johnson's advisers have been criticized for juxtaposing, in 1964, their favored option of bombing North Vietnam against two phony options: in effect, destroy the world or scuttle and run. Barack Obama criticized his advisers for a lack of viable options for the U.S. role in Afghanistan.

Bureaucratic Structure

The structure of administrative organizations is one of the factors that impede the flow of options and information to higher-level decision makers.

Hierarchy

Most bureaucracies have a hierarchical structure, whereby the information on which decisions are based usually passes from bottom to top. At each step in this ladder of communication, personnel screen the information from the previous stage. Such screening is necessary because the people at the top— presidents—cannot absorb all the detailed information that exists on an issue. They must have subordinates summarize and synthesize the information as it proceeds upward. The longer the communication chain, the greater the chance that judgments will replace facts, nuances or caveats will be excluded, subordinates will paint a positive face on a situation to improve their own or their organization's image, human error will distort the overall picture, and the speculations of "experts" will be reported as fact.

Screening, summarizing, and human error are not the only pitfalls in the transmission of information. When subordinates are asked to transmit information that can be used to evaluate their performance, they have a tendency to distort it in order to put themselves in the most favorable light. For example, many of the military's assessments of damage done to Iraqi forces and weaponry in the Gulf War turned out to be erroneous, having been inflated substantially by soldiers in the field.[120]

Subordinates sometimes distort facts by not reporting those that indicate danger. President Kennedy was not apprised of the following problems with the contingency plan for the invasion of the Bay of Pigs: The men participating in the invasion had not been told to flee to the mountains should the invasion fail; between the beach and the mountains, which supposedly offered refuge, was a large swamp; there was no good evidence that the Cuban people would rise up to support the invasion; and only one-third of the men had received guerrilla training. Instead, he was simply informed that if the invasion failed, the troops would retreat to the mountains, where they would carry out guerrilla warfare and win the support of the Cuban people. The CIA also failed to inform the president that a second U.S. air strike, which would have revealed the central American role in the invasion, would be necessary for success.[121]

At other times, subordinates may exaggerate the evidence in support of their favored options. George W. Bush administration officials who supported invading Iraq made assertions about the existence of WMDs that went beyond the evidence. The CIA itself was too assertive about the evidence of WMD in the *President's Daily Brief* (the highly classified intelligence report the president receives each morning) and in the National Intelligence Estimate on Iraq it produced in the fall of 2002.[122]

The president may attempt to compensate for the problems of hierarchy by sending personal aides or outsiders to assess a situation directly and propose options. However, the person assigned to the task, more than the situation itself, may determine the nature of the resulting report. Moreover, the president cannot bypass senior officials very often without lowering their morale and undercutting their operational authority.

President Kennedy's chief White House national security assistant, McGeorge Bundy, ordered that cables to the State Department, the CIA, and the Pentagon be sent directly to the White House and not just to the Washington headquarters of those departments, where they could be summarized and analyzed for transmittal to the president. However, this practice did not correct any distortion that may have gone into the cables in the first place, and someone still had to summarize and synthesize the tremendous volume of information before it reached the president. President Bush discovered the same problems when he asked for direct information channels from the field.

Decentralization

Even in a hierarchical executive branch, the president cannot assume that information will be centralized. There was a great deal of information pointing to the impending Japanese attack on Pearl Harbor, for example, but it was never fully organized. Similarly, there were many warnings about the possibility of terrorist attacks before September 11, 2001, but most did not reach the president. No one brings forward all the political, economic, social, military, and diplomatic considerations of a policy in a recognizable manner for the president's deliberation because the bureaucracy that is relevant to any policy is too decentralized and too large to coordinate it effectively. Moreover, the amount of information available is so vast that it cannot be collected, stored, retrieved, and analyzed in a single database or even a network of linked databases.

Before the 9/11 terrorist attacks, the FBI and the CIA did not adequately share the information they collected, did not assess the warning signs as a whole, and were slow to react to the significance of the intelligence they had obtained about the possibility of an attack. They also failed to comprehend the ominous rise of Osama bin Laden and his al-Qaeda network. Two years before the 9/11 attacks, the CIA suspected two of the hijackers of being terrorists and believed they held visas to enter the United States or that they were already in the country. However, the agency did not place the men on the government's terrorism watch list or notify the FBI that they might be in the United States. An FBI informant penetrated the circle of the two men but never received the CIA's information that they might be in al-Qaeda. The FBI failed to grasp the significance of a July 2001 communication sent from an agent in the bureau's Phoenix office that identified a pattern of Middle Eastern men, some with extreme anti-American beliefs, who were receiving pilot training at flight schools in the United States. The FBI also did not connect the Phoenix communication with the arrest in August 2001 of Zacarias Moussaoui, who was later indicted for complicity in the hijackings. The FBI and CIA did not assess the potential threat posed by Moussaoui in light of the heightened fears of a terrorist attack in the summer of 2001. Officials in the Department of Justice misunderstood and misapplied procedures for sharing information between intelligence and criminal investigations of the department, limiting sharing of information. Thus, the FBI did not tell the U.S. Attorney's office about Moussaoui because it felt it lacked probable cause to search his computer. The FBI also did not tell other agencies what it thought Moussaoui was up to, and no one acted on the general report its agents wrote. More broadly, no one organized law enforcement, immigration, visa, and intelligence information related to the hijackers to allow any agency to detect trends and patterns in their activities. No one was firmly in charge of managing terrorist information and able to draw relevant intelligence from anywhere in the government, assign responsibilities across agencies, track progress, and quickly bring obstacles up to the level where they could be resolved.[123]

As a result, in the words of the 9/11 Commission, "the system was blinking red" before the terrorist attacks, but no one connected the dots to identify the immediate threat. No one ordered domestic agencies to harden the borders, fortify transportation systems, target electronic surveillance, marshal state and local law enforcement, or warn the public. "The terrorists exploited deep institutional failings within our government,"[124] and President Bush did not make the organizational reforms necessary to combat terrorism more effectively until after the 9/11 attack.[125]

The lack of information sharing between the CIA and the FBI is only part of the president's intelligence problem. Table 7.1 lists the intelligence agencies that provide the White House with national security intelligence. Trying to coordinate the information flow from such a decentralized system is a massive task. In an effort to centralize the analysis of intelligence, Congress created a new national director of intelligence in 2004.

Table 7.1 Agencies with Responsibility for National Security Intelligence, 2013

Director of National Intelligence
Central Intelligence Agency
Department of Defense
    National Security Agency
    National Geospatial-Intelligence Agency
    National Reconnaissance Office
    Defense Intelligence Agency
    Army Intelligence and Security Command
    Office of Naval Intelligence
    Air Force Intelligence, Surveillance, and Reconnaissance Agency
    Marine Corps Intelligence Activity
Department of State
    Bureau of Intelligence and Research
Department of Treasury
    Office of Terrorism and Finance Intelligence
Department of Justice
    Counterterrorism Division, FBI
    Counterintelligence Division, FBI
    Directorate of Intelligence, FBI
    WMD Directorate, FBI
    Terrorist Screening Center, FBI
    Office of National Security Intelligence, DEA
Department of Energy
    Office of Intelligence and Counterintelligence
Department of Homeland Security
    Office of Intelligence and Analysis
    Domestic Nuclear Detection Office
    United States Secret Service
    United States Immigration and Customs Enforcement
    Coast Guard Intelligence

Umar Farouk Abdulmutallab was a Nigerian Islamist who attempted to detonate plastic explosives hidden in his underwear while on board a flight from Amsterdam to Detroit on December 25, 2009. The National Security Agency intercepted al-Qaeda operatives in Yemen talking about using a Nigerian man for an attack, and Abdulmutallab's father warned American diplomats in Nigeria about his son's radicalization in Yemen.

Nevertheless, security agencies could not integrate and understand the intelligence they possessed. Neither the State Department nor the National Counterterrorism Center (NCTC) discovered Abdulmutallab's U.S. visa until it was too late. The NCTC draws on streams of information from more than

80 databases and 28 computer networks across the government. Intelligence analysts are stymied, however, by computer systems that cannot easily search automatically—and repeatedly—for possible links. Using the search tools and databases they have, it is difficult for analysts to conduct dynamic searches to "connect the dots," which involve looking for multiple variables and terms scattered across databases. Further complicating the effort, many of the records in intelligence databases contain additional information in the form of written comments or notes attached to the main record. The notes and comments are not indexed, so the kinds of keyword searches that analysts perform cannot find them. It is often these subsets of information that contain the nuance, context, and interpretation that might be crucial to connecting the dots.

In some instances, no one has responsibility for providing critical information. As the 9/11 Commission put it:

> The September 11 attacks fell into the void between the foreign and domestic threats. The foreign intelligence agencies were watching overseas . . . the domestic agencies were waiting for evidence of a domestic threat from sleeper cells within the United States. No one was looking for a foreign threat to domestic targets.[126]

Standard Operating Procedures

Organizations use routines or standard operating procedures (SOPs) to gather and process information in a methodical fashion. However, the character of the SOPs may delay the recognition of critical information, distort the quality of information, and limit the options presented to policy makers. One reason that other agencies could not benefit from the FBI's information on possible terrorists is that the bureau did not produce intelligence reports like those other agencies routinely write and disseminate.[127]

In the case of the Cuban missile crisis, several weeks before the president was aware of the missiles, there was already a good deal of information in the U.S. intelligence system pointing to the presence of the missiles. However, the time required by SOPs to sort out raw information and verify it delayed recognition of the new situation. Organizational routines also masked signs forecasting the 1974 leftist coup in Portugal. Officials from the intelligence services of the CIA, the Defense Department, and the State Department testified after the event that their routines failed to focus much attention on Portugal and they could not shift personnel rapidly to a new area of concern.

SOPs affect not only if and when information is collected but also the substance of the information. In Vietnam, the military's concentration on the technical aspects of bombing caused it to substitute a set of short-run physical objectives for the ultimate political goals of the war. Military reports emphasized physical destruction per se rather than the political impact of such destruction. The enemy's capacity to recruit more men or rebuild a structure never seemed to enter into the calculations.

SOPs give disproportionate weight to information entering the system from regular channels. For example, the United States was highly dependent on the shah of Iran and Savak, the shah's secret police organization, for information about that nation. Up until a few months before the shah was deposed, they reported to the CIA and President Carter that there was no likelihood of revolution. The White House rejected more pessimistic reports from journalists and others outside the regular flow of information.

SOPs structure the process of decision making by preselecting those who will be asked for advice and predetermining when they will be asked. There are routine ways of invading foreign countries and determining agency budgets. Some people will be involved at earlier stages than others, and some will be viewed as having more legitimate and expert voices in policy discussions. When Lyndon Johnson limited his circle of personal advisers on the Vietnam War to a half-dozen top officials, those at a lower rung in the foreign policy hierarchy found it harder to have their dissent heard. In addition, there was little opportunity for others in the cabinet to challenge the war policy because they were not located in the proper decision-making channels.

SOPs also affect the nature of the alternatives proposed by bureaucratic units. Bureaucracies typically propose their standard ways of doing things rather than innovative solutions to problems. These standard policies may not be appropriate for the problem at hand, as when military commanders attempted to transplant to Indochina the operational methods of conventional warfare that had been successful in the European battle theaters of World War II instead of developing a strategy more appropriate for fighting a counterinsurgency effort in the jungles of Vietnam.[128] The 9/11 Commission complained of the narrow and unimaginative options for countering al-Qaeda that the bureaucracy presented to Presidents Clinton and George W. Bush.[129]

As a result of problems with established routines, presidents often create special task forces of "outside" experts to develop new programs, as President Clinton did with his health care proposal. Such bodies, when brought together for a new purpose, are less likely than established agencies to be blinded by SOPs.

Because only decision makers directly responsible for a policy are normally consulted on sensitive matters, fewer advisers contribute to secret deliberations than to debate on more open issues. This reduces the range of options that are considered in a secret decision and limits the analysis of the few options that are considered. For example, the secrecy of President Johnson's "Tuesday lunch group," which made the important decisions on the Vietnam War, prevented an advance agenda. Thus, decisions were made without a full prior review of the options.

Secrecy also makes it easier for those directly involved to dismiss (intentionally or unintentionally) the dissenting or offbeat ideas of outsiders as the products of ignorance. This is unfortunate because secret information is often inaccurate or misleading. President Kennedy wished he had not been successful in persuading the *New York Times* not to publish the plans for the Bay of Pigs invasion; afterward, he felt that publicity might have elicited some useful critiques.

CONCLUSION

Presidents face an enormously difficult and complex task in making decisions on a wide range of issues. They must work within the parameters of the national government's prior commitments and are further constrained by the limited time they can devote to considering options and information on any one policy. In addition, they face a number of other potential hazards in reaching decisions. The struggling facilitator, not the dominating director, is the description that generally matches the process of presidential decision making.

There are a variety of ways for presidents to organize the White House and acquire advice, but not all are equally useful in ensuring that presidents are presented with a full range of options, each supported with effective advocacy. Moreover, presidents may experience problems if their aides are reluctant to present candid advice, which may be aggravated by the aides' desire to increase their own influence and by the presidents themselves.

Bureaucratic politics also plays a role in determining the options and information that presidents receive and the forms in which these are presented. Agencies and their personnel inevitably have narrower perspectives than the White House and will desire to maintain and expand their programs, status, and influence. Those ambitions often bias the options and information presented to the White House. The ways in which bureaucratic units collect, process, and transmit options and information, and the secrecy that sometimes accompanies the process, may further distort what the president perceives.

It is important that presidents remain sensitive to the many obstacles to effective decision making and attempt to avoid or compensate for these obstacles as much as possible while realizing that perfectly rational decision making is unattainable.

Discussion Questions

1. It is convenient to argue that the president should examine all the options regarding an important policy issue, yet is it really possible for presidents to evaluate a wide range of options on all the policy questions with which they must deal? What do you think presidents really do? Do conservative presidents, for example, often consider liberal options, and vice versa? Give examples of contemporary presidents to support your answers.

2. We have seen that organizational parochialism may bias the information that bureaucratic units provide to the president. Is there a solution to this problem? Is it possible for committed, expert managers to run government agencies and still take a broad view of public policy and provide the president with information he may not want to hear?

3. A critical step in presidents' decision making is evaluating the consequences of the various options before them. How well can the White House do this? Is it possible to predict the consequences of choices that have not yet been made, such as levying sanctions against a country or cutting taxes for certain groups?

Web Exercises

1. Go to the White House website: http://www.whitehouse.gov/briefing-room/. Look at the wide range of issues on which the president made a decision in just one week. How much can one person know about all these issues? Is there a way for presidents to be better informed?

2. Select an issue that interests you from the White House website. How might the president's decisions on the issue have been different had there been no previous commitments restraining him? Were these previous commitments aids or hindrances to good policy? Go to http://www.whitehouse.gov/ and type a policy area that interests you (such as "education," "defense," or "health") in the search box.

Selected Readings

Allison, Graham, and Philip Zelikow. *Essence of Decision: Explaining the Cuban Missile Crisis,* 2nd ed. New York: Addison Wesley Longman, 1999.

Burke, John P. *Honest Broker?: The National Security Advisor and Presidential Decision Making.* College Station: Texas A&M University Press, 2009.

Burke, John P. "Organizational Structure and Presidential Decision-Making." In *Oxford Handbook of the American Presidency,* edited by George C. Edwards III and William G. Howell. Oxford: Oxford University Press, 2009, pp. 501–527.

Burke, John P., and Fred I. Greenstein. *How Presidents Test Reality: Decisions on Vietnam, 1954 and 1965.* New York: Russell Sage Foundation, 1989.

George, Alexander L., and Juliette L. George. *Presidential Personality and Performance.* Boulder, CO: Westview, 1998.

Halperin, Morton H., and Priscilla A. Clapp. *Bureaucratic Politics and Foreign Policy,* 2nd ed. Washington, DC: Brookings Institution, 2006.

Haney, Patrick J. *Organizing for Foreign Policy Crises.* Ann Arbor: University of Michigan Press, 1997.

Hult, Karen M., and Charles E. Walcott. "Influences on Presidential Decision-Making." In *Oxford Handbook of the American Presidency,* edited by George C. Edwards III and William G. Howell. Oxford: Oxford University Press, 2009.

Janis, Irving. *Groupthink,* 2nd ed. Boston: Houghton Mifflin, 1982.

Jervis, Robert. *Perception and Misperception in International Politics.* Princeton, NJ: Princeton University Press, 1976.

National Commission on Terrorist Attacks on the United States. *The 9/11 Commission Report.* New York: Norton, 2004.

Neustadt, Richard E. *Presidential Power and the Modern Presidents.* New York: Free Press, 1990.

Pious, Richard M. *Why Presidents Fail: White House Decision Making from Eisenhower to Bush II.* Lanham, MD: Rowman and Littlefield, 2008.

Porter, Roger B. "Gerald R. Ford: A Healing Presidency." In *Leadership in the Modern Presidency,* edited by Fred I. Greenstein. Cambridge, MA: Harvard University Press, 1988, pp. 199–227.

Notes

1. Quoted in John C. Donovan, *The Politics of Poverty,* 2nd ed. (Indianapolis, IN: Pegasus, 1973), p. 111.

2. On continuity in foreign policy despite changes in the occupant of the presidency, see William J. Dixon and Stephen M. Gardner, "Presidential Succession and the Cold War: An Analysis of Soviet-American Relations, 1948–1988," *Journal of Politics* 54 (February 1992): 156–175.

3. Quoted in Paul C. Light, *The President's Agenda: Domestic Policy Choice from Kennedy to Carter* (Baltimore, MD: Johns Hopkins University Press, 1982), p. 179.

4. Richard E. Neustadt, *Presidential Power and the Modern Presidents* (New York: Free Press, 1990), pp. 121–122.

5. James A. Baker III, *The Politics of Diplomacy* (New York: Putnam, 1995), p. 263.

6. Quoted in Burt Solomon, "Clinton Tinkers with His Staff . . . to Counter His Own Failings," *National Journal*, May 15, 1995, p. 1193.

7. *The 9/11 Commission Report* (New York: Norton, 2004), pp. 185–186, 208, 212–213; Richard A. Clarke, *Against All Enemies: Inside America's War on Terror* (New York: Free Press, 2004), pp. 26, 228, 230–231, 234–235, 237, 242–243, 254; Bob Woodward, *Plan of Attack* (New York: Simon and Schuster, 2004), pp. 80, 254.

8. George Tenet, *At the Center of the Storm: My Years at the CIA* (New York: HarperCollins, 2007), pp. 322–323.

9. Amy B. Zegart, *Spying Blind: The CIA, the FBI, and the Origins of 9/11* (Princeton: Princeton University Press, 2009), pp. 3–5.

10. Quoted in William Greider, "The Education of David Stockman," *Atlantic Monthly*, December 1981, p. 34.

11. Alexander L. George, "The Case for Multiple Advocacy in Making Foreign Policy," *American Political Science Review* 66 (September 1972): 766.

12. Bryce Harlow, quoted in Emmet John Hughes, *The Living Presidency: The Resources and Dilemmas of the American Presidential Office* (Baltimore, MD: Penguin, 1973), p. 345.

13. Henry Kissinger, *White House Years* (Boston: Little, Brown, 1979), p. 47; see also p. 1455.

14. Roger B. Porter, "Gerald Ford: A Healing Presidency," in Fred I. Greenstein, ed., *Leadership in the Modern Presidency* (Cambridge, MA: Harvard University Press, 1988), pp. 199–227.

15. Theodore C. Sorensen, *Decision-Making in the White House: The Olive Branch or the Arrows?* (New York: Columbia University Press, 1963), p. 3. See also Patrick J. Haney, *Organizing for Foreign Policy Crises* (Ann Arbor: University of Michigan Press, 1997).

16. President Ford wrote about this problem in *A Time to Heal: The Autobiography of Gerald R. Ford* (New York: Harper and Row, 1979), p. 147; see also p. 186.

17. Clark Clifford, *Counsel to the President* (New York: Random House, 1991), p. 636.

18. See Kissinger, *White House Years*, pp. 40, 602.

19. Interview with Henson Moore, White House Interview Program, October 15, 1999.

20. Hamilton Jordan, *Crisis: The Last Year of the Carter Presidency* (New York: Putnam, 1982), p. 42.

21. Sorensen, *Decision-Making in the White House*, p. 62.

22. Quoted in Light, *The President's Agenda*, p. 200.

23. On Obama, see Jonathan Alter, *The Promise: President Obama, Year One* (New York: Simon and Schuster, 2010), pp. 178, 194, 196, 198–199, 204–205, 218, 220, 315; Bob Woodward, *Obama's Wars* (New York: Simon & Schuster, 2010), pp. 168, 236–238, 258, 278–280, 298, 322; Ron Suskind, *Confidence Men: Wall Street, Washington, and the Education of a President* (New York: Harper, 2011), pp. 228, 279, 301–302, 323, 355–356, 364.

24. Kissinger, *White House Years*, p. 996.

25. See John P. Burke, "The Neutral/Honest Broker Role in Foreign-Policy Decision Making: A Reassessment," *Presidential Studies Quarterly* 35 (June 2005): 229–258.

26. Neustadt, *Presidential Power and the Modern Presidents*, chaps. 6–7.

27. Ron Suskind, *Confidence Men*, pp. 148–153, 214, 228, 277, 315–318, 340, 348, 377, 389; Alter, *The Promise*, pp. 190, 204–205, 207, 216, 218.

28. Richard N. Haass, *War of Necessity, War of Choice: A Memoir of Two Iraq Wars* (New York: Simon and Schuster, 2009), pp. 5–6, 212–216, 220, 234, 272; Bob Woodward, *The War Within* (New York: Simon and Schuster, 2008), 28, 50; Bob Woodward, *State of Denial* (New York: Simon and Schuster, 2006), p. 381; Michael Isikoff and David Corn, *Hubris: The Inside Story of Spin, Scandal, and the Selling of the Iraq War* (New York: Crown, 2006), p. 310; Ivo Daalder and I. M. Destler, "In the Shadow

of the Oval Office," *Foreign Affairs* 88 (January/February 2009): 125–126.

29. Donald Rumsfeld, *Known and Unknown* (New York: Penguin, 2011), pp. 318–319, 327, 329, 485, 491–492, 494, 498, 510–511, 517–519, 523, 525, 602; Douglas J. Feith, *War and Decision: Inside the Pentagon at the Dawn of the War on Terrorism* (New York: Harper, 2008), pp. 245, 273; Tenet, *At the Center of the Storm*, p. 308; Ron Suskind, *The One Percent Doctrine* (New York: Simon and Schuster, 2006), p. 224; Woodward, *State of Denial*, pp. 379–380, 404, 408, 455; Ron Suskind, *The Price of Loyalty* (New York: Simon and Schuster, 2004), pp. 121, 125–126, 144–149, 156, 273.

30. Rumsfeld, *Known and Unknown*, pp. 318–327.

31. Suskind, *The One Percent Doctrine*, p. 111; Barton Gellman, *Angler: The Cheney Vice Presidency* (New York: Penguin Press, 2008), chaps. 11–12.

32. Condoleezza Rice, *No Higher Honor: A Memoir of My Years in Washington* (New York: Crown Publishers, 2011), pp. 105–106; Gellman, *Angler*, pp. 81–90, 135–139, 162–173, 351; James P. Pfiffner, "Policy Making in the Bush White House," *Presidential Studies Quarterly* 39 (June 2009): 363–384.

33. Tenet, *At the Center of the Storm*, pp. 347, 356–358, 373; James Risen, *State of War: The Secret History of the CIA and the Bush Administration* (New York: Free Press, 2006), pp. 75–76; David L. Phillips, *Losing Ground* (Boulder, CO: Westview, 2005), pp. 60–61, 73, chap. 7; Gellman, *Angler*, pp. 222–225, 247; Jane Mayer, *The Dark Side: The Inside Story of How the War on Terror Turned into a War on American Ideals* (New York: Doubleday, 2008), p. 5.

34. Risen, *State of War*, pp. 64–65.

35. Rumsfeld, *Known and Unknown*, p. 323.

36. Rumsfeld, *Known and Unknown*, pp. 319, 326–327, 329, 485, 491–492, 494, 498, 510–511, 517–519, 523, 525, 602; Woodward, *State of Denial*, pp. 109, 190–191, 249, 241, 267; Risen, *State of War*, pp. 63–64, 66; Feith, *War and Decision*, pp. 143–144, 245, 250, 283–284, 439; Gellman, *Angler*, pp. 340–342; Mayer, *The Dark Side*, pp. 186–188; Peter W. Rodman,

Presidential Command (New York: Knopf, 2009), pp. 249–251, 256, 262–271.

37. Woodward, *Obama's Wars*, pp. 158–162.

38. Ronald Reagan, *An American Life* (New York: Simon and Schuster, 1990), pp. 540–541.

39. Woodward, *Bush at War*, pp. 136–137, 145, 168, 342. See also Suskind, *The Price of Loyalty*, pp. 165–166.

40. Woodward, *The War Within*, pp. 431, 433; Suskind, *The Price of Loyalty*, pp. 165–166; Scott McClellan, *What Happened: Inside the Bush White House and Washington's Culture of Deception* (New York: Public Affairs, 2008), pp. 127, 145, 203, 208. But see Karl Rove, *Courage and Consequence* (New York: Threshold Editions, 2010), p. 124.

41. Suskind, *The Price of Loyalty*, pp. 57–60, 107–109, 126, 148–149, 153, 295–306. A number of Bush's close associates thought the president asked probing questions. See Karen Hughes, *Ten Minutes from Normal* (New York: Viking, 2004), pp. 93, 282; Rumsfeld, *Known and Unknown*, pp. 319, 694; Rove, *Courage and Consequence*, p. 171.

42. Clarke, *Against All Enemies*, pp. 243–244; McClellan, *What Happened*, p. 145; Suskind, *The One Percent Doctrine*, p. 79; Paul R. Pillar, *Intelligence and U.S. Foreign Policy: Iraq, 9/11, and Misguided Reform* (New York: Columbia University Press, 2011), p. 13.

43. See *The 9/11 Commission Report*, pp. 260–262; Woodward, *Plan of Attack*, p. 80.

44. Woodward, *Plan of Attack*, pp. 249–250; Bob Woodward, *State of Denial*, p. 188; Pillar, *Intelligence and U.S. Foreign Policy*, p. 32. He did, however, ask his national security assistant to review the intelligence again. See, Rice, *No Higher Honor*, p. 200.

45. George W. Bush, *Decision Points* (New York: Crown, 2010), p. 242.

46. Pillar, *Intelligence and U.S. Foreign Policy*, pp. 14, 36, 41–42, 53–59.

47. Woodward, *State of Denial*, pp. 226, 237, 336–337, 419; Woodward, *Plan of Attack*, pp. 80, 149, 151; Isikoff and Corn, *Hubris*, p. 357; Suskind, *The Price of Loyalty*, pp. 57–60, 107–109, 126, 144–149, 153,

170–171, 295–306; Woodward, *The War Within*, p. 106.

48. Isikoff and Corn, *Hubris*, p. 310.

49. Haass, *War of Necessity, War of Choice*, pp. 5–6, 212–216, 220, 234, 272; Pillar, *Intelligence and U.S. Foreign Policy*, pp. 13–14.

50. Rumsfeld, *Known and Unknown*, p. 456; Woodward, *Plan of Attack*, pp. 251–252, 272, 416–417; Woodward, *State of Denial*, p. 90; Woodward, *The War Within*, p. 28.

51. Woodward, *Plan of Attack*, p. 272; Woodward, *State of Denial*, p. 90.

52. Bush, *Decision Points*, p. 251.

53. Woodward, *Plan of Attack*, p. 295; Thomas E. Ricks, *Fiasco: The American Military Adventure in Iraq* (New York: Penguin Press, 2006), p. 42.

54. Bush, *Decision Points*, pp. 199, 367.

55. Paul R. Pillar, "Intelligence, Policy, and the War in Iraq," *Foreign Affairs*, March/April 2006, pp. 24–25; Woodward, *Plan of Attack*, p. 139; Woodward, *The War Within*, pp. 106–107; Woodward, *State of Denial*, p. 260.

56. Rumsfeld, *Known and Unknown*, pp. 515–519; Rice, *No Higher Honor*, p. 238; Feith, *War and Decision*, p. 433; Woodward, *State of Denial*, pp. 197–198, 442; Woodward, *The War Within*, pp. 49–50; Tenet, *At the Center of the Storm*, pp. 426–428, 431, 437; Risen, *State of War*, p. 3; Michael R. Gordon, "Fateful Choice on Iraq Army Bypassed Debate," *New York Times*, March 17, 2008; Michael R. Gordon and Bernard E. Trainor, *Cobra II: The Inside Story of the Invasion and Occupation of Iraq* (New York: Pantheon Books, 2006), pp. 482–483; Edmund Andrews, "Envoy's Letter Counters Bush on Dismantling of Iraqi Army," *New York Times*, September 4, 2007; Ricks, *Fiasco*, p. 158.

57. Mayer, *The Dark Side*, pp. 34, 41–43, 52, 55, 64, 68–70, 80–89, 123–124, 186–188, 220–221, 234–236, 265, 268–269.

58. Bush, *Decision Points*, pp. 259–260.

59. Woodward, *The War Within*, p. 433.

60. Bush, *Decision Points*, p. 268.

61. Bush, *Decision Points*, pp. 371, 378.

62. Elisabeth Bumiller, "Casualty of Firestorm: Outrage, Bush and FEMA Chief," *New York Times*, September 10, 2005; Eric Lipton, "Hurricane Investigators See 'Fog of War' at White House," *New York Times*, January 28, 2006.

63. Woodward, *The War Within*, pp. 106, 320; Ricks, *Fiasco*, pp. 73, 99, 101.

64. Chester L. Cooper, *The Lost Crusade: America in Vietnam* (New York: Dodd, Mead, 1970), p. 223.

65. Ford, *A Time to Heal*, pp. 187–188; see also Reagan, *An American Life*, p. 536.

66. Melvyn P. Leffler, *For the Soul of Mankind* (New York: Hill and Wang, 2007), p. 232; Andrew Preston, *The War Council: MacGeorge Bundy, the NSC, and Vietnam* (Cambridge, MA: Harvard University Press, 2006), p. 181; Robert Dallek, *Flawed Giant: Lyndon Johnson and His Times, 1961–1973* (New York: Oxford University Press, 1998), p. 25.

67. George E. Reedy, *The Twilight of the Presidency* (New York: New American Library, 1970).

68. Pillar, "Intelligence, Policy, and the War in Iraq," p. 23; Woodward, *State of Denial*, pp. 224–225, 328, 370–371, 383; Tenet, *At the Center of the Storm*, pp. 317, 343; Risen, *State of War*, pp. 128–130, 145–147.

69. Ricks, *Fiasco*, pp. 99–100.

70. *Report of the Commission on the Intelligence Capabilities of the United States Regarding Weapons of Mass Destruction* (Washington, DC, 2005), p. 11ff.; Pillar, *Intelligence and U.S. Foreign Policy*, chap. 6; Richard K. Betts, *Enemies of Intelligence: Knowledge and Power in American National Security* (New York: Columbia University Press, 2007), pp. 94–95; Risen, *State of War*, pp. 23–25, 106, 110–119, 128–130, 145–147; Isikoff and Corn, *Hubris*, pp. 4–5, 61, 138–140, 410–411; Tenet, *At the Center of the Storm*, p. 302; Suskind, *The One Percent Doctrine*, pp. 189–190. But see Tenet, *At the Center of the Storm*, pp. 336, 342, 344; Gordon and Trainor, *Cobra II*, p. 127; and Robert Jervis, *Why Intelligence Fails* (Ithaca, NY: Cornell University Press, 2010), p. 134.

71. Dean Rusk, quoted in Leon V. Sigal, *Reporters and Officials: The Organization and*

Politics of Newsmaking (Lexington, MA: Heath, 1973), p. 147.

72. Irving Janis, *Groupthink*, 2nd ed. (Boston: Houghton Mifflin, 1982).

73. Larry Speakes, *Speaking Out* (New York: Scribner's, 1988), pp. 244–245.

74. "Mr. Secretary: On the Eve of Emeritus," *Life*, January 17, 1969, p. 62B.

75. Jack Valenti, *A Very Human President* (New York: Norton, 1975), pp. 115–116.

76. Woodward, *The War Within*, pp. 106–107.

77. Rice, *No Higher Honor*, pp. 16, 21; Woodward, *Plan of Attack*, pp. 148–152; Rumsfeld, *Known and Unknown*, p. 323.

78. John P. Burke and Fred I. Greenstein, *How Presidents Test Reality: Decisions on Vietnam, 1954 and 1965* (New York: Russell Sage Foundation, 1989); Robert S. McNamara, *In Retrospect: The Tragedy and Lessons of Vietnam* (New York: Times Books, 1995).

79. Richard K. Betts, *Surprise Attack: Lessons for Defense Planning* (Washington, DC: Brookings Institution, 1982).

80. Baker, *The Politics of Diplomacy*, p. 274. See also Haass, *War of Necessity, War of Choice*, pp. 272–273.

81. Jervis, *Why Intelligence Fails*, pp. 142, 176–177.

82. Tenet, *At the Center of the Storm*, p. 45.

83. Rumsfeld, *Known and Unknown*, pp. 464, 480–481, 517,664; Haass, *War of Necessity, War of Choice*, pp. 237, 254–258, 272–273; Woodward, *Plan of Attack*, pp. 415–416; Woodward, *State of Denial*, p. 455; Suskind, *The One Percent Doctrine*, pp. 62, 254; Mayer, *The Dark Side*, pp. 4–5.

84. Bush, *Decision Points*, p. 229; Rice, *No Higher Honor*, p. 198; Feith, *War and Decision*, pp. 238–239, 245–246, 274; Tenet, *At the Center of the Storm*, pp. 308–309, 322, 395; Suskind, *The Price of Loyalty*, pp. 76, 86, 96–97; Gordon and Trainor, *Cobra II*, pp. 14, 126; Ricks, *Fiasco*, pp. 42–43.

85. Pillar, "Intelligence, Policy, and the War in Iraq," p. 18; Haass, *War of Necessity, War of Choice*, pp. 5–6, 212–216, 220, 231, 234, 272.

86. Pillar, "Intelligence, Policy, and the War in Iraq," p. 18.

87. Isikoff and Corn, *Hubris*, pp. 32, 137, 295–296.

88. Kevin Woods, James Lacey, and Williamson Murray, "Saddam's Delusions: The View from the Inside," *Foreign Affairs*, May/June 2006.

89. Bush, *Decision Points*, pp. 224, 242, 245.

90. Haass, *War of Necessity, War of Choice*, p. 245.

91. Tenet, *At the Center of the Storm*, pp. 45–46, 330–332.

92. Leslie H. Gelb, with Richard K. Betts, *The Irony of Vietnam: The System Worked* (Washington, DC: Brookings Institution, 1979), pp. 190, 353–354, 365–367; see also McNamara, *In Retrospect*; Gordon M. Goldstein, *Lessons in Disaster: McGeorge Bundy and the Path to War in Vietnam* (New York: Holt, 2008), 190, 226.

93. John F. Harris and Dan Balz, "A Question of Balance," *Washington Post*, April 29, 2001, pp. A1, A6.

94. Kenneth T. Walsh, "Commander in Chief," *U.S. News and World Report*, December 31, 1990–January 7, 1991, p. 24.

95. Harding once complained to a friend:

John, I can't make a damn thing out of this tax problem. I listen to one side and they seem right, and then God! I talk to the other side and they seem just as right, and there I am where I started. I know somewhere there is a book that would give me the truth, but hell, I couldn't read the book. I know somewhere there is an economist who knows the truth, but I don't know where to find him and haven't the sense to know him and trust him when I did find him. God what a job!

Warren Harding, in William Allen White, *Masks in a Pageant* (New York: Macmillan, 1928), pp. 422–423.

96. George P. Schultz, *Turmoil and Triumph* (New York: Scribner's, 1933), pp. 263, 819.

97. Clarke, *Against All Enemies*, pp. 243–244.

98. O'Neill describes the president in meetings as silent and expressionless, uninformed and unengaged: "The only way I can describe it is that, well, the

President is like a blind man in a room of deaf people." Suskind, *The Price of Loyalty*, pp. 114, 149.

99. See, for example, Rumsfeld, *Known and Unknown*, 7221, 665, 667, 20; Haass, *War of Necessity, War of Choice*, pp. 272–273.

100. Rice, *No Higher Honor*, pp. 506–507.

101. George W. Bush, "Address," October 7, 2002.

102. Schultz, *Turmoil and Triumph*, pp. 263, 1133.

103. See, for example, Goldstein, *Lessons in Disaster*, pp. 172–173, 179–180, 186, 188–190, 215, 226.

104. Yuen Foong Khong, *Analogies at War: Korea, Munich, Dien Bien Phu, and the Vietnam Decisions of 1965* (Princeton: Princeton University Press, 1992).

105. Goldstein, *Lessons in Disaster*, pp. 138–140.

106. H. R. Haldeman, *The Ends of Power* (New York: Times Books, 1978), p. 34.

107. See Mark W. Huddleston and William W. Boyer, *The Higher Civil Service in the United States: Quest for Reform* (Pittsburgh, PA: University of Pittsburgh Press, 1996).

108. Richard M. Nixon, *Public Papers of the Presidents: Richard Nixon, 1972* (Washington, DC: Government Printing Office, 1974), p. 1150.

109. Graham Allison and Philip Zelikow, *Essence of Decision*, 2nd ed. (New York: Addison Wesley Longman), pp. 299–300.

110. Harry McPherson, *A Political Education* (Boston: Little, Brown, 1972), p. 298.

111. Mayer, *The Dark Side*, pp. 24–25; Thom Shanker, "Gates Wants to Shift $1.2 Billion to Bolster War Surveillance," *New York Times*, July 26, 2008; Thom Shanker, "Sharpened Tone in Debate over Culture of Military," *New York Times*, April 23, 2008.

112. Thom Shanker, "Defense Chief Criticizes Bureaucracy at the Pentagon," *New York Times*, September 30, 2008.

113. *The 9/11 Commission Report*, pp. 76–78.

114. Quoted in Haldeman, *The Ends of Power*, p. 107.

115. Goldstein, *Lessons in Disaster*, p. 43.

116. Rice, *No Higher Honor*, pp. 105–106.

117. Laurence E. Lynn, Jr., and David deF. Whitman, *The President as Policy-maker: Jimmy Carter and Welfare Reform* (Philadelphia: Temple University Press, 1981), pp. 116, 269.

118. Baker, *The Politics of Diplomacy*, p. 68.

119. Morton H. Halperin and Priscilla A. Clapp, *Bureaucratic Politics and Foreign Policy*, 2nd ed. (Washington, DC: Brookings Institution, 2006), pp. 85–86.

120. Betts, *Enemies of Intelligence*, pp. 23–24, 80–81, and sources cited therein.

121. Goldstein, *Lessons in Disaster*, p. 40.

122. Tenet, *At the Center of the Storm*, pp. 310, 315–316, 327–328, 334–335, 354, 358, 370; Ricks, *Fiasco*, pp. 54–55; Pillar, *Intelligence and U.S. Foreign Policy*, pp. 36, 142–143.

123. *The 9/11 Commission Report*, pp. 79, 91–92, 181–182, 267–269, 272–277, 352, 358, 400, 417, Mayer, *The Dark Side*, pp. 15–16, 112, 138.

124. *The 9/11 Commission Report*, pp. 263–265.

125. Zegart, *Spying Blind*, pp. 3–5.

126. *The 9/11 Commission Report*, p. 263.

127. *The 9/11 Commission Report*, p. 180.

128. McNamara, *In Retrospect*, pp. 211–212; Andrew F. Krepinevich Jr., *The Army and Vietnam* (Baltimore, MD: Johns Hopkins University Press, 1986). For an exception see Timothy J. McKeown, "Plans and Routines, Bureaucratic Bargaining, and the Cuban Missile Crisis," *Journal of Politics* 63 (November 2001): 1163–1190.

129. *The 9/11 Commission Report*, p. 350.

8

THE PRESIDENT AND THE EXECUTIVE BRANCH

Every president is dependent on the bureaucracy to achieve many of his goals. With divided government being the norm over the past three decades, presidents more than ever turn to the bureaucracy to accomplish changes in policy.[1] Public policies are rarely self-executing, however. They require a staff of experts who have an understanding of the substantive issues, institutional processes, and political implications involved in turning statutes, executive orders, and the like into services and benefits for the nation. These are the people who work in the executive branch. Some are civil servants, while others are political appointees, but both groups implement public policy.

The president sits atop the executive branch, the organization of which is illustrated in Figure 8.1. As the title of chief executive implies, the president has responsibility for executing or implementing government policies. Implementation includes issuing and enforcing directives; disbursing funds; making loans; awarding grants; signing contracts; collecting data; disseminating information; analyzing problems; assigning and hiring personnel; creating organizational units; proposing alternatives; planning for the future; and negotiating with private citizens, businesses, interest groups, legislative committees, bureaucratic units, and even other countries.

Because policy implementation is extremely complex, we should not expect presidents to accomplish it easily or exactly as they desire. Indeed, presidents are often frustrated in their efforts to meet their constitutional responsibilities to see that the laws are "faithfully executed." President Jimmy Carter complained: "Before I became president, I realized and I was warned that dealing with the federal bureaucracy would be one of the worst problems I would have to face. It has been even worse than I had anticipated."[2]

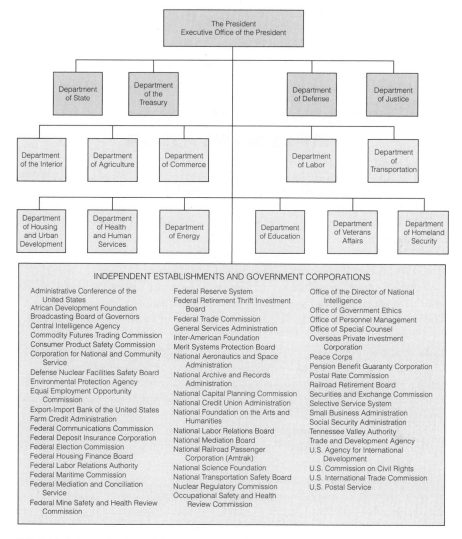

FIGURE 8.1 Organization of the Executive Branch

Source: Office of the Federal Register, *United States Government Manual 2012*
(Washington, DC: U.S. Government Printing Office, 2013).

In this chapter, we examine presidents' efforts, in conjunction with their subordinates in the executive branch, to implement public policies. Presidents fitting the director model dominate this process and ensure that policies are executed as they wish; presidents in the facilitator mold face just as great a challenge in leading the executive branch as in leading those who are not directly in their chain of command. We will find that, despite the unquestioned importance of implementation, it receives relatively low priority in the White House. We will also find that presidents face an uphill fight in implementing the policies for which they are responsible. Thus, we focus on the obstacles to effective policy implementation, including communication, resources, implementers' dispositions, bureaucratic structure, and executive follow-up, to better understand the difficulties the president faces.

LACK OF ATTENTION TO IMPLEMENTATION

Policy implementation has had a low priority in most administrations. Presidents have many obligations, of which implementing policy is only one. They must develop policies, make decisions, promote legislation, defuse or contain controversies, and court the public, to name only the most obvious tasks. Moreover, presidents—even former governors—generally lack experience in administration on the scale of the federal government and tend to find other tasks more compatible with their skills and interests.

Foreign affairs are always a top priority of the chief executive because of their importance, the president's unique constitutional responsibilities to deal with them, and the strong interest in international relations that many presidents bring to office. Besides, presidents often feel they can accomplish more in the international arena than at home, where they must wrestle over domestic issues with an unresponsive Congress or a recalcitrant executive branch. Ceremonial functions performed in the role of chief of state are traditions maintained by the president to broaden public support. All these activities typically take priority over implementation.

In addition, the incentives to invest time in implementation are few. Presidents have only a short time in office, and in their first terms they must constantly think about reelection. This encourages a short-run view in the White House, whereby presidents are more likely to try to provide the public with immediate gratification through passing legislation or giving speeches than with efforts to implement policies. As one Office of Management and Budget (OMB) official put it:

> The people in the White House are there for such a short time. The pressure is on making some impact and getting some programs passed. There is not enough time or reward in thinking carefully about effectiveness and implementation. The emphasis is really on quantity, not quality. The President could never be reelected on the effectiveness theme. "We didn't do much, but it is all working very well." Do you think a President could win with that?[3]

Presidents know that they will receive little credit if they manage policies well because it is very difficult to attribute effective implementation to them personally. Moreover, to most people, the functioning of government is seldom visible. When they pay attention to government at all, both citizens and the press are most interested in controversial scandals, the passage of new policies, or ceremonial functions. Policies such as Social Security reform or taxation, which can have a direct effect on people's lives, attract their attention; yet even here, the press and public are mainly concerned with the enactment of policies, not the process of their implementation. Although implementation directly influences the effectiveness of policies, this fact seems insufficient to entice the mass public and the press that caters to it to turn their attention to policy implementation. As a result of these incentives, presidents devote a comparatively small amount of their time to the task.

Similarly, policy makers devote too little consideration to problems of implementation in the formulation of policies.[4] Again, the proper incentives are missing. According to a Carter aide, "We all believe there should be more planning. The President has stressed the need for more caution. But when we fall behind, the President will impose a deadline. It is still a political system; and political systems are interested in results, not implementation."[5] As an aide to President Ronald Reagan commented, "It's unfortunately true that the management of the bureaucracy becomes one of the lowest priorities of almost every administration that comes to this city. Every administration pays a heavy price for it before it's over."[6]

The George W. Bush administration is a good example of paying the price. Its failure to plan adequately for the occupation of Iraq and to anticipate the insurgency that followed the toppling of Saddam Hussein cost it the public's trust. The president's hope to rely on Iraqi institutions such as the military and the police, to remove U.S. troops rapidly, to share the burden with allies, and to pay for reconstruction with Iraqi oil money but avoid massive reconstruction proved illusory.[7] As one commentator put it, "The Bush administration had goals for Iraq, but no coherent strategy for accomplishing them. Its policy was based on a combination of naïveté, misjudgment, and wishful thinking."[8] Similarly, the administration lacked a finished plan to guide its response to disasters such as Hurricane Katrina.

Massive budget deficits have placed a premium on using scarce public funds efficiently, however. Early in his tenure, President Bill Clinton launched a "National Performance Review" under Vice President Al Gore that emphasized cutting red tape, making government agencies more responsive to the needs of their clients, and cutting wasteful spending.[9] George W. Bush instituted his own performance-rating initiative, the Program Assessment Rating Tool or PART. Barack Obama has also committed his administration to efficiency and effectiveness in government programs. The White House launched the website Performance.gov to track progress on the administration's efforts to create a more effective, efficient, and responsive government and to share best practices across the government.

Despite these efforts, problems remain. The official who oversaw Bush's effort acknowledged that PART failed to achieve its main goals and received only cursory attention from policy makers. "There was frustration after eight years . . . that not enough agencies or program managers were actually using the results of the assessments to manage. Nor," he added, "was Congress—or, frankly, the administration—using the results to make significant budget decisions." He said, "You will never design a tool that will remove politics from the equation."[10]

COMMUNICATION OF PRESIDENTIAL DECISIONS

The first requirement for the effective implementation of presidential decisions or policies for which the president is responsible is that the individuals who are to implement a decision must know what they are supposed to do. Thus, presidents must transmit their decisions and implementation orders to the appropriate personnel. Naturally, these communications need to be accurate, and their implementers must accurately perceive them. Implementation directives must also be clear. If they are not, implementers may be confused about what they should do and will have the discretion to impose their own views on the implementation of policies (views that may differ from those of the president). Consistency in communicating directives is also crucial. Contradictory decisions confuse and frustrate administrative staff and constrain their ability to implement policies effectively.

Transmission

Before subordinates can implement a presidential decision, they must be aware that the president has made a decision and issued an order to implement it. This process is not always as straightforward as it may seem. Ignorance or misunderstanding of decisions frequently occurs. Although the executive branch has established highly developed lines of communication throughout the bureaucracy, this does not guarantee that communications will be transmitted successfully.

The 9/11 terrorist attacks presented many challenges to the U.S. government. Among them was the seemingly simple task of communicating orders. On the most basic level, the president found it difficult to speak with top officials in Washington because the phone line to the White House shelter conference room kept cutting off.

Even when the president's message was clear, his orders did not get through. Although the president and vice president ordered the North American Aerospace Defense Command (NORAD), which is responsible for defense of the nation's airspace, to shoot down planes suspected of having been hijacked, the order was not passed to the pilots in the skies over New York and Washington. One commander did not pass along the order "because he was unaware of its ramifications," while two other officers said "they were unsure how pilots would, or should, proceed with this guidance." As the chairperson of the 9/11 Commission put it: "When the president of the United States gives a shoot-down order, and the pilots who are supposed to carry it out do not get that order, then that's about as serious as it gets as far as the defense of this country goes." Perhaps even worse, an Air National Guard unit in Washington was operating under permissive rules of engagement that would have allowed pilots to shoot down planes, but the president, the vice president, and the military chain of command were unaware of this.[11]

There were also communication gaps between NORAD and the Federal Aviation Administration (FAA), which tracked the hijacked flights. They were unable to share information quickly or coherently as the terrorist attack unfolded, which prevented armed fighter jets from being scrambled fast enough. As a result of these communication problems, the last of the four hijacked planes had crashed before the vice president ordered the shoot downs. NORAD had nine minutes' notice on the first plane and did not know of other planes. In addition, within minutes of the second impact in New York, the FAA's Boston center instructed its controllers to inform all aircraft in its airspace of the events and to advise heightened cockpit security. It also asked for a similar alert nationwide. Neither occurred.[12]

Sometimes aides and other officials ignore presidential directives with which they disagree, primarily to avoid embarrassment for their chief. Such orders are generally given in anger and without proper consultation. For example, President Richard Nixon especially liked to let off steam by issuing outrageous orders. At one time, he instructed Secretary of State William Rogers to "fire everybody in Laos"; another time, he ordered everyone in the State Department to take lie detector tests. White House Chief of Staff H. R. Haldeman and other aides close to Nixon ignored these and similar outbursts, knowing the president would view things differently after he calmed down.[13]

In most instances, implementers have considerable discretion in interpreting their superiors' decisions and orders. Orders from the White House are rarely specific, and personnel at each rung in the bureaucratic ladder must use their judgment to expand and develop them. Obviously, this process invites the distortion of communications. Moreover, the further down in the bureaucracy presidential implementation directives go, the greater the potential for distortion becomes. In addition, subordinates may interpret the communications of their superiors in a manner that furthers their personal interests and those of their agencies rather than the goals of the president. Interest groups will also attempt to influence the interpretation of implementation orders at intermediate and low decision-making levels.

It is for these reasons that observers of the federal bureaucracy often recommend that presidents and other high officials make every attempt to commit their directives to writing (in detail where possible), use personalized communications where appropriate, and show persistence in attempting to convey their orders accurately to those who actually implement the policies. In an unusual move, Barack Obama personally dictated clear instructions for implementing his decisions regarding the war in Afghanistan.[14]

In general, the more decentralized the implementation of a public policy, the less likely it is to be transmitted accurately to its ultimate implementers. Decentralization usually means that a decision must be communicated through several levels of authority before it reaches those who will carry it out.

The more steps a communication must traverse from its original source, the weaker the signal that is ultimately received will be. A president can tell his secretary of state to go to another country and deliver a policy pronouncement to its prime minister with little concern that the message will be inaccurately transmitted. However, he cannot have the same confidence about messages aimed at caseworkers in a Social Security office or soldiers in the field. Here, the distance between the White House and the implementers is too great.

Moreover, the distance is increasing. Paul Light showed that a "thickening" of government has occurred over the past few decades. There are now more steps than ever through which information must flow to reach the individuals who actually implement a policy. As one frontline manager put it recently, "By the time an idea gets down here, it has been translated, reworked, and bureaucratized to the point where we just can't do it."[15]

In late 1983 and early 1984, President Reagan ordered reconnaissance flights over Lebanon. By the time the troops in the Middle East who were to implement the orders received them through the chain of command, however, they had been changed—undermining U.S. efforts to negotiate peace. In fact, the Pentagon canceled the flights at the very time when U.S. policy was to stand firm in Lebanon and then resumed the flights later, at a time when U.S. policy was to move toward withdrawal.[16]

Some presidents lack a personality that is suited to direct communication. Richard Nixon, who feared rejection and confrontation, adopted an indirect administrative style to avoid possible unpleasantness. He spoke elliptically to those who disagreed with him to avoid being rebuffed and typically failed to issue unambiguous orders directly to his subordinates. He did not like to say no personally or to discipline recalcitrant officials. When he found opposition within his administration, he tried to accomplish his objectives without his adversaries' awareness or he had intermediaries deliver either written or verbal orders. The president shunned personal efforts at persuading or inspiring subordinates.[17]

Nixon's unwillingness to communicate directly with his subordinates fostered an environment in which discipline and cohesion were often low. It also revealed a disunity in his administration that others could exploit, further eroding cohesion. Officials in positions of power, such as Secretary of State William Rogers, could increase their discretion by implementing orders with which they disagreed only when transmitted personally to them by the president—which they rarely were.[18] Secretary of State Donald Rumsfeld engaged in similar behavior during the George W. Bush administration.

The press also may serve as a means of more straightforward presidential communication. Individuals in the White House often believe that because most high-level bureaucrats read the *New York Times* and the *Washington Post*, they can communicate with these officials about policy matters more rapidly through news stories than through normal channels. The White House also uses other media outlets, such as television, newsmagazines, and specialized publications, to send messages to government officials.[19] Such messages may indicate a policy decision or position, or they may signal that an official White House statement was issued merely to appease special interests and should not be taken literally. However, the information provided in a story or as a response to a reporter's question is unlikely to be sufficient for guiding the implementation of a complex policy, and indeed, it may even be in error. Still, it is to the nuances contained in such communications that ears in Washington are often most attuned.

Clarity

If officials are to administer policies as presidents desire, White House implementation directives must be clear. However, the instructions transmitted to implementers are often vague and do not specify when or how a program is to be carried out. Lack of clarity provides implementers with the leeway to give new meaning to policies, which sometimes inhibits the intended change or brings about unintended consequences.

The lack of clarity about interrogation techniques in the George W. Bush administration set the stage for abuses in a number of prison settings.[20] Similarly, the president was not clear about who would hold power in Iraq in the aftermath of the U.S. invasion. According to Undersecretary of Defense for Policy Douglas Feith, "there was not a common, clear understanding of what the President wanted done."[21] Instead, the White House sent mixed signals to U.S. officials, which gave them substantial discretion and led to what many observers felt were disastrous policies.

There are several explanations for the lack of clarity in many implementation orders. Perhaps the most important is the sheer complexity of policy making. When they establish policy, neither presidents nor members of Congress have the time or expertise to develop and apply all the requisite details for how it will be carried out. They have to leave most (and sometimes all) of the details to subordinates (usually in the executive branch). Thus, although it is the president's responsibility to implement the policies of the national government no matter who initiates them, the White House must delegate much of this responsibility to others.

The difficulty in reaching consensus on policy goals also inhibits clarity in implementation directives. In the United States, we **share** wide agreement on the goals of avoidance of war, equal opportunity, and efficiency in government, but this consensus often dissolves when specific policy alternatives are under consideration. Lyndon Johnson once said, "If the full implications of any bill were known before its enactment, it would never get passed."[22]

Imprecise decisions make it easier for presidents to develop and maintain winning coalitions. Different people or groups can support the same policy for different reasons, as each may hold its own conception of the goal or goals the program is designed to achieve. Ambiguous goals also may make it less threatening for groups to be on the losing side of a policy conflict, which may reduce the intensity of their opposition.

The problems of starting up a new program may also produce confusion in the implementation instructions. Often, the passage of a new policy is followed by a period of administrative uncertainty in which a considerable time lag occurs before any information on the program is disseminated. This period is followed by a second phase in which rules are made but are then changed quickly as high-level officials attempt to deal with unforeseen problems of implementing the policy and of their own earlier directives.

A cynical yet realistic explanation for the lack of clarity in federal statutes is that Congress does not want them to be detailed. It would rather let the executive branch agencies provide the specifics, not because of the latter's expertise but because the agencies can later be assigned the blame for the rules that turn out to be unworkable or unpopular. One law affecting almost every college and university in the United States is Title IX of the Education Act Amendments of 1972, which states that "no person in the United States shall, on the basis of sex, be excluded from participation in, or be denied the benefits of, or be subject to discrimination under an education program or activity receiving Federal financial assistance." Such broad language allows Congress to sidestep many touchy questions and leave resolution to the president and his appointees. Moreover, individual members of Congress can gain credit with their constituents by intervening on their behalf regarding the application of regulations. In addition, if the goals are not precise, others cannot hold Congress accountable for the failure of its policies to achieve them. This imprecision adds to the president's burden in guiding the bureaucracy.

Sometimes Congress makes efforts to restrict the discretion of implementers. The Voting Rights Act reduced the discretion of local voting registrars by limiting the use of literacy tests and similar voter qualification devices. In some cases, the administration of voting registration was physically taken over by federal officials so that local officials could not inhibit voter registration. Congress has also invested a great deal of time in specifying eligibility requirements for government benefits ranging from social services and agricultural subsidies to grants for state and local governments.

Presidential decisions vary in specificity, and the White House often articulates them in policy statements expressing a sentiment or intention. They may indicate in general terms that certain actions should be taken but not specify exactly who should take them, or when or how they should take them.[23] One of Barack Obama's first acts as president was to send a memorandum to federal agencies ordering them to be as responsive as possible to Freedom of Information Act requests. The sentiment was genuine, but it is easy to see how much discretion this left for officials to interpret the order.

In addition, presidents seldom make a single, comprehensive decision covering a wide range of interrelated issues. More often, they decide a series of questions discretely and send a series of diffuse and, on some occasions, contradictory guidelines to the bureaucracy. Thus, no official receives just one order, but rather a stream of orders.[24]

It is generally easier for the president to reduce the discretion of officials via orders to stop doing something rather than instructions to start something. For example, an absolute ban on providing funds for abortions for poor women is more likely to be unambiguous and to be noticed if it is violated than an order to begin implementing a new policy. The implementation of most policies, however, requires positive actions rather than prohibitions. Moreover, in general, a series of positive actions extending over a long period of time and involving the technical expertise of numerous people throughout a bureaucratic hierarchy is necessary to implement a policy. The complexity of such policy making means it is very difficult for a president to communicate and enforce rules that effectively reduce the discretion available to most policy implementers.

Vague policy decisions often hinder effective implementation, but directives that are too specific may also adversely affect implementation. Implementers sometimes need the freedom to adapt policies to suit the situation at hand. A myriad of specific regulations can overwhelm and confuse personnel in the field and may make them reluctant to act for fear of breaking the rules. Apparently, this is what occurred in the Federal Emergency Management Agency (FEMA) as it tried to help the victims of Hurricane Andrew in 1992. During spring and summer 1993, President Clinton gave the same agency clearer direction and a shorter time frame in which to provide emergency assistance to Midwest flood victims, and the agency responded with greater dispatch and efficiency—which worked to the president's advantage.

Strict guidelines may also induce a type of goal displacement in which lower-level officials become more concerned with meeting specific requirements than with achieving the basic goals of the program. By rigidly adhering to the letter of a regulation, they may become so bogged down in red tape that the purpose of the rule is forgotten or defeated. Conversely, implementers sometimes simply ignore rigid regulations.

Consistency

Inconsistency as well as vagueness in guidance from the president may provide operating agencies with substantial discretion in the interpretation and implementation of policy, which they may not exercise to carry out a policy's goals. For example, before it was split into two agencies following the 9/11 terrorist attacks, the Immigration and Naturalization Service was often confronted with inconsistencies: The agency was supposed to keep out illegal immigrants but allow necessary agricultural workers to enter the country; it had to carefully screen foreigners seeking to enter the country but facilitate the entry of foreign tourists; and it had to find and expel illegal aliens yet not break up families, impose hardships, violate civil rights, or deprive employers of low-paid workers. As James Q. Wilson pointed out, "No organization can accomplish all of these goals well, especially when advocates of each have the power to mount newspaper and congressional investigations of the agency's failures."[25]

Similarly, the Forest Service is supposed to both help timber companies exploit the lumber potential in the national forests and preserve the natural environment. After the 2010 BP oil spill in the Gulf of Mexico, we learned that the Minerals Management Service (MMS), which regulated offshore drilling, had a dual role of both fostering and policing the industry—collecting royalty payments from the drilling companies while also levying fines on them for violations of law. It was split into two agencies the next year.

Many of the factors that produce unclear communications are also responsible for inconsistent directives. The complexity of public policies, the difficulties in starting up new programs, and the multiple objectives of many policies all contribute to inconsistency in policy communications. Another reason why decisions are often inconsistent is that the president and top officials constantly attempt to satisfy a diverse set of interests that may represent views on both sides of an issue. Consequently, policies that are not of high priority to the president may simply be left to flounder in a sea of competing demands.

RESOURCES

If the president lacks the resources necessary to carry out policies, implementation is likely to be ineffective. Important resources include money; staff of sufficient size and with the proper skills to carry out its assignments; and the information, authority, and facilities necessary to translate written proposals into functioning public services.

Money

Sometimes the problem the president faces in implementing policy and delivering services is simply a lack of money. From repairing the nation's transportation infrastructure to providing health care for the uninsured, from enrolling children in Head Start to buying new weapons systems, a program's budget determines the amount and often the quality of the service that government can provide.

Staff

Certainly, an essential resource in implementing policy is staff. "Big government" is often under attack, so it may seem surprising to learn that a principal source of implementation failure is inadequate staff. Although more than 4 million military and civilian personnel work full-time for the federal executive branch (see Table 8.1) and therefore for the president, there are still too few people with the requisite skills to do an effective job implementing many policies. We must evaluate the bureaucracy not only in terms of absolute numbers but also in terms of its capabilities to perform desired tasks.

The federal government provides a wide range of services—from national defense and immigration control to the maintenance of recreational facilities—through its own personnel. Each of these areas, and others like them, is labor intensive, and thus the quality of the services the bureaucracy provides is directly related to the size and skill of the staff available to the relevant agencies over which the president presides. However, there is substantial evidence that many agencies and departments are woefully understaffed.

Table 8.1 Federal Employment

Executive Departments	Number of Employees*
Defense (civilian, military functions)	765,000
Veterans Affairs	319,300
Homeland Security	191,000
Justice	117,700
Treasury	112,700
Agriculture	90,700
Health and Human Services Interior	72,600
Interior	69,800
Transportation	57,600
Commerce	43,000
State	33,200
Labor	17,500
Energy	15,900
Housing and Urban Development	9,200
Education	4,300
Larger Noncabinet Agencies	
U.S. Postal Service	546,203
Social Security Administration	65,300
Corps of Engineers—Civil Works	22,700
National Aeronautics and Space Administration	17,900
Environmental Protection Agency	16,900
Tennessee Valley Authority	13,300
General Services Administration	12,500
TOTAL Civilian Employees	2,681,151
Armed Forces	
Army	520,000
Navy	323,600
Air Force	327,600
Marines	190,200
Reserves	833,700
Total Active Forces	1,361,400
TOTAL Armed Forces	2,195,100

*Figures are for 2014.

SOURCES: Office of Management and Budget, *Budget of the United States Government, Fiscal Year 2014: Analytical Perspectives* (Washington, DC: U.S. Government Printing Office, 2013), Tables 10–2 and 10–3; and *Budget of the United States Government, Fiscal Year 2014: Appendix* (Washington, DC: U.S. Government Printing Office, 2013), pp. 233–234.

The U.S. Immigration and Customs Enforcement (ICE) in the Department of Homeland Security (DHS) lacks the personnel and technology to track most of the aliens who overstay their visas or who engage in suspicious activities. The ICE also lacks the resources even to identify, much less deport, more than 10 percent of the 200,000 convicted criminal aliens in the United States. Although 80 percent of the nation's drug supply and a large percentage of its medical devices and food are now imported, the Food and Drug Administration (FDA) lacks the personnel and computer systems to identify, much less inspect, the plants producing these items. Similarly, at a time when the use of low-cost generic drugs is one of the few ways to rein in skyrocketing health care costs, the FDA has a backlog of hundreds of applications to bring new generic products to the market.

Because of lack of personnel, it takes the Social Security Administration well over a year to process claims for Disability Insurance. There is a shortage of epidemiologists who are trained to recognize and investigate the outbreak of infectious disease. The Securities and Exchange Commission lacks the personnel to police companies and markets and thus protect investors against abuses in the marketplace such as occurred with Enron and the lending practices that led to the financial crisis in 2008. The army has lacked the personnel to fight active wars in both Iraq and Afghanistan, forcing defense officials to extend soldiers' tours and keep reservists on active duty longer than deemed wise. Similarly, there were far too few U.S. troops in Iraq after the invasion to prevent looting and violence. The Pipeline and Hazardous Materials Safety Administration is chronically short of inspectors, leaving much of the regulatory control in the hands of pipeline operators. The Fish and Wildlife Service lacks the personnel to evaluate requests for species to be protected.

Although staff size can be critical for almost every policy, it is more critical for some than for others. Insufficient staff is especially critical to implementation when the policy involved imposes unwelcome constraints on people, whether the requirements are those of grant policies, regulatory policies, or criminal law. Because such policies generally involve highly decentralized activities, sufficient staff must be available to monitor this behavior. It is much easier for the chief executive to implement a policy, such as Social Security, that distributes benefits that recipients desire. It requires more personnel to enforce limitations on people than to write checks to them.

The lack of staff makes compliance data difficult to obtain. Thus, the president and his subordinates often have to rely on information about compliance from those who are doing the complying such as those running schools, hospitals, pipelines, and mines. Quite naturally, this system of information raises questions about effective implementation. It should come as no surprise to us, then, when state and local governments misspend federal grants or hazardous wastes pollute the environment.

The fear of creating a totalitarian bureaucratic monolith and the pressures to allocate personnel to more direct services, such as the provision of agricultural expertise to farmers, keep the staff available to monitor implementation small. In addition, the scarcity of payroll funds, coupled with the irresistible urges of policy makers to provide public services (at least in form), ensure that staff size will often be inadequate to implement the programs. Moreover, in an age when "big government" is under attack, there are strong political incentives to downsize the bureaucracy.

Federal programs rely heavily on state agencies for their implementation. This reliance, however, does not solve the president's problem of lack of staff at the federal level; it merely transfers the problem to the states. Because this shortage of personnel exists at every level of government, delegating the implementation of a policy to a lower level rarely alleviates the problem. The federal government also contracts with private sector companies to provide many goods and services, but this approach is not appropriate for many federal government programs, ranging from fighting wars to prosecuting crimes.

Sometimes presidents turn limited staff size to their advantage. For example, the Reagan administration actually decreased staff in areas such as antitrust, civil rights, and environmental protection in an effort to reduce enforcement activities to which it was opposed.[26] The Republican Congress that was elected in 1995 attempted a similar strategy regarding the Environmental Protection Agency (EPA) but was unsuccessful. Such a strategy may be useful for stopping an activity, such as regulatory behavior, but it undermines efforts to take the positive actions that the administration may desire.[27]

Skill

In addition to numbers, skill is an important characteristic of implementation staff. The U.S. General Accounting Office reported that the federal government lacked employees with the necessary skills in information technology, science, economics, and management to run government programs soundly. For example, the Pentagon's financial statements are in such poor condition that they cannot be audited, and it has a critical shortage of engineers capable of managing complex weapons procurement programs.

Skill is especially critical and often in short supply when a government agency is carrying out or regulating highly technical activities. The Nuclear Regulatory Commission has difficulty finding nuclear engineers to monitor the safety of atomic power plants. As oil and gas companies took their drilling operations into deeper and riskier waters, the MMS had to rely on the expertise of those doing the drilling because it lacked the resources, personnel, training, and technology (as well as the enforcement tools, regulations, and legislation) that are critical to ensuring that offshore drilling is conducted in a safe and responsible manner. The agency frequently adopted industry-generated standards as federal regulations.

The terrorist attacks on September 11, 2001, dramatically showed that personnel with the proper skills are also often in short supply in the executive branch. We learned, for example, that the FBI and intelligence agencies had (and still have) only enough translators (especially in non-European languages) to interpret a small percentage of millions of pages of intercepted conversations. Only about fifty FBI agents can converse in Arabic. Because the FBI slashed its criminal investigative work force to expand its national security role after 9/11, it is now struggling to find enough agents and resources to investigate criminal wrongdoing tied to the country's economic crisis. Many Foreign Service officers in the Department of State lack the linguistic skills appropriate for their overseas postings. The government also lacked personnel with the right skills and capacity to deal with reconstructing Iraq.[28]

Similarly, in the wake of Hurricane Katrina, we learned that five of the eight top FEMA officials came to their posts with virtually no experience in handling disasters and that the agency's ranks of seasoned crisis managers had thinned dramatically. Before coming to FEMA, the director had been head of the International Arabian Horse Association, not usually a training ground for handling emergencies. The disastrous performance of this team followed naturally from its background.

Related to staff expertise is information. After the 9/11 terrorist attacks, we learned that the Immigration and Naturalization Service lacked information, such as terrorist watch lists, to prevent terrorists from entering the United States; the FAA did not receive information on flight training by suspected terrorists; and the FAA no-fly terrorist list contained the names of only twelve people (the agency did not receive information on terrorists from the FBI, CIA, or State Department).[29]

Sometimes the necessary personnel are very difficult to hire because of the higher incomes and greater flexibility that they can enjoy by working in the private sector. At other times, the needed staff may simply not exist, even in the private sector, and a government agency must invest in developing the expertise. The federal government's efforts to build a missile shield illustrate this problem. No one really knew how to build such a system, so it is not surprising that frequent failures have characterized the program.

Staff skills are especially critical for new policies or those involving technical questions. Routine functions, such as dispersing funds, building roads, training troops, hiring typists, providing building security, or purchasing goods, are relatively straightforward in their operation, and a wealth of information exists on how to carry them out. However, the implementers of policies such as controlling hospital costs or developing a missile shield do not share these advantages: They are being asked to meet goals no one has ever met. Thus, it is one thing for Congress or the White House to mandate a change in policy but something quite different for the executive branch officials who work for the president to figure out how to do it.

As a result, some responsibilities will simply not be met or else will not be met on time. Inefficiency is also likely to characterize the implementation of such policies. Some efforts will prove to be mistakes, and the implementers will have to try again. Moreover, regulations may be inappropriate, causing other government units or organizations in the private sector to purchase equipment, fill out forms, or stop certain activities unnecessarily. For example, before an agency acts to implement a law by ordering costly changes in an industry or its products (automobile emission standards, for instance), ideally the agency should be able to predict the effects of the change on the economic health of the industry in question. Such information, however, is frequently lacking, and the president may be severely criticized as a result.

Another response to limited staff is for the federal government to do most of its work through contracts, mandates to state and local governments, regulations on corporate and individual behavior, provisions of the tax code, and other indirect means. It is not easy to estimate the "true" size of government. One author concluded that well over 10 million jobs resulted from federal contracts or as a result of federal mandates to state and local governments.[30] Employing such techniques extends the range of government activity, but it also makes it more difficult for presidents to influence the implementation of policy directly and for others to hold them accountable for it.

Contractors have become a virtual fourth branch of government. Spending on federal contracts soared during the George W. Bush administration to more than $400 billion, and the estimated number of contractor jobs is nearly 8 million. This total far exceeds the number of people directly employed by the government.[31]

This growth was fuelled by the war in Iraq, domestic security, and Hurricane Katrina, and also by Bush's philosophy that encouraged outsourcing almost everything government does. Contractors build ships and satellites for the Department of Defense and intelligence agencies, but they also collect income taxes and develop agency budgets, fly pilotless spy aircraft, and take the minutes at policy meetings on the war. They sit next to federal employees at nearly every agency.

The contracting explosion raises questions. One argument for contracting out services is that the private sector will provide them at reduced cost because of competition to obtain the contracts. Yet most contracts have not been put up for full and open bidding, and the intended savings are scarce. Indeed, there are numerous official reports of billions of dollars of contractor waste and fraud, particularly in the rebuilding of Iraq.[32]

Contractors may not save money, and they also may not provide quality services. We learned on September 11, 2001, that the airport security personnel from the private sector carrying out federal policies lacked the training to protect airplanes from terrorist hijackings.

There is also almost always less public scrutiny of private companies than of government agencies, hiding government programs behind closed corporate doors. Companies, unlike government agencies, are not subject to the Freedom of Information Act. The lack of transparency is particularly problematic for firms exercising inherently governmental powers, such as providing security for U.S. personnel in Iraq or running prisons there. Some have been charged with abusing the use of force and engaging in illegal interrogations.

Authority

Authority is often a critical resource in policy implementation. Congress vests most of the authority in subordinate executive officials, but they, of course, work for the president. Sometimes agency officials simply lack the authority, even on paper, to implement a policy properly. For example, the policy being implemented may provide no sanctions against those violating the law, or the agency may lack authority to initiate administrative or judicial actions.

The Mine Safety and Health Administration lacks the power to subpoena mining company documents or to enforce effective penalties for safety violations. Until recently, the FDA lacked the power to order recalls of contaminated food. It also does no testing of drugs and medical devices on its own and must rely entirely on the test results submitted by manufacturers. Often, it even lacks access to potentially damaging company documents that reveal a manufacturer's involvement in product liability cases. The FDA also has no power to require drug makers to undertake new safety tests once a drug is approved.

When formal authority does exist, observers frequently mistake it for effective authority. However, authority on paper is one thing; authority effectively exercised is quite another. Executive branch officials may be reluctant to exercise authority for a number of reasons. One of the potentially most effective sanctions is the withdrawal of funds from a program. Cutting off funds is a drastic action. It may be embarrassing to all involved and antagonize the implementers of a program whose active support is crucial. Cutting off federal funds from projects also alienates the members of Congress who represent districts that are adversely affected by the elimination of government funds. Requiring states or cities to repay misspent funds can also have severe political consequences. In addition, terminating a project or withdrawing federal funds may hurt most those whom the policy is designed to aid. Schoolchildren, the elderly, or the poor are often the real victims of cutbacks. If a company loses federal contracts because of racial or sexual discrimination, it may be forced to lay off workers. Those with the least seniority may be the minorities the policy had tried to help. Similarly, cutting off federal funds for the educationally disadvantaged because of misallocation is most likely to hurt students from poor families. Local taxpayers ultimately pay fines for municipalities that violate the Safe Drinking Water Act.

The desire for self-preservation keeps many of the president's agencies from withdrawing funds. Agencies like the Federal Highway Administration and the Department of Education are primarily involved in channeling grants to other levels of government. To survive, they must give away money. If they fail to do so, they may look bad to Congress and superior executive officials and thus weaken future requests for budgets and authority. Thus, they may sacrifice the economic and social objectives of a program to the "maintenance" objectives of the bureaucratic unit.

Although executive officials often lack effective authority over other public officials, they have even less over private individuals, groups, and businesses, upon whom the successful implementation of policies often depends. Therefore, officials must make their policies attractive to the private sector. As a result of these efforts, for example, rules regarding safety in the workplace may not be issued; if they are, they rarely result in serious penalties for noncompliance. The federal government provided hundreds of billions of dollars to financial institutions in 2008 and 2009 so they would stay solvent and keep lending to prime the economy. Nevertheless, many of them failed to lend much of their new funds.

The president's authority to issue executive orders may play an important role in compensating for the lack of bureaucratic authority. Presidents have used executive orders for many important policy changes, including Franklin

D. Roosevelt's internment of Japanese Americans in World War II and his establishment of the Executive Office of the President, Harry Truman's desegregation of the armed services, John Kennedy's creation of the Peace Corps, Ronald Reagan's establishment of a process for OMB review of proposed regulations, and George W. Bush's declarations of emergency and the creation of the Office of Homeland Security and military tribunals to try terrorists captured abroad.[33] Barack Obama made important policy changes, ranging from education and student loans to mortgage repayments and prescription drugs, by executive order.

This authority has three sources: grants of constitutional power such as the powers of commander in chief, congressional delegation of its legislative authority through statutes, and the possibility that there exist inherent prerogative powers in the office. Congress delegates rule-making power to the president to set tariffs and impose trade restrictions, regulate industries, set agricultural marketing and production quotas, issue environmental protection rules, and specify aggravating factors for punishment under the Uniform Code of Military Justice. Only twice, both times in 1935, has the Supreme Court rejected a legislative delegation of power to the president.

Similarly, although Congress has the power to invalidate most executive orders, it rarely voids an important one. It did in 1998 when it prohibited Bill Clinton from spending to carry out an executive order on federalism. Sometimes the president backs down in the face of congressional opposition, such as Clinton did in 1993 when he contemplated ending the ban on gays and lesbians in the military. In general, however, executive orders provide the president an important policy-making power.

The judiciary has also given the president wide latitude in the issuance of executive orders. In the few instances in which the courts have reversed a presidential order, they have done so on the grounds that the order exceeded the president's constitutional or statutory authority. In the most notable example, the Supreme Court reversed Harry Truman's seizure of the steel mills to prevent a crippling lockout in the case of *Youngstown v. Sawyer* (1952). The Court held that the president had violated the Taft-Hartley Act because, in its deliberations on this legislation, Congress specifically rejected a provision that would have allowed the president to intervene directly in labor-management disputes.

One of the greatest obstacles to presidential direction of the bureaucracy is that the president shares authority over the bureaucracy. Congress passes the laws that establish and fund the programs that bureaucrats administer. With increasing frequency, courts issue orders that affect government regulations. In addition, agencies have extensive ties with external groups and congressional committees.[34] From one perspective, then, career civil servants have a strong political base from which to resist White House direction, including playing other political actors against each other to diminish presidential influence.[35]

At other times, the president's efforts to change the course of policy mobilizes opponents, as when Reagan's efforts to reduce enforcement activity in the EPA's Office of Water Quality encouraged citizen suits that had the effect of producing lower levels of political control in the long run.[36] More broadly, Reagan's (and to some extent George W. Bush's) efforts to reduce the rigor of EPA regulation reinvigorated a flagging environmental movement and infuriated the EPA's patrons in Congress, who resented what they saw as a blatant attempt to circumvent legislative intent by administrative action.[37]

Facilities and Equipment

Physical facilities may also be critical resources in policy implementation. Without the necessary buildings, equipment, supplies, and even green space, implementation will not succeed. U.S. troops in Iraq suffered from insufficient body armor and armored Humvees and trucks to protect them against roadside bombs. National Guard units have only a third of the equipment they need to respond to domestic disasters and terrorist attacks.

Frequently, there is also a shortage of sophisticated equipment. Computers are essential to the implementation of public policy. Nevertheless, the FBI lacks computers at its headquarters that allow it to search its own databases for multiple terms such as "aviation" and "schools." The FAA's air traffic control centers across the nation depend on aging, outdated equipment in the effort to direct the nation's air traffic. Similarly, the Internal Revenue Service (IRS) lacks the appropriate computer systems to integrate the dozens of databases that contain the information necessary to collect the $2 trillion in taxes that finance the federal government. The Customs Bureau lacks the computer system to monitor properly the flood of people and goods flowing into the United States every day. The computer system the EPA uses to track and control water pollution is obsolete, full of faulty data, and does not take into account thousands of significant pollution sources.

Although the president can request funds for new or additional facilities, both the White House and Congress hesitate to increase government spending to do so. In fact, increased spending in one area may come at the expense of decreased spending in another. Moreover, as is the case for staff, Congress often prefers to spread resources over many policies rather than to fund fewer programs adequately. Internal government procurement rules ("red tape") may add additional burdens to those trying to purchase expensive equipment such as computers.

DISPOSITIONS

We have seen that bureaucrats often operate with considerable discretion in their implementation of policy. Laws often permit agency heads wide latitude in influencing the rules, procedures, design, and substance of agency action.[38] This latitude provides implementers with the potential to give new meaning to policies, which may inhibit intended change or bring about unintended consequences. We also saw in Chapter 7 that bureaucrats may have views regarding the policies they are to administer that differ from the president's.

The fact that bureaucrats hold particular policy views and have discretion in the implementation of policy does not in itself pose problems for presidents.

If implementers are well-disposed toward a particular policy, they are likely to carry it out as the president intended. Other policies fall within a "zone of indifference." Lacking strong feelings about these policies, bureaucrats should implement them faithfully.

White House Distrust

The core of the tension between the White House and the career bureaucracy is the view that some recent administrations (including those of Bill Clinton[39] and George W. Bush) have brought to Washington: that the bureaucracy is not a neutral instrument. As the author of one prominent study put it:

> It is a rare political appointee . . . who does not take up his or her office convinced that senior career officials are . . . recalcitrant adversaries, saboteurs-in-waiting, obstinately committed to existing programs, and resistant to new policy initiatives.[40]

The new president and his staff believe that officials and the agencies they represent have interests of their own to advance and protect and may not necessarily view issues from the president's perspective.[41] If policies are in direct conflict with the policy views or personal or organizational interests of the implementers, they may exercise their discretion, sometimes in subtle ways, to hinder implementation. Moreover, bureaucrats "have resources of organization, time, and information that enable them to pursue those interests with vigor and persistence."[42]

As the size and scope of the federal government have grown since the 1960s, so has distrust, especially among Republican presidents and the general public. Richard Nixon told his cabinet, "We can't depend on people who believe in another philosophy of government to give us their undivided loyalty or their best work."[43] Similarly, Gerald Ford observed:

> There are bureaucratic fiefdoms out in the states or in various regions, and the people who occupy those pockets of power want to do things in their own way. They are pros at it. They have been disregarding Presidents for years, both Democratic and Republican.[44]

There is plenty of evidence that at times the ideologies of the White House and senior members of the civil service have clashed, although this potential for resistance to presidential initiatives has varied across agencies.[45] It is also the case that executive departments and independent agencies have agendas set by laws that predate the president's arrival in office and that serve as a force for continuity rather than change in response to the White House. In addition, it does not stretch the imagination to consider that how officials exercise their discretion depends to some degree on their dispositions about the policies and rules they administer.[46] National security assistant and secretary of state Henry Kissinger declared, "The outsider believes a Presidential order is consistently followed out. Nonsense. I have to spend considerable time seeing that it is carried out and in the spirit the President intended."[47]

There is some evidence that the policy predispositions of civil servants are critical to their compliance with their political principals.[48] B. Dan Wood and Richard Waterman found that the EPA maintained and even increased its inspections and citations of violations of environmental regulations in the face of strong efforts by the Reagan administration to constrain the enforcement of environmental protection laws.[49] Marissa Golden found some resistance to Reagan initiatives in the Civil Rights Division of the Justice Department.[50]

President Carter ordered federal agencies to discourage the development of low-lying areas that were in danger of damage from flooding. Twenty-five months later, however, only fifteen of the seventy-five agencies that had received the directive had issued regulations specifying how they were going to comply with the president's wishes. Forty-six of the agencies had not even taken the first step toward adopting the regulations. The primary reason for this lack of action was not bureaucratic indolence. Instead, it was the opposition of agencies to the substance of the president's order. Similarly, Ronald Reagan's efforts to build up special commando units for unconventional warfare and counterterrorist operations were hampered by the failure of the air force to provide adequate aircraft to deliver the forces and the army to provide the units with the proper equipment.

Differences in organizational viewpoints may also impede the cooperation between agencies that is so often necessary in policy implementation. The army requires aircraft, which belong to the air force (at its insistence), to transport troops. However, transporting troops is a low priority for the air force, which is more interested in flying strategic bombers and fighter planes. Thus, it typically does not fight for resources for troop transport planes or choose to allocate its scarce resources to that function, which undermines the ability of the army to carry out its own function. Similarly, in Iraq the army had to develop its own aerial surveillance capabilities, relying in part on civilian aircraft, because it felt the air force would not meet its surveillance needs. Secretary of Defense Robert Gates had to challenge the air force "to do more, much more" to send surveillance drones to collect more information on adversaries in Iraq and Afghanistan.

There may also be differences in viewpoints between presidential subordinates with different program responsibilities within a single agency. There was intra-agency conflict over the implementation of the National Environmental Policy Act. Secretaries of transportation, for example, had a difficult time getting development-oriented agencies in the department, such as the Federal Highway Administration, to consider seriously the environmental consequences of their projects.

Bureaucratic Responsiveness to the President

Although there is some evidence of bureaucratic resistance to presidential initiatives, there is good reason to expect the career bureaucracy to cooperate with the president's wishes. The professional norms of career civil servants offer political appointees considerable flexibility in directing agencies.[51] According to Francis Rourke, cases of bureaucratic challenge to presidential authority have been "a rare occurrence,"[52] and senior bureaucrats follow the election returns and defer to the president.[53] "What is surprising," agreed James Q. Wilson, "is not that bureaucrats sometimes can defy the president but that they support his programs as much as they do. The reason is simple: … bureaucrats want to do the right thing."[54]

Most studies have found that bureaucracies change their implementation of policy in line with the president's wishes, even in areas of political controversy. These studies cover a wide range of agencies in virtually every aspect of public policy.[55] As Richard Waterman and Kenneth Meier conclude, "All political-bureaucratic relationships are not a cauldron of conflict."[56]

It is also the case that the clashing of beliefs between career managers and political appointees has receded over time as the political views of the permanent bureaucracy shifted to the right and the senior civil service became more centrist. An increasing number of Republicans and Independents have moved into career managerial positions.[57]

Despite their initial suspicion and hostility, political appointees usually develop trust in the career executives who work for them. A "cycle of accommodation" characterizes the relationship between political appointees and career executives. This cycle occurs among most presidential appointees in all recent presidential administrations. Table 8.2 shows the results of surveys of appointees in the Johnson through the Clinton administrations. The figures in the table make clear that regardless of party, ideology, or administration, political appointees find that career executives are both competent and responsive.[58] As Paul Light put it, "In interview after interview, presidential appointees celebrate the dedication of their bureaucrats."[59]

Similarly, a survey of George H. W. Bush's political appointees found that they relied heavily on careerists for all aspects of their jobs, from formulating policy to implementing it. The political appointees also reported that they found career civil servants helpful in everything from mastering substantive policy details and anticipating policy implementation problems to providing liaisons with Congress and other components of the bureaucracy.[60] In Table 8.3, we can see the results from another survey of Bush political appointees. Most found that civil servants brought valuable experience to the job and had good leadership qualities and management skills. Equally important, these political appointees saw senior civil servants as working hard to carry out administration policies. Indeed, they perceived themselves as less likely to have valuable experience and be good managers than the civil servants who worked for them.

In sum, the bulk of the evidence supports a view that federal bureaucrats are "principled agents."[61] As Joel Aberbach and Bert Rockman point out, there is little evidence to support assertions of recalcitrant career civil servants when there is effective administrative leadership, including open channels of communication, willingness to listen to advice, clear articulation of goals, and mutual respect. Good management is compatible with good politics.[62] It is interesting that research has found that programs administered by careerists did better in PART evaluations under George W. Bush than those administered by political appointees.[63]

Table 8.2 Johnson–Clinton Appointees' Perception of Career Civil Servants

	Percentage Rating Careerists as Competent	Percentage Rating Careerists as Responsive
Party*		
Democratic	92	86
Independent	85	87
Republican	83	78
Ideology*		
Liberal	78	84
Moderate	90	85
Conservative	82	80
Administration		
Johnson	92	89
Nixon	88	84
Ford	80	82
Carter	81	86
Reagan	86	87
Bush	85	83
Clinton	82	78

*Johnson–Carter appointees only.

SOURCES: Johnson through Carter data: National Academy of Public Administration, Presidential Appointee Project, *Leadership in Jeopardy: The Fraying of the Presidential Appointments System* (Washington, DC: National Academy of Public Administration, 1985). This table is adapted from Paul C. Light, "When Worlds Collide: The Political-Career Nexus," in G. Calvin Mackenzie, ed., *The In-and-Outers: Presidential Appointees and Transient Government in Washington* (Baltimore, MD: Johns Hopkins University Press, 1987), p. 158. Reagan through Clinton data: Paul C. Light and Virginia L. Thomas, *The Merit and Reputation of an Administration: Presidential Appointees on the Appointments Process* (Washington, DC: Brookings Institution and Heritage Foundation, 2000), pp. 9, 31, 32.

Why do new administrations persist in the expectation of facing bureaucratic resistance in spite of strong evidence of bureaucratic responsiveness? Part of the answer may be that suspicions of the bureaucracy are fueled by presidential election campaigns, such as those of Jimmy Carter and Ronald Reagan, in which the winning candidate runs as a Washington outsider and engages in "bureaucrat bashing." (More recent presidents, however, have abstained from the temptation to criticize the bureaucracy in their campaigns and praised government employees.) In addition, most political appointees have viewed their positive experience with careerists as somehow unique, that their careerists were different from others.[64]

Staffing the Bureaucracy

The president's most straightforward response to implementation problems is to replace personnel who fail to implement policies the way the president desires with people who will cooperate. When presidents succeed in doing

**Table 8.3 George H. W. Bush Administration Appointees' Perception of
Career Civil Servants and Political Appointees**

	Percentage Agreement of Political Appointees about Civil Servants	Percentage Agreement of Political Appointees about Political Appointees
Bring valuable experience to the job	98	82
Have good leadership qualities	59	64
Have good management skills	61	55
Work hard to carry out administration initiatives and priorities	71	100

SOURCE: Adapted from Joel D. Aberbach and Bert A. Rockman, *In the Web of Politics: Three Decades of the U.S. Federal Executive* (Washington, DC: Brookings Institution, 2000), p. 123.

this, they can change the way in which a policy is implemented.[65] However, of the more than 4 million employees in the executive branch, the president and his designees appoint far less than 1 percent. Mid- and upper-level bureaucratic managers outnumber their political counterparts by almost 100 to 1, which places an obvious constraint on the ability of any administration to alter personnel.

Nominating Officials

Because the White House often distrusts the career bureaucracy, it invests a great deal of energy in its political appointments. A principal responsibility of political appointees is to elicit responsiveness of career officials to their directions. There are more than 4,000 political appointees in addition to the White House staff. These appointments fall into three categories. First, there are the Executive Schedule appointees, including the secretaries of cabinet departments, the heads of independent agencies and their deputies, and the heads of major departmental or agency bureaus or divisions such as assistant secretaries. There are also nominations for nearly 200 ambassadors, 94 U.S. attorneys, and 94 U.S. marshals, and also for many boards and commissions. These appointees are nominated by the president and confirmed by the Senate. There are over 1,100 presidential appointees requiring Senate confirmation.[66]

A second category of political appointees is comprised of noncareer senior executives and other officials. These appointees include senior staff in the immediate offices of cabinet secretaries, deputy secretaries, agency heads, and deputy assistant secretaries as well as members of some part-time boards and commissions. There are currently about 1,600 noncareer officials who are not subject to Senate confirmation. Lastly, the more than 1,500 Schedule C employees constitute the largest category of political appointees. Most hold titles such as "executive assistant" or "special assistant" and provide confidential support services to those in the Executive Schedule or to noncareer senior executives. A few hold management positions in special staff offices or small field offices. These officials are also not subject to Senate confirmation.[67]

After winning election, a president has less than three months to search for a new team to take over the government. Moreover, this selection must be done by the president-elect and the president's aides, all of whom will have been exhausted by the long, arduous election campaign and have many other demands on their time, such as preparing a budget and a legislative program. Members of the cabinet and other appointees usually have little advance notice of their selection and will be busy wrapping up their other responsibilities and doing preparation on the issues relevant to their new positions prior to their confirmation hearings. Thus, there is often slippage in the recruitment of the personnel at the top of the executive branch.

Presidents are also constrained politically in their appointments. Usually, they feel that such appointments must show a balance of geography, ideology, race, ethnicity, gender, and other demographic characteristics that are salient at the time. (Presidents Clinton, George W. Bush, and Barack Obama made substantial efforts to achieve diversity in their cabinet appointments.) Thousands of people seek appointments for themselves, and members of Congress and party officials urge thousands more on an administration. Few are qualified for the available jobs, yet due to political necessity the president will appoint some less-than-qualified individuals. Political favors may please political supporters, but they do not necessarily provide the basis for sound administration. Moreover, such appointments may result in incompatibilities with the president that lead to politically costly dismissals. Throughout a president's tenure in office, interest groups keep a watchful eye on who is appointed to what position.

A surprising limitation on personnel selection is that presidents often do not know of individuals who are qualified for the positions they have to fill. Following his election in 1960, John F. Kennedy told an aide: "For the last four years I spent so much time getting to know people who could help me get elected President that I didn't have time to get to know people who could help me, after I was elected, to be a good President."[68] Similarly, one close observer of the Obama White House found it striking how few top Democratic policy makers the new president knew as he selected his cabinet.[69] Thus, presidents often appoint people they do not know to the highest positions in the federal government.

In addition, many qualified people do not wish to undergo the loss of income and privacy and the partisan criticism that often accompany public service in senior positions. Such reluctance is not new. George Washington had five candidates in a row turn down appointment as secretary of state, so he moved Timothy Pickering from the Department of War to State and then had three turn down nomination as secretary of war. In addition, the first president had two persons, including John Marshall, turn down attorney general (and Alexander Hamilton turned down nomination as chief justice).[70]

In the past, early in their terms presidents did not typically impose their preferences for subcabinet-level officials on those whom they appointed to head the departments and agencies. The reason was partially the lack of organization in the personnel system. In addition, however, there was a concern that because top officials would be held accountable for the agencies' performances, they should be able to appoint subordinates whom they like and who would complement their own abilities and help them accomplish their jobs. Naturally, top officials generally requested this freedom. High officials also fought to name their subordinates because if they lost to the White House on personnel matters, their standing within their departments would drop.

The Reagan administration, in contrast, insisted on White House clearance of all subcabinet appointments. Although there is disagreement about the quality of the personnel appointed to high-level executive branch positions during this period, there is consensus on the view that Reagan's appointees were unusually loyal to the president and committed to his conservative ideology.

The George H. W. Bush administration reverted to the more common practice of giving department and agency heads discretion in making political appointments. It was more concerned with the competence and personal loyalty to the president of its political appointees than with their ideology. The presidents since Bush have cleared subcabinet appointments and placed a high priority on recruiting minorities and women to high office.

The George W. Bush administration, however, made the most systematic effort to politicize the bureaucracy, "both across the wider organization chart and deep down within the bureaucracy."[71] Sometimes the administration took political clearance to inappropriate lengths such as using political and ideological tests for hiring and promoting career lawyers in the Department of Justice or firing U.S. attorneys whom the White House saw as insufficiently responsive to its political needs.[72]

This process of political clearance, along with complex legal requirements regarding finances, security, and other matters, slowed these presidents' initial appointments. As a result, a large percentage of top departmental positions were still unfilled well into the first year of their tenures. After more than nine months in office, the Senate had not confirmed 40 percent of the top 505 positions in the George W. Bush administration.[73]

Similarly, seven months into his presidency, fewer than half of Barack Obama's top appointees were in place.[74] After 18 months, the president had filled only 79 percent of the key Senate-confirmed positions in his administration.[75] In addition to problems of political and financial vetting, the president faced the opposition of Senate Republicans. In several instances, the senators did not oppose a particular nominee but rather any nominee, so as to try to hamper the president's economic policies on prominent issues like housing, finance, foreign trade, and offshore drilling. In frustration, the president tested constitutional boundaries by making recess appointments while the Senate was technically in session.

As presidential terms extend from weeks into months and years, every White House experiences frustrating problems in policy implementation and tends to take a direct interest in personnel matters below the levels of department and agency heads. For example, in mid-1978 the Carter administration began a review of subcabinet officials with the object of weeding out those who were incompetent or disloyal. Tim Kraft was promoted to the position of assistant for political affairs and for personnel (indicating an appreciation for the linkage between the two), and Kraft and his staff began taking more interest in the appointees: "We have told the personnel people in the departments that we want to be consulted on all appointments, whether they are presidential appointments or appointments to high GS [civil service] positions."[76]

Limits on the Utility of Appointments

There has been a trend since the 1960s toward politicizing the bureaucracy and emphasizing the White House's operational control of the executive bureaucracy rather than traditional patronage. The number of political appointees at the top of the executive bureaucracy has increased substantially, as has the number of political appointees at lower ranks.[77] Presidents also make efforts to place political appointees in career positions just before leaving office.

Politicizing the bureaucracy has drawbacks, however. No matter how loyal to the president appointees are, they need to know what to do and how to do it once they obtain their positions. Studies have found that the preparation of appointed officials for their jobs, whether defined in terms of management experience, negotiating skills, congressional relations, or personal style, makes a difference. Good preparation for their jobs helps political appointees to mobilize the resources of the career bureaucracy.[78]

In addition, the design of policy implementation must be appropriate to the president's goals. Robert Durant challenges the assumption that presidents and their emissaries know what they are doing when they apply the tools of the administrative presidency. For example, the Reagan administration decreased staff in an effort to reduce enforcement activities to which it was opposed.[79] Such a strategy may have been useful for stopping an activity, such as regulatory behavior, but it undermined the administration's efforts to take more positive actions.[80]

It is difficult to recruit high-quality political appointees to some of the lower subcabinet positions, however, especially with the new financial reporting and divesting requirements and the visible and contentious nature of many confirmation hearings. Those that the president and his designees do appoint sometimes have policy expertise, but many are quite young, and few of them have managerial experience.[81]

The short tenure in the same job of typical political appointees[82] diminishes their ability to implement policy effectively, undermining the president's administrative strategy.[83] As administration becomes more politically and substantively complex, it takes appointees more time to learn their jobs and forge the relationships that make effective implementation possible. Appointees with short time horizons also have fewer incentives to deal with large but distant problems and may be more attentive to political and short-term considerations than to long-term program and agency management. Moreover, careerist agency managers believe that their efforts implementing appointee initiatives may be wasted, reducing their incentive to engage in long-term planning. As a civilian manager in the Department of Defense put it, "We start, we stop, we reverse, but we seldom move ahead for any period of time. One loses interest after a few years."[84]

Layering political appointees at the top of bureaucratic units complicates management and may separate the top executive from the bureaucracy and its services, thus decreasing the executive's opportunities to build personal support within the bureaucracy through communication, consultation, and access. Placing more political appointees at the top also undermines the motivation of the career service because it closes off the most senior positions to them.

The diffusion of responsibility that comes with a large number of decision points in a bureaucracy also increases the number of actors involved in policy implementation. Therefore, the costs of implementing presidential policy also increase because the White House and the president's top appointees have to influence more people in the implementation chain. Having more political checkpoints means there are more obstacles to innovation and barriers to employee involvement, which makes it more difficult to give frontline employees the authority to solve problems.

Despite its frequent use, political clearance is often a crude process. Many policy views fit under a party label. Democrats range from very liberal to very conservative, and the range for Republicans is nearly as great. Moreover, political appointees may be motivated by materialistic or selfish aims and not necessarily be responsive to the president. For example, a person may want the status of an ambassadorship, or a young lawyer may seek experience in the Justice Department or a regulatory agency in hope of cashing in on it later for a high-paying job in the private sector. Political appointees may also remain loyal to their home-state political organizations, interest group associations, or sponsors in Congress rather than to the White House. There are frequently unclear and tenuous links between the White House and political appointees, providing everyone with more discretion.[85]

Equally important, the president's appointees may disagree with him. Even George Washington had problems with his ambassador to France, James Monroe, after Monroe actively incited French anger over the Jay Treaty.[86] More recently, Richard Nixon ordered Secretary of Defense Melvin Laird to bomb a hideaway of Palestine Liberation Organization guerrillas, a move that Laird opposed. According to the secretary: "We had bad weather for 48 hours. The Secretary of Defense can always find a reason not to do something."[87] Thus, the president's order was stalled for days and eventually rescinded. President Reagan's national security assistant explained that the United States could not employ a strategy involving the selective use of force in order to support diplomatic efforts to keep peace in Lebanon because of the lack of cooperation between the Departments of State and Defense.[88]

It is sometimes difficult to fire recalcitrant appointees. Bill Clinton had disdain for FBI director William Freeh, who was not responsive to the president. Yet Clinton felt that dismissing Freeh would unleash denunciations by those claiming he was purging an enemy. Moreover, he feared such an act would generate comparisons to Richard Nixon's "Saturday Night Massacre," in which the president fired the Watergate special prosecutor and then had to endure the resignations of the two top officials in the Department of Justice.[89]

Turf fights among appointed officials over jurisdiction are not unusual in the executive branch. According to Richard Nixon, when presidential appointee J. Edgar Hoover directed the FBI, he "totally distrusted the other intelligence agencies—and, whenever possible, resisted attempts to work in concert with them."[90] At one point, the director cut off all liaison activities with the other intelligence agencies, including the Central Intelligence Agency, the Defense Intelligence Agency, and the National Security Agency.

Although recent presidents have placed many people who had favorable attitudes toward their administrations' policies in top career and politically appointed managerial positions, the number of vacancies they can fill remains limited.[91] Thus, filling vacancies is unlikely to be a sufficient strategy to alter the attitudes in the bureaucracy. The president must also influence those who are already holding their jobs.

Civil Service

Most executive branch employees rank below appointed officials in the federal hierarchy. Almost all civilian employees are covered by the protection of personnel systems designed to fill positions on the basis of merit. This system protects employees against removal for partisan political reasons. The military has a separate personnel system designed to accomplish the same goals.

If the president or a presidential appointee finds that a civil servant is obstructing implementation of the president's policies, he or she has some potential remedies. Those at the top of the civil service—in the Senior Executive Service (SES)—may be transferred and may be demoted more easily than in the past. Although members of the SES compose only a small percentage of the civil service (there are about 7,000 members of the SES), they are among the most powerful members of the career bureaucracy and the most crucial to implementing the president's policies.

Those below the SES are more difficult to move. It is possible to dismiss an incompetent or recalcitrant civil service employee, but this rarely happens. It takes more time, expertise, and political capital to fire a civil servant than most officials have or are willing to invest in such an effort. Transferring unwanted personnel to less troublesome positions is one of the most common means of quieting obstructive bureaucrats. In President Carter's words, it is "easier to promote and transfer incompetent employees than to get rid of them."[92]

Changing the personnel in government bureaucracies is difficult, and it does not ensure that the implementation process will proceed smoothly. Another potential technique that the president can use is to alter the dispositions of existing implementers through the manipulation of incentives. Because people generally act in their own interest, the manipulation of incentives by high-level policy makers may influence their subordinates' actions. Increasing the benefits or costs of a particular behavior may make implementers either more or less likely to choose it as a means of advancing their personal, organizational, or substantive policy interests.

The ability of top officials to exercise sanctions is severely limited. Rewards are the other side of the incentive coin, but they are even more difficult for executives to administer than penalties. Individual performance is difficult to reward with pay increases.[93] President Carter once complained that "more than 99 percent of all federal employees got a so-called 'merit' rating."[94] Ninety-eight percent of the 170,000 civilian employees under the Pentagon's new National Security Personnel System received 2009 performance-based pay increases. Raises are almost always given across the board, with everyone in the same category of employment receiving a similar percentage increase in salary, regardless of differences in performance. The Civil Service Reform Act of 1978 created the potential for awarding merit pay increases or bonuses to many managers, supervisors, and top executives in the federal civil service, but Congress has appropriated little money for these raises, and few civil servants have received them. Usually, personal performance can be rewarded only by promotions, which are, necessarily, infrequent. There may not be room at the top for qualified bureaucrats. Unlike a typical private business, a government agency cannot expand simply because it is performing a service effectively and efficiently. In addition, presidential subordinates who oppose or are indifferent to a policy are unlikely to employ incentives to further its implementation.

Limiting Discretion

In the absence of positive and negative incentives, the government relies heavily on rules to limit the discretion of implementers. As Vice President Al Gore explained in a report issued by the National Performance Review:

> Because we don't want politicians' families, friends, and supporters placed in "no-show" jobs, we have more than 100,000 pages of personnel rules and regulations defining in exquisite detail how to hire, promote, or fire federal employees. Because we don't want employees or private companies profiteering from federal contracts, we create procurement processes that require endless signatures and long months to buy almost anything. Because we don't want agencies using tax dollars for any unapproved purpose, we dictate precisely how much they can spend on everything from telephones to travel.[95]

Often, these rules end up creating new obstacles to effective and efficient governing, however. For example, in fall 1990, as U.S. forces were streaming toward the Persian Gulf to liberate Kuwait from Iraq, the air force placed an emergency order for 6,000 Motorola commercial radio receivers. However, Motorola refused to do business with the air force because of a government requirement that the company set up separate accounting and cost-control systems to fill the order. Ironically, the only way the air force could acquire the much-needed receivers was for Japan to buy them and donate them to the United States!

The White House has sought to constrain the exercise of bureaucratic discretion by requiring clearance of regulations and congressional testimony, limiting agency budgets, and establishing process restrictions on procurement and other spending.[96] The OMB reviews all regulations proposed by executive agencies (see Chapter 6), allowing the president to influence or block individual regulations. Agencies must also inform the OMB of upcoming regulations and documents providing guidance on the application of rules, aiding the White House in preempting or altering regulations and their applications before agencies propose them (when the political costs of opposition are less). Finally, the White House requires agencies to provide cost–benefit analyses of their proposed regulations and to have a regulatory policy office run by a political appointee to supervise the development of and evaluation of rules and documents providing guidance to regulated industries. Because cost–benefit analysis is often as much art as it is science, ideological preferences may determine the conclusions, which in turn may be used to resist regulations the administration opposes.[97]

Success in many policy areas often requires less bureaucratic rigidity, not more.[98] In addition, hierarchical control designed to limit bureaucratic discretion seems inappropriate for new approaches to public administration. Rather than being direct service providers or regulators, large elements of the federal service are becoming arrangers and monitors of proxy or third-party government, including services provided by state and local governments, private firms, and charitable organizations. Thus, the success of policy implementation now frequently depends on how adroitly federal agencies operate in nonhierarchical, loosely coupled networks of organizations that cut across the public, private, and nonprofit sectors, where discretion is either shared or shifts entirely to bureaucrats in the private and nonprofit sector.[99]

THE BUREAUCRATIC STRUCTURE

Policy implementers may know what to do and have sufficient desire and resources to do it, but they may still be hampered in implementation by the structures of the organizations in which they serve. Two prominent characteristics of bureaucracies are standard operating procedures (SOPs) and fragmentation, both of which may hinder presidential policy implementation.

Standard Operating Procedures

SOPs are routines that enable public officials to make numerous everyday decisions. They have many benefits for the chief executive. For one thing, they save time, and time is valuable. If a Social Security caseworker had to invent a new rule for every potential client and have it cleared at higher levels, few clients would be served. Thus, officials write detailed manuals to cover as many particular situations as they can anticipate. The regulations elaborating the Internal Revenue Code compose the bible of an IRS agent; similarly, a customs agent has binders filled with rules and regulations about what can and cannot be brought into the United States free of duty.

SOPs also bring uniformity to complex organizations. Justice is better served if officials apply rules uniformly, as in the implementation of welfare policies that distribute benefits to the needy or the levying of fines for underpayment of taxes. Uniformity also makes personnel interchangeable. Soldiers, for example, can be transferred to any spot in the world yet still do their job by referring to the appropriate manual, which is a substantial advantage for the commander in chief.

Although in theory SOPs are designed to make implementing policies easier, they may be inappropriate in some cases and even function as obstacles to action (see Chapter 7). Presidents have had many a plan thwarted by standard government practices. They certainly frustrated President Franklin D. Roosevelt, as he explained:

> The Treasury is so large and far-flung and ingrained in its practices that I find it is almost impossible to get the action and results I want. . . . But the Treasury is not to be compared with the State Department. You should go through the experience of trying to get any changes in the thinking, policy, and action of the career diplomats and then you'd know what a real problem was. But the Treasury and the State Department put together are nothing as compared with the Na-a-vy. . . . To change anything in the Na-a-vy is like punching a feather bed. You punch it with your right and you punch it with your left until you are finally exhausted, and then you find the damn bed just as it was before you started punching.[100]

SOPs may hinder policy implementation by inhibiting change. Because they are designed for typical situations, SOPs can be ineffective in new circumstances. For example, in 1962 the United States discovered the presence of Soviet missiles in Cuba and reacted by blockading the island. President John F. Kennedy was very concerned about the initial interception of Soviet ships, so he sent Secretary of Defense Robert McNamara to check on the procedures the Navy was following. McNamara stressed to Chief of Naval Operations George Anderson that the president did not want to follow the normal SOP, whereby a ship risked being sunk if it refused to submit to being boarded and searched, because Kennedy did not want to goad the Soviet Union into retaliation. However, McNamara found Admiral Anderson uncooperative. At one point in the discussion, he waved the Manual of Naval Regulations in the secretary's face and shouted, "It's all in here." To this, McNamara replied: "I don't give a damn what John Paul Jones would have done. I want to know what you are going to do, now."[101] The conversation ended after the admiral asked the secretary of defense to leave and let the navy run the blockade according to established procedures.

More recently, the FAA's protocols for hijackings assumed that the pilot of a hijacked aircraft would notify an air traffic controller that there had been a hijacking, that the FAA could identify the plane, that there would be time for the FAA and NORAD to address the issue, and that the hijacking would not be a suicide mission. As the 9/11 Commission put it, these SOPs were "unsuited in every respect" for the 9/11 terrorist hijackings.[102]

Sometimes SOPs cause organizations to take actions that superior officials do not desire, as the Cuban missile crisis dramatically illustrates. Despite President Kennedy's explicit order that the initial encounter with a Soviet ship not involve a Soviet submarine, the U.S. Navy, according to established procedure, used its "Hunter-Killer" antisubmarine warfare program to locate and float above Soviet submarines within 600 miles of the continental United States. Also following standard "Hunter-Killer" procedures, the navy forced several Soviet submarines to surface. Neither the president nor the secretary of defense ordered this drastic action. It came about because it was the programmed response to such a situation. The highest officials, who ostensibly had authority over the navy, never imagined that standard procedures would supplant their directives. Even worse, the commander of a Soviet submarine that the United States forced to surface had discretionary authority to fire its nuclear-tipped torpedo if attacked, and the crew pleaded with him to fire it.[103] Fortunately, he declined to do so. Clearly, SOPs can become deeply embedded in an organization and be difficult to control, even in times of crisis.

New policies are the most likely to require a change in organizational behavior and are therefore the most likely to have their implementation hindered by SOPs. For example, in October 1983, 241 U.S. marines were killed in their sleep during a terrorist attack on their barracks outside Beirut, Lebanon. A presidential commission appointed to examine the causes of the tragedy concluded that, among other factors contributing to the disaster, the marines in the peacekeeping force were "not trained, organized, staffed or supported to deal effectively with the terrorist threat."[104] In other words, they had not altered their SOPs regarding security (which are basic to any military unit) to meet the unique challenges of a terrorist attack.

Fragmentation

A second aspect of bureaucratic structure that may impede implementation is fragmentation—the dispersion of responsibility for a policy area among several organizational units. The more actors and agencies are involved with a particular policy and the more interdependent are their decisions, the less is the probability of successful implementation.

The resources and authority necessary for the president to attack a problem comprehensively are often distributed among many bureaucratic units. For example, the federal government has had as many as ninety-six agencies involved with the issue of nuclear proliferation. In his 2011 State of the Union address, President Obama pointed out that there are twelve different agencies that deal with exports, and there are at least five different agencies that deal with housing policy. The Interior Department is in charge of salmon while they are in fresh water, but the Commerce Department handles them when they are in saltwater.

Fifteen agencies regulate food safety. Cheese pizzas are the responsibility of the FDA, but pizzas with pepperoni on top fall under the purview of the Department of Agriculture (USDA). The USDA inspects commercially sold open-faced meat and poultry sandwiches, but the FDA is in charge of those sandwiches if they have two slices of bread. The FDA. oversees the safety of eggs still in their shells, but the Agriculture Department regulates liquid eggs that are used in industrial food production while also being responsible for chickens and the grading of eggs for quality.

The diffusion of responsibility in government makes the coordination of policies difficult but also essential. When the BP oil spill in the Gulf of Mexico occurred in 2010, we found that there were twenty-four separate offices and agencies with responsibility for making decisions about how to explore, map, preserve, exploit, and manage the ocean within U.S. territorial waters. This fragmentation led to delays, distractions, and disagreements over how to cap the well and defend the coastline.

In response to Hurricane Katrina, cities and states, the military, the Coast Guard, and the Department of Commerce, as well as private companies, offered to provide fresh water, diesel fuel, trucks, flat-bottomed boats, aircraft, and law enforcement officers to relieve people's suffering, keep the peace, and aid the rescue effort. Unfortunately, FEMA was incapable of accepting these offers and also had great difficulty coordinating federal relief and rescue efforts with those of the state of Louisiana.

On September 11, 2001, at least thirty-three departments and agencies had responsibility for protecting America's borders, focusing on threats ranging from illegal immigrants and chemical toxins to missiles and electronic sabotage. It is difficult to coordinate so many different agencies, especially when they lack a history of trust and cooperation. Moreover, there are often physical obstacles to cooperation, such as the largely incompatible computer systems of the Immigration and Naturalization Service and the Coast Guard. Once the borders have been breached and an attack has occurred, many other offices get involved in homeland security, including hundreds of state and local agencies.

To coordinate the implementation of a comprehensive national strategy to protect the United States from terrorist threats or attacks, Congress passed a massive reorganization of the government in 2002, including the creation of a new DHS. The success of this effort is unusual, however. It is difficult to organize government agencies around a single policy area. Broad policies, such as those dealing with environmental protection, are multidimensional and overlap with dimensions of other policies, such as agriculture, transportation, recreation, and energy. Similarly, any terrorist attack cuts across many areas. If people get sick because terrorists spray toxic chemicals on a portion of the food supply, the crime would not only be a case for the FBI but also for the Health and Human Services Department, the EPA, the FDA, and the USDA. In the absence of an attack, each of those departments and agencies has other responsibilities that overlap less than something as galvanizing as a terrorist attack.

The National Counterterrorism Center's (NCTC) mission is to gather information from across the government and assess terrorist threats facing the United States, then develop a plan for the government to combat them. To pan these streams of dots (about 12,000 pieces of information a day) for clues about terrorism, the center's analysts must access at least 28 computer networks maintained by other agencies, mostly through a time-consuming manual process. They cannot easily conduct dynamic searches, which involve looking for multiple variables and terms that are scattered across databases.

Moreover, the NCTC lacks authority to effectively coordinate counter-terrorism policy, and it cannot direct counterterrorism operations. It cannot investigate terrorist suspects in the United States (that is the FBI's job); it cannot conduct covert operations overseas (that is the CIA's sphere); it cannot intercept foreign communications (that is the National Security Agency's domain); and it cannot revoke visas (which is up to the State Department).

In 2004, Congress created the Office of the Director of National Intelligence (DNI) to coordinate the disparate parts of the intelligence community. However, the DNI lacks strict authority over the intelligence agencies because he does not completely control their budgets. As a result, the agencies still enjoy a large degree of autonomy. It is not surprising that the other agencies are still running largely disconnected and incompatible computer systems and that the Senate Select Committee on Intelligence concluded that the intelligence community failed to connect and appropriately analyze the information in its possession prior to December 25, 2009, that would have identified Umar Farouk Abdulmutallab (the "Christmas Day bomber") as a possible terrorist threat to the United States.[105]

A second obstacle to reorganization is Congress. Over the years, Congress has created many separate agencies and has favored categorical grants that assign specific authority and funds to particular agencies in order to oversee more closely and intervene more easily in policy administration. In addition, dispersing responsibility for a policy area also disperses "turf" to congressional committees. For example, in water resource policy, three committees in the House and three in the Senate have authority over the Army Corps of Engineers, the Soil Conservation Service, and the Bureau of Reclamation, respectively. None of these committees wants to relinquish its hold over these agencies, and therefore, the agencies and programs that deal with a common problem remain divided among three departments.

Like congressional committees, agencies are possessive about their jurisdictions. Usually department or agency heads will vigorously oppose executivebranch reorganizations that encroach on their sphere of influence. For example, when Tom Ridge, the director of the White House Office of Homeland Security, proposed consolidating some agencies involved in border security, such as the Immigration and Naturalization Service and the Coast Guard, his proposal was met with a storm of criticism from within the Bush administration, and Ridge had to back off. Similarly, when President Clinton proposed to merge the FBI with the Drug Enforcement Agency (DEA), both of which are units within the Justice Department, DEA officials were fearful of losing their agency identity (and perhaps their jobs) and mobilized sympathetic members of Congress to oppose the move.

Interest groups are a third force supporting fragmentation. They fear that a bureaucratic reorganization would jeopardize the close relationship they have with an agency. Interest groups also develop close working relationships with congressional committees and do not want to lose their special access in a reorganization of committee jurisdictions that might follow an executive-branch reorganization.

Often, combinations of interest groups, agencies, or legislative committees oppose reorganization. The Department of Education, which President Carter proposed, is composed almost exclusively of education programs from the old Department of Health, Education and Welfare. Head Start, Native American education, the school lunch program, GI bill benefits, job training, and some vocational and rehabilitation education programs remained where they were because of opposition to their being moved. For example, the Senate Agriculture Committee opposed any change out of fear of losing oversight responsibility for child nutrition programs, whereas the American Food Service Association opposed any change because it feared nutrition would not be a high priority with educators.

The FBI and CIA resisted having their counterterrorism units placed in the same agency, fearful that the new NCTC and its director would rob them of their powers. Civil libertarians, meanwhile, warned that putting the FBI, a domestic law enforcement agency, in such proximity to spies, who labor under fewer and different laws when working abroad, was a recipe for abuse.

Presidents have some resources in the battle over reorganization. When they cannot convince Congress to create an administrative agency that they want, presidents may strike out on their own. Over the past six decades, they have created half the new administrative agencies, using executive orders, department orders, and general reorganization authority (which they frequently possessed until the Supreme Court struck down the legislative veto in 1983) to create agencies like the National Security Agency, the Peace Corps, and the Environmental Protection Agency. These agencies tend to be smaller and less important than agencies that Congress creates with the president, but the president has more control over the personnel in them.[106]

In the past, Congress has often given presidents the right to propose reorganizations that would then receive a quick up or down vote. The polarization of politics in recent times has made such authority less likely. When President Obama asked for this "fast track" authority in 2012, Congress failed to act on his request.

Another approach is the increasingly common practice of presidential appointment of so-called executive-branch "czars" in the White House. For example, President Obama appointed officials to oversee economic reform, health care reform, energy and climate change, terrorism, nuclear nonproliferation, and urban policies.[107]

Duplication in the provision of public services is another result of bureaucratic fragmentation. President Carter complained, "There are . . . at least 75 agencies and 164,000 Federal employees in police or investigative work. Many of them duplicate or overlap state and local law enforcement efforts unnecessarily."[108] Even worse, duplication may spread the government's resources too thin. As the 9/11 Commission pointed out, there are too few experts in many areas of national security for us to be able to afford duplication of effort.[109]

Implementation may result in two or more agencies working at cross purposes. The United States is running out of helium-3, a rare gas crucial for detecting smuggled nuclear weapons materials, because one arm of the Energy Department has been selling the gas six times as fast as another arm could accumulate it, and the two sides failed to communicate for years.

Sometimes it is reorganization itself that encourages duplication and bureaucratic turf fights. In the years since the Bureau of Alcohol, Tobacco, Firearms, and Explosives (ATF) was moved into the Department of Justice to better coordinate the fight against terrorism with the FBI, the rival law enforcement agencies have fought each other for control, wasting time and money. The attorney general ordered them to merge their national bomb databases, but the FBI refused. The ATF has long trained bomb-sniffing dogs; the FBI started a competing program.[110]

Not only do such conflicts defeat the purposes of the programs involved, but they also force the president's highest-level aides and departmental executives to spend great amounts of time and energy negotiating with one another. This is wasteful, and it may result in compromises representing the lowest common denominators of the officials' original positions. Unfortunately, bold and original ideas may be sacrificed for intragovernmental harmony.

FOLLOW-UP

As a result of all the hindrances to effective policy implementation, it seems reasonable to suggest that implementation would be improved if presidents followed up on their decisions and orders to see that they have been properly implemented.

An incident that occurred during the Nixon administration illustrates the importance of follow-up. President Nixon ordered the CIA to destroy its stockpile of biological weapons. CIA Director Richard Helms relayed the president's order to the deputy director for plans (the head of the covert action division), who, in turn, relayed it to a subordinate. Five years later, however, officials discovered two lethal toxins hidden in a secret cache. A mid-level official had disobeyed the president's order and then retired, and his successor had assumed that the storage of the toxins had official approval. When called before Congress, Helms testified that he had undertaken no follow-up check on his own order, and when asked who told him the toxins had been destroyed, he replied, "I read it in the newspapers." Indeed, if the official who discovered the toxins had not received a directive from the new CIA director, William Colby, to be on the constant lookout for illegal action, he might not have checked on the legality of the toxins, and the cache would still have existed.[111]

Thus, a president must constantly check up on his orders, yet most recent presidents have not followed this advice. On the whole, follow-up has been haphazard. Presidents and their staffs have been too busy with crisis management, electoral politics, or encouraging the passage of legislation to delve into the details involved in monitoring policy implementation. Moreover, they lack systematic information about the performance of agencies. Some presidents are philosophically opposed to engaging in much follow-up. For example, Ronald Reagan believed that the chief executive should set broad policy goals and general ground rules and then appoint good people to accomplish the goals. He did not believe presidents should constantly monitor their subordinates.[112]

One technique that presidents can use to increase their capacity to follow up on their decisions is to enlarge the size of their personal staffs. Certainly, the executive staff is crucial to the president's ability to put his stamp on policy implementation. As Secretary of State George Shultz put it: "If the president's staff does not support a policy, the policy is not likely to succeed. The president by himself cannot make sure that a policy is being implemented, so the staff has to be brought along."[113]

Relying heavily on the White House staff for policy implementation can create additional burdens for the president, however—even if the staff supports a policy. Because chief executives can personally deal effectively with only a limited number of people, they are forced to relay implementation orders and receive feedback through additional layers of their own staffs. This, in turn, increases both the possibility of communication distortion and the burden of administration, which the staff is supposed to lighten. The more that authority is delegated to people at the top of a hierarchy, the more possibilities there are for inadequate coordination, interoffice rivalries, communication gaps, and other typical administrative problems to arise. Moreover, having a large number of aides with limited access to a top official such as the president increases the chance that they may carry out a presidential order given in anger. Individuals with limited access will be less likely to know the executive well enough or have enough confidence to hold back on implementing their supervisor's instructions.

Having a large implementation staff for a president has another drawback: Only a few people can credibly speak for the president. If too many people begin giving orders in the president's name, for example, they will undermine the credibility of all those claiming to speak for him. This credibility is important for aides trying to help the president implement policies. As one Carter aide explained: "If you are perceived by people in a given agency as being close to the president because you have an office in the West Wing, your phone calls will be returned more rapidly and your requests for information or action will be taken more seriously."[114]

Presidential assistants carry the contingent authority of the president, which is essential to accomplish anything at all because under the law, presidential assistants have no authority of their own. However, presidential authority is undermined if numerous people attempt to exercise it.

Excessively vigorous staff involvement in implementation decisions may cause other problems. For example, some observers of recent presidential administrations have concluded that as larger numbers of bright, ambitious, energetic assistants probe into the activities of departments and agencies, they will bring more issues to the president for decision making, which were formerly decided at lower levels in the bureaucracy. Bureaucrats will begin to pass the buck upward, and the White House must then make increasing numbers of decisions. This can easily make the Executive Office of the President top-heavy and slow. Involvement in the minutiae of government may also divert resources (including time) from the central objectives and major problems of a president's administration. In addition, if White House aides become intimately involved in the management of government programs, they may lose the objectivity necessary to evaluate new ideas regarding "their" programs.

Overcentralization of decision making at the highest levels may have other negative consequences: It may discourage capable people from serving in government posts where their authority is frequently undercut; it may lower morale and engender resentment and hostility in the bureaucracy, which may impede future cooperation; it may decrease respect for lower officials among their subordinates; it may reduce the time bureaucratic officials have for internal management because they must fight to maintain access to and support of the chief executive; and it may weaken the capability of agencies to streamline or revitalize their management. Similarly, too much monitoring of subordinates' behavior may elicit hostility or excessive caution and lack of imagination in administering policy.

Another factor inhibiting follow-up is secrecy. Secretly executed policies, such as those implemented by intelligence agencies, require few reports to Congress or superiors in the executive branch. Consequently, such officials' actions are not routinely monitored. Because members of Congress risk criticism for violating national security if they make public any secret information, they are reluctant to do so and have incentives to forgo their responsibility for the oversight and follow-up of certain secret policies. For example, when President Johnson's fear of leaks regarding decisions on the Vietnam War led him to restrict his direct communications to a few top officials (the Tuesday lunch group), he did so without a prearranged agenda or minutes of the meetings, which would have recorded decisions and made it possible to follow up on them.

The increasing number of management layers in government can also hamper follow-up. The thickening of government makes it more difficult to ascertain the locus of responsibility for policy implementation. Accountability is reduced when no one unit or individual can be held responsible for a lack of action or poor communication.

An organization's personnel may be aware of implementation problems yet fail to report them to the president or other administration officials. There are several reasons for this. An obvious one is that subordinates may fear that reporting implementation failures will reflect poorly on their own performance and also possibly anger their superiors. Additionally, employees may have a natural loyalty to their organization or to others in the organization who might be hurt by their negative reports. Further, the informal norms against reporting negative information may be very strong. Thus, employees may withhold information from their superiors to escape social ostracism in their peer groups. Finally, some bureaucrats may feel that the president is simply too busy to bother with matters of policy implementation.

Even when information indicating poor policy implementation is available to the president and other top executive officials, they may fail to use it. Information coming from the field is often fragmentary, circumstantial, inconsistent, ambiguous, and unrepresentative—in sum, it is very often unreliable. In addition, as noted in Chapter 7, such information may become lost in the huge volume of data circulating in the executive branch. It is very difficult for the president to have a clear idea of how a complex policy is actually implemented.

Organizations may fail to report problems in policy implementation for political reasons, such as the fear of losing public or legislative support for their programs. Also, within some organizations, rivalries between headquarters and field personnel make the latter reluctant to expose themselves to negative reactions to their implementation efforts.

Although there are limitations on performing follow-up properly, this does not mean that follow-up cannot work. Moreover, there is substantial evidence that it needs to be done. The Nixon administration's efforts to monitor and evaluate the actions of welfare caseworkers, and especially to review them for errors that allowed ineligible people to receive funds under the Aid to Families with Dependent Children program, had a significant influence on reducing the number of people receiving welfare. (Unfortunately, it appears that this approach also resulted in many eligible people not receiving welfare payments.)[115]

CONCLUSION

The president faces many obstacles in implementing public policies. Although the president is the chief executive, he has not typically been in a position to command the bureaucracy within the executive branch. Moreover, the president operates in an environment of scarce resources and few incentives to devote time and energy to implementation and will generally emerge from this process as a facilitator rather than a director.

Improving implementation is difficult as the roots of most implementation problems are embedded deeply in the fabric of American government and politics. Moreover, as long as presidents remain more concerned with shaping legislation to pass in the Congress than with the implementation of the law after it is passed, persist in emphasizing public relations rather than public policy, and allow crisis situations to continue to dominate their time, little progress is likely to be made in improving policy implementation. In addition, until there are more political incentives for officials to devote more attention to policy implementation and to develop better administrative skills, these priorities will probably not change. Given both the low visibility of many policy implementation activities and the lack of interest in them, the prospects for a change in incentives are not very favorable.

Discussion Questions

1. Since the 1970s, the American public has typically supported smaller government but no reduction in federal services. How should a president deal with the dilemma of making trade-offs between saving money and providing high-quality public services?

2. Some presidents such as Nixon, Reagan, and George W. Bush have emphasized bureaucratic responsiveness and made strong efforts to place administration loyalists throughout the bureaucracy. Other presidents, such as George H. W. Bush and Bill Clinton, have focused on efficiency and emphasized finding the most skilled people to fill administrative positions. Which strategy do you feel is best for the country? Why?

3. In the private sector, businesses and institutions use salary increases and bonuses to encourage effective job performance. Selective bonuses and substantial pay raises are relatively rare in the public sector, however. Should Congress appropriate more funds for the bureaucracy so that the president and his appointees can use economic incentives to make the bureaucracy more responsive to their policies, or would this be a waste of taxpayers' money?

Web Exercises

1. On January 24, 2003, President George W. Bush signed legislation that created the Department of Homeland Security (DHS), the largest department created since 1947. The department's mission is to secure the homeland, and Congress created the department to better coordinate the nation's homeland defenses and to emphasize the war on terrorism among the diverse roles of the department's component agencies. Go to the department's Website at www.dhs.gov to learn more about DHS. Then choose areas of DHS responsibility such as securing nuclear power plants or containers arriving by ship and search the Internet to determine whether you are satisfied with DHS's performance.

2. From the *United States Government Manual* (www.usgovernmentmanual. gov), you can obtain a good sense of how the executive branch is organized and some of the implications of the organization of the executive branch for implementing policy. For example, click on the Department of Agriculture in the Executive Branch: Departments category. Note that in addition to supporting agricultural research and directly aiding farmers, the department has responsibilities in nutrition, food safety, education, housing, civil rights, conservation, and international trade—areas also covered by other agencies and departments. Go to www.usgovernmentmanual.gov and list services that you might not expect in at least three departments. Then try to determine how well policy in these areas is coordinated in the federal government.

Selected Readings

Aberbach, Joel D., and Bert A. Rockman. *In the Web of Politics: Three Decades of the Federal Executive.* Washington, DC: Brookings Institution, 2000.

Allison, Graham, and Philip Zelikow. *Essence of Decision: Explaining the Cuban Missile Crisis,* 2nd ed. New York: Longman, 1999.

Arnold, Peri E. *Making the Managerial Presidency,* 2nd ed. Princeton, NJ: Princeton University Press, 1996.

Cooper, Phillip J. *By Order of the Executive.* Lawrence: University Press of Kansas, 2002.

Derthick, Martha. *Agency under Stress.* Washington, DC: Brookings Institution, 1990.

Durant, Robert F. *The Administrative Presidency Revisited.* Albany: State University of New York Press, 1992.

Edwards, George C., III. "Why Not the Best? The Loyalty–Competence Trade-Off in Presidential Appointments." In *Innocent until Nominated,* edited by G. Calvin Mackenzie. Washington, DC: Brookings Institution, 2000.

Howell, William G. *Power without Persuasion.* Princeton, NJ: Princeton University Press, 2003.

Lewis, David E. *Presidents and the Politics of Agency Design.* Stanford, CA: Stanford University Press, 2003.

Lewis, David E. *The Politics of Presidential Appointments.* Princeton, NJ: Princeton University Press, 2008.

Light, Paul C. *Thickening Government.* Washington, DC: Brookings Institution, 1995.

Mayer, Kenneth R. *With the Stroke of a Pen: Executive Orders and Presidential Power.* Princeton, NJ: Princeton University Press, 2001.

Warber, Adam L. *Executive Orders and the Modern Presidency.* Boulder, CO: Lynne Reinner, 2006.

Weko, Thomas L. *The Politicizing Presidency: The White House Personnel Office, 1948–1994.* Lawrence: University Press of Kansas, 1995.

Whitford, Andrew B. "The Pursuit of Political Control by Multiple Principals." *Journal of Politics* 67 (February 2005): 29–49.

Wood, B. Dan, and Richard W. Waterman. *Bureaucratic Dynamics.* Boulder, CO: Westview, 1994.

Notes

1. See, for example, Richard P. Nathan, *The Administrative Presidency* (New York: John Wiley and Sons, 1983); and Terry M. Moe, "The Politicized Presidency," in James P. Pfiffner, ed., *The Managerial Presidency,* 2nd ed. (College Station: Texas A&M University Press, 1999).

2. President Carter quoted in G. Calvin Mackenzie, "Personnel Appointment Strategies in Post-War Presidential Administrations" (paper presented at the Annual Meeting of the Midwest Political Science Association, Chicago, April 1980), introductory page.

3. Quoted in Paul C. Light, *The President's Agenda: Domestic Policy Choice from Kennedy to Carter* (Baltimore, MD: Johns Hopkins University Press, 1982), p. 145.

4. On this point, see Martha Derthick, *Agency under Stress* (Washington, DC: Brookings Institution, 1990), esp. pp. 66, 184.

5. Quoted in Derthick, *Agency under Stress,* p. 152.

6. David Gergen quoted in "How Much Can Any Administration Do?" *Public Opinion* (December/January 1982): 56.

7. Among the many studies of this issue, see Michael R. Gordon and Bernard E. Trainor, *Cobra II: The Inside Story of the Invasion and Occupation of Iraq* (New York: Pantheon Books, 2006); and Thomas E. Ricks, *Fiasco: The American Military Adventure in Iraq* (New York: Penguin Press, 2006). See also Condoleezza Rice,

No Higher Honor: A Memoir of My Years in Washington (New York: Crown Publishers, 2011), pp. 189–190.

8. David L. Phillips, *Losing Ground* (Boulder, CO: Westview, 2005), p. 156.

9. Al Gore, *From Red Tape to Results: Creating a Government That Works Better and Costs Less* (New York: Times Books, 1993).

10. Quoted in Shawn Zeller, "Performance Anxiety for 'New' Federal Standards," *CQ Weekly*, March 30, 2009, pp. 708–709.

11. *The 9/11 Commission Report* (New York: Norton, 2004), pp. 40–44; Philip Shenon and Christopher Marquis, "Panel Says Chaos in Administration Was Wide on 9/11," *New York Times*, June 18, 2004.

12. *The 9/11 Commission Report*, pp. 14–31.

13. See, for example, William Safire, *Before the Fall: An Inside View of the Pre-Watergate White House* (New York: Doubleday, 1975), pp. 112–113, 285–287, 353, 566–567; and H. R. Haldeman, *The Ends of Power* (New York: Times Books, 1978), pp. 58–59, 111–112, 185–187.

14. Bob Woodward, *Obama's Wars* (New York: Simon and Schuster, 2010), pp. 385–390.

15. Paul C. Light, *Thickening Government* (Washington, DC: Brookings Institution, 1995), p. 86.

16. George P. Shultz, *Turmoil and Triumph* (New York: Scribner's, 1993), pp. 228–229. See also Donald Rumsfeld, *Known and Unknown* (New York: Penguin, 2011), p. 15.

17. See, for example, Henry Kissinger, *White House Years* (Boston: Little, Brown, 1979), pp. 26, 28–29, 45–46, 48, 141–142, 158–159, 264, 482, 729, 806, 879, 887, 900, 909, 917, 994.

18. Ibid., pp. 28–29, 264, 900.

19. See Ted Sorensen, *Counselor: A Life on the Edge of History* (New York: Harper-Collins, 2008), p. 341, regarding John F. Kennedy using press conferences to speak to his own administration, especially those in middle and lower ranks.

20. Jane Mayer, *The Dark Side: The Inside Story of How the War on Terror Turned into a War on American Ideals* (New York: Doubleday, 2008), chap. 10.

21. Douglas J. Feith, *War and Decision: Inside the Pentagon at the Dawn of the War on Terrorism* (New York: Harper, 2008), pp. 436–440. See also Ricks, *Fiasco*, pp. 174–182.

22. Lyndon Johnson quoted in Doris Kearns, *Lyndon Johnson and the American Dream* (New York: Harper and Row, 1976), p. 137.

23. Morton H. Halperin and Priscilla A. Clapp, *Bureaucratic Politics and Foreign Policy*, 2nd ed. (Washington, DC: Brookings Institution, 2006), p. 243.

24. Ibid., pp. 244, 250.

25. James Q. Wilson, *Bureaucracy: What Government Agencies Do and Why They Do It* (New York: Basic Books, 1989), p. 158.

26. See, for example, B. Dan Wood and James E. Anderson, "The Politics of U.S. Antitrust Regulation," *American Journal of Political Science* 37 (February 1993): 1–39; B. Dan Wood and Richard W. Waterman, *Bureaucratic Dynamics* (Boulder, CO: Westview, 1994), chap. 4; and Evan J. Ringquist, "Political Control and Policy Impact in EPA's Office of Water Quality," *American Journal of Political Science* 39 (May 1995): 336–363.

27. Robert F. Durant, *The Administrative Presidency Revisited* (Albany: State University of New York Press, 1992).

28. Ahmed Rashid, *Descent into Chaos: The United States and the Failure of Nation Building in Pakistan, Afghanistan, and Central Asia* (New York: Viking, 2008), p. 194.

29. *The 9/11 Commission Report*, pp. 80–83.

30. Paul C. Light, *The True Size of Government* (Washington, DC: Brookings Institution, 1999), pp. 1, 44.

31. Paul C. Light, "Obama Has a Chance to Reverse Long Erosion of the Federal Service," *Washington Post*, November 19, 2008, p. A19.

32. Project on Government Oversight, *Bad Business: Billions of Taxpayer Dollars Wasted on Hiring Contractors* (Washington, DC: Project on Government Oversight, 2011).

33. The most complete treatments of executive orders can be found in William G. Howell, *Power without Persuasion* (Princeton, NJ: Princeton University Press, 2003); Kenneth R. Mayer, *With the Stroke*

of a Pen: Executive Orders and Presidential Power* (Princeton, NJ: Princeton University Press, 2001); Phillip J. Cooper, *By Order of the Executive* (Lawrence: University Press of Kansas, 2002); and Adam L. Warber, *Executive Orders and the Modern Presidency: Legislating from the Oval Office* (Boulder, CO: Lynne Rienner, 2006).

34. Scott R. Furlong, "Political Influence on the Bureaucracy: The Bureaucracy Speaks," *Journal of Public Administration Research and Theory* 8 (January 1998): 39–65.

35. Terry M. Moe, "Control and Feedback in Economic Regulation: The Case of the NLRB," *The American Political Science Review* 79 (December 1985): 1094–1116; Shep Melnick, *Regulation and the Courts: The Case of the Clean Air Act* (Washington, DC: Brookings Institution, 1983); George A. Krause, "Federal Reserve Policy Decision Making: Political and Bureaucratic Influences," *American Journal of Political Science* 38 (February 1994): 124–144; Richard W. Waterman, Amelia Rouse, and Robert Wright, "The Venues of Influence: A New Theory of Political Control of the Bureaucracy," *Journal of Public Administration Research and Theory* 8 (January 1998): 13–38; Richard W. Waterman and Kenneth J. Meier, "Principal-Agent Models: An Expansion?" *Journal of Public Administration Research and Theory* 8 (April 1998): 173–202; Jeff Worsham, Marc Allen Eisner, and Evan J. Ringquist, "Assessing the Assumptions: A Critical Analysis of Agency Theory," *Administration and Society* 28 (February 1997): 419–440.

36. See, for example, Ringquist, "Political Control and Policy Impact in EPA's Office of Water Quality."

37. Andrew B. Whitford, "The Pursuit of Political Control by Multiple Principals," *Journal of Politics* 67 (February 2005): 29–49; Richard A. Harris and Sidney M. Milkis, *The Politics of Regulatory Change: A Tale of Two Agencies* (New York: Oxford University Press, 1989), p. 276.

38. On administrative discretion, see Gary S. Bryner, *Bureaucratic Discretion* (New York: Pergamon Press, 1987).

39. See Lawrence R. Jacobs and Robert Y. Shapiro, *Politicians Don't Pander* (Chicago: University of Chicago Press, 2000),

pp. 88–89, on how the Clinton administration distrusted civil servants in developing their health care reform plan in 1993.

40. Mark W. Huddleston, *The Government's Managers* (New York: Priority Press, 1987), p. 61.

41. See, for example, Rosemary O'Leary, "The Bureaucratic Politics Paradox: The Case of Wetlands Legislation in Nevada," *Journal of Public Administration Research and Theory* 4, no. 4 (1994): 443–467.

42. David Lowery, "The Presidency, the Bureaucracy, and Reinvention: A Gentle Plea for Chaos," *Presidential Studies Quarterly* 30 (March 2000): 93.

43. Quoted in Carl M. Brauer, *Presidential Transitions: Eisenhower through Reagan* (New York: Oxford University Press, 1986), p. 150.

44. Gerald R. Ford, "Imperiled, Not Imperial," *Time*, November 10, 1980, p. 30.

45. See, for example, Joel D. Aberbach and Bert A. Rockman, "Clashing Beliefs within the Executive Branch: The Nixon Administration Bureaucracy," *American Political Science Review* 70 (June 1976): 456–468; Richard L. Cole and David A. Caputo, "Presidential Control of the Senior Civil Service: Assessing the Strategies of the Nixon Years," *American Political Science Review* 73 (June 1979): 399–413; Robert Maranto, "Still Clashing after All These Years: Ideological Conflict in the Reagan Executive," *American Journal of Political Science* 37 (August 1993): 681–698; Marissa Martino Golden, "Exit, Voice, Loyalty, and Neglect: Bureaucratic Responses to Presidential Control during the Reagan Administration," *Journal of Public Administration Research and Theory* 2 (January 1992): 29–62; Robert A. Maranto, *Politics and Bureaucracy in the Modern Presidency: Careerists and Appointees in the Reagan Administration* (Westport, CT: Greenwood Press, 1993); Judith E. Michaels, *The President's Call: Executive Leadership from FDR to George Bush* (Pittsburgh: University of Pittsburgh Press, 1997).

46. John Brehm and Scott Gates, *Working, Shirking, and Sabotage: Bureaucratic Responses to a Democratic Republic* (Ann Arbor: University of Michigan Press, 1997), p. 73, chap. 5.

47. Quoted in Halperin and Clapp, *Bureaucratic Politics and Foreign Policy*, p. 254.

48. See, for example, Hugh Heclo, *A Government of Strangers* (Washington, DC: Brookings Institution, 1977), pp. 171–172, 224–232.

49. B. Dan Wood, "Principals, Bureaucrats, and Responsiveness in Clean Air Enforcements," *American Political Science Review* 82 (March 1988): 213–234; B. Dan Wood and Richard W. Waterman, "The Dynamics of Political-Bureaucratic Adaptation," *American Journal of Political Science* 37 (May 1993): 497–528; Wood and Waterman, *Bureaucratic Dynamics.*

50. Golden, "Exit, Voice, Loyalty, and Neglect."

51. Robert Maranto and B. Douglas Skelley, "Neutrality: An Enduring Principle of the Civil Service," *American Review of Public Administration* 22 (September 1992): 173–188.

52. Francis Rourke, "Bureaucracy in the American Constitutional Order," *Political Science Quarterly* 102 (Summer 1987): 219.

53. Francis E. Rourke, "Grappling with the Bureaucracy," in Arnold J. Meltsner, ed., *Politics and the Oval Office: Towards Presidential Governance* (San Francisco: Institute for Contemporary Studies, 1981), p. 137.

54. Wilson, *Bureaucracy*, p. 275. See also Colin Campbell and Donald Naulls, "The Limits of the Budget-Maximizing Theory: Some Evidence from Officials' Views of Their Roles and Careers," in Andre Blais and Stephane Dion, eds., *The Budget-Maximizing Bureaucrat: Appraisals and Evidence* (Pittsburgh: University of Pittsburgh Press, 1991), pp. 85–118.

55. Terry M. Moe, "Regulatory Performance and Presidential Administration," *American Journal of Political Science* 26 (February 1982): 97–224; Moe, "Control and Feedback in Economic Regulation"; Wood, "Principals, Bureaucrats, and Responsiveness in Clean Air Enforcements"; Wood and Anderson, "The Politics of U.S. Antitrust Regulation"; B. Dan Wood and Richard W. Waterman, "The Dynamics of Political Control of the Bureaucracy," *American Political Science Review* 85 (September 1991): 801–828; Wood and Waterman, "The Dynamics of Political-Bureaucratic Adaptation"; Wood and Waterman, *Bureaucratic Dynamics;*

Ringquist, "Political Control and Policy Impact in EPA's Office of Water Quality"; Patricia W. Ingraham, "Political Direction and Policy Change in Three Federal Departments," in Pfiffner, ed., *The Managerial Presidency*, pp. 209–211; Steven D. Stehr, "Top Bureaucrats and the Distribution of Influence in Reagan's Executive Branch," *Public Administration Review* 57 (January/February 1997): 75–82; Marissa Martino Golden, *What Motivates Bureaucrats?* (New York: Columbia University Press, 2000), chap. 7.

56. Waterman and Meier, "Principal-Agent Models."

57. Joel D. Aberbach and Bert A. Rockman, with Robert M. Copeland, "From Nixon's Problem to Reagan's Achievement: The Federal Executive Reexamined," in Larry Berman, ed., *Looking Back on the Reagan Presidency* (Baltimore, MD: Johns Hopkins University Press, 1990); Joel D. Aberbach and Bert A. Rockman, "The Political Views of U.S. Senior Federal Executives, 1970–1992," *Journal of Politics* 57 (August 1995): 838–852; Joel D. Aberbach, "The Federal Executive under Clinton," in Colin Campbell and Bert A. Rockman, eds., *The Clinton Presidency: First Appraisals* (Chatham, NJ: Chatham House Publishers, 1996); Joel D. Aberbach, "The President and the Executive Branch," in Colin Campbell and Bert A. Rockman, eds., *The Bush Presidency: First Appraisals* (Chatham, NJ: Chatham House Publishers, 1991).

58. James P. Pfiffner, *The Strategic Presidency*, 2nd ed. (Lawrence: University Press of Kansas, 1996), pp. 78–81; James P. Pfiffner, "Political Appointees and Career Executives: The Democracy-Bureaucracy Nexus in the Third Century," *Public Administration Review* 47 (January/ February 1987): 57–65. See also Paul C. Light, "When Worlds Collide: The Political-Career Nexus," in G. Calvin Mackenzie, ed., The *In-and-Outers: Presidential Appointees and Transient Government in Washington* (Baltimore, MD: Johns Hopkins University Press, 1987); Robert Maranto, "Does Familiarity Breed Acceptance? Trends in Career-Noncareer Relations in the Reagan Administration,"

Administration and Society 23 (August 1991): 247–266.

59. Light, "When Worlds Collide," p. 166.

60. Michaels, *The President's Call*, pp. 234–235.

61. Brehm and Gates, *Working, Shirking, and Sabotage*, p. 202. They also found that federal employees do not shirk and are hard workers, chap. 5.

62. Joel D. Aberbach and Bert A. Rockman, "Mandates or Mandarins?" in Pfiffner, ed., *The Managerial Presidency*, p. 168.

63. David E. Lewis, *The Politics of Presidential Appointments* (Princeton, NJ: Princeton University Press, 2008), chap. 7.

64. Light, "When Worlds Collide," p. 160.

65. See, for example, Wood and Waterman, *Bureaucratic Dynamics*, chap. 3; and Ringquist, "Political Control and Policy Impact in EPA's Office of Water Quality."

66. The figures for presidential appointments come from Committee on Homeland Security and Governmental Affairs, United States Senate, 110th Congress, 2nd Session, *Policy and Supporting Positions* (Washington, DC: U.S. Government Printing Office, 2008).

67. See David Lewis and Richard W. Waterman, "The Invisible Presidential Appointments: An Examination of PAS, Schedule C, and SES Appointments to the Department of Labor," *Presidential Studies Quarterly* 43 (March 2013): 35–57.

68. John F. Kennedy quoted in Kenneth P. O'Donnell and David F. Powers, *Johnny, We Hardly Knew Ye: Memories of John Fitzgerald Kennedy* (New York: Pocket Books, 1972), p. 270.

69. Jonathan Alter, *The Promise: President Obama, Year One* (New York: Simon and Schuster, 2010), p. 45.

70. Ron Chernow, *Washington* (New York: Penguin Press, 2010), p. 735.

71. Andrew Rudalevige quoted in Charlie Savage, "For White House, Hiring Is Political," *New York Times*, July 31, 2008.

72. On techniques for politicizing the bureaucracy, see Lewis, *The Politics of Presidential Appointments*, pp. 26–43.

73. Presidential Appointee Initiative, Brookings Institution. The totals include appointments to full-time, Senate-confirmed posts in the cabinet departments and independent executive agencies (including regulatory commissions). The positions included in the total do not include ambassadors, U.S. attorneys, or U.S. marshals.

74. Peter Baker, "Obama's Team Is Lacking Most of Its Top Players," *New York Times*, August 24, 2009.

75. David E. Lewis, "Presidential Appointments in the Obama Administration: An Early Evaluation," in Andrew Dowdle, Dirk van Raemdonck, and Robert Maranto, eds., *The Obama Presidency: Change and Continuity* (New York: Routledge, 2011).

76. Tim Kraft quoted in Dom Bonafede, "Carter Sounds Retreat from 'Cabinet Government'," *National Journal*, November 18, 1978, pp. 1852–1857; see also "Rafshoon and Co.," *Newsweek*, January 29, 1979, p. 23.

77. See Light, *Thickening Government*; and Moe, "The Politicized Presidency."

78. Light, "When Worlds Collide." See also Paul C. Light and Virginia L. Thomas, *The Merit and Reputation of an Administration: Presidential Appointees on the Appointments Process* (Washington, DC: Brookings Institution and Heritage Foundation, 2000), p. 19; Laurence E. Lynn Jr., "The Reagan Administration and the Renitent Bureaucracy," in Lester M. Salamon and Michael S. Lund, eds., *The Reagan Presidency and the Governing of America* (Washington, DC: Urban Institute, 1985).

79. See, for example, Wood and Anderson, "The Politics of U.S. Antitrust Regulation"; Wood and Waterman, *Bureaucratic Dynamics*, chap. 4; and Ringquist, "Political Control and Policy Impact in EPA's Office of Water Quality."

80. Durant, *The Administrative Presidency Revisited*.

81. David M. Cohen, "Amateur Government," *Journal of Public Administration Research and Theory* 8 (October 1998): 450–497.

82. See Heclo, *A Government of Strangers*; Carolyn Ban and Patricia Ingraham, "Short-Timers: Political Appointee Mobility and Its Impact on Political-Career Relations in the Reagan Administration," *Administration and Society* 22 (May 1990): 106–124; Maranto, *Politics and Bureaucracy in the Modern Presidency*; Michaels, *The President's Call.*

83. See, for example, Ingraham, "Political Direction and Policy Change in Three Federal Departments," pp. 212–213.

84. Timothy B. Clark and Marjorie Wachtel, "The Quiet Crisis Goes Public," *Government Executive*, June 1988, p. 28.

85. Ibid., p. 211.

86. Ron Chernow, *Washington* (New York: Penguin Press, 2010), pp. 735, 744.

87. Melvin Laird quoted in Seymour M. Hersh, *The Price of Power: Kissinger in the Nixon White House* (New York: Summit, 1983), pp. 235–236.

88. Robert C. McFarlane, *Special Trust* (New York: Cadell and Davies, 1994), pp. 270–271.

89. John F. Harris, *The Survivor: Bill Clinton in the White House* (New York: Random House, 2005), p. 280.

90. Richard M. Nixon, *RN: The Memoirs of Richard Nixon* (New York: Grosset and Dunlap, 1978), pp. 472–473, 513.

91. See, for example, Cole and Caputo, "Presidential Control of the Senior Civil Service", pp. 399–413.

92. Jimmy Carter quoted in "Civil Service Reform," *Congressional Quarterly Weekly Report*, March 11, 1978, p. 660.

93. Brehm and Gates, *Working, Shirking, and Sabotage*, chaps. 4–5.

94. Jimmy Carter quoted in "Press Conference Text," *Congressional Quarterly Weekly Report*, March 11, 1978, p. 655.

95. Gore, *From Red Tape to Results*, p. 11.

96. William T. Gormley, *Taming the Bureaucracy: Muscles, Prayers, and Other Strategies* (Princeton, NJ: Princeton University Press, 1989); Paul C. Light, *The Tides of Reform: Making Government Work, 1945–1995* (New Haven, CT: Yale University Press, 1997); Peri Arnold, *Making the Managerial Presidency: Comprehensive Reorganization Planning, 1905–1996* (Lawrence: University Press of Kansas, 1998); William F. West, *Controlling the Bureaucracy* (Armonk, NY: M. E. Sharpe, 1995).

97. Joseph Cooper and William F. West, "Presidential Power and Republican Government: The Theory and Practice of OMB Review of Agency Rules," *Journal of Politics* 50 (November 1988): 864–895; William F. West, "The Institutionalization of Regulatory Review: Organizational Stability and Responsive Competence at OIRA," *Presidential Studies Quarterly* 35 (March 2005): 76–93.

98. Patrick J. Wolf, "Why Must We Reinvent the Federal Government? Putting Historical Developmental Claims to the Test," *Journal of Public Administration Research and Theory* 7 (July 1997): 353–388.

99. See Donald F. Kettl, *Sharing Power: Public Governance and Private Markets* (Washington, DC: Brookings Institution, 1993); Thad E. Hall and Laurence J. O'Toole, "Structures for Policy Implementation: An Analysis of National Legislation, 1965–1966 and 1993–1994," *Administration and Society* 31 (January 2000): 667–686.

100. Franklin D. Roosevelt quoted in M. S. Eccles, *Beckoning Frontiers* (New York: Knopf, 1951), p. 336.

101. Quoted in Deborah Shapely, *Promise and Power* (Boston: Little, Brown, 1993), p. 177. For a slightly different version of this confrontation, see Dino A. Brugioni, *Eyeball to Eyeball* (Random House, 1991), p. 474. See also Michael Dobbs, *One Minute to Midnight; Kennedy, Khrushchev, and Castro on the Brink of Nuclear War* (New York: Knopf, 2008), pp. 71–72.

102. *The 9/11 Commission Report*, pp. 17–18.

103. Sorensen, *Counselor*, p. 305. See also Dobbs, *One Minute to Midnight*, pp. 94, 303.

104. *Report of the DOD Commission on Beirut International Airport Terrorist Act*, October 23, 1983 (Washington, DC: Government Printing Office, December 20, 1983), p. 133.

105. Senate Select Committee on Intelligence, *Report on the Attempted Terrorist*

Attack on Northwest Airlines Flight 253, May 18, 2010.

106. William G. Howell and David E. Lewis, "Agencies by Presidential Design," *Journal of Politics* 64 (November 2002): 1095–1114.

107. See, for example, Justin S. Vaughn and José D. Villalobos, "The Policy Czar Debate," in Robert P. Watson, Jack Covarrubias, Thomas Lansford, and Douglas M. Brattebo, eds., *The Obama Presidency: A Preliminary Assessment* (Albany, NY: SUNY Press, 2012); and Mark J. Rozell and Mitchel A. Sollenberger, "Obama's Executive Branch Czars: The Constitutional Controversy and a Legislative Solution," *Congress & the Presidency* 39 (January–April 2012): 74–99.

108. "Carter Criticizes Federal Bureaucracy," *Congressional Quarterly Weekly Report*, June 3, 1978, p. 1421.

109. *The 9/11 Commission Report*, p. 401.

110. Jerry Markon, "FBI, ATF Battle for Control of Cases; Cooperation Lags Despite Merger," *Washington Post*, May 2008.

111. William Colby, *Honorable Men: My Life in the CIA* (New York: W. W. Norton, 1975), pp. 440–441; "Intelligence Failures, CIA Misdeeds Studied," *Congressional Quarterly Weekly Report*, September 20, 1975, p. 2025.

112. Ronald Reagan, *An American Life* (New York: Simon and Schuster, 1990), p. 161.

113. Shultz, *Turmoil and Triumph*, p. 166.

114. Quoted in Stephen J. Wayne, "Working in the White House: Psychological Dimensions of the Job" (paper presented at the annual meeting of the Southern Political Science Association, New Orleans, November 1977), pp. 16–17.

115. Ronald Randall, "Presidential Power versus Bureaucratic Intransigence: The Influence of the Nixon Administration on Welfare Policy," *American Political Science Review* 73 (September 1979): 795–810.

9

THE PRESIDENT
AND CONGRESS

I f one were to write a job description of the presidency, near the top of the
list of presidential responsibilities would be that of working with Congress.
According to Lyndon Johnson, "There is only one way for a President to
deal with Congress, and that is continuously, incessantly, and without inter-
ruption."[1] Because our system of separation of powers is really one of shared
powers, presidents can rarely operate independently of Congress. Although
they require the cooperation of Congress, they cannot depend on it. Thus,
one of the president's most difficult and frustrating tasks is trying to persuade
Congress to support his policies.

The differences in our contrasting views of presidential leadership are
perhaps most clear in the area of executive–legislative relations. A director president would dominate Congress, reliably obtaining its support for his policies
and precluding legislative initiatives he opposes. Facilitators, conversely, would
find the going much tougher. They would often fail to achieve their legislative
goals and almost always have to struggle to win at all. Congress may pass major
legislation over their opposition, and frustration and stalemate may characterize such a presidency much of the time.

In this chapter, we examine the president's leadership of Congress. Because it is important to understand the context of presidential–congressional
interaction, we begin with a discussion of the president's formal legislative
powers and the inevitable sources of conflict between the two branches.
We then move to an examination of the potential sources of presidential influence in Congress, including party leadership, public support, and
legislative skills. In our discussion, we emphasize both how presidents attempt to persuade members of Congress and the utility of each source of
influence.

FORMAL LEGISLATIVE POWERS

Presidents today have a central role in the legislative process. They are expected to formulate and promote policies. They are expected to coordinate them within the executive branch, to introduce them to Congress, and to mobilize support for them on Capitol Hill and, increasingly, with the general public.

These expectations suggest a broad scope of legislative authority for the president. In actuality, however, the constitutional basis for this authority is quite limited. Only four duties and responsibilities were designated by Article 2: (1) to inform Congress from time to time on the state of the union, (2) to recommend necessary and expedient legislation, (3) to summon Congress into special session and adjourn it if the two houses cannot agree on adjournment, and (4) to exercise a qualified veto.

With the exception of the veto, these responsibilities stem primarily from the president's unique position within the political system—as the only official other than the vice president who was to have continuous tenure, a national perspective, and the ability to respond quickly and decisively to emergencies. As the framers of the Constitution saw it, these job-related qualifications placed the president in a unique position to inform Congress, recommend legislation, and summon Congress into session if necessary.

The rationale for the veto was different. Justified within the Constitutional Convention as a defensive weapon, the veto was proposed as a device by which the president could prevent the legislature from usurping executive powers. The founders feared that the institutional balance would become undone and that the Congress would be the likely perpetrator. We examine later in this chapter the extent to which their fears were justified and how the veto has been used as a political and constitutional weapon.

Over the years, presidents have employed their legislative responsibilities to enlarge their congressional influence. The State of the Union address is a good example. In the nineteenth century, it was a routine message dealing primarily with the actions of the executive departments and agencies for the previous year. Beginning with Thomas Jefferson and continuing through William Howard Taft, the White House sent the address to the Congress to be read by the clerk of the House and then distributed to the members. Woodrow Wilson revived the practice of the first two presidents and delivered the speech himself. Subsequently, however, presidents have timed the address to maximize its public exposure, and today it is an important vehicle by which presidents can articulate the legislative goals of their administrations, recite their accomplishments, present their agendas, and try to mobilize support for their programs.

Similarly, presidents have transformed their responsibility to recommend necessary and expedient legislation into an annual agenda-setting function.

Although nineteenth-century presidents formulated some legislative proposals and even drafted bills in the White House, it was not until the twentieth century that the practice of presidential programming developed on a regular basis. Theodore Roosevelt, Woodrow Wilson, and Franklin Roosevelt submitted comprehensive legislative proposals to Congress. Harry Truman packaged them in the State of the Union address. With the exception of Dwight Eisenhower in his first year in office, every subsequent president has followed the Truman tradition.

To some extent, Congress has found the president's legislative initiatives advantageous, and in some cases it has insisted on them. For example, the 1921 Budget and Accounting Act, the 1946 Employment Act, and the 1974 Budget Act require the president to provide Congress with annual reports and an annual executive budget.

The calling of special sessions by the president has fallen into disuse. The length of the current legislative year, combined with changes in the calendar, has made this function largely obsolete. The last special session occurred in 1948. In the past, however, presidents frequently would call special sessions after their inauguration to gain support for their objectives and to initiate "their" Congress. Until the passage of the Twentieth Amendment in 1933, Congress began its session on or about December 1. This made every other session of Congress a "lame duck" session and forced a newly elected president to wait nine months for the newly elected Congress. Between the Lincoln and Franklin Roosevelt administrations, there were nineteen special sessions.[2]

SOURCES OF CONFLICT BETWEEN THE EXECUTIVE AND LEGISLATURE

Presidents must influence Congress because they generally cannot act without its consent. Under the constitutional system of separation of powers, Congress must pass legislation and can override vetoes, and the Senate must ratify treaties and confirm presidential appointments to the cabinet, the federal courts, regulatory commissions, and other high offices. The bicameral structure of Congress further complicates the process by requiring the president to build not one but two coalitions from among quite different sets of representatives. In addition, the requirement that the Senate ratify treaties by a two-thirds vote is a constitutional provision that increases the burden of coalition building because it forces the president to achieve a supermajority to achieve ratification. The use of the filibuster in the Senate has a similar effect, requiring sixty votes to stop debate.

However, these overlapping powers and constitutional requirements do not explain the president's need to influence Congress. Theoretically, the two branches could be in agreement. In fact, the president and some members of Congress will always disagree because of their personalities or past histories, yet these differences are not the source of systematic conflict. Rather, the source lies in the structure and processes of American politics.

Constituencies

In *The Federalist No. 46,* James Madison focused on the greatest source of conflict between the president and Congress—their different constituencies:

> The members of the federal legislature will likely attach themselves too much to local objects. . . . Measures will too often be decided according to their probable effect, not on the national prosperity and happiness, but on the prejudices, interests, and pursuits of the governments and the people of the individual states.[3]

Only presidents (and their vice presidential running mates) are chosen in a national election. Each member of Congress is elected by only a fraction of the populace. Inevitably, presidents must form a broader electoral coalition in order to win their office than any member of Congress. Moreover, two-thirds of the senators are not elected at the same time as the president, and the remaining senators and all the House members seem to be increasingly insulated from the causes of presidential victories. In addition, the Senate overrepresents rural states because each state has two senators regardless of its population. Thus, the whole that the president represents is different from the sum of the parts represented by each legislator. Each member of Congress will give special access to the interests that he or she represents, but Congress as a body has more difficulty in representing the nation as a whole.

Internal Structures

The internal structures of the executive and legislative branches also cause differences between the president and Congress. The executive branch is hierarchically organized, facilitating the president examining a broad range of viewpoints on an issue and then weighing and balancing various interests. This structure also helps the president to view the trade-offs among various policies. Because one person, the president, must support all the major policies emanating from the executive branch, he is virtually forced to take a comprehensive view of those policies.

In comparison to the presidency, the houses of Congress are highly decentralized. The party structure is not always sufficient to unify their decision-making processes. Committee memberships are frequently unrepresentative of each chamber,[4] and members of each committee may defer to members of the other committees. Thus, members representing special interests have a disproportionate say over policy regarding those interests.

Although the decentralized structure of Congress ensures that a diversity of views will be heard and that many interests will have access to the legislative process, it does not follow that *each* member will hear all the views and see the proponents of each interest. Indeed, the decentralization of Congress almost guarantees that the information available to it as a whole is not a synthesis of the information available to each legislator. The Congress as a whole does not ask questions; individual members do. Thus, not all of its members receive the answers.

One of the functions of decentralizing power and responsibility in Congress is to allow for specialization in various policy areas. However, because of specialization, legislators make decisions about many of the policies with which Congress must deal in form only. In actuality, they tend to rely on the cues of party leaders, state party delegations, relevant committee leaders of their party, and other colleagues to decide how to vote. These cue givers, however, are chosen because they represent constituencies or ideologies that are similar to those of the member who is consulting them. They do not represent a cross section of viewpoints.[5]

Besides not considering the full range of available views, members of Congress are not generally in a position to make trade-offs between policies. Because of its decentralization, Congress usually considers policies serially—that is, without reference to other policies. Without an integrating mechanism, members have few means by which to set and enforce priorities and emphasize the policies with which the president is most concerned, especially when the opposition party controls Congress. In addition, Congress has little capability, except within the context of the budget, to examine two policies, such as education and health care, in relation to each other. Not knowing that giving up something on one policy will result in a greater return on another policy, members have little incentive to engage in trade-offs.

Similarly, the decentralization of Congress limits its ability to deal comprehensively with major policy domains. Congress distributes its workload among committees, but committee jurisdictions do not usually cover entire policy areas. For example, no one congressional committee handles health, economic stability, or national security (the last requiring a coordination of defense policy and diplomacy). Conflict with the president may occur because the more centralized nature of the presidency encourages the White House to evaluate legislation in terms of its relationship to related issues in policy domains.

The hierarchical structure of the executive branch, with the president at the pinnacle, forces the president to take responsibility for the entire executive branch. Moreover, when the president exercises power, it is clear who is acting and who should be held accountable. Congress, in contrast, is not responsible for implementing policies, and each member is relatively obscure compared with the president. Because Congress is so decentralized, any member can disclaim responsibility for policies or their consequences. Members of Congress, therefore, can and do make irresponsible or self-serving decisions and then let the president take the blame.

All this can be very frustrating to the president. Gerald Ford, who spent most of his adult life in Congress, wrote the following after leaving the White House:

> When I was in the Congress myself, I thought it fulfilled its constitutional obligations in a very responsible way, but after I became President, my perspective changed. It seemed to me that Congress was beginning to disintegrate as an organized legislative body. It wasn't answering the nation's challenges domestically because it was too fragmented. It responded too often to single-issue special interest groups and it therefore wound up dealing with minutiae instead of attacking serious problems in a coherent way.[6]

Information and Expertise

The different internal structures of the president and Congress influence the amount and quality of the information available to them for decision making, further encouraging the two branches to see issues from different perspectives. Members of Congress rarely have available to them expertise of the quantity and quality that is available to the president.

Aside from the fact that the executive branch includes more than 4 million civilian and military employees plus hundreds of advisory committees while Congress employs only a few thousand people (many of whom work in supporting agencies, including the Library of Congress), the expertise of the two branches differs. Members of Congress tend to hire generalists, even on committee staffs. Sometimes these individuals develop great expertise in a particular field, but others may only be amateurs compared with their counterparts in the executive branch. Many are selected to serve legislators' needs and desires that have little to do with policy analysis, and neither house has a merit system, a tenured career service, or a central facility for recruiting the best available talent. Congress is especially at a disadvantage in national security policy, where the president relies on classified information that is generally unavailable to Congress.

Time Perspectives

The differences in the length of terms of presidents and members of Congress encourage them to adopt different time perspectives. Presidents fear that their mandates (most presidents feel they obtained one in their election) are short-lived, and they know their tenures will be short. Thus, they can waste no time in pushing for the adoption of their policies. (Presidents, of course, can procrastinate in proposing or reacting to others' solutions to national problems, and they may focus on short-term political gains. The issue is one of institutional tendencies.)

Congress has a different timetable. Its members tend to be careerists and therefore do not have the same compulsion to enact policies rapidly. This lethargic approach is aggravated by the decentralization of Congress, which ensures that a great deal of negotiating and compromising must take place on all but a few noncontroversial (and usually unimportant) issues. This process can, and often does, take years. President Richard Nixon proposed revenue sharing in 1969; it passed in 1972. President Truman proposed a national health plan in 1948; a limited version (Medicare) was passed in 1965. President Ronald Reagan initiated the idea of a free trade area in North America, but it was not enacted until the Clinton administration. One consequence of Congress's frequent sluggishness in handling legislation is that the president is not likely to get much of what he wants until later, if at all. A second consequence is that presidential policies may be passed too late to become fully effective.

At the same time that differences in tenures encourage the president and Congress to process legislation at different speeds, they also invite them to adopt different time perspectives on policy issues. A president, especially one in his second term, may choose to tackle long-term issues such as Social Security financing or tax reform. They are more worried about their legacies than about providing short-term benefits to voters that will serve electoral needs. Conversely, most members of Congress, especially those in the House, are constantly facing election. As one representative put it during the Reagan presidency, "My neck's on the chopping block—not Reagan's. He can talk about longer-term solutions to interest rates and unemployment. I can't. I need something to tell my people now."[7]

We have seen that the structure of American government exerts strong pressure on the two branches to represent different sets of interests and to view policies differently. These differences set the stage for conflict and virtually compel a president to try to influence Congress.

AGENDA SETTING

Attaining agenda status is a necessary prelude to the passage of a bill, and thus obtaining agenda space for his most important proposals is at the core of every president's legislative strategy. The burdens of leadership are considerably less at the agenda stage than at the floor stage, where the president must try to influence decisions regarding the political and substantive merits of a policy. At the agenda stage, in contrast, the president only has to convince members that his proposals are important enough to warrant attention. The White House generally succeeds in obtaining congressional attention to its legislative proposals.[8] Thus, the agenda-setting stage of the legislative process rarely poses an insurmountable barrier to the president.[9]

PARTY LEADERSHIP

"What the Constitution separates our political parties do not combine."[10] Richard Neustadt wrote these words more than four decades ago to help explain why presidents could not simply assume support from the members of their party in Congress. The challenge of presidential party leadership in Congress remains just as great and is just as important today as it was when Neustadt wrote his famous treatise on presidential power.

Party Support of the President

Representatives and senators of the president's party are almost always the nucleus of coalitions supporting the president's programs. As one White House aide put it, "You turn to your party members first. If we couldn't move our own people, we felt the opportunities were pretty slim."[11] No matter what other resources presidents may have, without seats in Congress held by their party, they will usually find it very difficult to move their legislative programs through Congress. Thus, leading their party in Congress is the principal task of all presidents as they seek to counter the tendencies of the executive and legislative branches toward conflict inherent in the system of checks and balances.

Table 9.1 shows the support given presidents by members of each party on roll-call votes on which the presidents took a stand. Clearly, there is a substantial difference between the levels of support presidents receive from members of the two parties, with the gap averaging more than 60 percentage points in recent years. Although the presidents of each party varied considerably in their policies, personalities, and political environments, their fellow partisans in Congress gave them considerably more support than they gave presidents of the opposition party. This is one reason that scholars have found that presidents are more likely to engage in major uses of force in international relations when their party has a majority in Congress.[12]

With a president of their own in the White House, party members in Congress may alter their voting tendencies. For example, Republicans have a tendency to be more supportive of internationalist foreign policies and are more likely to accept governmental economic activity when a Republican is president. Democrats, in contrast, have a tendency to move in the opposite direction when there is a Republican in the White House. In 1981, with a conservative Republican as president, many Republicans in Congress shifted to supporting foreign aid and increasing the national debt ceiling, even though they had opposed these policies under the previous Democratic administration of Jimmy Carter. A similar tendency occurred in 2001 when Republican George W. Bush replaced Democrat Bill Clinton. Likewise, some members of the president's party who voted for a bill when it was originally passed will switch and vote against the same legislation if their party leader vetoes it.[13]

Although the president receives more support from members of his party than from the opposition, this is not necessarily the result of party affiliation. It is difficult to tell whether a member of the president's party votes for the president's policies because of shared party affiliation, basic agreement with those policies, or some other factor. Undoubtedly, members of the same party share many policy preferences and have similar electoral coalitions supporting them.

Despite the proclivity of members of Congress to support presidents of their party, the White House may also experience substantial slippage in party cohesion in Congress. Table 9.1 shows that presidents cannot always count on

Table 9.1 Presidential Support in Congress by Party, 1953–2012

President	President's Party	House of Representatives Percentage Support*			Senate Percentage Support		
		President's Party	Opposition Party	Difference in Support[†]	President's Party	Opposition Party	Difference in Support[†]
Eisenhower	Republican	63	42	21	69	36	33
Kennedy	Democrat	73	26	47	65	33	32
Johnson	Democrat	71	27	44	56	44	12
Nixon/Ford	Republican	64	39	25	63	33	30
Carter	Democrat	63	31	32	63	37	36
Reagan	Republican	70	29	51	74	31	43
G. H. W. Bush	Republican	73	27	44	75	29	46
Clinton	Democrat	75	24	51	83	22	61
G. W. Bush	Republican	84	20	64	86	18	68
Obama	Democrat	85	18	67	94	21	73

*On roll-call votes on which the winning side was supported by fewer than 80 percent of those voting.

[†]Differences expressed as percentage points.

their own party members for support (this is also true on key votes). This slippage forces presidents to adopt an activist orientation toward party leadership and devote as much effort to converting party members to support them as to mobilizing members of their party who already agree with them.

Leading the Party

That members of the president's own party are more open than the opposition to presidential influence is clear. Members of the president's party typically have personal loyalties or emotional commitments to their party and their party leader, which the president can often translate into votes when necessary. Thus, members of the president's party vote with him when they can, thereby giving him the benefit of the doubt, especially if their own opinion on an issue is weak. Moreover, this proclivity for supporting the president increases the effectiveness of other sources of party influence.

One of these sources is the desire of members of the presidential party to avoid embarrassing "their" administration. This attitude stems from two motivations. The first is related to the sentiments already discussed, but the second is more utilitarian. Members of the president's party have an incentive to make the president look good because his standing in the public may influence their own chances for reelection. They also want a record of legislative success to take to the voters. In 2003, Republicans overcame their distaste for social welfare programs and supported a prescription drug program under Medicare to show that they could deliver when they had power and to give President George W. Bush a victory to aid his reelection in 2004.

Thus, the willingness of members of Congress to support a policy may depend on who proposes it. Presidential agenda items tend to exacerbate partisan disagreement in Congress. Democrats concurred but Republicans balked in 1993 when Bill Clinton proposed Goals 2000, providing for voluntary testing for students in elementary and secondary schools. In 2001, the parties reversed their stances when George W. Bush proposed a more ambitious educational assessment program.[14]

Thus, presidential leadership itself demarcates and deepens cleavages in Congress. The differences between the parties and the cohesion within them on floor votes are typically greater when the president takes a stand on issues. When the president adopts a position, members of his party have a stake in his success, while opposition party members have a stake in the president losing. Moreover, both parties take cues from the president that help define their policy views, especially when the lines of party cleavage are not clearly at stake or already well established.[15]

Presidents may also find it easier to obtain party unity behind their programs if their party regains control of one or both houses of Congress at the time of their election. Many new members may feel a sense of gratification for the president's coattails. Moreover, the prospect of exercising the power to govern may provide a catalyst for party loyalty, while the loss of power may temporarily demoralize the opposition party. All the motivations to support the president are, of course, buttressed by a basic distrust of the opposition party.

Working with Congressional Leaders

Each party has a set of floor and committee leaders in the House and Senate who, in theory, should be a valuable resource for their party's leader in the White House. The president needs both their advice and their resources for making head counts and other administrative chores. Because of their role perceptions, because their reputations for passing legislation give them a clear stake in the president's success, and because they are susceptible to the same sentiments and pressures toward party loyalty as are other members of Congress, floor leaders of the president's party in Congress are usually very supportive of the White House.

Committee leaders of the president's party usually have a similar orientation. Representative Daniel Rostenkowski, chair of the House Ways and Means Committee, told President Clinton, "You send the proposals, and I'll be the quarterback." Senator Daniel Patrick Moynihan, the chair of the Senate Finance Committee, declared, "The most important thing for me coming to the job . . . is that I want to get the president's agenda through."[16]

However, party floor leaders are not always dependable supporters, and they certainly are not simply extensions of the White House. Shortly before Barack Obama's inauguration, House Majority Leader Steny Hoyer dismissed a reporter's suggestion that Democrats would go easy on oversight of the administration. To make his point, he held up a copy of the congressional newspaper *The Hill*, its headline blaring "I Don't Work for Obama," a reference to a comment by Senate Majority Leader Harry Reid.[17] House Majority Leader Richard Gephardt and House Majority Whip David Bonior broke with President Clinton over several important trade bills and led the opposition to them. There is little the White House can do in such a situation. Presidents do not lobby for candidates for congressional party leadership positions, and they virtually always remain neutral during the selection process. They have no desire to alienate important members of Congress whose support they will need.

Similarly, seniority usually determines committee chairs and ranking minority members. Furthermore, the chairs always come from the majority party in the chamber, which often is not that of the president. It is unusual for the president to influence who holds these important positions. Moreover, the norm of supporting a president of one's party is weaker for committee leaders than for floor leaders.

Presidents and their staff typically work closely with their party's legislative leaders, meeting weekly for breakfast when Congress is in session. (Sometimes these meetings include the leaders of the opposition party as well.) These gatherings provide opportunities for an exchange of views and for the president to keep communication channels open and maintain morale. The significance of these efforts has varied, however. At one extreme, Richard Nixon's meetings were often pro forma, serving more as a symbolic ritual than a mechanism for leadership. At the other, Lyndon Johnson used them as strategy sessions to integrate congressional leaders into the White House legislative liaison operation.

Equally as important as the congressional party leaders' relations with the president are their relations with their party colleagues in Congress. Larger congressional staffs and an explosion in the number of lobbyists, independent policy analysts, and congressional work groups and caucuses have made it easier for members of Congress to inform themselves, challenge the White House (and congressional leadership), and provide alternatives to the president's policies. The increased number of roll-call votes and, thus, the increased visibility of representatives' voting behavior generated more pressure on House members to abandon party loyalty, which made it more difficult for the president to gain passage of legislation. Reforms that opened committee and subcommittee hearings to the public had the same effect. There has also been a heavy turnover in the congressional personnel in recent years, and new members have brought with them new approaches to legislating. They are less likely to adopt the norms of apprenticeship and specialization than were their predecessors in their first terms. Instead, they have eagerly taken an active role in all legislation. They place a heavy emphasis on individualism and showmanship, and usually much less on party regularity.

Thus, congressional party leaders now have more decision makers to influence than they did under, say, Lyndon Johnson in the 1960s. They can no longer rely on dealing with the congressional aristocracy and expect the rest of the members to follow. As Reagan's lobbyist Kenneth Duberstein put it, "For most issues you have to lobby all 435 Congressmen and almost all 100 Senators."[18]

Nevertheless, beginning with the Republican takeover of the House in 1995, Speakers of the House of both parties have recentralized some power in the hands of the party leadership. As the party contingents have become more homogeneous, there has been more policy agreement within the parties and thus more party unity in voting on the floor. Increased agreement has made it easier for Speakers to exercise their prerogatives regarding the assignment of bills and members to committees, the rules under which the House considers legislation on the floor, and the use of an expanded whip system—all developments that have enabled the parties to advance an agenda that reflects party preferences and work on behalf of a president of the same party. In addition, the rules in the House make control of the agenda by the majority party much easier than in the more decentralized Senate.

Committee chairs have less discretion than in previous decades because of limits on their terms, and the leadership has placed them on notice that to maintain their positions they have to support the party program. In several instances, the majority party has ignored seniority and named the Speaker's allies as committee chairs, and the leadership has played the predominant role in selecting members to the committees. In addition, to write major legislation, they have sometimes displaced committees with ad hoc task forces of their choosing.

As a result, the House leadership can be quite effective in supporting a president of its party, as it was for George W. Bush in 2001–2006 and Barack Obama in 2009–2010. Conversely, centralized power does little to help the president if the opposition is in the majority, as it frequently is. It only makes the opposition more effective, as when Republicans dominated the agenda-setting process in Congress under Bill Clinton in 1995–2000 and Barack Obama in 2011–2014 or when Democrats had the majority under George W. Bush in 2007–2008.

Although the party leadership, at least in theory, possesses sanctions that it can exercise to enforce party discipline (including exercising discretion on committee assignments, patronage, campaign funds, trips abroad, and aid with members' pet bills), in reality this discretion exists primarily on paper. Members of Congress consider most rewards a matter of right, and it is the leadership's job to see that they are distributed equitably. Party leaders usually do not dare to withhold benefits because they fear being overturned by the rank and file. (Senate Majority Leader Robert Dole sometimes termed his position that of "majority pleader.") Threats of sanctions in such a situation are unconvincing and thus rarely occur. When Speaker Newt Gingrich removed a recalcitrant member from a committee, many Republicans rebelled, and the Speaker had to compensate the member with a prestigious committee assignment. In addition, few representatives were impressed when Gingrich refused to campaign for those who had failed to provide him reliable support.

Obstacles to Party Unity

The primary obstacle to party cohesion in support of the president is lack of a consensus among members of the president's party on policies. This diversity of views often reflects the diversity of constituencies represented by party members. The frequent defection from support of Democratic presidents by the conservative Southern Democrats, or "boll weevils," was one of the most prominent features of American politics. Republican presidents often lack stable coalitions as well. George W. Bush received nearly unanimous support from his party for his proposals to reduce taxes, but when it came time to reform Social Security or immigration, things were different. Republicans were not enthusiastic and were sometimes in the forefront of the opposition to these policies.

Although in recent years the parties in Congress have become more homogeneous (as conservative constituencies increasingly elect Republicans, especially in the House),[19] there is still a substantial range of opinion within each party. When constituency opinion and the president's proposals conflict, members of Congress are more likely to vote with their constituencies, to whom they must return for reelection. For example, Bill Clinton found it very difficult to obtain party support for policies designed to encourage international trade because of the opposition of blue-collar interests, the traditional base of the Democratic Party.

Yet other obstacles may confront a president trying to mobilize his party in Congress. If the president's party has just regained the presidency but remains a minority in Congress, its members need to adjust from their past stance as the opposition minority to one of a "governing" minority. This is not always easily done, however, as Richard Nixon found when he sought Republican votes for budget deficits.

Further difficulties may stem from the fact that the winning presidential candidate may not be the natural leader of the party. Indeed, as in the case of Jimmy Carter and to a lesser extent Bill Clinton, some presidents campaign against the party establishment and are not identified with the Democratic Party program as it exists at the time. Naturally, when a new president arrives in Washington under these conditions, intraparty harmony is not likely to materialize overnight, and appeals for party loyalty may fall on less-than-receptive ears.

The constant opposition he faced from the vocal and powerful liberal wing of his own party undermined Carter's ability to promote his policies. In 1980, the president had to deal with the challenge of Senator Edward Kennedy for the Democratic nomination for president. As Carter reflected more than a quarter century after leaving the White House, "The Democratic party was never mine. . . . I was never able to consolidate support in the Democratic party, particularly after Kennedy decided to run for president."[20] In the absence of a party consensus on policy, Carter's White House had to rely on forming discrete coalitions.

Midterm Election Campaigning

Members of Congress who are of the president's party are more likely to support the president than are members of the opposition party, and presidents do their best to exploit this potential of partisan support. Nevertheless, such actions are inevitably at the margins of coalition building because they take place within the confines of the partisan balance of the Congress. To exploit the benefits of party leadership fully, presidents need as many of their fellow partisans in Congress as possible. Once members of Congress have been elected, however, they rarely change their party affiliation, and the few instances when they have changed have not resulted from presidential persuasion. (Indeed, under Democrat Bill Clinton, five members of the House and two in the Senate switched from Democrat to Republican.) Thus, if presidents are to alter the party composition of Congress, they must help to elect additional members of their party. One way to try to accomplish this goal is to campaign for candidates in midterm congressional elections.

There are a number of limitations to such a strategy, however. Sometimes presidents are so unpopular that the candidates of their party do not want their support. For example, President Johnson adopted a low profile during the 1966 campaign because of his lack of public support (below 50 percent in the Gallup Poll). Similarly, in 1974, before he resigned, President Nixon wanted invitations to campaign for Republicans to prove that he was not political poison, but he received few offers as the Watergate crisis reached a head. Some candidates asked Ronald Reagan to stay away because of the recession in 1982, with which many voters identified him; in 1994, opposition to Bill Clinton was a primary cause of the Democrats' loss of both houses of Congress; and in 2006, the tables were turned and opposition to George W. Bush was at the core of the Democrats retaking both houses. In 2010, public antagonism toward Barack Obama led to a stinging defeat for Democrats.

Nevertheless, modern presidents have often taken an active role in midterm congressional elections, and there is evidence that those for whom they campaign show their gratitude in increased support—if they win.[21] Often, however, presidents have little impact on the results of congressional elections.[22] As Table 9.2 shows, a recurring feature of American politics is the *decrease* in representation of the president's party in Congress in midterm congressional elections. In 2010, the Democrats lost six seats in the Senate and sixty-three seats in the House, depriving President Obama of a majority. We can trace this phenomenon back further in U.S. history to Woodrow Wilson's midterm campaigning in 1918, which was rewarded by the loss of both houses of Congress. (Even George Washington's Federalists lost seats in the House in the first midterm election, in 1790.)

Recently, there have been exceptions, however. In 1998, the Democrats gained five seats in the House, an election that occurred in the context of the widely unpopular effort by Republicans to impeach Bill Clinton.[23] In 2002, Republicans made small gains in both houses. In this election, George W. Bush engaged in the most active midterm campaigning of any president in history, and the Republican gains were the result of both heavy turnout among Republicans, who responded to the president who was extraordinarily popular in the face of the 9/11 attacks, and favorable redistricting following the 2000 census. In 2006, however, George W. Bush's Republicans lost majorities in both houses of Congress.

Table 9.2 Changes in Congressional Representation of the President's Party in Midterm Elections

Year	President	House	Senate
1954	Eisenhower	−18	−1
1958	Eisenhower	−47	−3
1962	Kennedy	−4	+3
1966	Johnson	−47	−4
1970	Nixon	−12	+2
1974	Ford	−47	−5
1978	Carter	−15	−3
1982	Reagan	−26	0
1986	Reagan	−5	−8
1990	G. H. W. Bush	−9	−1
1994	Clinton	−52	−8
1998	Clinton	+5	0
2002	G. W. Bush	+6	+2
2006	G. W. Bush	−30	−6
2010	Obama	−63	−6

Presidential Coattails

Another potential means by which presidents may influence the partisan composition of Congress is through their coattails. Presidential coattails are part of the lore of American politics. Politicians project them in their calculations, journalists attribute them in their reporting, historians recount them, and political scientists analyze them. However, we have limited understanding of how they affect the outcomes in congressional elections. (A coattail victory is a victory for a representative of the president's party in which presidential coattail votes provide the increment of the vote necessary to win the seat.)

Coattail victories, whether they bring in new members or preserve the seats of incumbents, can have significant payoffs for the president in terms of support for the administration's programs. Those members of the president's party who won close elections may provide an extra increment of support out of a sense of gratitude for the votes they perceive were received due to presidential coattails or out of a sense of responsiveness to their constituents' support for the president.

However, research has found that the outcomes of very few congressional races are determined by presidential coattails.[24] Winning presidential candidates run behind all but a handful of members of Congress in their states or districts. George W. Bush's Republicans lost four seats in the Senate and two in the House in the elections of 2000.

The change in party balance that usually emerges when the electoral dust has settled following a presidential election is strikingly small. In the sixteen presidential elections between 1952 and 2012, the party of the winning presidential candidate gained an average of 8 seats (out of 435) per election in the House. In the Senate, the opposition party actually gained seats in seven of the elections (1956, 1960, 1972, 1984, 1988, 1996, and 2000), and there was no change in 1976 and 1992. The net gain for the president's party in the Senate averaged about one seat per election. The results of elections over the past sixty years are shown in Table 9.3.

Such losses are nothing new. In 1792, George Washington easily won reelection, but the opposition Democrat-Republicans captured the House of Representatives. Most House seats are too safe for a party, and especially for an incumbent, to have the election outcome affected by the presidential election. Senate elections are more affected by the president's standing with the public, but the president's party typically gains only one seat in a presidential election year.[25]

Thus, presidents cannot expect personally to carry like-minded running mates into office to provide additional support for their programs. On the contrary, rather than being amenable to voting for the president's policies due to shared convictions, representatives are free to focus on parochial matters and respond to narrow constituency interests. Similarly, although we cannot know the extent to which representatives have felt gratitude to presidents for their coattails, and thus have given them additional legislative support in the past, we do know that any such gratitude is rarely warranted. The more representatives are aware of the independence of their elections from that of the president, the less likely they are to feel that they must "thank" the president with an additional increment of support.

Table 9.3 Changes in Congressional Representation of the President's Party in Presidential Election Years

Year	President	House	Senate
1952	Eisenhower	+22	+1
1956	Eisenhower	−2	−1
1960	Kennedy	−22	−2
1964	Johnson	+37	+1
1968	Nixon	+5	+6
1972	Nixon	+12	−2
1976	Carter	+1	0
1980	Reagan	+34	+12
1984	Reagan	+14	−2
1988	G. H. W. Bush	−3	−1
1992	Clinton	−10	0
1996	Clinton	+9	−2
2000	G. W. Bush	−2	−4
2004	G. W. Bush	+4	+4
2008	Obama	+21	+8
2012	Obama	+8	+1

Bipartisanship

On July 27, 1981, President Reagan delivered an exceptionally important and effective televised address to the nation seeking the public's support for his tax-cut bill and going to great lengths to present his plan as "bipartisan." It was crucial that he convince the public that this controversial legislation was supported by members of both parties and was therefore, by implication, fair. Thus, he described it as "bipartisan" a full eleven times in the span of a few minutes. No one was to miss the point. The president required the votes of Democrats in the House to pass his bill, and he wanted their constituents to apply pressure to them to support it.

Despite the advantage that presidents have in dealing with members of their party in Congress, they are often forced to solicit bipartisan support. The opposition party may control one or both houses of Congress, so even if all members of the president's party supported the administration on its key initiatives, that would not be sufficient. Between 1953 and 1992, Republican presidents faced a Democratic House of Representatives for twenty-six years and a Democratic Senate for twenty years. George W. Bush enjoyed Republican Party control of both houses of Congress for less than five months in 2001 before the Democrats gained a majority in the Senate, and the Democrats had majorities in each house for his last two years in office. President Clinton faced a Republican House and Senate from 1995 through 2000. Without Republican support, he would not have obtained passage of the North American Free Trade Agreement (NAFTA) and the General Agreement on Trade and Tariffs (GATT) or the line-item veto. Barack Obama faced a Republican-controlled House in 2011–2014.

A second reason for bipartisanship is that presidents cannot depend on all the members of their party to support them on all issues. Table 9.1 showed clearly that members of the president's own party frequently oppose the president. Jimmy Carter may have been exaggerating a bit when he wrote, "I learned the hard way that there was no party loyalty or discipline when a complicated or controversial issue was at stake—none."[26] Nevertheless, presidents cannot take party support for granted.

Not only do partisan strategies often fail, but they also may provoke the other party into a more unified posture of opposition. When there is confrontation, there can be no consensus, and consensus is often required to legislate changes on important issues. Presidents are also inhibited in their partisanship by pressures to be "president of all the people" rather than a highly partisan figure. This role expectation of being somewhat above the political fray may constrain presidents in their role as party leader.

Despite the frequent necessity of a bipartisan strategy, it is not without costs. Bipartisanship often creates a strain with the extremes within the president's party, as a Republican president tries to appeal to the left for Democratic votes and a Democratic president to the right for Republican votes. Although it is true that the Republican right wing and Democratic left wing may find it difficult to forge a coalition in favor of alternatives to their own president's policies, it is not true that they must therefore support their president. Instead, they may complicate a president's strategy by joining those who oppose administration policies.

As Table 9.1 demonstrated, the ultimate limitation on a bipartisan strategy is that the opposition party is generally not a fertile ground for obtaining policy support. Democratic presidents have often been frustrated in their efforts to deal with Republicans. Presidents Clinton and Obama faced virtually unanimous Republican opposition to their economic, budget, and health care proposals.[27] Republican presidents also face obstacles to obtaining bipartisan support. Only twenty-three House Democrats supported Ronald Reagan on both the important budget and tax votes in 1981, despite the president's persuasive efforts, the perception that the president had a mandate, and the pull of ideology. Similarly, few Democrats supported George W. Bush's tax cut proposals or the budget on which they were based. Moreover, the president's efforts to exploit bipartisan support for the war on terrorism to increase support for his domestic policies were generally unsuccessful. Nevertheless, presidents cannot ignore the opposition party, and even a few votes may be enough to bring them a majority.

PUBLIC SUPPORT

Although congressional seats held by members of the president's party may be a necessary condition for presidential success in Congress, they are not a sufficient one: The president needs public support as well. In the words of Eisenhower aide and presidential authority Emmet John Hughes, "Beyond all tricks of history and all quirks of Presidents, there would appear to be one unchallengeable truth: the dependence of Presidential authority on popular support."[28]

Public Approval

In his memoirs, President Johnson wrote, "Presidential popularity is a major source of strength in gaining cooperation from Congress."[29] Thus, following his landslide electoral victory, he assembled the congressional liaison officials from the various departments and told them that his victory at the polls "might be more of a loophole than a mandate." Moreover, as his popularity could decrease rapidly, they would have to use it to their advantage while it lasted.[30]

President Carter's aides were quite explicit about the importance of public approval in their efforts to influence Congress. One stated that the "only way to keep those guys [Congress] honest is to keep our popularity high."[31] The president's legislative liaison officials generally agreed that their effectiveness with Congress ultimately depended on the president's ability to influence public opinion. As one of them said, "When you go up to the Hill and the latest polls show Carter isn't doing well, there isn't much reason for a member to go along with him. There's little we can do if the member isn't persuaded on the issue."[32] The Reagan administration was especially sensitive to the president's public approval levels. According to one top aide, "Everything here is built on the idea that the president's success depends on grassroots support."[33]

Why is presidential approval or popularity such an important source of influence in Congress? According to a senior aide to President Carter:

> When the President is low in public opinion polls, the Members
> of Congress see little hazard in bucking him. . . . After all, very few
> Congressmen examine an issue solely on its merits; they are politicians
> and they think politically. I'm not saying they make only politically
> expedient choices. But they read the polls and from that they feel
> secure in turning their backs on the President with political impunity.
> Unquestionably, the success of the President's policies bears a tremendous
> relationship to his popularity in the polls.[34]

The public's evaluations of the president may serve as an indicator of broader opinions on politics and policy. Moreover, members of Congress must anticipate the public's reaction to their decisions to support or oppose the president and his policies. Depending on the president's public standing, they may choose to be close to him or independent from him to increase their chances of reelection. As analyst William Schneider put it, "popularity is power. Members of Congress are all in business for themselves. If a President is popular, they'll support him because they want to be with a winner. If he starts losing popularity, they'll abandon him. Even members of his own party don't want to be associated with a loser."[35]

It is prudent for members of Congress to anticipate voters' reactions to their support for the president. Their constituents hold them accountable for their legislative voting, especially on salient issues such as those on which the president has taken a stand.[36] Strong supporters of unpopular presidents in competitive districts are particularly at risk because senators and representatives who support the president more than constituents prefer are more likely to lose.[37] In 1994, Democratic candidates were more likely to be defeated in districts where Bill Clinton was weak.[38] Opinions about George W. Bush's job performance and his decision to invade Iraq were exceptionally strong predictors of individual vote choices in the 2006 congressional elections.[39] Nearly 40 percent of voters cast ballots to oppose the president.[40] In 2010, Barack Obama was low in the approval polls, and opposition to his initiatives, particularly health care reform, cost Democrats their majority in the House and greatly reduced their majority in the Senate.[41]

Members of Congress may also use the president's standing in the polls as an indicator of his ability to mobilize public opinion against his opponents. As Richard Nixon put it, "An even greater incentive for members [of Congress to support the president] is the fear that a popular president may oppose them in the next election."[42]

Public approval operates mostly in the background and sets the limits of what Congress will do for, or to, the president. Widespread support gives a president leeway and weakens resistance to the administration's policies. Moreover, it provides a cover for members of Congress to cast votes to which their constituents might otherwise object, as they can defend their votes as support for the president rather than on substantive policy grounds alone.

Lack of public support strengthens the resolve of those who are inclined to oppose the president and narrows the range in which he receives the benefit of the doubt, as Bill Clinton discovered when his approval ratings dipped into the 35 percent range in mid-1993. In addition, low ratings in the polls may create incentives to attack the president, further eroding an already weakened position. For example, after the arms sales to Iran and the diversion of funds to the Contras became a cause célèbre in late 1986, it became more acceptable in Congress and in the press to raise questions about Ronald Reagan's capacities as president. Disillusionment is a dangerous phenomenon for the White House. As a chief of the White House congressional relations office put it, "When the president's approval is low, it's advantageous and even fun to kick him around."[43]

The impact of presidential approval on presidential support occurs at the margins of coalition building, within the confines of other influences. No matter how low a president's standing in public polls falls or how close it is to the next election, he or she will still receive support from a substantial number of senators and representatives. Similarly, no matter how high approval levels climb or how large a president's winning percentage of the vote, a significant portion of the Congress may still oppose his policies. Members of Congress are unlikely to vote against the clear interests of their constituents or the firm tenets of their ideology, even out of deference to a widely supported chief executive. George W. Bush's very high approval levels in the months following the 9/11 attacks did not engender similarly high support among Democrats in Congress for his domestic policy proposals.[44] Thus, widespread support should give presidents leeway and weaken resistance to their policies, giving them, at best, leverage but not control.[45] In contrast, when presidents lack popular support, their options are reduced, their opportunities are diminished, and their room for maneuver is checked.

As the most volatile leadership resource, public approval is the factor most likely to determine whether an opportunity for policy change exists. Public approval makes other resources more efficacious. If the chief executive is high in public esteem, the president's party is more likely to be responsive, the public is more easily moved, and legislative skills become more effective. Thus, public approval is the resource that has the most potential to turn a typical situation into one favorable for change, which provides a strong incentive for the president to try to gain popular support. However, as we have seen, presidential approval cannot be easily manipulated.

Public approval is a necessary, but not a sufficient, source of influence in Congress. It is most useful in combination with party supporters in each house. If either approval or seats are lacking, the president's legislative program will be in for rough going.

Mandates

Another indicator of the public's opinion of the president is the results of the presidential election. Electoral mandates can be powerful symbols in American politics, as they accord added legitimacy and credibility to the newly elected president's proposals. Moreover, concerns for both representation and political survival will encourage members of Congress to support the president if they feel the people have spoken.[46]

More importantly, mandates change the premises of decisions. Following the 1932 election, the essential question became how government should act to fight the Depression rather than whether it should act. Similarly, following the 1964 election, the dominant question in Congress was not whether to pass new social programs but, rather, how many to pass and how much to increase spending. In 1981, however, the tables were turned. Ronald Reagan's victory placed a stigma on big government and exalted the unregulated marketplace and large defense efforts. Reagan had won a major victory even before the first congressional vote.

Although presidential elections can structure choices for Congress, merely winning an election does not give a president a mandate. Every election produces a winner, but mandates are much less common. Even large electoral victories such as Richard Nixon's in 1972 and Ronald Reagan's in 1984 carry no guarantee that Congress will interpret the results as mandates from the people to support the president's programs, especially if the voters also elect majorities in Congress from the other party.

The winners in presidential elections usually claim to have been accorded a mandate,[47] of course, but in the absence of certain conditions, few observers accept these assertions at face value. Conditions that promote the perception of a mandate include a large margin of victory, the impression of long coattails, hyperbole in the press analyses of the election results that exaggerates the one-sidedness of the victory, a surprisingly large victory accompanying a change in parties in the White House, a campaign oriented around a major change in public policy, consistency of the new president's program with the prevailing tides of opinion in both the country and his party, or a sense that the public's views have shifted.[48] In 2004, George W. Bush won with less than 51 percent of the vote, lacked substantial coattails, and did not emphasize specific policy proposals in his campaign. Thus, his claims of a mandate lacked credibility—as he soon discovered when the public and Congress were unresponsive to his proposals for reforming Social Security.

Because it is unusual for these conditions to be met, perceptions of mandates are rarely strong. Presidents can do little about these perceptions. Some are simply elected under more favorable conditions for legislative leadership than are others. When mandates do occur or are effectively claimed, the issue becomes one of exploiting the special opportunities they provide.

EVALUATING STRATEGIC POSITION

The first step a new administration should take to ensure success with Congress is to assess its strategic position accurately so it understands the potential for change and will not overreach or underachieve. Presidents must largely play with the hands that the public deals them through its electoral decisions on the presidency and Congress, as well as its evaluations of the chief executive's handling of his job. Presidents are rarely in a position to augment substantially their political capital, especially when just taking office.

The early periods of new administrations most clearly etched on our memories as notable successes were those in which presidents properly identified and exploited conditions for change. When Congress first met in special session in March 1933 after Franklin D. Roosevelt's inauguration, it rapidly passed, at the new president's request, bills to control the resumption of banking, repeal Prohibition, and effect government economies. This is all Franklin D. Roosevelt originally planned for Congress to do; he expected to reassemble the legislature when permanent and more constructive legislation was ready. Yet the president found a situation ripe for change, and he decided to exploit this favorable environment and strike repeatedly with hastily drawn legislation before sending Congress home. This period of intense activity came to be known as the Hundred Days.

Lyndon Johnson also knew that his personal leadership could not sustain congressional support for his policies. He realized that the assassination of President Kennedy and the election of 1964 provided him a unique chance to pass his Great Society legislation and moved immediately to exploit it. Similarly, the Reagan administration recognized that the perceptions of a mandate and the dramatic elevation of Republicans to majority status in the Senate provided it with a window of opportunity to effect major changes in public policy but that it had to concentrate its focus and move quickly before the environment became less favorable. Moreover, within a week of the March 30, 1981, assassination attempt on Reagan, Michael Deaver convened a meeting of other high-ranking aides at the White House to determine how best to take advantage of the new political capital the shooting had created.

If the White House misreads its strategic position, the president may begin his tenure with embarrassing failures in dealing with Congress. Moreover, the greater the breadth and complexity of the policy change a president proposes, the more opposition it is likely to engender—and thus the stronger the president's strategic position must be to succeed. In an era when a few opponents can effectively tie up bills, the odds are clearly against the White House.

Bill Clinton overestimated the extent of change that a president elected with a minority of the vote could make, especially when the public is dubious and well-organized interest groups are fervently opposed. Nevertheless, the president proposed, without Republican support, perhaps the most sweeping, complex prescriptions for controlling the conduct of state governments, employers, drug manufacturers, doctors, hospitals, and individuals in American history. The foundation was lacking for change of this magnitude. The consequences of the bill's failure were greater than disappointment, however. Because Clinton declared health care reform to be the cornerstone of his efforts to change public policy, his handling of the bill became a key indicator of the administration's competency at governing. The bill's death throes occurred only a few months before the 1994 elections, the greatest midterm electoral disaster for the Democrats in the previous fifty years.

George W. Bush faced an especially unusual beginning to his presidency, but he made the most of his situation. Bush was not intimidated by the lack of a plurality in his election, the nature of its resolution, or the loss of Republican seats in both houses of Congress. He ignored those who urged him to strike a bipartisan posture and hold off on his major initiatives. The White House understood that the one policy that both unified and energized Republicans was tax cuts. Although most congressional Democrats would oppose the cuts, a majority of the public, including Independents and even some Democrats, would support or at least tolerate them. Equally important, tax cuts, unlike most other major policies, could be considered under rules that prohibited a filibuster. Thus, a united, although slender, majority could—and did—prevail.

Barack Obama campaigned on a platform of major change in policy, enjoyed substantial Democratic majorities in both houses of Congress, and thought his rhetorical skills would allow him to maintain the public's support for his major initiatives. He did get several significant pieces of legislation through Congress, but he also disappointed his supporters by failing to pass reforms of tax policy, immigration, environmental protection and climate change, and other key issues. He had misestimated his ability to win support from the public and congressional Republicans. Like Bill Clinton, he led the Democrats to a major defeat in the 2010 midterm elections, losing his majority in the House.[49]

PRESIDENTIAL LEGISLATIVE SKILLS

In this section of our discussion of presidential influence in Congress, we examine other White House efforts to persuade members of Congress to support the president's legislative proposals. Some of these activities are aimed at building goodwill in the long run and others at obtaining votes from individual members of Congress on specific issues. Whatever the immediate goal, the nature of the legislative process in America demands that presidents apply their legislative skills in a wide range of situations. In the words of one presidential aide:

> Senator A might come with us if Senator B, an admired friend, could be persuaded to talk to him. Senator C wanted a major project out of Chairman D's committee; maybe D, a supporter of our bill, would release it in exchange for C's commitment. Senator E might be reached through people in his home state. If Senator F could not vote with us on final passage, could he vote with us on key amendments? Could G take a trip? Would the President call Senator H?[50]

Congressional Liaison

Although the Constitution establishes separate institutions, the operation of the government requires those institutions to work together. We expect presidents to propose legislation and to get it enacted into law. Clearly, they need all the help they can get. To assist them in these efforts as well as with their other ongoing legislative responsibilities, a White House congressional liaison staff has operated since 1953.

In addition to representing the president's views to members of Congress, the office now caters to the constituency needs of members, gathers intelligence on members' views on legislation, tracks the progress of legislation through the congressional labyrinth, coordinates department and agency legislative efforts, and works closely with the congressional leadership of the president's party. Supplementing these efforts, the White House political office handles patronage and other party-related matters, while the intergovernmental affairs office orchestrates state and local officials behind other administration initiatives.

Congressional liaison has developed and expanded because it serves the needs of both the executive and legislative branches. For Congress, it helps integrate legislative views into executive policy making, services constituency needs, forces presidents to indicate their legislative priorities, provides channels for reaching compromises, and helps the leadership to form majority coalitions. For presidents, it enables them to gain a congressional perspective, communicate their views to Congress, mobilize support for their programs, and reach accommodations with the legislature. Such efforts to bridge the constitutional separation have helped to overcome some of the hurdles in the formulation of public policy.

The White House also established a public liaison office to organize outside groups and community leaders into coalitions backing the administration's proposals.[51] Once established, the White House orchestrates these coalitions to mount grassroots efforts directed toward Congress. The public liaison office identifies the positions of members on key issues, targets those who are wavering, and has group representatives from their own constituencies contact them. It also organizes mass letter-writing and telephoning campaigns. These constituency-based pressures are designed to make it easier for members of Congress to vote with the president, regardless of their party affiliation, by providing them political cover.

We now turn from institutionalized efforts to deal with Congress to the particular legislative techniques that presidents and their liaison aides must utilize in their efforts to win support for the administration's proposals on Capitol Hill.

Personal Appeals

A special aspect of presidential involvement in the legislative process is the personal appeal for votes. According to presidential scholar Richard Neustadt, "When the chips are down, there is no substitute for the President's own footwork, his personal negotiation, his direct appeal, his voice and no other's on the telephone."[52] Members of Congress are as subject to flattery as other people, and they are equally impressed when the president calls.

Calls from the president must be relatively rare to maintain their usefulness and will have less impact if they are made too often. Moreover, members might begin to expect calls, for which the president has limited time, or they might resent too much high-level pressure being applied to them. In contrast, they might exploit a call by saying they are uncertain about an issue in order to extract a favor from the president.

Presidents become intensely involved only after the long process of lining up votes is almost done and their calls are needed to win on an important issue (a situation that arises only a few times a year). A good example occurred on the final House vote on President Obama's health care plan in March 2010. After studying the head counts prepared by the White House congressional liaison and the congressional party whips' offices, he focused on representatives who were uncommitted or weakly committed in either direction. Obama engaged in a round-the-clock effort in which he delved into arcane policy discussions, promised favors, and mapped out election strategy. He met with or called dozens of lawmakers,[53] including ninety-two in the week before the final House vote in March 2010.[54] As one Washington reporter put it, "Some fence-sitters nearly drowned in presidential attention."[55] As a result, the president, with the invaluable aid of Speaker Nancy Pelosi, was able to garner enough votes to eke out a narrow victory.

Despite the prestige of their office, their invocations of national interest, and their persuasiveness, presidents often fail in their personal appeals. For example, President Eisenhower liked to depend heavily on charm and reason. In 1953, he tried to persuade Republican chairman Daniel Reed of the House

Ways and Means Committee to support the continuance of the excess profits tax and to oppose a tax cut. "I used every possible reason, argument, and device, and every kind of personal and indirect contact," he wrote, "to bring Chairman Reed to my way of thinking." Nonetheless, he failed.[56] Similarly, Lyndon Johnson was renowned for his persuasiveness but nevertheless failed on many issues, ranging from civil rights and education to Medicare and the Panama uprising. "No matter how many times I told Congress to do something," he wrote, "I could never force it to act."[57] If Eisenhower and Johnson often failed in their efforts at persuasion, we should not be surprised that other presidents have failed as well.

Bargaining

It is part of the conventional wisdom that the White House regularly "buys" votes through bargains struck with members of Congress. There can be no question that many bargains occur and that they take a variety of forms. Reagan's budget director, David Stockman, recalled that "the last 10 or 20 percent of the votes needed for a majority of both houses [on the 1981 tax cut] had to be bought, period." "The hogs were really feeding," he declared. "The greed level, the level of opportunism, just got out of control."[58]

Winning the votes of wavering lawmakers and the support of powerful industries for ambitious energy and climate-change legislation required the Obama White House to make many compromises and outright gifts. The biggest concessions went to utilities, which wanted assurances that they could continue to operate and build coal-burning power plants without shouldering new costs. They also won a weakening of the national mandate for renewable energy. A series of compromises was reached with rural and farm-state members that would funnel billions of dollars in payments to agriculture and forestry interests. Automakers, steel companies, natural gas drillers, refiners, universities, and real estate agents all got in on the action. The deal making continued right up until the final minutes, with the bill's coauthor, Henry Waxman, doling out billions of dollars in promises on the House floor to secure the final votes needed for passage.[59]

Nevertheless, bargaining, in the form of trading support on two or more policies or providing specific benefits for representatives and senators, occurs less often and plays a less critical role in the creation of presidential coalitions in Congress than one might think. For obvious reasons, the White House does not want to encourage the type of bargaining Stockman described.

The president cannot bargain with Congress as a whole because it is too large and decentralized for one bargain to satisfy everyone. In addition, the president's time is limited, as are the administration's resources—only a certain number of appointive jobs are available, and the federal budget is limited. Moreover, funding for public works projects is in the hands of Congress. Thus, most of the bargains that are reached are implicit. The lack of respectability surrounding bargaining also encourages implicitness.

In addition, if many direct bargains are struck, word will rapidly spread, everyone will want to trade, and persuasive efforts will fail. A good example occurred in 1993 when President Clinton proposed to increase user fees for grazing and mineral rights on federal land. Following protests from Western senators, whose votes he needed for his budget, the president told them he would remove the fees from his budget and deal with them separately in a bill later in the session. His decision opened a Pandora's box because it signaled to every interest group in Washington that he would cave in to pressure. He was quickly inundated with requests to change his budget in other ways. The word was out that the president could be "rolled."

Fortunately for the president, bargaining with everyone in Congress is not necessary. Except on vetoes and treaties, only a simple majority of those voting is needed (or 60 votes in the Senate of avoid a filibuster), and thus a large part of Congress can be "written off" on any given vote. Moreover, presidents generally start with a substantial core of party supporters and then add to this number those of the other party who agree with their views on ideological or policy grounds. Others may provide support on the basis of goodwill that a president has generated through White House services, constituency interest, or high levels of public support. Thus, the president needs to bargain only if all these groups fail to provide a majority for crucial votes, and bargaining is needed only with enough people to provide that majority.

Because resources are scarce, presidents usually try to use them for bargaining with powerful members of Congress, such as committee chairs or those whose votes are most important. There is no guarantee that a tendered bargain will be accepted, however. The members may not desire what the president offers, or they may be able to obtain what they want on their own. This is, of course, particularly true of the most powerful members, whose support the president needs most. Sometimes, members of Congress do not want to trade at all because of constituency opinion or personal views. At other times, the president may be unwilling to bargain.

Most of the pressure for bargaining actually comes from Capitol Hill. When the White House calls and asks for support, representatives and senators frequently raise a question regarding some request that they have made. In the words of a presidential aide, "Every time we make a special appeal to a Congressman to change his position, he eventually comes back with a request for a favor ranging in importance from one of the President's packages of matches to a judgeship or cabinet appointment for a 'worthy constituent.'"[60]

More general bargains also take place. In the words of Nixon's chief congressional aide William Timmons, "I think they [members of Congress] knew that we would try our best to help them on all kinds of requests if they supported the President, and we did. It kind of goes without saying." His successor in the Ford administration, Max Friedersdorf, added his assurance that people who want things want to be in the position of supporting the president. This implicit trading on "accounts" is more common than explicit bargaining.[61]

For the White House, a member of Congress indebted to the president is easier to approach and ask for a vote. For the member, previous support increases the chances of a request being honored. Thus, officeholders at both ends of Pennsylvania Avenue want to be in each other's favor. The degree of debt determines the strategy used in presidential requests for support. Although services and favors increase the president's chances of obtaining support, they are not usually exchanged for votes directly. They are strategic, not tactical, weapons.

Services and Amenities

As a member of Congress who is indebted to the president is easier to approach to ask for a vote, the White House provides many services and amenities for representatives and senators. Although it may bestow these favors on any member of Congress, they actually go disproportionately to members of the president's party. "The White House certainly remembers who its friends are," Lawrence F. O'Brien, head of the congressional liaison office, both warned and promised legislators early in the Kennedy administration.[62] Personal amenities used to create goodwill include social contact with the president, flattery, rides on Air Force One, visits to Camp David, birthday greetings, theater tickets for the presidential box at the Kennedy Center, invitations to bill-signing ceremonies, pictures with the president, briefings, and a plethora of others, the number and variety of which are limited only by the imagination of the president and his staff.

In addition, the White House often helps members of Congress with their constituents. A wide range of services is offered, including greetings to elderly and other "worthy" constituents, signed presidential photographs, presidential tie clasps and other White House memorabilia, reprints of speeches, information about government programs, White House pressure on agencies in favor of constituents, passing the nominations of constituents on to agencies, influence on local editorial writers, ceremonial appointments to commissions, meetings with the president, and arguments to be used to explain votes to constituents. The president may also help members of Congress please constituents through patronage, pork-barrel projects and government contracts, and aid with legislation that is of special interest to particular constituencies. Districts and counties receive systematically more federal outlays when legislators in the president's party represent them.[63]

Campaign aid is yet another service that the White House can provide to party members, and the president may dangle it before them to entice support. This aid may come in various forms, including campaign speeches by the president and executive officials for congressional candidates, funds and advice from the party national committees, presidential endorsements, pictures with the president, and letters of appreciation from the president. Recent presidents have been especially active in directly raising funds for their parties' candidates.

All administrations are not equally active in providing services and amenities for members of Congress. The Johnson and Reagan White Houses fall at the "active" end of this spectrum, while the Nixon and Carter presidencies fall at the other end. However, any such differences are relatively small in comparison with the efforts made by every recent administration to develop goodwill among its party members in Congress. Although this activity is to the advantage of all presidents and may earn them a fair hearing and the benefit of the doubt in some instances, party members consider it their right to receive benefits from the White House and are unlikely to be especially responsive to the president as a result.

Pressure

Just as presidents can offer the carrot, they can also wield the stick. Moreover, the increased resources available to the White House in recent years provide increased opportunities to levy sanctions in the form of the withholding of favors. As the deputy chairman of the Republican National Committee said, there is more money than ever "to play hardball with. We're loaded for bear."[64] The threats of such actions are effective primarily with members of the president's party, of course, because members of the opposition party do not expect to receive many favors from the president.

Although sanctions or threats of sanctions are far from an everyday occurrence, they do happen. These may take the form of excluding a member from White House social events, denying routine requests for White House tour tickets, or shutting off access to the president. Each of these personal slights sends a signal of presidential displeasure. More dramatically, after Senator Richard Shelby complained about President Clinton's budget package, the White House announced that it was moving the management team for a space shuttle contract from Alabama to Texas, which constituted a loss of jobs for the senator's state. To add insult to injury, Senator Shelby was given one ticket to the White House ceremony honoring the University of Alabama football team; Senator Howell Heflin, Alabama's other senator, received eleven.

Senator James Jeffords of Vermont irritated the George W. Bush administration by his lack of support of some of the president's principal initiatives. The White House did not invite the senator to a ceremony honoring a Vermont teacher, cut Jeffords (chairman of the Senate Education Committee) out of the loop on the administration's education proposal, withheld its support for a Northeastern dairy compact important to him, and passed the word to reporters that Jeffords would learn to rue his rebelliousness.

Heavy-handed arm twisting is unusual, however, because it can be costly for the president. The White House backtracked on moving the National Aeronautics and Space Administration (NASA) team from Alabama, but Senator Shelby later switched parties and became a Republican. Similarly, Senator Jeffords left the Republican Party and became an Independent in 2001, giving Democrats control of the Senate.

More typical is the orchestration of pressure by others. The Reagan White House was especially effective in this regard. By operating through party channels, its Political Affairs Office, and its Office of Public Liaison, the administration was able to generate pressure from party members' constituents, campaign contributors, political activists, business leaders, state officials, interest groups, and party officials.

Despite the resources available to presidents, if members of Congress wish to oppose them, there is little the White House can do to stop them. This is true for those in the president's party as well as those in the opposition. The primary reason is that the parties are highly decentralized, and thus national party leaders do not control those aspects of politics that are of vital concern to members of Congress—namely, nominations and elections. Members of Congress are largely self-recruited, gain their party's nominations by their own efforts and not those of the party, and provide most of the money and organizational support needed for their elections. Presidents can do little to influence the results of these activities; usually, they do not even try. As President Kennedy said in 1962, "Party loyalty or responsibility means damn little. They've got to take care of themselves first. They [House members] all have to run this year—I don't and I couldn't hurt most of them if I wanted to."[65]

Consultation

Consulting with members of Congress on legislation can be advantageous for the White House. Members of Congress appreciate advance warning of presidential proposals, especially those that affect their constituencies directly. No official, especially an elected one, wants to be blindsided. Politicians quite naturally want to be prepared to take credit or avoid blame. Moreover, when a policy fails, members of Congress are unlikely to support the president in the perilous landing of the policy if they are not involved in the take-off.

Consultation before announcing a bill may also be useful in anticipating congressional objections. It may, in fact, be possible to preempt some of the opposition with strategic compromises and to garner some advance commitments. At the very least, members of Congress will feel they have had an opportunity to be heard. They take pride in their work and may be offended if they feel the White House has not taken them seriously.

Despite these advantages, presidential consultation with Congress has often played a modest role in presidential–congressional relations.[66] Consultation is not easy to accomplish. Arriving at a common position within the executive branch may tax the resources and patience of the White House, particularly at a time when other exigencies press on the president and senior staff. Extending the negotiations to the legislature (and thus the public) and broadening the conflict may render the process of policy formulation unmanageable and increase its costs significantly. White House officials often are also concerned with the nature of Congress, which they frequently view as parochial, sieve-like, and prone to transform important matters of state into pork-barrel issues.

An additional challenge is determining with whom the White House should consult. The decentralization of power within Congress presents a substantial burden to executive branch officials wishing to consult with all the relevant members, especially on jurisdictionally complex matters. In some cases, even identifying the appropriate senators and representatives is difficult.

Time is an ever-present factor in White House operations, and it influences consultation with Congress as well. At least fifty congressional staff members of Democratic members of Congress participated in President Clinton's task force on health care, which took eight months to formulate. If severe deadlines are imposed on the production of a presidential initiative (such as the 1977 energy proposal), consultation may be difficult. In addition, a president with an extensive legislative agenda may send a large number of bills to Congress, restricting the time officials can devote to consulting on any one of them.

A president with firm ideas on policy or with a proposal that might engender opposition is unlikely to relish consulting with Congress in order to make compromises to satisfy congressional desires. In addition, some presidential proposals are designed by the White House to assuage constituency groups or fulfill campaign promises, which significantly constrains the possibilities of modifying these bills in response to congressional consultation.

Some observers propose that the White House involve relevant members of Congress in the process of developing the president's legislative program, the rationale being that those who have been involved in formulating a bill are more likely to support it after it is sent to the Hill. This process is not typical, however, because chief executives have found it too cumbersome to include members of Congress, especially those of the opposition party, in writing legislation, and most members of Congress prefer to protect their status as members of an independent branch.

Setting Priorities

An important aspect of a president's legislative strategy can be establishing priorities among legislative proposals. The goal of this effort is to set the congressional agenda. If the president is not able to focus the attention of Congress on his priority programs, these bills may become lost in the complex and overloaded legislative process. Congress needs time to digest what the president sends, to come up with independent analysis, and to schedule hearings and markups of bills. Unless the president gives some indication of what is most important, Congress will simply put the proposals in a queue where they will compete with each other for attention, often with disastrous results for the president.

Queuing is especially likely to be a problem if much of the president's program must go through a single committee, as was the case for Jimmy Carter and the House Ways and Means Committee in 1977. Thus, it may be wise to spread legislative proposals among several committees so that they can work on different parts of the president's agenda at the same time.

Setting priorities is also important because presidents and their staff can lobby effectively for only a few bills at once. Moreover, the president's political capital is inevitably limited, so it is sensible to focus it on the issues the administration cares about most. In 1977, Jimmy Carter spent his political capital on ending pork-barrel water projects, which was not one of his priority items. Similarly, in 1993 Bill Clinton risked losing focus on his economic and health care programs by proposing a host of controversial policies on abortion, homosexuals in the military, campaign reform, and environmental protection, among others. Many of these policies were initiated in response to pressures from segments of his party for action following twelve years of Republican presidents.

Tax cuts, education reform, an overhaul of defense policy, and greater federal support for faith-based social welfare programs were the top priorities of the new George W. Bush administration. The president spoke extensively about each initiative, and the administration went to considerable lengths to focus attention on these priority proposals. The faith-based initiative received attention in the week after the inauguration, followed in successive weeks by education, tax cuts, and defense. Similarly, the president focused on a few initiatives, including reforming Social Security, the tax code, and personal injury lawsuits, in his second term.

Setting priorities in the early weeks of a new administration is also important because, during his first months in office, the president has the greatest latitude in focusing on priority legislation. The White House can put off dealing with the full spectrum of national issues for a period of months at the beginning of the term of a new president, but it cannot do so indefinitely. Eventually it must decide on them. By the second year, the agenda is full and more policies are in the pipeline as the administration attempts to satisfy its constituencies and responds to unanticipated, or simply overlooked, problems, including international crises. These issues affect simultaneously the attention of the public and the priorities of Congress and thus the White House's success in focusing attention on its priority issues.[67]

In addition, presidents themselves may distract from their own legislative priorities. The more the White House tries to do, the more difficult it is to focus the country's attention on a few priority items. As we saw in Chapter 4, presidents have so many demands to speak and decide on issues that it is impossible for White House planners to organize their schedules to focus the attention of Congress and the public for an extended period of time on their major goals.

Focusing attention on priorities is considerably easier for a president with a short legislative agenda, such as Ronald Reagan, than it is for one with a more ambitious agenda, such as Barack Obama. Obama began proposing his large agenda immediately after taking office. Moreover, Democrats had a laundry list of initiatives that George W. Bush had blocked, ranging from gender pay equity and children's health insurance to tougher tobacco regulations and a new public service initiative. In addition, there were recession-related efforts to provide mortgage relief and curb predatory banking practices to complement the president's economic stimulus measure. The more the White House tried to do, the more difficult it was to focus the country's attention on priority issues. Once the administration had put in place policies to deal with the worst of the crises Obama inherited, it moved on to health care, climate change, Afghanistan, and other major initiatives. The result was a perception in the public about a loss of focus on unemployment, prompting a shift back to the economy at the beginning of the president's second year in office.

The president communicates with the public in a congested communications environment clogged with competing messages from a wide variety of sources, through a wide range of media, and on a staggering array of subjects.[68] Congress is quite capable of setting its own agenda and is unlikely to defer to the president for long, especially if the opposition party controls one or both chambers. A year into Barack Obama's tenure, White House communications director Dan Pfeiffer declared, "It was clear that too often we didn't have the ball—Congress had the ball in terms of driving the message."[69]

Moving Quickly

The president must move quickly to exploit the honeymoon atmosphere that typically characterizes the early months of a new administration. First-year proposals have a better chance of passing Congress than do those sent to the Hill later in an administration. Lyndon Johnson explained, "You've got to give it all you can in that first year. . . . You've got just one year when they treat you right."[70] Despite a severely truncated transition because of the disputed election results, George W. Bush lost no time in sending priority bills to Congress. Proposals for a large cut in income taxes, education reform, and increased support for faith-based charities went to Congress in short order. Barack Obama began promoting his economic stimulus program during the transition period so that Congress would be in a position to pass it shortly after he took office.

The failure to be ready to propose priority legislation can be costly. A policy vacuum existed in the approximately ten months between Bill Clinton's inauguration and the arrival of a complete health care reform proposal on Capitol Hill. In this vacuum, issues of relatively low priority such as the homosexuals in the military issue received disproportionate attention in the press and may have cost the administration vital goodwill that it needed in its search for support for its cornerstone policy. In addition, the president was forced to raise health care reform in the context of major expenditures of political capital in battles on behalf of his budget and NAFTA.

The danger, of course, is in proposing a policy without thorough analysis in order to exploit this favorable political climate. This appears to have occurred with the budget cuts that Reagan proposed in early 1981. In this case, the departments, including cabinet members, and their expertise were kept at a distance in the executive decision-making process. Although taking time to draft proposals does not guarantee that they will be well conceived, it is by no means clear that the rapid drafting of legislation is in the best interests of the nation.

It is easier for a president who has a small agenda with an essentially negative character, such as Ronald Reagan's agenda of cutting taxes or domestic spending, to move rapidly to exploit the honeymoon. It is much more difficult to draft complex legislation rapidly, a problem Jimmy Carter faced in his first year when he tried to deal with issues such as energy, welfare reform, and the containment of health costs. Bill Clinton and Barack Obama faced similar problems with their health care reform programs. In contrast, Kennedy and Johnson had the advantage of a party program that had been building up during the 1950s when the Democrats were not in the White House.

Structuring Choice

Framing issues in ways that favor the president's programs may set the terms of the debate and thus the premises on which members of Congress cast their votes. The key vote on Ronald Reagan's budget cuts in 1981 was on the rule determining whether there would be a single vote of yea or nay in the House. Once the rule was adopted, the White House could frame the issue as a vote for or against the popular president, and the broad nature of the reconciliation bill shifted the debate from the losses of individual programs to the benefits of the package as a whole. Although Reagan could not win an important individual vote on cutting a social welfare program, by structuring the choice facing Congress, he was required only to win one vote and could avoid much of the potential criticism for specific reductions in spending.

Portraying policies in terms of criteria on which there is a consensus, and playing down divisive issues, are often at the core of efforts to structure choices for Congress. For example, federal aid to education had been a divisive issue for years before President Johnson proposed the Elementary and Secondary Education Act in 1965. To blunt opposition, he successfully changed the focus of debate from teachers' salaries and classroom shortages to fighting poverty, and from the separation of church and state to aiding children. This change in the premises of congressional decision making eased the path for the bill.

Although the structuring of choices can be a useful tool for the president, there is no guarantee that it will succeed, and opponents of the president's policies are unlikely to defer to an administration's attempts to structure choices on the issues. On President Clinton's first major legislative proposal—his fiscal stimulus package—Republicans succeeded in defining his economic program in terms of pork-barrel spending instead of increasing employment. In response to his first budget, the Republicans focused public debate on tax increases rather than economic growth or deficit reduction. Clinton attempted to depict his health care plan in comforting, affordable terms. His opponents did not simply submit, however, and launched an aggressive advertising campaign that characterized the president's plan as expensive, experimental, providing lower quality and rationed care, costing jobs, and bringing a lot more government and red tape to health care. In the end, public debate focused on the reform's pitfalls. The president's difficulty in defining himself and his policies frustrated him. As Clinton reflected: "The thing that has surprised me most is how difficult it is . . . to really keep communicating what you're about to the American people."[71]

The Context of Influence

In our discussion of the president's legislative skills, it is important to keep in mind the general context in which a president is forced to operate today—a period characterized by congressional assertiveness. The diminished deference to the president by individual members of Congress and the institution as a whole naturally makes presidential influence more problematic.

The Kennedy–Johnson years were characterized by stable prices, sustained economic growth, and expansive government. The prosperity of the 1960s provided the federal government with the funds for implementing new policies with little risk. Taxes did not have to be raised and sacrifices did not have to be made in order to help the underprivileged. The late 1970s to the late 1990s, however, was a period in which government resources were scarce—in part because of the continuing cost of the programs enacted in the 1960s. Such a condition made the passage of expensive new programs more difficult. When resources are scarce, presidents are faced with internal competition for them and the breakdown of supporting coalitions. They must choose between policies rather than building coalitions for several policies through logrolling.

George W. Bush was the first president in nearly forty years to begin his tenure with slack resources, easing the path for passage of a large tax cut. Barack Obama took office under conditions of a financial crisis in which the government was running huge deficits. The desperation of the country, however, created conditions for the passage of a massive stimulus bill.

The Impact of Legislative Skills

In general, presidential legislative skills must compete, as does public support, with other, more stable factors that affect voting in Congress, including party, ideology, personal views and commitments on specific policies, and constituency interests. By the time a president tries to exercise influence on a vote, most members of Congress have made up their minds on the basis of these other factors.

Systematic quantitative studies have found that, once we control for the status of their party in Congress and their standing with the public, presidents renowned for their legislative skills (such as Lyndon Johnson) are generally no more successful in winning votes (even close ones) or obtaining congressional support than those, such as Jimmy Carter, who are considered to have been less adept in dealing with Congress.[72] Even skilled presidents cannot change the contours of the political landscape and create opportunities for change very much. However, they can recognize favorable configurations of political forces, such as those that existed in 1933, 1965, and 1981, which they can effectively exploit to embark on major shifts in public policy. Franklin D. Roosevelt, Lyndon Johnson, and Ronald Reagan were particularly effective in exploiting their resources in their early years in office; Jimmy Carter and Bill Clinton were not.

THE VETO

Sometimes, presidents not only fail to win passage of their proposals but Congress also passes legislation to which they are strongly opposed. Because all bills and joint resolutions, except those proposing constitutional amendments, must be presented to the president for approval, he has another opportunity to influence legislation: the veto.

When Congress passes an item that must be submitted to the president, he has several options. Within ten days (Sundays excepted) of its presentation, the president may (1) sign the measure, in which case it becomes the law of the land, (2) not sign the measure and return it to the house in which it originated with a message stating the reasons for withholding approval, or (3) do nothing.

A bill or joint resolution that the president returns to Congress has been vetoed. It can then become law only if each house of Congress repasses it by a two-thirds majority of those present. Congress may override the presidential veto at any time before it adjourns *sine die* (that is, before the end of that particular Congress).

The veto's origin in America stems from the British colonial experience, where the veto served as a means by which colonial governors could protect the interests of the Crown. The clashes with the local assemblies that the exercise of the veto produced led the Constitution's framers to qualify the exercise of the veto by allowing two-thirds of both houses to override it.

Early presidents exercised their veto power sparingly; the first six presidents vetoed a total of eight bills. However, the seventh president, Andrew Jackson, vetoed twelve, and his successors have followed his example. Once partisan competition before a broad electorate had developed in Jackson's era, there was a greater incentive for presidents to use the veto power to stake out positions and for Congress to take positions by passing legislation it knew the president would veto.[73]

The president can veto only an entire bill. Unlike most state governors, presidents do not have an item veto, which would allow them to veto specific provisions of a bill. As a result of this constraint, members of Congress use a number of strategies to avoid a possible veto of a particular proposal. For example, Congress may add increased appropriations or riders (that is, nongermane provisions) that the White House might not want to bills that it otherwise desires, thus forcing the president to decide whether to accept these unattractive provisions in order to gain the legislation. In most such cases, presidents desist from using their vetoes. For example, after President Carter vetoed a bill providing for increased salaries for Public Health Service physicians, Congress added the pay raise to mental health services legislation, a pet project of First Lady Rosalynn Carter, and the president signed the bill.

In 1987, Congress passed the entire discretionary budget of the federal government in one omnibus bill. Consequently, the president had to accept the whole package or else lose appropriations for the entire government. President Reagan frequently called for a constitutional amendment giving the president an item veto, and Presidents Bush and Clinton followed his example. They argued that an item veto would allow the president to stop unnecessary spending within massive appropriations bills and thus help to bring the budget under control.

In 1996, Congress heeded their call with a bill that created an elaborate mechanism for the president to veto specific items in legislation. President Clinton cast eighty-two such vetoes, but opponents challenged the line-item veto in the courts. They charged that under Article 1 of the Constitution, all legislative power is vested with Congress; the president can only accept or reject bills in their entirety. The new veto, the lawsuits argued, gave the president the power to change a law—or amend it—after he has signed it. In 1998, the Supreme Court agreed, finding the bill to be unconstitutional in *Clinton v. New York City.*

If the president does nothing after receiving a measure from Congress, it becomes law after ten days (Sundays excepted), provided Congress remains in session. If it has adjourned during the ten-day period, thus preventing the president from returning the bill to the house of its origination, the bill is pocket vetoed. A pocket veto kills a piece of legislation just as a regular veto does. Historically, somewhat fewer than half of all vetoes have been pocket vetoes. Table 9.4 presents data on the vetoes by recent presidents.

Presidents have sometimes attempted to use the pocket veto by taking no action on measures sent to them just before Congress went into a temporary recess and claiming that the recess prevented them from returning their veto for congressional consideration. (In 1964, President Johnson pocket vetoed a bill during a congressional recess and then recalled and signed it.) However, in 1976, after the Nixon and Ford White Houses had lost litigation on the issue, the Ford administration promised that the president would not use the pocket veto during congressional recesses as long as an official of Congress was designated to be on hand to receive his vetoes. Since Congress is in session nearly all year, most people thought that only an adjournment *sine die* would provide the opportunity for a pocket veto.

Ronald Reagan used the pocket veto during a recess at the end of the 1981 session without apparent problems, but thirty-three House Democrats filed suit in federal court to challenge his pocket veto during the congressional recess at the end of 1983 of a bill making aid to El Salvador dependent on

Table 9.4 Regular and Pocket Vetoes

President	Regular Vetoes	Pocket Vetoes	Total Vetoes
Eisenhower	73	108	181
Kennedy	12	9	21
Johnson	16	14	30
Nixon	26	17	43
Ford	48	18	66
Carter	13	18	31
Reagan	39	39	78
G. H. W. Bush	29	15	44
Clinton	37	1	38
G. W. Bush	12	0	12
Obama*	2	0	2

*As of March 2013.

human rights progress. As a result, in 1984 a federal appeals court ruled against the president. Presidents since Reagan have claimed to have pocket vetoed some bills during congressional recesses, but Congress has treated them like regular vetoes.[74]

The last column in Table 9.4 indicates that vetoes are infrequently used (George W. Bush issued no vetoes during his entire first term in office and Barack Obama issued only two). Not only are the absolute numbers low, but also less than 1 percent of the bills passed by Congress (which typically number several hundred per session) are vetoed. The table also shows that presidents who face Congresses controlled by the opposition party (Eisenhower, Nixon, Ford, Reagan, and Bush) used more vetoes, as we would expect. These presidents were more likely to be presented with legislation that they opposed.

Table 9.5 illustrates another important fact about vetoes—the tendency of Congress to sustain them. Congress does occasionally override a veto, however, especially when the president's party is in the minority in Congress. George W. Bush lost an unusually high percentage of vetoes after the Democrats regained control of Congress in the 2006 election. Some very important legislation has been passed over the president's veto. In the post–World War II era, such legislation includes the Taft-Hartley Labor Relations Act (1947), the McCarran-Walter Immigration Act (1952), the McCarran-Wood Internal Security Act (1950), and the War Powers Resolution (1973).

Sometimes presidents choose not to veto a bill, either because they feel that the good in it outweighs the bad or because they do not want their veto to be overridden. Thus, when Congress passed an amendment to a foreign aid authorization bill imposing new sanctions on China by such large margins that it was impossible to sustain a veto, President George H. W. Bush, who was opposed to it, nonetheless reluctantly signed the measure.

Table 9.5 Vetoes Overridden

President	Regular Vetoes	Vetoes Overridden	Percentage Vetoes Overridden
Eisenhower	73	2	3
Kennedy	12	0	0
Johnson	16	0	0
Nixon	26	7	27
Ford	48	12	25
Carter	13	2	15
Reagan	39	9	23
G. H. W. Bush	29	1	3
Clinton	37	2	5
G. W. Bush	12	4	33
Obama*	2	0	0

*As of March 2013.

When a bill is introduced in either house of Congress, the chamber's parliamentarian classifies it as public or private. Generally, public bills relate to public matters and deal with individuals by classifications or categories, such as college students or the elderly. A private bill, in contrast, names a particular individual or entity that is to receive relief, such as through payment of a pension or a claim against the government or the granting of citizenship. Up until 1969, presidents usually vetoed more private than public bills. Recent presidents have vetoed very few private bills, however, reflecting the general decrease in private bills in Congress.

Sometimes the president uses the veto to stop legislation from passing at all. At other times the White House uses the threat of a veto to shape legislation more to its liking. Presidents frequently threaten to veto bills unless certain provisions are removed or altered, and they usually receive concessions from Congress when they do.[75] For example, George H. W. Bush, a Republican facing large Democratic majorities in Congress, repeatedly made strategic use of the veto to move Congress in his direction. In a typical example, he vetoed a substantial increase in the federal minimum wage in 1989. This encouraged Congress to pass a more modest increase, which was acceptable to the president. President Clinton threatened to veto a large transportation bill in 1998 because it violated his 1997 budget agreement with Congress. Clinton's threatened veto gave leverage to members of Congress who wanted to trim the legislation, and they were successful.

George W. Bush focused his veto threats on appropriations that exceeded his budget and proposals that would alter his key policy initiatives. Usually, his veto threats succeeded in thwarting legislation he opposed, but his reluctance to veto appropriations bills undermined the credibility of his threats on spending measures.

In a more unusual situation, in 1987 President Reagan threatened to veto the omnibus appropriations bill, which contained the money necessary for running the government for the following year, if Congress did not include certain provisions that he favored. Fearing a shutdown of the government, Congress acquiesced. Bill Clinton followed a similar strategy numerous times after he won a major battle with congressional Republicans that led to two unpopular government shutdowns in 1995–1996. Because the president succeeded in assigning to the Republicans culpability for the shutdowns, his threat to veto legislation that did not provide as much funding as he sought provided him important leverage in future budget negotiations.

Signing Statements

For nearly two centuries, presidents have issued *signing statements* addressing constitutional or other legal questions when signing bills into law after failing to convince Congress to modify legislative provisions that they oppose. Often such statements have not been controversial and have been used for rhetorical or hortatory purposes.[76] Yet presidents in the period since the New Deal, especially following the congressional resurgence of the 1970s, have used these statements to attempt to nullify legislative provisions.[77] The White House is most likely to object to a bill when the ideological distance between president and Congress is great.[78]

In *INS v. Chadha* (1983) the Supreme Court held unconstitutional provisions in legislation providing for a veto of executive action by one house of Congress. This decision also voided by implication committee vetoes and reporting requirements that Congress often requires before executive actions can be taken. The Court's decision, however, has not stopped Congress from writing such provisions into legislation and from informally requiring the executive to abide by them. In response to what they see as a violation of the separation of powers, presidents, beginning with Reagan, began to identify such provisions and note their "unconstitutionality" when they signed legislation into law.[79] Reagan and his successors have also used the statements to keep department and agency officials in line with the president's views on how the law should be implemented.

More generally, recent presidents have used signing statements to challenge congressional provisions that interfered with the president's responsibility to "to take care that the laws be faithfully executed" or his constitutional authority in foreign affairs, such as language that directs presidents in negotiations and discussions with international organizations and foreign governments and prohibits them from performing certain military missions.[80] George W. Bush was particularly active in the use of signing statements,[81] while Barack Obama has continued the practice, albeit at a lesser pace.

Perhaps the most contentious of Bush's signing statements concerned the 2005 Detainee Treatment Act, which prohibited U.S. personnel from using torture on enemy combatants and other foreign prisoners as a means of exacting information about terrorist activities. The president had opposed a blanket restriction against the use of torture, claiming that U.S. interrogators needed flexibility to extract difficult-to-obtain information necessary to protect the United States against further acts of terrorism. He threatened to veto any legislation that contained such a provision. After Republican leaders in Congress informed Bush that a veto would likely be overturned by Congress, the president backed off his threat, agreed to some compromise language, and said he would approve the legislation. However, when he did so, Bush reiterated his contention that the part of the legislation that instructed the executive branch on how to execute the law was unconstitutional and therefore unenforceable.[82]

CONCLUSION

Presidents face an uphill battle in dealing with Congress.[83] Their formal powers of recommending legislation and vetoing bills help set the legislature's agenda and prevent some legislation from passing. However, these prerogatives are of only marginal help in obtaining what they want. Conflict between the executive and legislative branches is inherent in the U.S. system of government. The overlapping powers of the two branches, their representation of different constituencies, and the contrast of the hierarchical, expert nature of the executive and the decentralized, generalist Congress guarantee that, except in extraordinary circumstances, conflict between them will remain a central feature of American politics.

The chief executive's assets in dealing with Congress do not provide silver bullets for the White House. Party leadership is a potential source of influence in Congress, and presidents receive considerably more support from members of their party than from the opposition. Much, or even most, of this support is the result of members of the same party sharing similar policy views rather than the influence of the president's party leadership. Nevertheless, presidents work closely with their party and its leaders in Congress and tend to gain some increment of support as a result of party loyalty. Party support is undependable, however, as constituency interests, a lack of policy consensus, and other factors intervene and diminish the importance of the party label. Congressional party leaders are often in weak positions to move their troops in the president's direction. Ideally, presidents could influence the election of members of their party to Congress, but presidential coattails are short and midterm campaigning seems to have limited payoffs. Thus, presidents generally have to seek support from opposition party members, but their efforts at bipartisanship, although necessary, may strain relations with the less moderate wing of their own party.

Presidents are more likely to receive support in Congress when they have the public's approval than when they sit low in the polls. However, as we saw in Chapter 4, they cannot depend on the public's support nor can they be sure of being able to mobilize new support. Moreover, public approval is usually a necessary, but not a sufficient, source of influence. Even when presidents are high in the polls, they will find it difficult to pass their programs if their party lacks a majority of congressional seats.

The White House engages in a large-scale legislative liaison effort to create goodwill and influence votes on a more personal level. Presidents consummate bargains, provide services and amenities, twist arms, call members of Congress, and consult with them in advance. However, there are severe limits on a president's time and resources. Presidents can increase the chances of their success by moving programs early in their tenure and not letting those programs clog the legislative process. Many find it difficult or impossible to control the congressional agenda so neatly, however. Although presidential legislative skills are crucial in winning some votes, their importance is often exaggerated. Thus, presidents must constantly struggle to succeed in having their policies enacted into law.

Presidential leadership of Congress is at the margins most of the time. In general, successful presidential leadership of Congress has not been the result of the dominant chief executive of political folklore, who reshapes the contours of the political landscape to pave the way for change. Rather than creating the conditions for important shifts in public policy, the effective president is the less heroic figure of the facilitator, who works at the margins building coalitions to recognize and exploit opportunities presented by a favorable configuration of political forces.

Discussion Questions

1. Some argue that members of the president's party in Congress should simply vote their consciences and pay little attention to party loyalty to their leader. Others say that the only way that election promises can be implemented, and thus be made meaningful to the majority of voters, is for the party to stick together and pass legislation. Should members of Congress defer principally to their party, to the president, or to their constituencies' interests?

2. Many people seem to think that divided government is good for the country because it prevents the president from concentrating too much power in the executive branch. Others view divided government as an obstacle to bringing about change because different parties control the Congress and the White House. What do you think? Is it good for people to split their tickets and vote for a president of one party and members of the House or Senate from the other party? What are the advantages and costs of divided government?

3. What can Barack Obama do to overcome congressional resistance to his major legislation? Which of the president's legislative activities have been most successful, and why were they successful?

Web Exercises

1. One measure of presidential influence is the extent to which presidents can get Congress to enact bills they support. Go to the OMB website at http://www.whitehouse.gov/omb/ and click on "Legislative Information" and then "Statements of Administration Policy" to determine the president's position on pending legislation. Follow the legislation to the relevant congressional committee using the Thomas website at http://Thomas.loc.gov. Determine if hearings have been held, whether administration officials have been called to testify, and whether the committees have marked up the bill and sent it to the floors of their respective houses. Of the legislation that reaches the floor, for which do you think the White House will lobby hardest? Predict whether the president will be successful in passing legislation he supports or stopping legislation he opposes.

2. Look at the items President Clinton vetoed with the line-item veto at http://www.access.gpo.gov/nara/nara004.html. Did these vetoes make an important contribution to public policy? Do you agree with the Supreme Court's decision in *Clinton v. New York City* (1998) that Congress had delegated power to the president unconstitutionally?

3. Every president, including Barack Obama and George W. Bush, takes office articulating a desire for bipartisanship. Go to http://voteview.com/Polarized_America.htm and look at the level of polarization in Congress over time. How much potential is there for President Obama to obtain bipartisan support for his initiatives? Is he likely to be more successful in some policy areas than in others?

Selected Readings

Coleman, John J., and David C. W. Parker. "The Consequences of Divided Government." In *Oxford Handbook of the American Presidency*, edited by George C. Edwards III and William G. Howell. Oxford: Oxford University Press, 2009, pp. 383–402.

Edwards, George C., III. *At the Margins: Presidential Leadership of Congress.* New Haven, CT: Yale University Press, 1989.

Edwards, George C., III. "Presidential Approval as a Source of Influence in Congress." In *Oxford Handbook of the American Presidency*, edited by George C. Edwards III and William G. Howell. Oxford: Oxford University Press, 2009.

Edwards, George C., III. *Overreach: Leadership in the Obama Presidency.* Princeton, NJ: Princeton University Press, 2012, pp. 338–361.

Edwards, George C., III. *The Strategic President: Persuasion and Opportunity in Presidential Leadership.* Princeton, NJ: Princeton University Press, 2009.

Fisher, Louis. *Constitutional Conflicts between Congress and the President*, 5th rev. ed. Lawrence: University Press of Kansas, 2007.

Grossback, Lawrence J., David A. M. Peterson, and James A. Stimson. *Mandate Politics.* Cambridge, UK: Cambridge University Press, 2006.

Jones, Charles O. *The Presidency in a Separated System*, 2nd ed. Washington, DC: Brookings Institution, 2005.

Kriner, Douglas L. *After the Rubicon: Congress, Presidents, and the Politics of Waging War.* Chicago: University of Chicago Press, 2010.

Krutz, Glen S., and Jeffrey S. Peake. *Treaty Politics and the Rise of Executive Agreements.* Ann Arbor: University of Michigan Press, 2009.

Lee, Frances E. *Beyond Ideology: Politics, Principles, and Partisanship in the U.S. Senate.* Chicago: University of Chicago Press, 2009.

Neustadt, Richard E. *Presidential Power and the Modern Presidents.* New York: Free Press, 1990.

Rhode, David W., and Meredith Barthelemy. "The President and Congressional Parties in an Era of Polarization." In *Oxford Handbook of the American Presidency*, edited by George C. Edwards III and William G. Howell. Oxford: Oxford University Press, 2009.

Wayne, Stephen J. "Legislative Skills." In *Oxford Handbook of the American Presidency*, edited by George C. Edwards III and William G. Howell. Oxford: Oxford University Press, 2009.

Notes

1. Lyndon Johnson quoted in Doris Kearns, *Lyndon Johnson and the American Dream* (New York: Harper and Row, 1976), p. 226.

2. Occasionally, Congress may continue its session after the elections. The 103rd Congress did that in 1994 in order to consider the General Agreement on Tariffs and Trade (GATT). The president supported GATT, but some members of Congress did not wish to vote on it until after the midterm elections. In 2008, Congress reconvened after the presidential election to attempt to deal with the financial crisis. Special sessions occur only after Congress has adjourned.

3. James Madison, "The Federalist, No. 46," in *The Federalist* (New York: Modern Library, 1937), p. 307.

4. E. Scott Adler and John S. Lapinski, "Demand-Side Theory and Congressional Committee Composition: A Constituency Characteristics Approach," *American Journal of Political Science* 41 (July 1997): 895–918; William T. Bianco, "Reliable Source or Usual Suspects? Cue-Taking, Information Transmission, and Legislative Committees," *Journal of Politics* 59 (August 1997): 913–924; Tim Groseclose, "Testing Committee Composition Hypotheses for the U.S. Congress," *Journal of Politics* 56 (May 1994): 440–458; Christopher J. Deering

and Steven S. Smith, *Committees in Congress*, 3rd ed. (Washington, DC: Congressional Quarterly Press, 1997); Richard L. Hall and Bernard Grofman, "The Committee Assignment Process and the Conditional Nature of Committee Bias," *American Political Science Review* 84 (December 1990): 1149–1166; John Londregan and James M. Snyder, "Comparing Committee and Floor Preferences," *Legislative Studies Quarterly* 19 (May 1994): 233–266; Geoffrey D. Peterson and J. Mark Wrighton, "The Continuing Puzzle of Committee Outliers: A Methodological Reassessment," *Congress and the Presidency* 25 (Spring 1998): 67–78; Kenneth A. Shepsle, *The Giant Jigsaw Puzzle: Democratic Committee Assignments in the Modern House* (Chicago: University of Chicago Press, 1978); James M. Snyder, "Artificial Extremism in Interest Group Ratings," *Legislative Studies Quarterly* 17 (August 1992): 319–345. But see Keith Krehbiel, "Are Congressional Committees Composed of Preference Outliers?" *American Political Science Review* 84 (March 1991): 149–163; and Keith Krehbiel, "Deference, Extremism, and Interest Group Ratings," *Legislative Studies Quarterly* 19 (February 1994): 61–77.

5. See, for example, John W. Kingdon, *Congressmen's Voting Decisions*, 3rd ed. (Ann Arbor: University of Michigan Press, 1989); and Donald R. Matthews and James A. Stimson, *Yeas and Nays* (New York: Wiley, 1975).

6. Gerald R. Ford, *A Time to Heal: The Autobiography of Gerald R. Ford* (New York: Harper and Row, 1979), p. 150.

7. Quoted in Norman J. Ornstein, "Assessing Reagan's First Year," in Norman J. Ornstein, ed., *President and Congress: Assessing Reagan's First Year* (Washington, DC: American Enterprise Institute, 1982), pp. 102–103.

8. George C. Edwards III and Andrew Barrett, "Presidential Agenda Setting in Congress," in Jon R. Bond and Richard Fleisher, eds., *Polarized Politics: Congress and the President in a Partisan Era* (Washington, DC: CQ Press, 2000).

9. See, however, George C. Edwards III and B. Dan Wood, "Who Influences Whom? The President, Congress, and the

Media," *American Political Science Review* 93 (June 1999): 327–344.

10. Richard E. Neustadt, *Presidential Power and the Modern Presidents* (New York: Free Press, 1990), p. 29.

11. Quoted in Paul C. Light, *The President's Agenda: Domestic Policy Choice from Kennedy to Carter* (Baltimore, MD: Johns Hopkins University Press, 1982), p. 135.

12. William G. Howell and Jon C. Pevehouse, "Presidents, Congress, and the Use of Force," *International Organization* 59 (Winter 2005): 209–232.

13. See Keith Krehbiel, *Pivotal Politics: A Theory of U. S. Lawmaking* (Chicago: University of Chicago Press, 1998); Terry Sullivan, "Bargaining with the President: A Simple Game and New Evidence," *American Political Science Review* 84 (December 1990): 1167–1196; and Glen Biglaiser, David J. Jackson, and Jeffrey S. Peake, "Back on Track: Support for Presidential Trade Authority in the House of Representatives," *American Politics Research* 32 (November 2004): 679–697, concerning party members switching to support the president of their party.

14. Francis Lee, "Dividers, Not Uniters: Presidential Leadership and Senate Partisanship, 1981–2004," *Journal of Politics* 70 (October 2008): 914–928.

15. Frances E. Lee, *Beyond Ideology: Politics, Principles, and Partisanship in the U.S. Senate* (Chicago: University of Chicago Press, 2009), chap. 4.

16. Moynihan quoted in "Recasting Senate Finance: Moynihan to Take Helm," *Congressional Quarterly Weekly Report*, December 12, 1992, p. 3796.

17. Shailagh Murray and Paul Kane, "Democratic Congress Shows Signs It Will Not Bow to Obama," *Washington Post*, January 11, 2009, p. A5.

18. Quoted in Steven R. Weisman, "No. 1, the President Is Very Result Oriented," *New York Times*, November 12, 1983, pp. 10, 85. See also Shirley Elder, "The Cabinet's Ambassadors to Capitol Hill," *National Journal*, July 29, 1978, p. 1196.

19. David W. Rohde, *Parties and Leaders in the Postreform House* (Chicago: University of Chicago Press, 1991).

20. George C. Edwards III, "Interview with President Jimmy Carter," *Presidential Studies Quarterly* 38 (March 2008): pp. 2, 5–6.

21. Paul Herrnson, Irwin Morris, and John McTague, "The Impact of Presidential Campaigning for Congress on Presidential Support in the U.S. House of Representatives," *Legislative Studies Quarterly* 36 (February 2011): 99–122.

22. See Jeffrey E. Cohen, Michael A. Krassa, and John A. Hamman, "The Impact of Presidential Campaigning on Midterm U.S. Senate Elections," *American Political Science Review* 85 (March 1991): 165–180.

23. Benjamin Highton, "Bill Clinton, Newt Gingrich, and the 1998 House Elections," *Public Opinion Quarterly* 66 (Spring 2002): 1–17.

24. George C. Edwards III, *The Public Presidency* (New York: St. Martin's, 1983), pp. 83–93; Gregory N. Flemming, "Presidential Coattails in Open-Seat Elections," *Legislative Studies Quarterly* 20 (May 1995): 197–212; Barry C. Burden and David C. Kimball, *Why Americans Split Their Tickets: Campaigns, Competition, and Divided Government* (Ann Arbor: University of Michigan Press, 2002).

25. James E. Campbell and Joe A. Sumners, "Presidential Coattails in Senate Elections," *American Political Science Review* 84 (June 1990): 513–524; Alan I. Abramowitz and Jeffrey A. Segal, *Senate Elections* (Ann Arbor: University of Michigan Press, 1992), pp. 121, 233, 238.

26. Jimmy Carter, *Keeping Faith: Memoirs of a President* (New York: Bantam, 1982), p. 80.

27. See George C. Edwards III, *Overreach: Leadership in the Obama Presidency* (Princeton, NJ: Princeton University Press, 2012), chaps. 4–6, for Obama's efforts to obtain bipartisan support and his lack of success in doing so.

28. Emmet John Hughes, *The Living Presidency* (Baltimore, MD: Penguin, 1974), p. 68.

29. Lyndon B. Johnson, *The Vantage Point: Perspectives of the Presidency, 1963–1969* (New York: Popular Library, 1971), p. 443.

30. Ibid., p. 323.

31. Quoted in "Run, Run, Run," *Newsweek*, May 2, 1977, p. 38.

32. Quoted in "Carter Seeks More Effective Use of Departmental Lobbyists' Skills," *Congressional Quarterly Weekly Report*, March 4, 1978, p. 585.

33. Quoted in Sidney Blumenthal, "Marketing the President," *New York Times Magazine*, September 13, 1981, p. 110.

34. Quoted in Dom Bonafede, "The Strained Relationship," *National Journal*, May 19, 1979, p. 830.

35. William Schneider, "It's Payback Time for GOP and Press," *National Journal*, March 19, 1994, p. 696.

36. Brandice Canes-Wrone, David W. Brady, and John F. Cogan, "Out of Step, Out of Office: Electoral Accountability and House Members' Voting," *American Political Science Review* 96 (March 2002): 127–140.

37. Paul Gronke, Jeffrey Koch, and J. Matthew Wilson, "Follow the Leader? Presidential Approval, Presidential Support, and Representatives' Electoral Fortunes," *Journal of Politics* 65 (August 2003): 785–808; Burden and Kimball, *Why Americans Split Their Tickets*; David W. Brady, Brandice Canes-Wrone, and John F. Cogan, "Differences between Winning and Losing Incumbents," in David W. Brady, John F. Cogan, and Morris P. Fiorina, eds., *Change and Continuity in House Elections* (Stanford, CA: Stanford University Press, 2000); David W. Brady, John F. Cogan, Brian Gaines, and R. Douglas Rivers, "The Perils of Presidential Support: How the Republicans Captured the House," *Political Behavior* 18 (December 1996): 345–368.

38. Brady et al., "The Perils of Presidential Support."

39. Gary C. Jacobson, "The War, the President, and the 2006 Midterm Congressional Elections," paper delivered at the Annual Meeting of the Midwest Political Science Association, April 12–15, 2007.

40. Pew Research Center for the People & the Press, "October 2006 Survey on Electoral Competition: Final Topline October 17–22," 2006.

41. See Edwards, *Overreach*, chap. 7.

42. Richard M. Nixon, *In the Arena: A Memoir of Victory, Defeat and Renewal* (New York: Simon and Schuster, 1990), p. 282.

43. William E. Timmons, *Memorandum for the President*, December 31, 1973, p. 3.

Folder: Executive–Legislative Relations—93rd Congress, 1st Session, William E. Timmons Files, Box 3, Gerald R. Ford Library, p. 3. See also George W. Bush, *Decision Points* (New York: Crown, 2010), p. 330.

44. Michael S. Rocca, "9/11 and Presidential Support in the 107th Congress," *Congress & the Presidency* 36, no. 2 (2009): 272–296.

45. Stephen A. Borrelli, J. Mark Wrighton, and Chad Bryan, "Policy-Specific Approval Ratings and Presidential Success on Roll Calls: An Exploration," *American Review of Politics* 19 (Fall 1998): 267–282; George C. Edwards III, "Aligning Tests with Theory: Presidential Approval as a Source of Influence in Congress," *Congress and the Presidency* 24 (Fall 1997): 113–130.

46. Lawrence J. Grossback, David A. M. Peterson, and James A. Stimson, *Mandate Politics* (New York: Cambridge University Press, 2006).

47. Patricia Heidotting Conley, *Presidential Mandates* (Chicago: University of Chicago Press, 2001).

48. George C. Edwards III, *At the Margins: Presidential Leadership of Congress* (New Haven, CT: Yale University Press, 1989), chap. 8; Lawrence J. Grossback and David A. M. Peterson, "Comparing Competing Theories on the Causes of Mandate Perceptions," *American Journal of Political Science* 49 (April 2005): 406–419.

49. See Edwards, *Overreach*.

50. Harry McPherson, *A Political Education* (Boston: Little, Brown, 1972), p. 192.

51. On the office's organization of outside groups, see Mark A. Peterson, "The Presidency and Organized Interests: White House Patterns of Interest Group Liaison," *American Political Science Review* 86 (September 1992): 612–625.

52. Richard E. Neustadt, "Presidency and Legislation: Planning the President's Program," in Aaron Wildavsky, ed., *The Presidency* (Boston: Little, Brown, 1969), p. 596.

53. Sandhya Somashekhar and Paul Kane, "Democrats Yet to Decide on Health-care Bill Bear the Weight of Washington," *Washington Post*, March 18, 2010; Sheryl Gay Stolberg, Jeff Zeleny, and Carl Hulse,

"The Long Road Back," *New York Times*, March 21, 2010; Jonathan Alter, *The Promise: President Obama, Year One* (New York: Simon and Schuster, 2010), pp. 409, 432.

54. Brien Friel et al., "So, Who Won?" *National Journal*, March 27, 2010, p. 20.

55. These examples come from Ceci Connolly, "How Obama Revived His Health-care Bill," *Washington Post*, March 23, 2010.

56. Dwight D. Eisenhower, *Mandate for Change, 1953–1956* (New York: Signet, 1963), pp. 254–255.

57. Johnson, *The Vantage Point*, p. 40.

58. David Stockman, *The Triumph of Politics* (New York: Harper and Row, 1986), pp. 251, 253, 260–261, 264–265; see also William Greider, "The Education of David Stockman," *Atlantic Monthly*, December 1981, p. 51.

59. John M. Broder, "With Something for Everyone, Climate Bill Passed," *New York Times*, July 1, 2009.

60. Quoted in Gary W. Reichard, *The Reaffirmation of Republicanism: Eisenhower and the Eighty-Third Congress* (Knoxville: University of Tennessee Press, 1975), p. 173.

61. William Timmons and Max Friedersdorf quoted in "Turning Screws: Winning Votes in Congress," *Congressional Quarterly Weekly Report*, April 24, 1976, pp. 952–953.

62. Quoted in Neil McNeil, *Forge of Democracy* (New York: McKay, 1963), p. 260.

63. Christopher R. Berry, Barry C. Burden, and William G. Howell, "The President and the Distribution of Federal Spending," *American Political Science Review* 104 (November 2010): 783–799.

64. Quoted in "Turning Screws," pp. 952–953.

65. Quoted in Theodore Sorensen, *Kennedy* (New York: Bantam, 1966), p. 387.

66. See Mark A. Peterson, *Legislating Together* (Cambridge, MA: Harvard University Press, 1990).

67. See an interview with Bill Clinton by Jack Nelson and Robert J. Donovan, "The Education of a President," *Los Angeles Times Magazine*, August 1, 1993, p. 39.

See also Bill Clinton, *My Life* (New York: Knopf, 2004), p. 556.

68. See George C. Edwards III, *The Strategic President: Persuasion and Opportunity in Presidential Leadership* (Princeton, NJ: Princeton University Press, 2009), pp. 96–104.

69. Quoted in Michael D. Shear, "White House Revamps Communications Strategy," *Washington Post*, February 15, 2010.

70. Quoted in McPherson, *A Political Education*, p. 268.

71. Clinton quoted in Bob Woodward, *The Agenda: Inside the Clinton White House* (New York: Simon and Schuster, 1994), p. 313.

72. Edwards, *At the Margins*, chap. 9. See also Richard Fleisher, Jon R. Bond, and B. Dan Wood, "Which Presidents Are Uncommonly Successful in Congress?" in Bert Rockman and Richard W. Waterman, eds., *Presidential Leadership: The Vortex of Presidential Power* (New York: Oxford University Press, 2007).

73. Nolan McCarty, "Presidential Vetoes in the Early Republic: Changing Constitutional Norms or Electoral Reform?" *Journal of Politics* 71 (April 2009): 369–384.

74. Robert J. Spitzer, "The Historical Presidency: Growing Executive Power: The Strange Case of the 'Protective Return' Pocket Veto," *Presidential Studies Quarterly* 42 (September 2012): 637–655.

75. Charles M. Cameron, *Veto Bargaining: Presidents and the Politics of Negative Power* (New York: Cambridge University Press, 2000). See also Rebecca E. Deen and Laura W. Arnold, "Veto Threats as a Policy Tool: When to Threaten?" *Presidential Studies Quarterly* 32 (March 2002): 44.

76. Christopher S. Kelley and Bryan W. Marshall, "The Last Word: Presidential Power and the Role of Signing Statements," *Presidential Studies Quarterly* 38 (June 2008): 248–267.

77. Richard S. Conley, "The Harbinger of the Unitary Executive? An Analysis

of Presidential Signing Statements from Truman to Carter," *Presidential Studies Quarterly* 41 (September 2011): 546–569; Kevin A. Evans, "Looking before Watergate: Foundations in the Development of the Constitutional Challenges within Signing Statements, FDR–Nixon," *Presidential Studies Quarterly* 42 (June 2012): 390–405.

78. Andrew B. Whitford, "Signing Statements as Bargaining Outcomes: Evidence from the Administration of George W. Bush," *Presidential Studies Quarterly* 42 (June 2012): 343–362. See also Kevin Evans, "Challenging Law: Presidential Signing Statements and the Maintenance of Executive Power," *Congress & the Presidency* 38, no. 2 (2011): 217–234.

79. Michael J. Berry, "Controversially Executing the Law: George W. Bush and the Constitutional Signing Statement," *Congress & the Presidency* 36, no. 2 (2009): 244–271.

80. Go to *The American Presidency Project*, University of California at Santa Barbara, http://www.presidency.ucsb.edu /signingstatements.php?year=2010&Sub mit=DISPLAY#axzz282wCwcpS, to see examples of signing statements.

81. Phillip J. Cooper, "George W. Bush, Edgar Allan Poe, and the Use and Abuse of Presidential Signing Statements," *Presidential Studies Quarterly* 35 (September 2005): 515–532.

82. James P. Pfiffner, *Power Play: The Bush Presidency and the Constitution* (Washington, DC: Brookings Institution, 2008), pp. 159–160. More broadly, see Christopher S. Kelley and Bryan W. Marshall, "Assessing Presidential Power: Signing Statements and Veto Threats as Coordinated Strategies," *American Politics Research* 37 (May 2009): 508–533.

83. See David R. Mayhew, *Partisan Balance: Why Political Parties Don't Kill the U.S. Constitutional System* (Princeton, NJ: Princeton University Press, 2011), pp. 57–79.

10

THE PRESIDENT
AND THE
JUDICIARY

he president's interactions with Congress and the bureaucracy are
constant, and they receive considerable attention. Relations with the
third branch of government, the judiciary, however, are in many ways
more intermittent and less visible. Nevertheless, chief executives have important
relationships with the courts, and it is through their nominations to the bench
that they have opportunities to influence public policy for years to come. The executive branch, operating through the solicitor general's office, is also a frequent
litigant in the federal courts, especially at the Supreme Court level. Such litigation
provides another opportunity for the president to influence judicial decisions.

In addition, presidents may end up with responsibility for enforcing court
decisions even though they were not directly involved in them. Sometimes,
enforcing the law actually means complying with decisions directed at the
White House. Although such instances are not common, they may provide
moments of high political drama and have important consequences for our
political system. Finally, the Constitution gives the president the right to
exercise some judicial powers directly through the granting of pardons, amnesty, and clemency for individuals who are accused or convicted of federal
crimes.

The distinction between the director and facilitator presidential types is
less clear in relationships with the judiciary than with Congress. Although
both presidential types would take advantage of the opportunity to nominate
compatible judges to the federal bench, it is theoretically possible that
dominant presidents would be able to mold the courts more, moving jurists to
reach decisions of which they approve and to overturn previous decisions that
they oppose. Facilitators will be more constrained in placing their first choices
on the bench and will not dominate their judicial decision making. Their
victories will result from the views of the judges they nominate to the bench
rather than their influence over these judges once they don their judicial robes.

JUDICIAL SELECTION

The president's primary means of exercising leadership of the judicial branch is through the nomination of federal judges. In this section, we examine the process of judicial selection for the federal courts and the types of people who become federal judges.

Selection of Lower-Court Judges

We begin with the federal district courts and the courts of appeals, which include most federal judges and handle most federal cases. The president nominates people to fill these slots for lifetime service, and the Senate must confirm each nomination by a majority vote. Because of the Senate's role, the president's discretion ends up being much less than it appears.

Senatorial courtesy is the customary manner in which the Senate disposes of state-level federal nominations for such positions as judgeships and U.S. attorneys.[1]

- For district court positions, the Senate does not confirm nominees if they are opposed by a senator of the president's party from the state in which the nominee is to serve.

- For courts of appeals positions, the Senate does not confirm nominees opposed by a senator of the president's party from the state of the nominee's residence.

To invoke the right of senatorial courtesy, the relevant senator usually simply states a general reason for opposition. Other senators then honor their colleague's views and oppose the nomination, regardless of their personal evaluations of the candidate's merits.

Because of the strength of this informal practice, presidents usually check carefully with the relevant senator or senators ahead of time to avoid making a nomination that the Senate will not confirm. In many instances, this is tantamount to giving the power of nomination to these senators. Typically when there is a vacancy for a federal district judgeship, the relevant senator or senators from the state where the judge will serve suggest one or more names to the attorney general and the president. If neither senator is of the president's party, then the party's state congresspersons or other state party leaders may make suggestions. Other interested senators may also try to influence a selection.[2]

The first instance of senatorial courtesy occurred in 1789, when President George Washington failed to obtain confirmation of Benjamin Fishbourn as naval officer of the port of Savannah because of the opposition of Georgia's two senators, and since that time, senatorial courtesy has become a well-established tradition. By 1840, senators were virtually naming federal district court judges by providing the president with a list of "acceptable" choices from which the administration could choose.

In early 2009, Senate Republicans added a new element to senatorial courtesy when they sent President Obama a letter in which they vowed to prevent the confirmation of judicial nominees in instances where the White House did not properly consult Republican home-state senators. The implication of this letter is that members of the opposition party would have a de facto veto power, something without precedent in the history of judicial selection. Obama did consult with Republican home-state senators and did not nominate judges opposed by these senators.[3]

The White House, the Department of Justice, and the Federal Bureau of Investigation conduct competency and background checks on persons suggested for judgeships, and the president usually selects a nominee from those who survive the screening process. If a senator to whom senatorial courtesy is due recommended one of these survivors, it is difficult for the president to reject the recommendation in favor of someone else who survived the process. Thus, senatorial courtesy turns the Constitution on its head; in effect, the Senate ends up making nominations, and the president then approves them.

Presidents possess assets in such a situation, but they rarely find it worthwhile to fight a senator over a district court judgeship. These judges seldom interfere with their policies. If they desire to do so, presidents can refuse to nominate anyone to the position in an attempt to pressure a senator into supporting their nominee in order to avoid a backlog of federal cases in the state. Alternately, they may make an appointment during a congressional recess at the end of a session. Although the nominee must still be confirmed in the next session of Congress, by then he or she may have had an opportunity to demonstrate such exemplary capabilities on the bench that the Senate will look more favorably on the appointment.

Typically, the attorney general asks the Standing Committee on the Federal Judiciary of the American Bar Association (ABA) for its evaluation of potential nominees. The George W. Bush administration was an exception (but the ABA still evaluated candidates after the president nominated them). Other individuals have input in judicial selection as well. The Department of Justice may ask sitting judges, usually at the federal level, to evaluate prospective nominees. Sitting judges may also initiate recommendations to advance or retard someone's chances of being nominated. In addition, candidates for the nomination are often active on their own behalf. They have to alert the relevant parties that they desire the position and orchestrate a campaign of support for themselves. As one appellate judge observed, "People don't get judgeships without seeking them. Anybody who thinks judicial office seeks the man is mistaken. There's not a man on the court who didn't do what he thought needed to be done."[4]

Presidents usually have more influence in the selection of judges to the federal courts of appeals than to federal district courts. Because the decisions of appellate courts are generally more significant than those of lower courts, the president naturally takes a greater interest in appointments to the former. At the same time, individual senators are in a weaker position to determine who the nominee will be because the jurisdiction of an appeals court encompasses several states. Although custom and pragmatic politics require that these judgeships be apportioned among the states, the president has discretion in how this is done and therefore has a greater role in recruiting appellate judges than district court judges. Even here, however, senators from the state in which the candidate resides may be able to veto a nomination.

The Reagan White House created an institutional apparatus to ensure that the president's judicial nominees shared the philosophical and policy orientation of the president. The President's Committee on Judicial Selection was a joint White House–Justice Department committee chaired by the White House Counsel, and it has been continued under Ronald Reagan's successors. Presidential aides survey candidates' decisions (if they have served on a lower court),[5] speeches, political stands, writings, and other expressions of opinion. They also turn for information to people who know the candidates well. Although it is considered improper to question judicial candidates about upcoming court cases, it is appropriate to discuss broader questions of political and judicial philosophy. The Reagan administration was especially concerned about such matters and had each potential nominee (for all judicial vacancies) fill out a lengthy questionnaire and be interviewed by administration officials.[6] The George H. W. Bush administration, which was also attentive to nominating conservative judges, continued this practice.[7]

When Bill Clinton took office, many supporters hoped he would quickly begin undoing a major legacy from twelve years of Republican control of the White House: a federal judiciary populated with conservative judges. He did not meet these expectations, however. Although Clinton nominated a record number of women and minorities to the federal bench, and although his nominees had impressive credentials, he had little interest in ensuring that his nominees were ideologically liberal. The president was slow to nominate judges and was unwilling to spend political capital to win Senate confirmation for nominees labeled as liberal, especially after the Republicans took control of Congress following the 1994 congressional elections. As a result, Clinton's judges were decidedly less liberal than those of other modern Democratic presidents.[8]

While campaigning for the presidency in 2000, George W. Bush committed himself to naming judges like Justices Antonin Scalia and Clarence Thomas, two of the most conservative justices on the U.S. Supreme Court. As president, Bush stated bluntly that he was looking to appoint conservatives to the courts.[9] His administration followed through, and almost all of his nominees to the lower federal courts can fairly be characterized as conservatives who shared the president's judicial philosophy. To an even greater extent than during the Reagan and George H. W. Bush administrations, the White House Counsel's Office took responsibility for philosophically screening potential candidates, including conducting interviews.[10]

The Obama administration did not see nominating judges as a priority and has been slow to send nominees to the Senate. Obama followed the pattern of Bill Clinton and has not been as rigorous in ideological screening as his Republican predecessors. The president has often nominated political moderates to the bench, although not conservative activists or ideologues.[11]

Traditionally, the Senate confirmed lower federal court nominations swiftly and unanimously.[12] However, the increasing polarization of partisan politics in recent years has affected judicial nominations, especially those for the courts of appeals.[13] Increasingly, lower-court confirmations have become lengthy and contentious proceedings. Any senator can now exploit the opportunities for delay and gain influence in the nomination process. Filibusters have become routine.[14] As a presidential election nears, the party that controls the Senate has an incentive to delay confirmations in the hope that it will gain control of the White House.[15] As a result, there has been a dramatic increase in the time for confirmation,[16] which in turn has decreased the chances of confirmation. Since 1992, the Senate has confirmed only 60 percent of nominees to the courts of appeals.[17]

The confirmation process has become more contentious because the trend in judicial selection has been to move away from primarily patronage concerns to concerns about furthering the president's policy agenda through judicial appointments. Since the 1980s, senators have felt free to oppose judicial nominees on policy and judicial philosophy grounds. If the president uses ideological criteria to make nominations,[18] then senators think they are entitled to do the same when considering confirmation of those nominees.[19] The greater the ideological difference between the president and the opposing party, or between the president and the home-state senators, the longer and more contentious the nomination process. Divided party government, the potential for nominees to tip the ideological balance on a circuit court of appeals, and proximity to a presidential election also contribute to slower and lower confirmation rates.[20] In addition, interest groups opposed to nominations have raised the salience of confirmations by increasing their activity and encouraging senators aligned with them to delay and block nominations.[21]

George H. W. Bush experienced an especially difficult time obtaining the confirmation of lower-court judges from the Democratic-controlled Senate. Bill Clinton suffered even greater frustrations with the Republican Senate after 1995. The Senate confirmed only 61 percent of his nominees to the courts of appeals and only 81 percent of his nominees to the district courts.[22] As a result of Republican obstructionism, Clinton had to negotiate agreements with Republican senators, giving some of them a role in the selection of judges equivalent to that accorded his fellow Democrats. He also made a recess appointment of a court of appeals judge shortly before leaving office. Such appointments are unusual and good only for the remainder of a congressional term.

George W. Bush faced stiff partisan opposition to some of his nominations and in response made two recess appointments to courts of appeals. Infuriated at what they viewed as a misuse of the recess appointment power and an attempt to bypass the Senate's confirmation responsibilities, Democratic senators shut down the confirmation process for several months in 2004. After the Republicans nearly voted to end the possibility of filibustering judicial nominations, fourteen senators from both parties forged a deal without White House approval that allowed some—but not all—of Bush's stalled judicial nominees to receive floor votes. The White House pledged not to bypass the Senate with any more recess appointments of judges.

Nevertheless, partisan conflict over nominations continued as the Republican minority used secret holds, threats of filibusters, and various Senate procedures to delay and often stymie Barack Obama's judicial nominations to the courts of appeals, even at the district court level—a new element in the partisan battle.

Backgrounds of Lower-Court Judges

What type of individual becomes a judge through this process? The data in Tables 10.1 and 10.2 show that federal judges are not a representative sample of the American people. They are all lawyers (although this is not a constitutional requirement), and they are overwhelmingly white and male. Only Presidents Obama, Clinton, Carter, and both Bushes have nominated a substantial number of women to the federal bench. Only Obama, Clinton, Carter, and, to a lesser extent, George W. Bush have nominated a significant percentage of minorities. Barack Obama's record of nominating women and minorities to the federal bench is in a class by itself.

Federal judges have typically held office as judges or prosecutors, and often they have been involved in partisan politics. This involvement is generally what brings them to the attention of senators and the Department of Justice when they seek nominees for judgeships. As Griffin Bell, a former U.S. attorney general and circuit court judge, once remarked:

> For me, becoming a federal judge wasn't very difficult. I managed John F. Kennedy's presidential campaign in Georgia. Two of my oldest and closest friends were two senators from Georgia. And I was campaign manager and special, unpaid counsel for the governor.[23]

Perhaps the most striking finding in Tables 10.1 and 10.2 is the fact that presidents rarely appoint someone to a judgeship who does not share their party affiliation. Merit considerations obviously occur after partisan screening. Judgeships are patronage plums that may serve as rewards for political service to either the president or senators of the president's party, as consolation prizes for unsuccessful candidates, or even to "kick upstairs" an official in order to remove him or her from an executive-branch post. When presidents nominate someone of the other party for a judgeship, it is usually because of ideological congruity with the nominee or to obtain support in a state where his or her party is weak.

Partisanship also plays a role in the creation of judgeships. Because of their keen interest in them, members of Congress are reluctant to create judicial positions to be filled by a president of the minority party in Congress.[24] For example, Democrats in Congress rejected President Dwight Eisenhower's efforts to create new judgeships in every year of his second term (1957–1960), even though he offered to name Democrats to half the new positions. In 1962, however, a similar bill easily passed Congress with Democrat John Kennedy in the White House. This partisan behavior was nothing new. In 1801, the newly elected Jeffersonians repealed a law creating separate judges for the circuit courts of appeal passed by the outgoing Federalists a few months earlier.

Although women and people of different ethnicities and religions may desire to have people in their group appointed to the federal bench—at the

Table 10.1 Backgrounds of Recent Federal Appeals Court Judges

	Administration					
	Obama*	G. W. Bush	Clinton	G. Bush	Reagan	Carter
No. of nominees	15	59	61	37	78	56
Experience (percentage)						
Judicial	80	61	59	62	60	54
Prosecutorial	73	34	38	30	28	30
Neither one	7	25	30	32	35	39
Party (percentage)						
Democrat	93	7	85	3	—	82
Republican	—	92	7	89	96	7
Independent	7	2	8	8	3	11
Past party activism (percentage)	40	68	54	70	67	73
Ethnicity or race (percentage)						
White	47	85	74	89	97	79
African American	33	10	13	5	1	16
Hispanic	13	5	12	5	1	4
Asian	7	—	2	—	—	2
Gender (percentage)						
Male	67	75	67	81	95	80
Female	33	25	33	19	5	20
Average age	54	50	51	49	50	52

*As of January 1, 2011.

SOURCE: Adapted from Sheldon Goldman, Elliot Slotnick, and Sara Schiavoni, "Obama's Judiciary at Midterm," *Judicature* 94 (May–June 2011): 297. Used with permission, American Judicature Society.

very least, judgeships have symbolic importance for them[25]—the real question is what, if any, policy differences result. There is some evidence that female judges on the courts of appeals are more likely than are male judges to support charges of sex discrimination and sexual harassment, and they seem to influence the male judges deciding the cases with them.[26] Similarly, racial and ethnic minority judges on these courts are more likely to find for minority plaintiffs in voting rights cases and also to influence the votes of white judges sitting with them.[27] At the level of the Supreme Court, conservative Justice Antonin Scalia has said that Justice Thurgood Marshall "could be a persuasive force just by sitting there. He wouldn't have to open his mouth to affect the nature of the conference and how seriously the conference would take matters of race."[28] It is true, of course, that Justice Clarence Thomas, the second African American justice, is one of the most conservative justices since the New Deal, illustrating that not everyone from a particular background has a particular point of view.

Many members of each party have served, of course, and it appears that Republican judges in general are somewhat more conservative than are Democratic judges. Former prosecutors serving on the Supreme Court have tended to be less sympathetic toward defendants' rights than have other justices. It seems, then, that background does make some difference,[29] yet for reasons that we examine in the following sections, on many issues party affiliation and other characteristics are imperfect predictors of judicial behavior.

Selection of Supreme Court Justices

As with lower-court judges, a majority of those voting in the Senate must confirm justices of the Supreme Court. There have been no recess appointments to the Court since the Senate voiced its disapproval of the practice in 1960. When the chief justice's position becomes vacant, the president may either nominate someone already on the Court or someone from outside it to fill the position. Usually, presidents choose the latter course in order to widen

Table 10.2 Backgrounds of Recent Federal District Court Judges

	Administration					
	Obama*	G. W. Bush	Clinton	G. Bush	Reagan	Carter
No. of nominees	44	261	305	148	290	202
Experience (percentage)						
Judicial	55	52	52	47	46	54
Prosecutorial	48	47	41	39	44	38
Neither one	30	25	29	32	29	31
Party (percentage)						
Democrat	89	8	88	6	5	91
Republican	—	83	6	89	92	5
Independent	11	9	6	5	3	5
Past party activism (percentage)	55	53	50	64	60	61
Ethnicity or race (percentage)						
White	59	83	75	89	92	79
African American	25	6	17	7	2	14
Hispanic	5	11	6	4	5	7
Asian	11	1	1	—	1	1
Gender (percentage)						
Male	46	79	72	80	92	86
Female	55	21	29	20	8	14
Average age	50	50	50	48	49	50

*As of January 1, 2011.

SOURCE: Adapted from Sheldon Goldman, Elliot Slotnick, and Sara Schiavoni, "Obama's Judiciary at Midterm," *Judicature* 94 (May–June 2011): 296. Used with permission, American Judicature Society.

their range of options, but if they decide to elevate a sitting associate justice, as President Reagan did with William Rehnquist in 1986, he or she must go through a new confirmation by the Senate.

Although many of the same actors are present in the case of Supreme Court nominations, their influence is typically quite different. The president is vitally interested in the Court because of the importance of its work, which includes making decisions on the scope of presidential powers, and will generally be intimately involved in the recruitment process. Unlike the case of federal judges, presidents have been personally acquainted with many of the people they have nominated to the Supreme Court (reflecting their involvement in the selection process), and it is not unusual for an administration official to receive a nomination. Presidents also often rely on the attorney general and the Justice Department to identify and screen candidates for the Court.

There are few matters as important to justices on the Supreme Court as the ideology, competence, and compatibility of their colleagues, and thus it is not surprising that they (especially chief justices) often try to influence nominations to the Court. Chief Justice William Howard Taft, who was a former president, was especially active during his tenure in the 1920s, and Warren Burger played a prominent role in the Richard Nixon administration.[30] Nevertheless, although presidents will listen to recommendations from justices, they feel no obligation to follow them.

Senators play a much less prominent role in the recruitment of Supreme Court justices than in the selection of lower-court judges, especially for the district courts. No senator can claim that the jurisdiction of the Supreme Court falls within the realm of his or her special expertise, interest, or sphere of influence. Thus, presidents typically consult with senators from the state of residence of a nominee after they have decided whom to select. At this point, senators are unlikely to oppose a nomination because they like having their state receive the honor and are well aware that should they reject the nominee, the president can simply select someone from another state.

Candidates for nomination are also much less likely to play a significant role in the recruitment process. Although there have been exceptions, most notably William Howard Taft, people seldom campaign for a position on the Court. They can accomplish little through such activity, and because of the Court's standing, it might offend those who do play important roles in selecting nominees.

The ABA's Standing Committee on the Federal Judiciary has played a varied, but typically modest, role at the Supreme Court, and the White House usually has asked it to evaluate candidates for the Supreme Court only after the president had nominated them. The committee has never found a nominee unqualified to serve on the Court. In 2001, the Bush administration decided not to ask its advice, but the Obama administration revived the practice.

Through 2012, there have been 153 nominations to the Supreme Court, and 112 people have served. Of those, four people were nominated and confirmed twice, eight declined appointments or died before beginning service on the Court, and twenty-nine failed to secure Senate confirmation.

Presidents, then, have failed 20 percent of the time to appoint the nominees of their choice to the Court—a percentage much higher than that for any other federal position.

Thus, although home-state senators do not play prominent roles in the selection process for the Court, the Senate as a whole does. In fact, through its Judiciary Committee the Senate may probe a nominee's judicial philosophy in great detail.

For most of the twentieth century, Supreme Court nominations were routine affairs. Of the eight nominees that failed to receive Senate confirmation in that century (see Table 10.3), seven occurred since the presidency of John F. Kennedy. The 1960s were tumultuous times, which bred ideological conflict. Although Kennedy had no trouble with his two nominations to the Court (Byron White and Arthur Goldberg), his successor, Lyndon Johnson, was not so fortunate. He had to withdraw his nomination of Abe Fortas (already serving on the Court) to serve as chief justice, and therefore the Senate never voted on Homer Thornberry, Johnson's nominee to replace Fortas as an associate justice. Richard Nixon, the next president, had two nominees rejected in a row following bruising battles in the Senate.

Two failed nominations occurred in 1987. On June 26, Justice Lewis Powell announced his retirement from the Supreme Court. President Reagan had already been able to elevate Justice William Rehnquist to chief justice and also had appointed Sandra Day O'Connor and Antonin Scalia. With yet another appointee, he would have a solid bloc of conservative votes on the Court for years to come.

Reagan nominated Judge Robert H. Bork to fill the vacancy. Everyone agreed that Bork was an intelligent and serious legal scholar, and he had also served in the Justice Department. (He was the individual who had fired special prosecutor Archibald Cox in the "Saturday Night Massacre" of Watergate fame.) At this point, agreement on his qualifications ended, however.

Table 10.3 Senate Rejections of Supreme Court Nominees

Nominee	Year	President
John J. Parker	1930	Hoover
Abe Fortas*	1968	Johnson
Homer Thornberry†	1968	Johnson
Clement F. Haynsworth Jr.	1969	Nixon
G. Harrold Carswell	1970	Nixon
Robert H. Bork	1987	Reagan
Douglas H. Ginsburg*	1987	Reagan
Harriet Miers*	2005	G. W. Bush

*Nominations were withdrawn. (Fortas was serving on the Court as an associate justice and was nominated to be chief justice.)

†The Senate took no action on Thornberry's nomination.

Bork testified before the Senate Judiciary Committee for twenty-three hours. At the end, his supporters portrayed him as a distinguished scholar who would practice "judicial restraint," deferring to Congress and the state legislatures and adhering to the precedents of the Supreme Court. Conversely, his opponents saw him as an extreme judicial ideologue who would use the Supreme Court to achieve conservative political ends, thus reversing decades of court decisions. A wide range of interest groups entered the fray, mostly in opposition to the nominee, and in the end, following a bitter floor debate, the Senate rejected the president's nomination by a vote of 58 to 42.

Six days after the Senate vote on Bork, the president nominated Douglas H. Ginsburg to the high court. Just nine days later, however, Ginsburg withdrew his nomination following disclosures that he had smoked marijuana at parties while a law professor at Harvard. Not until the spring of 1988 did Reagan finally succeed in filling the vacancy, with Anthony Kennedy.

In June 1991, at the end of the Supreme Court's term, Associate Justice Thurgood Marshall announced his retirement from the Court. Shortly thereafter, President Bush announced his nomination of another African American federal appeals judge, Clarence Thomas, to replace Marshall. Because Thomas was a conservative, this decision was consistent with the Bush administration's emphasis on placing conservative judges on the federal bench.

The president claimed that he was not employing quotas when he chose another African American to replace the only African American ever to sit on the Supreme Court and argued that Thomas was simply the most qualified person for the job. This placed liberals in a dilemma. On the one hand, they favored having a minority group member serving on the nation's highest court. On the other hand, however, Thomas was unlikely to vote the same way as Thurgood Marshall. Instead, the new justice presented the prospect of strengthening the conservative trend in the Court's decisions. In the end, this ambivalence inhibited spirited opposition to Thomas, who was circumspect about his judicial philosophy in his appearances before the Senate Judiciary Committee, which sent his nomination to the Senate floor on a split vote.

Just as the Senate was about to vote on the nomination, however, charges of sexual harassment leveled against Thomas by University of Oklahoma law professor Anita Hill were made public. Hearings were reopened on the charges in response to criticism that the Senate was sexist for not seriously considering them in the first place. For several days, citizens sat transfixed before their television sets as Professor Hill calmly and graphically described her recollections of Thomas's behavior. Thomas then emphatically denied any such behavior and charged the Senate with racism for raising the issue. Ultimately, public opinion polls showed that more people believed Thomas than Hill, and the Senate confirmed him by a vote of 52 to 48, the closest vote on a Supreme Court nomination in more than a century.

The Senate's response to President Clinton's nominees harkens back to the Kennedy era. Neither Ruth Bader Ginsburg nor Stephen Breyer caused much controversy. The Clinton administration undertook detailed background checks of potential nominees and floated several names to test public reaction prior to the president's announcements of his choices.[31] The Senate also easily confirmed George W. Bush's nomination of John Roberts as chief justice. Indeed, he was difficult to oppose. His pleasing and professional personal demeanor and his disciplined and skilled testimony before the Senate Judicial Committee gave potential opponents little basis for opposition.

Attention immediately turned to George W. Bush's nomination of White House counsel Harriet Miers in October 2005 to replace Justice O'Connor. Bush apparently thought Miers's lack of a published record would make it easier to push her nomination through. What looked like an adroit political decision soon turned sour, however. Many of the president's most passionate supporters had hoped and expected that he would make an unambiguously conservative choice to fulfill their goal of clearly altering the Court's balance, even at the cost of a bitter confirmation battle. By instead settling on a loyalist with no experience as a judge and little substantive record on abortion, affirmative action, religion, and other socially divisive issues, the president shied away from a direct confrontation with liberals and in effect asked his base on the right to trust him on his nomination. Many conservatives were bitterly disappointed and highly critical of the president. They demanded a known conservative and a top-flight legal figure. The nomination also smacked of cronyism, with the president selecting a friend and a loyalist rather than someone of obvious merit. The comparison with Roberts only emphasized the thinness of Miers's qualifications. In short order, Miers withdrew from consideration, and the president nominated Samuel Alito.

Alito was clearly a traditional conservative and had a less impressive public presence than Roberts. Response to him followed party lines, but the nominee appeared too well qualified and unthreatening in his confirmation hearings to justify a filibuster, and without one, his confirmation was assured. The Senate confirmed Alito by a vote of 58 to 42.

President Obama made his first nomination to the Court in 2009, selecting Sonia Sotomayor. Although conservatives raised questions about some of her previous statements and decisions, the Senate confirmed here by a vote of 68 to 31, largely along party lines. When she took the oath of office, she became the first Hispanic justice. In 2010, the president nominated solicitor general Elena Kagan to the Court. She was confirmed by a vote of 63 to 37, once again largely along party lines.

The history of recent failed nominations indicates that presidents are most likely to run into trouble under certain conditions. Presidents whose parties are in the minority in the Senate or who make a nomination at the end of their term face a greatly increased probability of substantial opposition. This is also the case for those who have the opportunity to nominate a justice whose confirmation would result in important shifts in the coalitions on the Court and thus affect policy outcomes. Equally important, to defeat a nomination, opponents must usually credibly question a nominee's competence (Carswell and Miers) or ethics (Fortas, Haynsworth, and Carswell) to attract moderate senators to their side and make ideological protests seem less partisan. A charge of scandal will weaken support for a nomination among the president's copartisans and galvanize the opposition. Opposition based on a nominee's ideology alone is generally not considered a valid reason to vote against confirmation, although ideology is the primary concern of senators.[32] As long as Americans are polarized around social issues and as long as the Court makes critical decisions about these issues, the potential for conflict over the president's nominations is always present.[33]

Characteristics of Justices

Competence and ethical behavior are important to presidents for reasons beyond merely obtaining Senate confirmation of their nominees to the Court. Skilled and honorable justices reflect well on the president and will likely do so for many years. Moreover, they are more effective advocates and thus can better serve the president's interests. In addition, presidents usually have enough respect for the Court and its work that they do not want to saddle it with a mediocre justice. Although the criteria of competence and character screen out some possible candidates, there is still a wide field from which the president may choose. Other characteristics then play prominent roles.

As with their colleagues on the lower federal courts, Supreme Court justices share many characteristics that are quite unlike those of the typical American. All have been lawyers, and all but six (Thurgood Marshall, nominated in 1967; Sandra Day O'Connor, nominated in 1981; Clarence Thomas, nominated in 1991; Ruth Bader Ginsburg, nominated in 1993; Sonia Sotomayor, nominated in 2009; and Elena Kagan, nominated in 2010) have been white males. Most have been in their fifties and sixties when they took office, from the upper-middle to upper class, and Protestants. (See Table 10.4 for some background information on the current Supreme Court.)

Race and gender have become more salient criteria in recent years. In the 1980 presidential campaign, Ronald Reagan promised to appoint a woman

Table 10.4 Supreme Court Justices, 2013

Justice	Birth Year	Previous Position	Nominating President	Year of Appointment
John G. Roberts Jr.	1955	U.S. Court of Appeals	G. W. Bush	2005
Antonin Scalia	1936	U.S. Court of Appeals	Reagan	1986
Anthony M. Kennedy	1936	U.S. Court of Appeals	Reagan	1988
Clarence Thomas	1948	U.S. Court of Appeals	G. Bush	1991
Ruth Bader Ginsburg	1933	U.S. Court of Appeals	Clinton	1993
Stephen G. Breyer	1938	U.S. Court of Appeals	Clinton	1994
Samuel A. Alito Jr.	1950	U.S. Court of Appeals	G. W. Bush	2006
Sonia Sotomayor	1954	U.S. Court of Appeals	Obama	2009
Elena Kagan	1960	U.S. Solicitor General	Obama	2010

to a vacancy on the Court should he be elected. Geography once was a prominent criterion for selection to the Court but is no longer very important. Presidents do like to spread the slots around, however, as when Richard Nixon decided that he wanted to nominate a southerner. At various times, there have been what some have termed a "Jewish seat" and a "Catholic seat" on the Court, but these are not binding on the president. For example, after a half-century of having a Jewish justice, there was none between 1969 and 1993, until President Clinton nominated Ruth Bader Ginsburg to the Court. She was followed by another Jewish nominee, Stephen Breyer. By 2012, all the justices were either Roman Catholic or Jewish.

Although presidents have often selected Supreme Court justices at least in part for their symbolic appeal to geographic, gender, racial, and religious interests, such appointees may not actually provide these groups with much policy representation. There is evidence that most symbolic appointees do not vote for their own group's policy attitudes any more than do other members of the Court.[34]

Partisanship remains an important influence on the selection of justices; only 13 of 112 members were nominated by presidents of a different party. Moreover, many of the thirteen exceptions were actually close to the president in ideology, as was the case in Richard Nixon's appointment of Lewis Powell. Herbert Hoover's nomination of Benjamin Cardozo seems to be one of the few cases where partisanship was completely subjugated to merit as a criterion for selection. However, usually about 90 percent of presidents' judicial nominations are of members of their own party.

The role of partisanship is not really surprising even at the level of the highest court. Most of the presidents' acquaintances are in their own party, and there is usually a certain congruity between party and political views. The president may also use Supreme Court nominations as a reward, as when President Eisenhower nominated Earl Warren as chief justice. As leader of the California delegation to the 1952 Republican convention, Warren had played a crucial role in Eisenhower's successful bid for the Republican nomination for president. Many justices at one time were active partisans, which gave them visibility and helped them obtain the positions from which they moved to the Court.

Typically, justices have held high administrative or judicial positions before moving to the Supreme Court. All but one member of the current Court served on a federal court of appeals (Table 10.4), where they created records that the White House could review. Most justices have had some experience as judges, often at the appellate level, and many have worked for the Department of Justice. Some have held high elected office, and a few have had no government service but rather have been distinguished attorneys. The fact that not all justices, including many of the most distinguished ones, have had previous judicial experience may seem surprising, but the unique work and environment of the Court renders this background much less important than it might be for other appellate courts.

PRESIDENT–SUPREME COURT RELATIONS

At the top of two complex branches of government stand the president and the Supreme Court. Each has significant powers. In a system of shared powers such as ours, it is not surprising that the president is interested in influencing the Court. In this section, we examine efforts of the White House to mold the Court through filling vacancies, setting its agenda, and influencing and enforcing its decisions. We also look at interbranch relations that involve advising and other services.

Molding the Court

One of the most significant powers of the president lies in molding the Supreme Court through nominations. In effect, all presidents try to "pack" the courts.[35] They want more than "justice"; they want policies with which they agree. Because justices serve for life, the impact of a president's selections will generally be felt long after that president has left office. As a result, the White House typically makes substantial efforts to ascertain the policy preferences of candidates for the Supreme Court.

As a result of all this effort, presidents are generally satisfied with the actions of their nominees, especially those who had prior judicial experience to examine.[36] Given the discretion that justices often have in making decisions, it is not surprising that consistent patterns related to their values and ideology—to conservative versus liberal positions—are often evident in their decisions.[37] Thus, the right nominations can reinforce, slow, or alter trends in the Court's decisions. Franklin Roosevelt's nominees substantially liberalized the Court, whereas Richard Nixon's choices turned it in a basically conservative direction. Although precedent, legal principles, and even political pressures from the public, Congress, and the White House constrain justices' discretion,[38] justices usually arrive at a decision consistent with their policy preferences.

Nevertheless, it is not always easy to identify the policy inclinations of candidates, and presidents have been disappointed in their selections about a quarter of the time. President Eisenhower, for example, was displeased with the liberal decisions of both Earl Warren and William Brennan. Once, when asked whether he had made any mistakes as president, he replied, "Yes, two, and they are both sitting on the Supreme Court."[39] Earlier, Woodrow Wilson was shocked by the very conservative positions of one of his nominees, James McReynolds. On a more limited scale, Richard Nixon was certainly disappointed when his nominee for chief justice, Warren Burger, authored the Court's decision calling for immediate desegregation of the nation's schools shortly after his confirmation. This did little for the president's "Southern strategy."

There are several reasons presidents may make what, in their view, are errors in nominations to the Court. They and their aides may have done a poor job of probing the views of candidates. Moreover, once on the Court, justices may change their attitudes and values over time because of new insights gained in their position, the normal process of aging, or the influence of other members of the Court. (Virtually all justices between 1801 and 1835 were strongly affected by Chief Justice John Marshall.) Justices are also often constrained by their obligation to follow precedents (when they are clear).

Some presidents have been relatively unconcerned with ideology in their nominations. In periods of relative political and social calm, or when there is a solid majority on the Court that shares their views and is likely to persist for several years, presidents might give less weight to policy preferences than to other criteria in choosing justices. In contrast, political polarization led President Clinton to deemphasize ideology in his nominations.

Presidents cannot have much impact on the Court unless they have vacancies to fill, of course. Although, on the average, there has been an opening on the Supreme Court every two years, there is a substantial variance around this mean.[40] Franklin D. Roosevelt had to wait five years before he could nominate a justice, all the while facing a Court that found much of his New Deal legislation unconstitutional. In more recent years, Jimmy Carter was never able to nominate a justice; indeed, between 1972 and 1984 there were only two vacancies on the Court. George W. Bush did not have the opportunity to nominate a justice in his first term. Conversely, Richard Nixon was able to nominate four justices in his first three years in office.

Sometimes, Congress or the president takes unusual steps to enhance or limit a president's ability to fill vacancies. The legislature altered the size of the Supreme Court many times between 1801 and 1869. In 1801, the Federalists reduced the Court from six to five members, and the Jeffersonians increased it back to six the following year. In 1863, Abraham Lincoln got Congress to increase the number of justices from nine to ten after the Court upheld the legality of measures to fight the Civil War by only a 5 to 4 vote.

In 1866, the Radical Republicans in Congress reduced the size of the Court from ten to seven members to prevent Andrew Johnson from nominating new justices. When President Grant took office, Congress increased the number to nine because it had confidence Grant would nominate members to its liking. This number has remained unchanged since then, and it now seems inviolate.

Franklin D. Roosevelt attempted to "pack" the court in 1937, when he proposed to add a justice to the Court for every justice currently serving who was over age seventy and had served ten years. This proposal was an obvious attempt to change the direction of Court decisions on his economic policies, and, after a prolonged political battle, Congress refused to approve it. The effort was politically costly to Roosevelt,[41] but the president at least had the satisfaction that the Court was already beginning to approve liberal legislation.

The president's role in Supreme Court judicial selection is not limited to the nomination of justices; it extends to the creation of positions as well. Justices are typically not prone to retirement, but presidents are sometimes frustrated enough at Court decisions to attempt to accelerate the creation of vacancies. Thomas Jefferson and his supporters tried to use impeachment to remove justices and thus gain control of the judiciary, which was largely Federalist (and thus anti-Jeffersonian). They abandoned this strategy, however, when the Senate failed to convict Justice Samuel Chase in 1805, who had made himself vulnerable with his partisan activities off the bench and injudicious remarks on it.

More often, presidents have relied on less direct forms of pressure. Theodore Roosevelt resorted to leaks in the press in an unsuccessful effort to induce two justices to resign. More recently, the Nixon administration orchestrated a campaign to force liberal justice Abe Fortas to resign after he was accused of financial improprieties.

Justices also play the game of politics, of course, and may try to time their retirements so that a president with compatible views will choose their successor.[42] This is one reason why justices remain on the Court for so long even when they are clearly infirm. William Brennan and Thurgood Marshall, the most senior justices on the Court in the 1980s, stayed through the Reagan years because their liberal views contrasted sharply with those of the president. William Howard Taft, a rigid conservative, even feared conservative Republican Herbert Hoover naming his successor.

Such tactics do not always succeed. In 1968, Chief Justice Earl Warren submitted his resignation to President Johnson, whom he felt would select an acceptable successor. When Johnson's choice of Abe Fortas failed to win confirmation, however, the opportunity to nominate the new chief justice passed to Warren's old California political rival, newly elected President Richard Nixon.

Arguments in the Courts

The president may influence what cases the courts hear as well as who hears them. The solicitor general is a presidential appointee who must be confirmed by the Senate and serves in the Department of Justice.[43] It is he or she (not the attorney general) who supervises the litigation of the federal executive branch. In this position, the solicitor general plays a major role in determining the agenda of federal appellate courts. Although able to exercise wide discretion, the solicitor general is subject to the direction of the attorney general and the president, with the latter playing a role in major cases.

The solicitor general decides which of the cases lost by the federal government in the federal district courts or the courts of appeals will be appealed to the next higher court. The courts of appeals must hear properly appealed cases, but the Supreme Court, for all practical purposes, has complete control over its own docket. Thus, it is significant that the Court is far more likely to accept cases that the solicitor general wants to have heard than those from any other party.[44] Moreover, the amount of litigation involved is quite large. In recent years, the federal government has been a party to about half the cases heard in federal courts of appeals and the Supreme Court.

In rare instances the president may decide not to defend laws passed by Congress against charges that they are unconstitutional. In 1990, the Bush administration refused to defend a Federal Communications Commission affirmative-action program because it viewed the law as unconstitutional. Similarly, the Obama administration declared it would no longer defend the part of the Defense of Marriage Act that denies federal benefits to gay and lesbian couples married in states that recognize such unions, and it did not defend the constitutionality of statutes blocking same-sex military spouses from receiving marriage benefits—including rights to visitation in military hospitals, survivor benefits, and burial together in military cemeteries.

The executive branch also participates in cases to which it is not directly a party. The solicitor general files *amicus curiae* (friend of the court) briefs supporting or opposing the efforts of other parties before the Court.[45] These cases range from affirmative action to abortion rights and equal pay for women. Once again, the Court usually grants the government's request to participate in this way. Indeed, the Court wants to know the president's preferences,[46] although it does not necessarily support them.[47]

When a case reaches the Supreme Court, the solicitor general supervises the preparation of the government's arguments in support of its position, whether it is a direct party or an amicus. Court decisions often reflect these arguments[48] and thus they become the law of the land. Because the government has participated in almost every major controversy decided by the courts in the past fifty years, the potential influence of the executive branch on public policy through the courts is substantial. Moreover, both as a direct party and as an amicus, the federal government wins a clear majority of the time.[49]

The government's success is due to several factors. The solicitor general builds credibility with the Court by not making frivolous appeals and, in a few instances, even by telling the Court that the government should not have won cases in lower courts. Equally important, the solicitor general and his or her staff (again, not the attorney general) develop more expertise in dealing with the Court than anyone else because they appear before it more frequently, and they use the resources of the Justice Department to provide the Court with high-quality briefs. In addition, it appears that individual members of the Court are more receptive to the views of the solicitor general when they share general ideological predispositions with him.[50]

On a very rare occasion, the president may directly attempt to influence a Court decision. James Buchanan, while president-elect, pushed for a decision on the *Dred Scott* case and lobbied a justice to join the Court's southern majority.[51] In a very unusual move in 1969, Department of Justice officials visited Justice Brennan and Chief Justice Warren to alert them that the administration was worried about the outcomes of some wiretapping cases on the Court's agenda. The administration was concerned that the Court's decisions would force the discontinuance of its surveillance of embassies or its prosecutions based on the information obtained from them. According to Warren, this visit had no influence on the Court's decision making.[52]

Enforcing Court Decisions

Another important relationship between the judicial and executive branches involves enforcing court decisions. Although the executive branch provides the federal courts with U.S. marshals, they are too few and lack sufficient authority to be of systematic aid, especially if a court order is directed against a coordinate branch of government. Thus, the courts must often rely on the president to enforce their decisions, especially their more controversial ones.

The Constitution is, not surprisingly, ambiguous as to the president's responsibility for aiding the judicial branch. Although it never explicitly discusses the point, it does assign the president the responsibility to "take care that the laws be faithfully executed." Typically, presidents have responded to support the courts or, at least, the rule of law. On several occasions, such as during the efforts of President Eisenhower and President Kennedy to integrate educational institutions, presidents have gone so far as to deploy federal troops to ensure compliance with court orders.

Presidents may use the carrot as well as the stick to encourage others to comply with Court decisions. One of the most significant and controversial Supreme Court decisions of this century was *Brown v. Board of Education* (1954), which called for an end to segregation in public schools. Compliance with this decision was a long and tortuous process, but it was aided by the

"Do you ever have one of those days when everything seems un-Constitutional?"

passage of laws that provided federal aid only for school districts that do not segregate and that provided schools with extra funds to help ease the process of desegregation.

There have been exceptions to presidential cooperation, however. In *Worcester v. Georgia* (1832), the Court found that the state of Georgia had no authority over Cherokee Indian lands and that missionaries arrested there by the state should be released. The Court also implied that it was the president's responsibility to enforce its decision. Georgia refused to comply with the decision, however, and President Andrew Jackson took no actions to enforce it. He is reputed to have stated, "Well, [Chief Justice] John Marshall has made his decision, now let him enforce it."

Other Relationships

In the earliest years of our nation, the line of separation between the executive and judicial branches was vague and was often crossed. President George Washington consulted with the chief justice on a range of matters and received written advisory opinions on matters of law. Washington even used the first two chief justices as diplomats to negotiate with other countries. The chief justice also served on a commission to manage the fund for paying off the national debt.[53]

This interbranch cooperation did not last long, however. Many critics spoke out against the diplomatic efforts of justices, the Court decided against providing further advisory opinions, and the frequency of informal consultation between the White House and justices declined. The Court also refused to examine pension claims for the secretary of the treasury. Hostility between the president and the judiciary, which was populated primarily by his Federalist political enemies, marked the years of Jefferson's presidency.

In the twentieth century, William Howard Taft often conferred with President Calvin Coolidge and members of his cabinet.[54] The most notable formal exceptions to a strict separation between the two branches have been Justice Owen Roberts's chairing a presidential commission on the attack on Pearl Harbor, Justice Robert Jackson's service as chief American prosecutor at the Nuremberg trials of Nazi leaders following World War II, and Chief Justice Earl Warren's chairmanship of the commission investigating the assassination of President Kennedy. President Johnson turned to Justices Arthur Goldberg[55] and especially Abe Fortas for advice. Fortas received a great deal of criticism for his service as an informal adviser to Johnson on a wide range of issues. While on the court, in the words of one biographer, "Fortas served as political advisor, speechwriter, crisis manager, administration headhunter, legal expert, war counselor, or just plain cheerleader."[56]

This type of relationship has occurred from time to time, however (principally between justices and the presidents who appointed them), continuing a pattern established before the justice reached the Court. Felix Frankfurter continued to advise Franklin D. Roosevelt after he took his seat on the court, as did Louis Brandeis for Woodrow Wilson,[57] Chief

Justice Fred Vinson for Harry Truman,[58] and a number of others through-out U.S. history.

More striking perhaps is the fact that Chief Justice Warren Burger appears to have discussed the Court's internal activities and issues pending before it with President Nixon and other top administration officials.[59] This behavior would seem to be a breach of the separation of powers. Burger also appears to have asked Nixon to use his influence with congressional Republicans to dis-courage them from proceeding with their attempt to impeach Justice William O. Douglas. However, it is also possible that the chief justice delayed circulating his concurring opinion in *Roe v. Wade* to spare Nixon the embarrassment at his second inauguration.[60]

COMPLYING WITH THE COURT

It is one thing for the White House to enforce a court decision against some-one else and something quite different for it to comply with an order directed at the president after he has lost a case in the Supreme Court. At that point, interesting constitutional questions arise that have the potential for substan-tial interbranch conflict. However, presidents typically do comply with court orders, a task made easier by the general deference of the courts to the chief executive.[61]

Presidential Compliance

The Constitution is ambiguous about which branch shall have the final say in interpreting it. The Supreme Court made some progress in resolving this question in *Marbury v. Madison* (1803), in which it voided an act of Congress for the first time and asserted its right to make the final judgment on the constitutionality of actions of the other branches of government. *Marbury* did not really settle the question of the president's obligation to accept and follow the Court's interpretation of the Constitution, however, because the president could argue that the law the Court had voided actually pertained directly only to the Court's own branch, the judiciary. It was not until *Scott v. Sanford* (1857) that the Court again declared an act of Congress unconstitutional; this time, the law was not directly related to the judiciary.

Presidents typically have obeyed Court decisions even when it has been costly to do so. During the Korean War, the United Steelworkers of America gave notice of an industry-wide strike. Concerned about steel production during wartime, President Truman ordered the secretary of commerce to seize and op-erate the steel mills. The steel companies then asked the courts to find the presi-dent's actions unconstitutional. In *Youngstown Sheet and Tube Co. v. Sawyer* (1952), the Supreme Court did so. It found that the president lacked inherent power un-der the Constitution to seize the steel mills and that Congress had chosen not to give him statutory power to do so. Thus, in a rare occurrence, the Court ordered the president to reverse his actions, and Truman immediately complied.

The courts held that President Nixon could not impound funds appropriated by Congress, engage in electronic surveillance without a search warrant, or prevent the publication of the *Pentagon Papers*. He complied with each decision. In 2008 (*Medellin v. Texas*), the Supreme Court declared that President George W. Bush lacked the power to order the state of Texas to reopen the murder case of a Mexican who had been sentenced to death without being told he had a right to contact the Mexican consulate. That decision ended the matter.

The Watergate scandal produced another important case involving presidential prerogatives. The special prosecutor, Leon Jaworski, subpoenaed tapes and documents relating to sixty-four conversations between President Nixon and his aides and advisers. Jaworski needed the material for the prosecution of Nixon administration officials, but the president claimed that executive privilege protected his private conversations with his assistants and refused to produce the subpoenaed material. Thus, the case worked its way quickly to the Supreme Court.

In *United States v. Nixon* (1974), the Court unanimously ordered the president to turn the subpoenaed material over to the special prosecutor. Although Nixon had threatened not to comply with anything less than a "definitive" decision, he obeyed the Court. The Court held that a claim of executive privilege unrelated to military, diplomatic, or national security matters cannot be absolute and in this case must give way to considerations of due process of law in criminal proceedings. Moreover, the justices reaffirmed that it was they, and not the president, who would make the final judgment in such matters. Nixon resigned the presidency about two weeks later.

Although the Constitution does not discuss immunity for the president from lawsuits, there has always been a concern that unless executive employees enjoy immunity for their official actions, they would be constantly looking over their shoulders for possible lawsuits and could not administer laws vigorously and effectively. In response, the federal courts have developed a doctrine of official immunity for the president and other executive officials. In 1982, the Supreme Court held that the president is entitled to absolute immunity, in civil suits, regarding his official acts (*Nixon v. Fitzgerald*).

Paula Jones raised a different issue. She sued Bill Clinton over "abhorrent" sexual advances that she claimed he made to her while he was governor of Arkansas and over punishment that she claimed she received from her supervisors in her state job after she rejected the governor's advances. The White House, fearing a media circus surrounding the embarrassing charges, claimed that while in office, the president was immune from private civil litigation arising out of *unofficial* acts committed in a personal capacity before he took office.

The Supreme Court saw things differently and, in *Clinton v. Jones* (1997), held that the president enjoyed no such immunity. It also opined that the case could move ahead without substantially burdening President Clinton. Preparations for the trial went forward, but the presiding judge dismissed the case as frivolous shortly before it was scheduled to begin in 1998. Jones appealed this decision, and on November 13, 1998, she agreed to accept $850,000 to settle with Clinton.

In the meantime, the president complied with the Court's decision and provided pretrial testimony for the Jones case, giving his political opponents, who were funding the case, the opportunity to ask embarrassing questions about his relationship with White House intern Monica Lewinsky (who also provided testimony). Clinton's supporters argued that these questions provided the potential for a perjury trap because the president was naturally reluctant to give complete or fully accurate answers. These responses, in turn, provided the Republicans with ammunition to charge that the president had committed perjury, suborned witnesses, and obstructed justice, leading to the House impeaching him in 1998.

The war on terrorism has presented new challenges for judicial oversight of the presidency. The Court limited the president's powers when it found that detainees held in the United States and at the naval base at Guantánamo Bay, Cuba, had the right to challenge their detention before a judge or other neutral decision maker (*Hamdi v. Rumsfeld*, *Rasul v. Bush*, 2004). In another historic decision, *Hamdan v. Rumsfeld* (2006), the Supreme Court held that the procedures President George W. Bush had approved for trying prisoners at Guantánamo Bay lacked congressional authorization and violated both the Uniform Code of Military Justice and the Geneva Conventions. The flaws the Court cited were the failure to guarantee defendants the right to attend their trial and the prosecution's ability under the rules to introduce hearsay evidence, unsworn testimony, and evidence obtained through coercion. Equally important, the Constitution did not empower the president to establish judicial procedures on his own.

Challenging the Courts

Presidents are not always compliant with Court decisions, however. In *United States v. Burr* (1807), President Jefferson was subpoenaed to appear at the treason trial of Aaron Burr and to produce a certain letter. Jefferson refused to appear at the trial, but he did provide the document, while stressing that he did so voluntarily and not because of judicial writ. Similarly, President James Monroe was subpoenaed as a witness in a trial, but he sent a written response instead.[62]

The Civil War raised many difficult constitutional questions for the Court and the president. One set of cases found President Abraham Lincoln simply ignoring court orders. The president had suspended the writ of habeas corpus, which requires the government to explain why a person has been detained, and in the most famous of these cases, a citizen held prisoner by the military sued for his freedom. Chief Justice Roger Taney ordered his release, but Lincoln refused to give him up to the U.S. marshal sent to bring him into court. The chief justice (on circuit court duty) then held, in *Ex parte Merryman* (1861), that the president had exceeded his constitutional authority (the Constitution seems to give only Congress the power to suspend habeas corpus), but Lincoln simply ignored the decision, and Merryman remained under arrest. Lincoln argued that he had not violated the Constitution but that, in any case, it would be better for the president to violate a single provision to a limited extent than to incur anarchy because of failure to suppress the rebellion in the South.

Another aspect of presidential compliance with Court decisions is the administration of laws that the Court has approved and that the president opposes. This issue has arisen most directly with the claims of some presidents to the right to decide not to execute laws that they view as unconstitutional, even if those laws have received court approval. Jefferson's opposition to the Alien and Sedition Acts, which were passed under his predecessor John Adams and upheld by the courts, led him to stop all prosecutions and pardon all those who had been convicted under these laws when he took office. Similarly, Andrew Jackson dismantled the Bank of the United States although the Court had approved it as constitutional.

This issue has never really been resolved, and presidents have often been lax in administering laws that they oppose. Federal courts ordered the Nixon administration to more strictly enforce laws to eliminate segregation and sex discrimination in public educational institutions. Such court orders are rare, however.

Recent presidents, especially George H. W. Bush and George W. Bush, have declared many sections of bills that they signed into law to be unconstitutional and therefore unenforceable. Their objections have generally focused on protecting areas of traditional presidential influence (foreign policy and defense) and to combat various forms of congressional oversight, especially legislative vetoes of administrative action.[63] These actions have not resulted in court battles.

If presidents are dissatisfied with Supreme Court decisions, their first thoughts are usually directed toward appointing new members with views similar to their own. There are some other options, however. They may join in congressional efforts to remove certain types of cases from the Court's appellate jurisdiction.[64] Congress has succeeded in such an action only once, however—on jurisdiction to hear appeals on certain writ of habeas corpus cases following the Civil War—and in this case (*Ex parte McCardle*, 1828) the president supported the Court.

George W. Bush asked Congress to strip the federal courts of jurisdiction to hear habeas corpus petitions from detainees seeking to challenge their designation as enemy combatants or who were waiting for the government to determine whether they were enemy combatants. This portion of a broader law allowed the U.S. government to detain such aliens indefinitely without prosecuting them in any manner. However, in 2008, the Supreme Court in *Boumediene v. Bush* voided that provision and held that foreign terrorism suspects in custody at Guantánamo Bay have constitutional rights to challenge their detention in U.S. courts. "The laws and Constitution are designed to survive, and remain in force, in extraordinary times," the Court proclaimed. The Court also found that the procedure established for reviewing enemy combatant status failed to offer the fundamental procedural protections of habeas corpus.[65]

Alternatively, presidents might support efforts to pass a constitutional amendment to overturn a Court interpretation of the Constitution, as George H. W. Bush did when the Court held that the burning of the American flag was a form of protected speech. President Reagan supported amendments to allow prayer in public schools and to prohibit abortions. Such efforts rarely succeed, however, and these did not.

In contrast, when the Court has made a statutory interpretation in which it interprets an act of Congress, Congress can reverse the decision simply by changing the law to clarify the intentions of those supporting the policy.[66] In a notable example, in 1953 President Eisenhower supported legislation that deeded federal mineral rights on offshore lands to the states even though the Court had held in 1951 that the federal government owned the rights.

Deference to the President

A principal reason why complying with judicial decisions has rarely posed a problem for the president is the small number of instances in which the courts have held presidential actions to be in violation of the Constitution. Rarely have even these decisions interfered significantly with the president's policies (the *Youngstown* case was a major exception). More typically, these cases have dealt with matters such as presidential instructions to customs officials or the suspension of the writ of habeas corpus.

Several presidents, including Thomas Jefferson, Abraham Lincoln, and Franklin D. Roosevelt, threatened privately to disobey Court decisions that went against them, but in each case, defiance was unnecessary because the Court supported them. The most blatant instance of a president's threatening to disobey a Court order occurred in a case in which the Court was asked to enjoin President Andrew Johnson from administering military governments in Southern states following the Civil War. In oral argument before the Court, the president, speaking through his attorney general, let it be known that he would not comply with a decision enjoining him from implementing the laws. The Court, in turn, found in *Mississippi v. Johnson* (1867) that it lacked jurisdiction to stop the president from performing official duties that required executive discretion; consequently, the issue failed to come to a head. We should also note that Johnson had vetoed these bills when Congress passed them, yet once they were passed, the president faced impeachment if he failed to execute them.

Most presidential actions are not based on the president's prerogatives under the Constitution and therefore do not lend themselves to constitutional adjudication. Effective opposition to most presidential policies must focus on the broader political arena. Moreover, it is especially difficult to prevent the president from acting. Most challenges occur only after the fact. On some occasions it is possible to oppose the president by challenging the constitutionality of laws he supported and Congress passed. Such efforts are rarely successful, but they were important during the early years of the New Deal. In the end, however, President Roosevelt prevailed.

In the area of foreign and defense policy, the Court has interpreted the Constitution and statutes so as to give the president broad discretion to act. In general, the history of litigation regarding challenges to the president's actions in the field of national security policy has been one of avoidance, postponement of action, or deference to the chief executive, particularly during the time frame in which the action occurs. The judiciary has been content to find that discretionary actions of the executive branch were beyond its competence to adjudicate.[67]

Since the Civil War, presidents have been allowed especially broad powers in wartime. During the Civil War, the Supreme Court approved President Lincoln's deployment of troops during hostilities in the absence of a declaration of war and gave the chief executive discretion to determine the extent of force the crisis demanded and when an emergency existed. Similarly, it upheld the president's blockade of the South, the expansion of the army and navy beyond statutory limits, the calling out of the militia, and most of his suspensions of habeas corpus. He spent public funds without appropriations, declared martial law in various areas, ordered people arrested without warrant, tried civilians in military courts, closed the use of the Post Office for "treasonable" correspondence, seized property, and emancipated slaves—all without interference from the courts.[68]

During World War I, Congress delegated President Woodrow Wilson broad authority to regulate commissions, transportation, and the economy; to draft soldiers; and even to censor criticism—all with the approval of the Court. Franklin D. Roosevelt exercised even broader economic powers during World War II. He ordered the removal of Japanese Americans from the West Coast to relocation centers and confiscated their property, and the Court upheld his action in *Korematsu v. United States* (1944). He also bypassed the courts to establish special military commissions to try Nazi saboteurs, again with the Court's approval in *Ex Parte Quirin* (1942).

During the period of U.S. military involvement in Vietnam, no declaration or other formal congressional authorization for the war was ever issued. Many people, including many legal authorities, felt that this country's participation in the war without a formal declaration by Congress was unconstitutional, and several dozen cases were brought in federal court by opponents of the war to challenge various aspects of its legality. However, the Supreme Court simply refused to hear all but one of these cases and never issued a written opinion regarding the war. A combination of deference to the president and pragmatic politics (one wonders what would have happened had the war been declared unconstitutional while troops were engaged in combat) rendered the Court irrelevant to the issue.[69]

Similarly, a district court refused to hear a suit brought by several members of Congress that challenged George Bush's expansion of U.S. forces in the Persian Gulf in 1991 as a prelude to war. In this case, the court simply found that the country was not yet at war, and thus there was no basis for the suit. Another court also found the military to be within its rights to inoculate members of the armed forces against biological weapons, even without their permission, so as to facilitate the preparation for war in the Gulf.

It is interesting that in times in which presidents are most likely to stretch their power (that is, in wartime), the courts are the least likely to intervene. When they finally do, the war may already be over. For example, following both the Civil War (*Ex parte Milligan,* 1866) and World War II, the Supreme Court held that military tribunals could not try civilians while the civilian courts were open. In each case, however, the president at whom the decision was directed was no longer living.

In the aftermath of the 9/11 terrorist attacks, the FBI detained more than 1,200 people as possible dangers to national security. Of these detainees, 762 were illegal aliens (mostly Arabs and Muslims), and many of them languished in jail for months until cleared by the FBI. For the first time in U.S. history, the federal government withheld the names of detainees, reducing their opportunities to exercise their rights to access to the courts and to counsel. The government argued that releasing the names and details of those arrested would give terrorists a window on the terror investigation. For similar reasons, the president also claimed the right to deny suspected terrorists or captured prisoners the normal rights in the judicial process. In 2004, the Supreme Court refused to consider whether the government properly withheld names and other details about these prisoners. However, we have seen that the Court did overrule the president regarding the rights of detainees to challenge their detentions before a neutral official and the procedures for trying prisoners.

During peacetime, the courts have found that presidents also have substantial discretion to act in the areas of foreign affairs and defense. They have broad prerogatives to act in negotiating and executing international agreements, withholding state secrets from the public, allocating international airline routes, terminating treaties, making executive agreements, recognizing foreign governments, using military activities to protect American interests abroad, punishing foreign adversaries, and acquiring and divesting foreign territory.

In the domestic sphere, the president's prerogatives are closely linked to maintaining order. Thus, presidents have discretion to declare and terminate national emergencies and even martial law. They may also call out the militia or the regular armed forces to control internal friction and keep the peace.

It is not unusual for courts to find the actions of executive branch officials to be violations of statutes passed by Congress, usually for exceeding the discretionary limits in the law. In these situations, the judiciary generally finds that the law, not the Constitution, must be changed (or perhaps just clarified) before the president's agents can take certain actions. Depending on the prevailing view in Congress, this may pose little problem for the president. At any rate, rarely are the issues involved central to his program.

JUDICIAL POWERS

In addition to enforcing court orders, presidents have some judicial instruments of their own. For example, they can issue pardons, commute sentences, grant clemency, and proclaim amnesty. These powers are exclusively theirs.

Over the years, the exercise of this judicial authority by presidents has sparked controversy. Critics accused both Thomas Jefferson and Abraham Lincoln of favoring their friends and Harry S. Truman of avoiding the usual scrutiny of pardons in the Department of Justice. Gerald Ford's unconditional pardon of Richard Nixon in 1974 became a major political issue that adversely affected Ford's electability two years later. Issued prior to a conviction or even an indictment of the former president, the pardon, "for all offenses against the United States which Richard Nixon has committed or may have committed or taken part in during the period from January 20, 1969, through August 9, 1974," precluded any criminal prosecution. Although critics accused Ford of subverting the legal process, they did not dispute his power to issue the pardon.[70] Whether Nixon's acceptance of it amounted to an admission of guilt has also been unclear.

On December 24, 1992, twelve days before former Secretary of Defense Caspar Weinberger was to go to trial for perjury in the Iran-Contra scandal, George H.W. Bush pardoned him. In issuing pardons to Weinberger and five other Iran-Contra defendants from the Reagan years, President Bush charged that Independent Counsel's prosecutions represented the "criminalization of policy differences." The other people pardoned included former national security assistant Robert C. McFarlane, former Assistant Secretary of State Elliott Abrams, and three CIA officials. The Weinberger pardon marked the first time a president ever pardoned someone in whose trial he might have been called as a witness (the president was knowledgeable of factual events underlying the case).

In 2007, George W. Bush commuted the sentence of Vice President Dick Cheney's former chief of staff, Scooter Libby, who was found guilty of perjury and obstruction of justice in the case of the leaking the identity of CIA undercover operative Valarie Plame. The president's action was highly controversial and added fuel to the intense political polarization of the time.

In addition to the issuance of unconditional pardons, presidents may grant conditional reprieves. In 1954, the Supreme Court upheld President Eisenhower's commutation of a death sentence, provided that the individual never be paroled; in 1972, President Nixon granted executive clemency to former labor leader James Hoffa on the condition that he refrain from further union activities. In 1999, President Clinton granted clemency to eleven Puerto Rican terrorists on the condition that they renounce the use of violence and that they stay away from each other.

Presidents may also issue general amnesty. George Washington did so for hundreds of participants in the Whiskey Rebellion. Abraham Lincoln exercised this authority in 1863 in an effort to persuade Southern deserters to return to the Union. In order to heal the wounds of the Civil War, his successor, Andrew Johnson, in 1868 granted universal amnesty to all those who had participated in the insurrection. Twentieth-century presidents have used this power to pardon those individuals who were convicted of crimes and subsequently served in the military and to prevent the imposition of wartime penalties (still on the books) on those who failed to register for the draft during peacetime. Harry S. Truman pardoned 9,000 people who had been convicted of desertion in peacetime.

The most sweeping and controversial amnesty proclamation in recent times occurred in 1977 when—implementing one of his campaign promises—President Carter pardoned all Vietnam draft resisters and asked the Defense

Department to consider, on an individual basis, the cases of military deserters during that war. Congress attempted to undercut Carter's general pardon by prohibiting the use of funds to execute his order but was unsuccessful because the president's directive to the Justice Department did not require a separate appropriation.

President Clinton issued nearly 40 percent of all his pardons on his last day in office in 2001, and several of these pardons raised a storm of controversy. Among those he pardoned were a fugitive on the FBI's Ten Most Wanted list, a crack cocaine drug lord, and a baldness-cure scam artist whose patrons had paid Clinton's brother-in-law Hugh Rodham $400,000. (Rodham paid it back after the press found out.) The pardon that attracted the most attention, however, was of billionaire Marc Rich, who was accused of tax fraud and illegally doing business with hostile nations. Rich had lived abroad as a fugitive for many years and even renounced his U.S. citizenship, and he employed prominent attorneys with connections to Clinton to make the case for his pardon. Critics charged that in making some of his decisions regarding pardons, the president had circumvented the regular review process in the Department of Justice and responded to inappropriate back-channel lobbying from those who were politically well connected and to some who had made large donations to his presidential library and the Democratic Party.

George W. Bush also granted clemency to several people who circumvented the normal review process. Bush even withdrew one grant of clemency the day after he granted it when more information about the recipient came to light. Table 10.5 shows the number of pardons, commutations, and rescinded convictions issued by recent presidents.

Table 10.5 Presidential Pardons, Commutations, and Rescinded Convictions

President	Years in Office	Number of Pardons, Commutations, and Rescinded Convictions
Eisenhower	1953–1961	1,157
Kennedy	1961–1963	575
Johnson	1965–1969	1,187
Nixon	1969–1974	926
Ford	1974–1977	409
Carter	1977–1981	566
Reagan	1981–1989	406
Bush	1989–1993	77
Clinton	1993–2001	456
GW Bush	2001–2009	200
Obama*	2009–	40

*Through January 2013.

SOURCE: University of Pittsburgh Law School, "Presidential Clemency Actions, 1789–2001," accessed at http://jurist.law.pitt.edu/pardonspres1.htm. Updated by the authors.

CONCLUSION

Presidents are involved in vital relationships with the judicial branch, especially with the Supreme Court. They attempt to influence its decisions through the process of selecting judges and justices and through the arguments of their subordinates before the courts. There are strong congressional constraints on them in the selection of judges, however, and presidents sometimes err in their choice of nominees. Although the executive branch has skilled litigators before the federal appellate courts and a clear record of success, the chief executive is ultimately dependent on the judgment of members of a branch of government that is much more autonomous than the legislature. The president is once again a facilitator, not a director, of change.

A judicial decision does not end a president's relationship with the courts on an issue; in the capacity as chief executive, a president may be obliged to enforce judicial decisions (a responsibility that sometimes conflicts with policy goals). Moreover, although the judiciary is generally deferential to presidents, the courts may order a president to comply with a holding against a presidential action. Such decisions do not affect most of what presidents do, but in some instances they do hamper their actions. Thus, both conflict and harmony characterize the president's relations with the courts, and influencing judicial decisions remains an important, but at times frustrating, priority for the White House.

Discussion Questions

1. Presidents often face considerable opposition to their judicial nominees. What should be the role of the Senate in the confirmation process? Should an opposition-controlled Senate oppose nominees who share the president's views, or should the Senate simply be a check on the nominees' basic qualifications?

2. What criteria should the president employ when choosing judicial nominees? Are race, gender, and partisanship legitimate criteria? What should be the role of ideological considerations, such as whether a nominee believes in judicial activism or restraint?

3. Should the president be immune from civil lawsuits from private individuals while serving in office? Was the Supreme Court correct to state that such suits would not be a drain on the president's time and energy and that there would not be many frivolous suits? Did the Paula Jones suit, followed by the Kenneth Starr investigation, distract President Clinton from his presidential duties or encourage him to be more presidential in behavior?

Web Exercises

1. Listen to the oral arguments before the Supreme Court in the case of *Clinton v. Jones* (1997). You can also read the transcript of the argument and the Court's decision. Go to http://www.oyez.org

/cases/1990–1999/1996/1996_95_1853. Did the Court make the right decision? Was it correct that lawsuits will distract the president from the core business of the presidency?

2. Read the Supreme Court's decision in *United States v. Nixon* (1974). Note how the Court denied the president's claim of executive privilege while at the same time establishing the principle of executive privilege for the first time in a Supreme Court case. Go to http://www.oyez.org /cases/1970–1979/1974/1974_73_1766. What does the case tell us about the relationship between the judiciary and the president?

3. Examine the Supreme Court's decision in *Bush v. Gore*. Go to http://www .oyez.org/cases/2000–2009/2000/2000_00_949. Should the Court have become involved in the Florida election controversy? If so, why? If not, why not? Do you think the Court's prestige increased or decreased as a result of the decision in this matter?

Selected Readings

Abraham, Henry J. *Justices, Presidents, and Senators: A History of U.S. Supreme Court Appointments from Washington to Bush II*, 5th ed. Lanham, MD: Rowman and Littlefield, 2007.

Binder, Sarah A., and Forrest Maltzman. *Advice and Dissent: The Struggle to Shape the Federal Judiciary.* Washington, DC: Brookings Institution, 2009.

Epstein, Lee, and Jeffrey A. Segal. *Advice and Consent.* Oxford: Oxford University Press, 2005.

Epstein, Lee, and Jeffrey A. Segal. "Nominating Federal Judges and Justices." In *Oxford Handbook of the American Presidency*, edited by George C. Edwards III and William G. Howell. Oxford: Oxford University Press, 2009, pp. 625–645.

Fisher, Louis. "Judicial Review of the War Power." *Presidential Studies Quarterly* 35 (September 2005): 466–495.

Goldman, Sheldon. *Picking Federal Judges.* New Haven, CT: Yale University Press, 1997.

Moraski, Bryon J., and Charles R. Shipan, "The Politics of Supreme Court Nominations: A Theory of Institutional Constraints and Choices." *American Journal of Political Science* 43 (October 1999): 1069–1095.

Rowland, C. K., and Bridget Jeffery Todd, "Where You Stand Depends on Who Sits: Platform Promises and Judicial Gatekeeping in the Federal District Courts." *Journal of Politics* 53 (February 1991): 175–185.

Whittington, Keith E. "Judicial Checks on the President." In *Oxford Handbook of the American Presidency*, edited by George C. Edwards III and William G. Howell. Oxford: Oxford University Press, 2009, pp. 646–664.

Yalof, David A. *Pursuit of Justices: Presidential Politics and the Selection of Supreme Court Nominees.* Chicago: University of Chicago Press, 1999.

Notes

1. See Sarah A. Binder and Forrest Maltzman, *Advice and Dissent: The Struggle to Shape the Federal Judiciary* (Washington, DC: Brookings Institution, 2009) on the history and procedures regarding judicial nominations.

2. Sarah Binder and Forrest Maltzman, "The Limits of Senatorial Courtesy," *Legislative Studies Quarterly* 29 (February 2004): 5–22. Michael A. Sollenberger, "The Blue Slip: A Theory of Unified and Divided Government, 1979–2009,"

Congress & the Presidency 37 (May–August 2010): 125–156; Brandon Rottinghaus and Chris Nicholson, "Counting Congress In: Patterns of Success in Judicial Nomination Requests by Members of Congress to Presidents Eisenhower and Ford," *American Politics Research* 38 (July 2010): 691–717.

3. Sheldon Goldman, Elliot Slotnick, and Sara Schiavoni, "Obama's Judiciary at Midterm," *Judicature* 94 (May–June 2011): 262–303.

4. Quoted in J. Woodford Howard Jr., *Courts of Appeals in the Federal Judicial System* (Princeton, NJ: Princeton University Press, 1981), p. 101.

5. One study found, however, that judicial experience is not related to the congruence of presidential preferences and the justices' decisions on racial equality cases. See John Gates and Jeffrey Cohen, "Presidents, Supreme Court Justices, and Racial Equality Cases: 1954–1984," *Political Behavior* 10, no. 1 (1988): 22–35.

6. David M. O'Brien, "The Reagan Judges: His Most Enduring Legacy?" in Charles O. Jones, ed., *The Reagan Legacy* (Chatham, NJ: Chatham House, 1988), pp. 60–101.

7. Sheldon Goldman, "The Bush Imprint on the Judiciary: Carrying on a Tradition," *Judicature* 74 (April/May 1991): 294–306.

8. See David M. O'Brien, "Judicial Legacies: The Clinton Presidency and the Courts," in Colin Campbell and Bert A. Rockman, eds., *The Clinton Legacy* (New York: Seven Bridges Press, 2000).

9. Elisabeth Bumiller, "Bush Vows to Seek Conservative Judges," *New York Times*, March 29, 2002, p. A24.

10. Sheldon Goldman, "Do We Have a Crisis in Judicial Selection?" in George C. Edwards III, ed., *Presidential Politics* (Belmont, CA: Wadsworth, 2005).

11. Goldman et al., "Obama's Judiciary at Midterm," pp. 262–303.

12. Binder and Maltzman, *Advice and Dissent*, chaps. 1–2.

13. Scott Basinger and Mark Maxwell, "The Changing Politics of Federal Judicial Nominations," *Congress & the Presidency* 37 (May–August 2010): 157–175; Sollenberger, "The Blue Slip," pp. 125–156;

Ryan C. Black, Anthony J. Madonna, and Ryan J. Owens, "Obstructing Agenda-Setting: Examining Blue Slip Behavior in the Senate," *The Forum* 9, no. 4 (2011).

14. Binder and Maltzman, "The Limits of Senatorial Courtesy," pp. 5–22.

15. Wendy L. Martinek, Mark Kemper, and Steven R. Van Winkle, "To Advise and Consent: The Senate and Lower Federal Court Nominations, 1977–1998," *Journal of Politics* 64 (May 2002): 337–361.

16. Binder and Maltzman, *Advice and Dissent*, pp. 4–6, chaps. 2, 4; Jon R. Bond, Richard Fleisher, and Glen S. Krutz, "Malign Neglect: Evidence That Delay Has Become the Primary Method of Defeating Presidential Appointment," *Congress & the Presidency* 36 (Fall 2009): 226–243; and Lauren Cohen Bell, "Senatorial Discourtesy: The Senate's Use of Delay to Shape the Federal Judiciary," *Political Research Quarterly* 55 (September 2002): 589–607.

17. Binder and Maltzman, *Advice and Dissent*, pp. 2–4, chap. 4.

18. On this point, see Elisha Carol Savchak, Thomas G. Hansford, Donald R. Songer, Kenneth L. Manning, and Robert A. Carp, "Taking It to the Next Level: The Elevation of District Court Judges to the U.S. Court of Appeals," *American Journal of Political Science* 50 (April 2006): 478–493.

19. Goldman, "Do We Have a Crisis in Judicial Selection?"

20. Binder and Maltzman, *Advice and Dissent*, chaps. 3–4.

21. Nancy Scherer, Brandon L. Bartels, and Amy Steigerwalt, "Sounding the Fire Alarm: The Role of Interest Groups in the Lower Federal Court Confirmation Process," *Journal of Politics* 70 (October 2008): 1026–1039.

22. Elizabeth Palmer, "For Bush's Judicial Nominees, A Tough Tribunal Awaits," *CQ Weekly*, April 28, 2001, pp. 898–902.

23. Griffin Bell quoted in Nina Totenberg, "Will Judges Be Chosen Rationally?" *Judicature* 60 (August/September 1976): 93.

24. See Binder and Maltzman, *Advice and Dissent*, chap. 5; Jon R. Bond, "The Politics of Court Structure: The Addition of New

Federal Judges, 1949–1978," *Law and Policy Quarterly* 2 (April 1980): 181–188.

25. See, for example, the important role that African American support played in the confirmation of Clarence Thomas even though he was likely to vote against the wishes of leading civil rights organizations. L. Marvin Overby, Beth M. Henschen, Julie Walsh, and Michael H. Strauss, "Courting Constituents: An Analysis of the Senate Confirmation Vote on Justice Clarence Thomas," *American Political Science Review* 86 (December 1992): 997–1003.

26. Jennifer L. Peresie, "Female Judges Matter: Gender and Collegial: Decisionmaking in the Federal Appellate Courts," *Yale Law Journal* 114 (May 2005): 1759–1790.

27. Adam B. Cox and Thomas J. Miles, "Judging the Voting Rights Act," *Columbia Law Review* 108 (January 2008): 1–54.

28. Quoted in Adam Liptak, "The Waves Minority Judges Always Make," *New York Times*, May 1, 2009.

29. On the impact of the background of members of the judiciary, see Robert A. Carp, Donald Songer, C. K. Rowland, Ronald Stidham, and Lisa Richey-Tracy, "The Voting Behavior of Judges Appointed by President Bush," *Judicature* 76 (April/May 1993): 298–302; C. K. Rowland and Bridget Jeffery Todd, "Where You Stand Depends on Who Sits: Platform Promises and Judicial Gatekeeping in the Federal District Courts," *Journal of Politics* 53 (February 1991): 175–185; C. K. Rowland, Donald R. Songer, and Robert A. Carp, "Presidential Effects on Criminal Justice in the Lower Federal Courts: The Reagan Judges," *Law and Society Review* 22, no. 1 (1988): 191–200; Timothy B. Tomasi and Jess A. Velona, "All the President's Men? A Study of Ronald Reagan's Appointments to the U.S. Courts of Appeals," *Columbia Law Review* 87 (May 1987): 766–793; John Gottschall, "Reagan Appointments to the United States Court of Appeals: The Continuation of a Judicial Revolution," *Judicature* 70 (June/July 1986): 48–54; Thomas G. Walker and Deborah J. Barrow, "The Diversification of the Federal Bench: Policy and Process Ramifications," *Journal of Politics* 47 (May 1985): 596–617; and sources cited therein.

30. See John W. Dean, *The Rehnquist Choice* (New York: Free Press, 2001).

31. See John Anthony Maltese, *The Selling of Supreme Court Nominees* (Baltimore, MD: Johns Hopkins University Press, 1995).

32. See Lee Epstein, René Lindstädt, Jeffrey A. Segal, and Chad Westerland, "The Changing Dynamics of Senate Voting on Supreme Court Nominees," *Journal of Politics* 68 (May 2006): 296–307; John Massaro, *Supremely Political* (Albany: State University of New York Press, 1992); Charles M. Cameron, Albert D. Cover, and Jeffrey A. Segal, "Senate Voting on Supreme Court Nominees: A Neoinstitutional Model," *American Political Science Review* 84 (June 1990): 525–534; Jeffrey Segal, "Senate Confirmation of Supreme Court Justices: Partisan and Institutional Politics," *Journal of Politics* 49 (November 1987): 998–1015; and P. S. Ruckman, Jr., "The Supreme Court, Critical Nominations, and the Senate Confirmation Process," *Journal of Politics* 55 (August 1993): 793–805.

33. See also Scott Basinger and Maxwell Mak, "The Changing Politics of Supreme Court Confirmations," *American Politics Research* 40 (July 2012): 737–763.

34. Thomas R. Marshall, "Symbolic versus Policy Representation on the U.S. Supreme Court," *Journal of Politics* 55 (February 1993): 140–150.

35. See Bryon J. Moraski and Charles R. Shipan, "The Politics of Supreme Court Nominations: A Theory of Institutional Constraints and Choices," *American Journal of Political Science* 43 (October 1999): 1069–1095.

36. Robert Scigliano, *The Supreme Court and the Presidency* (New York: Free Press, 1971). This is also true for nominees to the courts of appeals. See Ashlyn Kuersten and Donald Songer, "Presidential Success through Appointments to the United States Courts of Appeals," *American Politics Research* 31 (March 2003): 107–137; Donald R. Songer and Martha Humphries Ginn, "Assessing the Impact of Presidential and Home State Influences on Judicial Decisionmaking in the United States Courts of Appeals," *Political Research Quarterly* 55 (June 2002): 299–328; and Micheal W. Giles, Virginia A. Hettinger, and Todd

Peppers, "Picking Federal Judges: A Note on Policy and Partisan Selection Agendas," *Political Research Quarterly* 54 (September 2001): 623–641.

37. See, for example, Jeffrey A. Segal and Harold J. Spaeth, *The Supreme Court and the Attitudinal Model* (Cambridge, UK: Cambridge University Press, 1993); Jeffrey A. Segal and Albert O. Cover, "Ideological Values and the Votes of U.S. Supreme Court Justices," *American Political Science Review* 83 (June 1989): 557–566; Tracey E. George and Lee Epstein, "On the Nature of Supreme Court Decision Making," *American Political Science Review* 86 (June 1992): 323–337; and Jeffrey A. Segal and Harold J. Spaeth, "The Influence of *Stare Decisis* on the Votes of United States Supreme Court Justices," *American Journal of Political Science* 40 (November 1996): 971–1003.

38. Michael A. Bailey and Forrest Maltzman, *The Constrained Court: Law, Politics, and the Decisions Justices Make* (Princeton, NJ: Princeton University Press, 2011); **Brandon L. Bartels**, "Choices in Context: How Case-Level Factors Influence the Magnitude of Ideological Voting on the U.S. Supreme Court," *American Politics Research* 39 (January 2011): 142–175; and Brandon L. Bartels, "The Constraining Capacity of Legal Doctrine on the U.S. Supreme Court," *American Political Science Review* 103 (August 2009): 474–495.

39. Dwight Eisenhower quoted in Henry J. Abraham, Justices, Presidents, and Senators: A History of U.S. Supreme Court Appointments from Washington to Clinton (Lanham, MD: Rowman and Littlefield, 1999), p. 200.

40. See Gary King, "Presidential Appointments to the Supreme Court: Adding Systematic Explanation to Probabilistic Description," *American Politics Quarterly* 15 (July 1987): 373–386.

41. See George C. Edwards III, *The Strategic President: Persuasion and Opportunity in Presidential Leadership* (Princeton, NJ: Princeton University Press, 2009), pp. 193–195.

42. On the importance of ideology and partisanship considerations in judicial retirement and resignation decisions, see

Kjersten R. Nelson and Eve M. Ringsmuth, "Departures From the Court: The Political Landscape and Institutional Constraints," *American Politics Research* 37 (May 2009): 486–507; Deborah J. Barrow and Gary Zuk, "An Institutional Analysis of Turnover in the Lower Federal Courts, 1900–1987," *Journal of Politics* 52 (May 1990): 457–476; and Gary Zuk, Gerard S. Gryski, and Deborah J. Barrow, "Partisan Transformation of the Federal Judiciary, 1869–1992," *American Politics Quarterly* 21 (October 1993): 439–457.

43. See Rebecca Mae Salokar, *The Solicitor General* (Philadelphia: Temple University Press, 1992); and Lincoln Caplan, *The Tenth Justice: The Solicitor General and the Rule of Law* (New York: Random House, 1987).

44. On the Court's acceptance of cases, see H. W. Perry, Jr., *Deciding to Decide: Agenda Setting in the United States Supreme Court* (Cambridge, MA: Harvard University Press, 1991); Doris Marie Provine, *Case Selection in the United States Supreme Court* (Chicago: University of Chicago Press, 1980); and Stuart H. Teger and Douglas Kosinski, "The Cue Theory of Supreme Court Certiorari Jurisdiction: A Reconsideration," *Journal of Politics* 42 (August 1980): 834–846.

45. Chris Nicholson and Paul M. Collins Jr. "The Solicitor General's Amicus Curiae Strategies in the Supreme Court," *American Political Research* 36 (May 2008): 382–415.

46. See Timothy R. Johnson, "The Supreme Court, the Solicitor General, and the Separation of Powers," *American Politics Research* 31 (July 2003): 426–451.

47. Rebecca E. Deen, Joseph Ignagni, and James Meernik, "Executive Influence on the U.S. Supreme Court: Solicitor General *Amicus* Cases, 1953–1997," *American Review of Politics* 22 (Spring 2001): 3–26.

48. Bailey and Maltzman, *The Constrained Court*, chaps. 6–7; James F. Spriggs and Paul J. Wahlbeck, "Amicus Curiae and the Role of Information in the Supreme Court," *Political Research Quarterly* 50 (June 1997): 365–386.

49. On the solicitor general's success, see Jeffrey A. Segal, "Courts, Executives, and Legislatures," in John B. Gates and

Charles A. Johnson, eds., *The American Courts* (Washington, DC: Congressional Quarterly Press, 1991), pp. 376–382.

50. Michael A. Bailey, Brian Kamoie, and Forrest Maltzman, "Signals from the Tenth Justice: The Political Role of the Solicitor General in Supreme Court Decision Making," *American Journal of Political Science* 49 (January 2005): 72–85.

51. Burt Solomon, *FDR v. The Constitution* (New York: Walker and Co., 2009), p. 10.

52. Earl Warren, *The Memoirs of Chief Justice Earl Warren* (Garden City, NY: Doubleday, 1971), pp. 337–342.

53. William Castro, *The Supreme Court in the Early Republic* (Columbia: University of South Carolina Press, 1995), chap. 6.

54. Solomon, *FDR v. The Constitution*, p. 10.

55. Robert A. Caro, *The Passage of Power* (New York: Knopf, 2012), pp. 368, 407.

56. Bruce Allen Murphy, *Fortas* (New York: William Morrow, 1988), p. 235. Murphy chronicles the Johnson–Fortas relationship in great detail. See also Joseph A. Califano, Jr., *The Triumph and Tragedy of Lyndon Johnson* (New York: Simon and Schuster, 1991), pp. 95–96, 118, 120, 153–154, 161–163, 189, 191, 205, 213–218, 298, 306, 312–315.

57. Bruce Allen Murphy, *The Brandeis/ Frankfurter Connection: The Secret Political Activities of Two Supreme Court Justices* (New York: Oxford University Press, 1982).

58. See Clark Clifford, *Counsel to the President* (New York: Random House, 1991), p. 215; and David McCullough, *Truman* (New York: Simon and Schuster, 1992), p. 897.

59. John Ehrlichman, *Witness to Power: The Nixon Years* (New York: Simon and Schuster, 1982), p. 133.

60. Linda Greenhouse, *Becoming Justice Blackmun* (New York: Times Books, 2005), pp. 99–100, 127.

61. But see Ryan J. Owens, "The Separation of Powers and Supreme Court Agenda Setting," *American Journal of Political Science* 54 (April 2010): 412–427.

62. Grant, Nixon, Ford, Carter, and Clinton also responded to court orders to provide testimony and other information.

63. Andrew B. Whitford, "Signing Statements as Bargaining Outcomes: Evidence from the Administration of George W. Bush," *Presidential Studies Quarterly* 42 (June 2012): 343–362; Kevin A. Evans, "Looking before Watergate: Foundations in the Development of the Constitutional Challenges within Signing Statements, FDR–Nixon," *Presidential Studies Quarterly* 42 (June 2012): 390–405; Richard S. Conley, "The Harbinger of the Unitary Executive? An Analysis of Presidential Signing Statements from Truman to Carter," *Presidential Studies Quarterly* 41 (September 2011): 546–569; Michael J. Korzi, "'A Legitimate Function': Reconsidering Presidential Signing Statements," *Congress & the Presidency* 38, no. 2 (2011): 195–216; Kevin Evans, "Challenging Law: Presidential Signing Statements and the Maintenance of Executive Power," *Congress & the Presidency* 38, no. 2 (2011): 217–234; Michael J. Berry, "Controversially Executing the Law: George W. Bush and the Constitutional Signing Statement," *Congress & the Presidency* 36 (Autumn 2009): 244–271; Charles Tiefer, *The Semi-Sovereign Presidency* (Boulder, CO: Westview, 1994), chap. 3; Christopher S. Kelley and Bryan Marshall, "The Last Word: Presidential Power and the Role of Signing Statements," *Presidential Studies Quarterly* 38 (June 2008): 248–267; and Phillip J. Cooper, "George W. Bush, Edgar Allan Poe, and the Use and Abuse of Presidential Signing Statements," *Presidential Studies Quarterly* 35 (September 2005): 515–532.

64. Congress has succeeded in such an action only once, however—on jurisdiction to hear appeals on certain writ of habeas corpus cases following the Civil War—and in this case, the president supported the Court. The case was *Ex parte McCardle* (1828).

65. Congress has frequently passed legislation to strip lower-court jurisdiction. See Dawn M. Chutkow, "Jurisdiction Stripping: Litigation, Ideology, and Congressional Control of the Courts," *The Journal of Politics* 70 (October 2008): 1053–1064.

66. William N. Eskridge, "Overriding Supreme Court Statutory Interpretation Decisions," *Yale Law Journal* 101 (1991): 331–455; Joseph Ignagni and James

Meernik, "Explaining Congressional Attempts to Reverse Supreme Court Decisions," *Political Research Quarterly* 10 (June 1994): 353–372. See also R. Shep Melnick, *Between the Lines: Interpreting Welfare Rights* (Washington, DC: Brookings Institution, 1994).

67. See, for example, Craig R. Ducat and Robert L. Dudley, "Federal District Judges and Presidential Power during the Postwar Era," *Journal of Politics* 51 (February 1989): 98–118.

68. Forrest McDonald, *The American Presidency: An Intellectual History* (Lawrence: University Press of Kansas, 1994), pp. 398–402.

69. Anthony A. D'Amato and Robert M. O'Neil, *The Judiciary and Vietnam* (New York: St. Martin's, 1972); Louis Fisher, "Judicial Review of the War Power," *Presidential Studies Quarterly* 35 (September 2005): 466–495.

70. There were many allegations of a deal between the two men, and some observers even accused Ford of having agreed to the pardon in exchange for his nomination as vice president by Nixon. However, in sworn testimony before the House Judiciary Committee in 1974, Ford vehemently denied that he had made such an agreement.

11

DOMESTIC
POLICY MAKING

The framers of the Constitution gave presidents a policy role, but they did not expect them to dominate that policy. Yet that is precisely what chief executives have tried to do. Seizing on the initiative that the Constitution provides—and which their central perspective, institutional structure, and political support facilitate—presidents have become chief policy makers. Today, the public expects them to propose and achieve national goals. They are expected to redeem campaign promises, respond to emergencies in policy, and propose solutions to the country's social, economic, and political ills as they occur. Failure to address critical issues and rectify national problems usually results in public criticism, increasing job disapproval, and even electoral defeat should unsatisfactory conditions persist.

The problem that presidents face in performing their leadership role is that public expectations often exceed their institutional and political resources to achieve them. They have at their disposal significant policy expertise, but the experts are not always in agreement on what to do or how to do it. They have considerable institutional resources in their presidential office and the executive branch, but they cannot control the behavior of those in other branches of government, much less those outside the government who affect that behavior. They have difficulty even overseeing the actions of those who are presumably subordinate to them. They have political clout, but that clout varies with time and circumstances. The economic, social, and political conditions may not be amenable to easy and quick policy solutions. Thus, the president's policy role is complex and often difficult to exercise successfully even though the initiation and execution of that policy may be critical to how presidents are evaluated by the public, news media, and government officials with whom they must interact.

The president's domestic policy role did not evolve gradually; it developed primarily as a response to policy problems during the twentieth and twenty-first centuries. The first part of this chapter chronicles the growth of the president's domestic policy-making role; the second part looks at campaign promises and how they frame an administration's initial policy priorities; and the third part examines the structure and processes for converting those priorities into legislative policy proposals. Here we focus on roles of the policy staffs in the White House and the Office of Management and Budget (OMB). In the fourth section of the chapter, we turn to the strategies president use for converting their agendas into public policy. Throughout the chapter, we note shifts in power from the executive departments and agencies to the White House.

THE DEVELOPMENT OF A DOMESTIC POLICY-MAKING ROLE

Although the framers of the Constitution did not envision the president as chief domestic policy maker, they did anticipate that the executive would participate in the policy-making process. Within the framework of the separation of powers, the president was given the duty to recommend necessary and expedient legislation and latitude in the execution of the law. Taken together, this duty and that latitude provide the constitutional basis upon which a substantial domestic policy-making role has been built.

For the first one hundred years, presidents recommended measures, took positions, and occasionally even drafted bills, but they did not formulate policy within the domestic policy sphere on a regular basis—that was considered the responsibility of the Congress. Beginning with Theodore Roosevelt and continuing with Woodrow Wilson, the president's domestic policy-making role became more regularized. Both presidents proposed comprehensive legislative programs. Roosevelt's Square Deal included antitrust, consumer protection, and environmental legislation; Wilson's New Freedoms consisted of proposals to help farmers and industrial workers as well as tariff and banking reform. During Wilson's presidency, the Federal Trade Commission and the National Park Service were created. He also introduced legislation that led to the creation of the Federal Reserve System.

Wilson's Republican successors (Harding, Coolidge, and Hoover) did not follow in his footsteps. Their conservative philosophy undoubtedly influenced their conception of a more limited presidential role within the domestic policy sphere. From the perspective of the 1920s, the Republican interlude was a return to "normalcy," as Warren Harding termed it, in which Congress proposed and the president disposed. From today's perspective, it was a brief respite in the growth of the president's domestic expectations and responsibilities.

Franklin Roosevelt, more than any other president, enlarged policy-making expectations. Coming into office in the throes of the Great Depression, Roosevelt believed it was absolutely essential for the president to take the initiative. With a sizable Democratic majority inclined to support his proposals, Roosevelt used his personal influence to get them enacted into law. He was particularly active in the first hundred days of his administration, formulating legislation to address the nation's most pressing economic problems.

By the end of the Roosevelt era, the president's role as domestic policy maker was firmly established. In fact, when Harry S Truman, Roosevelt's successor, asked Congress for legislation to combat inflation, Republican legislative leaders criticized him for not presenting a draft bill. When Dwight D. Eisenhower failed to propose a legislative program during his first year as president, he was criticized from both sides of the aisle. "Don't expect us to start from scratch on what you people want," an irate member of the House Foreign Affairs Committee told an Eisenhower official. "That's not the way we do things here. You draft the bills and we work them over."[1]

Whereas Roosevelt extended presidential initiatives primarily into the economic sphere, Presidents John Kennedy and Lyndon Johnson expanded them into the social realm. Medical aid to the elderly, public housing, community health, minimum wages, and conservation and education programs, plus a variety of civil rights policies, were crafted during their administrations.

Richard Nixon did not seek to reverse Kennedy and Johnson's policy initiatives, although he did try to reduce some of the spending that the Democratic Congress had appropriated. But he also proposed domestic programs of his own, including a large revenue-sharing program with the states, an executive order known as the Philadelphia Plan that required government contractors to subcontract with minority-owned businesses, and cost-of-living adjustments to the major entitlement programs.

By the end of the Nixon period, the president's role as chief policy initiator had been firmly established. Presidential candidates set their first-year agenda during the electoral campaigns and then devoted their first and second years in office to converting that agenda into public policy. As time wore on, they were increasingly expected to mobilize public support and build policy coalitions outside of government to pressure Congress to enact their domestic policy goals.

In the 1970s, the liberal environment that contributed to an expansive government role within the domestic policy arena began to change. A weaker economy, the war in Vietnam, and the persistence of social issues that civil rights and social welfare legislation had not rectified raised doubts about the government's ability to address these issues, much less the wisdom of its trying to do so. Ronald Reagan articulated these concerns in his victorious 1980 campaign. For Reagan, government was not the solution. It had become the problem.

The Reagan administration reduced discretionary domestic spending and wished to cut back on entitlement programs, but could not gain sufficient support in Congress to do so. It was successful in lowering taxes and increasing defense expenditures, both of which helped stimulate the economy but also contributed to large budget deficits and a growing national debt.[2] Concern about this "red ink" prompted Congress and Reagan's successor, George H. W. Bush, to agree on a major deficit reduction plan that enhanced revenue, much to the dismay of conservative Republicans, and lowered expenditures. Divisions within the Republican Party combined with another economic downturn to lead to Bush's defeat in the 1992 election.

Despite Clinton and the Democrats' victory in that election, the public mood remained conservative, and confidence in government declined. With the economy still in recession, the budget unbalanced, and federal debt ballooning, another deficit reduction bill, enacted in 1993, cut back further in government spending. Hard hit were popular social programs, such as Head Start for preschoolers and student grants for national service. The president's major initiative to reform national health care died in Congress.

The effort to reduce the size and reach of the federal government still further was accelerated after the Republicans gained control of Congress in 1995. Pursuing the policy objectives in their "Contract with America" to balance the budget; eliminate federal entitlements in welfare, Medicaid, and farm subsidies; and devolve responsibilities for these social needs to the states (initially funding them with a bloc grant), the Republican Congress put the president on the policy defensive. Clinton responded by threatening to veto any bills that shortchanged the educational, environmental, and social programs that his administration and the Democrats strongly supported. Although most of the proposals in the Republican Contract did not become law, a major reform of the welfare system that included new work rules for recipients and limitations on payments did. After vetoing two welfare reform proposals, the president finally approved the legislation, fearing another veto might jeopardize his reelection. The confrontation between a Republican Congress and Democratic president continued over the course of Clinton's second term although the economy improved and budget surpluses replaced deficits.

George W. Bush began his presidency with an agenda that concentrated largely on domestic issues: first and foremost, a large tax cut that reduced government revenue and made the taxing structure less progressive. His proposals to reform education and provide benefits for prescription drugs also became public policy, but the administration's focus shifted to national security after the terrorist attacks on September 11, 2001. Although the president was reelected, his domestic policy initiatives to privatize Social Security, simplify the tax code, and reform immigration policy failed to gain much public or even Republican support. As the administration became mired in the wars in Afghanistan and Iraq, the economy weakened, deficits soared, and the president's popularity sank. A major financial crisis in the fall of 2008 sent the economy into further tailspin and contributed to Barack Obama's victory in the 2008 presidential election.

Responding to the economic emergency, Obama proposed a massive spending bill to stimulate the economy and "invest in America's future" with programs to rebuild the nation's infrastructure, computerize health care records, produce more renewable energy, and provide additional funds for education and mass transit, all of which were achieved without a single Republican vote. But it was the president's proposal to reform health care that generated the most partisan and vocal opposition. Its enactment, along with a tepid economic recovery, persistently high unemployment, low real estate prices, and even larger budget deficits, resulted in a Republican victory in the 2010 midterm elections and a legislative stalemate for the remainder of the president's first term in office.

CAMPAIGNING AND GOVERNING: SETTING POLICY GOALS

The presidential campaign begins the presidential phase of the policy-making process. To get elected, candidates pledge to achieve broad goals and, increasingly, specific policies. Kennedy promised to get the country moving again in 1960; Johnson fashioned much of his Great Society and civil rights legislation from his 1964 campaign; Nixon said that he would bring a divided nation together in 1968 and keep it together in 1972; and Carter, in the aftermath of Watergate, said that his would be an honest, open, and responsive presidency in contrast to the imperial and seemingly corrupt style of his predecessor. In 1980, Reagan urged Americans to return to their traditional values of economic individualism and political freedom; in 1984, he promised to continue his strong leadership at home and abroad. His vice president, George H. W. Bush, said he would continue Republican policies of less government, lower taxes, and maintaining a strong military, but do so "in a kinder and gentler way" than his predecessor. Clinton pledged to stimulate the economy, reduce the deficit, cut middle-class taxes, reform health care, and change welfare "as we know it." Four years later, in 1996, he promised to balance the budget without hurting education, the environment, or the Medicare and Social Security systems.

In 2000, George W. Bush said he would reform education, revitalize the military, cut taxes, and pursue a foreign policy based on U.S. national security interests and democratic values. In 2004, he emphasized the continuing war against terrorism plus domestic priorities that had to be shelved after the 2001 attacks: partial privatization of Social Security, tort reform, tax simplification, and a national energy policy.

In 2008, Barack Obama called for transformational change in policy and politics. He advocated that government serve as a positive force, providing opportunities for those who needed them the most. He also railed against the strident, ideological partisanship that had divided the country since the 1980s. Initially forced to focus on the economy, he relied on his party's partisan advantage in Congress to achieve his policy goals. This reliance undercut his bipartisanship message and further reinforced the partisan divide. It also created wedge issues which worked to the president's and his party's political advantage in the 2012 elections. In that campaign, the president asked for more time to complete the economic recovery and protect middle class interests and values. He elaborated on his policy proposals in his second Inaugural address and the State of the Union message that followed it.

What candidates promise matters because, if elected, they do try to deliver on them. Their campaign promises and their party's platform become the new administration's policy agenda and the criteria by which its success or failure will be initially evaluated. Campaigns also affect governance through the personnel who are recruited for key administration positions. Campaign aides who drafted position papers and policy pronouncements and helped with speech and debate preparation are frequently rewarded with top policy-making jobs in the new administration, jobs that allow them to remain on the winning team and put their ideas for new public policy into practice.

STRUCTURE AND PROCESS

The centralization of policy making in the White House began in the 1960s. The desire of Presidents Kennedy and Johnson to generate new initiatives, combined with their view of the bureaucracy as a pretty conservative place in which innovative ideas were not likely to originate, resulted in a shift of power from the departments and agencies to the Executive Office of the President (EOP).

The Growth of White House Policy Staffs

Kennedy and Johnson set up task forces composed of campaign supporters, academics, and business and labor leaders to investigate problems and devise possible solutions. The large number of task forces forced an expansion in the White House personnel who regularly dealt with domestic policy matters. By the mid-1960s, separate White House staffs had been created in the national security and domestic policy spheres. These staffs were enlarged and institutionalized by President Nixon and have remained active since then.

The influence of these staffs has varied, however, with the operating style and policies goals of presidents. During the administration of Gerald Ford, the White House staff did not play a major role in policy development until the president began his 1976 election campaign; during Carter's presidency, it did. The president depended on his domestic policy advisers to detail the principal legislative initiatives Carter proposed to Congress. Although Ronald Reagan turned to his department secretaries individually and collectively for their advice, he also relied heavily during his first term on his counselor, Edwin Meese, who was charged with coordinating and overseeing the implementation of the president's major domestic initiatives.

During the Clinton and George W. Bush administrations, it was the White House staff that designed legislative proposals in areas of health, education, energy, campaign finance, and electoral reform. However, the personal scandals that plagued the Clinton White House and the declining popularity of Bush during his second term magnified the difficulties both presidents encountered in getting congressional approval.

Barack Obama began his presidency with a flourish of legislative activity. He appointed eight senior aides, whom the press referred to as policy czars, to help him fashion initiatives that cut across agency jurisdictions. Obama's proliferation of White House policy units led to complaints from his department and agency heads that they had been left out of the loop. After the Republican victory in the 2010 midterm elections, the president dismantled some of these staffs and gave greater responsibilities to cabinet secretaries. However, the slow pace of the economic recovery and sizable budget deficits combined with

Republican opposition to new domestic policy initiatives forced him to rely on executive rule making rather than legislation to shape public policy.

The Roles of the Office of Management and Budget

The Bureau of the Budget (BOB), the predecessor to the OMB, was established in 1921 to help the president prepare an annual budget and submit it to Congress. In performing this function, the budget agency annually reviewed requests for funds from the executive departments and agencies. Beginning in the 1930s, this centralized clearance process was extended to include all executive branch requests for legislation, regardless of whether money would be expended. In each case, the budget officials had to decide whether or not the proposal was in accordance with the president's program, consistent with the president's objectives, or at the very least not opposed by the president. Any proposal that conflicted with presidential policy could not be initiated or supported by the departments or agencies.

Legislative Clearance

In making their judgments, the analysts in the BOB relied on presidential campaign statements, major addresses and reports, and special messages to Congress. If the BOB officials were uncertain about the president's program, they would consult with their counterparts in the White House, although such consultation tended to be the exception, not the rule. The BOB's decision was usually final. Although appeals could be made to the president by the departments and agencies, they were not encouraged. The White House wanted the clearance procedure to work, and it did.

In fact, the process worked so well that it was extended to the positions that departments and agencies took on pending legislation and the testimony their officials presented to Congress. Beginning in 1947, standing committees of both legislative bodies requested that the BOB indicate the president's position on any legislation that did not originate in the executive departments and agencies.

From the president's perspective, the central clearance process offered a number of benefits: (1) It provided a mechanism for imprinting a presidential seal of approval on those proposals that the administration supported and withholding it from those it opposed; (2) it made the departments and agencies aware of each other's views; and (3) it helped resolve interagency disputes and promoted internal coordination. For these reasons, central legislative clearance has remained the standard operating procedure for contemporary presidents. It is run by the Office of Management and Budget (OMB), which President Nixon restructured and retitled in 1970 to replace the BOB.

One of the most important functions of the clearance process is the resolution of conflict. Rather than killing a proposal, the OMB removes the objectionable parts and mediates the differences between the agencies. From the department's perspective, however, the clearance requirement is often seen as a constraint and the OMB as the policing agency.

As part of its coordinative role, the OMB also prepares statements of administration policy (SAPs) on most bills approved by congressional committees and awaiting floor consideration. The SAP, which is drafted by the relevant department or agency or occasionally by the OMB, is then coordinated and cleared within the executive branch and approved by White House policy and legislative liaison aides. The purpose of such statements is to inform members of Congress of the administration's position on the legislation with the ultimate goal of influencing congressional deliberations in accordance with the president's policy goals.

Although presidents cannot dictate to Congress, they can usually prevent the enactment of bills they oppose. By threatening a veto if certain provisions are or are not included, presidents exercise leverage with Congress, especially over the content of legislation that needs to be passed, such as appropriations, the reauthorization of popular programs, or bills that certain members of Congress desire. President Clinton used the veto threat very effectively against the Republicans on appropriation bills after the closure of government in the winter of 1995–1996. George W. Bush employed the veto threat in much the same manner against the Democratically-controlled Congress in the last two year of his administration. Throughout his presidency, President Obama threatened to veto any bill that reversed the health care reform legislation enacted in 2010. In his first term, however, he vetoed only two, relatively minor bills, neither of which concerned health care.[3] Veto threats occur less frequently when the president's party controls Congress.

Whereas the OMB formulates the SAP, the president's legislative agents work with the congressional leadership of the president's party to render a veto unnecessary. The OMB takes the lead in lobbying for the president's budget and the appropriations that follow from it, while the Department of the Treasury handles revenue bills for the administration.

Once legislation is enacted, the OMB coordinates the process that advises the president whether to approve or disapprove it, circulating the bill that Congress has enacted to all executive branch units that have been involved in its development, would be involved in its implementation, or have a substantive interest in the legislation. The departments and agencies have forty-eight hours in which to make a recommendation to the president. Their recommendations, accompanied by supporting arguments and frequently by drafts of signing or veto statements, are then summarized by the OMB, which adds a recommendation of its own and sends the entire file to the White House, usually within the first five days of the ten-day period (excluding Sunday) granted to the president by the Constitution to approve or disapprove legislation Congress has passed. A similar process designed to solicit the views of key presidential advisers occurs within the White House. A diagram of the central clearances and enrolled bill processes is shown in Figure 11.1.

With limited time and expertise of their own, presidents usually follow the advice they receive in this clearance process, particularly when there is a consensus among the executive branch agencies. If there is not a consensus, presidents often rely on the OMB and the judgment of the principal agency under whose jurisdiction the implementation of the legislation would fall.

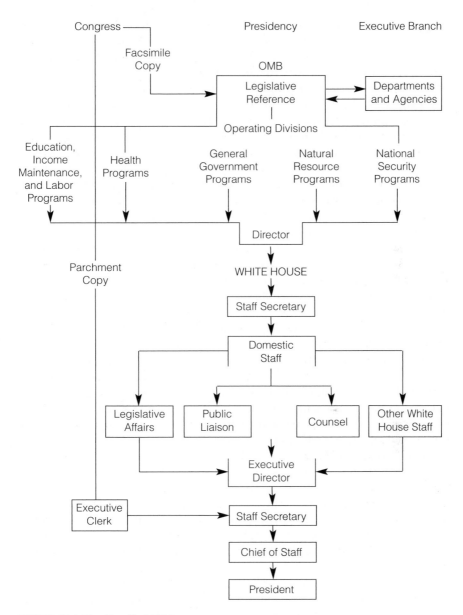

FIGURE 11.1 The Enrolled Bill Process

An OMB recommendation to approve a bill is almost always accepted. As the agency that says "no" most often, its advice to the president to approve legislation seems to be regarded by the White House as an all-clear signal. Conversely, the OMB's advice to veto may be ignored if there is significant political pressure in favor of the legislation.

Regulatory Review

After the president approves legislation, the executive branch departments and agencies are charged with its implementation. They do so by establishing regulations by which the legislative policy is to be put into effect. Here, too, the OMB performs an important clearance function. A presidential regulatory review process was instituted during Reagan's tenure in 1981. In order to decrease the number of federal regulations that federal agencies promulgate to implement public policy, the Reagan administration required that all significant regulations be reviewed by the OMB to make sure that they were necessary, cost effective, and consistent with the goals of the administration. Presidents that have succeeded Reagan have continued this process.[4]

Today, the procedures for reviewing agency regulations begin when executive departments and agencies issue a pending rule. The opinions of nongovernmental groups that would be affected by the rule are then solicited. On the basis of their opinions and recommendations, the agencies initiating the regulation refine it and submit it to the OMB for its review. In support of their proposed regulation, federal agencies must provide quantitative data that estimates its costs and benefits.

The regulatory review process has increased the OMB's influence at the expense of the rest of the executive branch as well as that of Congress. It circumvents the "iron triangle" relationship that had traditionally existed among the executive branch agencies, the congressional committees that oversee them, and outside interest groups. Regulatory review puts the OMB in a position to negate or modify the political compromises that may have been made among these parties. Working behind the scenes, the OMB has become the presidency's principal naysayer, coordinator, and management overseer of the executive branch departments and agencies.

Executive Orders

Another increasingly important function of the OMB is reviewing executive orders prior to their promulgation by the president. It is the OMB's job to make sure that the orders conform to legal precedent, do not violate constitutional or statutory law, and fall within the scope of the president's executive authority. The specifics of the orders are usually drafted by the department or agency with the most policy expertise on the matter—the same executives that will be charged with implementing them.

Here, too, the OMB's decisions are final. Appeals to the president to reject these decisions are discouraged, and end runs to Congress by executive departments and agencies are prohibited. Within the OMB, final decisions are made by political appointees in consultation with the White House. The OMB's top officials are housed with the president's policy staffs in the Eisenhower Executive Office Building that is next to the West Wing of the White House.

Organizational Trends

Two structural trends in presidential policy making stand out: power has become more centralized in the White House; and policy is shaped more by
political appointees and not by the civil servants that have the longest tenure,
the most experience, and are likely to have the most specific knowledge of
policy within their areas of expertise. Are these trends good or bad? Some
students of public administration see them as necessary to achieve a more
responsive federal bureaucracy, one that conforms to the judgment of the electorate as expressed in the last presidential election.[5] Others, however, believe
that they lead to a rush to judgment by officials driven more by partisan presidential interests than the merits of sound public policy judgments.[6]

The centralization of power in the White House has reduced the policy-
making role of the president's cabinet. In a top-down system, influential advisers
filter and broker ideas and then funnel them to the president. Their influence
stems primarily from their control over the information and from the analytic
network on which that information rests as well as their access to the president.
The senior advisers tend to be advocates as well as mediators. That presidents
rely on them enhances their status and influence, not only with the president
but also with others who wish to affect the president's policy judgments.

Any policy-making apparatus has its strengths and weaknesses. The centralization of it in the White House is no exception. It enables presidents to
exercise more control over the content, timing, and promotion of their policy
initiatives. They can act quickly and decisively, translate their campaign promises into policy proposals in the manner they desire, and make sure that the
costs of the policy coincide with their budget requests. Moreover, a centralized policy-making process in the White House can minimize the pressures
of Congress, party, and nonparty groups; employ a national perspective rather
than be forced to take parochial interests into account; and make policy decisions that accord with an administration's political beliefs. A centralized system
facilitates an action orientation, can demonstrate a president's leadership skills,
and may provide the president more bargaining leverage with Congress and
others who stand in the way of achieving the administration's policy goals.[7]

But there are often problems associated with moving too quickly, with too
little input from too few sources on too few options. In a constitutional system of separate institutions sharing powers, in a political system with a multi-
plicity of interested groups and organizations, and in a government in which
electoral support must be expanded to convert campaign promises into public
policy, the centralization of policy making often impedes rather than facilitates
successful policy outcomes. According to Andrew Rudalevige, congressional
support is harder to achieve when the formulation of policy is restricted to a
small group within a highly centralized presidency.[8]

There are other difficulties. The information that the president receives may
be incomplete or inaccurate; policy decisions in one area may impact those in
other areas with unintended consequences. Complex policy may be difficult to

explain to a general public. Members of Congress are more sensitive to pressures from their constituencies; they tend to take a narrower perspective than do presidents and their advisers.

The inverse relationship of policy centralization to a successful legislative outcome places contemporary presidents in a dilemma. They can formulate policy they prefer but may not get it through Congress, or they can consider other interests and perspectives that members of Congress bring to the table that may dilute their policy objectives but improve the chances of passage. Presidents must remember that coalition building inside and outside of government is the key to successful legislative outcomes. The need to reach out and promote their policy is what has led contemporary White Houses to place greater emphasis on public relations.

In addition to structure and process, presidents' policy goals and personal styles have also affected policy making. The desire for innovative policy, which was particularly evident during the Kennedy, Johnson, Clinton, and Obama presidencies, spurred the development of new sources for ideas and programs. All four presidents turned to individuals and groups outside the government to supplement the input they received from those inside their administrations. In contrast, the goals of retrenchment and consolidation, which were particularly evident during the Reagan and George W. Bush administrations, turned the focus back to executive officials appointed by the president who shared their administration's ideological and policy perspectives.

STRATEGIES FOR POLICY MAKING

The organizational component is only one aspect of policy making. Presidents obviously need a mechanism to help them design and coordinate their programs, but that mechanism alone cannot ensure the program's success. Policy must be strategically accomplished. External interests must be accommodated, agendas must be artfully constructed and packaged, and long-term national objectives must be maintained despite the persistence of parochial perspectives and short-term goals.

Building a Policy Agenda

The changing institutional and political environment for policy has also affected the content of agendas. In recent presidencies, with the exception of Barack Obama's first two years in office, the scope of these agendas has become more modest. Domestic policies, however, have become more complex, resulting in larger and larger legislative bills.

In the past, agendas tended to be laundry lists of proposals designed to appeal to as broad a segment of electoral supporters as possible. Franklin Roosevelt's New Deal, Truman's Fair Deal, Kennedy's New Frontier, Johnson's

Great Society, and even Nixon's New Federalism programs are examples. The depressed American economy of the 1930s, the increasing social consciousness of the 1960s, and the democratizing of the nomination process in the 1970s all contributed to the demands for a large and diverse policy agenda.

So have the ways in which presidents have formulated their domestic programs. By soliciting proposals from a variety of sources and established interests, presidents have generated multiple pressures on their own programs. The most effective way to deal with these pressures has been to accommodate them in packages that included something for almost everyone.

Although these pressures have persisted and even increased, the president's ability to achieve them has diminished. The environment for new policy initiatives has become more hostile. The population has become less supportive of expansive and expensive government programs. Budgetary constraints combined with divided government in an age of political polarization have increased the hurdles that presidents have to overcome to convert their policy proposals into law.

One consequence of increasing costs and decreasing resources has been the need to limit items, particularly high-cost items, in the domestic agenda, prioritize them more clearly, and cycle them more effectively over the congressional calendar, rather than overwhelming Congress with too many proposals too quickly.[9] Another has been the need to package and promote the proposals in such a way as to maximize their public appeal and minimize their initial political cost. A third imperative for contemporary presidents has been to avoid excessive involvement in the specifics of policy, an involvement that often causes them to lose sight of a broader and longer-term national perspective but also allows them to tailor the program according to their wishes. Excessive delegation has its costs, but involvement also requires time, a commodity in short supply in the White House.

Limiting the Items

Limiting items in their agenda helps presidents set the pace and tone of public debate and frame the issues to their political advantage. It helps them direct public attention to certain presidential activities, thereby contributing to the perception that they are in command. It also enables them to concentrate resources behind their administration's priorities rather than have them dissipated in accordance with numerous wish lists that emanate from the Congress, the executive departments and agencies, and outside groups.[10]

There is, of course, a negative side to limiting the agenda. Some people's expectations will not be realized. For the Reagan administration, it was the social objectives of the conservatives that were largely abandoned; for the succeeding George H. W. Bush administration, it was the fiscal conservatives that lost out. Both Clinton and Obama were criticized by liberal Democrats for compromises that tilted against the needy.[11]

Another problem with limiting the agenda is that legislative defeats will appear to be more serious leadership failures. Clinton was unable to obtain the enactment of two of his three legislative priorities, economic stimulus plan and health care, in his first two years when his own party controlled both house of Congress; similarly, George W. Bush could not persuade Republican legislators to reform Social Security, immigration, and the tax system, three policy priorities he declared after his reelection.

Cycling Legislative Proposals

Another strategic consequence of the increased costs of domestic policy making is that an administration's priorities must be cycled over the course of the congressional calendar. Presidents cannot wait several months before making their initial proposals, nor should they inundate Congress with them all at once.

Moving quickly on the most controversial items is important for several reasons. Electoral cycles, department pressures, and public moods tend to decrease presidential influence over time. As members of Congress position themselves for the next election, as bureaucrats and their clientele begin to assert their claims on political appointees, as segments of the winning electoral coalition become disillusioned, and as the out party begins to coalesce around an opposing candidate, it is more difficult for a president to achieve domestic policy goals.

There tends to be a honeymoon period when a new president takes office in which partisan opposition may be muted or silenced. Presidents need to take advantage of whatever good feelings and cooperative attitudes are extended toward the new administration because they probably will not last.[12]

But moving too quickly, failing to consider other factors that may impact on the policy decision or not considering the opinions of a broad range of groups and individuals can generate problems with the policy solution not being acceptable to those who were not consulted yet may be directly affected by the proposal.

Reputations are built early and tend to persist longer than does a president's ability to achieve successful policy outcomes. Carter found this out the hard way. He used his first six months in office to design policies to implement his election promises. By the time these proposals were readied for Congress, his honeymoon had ended and his policies got stuck in a legislative labyrinth. Many were not enacted.

The same thing happened to Clinton during his first two years in office. He delayed his health care proposal until September 1993 to avoid overwhelming Congress with too many complex issues too soon. He did not want to dilute his administration's efforts to get its deficit reduction plan through Congress. But when health care was introduced, it consumed the congressional agenda, delaying consideration of other administration initiatives. And when it failed, there was insufficient time and the president had insufficient clout to deal effectively with other measures. His party suffered accordingly in the 1994 midterm elections.

In contrast, the Reagan and George W. Bush administrations had their agendas in place prior to taking office. Seizing on his unexpectedly large electoral victory in 1980, Reagan claimed a mandate for his economic program and then moved quickly and successfully to obtain its enactment. As president-elect, Barack Obama used the economic crisis and momentum from his election to urge congressional Democrats to vote for the release of the second stage of bail-out funds in 2008 and to speed passage of the American Recovery and Reinvestment Act as well as other economic and social legislation in 2009 and 2010. Once the political climate changed with Obama party's defeat losses in the 2010 midterm elections, he was much less active in the legislative arena.

The dilemma presidents often face is that their influence tends to be greatest when their knowledge of substantive policy issues is least. According to Paul Light, declining influence requires presidents to look for available alternatives among existing options and take the first acceptable one.[13] There is a danger here as well: the danger that incomplete information, inexperience, and incompetence can produce.

Haste can also make waste, as Obama found out with his stimulus package. There were not sufficient "shovel ready" projects on which to spend, not enough time for competitive bidding to occur, and difficulty in targeting projects to areas in which unemployment was highest. These factors reduced the impact of the policy and generated criticism from its conservative opponents.

Administrations needed to take advantage of items that have been under consideration for some time, especially items carried over from one legislative calendar to the next. Backing proposals that already have garnered support in Congress and with the general public can enhance an administration's early legislative record and reputation, although it obviously limits a president's personal impact on this legislation and the credit received from its enactment. Thus President Obama backed the Children's Health Insurance Reauthorization Act, and Clinton supported legislation requiring employers to provide for parental leave, helping states to ease voter registration procedures, and permitting federal workers to become more involved in political activities, all bills that their predecessors had vetoed.

In short, the opportunities for quick victories, the need to redeem campaign promises and platform planks, and the desire to placate groups in Congress that have supported certain legislative initiatives in the past are inducements for presidents to pursue programs that have been percolating certain legislative initiatives for some time. Political scientist Charles O. Jones contends that the greater the congruity between the president's agenda and that of Congress, the more likely a president can gain major legislative successes.[14] The elections of 1964, 1980, and 2008 all generated strong legislative congruity with the president, setting the stage for significant policy achievements in the first two years of the Johnson, Reagan, and Obama administrations.

Presidential discretion also varies with the policy time frame. Presidents tend to have more discretion on long-term issues than short-term ones.[15] They have more leeway when they replace a president of the opposite party than when they succeed one of their own.

Packaging and Promoting Legislative Priorities

It is necessary for administrations to prioritize items in their legislative agenda and package them artfully in the context of the political environment in which they find themselves. Presenting a few key proposals rather than a comprehensive list of them reduces the task of coalition building, but it may also disappoint individuals and groups whose pet projects are not included. Similarly, presenting presidential initiatives as either/or propositions may lessen the chances that they will be modified, but it also may increase their chances for defeat.

The Reagan, Clinton, and George W. Bush experiences are instructive here. In 1981, Reagan presented Congress with a "take it or leave it" budget reconciliation plan. In 2001, Bush also stood firm on his budget and tax proposals, but Clinton did not. In 1993, he gave the Democratic Congress a third option, declaring that if legislators did not like his proposed combination of spending cuts and tax increases in his deficit reduction plan, they could change them. They did, jettisoning the president's proposed energy tax and increasing cuts in his domestic spending priorities. Moreover, Clinton's willingness to accept changes encouraged members of Congress to bargain with him; the Reagan and Bush strategy discouraged bargaining.

The Obama administration worked with Democratic leaders in Congress to minimize changes in the president's first budget by using the reconciliation process to reduce the number of votes needed in the Senate for passage. Such a procedure helped the president achieve health care reform, but it also reduced the influence he had in shaping the final legislative package.

The fewer the roll-call votes on a legislative proposal, the easier it is for a president to concentrate resources and mobilize a winning coalition. Reagan successfully pursued this strategy in his 1981 and 1982 budget battles with the Democrats in Congress. The packaging of a large personal and corporate income tax cut in 1981, a Social Security compromise in 1983, and a tax reform program in 1986 were critical to the enactment of each of these proposals in the form and with the speed that the president desired.

One of the reasons why the Reagan administration was so effective was the president's ability to promote his priorities within the Congress and among the general public simultaneously. To gain congressional support, it is necessary for the White House to convince members of Congress that the president's proposals are supported by their constituents. Generating a constituency-based response on the basis of a prime-time television appeal or massive Internet communication are ways to achieve that objective. Showing an economic benefit for a particular area, group, or electoral constituency is another. Evidencing political muscle and implicitly holding out the possibility of retribution from the voters is a third.

Conversely, it may be difficult for a president to explain, much less convince the American people of his policy's merits. Much depends on the time, place, and environment, over which presidents have little control. Presidents Bill Clinton and George W. Bush each conducted large-scale public relations campaigns for their health care and Social Security proposals but were unsuccessful. President Obama was unable to persuade a plurality of Americans to support the health care legislation Congress was considering.[16] Nonetheless, he was successful in getting it enacted because of his party's large partisan majority and because its electoral base strongly supported the legislation.[17]

Professor Matthew W. Beckman contends that presidents must engage congressional leaders early to move their legislation forward.[18] In studying presidentially initiated domestic policy proposals from 1953 to 2004, Beckman found that presidents that lobbied for their initiatives were twice as likely to get bills they supported than those that did not.[19] President Obama's hands-on approach to health care reform supports Beckman's thesis.

BOX 11.1 THE PRESIDENCY IN ACTION: OBAMA'S LOBBYING ON HEALTH CARE REFORM

On the evening of January 19, 2010, well before the actual results of the Massachusetts special election to fill the late Ted Kennedy's Senate seat, President Obama met with House Speaker Nancy Pelosi and Senate Majority Leader Harry Reid at the White House. The topic was health care or, more precisely, what to do about it in the light of the political defeats the Democrats had suffered in the gubernatorial elections of 2009 and in Massachusetts. Pelosi and Reid each had built a majority and enacted legislation only to find themselves and their partisan supporters at odds with the other house's bill. They were dispirited, and the president was frustrated. Not only had Obama's legislative strategy not produced the desired outcome, but Democrats were questioning his resolve, specifically his failure to take charge and twist the arms of members of Congress. Some of the president's advisers believed that the White House had delegated too much of the bill-drafting responsibility; his chief of staff, Rahm Emmanuel, was urging restraint and recommending that Obama reopen the health care packages, salvaging what he could from them. But the president did not want to give up when he had gotten so close. He had told his cabinet in January that he was on the two-yard line and did not intend to settle for a field goal.

Obama was scheduled to attend a House Republican caucus in Baltimore at the end of January, part of which was to be televised. By most accounts, the president did well debating his opponents on health care, so well that he scheduled a bipartisan White House summit on health care several weeks later to keep the initiative alive, much to the dismay of Democrats who saw little hope of achieving acceptable compromises with the Republicans.

The event, held at the Blair House across the street from the White House, lasted seven hours and attracted media attention. Although the president accepted about twenty GOP suggestions, he won no converts. But the meeting energized him. A proposed rate hike of 40 percent by Anthem Blue Cross in California also gave him a concrete example to explain why the status quo was unacceptable.

Stimulated by his own rhetoric and by polls showing some shift in public sentiment, Obama, congressional leaders, and lobbyists representing groups that favored the legislation—labor unions, the pharmaceutical

(continued)

(continued)

industry, the AARP, and Moveon. Org—began to work Capitol Hill. They identified reluctant and on-the-fence Democrats, mounted a $6 million advertising campaign directed at these representatives' electoral constituencies, and organized an outreach effort in which prominent constituents were urged to contact their representatives to support the legislation.[20]

The president himself met or spoke with sixty-four members of the House in the month following the White House summit. To conservative "Blue Dog" Democrats, he emphasized the deficit savings that the Congressional Budget Office said the legislation would produce; to the liberals, he warned of the political damage that a health care defeat would wreak on their other priorities as well as their party in the midterm elections of 2010.[21]

During his campaign, Obama's most important convert was Dennis Kucinich (D-Ohio), a liberal activist unhappy with the absence of a government insurance option in the Senate plan. Obama convinced him on a flight on Air Force One from Washington, D.C., to his congressional district in Cleveland, Ohio, to support a compromise with the Senate. Kucinich's backing led others to join the bandwagon. Momentum was shifting among Democrats to support the Senate bill and then modify it by using the reconciliation process in which only a simply Senate majority was required. There was little Republicans could do but cry foul and threaten retaliation at the polls. Congressional Republicans had used similar procedures when their party controlled Congress during the Bush administration.

Obama, his cohorts, and Speaker Pelosi snatched victory from defeat.[22] The president had gotten personally involved, albeit late in the game, and showed what hands-on lobbying could achieve. Health care reform was enacted, although public opinion on the merits of the legislation did not change and the Democrats suffered a major defeat in the 2010 midterm elections. But President Obama achieved his policy objectives and what he hoped would become a major part of his presidential legacy.

The inside and outside lobbying efforts should be synchronized with each other, taking into account the time frame in which Congress is considering the legislation. During the committee stage, White House orchestration of interest group support is vital; if the legislation reaches the floor, a broader public campaign may be necessary. The key is to direct public support where it will do the most good. Mails, e-mails, telephone calls, and personal visits from prominent citizens, contributors, interest group representatives, and company executives and union leaders can be effective if they demonstrate constituency preferences or the economic impact the legislation would have on that member's electoral base.

Discerning the Forest from the Trees

Constraints on time and energy suggest another lesson for contemporary presidents. They should not involve themselves too deeply in the details of policy making, although they need to provide general guidance. Jimmy Carter is a case in point. Finding it difficult to delegate to others, he spent considerable time becoming an expert on the various policy issues in which he was interested or that came to his attention. At the beginning of his administration, he read upward of 400 pages of papers and memos a day![23] Bill Clinton evidenced similar involvement in the policy specifics as well as mid-level personnel selections.

In contrast to Carter and Clinton, Reagan and George W. Bush left most of the policy-making details to their senior White House aides, cabinet officials, and Republican leaders in Congress. This practice exposed them to the charge that they were overly dependent on others for the decisions they had to make, the time frame in which they had to make them, and the range of options from which they had to choose; but they could also shift some blame to staff aides if parts of the policy were ill-conceived or controversial, whereas Carter and Clinton had more difficulty doing so.

Obama's decision-making style is to encourage a diversity of perspectives, have his advisers debate policy options, ask tough questions throughout the process, and then make the final judgment. But he also delegates a lot of the day-to-day negotiations with Congress to his White House aides and desires congressional leaders to work out the necessary compromises on legislation. As a consequence, he is stuck with the final product they produce.

Sustaining a National Perspective

Reagan's ideological perspective helped him tackle another policy-making problem that often besets contemporary presidents: how to sustain a national perspective in the light of continuous parochial pressures that are exerted on almost every policy issue. A strong, consistent ideological orientation provides rationale for including (and excluding) certain items in a policy agenda and linking them to one another in a way that makes sense to partisan supporters. It helps transform an electoral coalition into a policy coalition. It is also useful in overcoming tendencies that frequently lead executive branch officials to advocate interests that may be at variance with the president's.

The Reagan and George W. Bush administrations employed ideology in converting electoral promises into tangible goals. They also used ideology as a criterion for appointment. Cabinet and subcabinet officials were nominated in part because they shared the president's political and policy views. They were expected to impose those views on the agencies in which they worked.

Ideology, or a set of coherent policy views, in short, can be a unifying tool. It can build support by simplifying and focusing. It can also give people a sense of where the president is coming from and going to. But ideology is not without its limits. Rigid adherence to a certain perspective or issue position makes compromise difficult. As it unifies supporters, so too can it unify opponents, polarize the political environment, and inhibit compromise. The budget debates between Clinton and the Republican Congress in 1995–1996 and between Obama and a divided Congress between 2011-2013 provide examples of two sides digging in their heels and extending decision making to the brink—and in Clinton's case, beyond it, when the government was forced to close not once but twice.

The absence of an overarching policy framework can also produce problems. Critics have contended that policy inconsistencies in the Carter administration were due in part to this dilemma. As James Fallows, a former Carter speechwriter, observed:

> I came to think that Carter believes fifty things, but no one thing. He holds explicit, thorough positions on every issue under the sun, but he has no large view of the relations between them, no line indicating which goals (reducing unemployment? human rights?) will take precedence over which (inflation control? a SALT [Strategic Arms Limitation Talks] treaty?) when the goals conflict.[24]

The same criticism was directed at Clinton, especially during his first two years in office, and at Obama by members of their own party.

Maintaining a Long-Range View

Another problem related to policy consistency is maintaining a long-range perspective. In making policy, everyday emergencies tend to drive out long-term planning, thereby restricting the outlook of those involved in policy making to the short term and rarely beyond the next election.

Contemporary White Houses have attempted from time to time to design a longer-range domestic planning capability, but usually without much success. In 1975, President Ford asked Vice President Rockefeller to provide leadership and direction for the establishment of social goals. However, Rockefeller's decision not to run for office one year later abruptly ended that effort. The Reagan administration created a long-range policy-making unit in the White House, but it lasted only two years. The administration of George W. Bush was initially guided by a strategic plan designed by his principal political adviser, Karl Rove. Early on, however, the administration had to confront a variety of unexpected events that created more pressing goals and necessitated new strategies for accomplishing them.

Accommodating External Forces

Initiating a policy agenda is only half the battle; transforming it into public policy is the other. To achieve this objective, presidents need to convert their electoral coalition into a governing majority and do so on an issue-by-issue basis.

Changes within the political and institutional environment have increased the difficulty of accomplishing this task. The decentralization of power in Congress, the growth of single-issue groups, the partisan rhetoric and ideological polarization that has dominated Congress since the 1990s, and divided government for much of this period have created additional hurdles for presidents and required them to be more sensitive to outside interests and devote more personal and institutional resources to coalescing these interests into governing coalitions.

Since the 1970s, an increasing number of groups have tried to influence the formulation and execution of public policy. Seeing allies as well as opponents among these groups, presidents began to mobilize organized interests in support of their policy objectives. In doing so, they invited interest group and community leaders to the White House for policy briefings. A separate office, public liaison, was set up in 1978 to lobby the lobbyists. Initially, this office functioned as a conduit, providing White House access to those outside the government and public relations opportunities for presidents to promote their policy agendas. This practice has continued despite negative public perceptions of special interest politics. Contemporary presidents have also criticized these sources of influence peddling yet have been forced to deal with them, as Obama did on health care reform.

The expansion of group representatives in Washington and their involvement in a range of issues has forced contemporary White Houses to devote considerable time, energy, and staff to interest group persuasion and coordination. One potentially pernicious effect of the expansion of presidential–interest group relations has been the extension of "revolving-door politics"—the practice of public officials leaving the government, obtaining jobs in the private sector, and cashing in on their political connections and know-how. A relatively large percentage of interest group leaders have been former members and staff of Congress, the White House, or the departments and agencies. Naturally, they use their experience in government to further the interests of the groups they for whom they work in the private sector. If they return to government, their impartiality in matters that affect those groups is likely to be challenged.

To minimize conflicts of interest among current and former government officials, Congress enacted legislation to prohibit former government officials from working on any issue in the private sector in which they were involved in government. The law also imposes a one-year moratorium on contacts by ex-government executives as lobbyists with the government office in which they worked. The Obama administration increased the moratorium to two years. Obama prohibited members of his staff from working on matters they had previously lobbied on or from approaching agencies that they once targeted.

But these prohibitions have not stopped revolving-door politics; they have not prevented former government officials from advising clients and others on the basis of their experience and personal contacts, nor have they prevented them from enriching themselves after they have left office.[25]

The particular strategies presidents have used to interact with interest groups have varied with their administrations' goals. According to Mark Peterson, who has studied the White House–interest group connection, Franklin Roosevelt mobilized groups to support his program; Lyndon Johnson was more concerned with building a broad-based public consensus; and Jimmy Carter at first reached out to those who lacked effective representation but later toward groups that could more effectively help him get his proposals through Congress. The Reagan administration appealed to both sympathetic and unsympathetic groups in order to cast the president in a more favorable light and to meet expectations of greater access to the administration and service from it.[26]

Bill Clinton had mixed success in getting outside groups to support his policies. In the arena of international trade, his administration worked closely with business lobbyists to pressure Congress to support the North American Free Trade Agreement (NAFTA); in the health care sphere, however, interest groups helped to stall and eventually kill the administration's proposal. The exclusion of prominent medical groups from the task forces that formulated the plan, the attacks against the insurance and pharmaceutical industries by Hillary Rodham Clinton and other senior officials, and the inability of the White House to coordinate an inside-the-Beltway coalition of lobbyists as it did for NAFTA led to the demise of its health care reform.[27]

President George W. Bush also tried to mobilize sympathetic groups behind his administration's energy proposals, faith-based initiatives, and war in Iraq. He was successful in doing so during his first term but much less so during his second, when many groups tried to distance themselves from an increasingly unpopular president and unpopular war.

Barack Obama began his first term by inviting suggestions from individuals and groups around the country on the substance and scope of his policy initiatives. During the transition, his advisers established a website to solicit opinions and recommendations on major policy issues. In designing the principal components of its legislative package on health care, the administration reached out to health care groups directly through their Washington representation. Deals were made with the pharmaceutical industry and hospital associations. In return for their support of the president's reform initiative, the pharmaceutical industry was promised that the administration would continue to oppose the importation of prescription drugs and would not use Medicare to bargain for lower prices. Similarly, the hospitals were told that government subsidies would continue. These decisions were approved by a president who had campaigned against special interest politics in 2008 and who initially said that his administration would not hire former and current lobbyists.

The Obama administration's attempt to convert its campaign organization into an effective governing organization also was not successful. Despite maintaining a website for the new group, Organizing for America, the White House was unable to turn out policy supporters as it had during the 2008 election campaign despite e-mail correspondence, online press conferences, and the use of Twitter, Facebook, and other noteworthy popular sites. It changed the name to Organizing for Action, and updated the files of this group in the second term.

CONCLUSION

Presidents have become national policy makers. This role developed primarily in the twentieth century and evolved largely as a consequence of social, economic, and political problems that required solutions by the federal government. With a national perspective, a large staff structure, and the ability to focus public attention and mobilize support, presidents have been placed in the position in which they can initiate policies and then use their institutional and personal resources to get them adopted. The electoral process has provided them with further incentives to do so. Congress, the executive branch, and the public frequently look to them for leadership.

The mechanism for presidential policy making has taken form since the middle of the twentieth century. Once the EOP was created in 1939, a unit within it, then known as the Bureau of the Budget provided the resources and managed the executive branch's decision-making processes, with its senior civil servants working closely with the White House to develop, coordinate, and clear initiatives emanating from the departments and agencies. As presidents turned from departments and agencies to other sources for policy ideas, a two-track programming system evolved, with the White House on the top tier and the departments and agencies on the secondary one.

The president's chief policy aides began to dominate the process. They, in turn, depended on political appointees in the OMB and the civil servants that worked for them to monitor and integrate the input of the executive branch agencies. The White House became the focal point for building support for these priorities. These developments have enhanced the institutional presidency's influence but not necessarily that of individual presidents, who have become increasingly dependent on their staff for deciding when they should become involved, what options they should consider, and how those options should be presented, articulated, and promoted, both within and outside the government.

Competing demands, complex issues, and confrontational politics have made domestic policy making more difficult. Performance expectations exceed the presidency's institutional resources most of the time. Presidents cannot dictate policy outcomes, but they can affect them through their policy-making strategies.

To exert leadership today, presidents must limit their priorities, cycle and carefully package their issues, establish and maintain a long-term national perspective, and move quickly when they have the greatest strategic advantage, political capital, and public support, usually at the beginning of their terms in office. It important that they develop and move key parts of their legislative agenda early not only because their chances for legislative success are better but also because early successes enhance presidents' reputations and increase their political capital for subsequent policy battles.

Public relations has become an important component of domestic policy making. An administration must accommodate external forces and mobilize them into a policy coalition. It must also generate support at the grassroots level because members of Congress respond more to their political constituencies than to a generic presidential appeal. All of this effort requires a substantial policy-building structure in the White House and effective communications from and to that White House.

These tasks are not easy. They are time-consuming, labor intensive, and fraught with danger; particularly if an opposition mobilizes, the public loses focus, and the president raises the stakes by going public.

The diversity of interests within the domestic arena, the impact that domestic policy has on society, and the intensity with which groups fight for their economic and social interests usually make domestic policy making more difficult than foreign policy making for presidents. Domestic policy making tends to be more partisan, requires more compromise, and has shorter-term political con-sequences. These difficulties create incentives over time for presidents to find other ways and other arenas in which to enhance their leadership image.

Discussion Questions

1. What are the principal limitations on a president's ability to set a domestic policy agenda? Discuss these limitations and indicate their impact on recent presidencies.

2. Describe the institutional mechanisms and practices that have been developed to help presidents perform their policy-making role. Do they enhance or reduce the president's personal influence?

3. Every president tries to leave an imprint on the nation; Ronald Reagan, Bill Clinton, George W. Bush, and Barack Obama are no exceptions. Discuss their domestic policy legacies. Which of these presidents do you think has or will have left a more enduring legacy? Briefly explain your answer.

 ## Web Exercises

1. Go to the White House website at http://www.whitehouse.gov. Indicate the principal policy positions the president has taken on recent issues and the ways in which he has tried to gain public attention and support for these positions (via his announcements, meetings, press conferences, ceremonies, and especially travels).

2. Go to the White House website and access the president's inaugural address or his last State of the Union address. From the address, list the president's principal domestic priorities. Then search the White House and congres-sional websites (http://thomas.loc.gov) to see which of them have been proposed as legislation and which of those have been enacted, defeated, or are still pending? Which priorities has the president tried to implement through executive authority?

3. Go to the OMB website at http://www.whitehouse.gov/omb and discern the president's position on legislation introduced by members of Congress from your home state. Then follow the legislation as it goes through the House and Senate: http://www.house.gov and http://www.senate.gov. Do you think that the president's position will have anything to do with the success or failure of the bill?

Selected Readings

Beckman, Matthew N. *Pushing the Agenda: Presidential Leadership in U.S. Lawmaking, 1953–2004.* Cambridge, UK: Cambridge University Press, 2010.

Bush, George W. *Decision Points.* New York: Random House, 2010.

Cohen, Jeffrey E. *Presidential Responsiveness and Public Policy Making: The Publics and the Policies That Presidents Choose.*

Ann Arbor: University of Michigan Press, 1997.

Dickinson, Matthew. "Agenda and Unilateral Action: New Insights on Presidential Power." *Congress and the Presidency* 31 (Spring 2004): 99–109.

Edwards, George C., III. *The Strategic Presidency*. Princeton, NJ: Princeton University Press, 2009.

Edwards, George C., III, and Andrew Barrett, "Presidential Agenda Setting in Congress." In *Polarized Politics*, edited by Jon R. Bond and Richard Fleisher. Washington, DC: Congressional Quarterly, 2000, pp. 109–133.

Foreman, Christopher H., Jr. "Ambition, Necessity, and Polarization in the Obama Domestic Agenda." In *The Obama Presidency: Appraisals and Prospects*, edited by Colin Campbell, Bert A. Rockman, and Andrew Rudalevige. Washington DC: CQ Press, 2012, pp. 244–267.

Graham, John D. *Bush on the Home Front*. Bloomington, IN: Indiana University Press, 2010.

Jacobs, Lawrence R. "The Privileges of Access: Interest Groups and the White House." In *The Obama Presidency: Appraisals and Prospects*, edited by Colin Campbell, Bert A. Rockman, and Andrew Rudalevige. Washington DC: CQ Press, 2012, pp.149–170.

Jacobs, Lawrence R., and Theda Skocpol. *Health Reform and American Politics*. New York: Oxford University Press, 2010.

Light, Paul C. *The President's Agenda: Domestic Policy Choice from Kennedy to Clinton*. Baltimore, MD: Johns Hopkins University Press, 1999.

Peterson, Mark A. "The Presidency and Organized Interests: White House Patterns of Interest Group Liaison." *American Political Science Review* 86 (September 1992): 612–625.

Rudalevige, Andrew. *Managing the President's Program*. Princeton, NJ: Princeton University Press, 2002.

_____. "Rivals or a Team? Staffing and Issue Management in the Obama Administration." In *The Obama Presidency: Appraisals and Prospects*, edited by Colin Campbell, Bert A. Rockman, and Andrew Rudalevige. Washington DC: CQ Press, 2012, pp. 171–197.

Sinclair, Barbara. *Party Wars: Polarization and the Politics of National Policy Making*. Norman, OK: University of Oklahoma, 2006.

Warshaw, Shirley Anne. *The Domestic Presidency: Policy Making in the White House*. Boston: Allyn and Bacon, 1997.

Wayne, Stephen J. *The Legislative Presidency*. New York: Harper and Row, 1978.

Notes

1. Richard E. Neustadt, "Presidency and Legislation: Planning the President's Program," *American Political Science Review* 49 (December 1955): 1015.

2. Democrats contended that the real design of these budget policies was to ensure that there would not be sufficient funds available to launch new domestic policy initiatives after Reagan left office.

3. One was a bill that appropriated money for Congress to operate before other appropriations that funded the government were enacted. The other was legislation on notarization of legal documents by states after information became public that lenders had been circumventing legal procedures on foreclosure documents.

4. Significant was defined as any regulation that had an annual cumulative effect on the economy of $1 million or more.

5. Terry M. Moe, "The Politicized Presidency," in John Chubb and Paul E. Peterson, eds., *New Directions in American Politics* (Washington, DC: Brookings Institution, 1985), pp. 235–271.

6. David E. Lewis, *The Politics of Presidential Appointments* (Princeton, NJ: Princeton University Press, 2008), pp. 202–219.

7. Presidents who lack leverage with the public are more apt to centralize policy

making than those who have broad-based public support for the initiatives they are promoting. Daniel E. Ponder, "Presidential Leverage and the Politics of Policy Formulation," *Presidential Studies Quarterly* 42 (June 2012): 301, 317.

8. Andrew Rudalevige, *Managing the President's Program* (Princeton, NJ: Princeton University Press, 2002), p. 114.

9. Paul C. Light, *The President's Agenda* (Baltimore, MD: Johns Hopkins University Press, 1982), p. 217.

10. As mentioned in Chapter 9, presidents can usually get Congress to consider their legislative policy requests but have less success in getting them enacted into law. See George C. Edwards III and Andrew Barrett, "Presidential Agenda Setting in Congress," in Jon R. Bond and Richard Fleisher, eds., *Polarized Politics* (Washington, DC: CQ Press, 2000), pp. 265–287.

11. Clinton's approval of welfare reform that increased work requirements and reduced the period during which people could receive benefits was strongly opposed by liberal Democrats. Obama's openness to Medicare and Social Security reform and his concessions tax increases for the wealthy also incurred Democratic wrath.

12. Matthew N. Beckman and Joseph Godfrey, "The Policy Opportunities in Presidential Honeymoons," *Political Research Quarterly* 60 (June 2007): 250–262.

13. Light, *President's Agenda*, p. 218.

14. Charles O. Jones, "Presidents and Agendas: Who Defines What for Whom?" in James P. Pfiffner, ed., *The Managerial Presidency* (Pacific Grove, CA: Brooks/Cole, 1991), pp. 197–213.

15. Fengyan Shi, "Agenda Setting: What Influence Do Presidents Actually Have?" Paper presented at the annual meeting of the American Political Science Association, Washington, DC, September 1993.

16. "Trends A-Z: Healthcare System," *Gallup Poll*. http://www.gallup.com /poll/4708/healthcare-System.aspx (accessed August 16, 2012).

17. After the House vote, 81 percent of Democrats said that it was a good thing that Congress passed the legislation, while only a minority of Republicans (11 percent) and Independents (43 percent) said it was good. March 29, 2010. Lydia Saad, "One Week Later, Americans Divided on Healthcare," *Gallup Poll*, March 2010. http://www.gallup. com/poll/127025/One-Week-Later-Americans-Divided-Healthcare.aspx.

18. Matthew W. Beckman, *Pushing the Agenda: Presidential Leadership in U.S. Lawmaking, 1953–2004* (Cambridge, UK: Cambridge University Press, 2010), p. 14.

19. Ibid., p. 148.

20. Jonathan Cohn, "How They Did It: The Inside Account of Health Care Reform's Triumph," *New Republic*, June 10, 2010, p. 24.

21. Jeff Zeleny, "Millions Spent to Sway Democrats on Health Care," *New York Times*, March 14, 2010. http://www .nytimes.com/2010/03/15/health /policy/15health.html.

22. Sheryl Gay Stolberg, Jeff Zeleny, and Carl Hulse, "Health Vote Caps a Journey Back from the Brink," *New York Times*, March 20, 2010. http://www .nytimes.com/2010/03/21/health /policy/21reconstruct.html.

23. James Fallows, a former Carter speechwriter, described his boss as "the perfectionist accustomed to thinking that to do a job right you must do it yourself." Fallows illustrated his point:

> He [Carter] would leave for a weekend at Camp David laden with thick briefing books, would pore over budget tables to check the arithmetic, and during his first six months in office, would personally review all requests to use the White House tennis court. ... After six months had passed, Carter learned that this was ridiculous, as he learned about other details he would have to pass by if he was to use his time well. But his preference was still to try to do it all.

James Fallows, "The Passionless Presidency," *Atlantic Monthly*, May 1979, p. 38.

24. Ibid., p. 42.

25. Graham K. Wilson, "The Clinton Administration and Interest Groups," in

Colin Campbell and Bert A. Rockman, eds., *The Clinton Presidency: First Appraisals* (Chatham, NJ: Chatham House, 1996), pp. 225–230.

26. Mark A. Peterson, "The Presidency and Organized Interests: White House Patterns of Interest Group Liaison," *American Political Science Review* 86 (September 1992): 612–616.

27. Haynes Johnson and David Broder, *The System* (Boston: Little, Brown, 1996); Lawrence R. Jacobs and Robert Y. Shapiro, *Politicians Don't Pander: Political Manipulation and the Loss of Democratic Responsiveness* (Chicago: University of Chicago Press, 2000).

12

BUDGETARY
AND ECONOMIC
POLICY MAKING

Presidents have always been concerned about the costs of government
and the state of the economy, but that concern has never been greater
than it is today. With a budget of approaching $4 trillion; with a national
debt of almost $17 trillion and growing; with much of that debt currently
owed to foreign nationals, companies, and governments; with federal revenues
tied to economic conditions and interest rates; and with the private sector sensitive to public expenditures, particularly when the economy is sluggish, almost
any substantive policy decision a president makes has significant budgetary and
economic implications for the country as a whole as well as important political
consequences.

Moreover, budgetary and economic decisions are interrelated. Budgetary
problems are magnified by a weak economy and diminished by a strong one.
Large and continuing budget and trade deficits can have both long- and short-
term effects on the economy, as can a surplus in either of these accounts.

These factors make budgetary and economic policy making one of the
most critical, complex, and contentious spheres for the exercise of presidential
leadership. Although the president is expected to present a budget, the con-
tents of that budget are shaped by the commitments of past administrations
and Congresses; the obligation to pay interest on the national debt and meet
the statutory requirements of other legislative programs, particularly those that
entitle people to benefits; and the costs of operating the government. Nor can
presidents determine economic policy on their own. Congress enacts laws to
authorize programs, raise revenue, and appropriate funding.

Thus, presidents are expected to meet the country's ever-changing economic needs, but often lack the power to do so. Directing change under these
circumstances is extremely difficult, although it is not impossible, as Franklin
Roosevelt, Ronald Reagan, and Barack Obama demonstrated at the outset of

their presidencies. Nonetheless, being a facilitator rather than a director tends to be the best presidents can do most of the time, at least as far as budget and economic policy making are concerned; and even in the facilitator role, the task is not easy.

THE FEDERAL BUDGET

The budget is a document that forecasts revenue and estimates expenditures of the federal government. It does so for a fiscal year—a twelve-month period beginning October 1 and continuing through the following September 30. The primary purpose of the budget is to allocate limited funds, but that allocation is highly political, as the recent confrontations between the Republicans and Democrats and Congress and the presidency attest.

A Brief History

A presidential budget has been required since 1921. Prior to that time, departments and agencies went directly to Congress for their appropriations. Their requests were compiled in a "Book of Estimates," but neither the president nor the treasury secretary made any systematic attempt to coordinate total revenues, although they exercised oversight of their budget estimates.[1] However, with revenues, primarily from custom duties, exceeding expenditures during most of the nineteenth century, the lack of centralized planning was not perceived to be much of a problem.

Expenditures rose at the end of the century and the beginning of the next, and modest surpluses turned into deficits. Concerned about them, Congress enacted legislation in 1905 to ensure that the government spent money more prudently. It gave the president the statutory responsibility and authority to prevent unwise and unnecessary expenditures.[2] The costs of World War I, however, vastly increased federal government spending, produced sizable budgetary deficits, and led Congress to enlarge the president's budgetary responsibilities to improve efficiencies and control spending.[3]

The Budget and Accounting Act of 1921 required the president to present an annual executive branch budget. The legislation also established a bureau within the Department of the Treasury to handle these new administrative responsibilities. Acting as a surrogate for the president, the Bureau of the Budget (BOB) organized and ran a process that solicited yearly expenditure estimates from the departments and agencies, evaluated and adjusted them according to the president's policy goals, and combined them into a comprehensive executive budget. Departments and agencies were prohibited from submitting their financial requests directly to Congress unless specifically requested to do so. An office, now known as the General Accountability Office (GAO), was created to help Congress oversee the executive branch's expenditure of appropriated monies. This budget process cycle has continued through the years, although the budget itself and Congress's consideration of it have changed dramatically.

In its early years, the president's budget was relatively small by contemporary standards, oriented toward the executive agencies, and utilized primarily as a vehicle for consolidating government spending.[4] Before the 1930s, most of the money went directly to the departments and agencies for the costs of running the government. There were relatively few public works projects that required additional funding.

The Great Depression of the 1930s had a major effect on the budget, increasing demands for government services. Franklin Roosevelt responded to these demands by proposing a series of programs that provided jobs, helped protect savings, and in 1937, led to the creation of the Social Security system.

Followed by World War II and the cold war with the Soviet Union, the government's spending in domestic and defense areas continued to increase as new entitlement programs, Medicare and Medicaid, were enacted into law. These programs consumed an ever-increasing proportion of government expenditures and were not subject to presidential control. They legally entitle people to benefits as long as they meet eligibility requirements (for example, age for Social Security and Medicare, income for Medicaid, or military service for veterans' benefits). These entitlements are independent of specific appropriations by Congress. In 1974, Congress decided to peg Social Security payments to the Consumer Price Index, thereby removing decisions even on the levels of benefits. It requires an act of Congress to change the payments.[5]

Even within the so-called discretionary part of the budget—that is, the part of the budget for which annual appropriations are necessary—many of the expenditures are for big-ticket items, such as the salaries and benefits for civil servants and military personnel, scientific research, development and production of intelligence and national security processes and highly sophisticated communication systems, defense weapons and material, and government construction projects, items that cannot be reduced or eliminated without basic changes in policy and/or significant cost to the taxpayer if design and production are already underway. These annual needs and entitlement programs have left presidents with discretion only over a relatively small portion of the total budget, a little more than one-third of it.

Instead of primarily affecting departments and agencies, the budget now has a direct impact on many people and groups outside the government. As a consequence, constituencies composed of veterans, senior citizens, industry representatives, labor, and others have organized to protect and extend their benefits. The pressures they exert also reduce the range of acceptable options for those in power.

The regular involvement of interest groups on budgetary politics has made it more difficult for the president and Congress to use the budget as a device for controlling spending. By the late 1970s, the budget demonstrated more of the presidency's weaknesses than its strengths; presidents were responsible for most of it yet controlled only part of it.

In the 1980s, the primary objective of presidential budgeting began to change. Seeds of this change were sown in the economic problems of the previous decade: the decline in the nation's productivity and its industrial

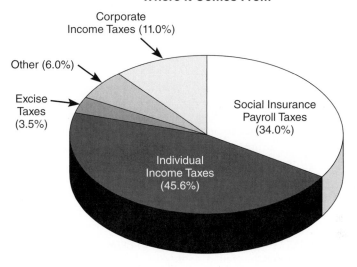

Where It Comes From

Corporate
Income Taxes (11.0%)

Other (6.0%)

Excise
Taxes
(3.5%)

Social Insurance
Payroll Taxes
(34.0%)

Individual
Income Taxes
(45.6%)

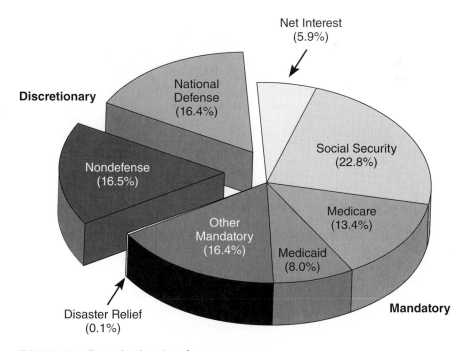

Where It Goes

Net Interest
(5.9%)

Discretionary

National
Defense
(16.4%)

Social Security
(22.8%)

Nondefense
(16.5%)

Other
Mandatory
(16.4%)

Medicare
(13.4%)

Medicaid
(8.0%)

Disaster Relief
(0.1%)

Mandatory

FIGURE 12.1 The Federal Budget for 2014.

Source: United States Office of Management and Budget, Budget Fiscal Year 2014.
http://www.whitehouse.gov/sites/default/files/omb/budget/Fy2014/assests/tables.pdf

competitiveness, and the rise in inflation and unemployment, especially during the 1970s. These factors, along with a steadily increasing national debt and sizable annual deficits, led those inside and outside the government to question the wisdom of ever-increasing government spending that resulted in large and continuing budget deficits.

The Reagan Revolution

Upon taking office, President Reagan took the lead in reordering national priorities, using the budget to achieve his policy goals. He reduced the proportion of annual government expenditures devoted to domestic discretionary spending and almost doubled the proportion for defense. President Reagan also wanted to cut back substantially on the popular entitlement programs, but with the exception of an adjustment made to Social Security in 1983 that gradually increased the retirement age and the amount of income subject to its payroll tax, Congress refused to reduce the benefits of these popular program. Federal income tax rates were also cut; deficits persisted and grew.

Congress attempted, but failed, to impose discipline on government spending by enacting legislation that automatically triggered cuts if expenditures exceeded revenues by a certain amount. The first of these legislative acts, the Balanced Budget and Emergency Deficit Control Act of 1985—known by the names of three of its sponsors, senators Phil Gramm, Warren Rudman, and Ernest Hollings—required a balanced budget within five years of its passage (subsequently extended to eight), set specific deficit targets to be met over this period, and authorized automatic cuts in some domestic and defense programs to bring the deficit to the required levels if the targets were not met.[6] By authorizing automatic cuts, Congress acknowledged its own inability to make tough and potentially unpopular budgetary decisions.

The legislation, however, did not achieve its objective. To stay within the targets prescribed by the law but not suffer political retribution for steep cuts in popular programs, Congress and the president devised a variety of accounting and reporting techniques that ostensibly met the goals but actually evaded them. These included overly optimistic forecasts of revenue, underestimation of automatic government payments, the extension of expenditures into the next fiscal year, the pulling of revenues into the current year from the next one, and the enactment of supplemental spending bills not included in the Gramm-Rudman-Hollings targets. The government even sold some of its assets to stay within the guidelines of the legislation. The need to bail out the savings and loan associations at the end of the 1980s further aggravated the spending problem.

President George H. W. Bush and the Democratically-controlled Congress tried to halt the red ink in 1990 by raising additional revenue and imposing constraints on future spending. The Budget Enforcement Act of 1990 placed specific limits on discretionary expenditures and set overall spending targets within three broad categories: defense, international affairs, and domestic programs. There was also a pay-as-you-go (PAYGO) provision that required

Congress to pay for the cost of any new program by obtaining savings from existing programs and to pay for any new tax reductions by obtaining additional revenues. Despite these efforts, however, annual deficits continued and the national debt increased to over $4 trillion.

Clinton and the Politics of a Balanced Budget

After the 1992 election, Clinton, who promised that deficit reduction would be a major priority of his administration, proposed a plan to do so that contained new taxes and cuts. The Democratic Congress modified Clinton's plan, increasing spending cuts and decreasing tax increases, and then enacted it by the barest of margins. The legislation, the Omnibus Budget Reconciliation Act of 1993, along with the rapid growth of the economy, spurred on by the technological revolution in communications, had the desired effect. It substantially reduced the deficit and eventually turned it into a surplus. Before the deficit was eliminated, however, the Republicans, who won control of Congress in the 1994 midterm election and attempted to enact a constitutional amendment that would have required Congress to enact balanced budgets. Their amendment failed by only one vote in the Senate.

Throughout the fall of 1995 and into the winter of 1996, Congress and the president battled over these budget issues. As a consequence of this battle and the refusal of each side to compromise with the other, the government was forced to close down, not once but twice. Eventually, through the skillful use of his bully pulpit, President Clinton turned public opinion against the Republicans, forcing the GOP to back down. Finally, in 1997, both sides agreed to legislation that would balance the budget. Within a year, the deficit turned into a surplus. The problem had been solved, but only temporarily.

The End of Budget Surpluses

When George W. Bush became president, the Congressional Budget Office predicted a huge surplus over the next decade. Lower taxes and a war on terrorism fought in Afghanistan, Iraq, and elsewhere around the world, combined with expanded intelligence and security needs at home, quickly undermined that prediction. Increases in farm subsidies, veterans' benefits, and Medicare expenses in the form of a new prescription drug program added to the red ink. By the end of the final year of the Bush administration, the debt was almost $10 trillion.

The economy fell into recession in the spring of 2008. In the fall of that year, a major financial crisis, fueled by speculative real estate investments, plunged the country into a severe economic downturn. Fearful that banks, several big Wall Street investment firms, and a major insurer, American Insurance Group (AIG), would be unable to meet their financial obligations and go under, Treasury Secretary Henry Paulsen, a former head of one of these investment firms, proposed a $700 billion bailout program for these "too-big-to-fail" companies. The Democratic Congress and both major presidential candidates supported the proposal; the general public did not, strongly objecting to the taxpayers bailing out the firms (and their well-paid corporate executives) that caused the problems that contributed to millions of Americans losing their jobs, homes, and savings. Bailout funds were also used to help two of the big three American automobile producers, General Motors and Chrysler, get back to profitability.

The financial crisis aggravated the already weak economy. Unemployment soared, real estate prices plummeted, and the stock market lost almost half of its value over a six-month period. The magnitude of these economic problems prompted president-elect Obama to urge the new Democratic Congress to enact a large spending bill that would stimulate the economy and make a down payment on the promises he had made during the campaign. The legislation provided for an additional $787 billion in government spending. Subsequently, Congress also decided to maintain the tax cuts that were initiated in the first year of the Bush administration. As a consequence of these expenditures, the wars in Iraq and Afghanistan and lower revenues resulting from the recession and the continuation of the tax cuts, the government experienced massive deficits and a huge increase in its national debt (see Table 12.1).

Combined with the slow economic recovery and a health care debate that divided the country, these deficits and the debt became a major issue in the 2010 midterm elections. Prior to those elections, a new political movement, known as the Tea Party,[7] mobilized opposition to what some believed to be out-of-control spending by the government. Mistrust of that government resulted in the defeat of some Republican incumbents in the 2010 primaries and many Democrats in the general election. The new Republican majority in the House of Representatives interpreted their mandate to be cutting government spending significantly.

The first vote on which they could try to impose this mandate was on raising the amount of money that the government could borrow. When the treasury reached the $14.3 trillion limit that legislation had imposed, House Republicans insisted that any rise in that limit be accompanied by cuts of a similar amount. Their insistence led to a confrontation with the Democratically controlled Senate and the White House in August, 2011.

Table 12.1 The Budget, Deficit/Surplus, and the National Debt (in Millions), 1960–2015

Year	Receipts	Outlays	Surplus/Deficit (–)	Gross National Debt
1960	$ 92,942	$ 92,191	$ 301	$ 290,525
1970	192,807	195,649	–2,842	380,921
1980	517,112	590,541	–73,830	909,041
1990	1,031,958	1,252,944	–221,036	3,206,290
2000	2,025,191	1,788,950	–236,241	5,628,700
2010	2,162,724	3,456,213	1,293,489	13,528,807
2015*	3,332,000	3,908,000	576,000	19,148,000

*Estimated in Fiscal 2014 Budget
SOURCE: United States Budget, FY 2014.

With both sides adhering to their partisan positions, an impasse that would prevent the United States from meeting its debt obligations loomed. In the final hours before a debt default could occur, a compromise was reached in which the budget was cut substantially and the debt limit raised. Half of the cut was taken out of future spending and the other half was to be determined by a joint bipartisan committee. In the event the committee could not reach an agreement, the president was ordered to sequester the additional funds with an across-the-board spending cut to take effect in December 2012, a date Congress subsequently extended for three months. With the 2001 tax cuts set to expire at the end of 2012, the debt limit reaching its congressionally imposed maximum of $16.4 trillion, and annual budget deficits exceeding $1 trillion for four years in a row, the country was approaching a fiscal cliff. It was averted by a last-minute deal that raised tax rates for the top one percent of wage earners (individuals making in $400,000 or more and families $450,000 or more), maintained the Bush tax cuts for the rest of the taxpayers, and returned the Social Security payroll tax, which had been cut by 2 percent, to its prerecession level. $1.2 trillion in government spending was to be forcibly cut through sequestration over a 10-year period with further debt limit issues looming.

In summary, the evolution of the budget explains why it no longer is an effective instrument of presidential power. Not only are presidents and members of Congress constrained by previous commitments, existing legislation, and their campaign promises, but they are also subject to strong clientele and constituency pressures as well as to fluctuations in the economy that may prevent them from imposing spending discipline or repealing popular tax benefits. Confrontation, negotiation, and compromise, not dictation and domination, describes the relationship between the presidency and Congress on budgetary matters most of the time.

THE BUDGET MAKERS

The President

As we have noted, presidents bear the primary responsibility for the executive phase of the budget and normally play a major role in the legislative process as well, but they have only limited influence to affect desired outcomes. Their goals dictate budget priorities and shape its initial guidelines; their policies determine the new big-ticket expenditures; and their decisions resolve interagency disputes. They can also decrease or eliminate funding for duplicative programs or those that they believe are no longer necessary.[8]

In shaping the budget, presidents can get involved in detailed decision making if they desire. Some have done so, such as Gerald Ford and Jimmy Carter, while others, such as Richard Nixon, Ronald Reagan, and George W. Bush, have not. At times, Bill Clinton and Barack Obama got involved in detailed budget decision making, but both also had strong Office of Management and Budget (OMB) directors on whom they relied.

The Office of Management and Budget

The OMB is the principal institutional entity that runs the budget review process. Created in 1921 to "assemble, correlate, revise, reduce, or increase the estimates of the several departments or establishments,"[9] the Budget Bureau, as it was originally called, was charged with making decisions on the amount of funding requested for executive departments and agencies. Moved to the Executive Office of the President in 1939, the office continues to run the budget review process on the president's behalf.

In 1970 President Nixon reorganized the Budget Bureau. In addition to adding management to its title and functions, Nixon also increased the number of political appointees that ran this presidential agency. The politicization has continued under subsequent administrations. Today, there are around twenty political appointees in top positions in the OMB.

New oversight and coordination functions have also been added. President Carter set up a division within the OMB to oversee reorganization efforts; Reagan charged that agency with regulatory review. George W. Bush used it to assess how well executive departments and agencies were performing; Barack Obama has ordered it to oversee and reevaluate existing regulatory authority. All contemporary presidents beginning with Ronald Reagan have relied on their budget directors to negotiate spending agreements with Congress.

In recent times, the OMB's political sensitivities and its expanded role have contributed to its influence. The willingness of presidents to use the agency to promote their policy objectives has worked to the same end. The OMB's clout in the budget review process has increased, allowing it (in conjunction with the White House) to shift major allocations from agency to agency in accordance with the president's wishes.

The OMB's ability to effect change does vary, however, over the course of an administration. In the beginning, its institutional resources, particularly its access to information and expertise, are most valuable in overcoming traditional departmental interests and congressional resistance to new presidential initiatives. How the Reagan administration obtained its 1981 budget cuts illustrates the advantage the OMB can give a president in his first year in office. In January 1981, before many of the departments were fully staffed and their secretaries had been fully briefed about their budget needs, the OMB proposed major reductions in domestic programs. Almost immediately, budget working groups were established. Composed of key White House personnel, budget officials, and appropriate department secretaries and their aides, the groups reviewed the proposed cuts and made recommendations to the president. In most cases, the recommendations supported the cuts because Reagan had stated his goals, the OMB had a near monopoly over budget information, and the composition of the budget working groups was stacked against the departments. The secretaries were not had a position to advocate their departments' interests even if they wanted to do so.[10]

Director	
Deputy Director	**Deputy Director for Management**
Executive Associate Director	
OMB-Wide Support Offices	**Statutory Offices**
General Counsel Economy Policy Legislative Reference Budget Review Legislative Affairs Management and Operations Performance and Personnel Management Strategic Planning and Communications	Federal Financial Management Federal Procurement Policy E-Government & Information Technology Information & Regulatory Affairs Intellectual Property Enforcement
Resource Management Offices	
Natural Resources Education, Income Maintenance and Labor Health General Government National Security	

FIGURE 12.2 The Organization of the Office of Management and Budget (OMB)

Source: The Office of Management and Budget.
http://www.whitehouse.gov/sites/default/files/omb/assets/about_omb/omb_org_chart_0.pdf.

Over time, however, the advantages that the OMB can give a president decline. The inevitability of pressure to maintain existing benefits, the relatively small amount of discretionary spending, and the tendency of departments to develop their own constituency-oriented programs limit the OMB's ability to effect major change, particularly in the last years of an administration. Figure 12.2 lists the current organizational structure of the OMB.

Other Executive Departments and Agencies

Although the OMB is the principal participant in the executive phase of the budgetary process, it is not the only one. In one way or another, every executive agency has an impact on the budget, mostly its own.

Departments and agencies are asked to submit yearly estimates for their programs and operational costs. They are expected to defend these estimates before the OMB and Congress. They may also have to appeal to the president if funding for a particular program is cut or substantially reduced.

Most agencies have a division that coordinates their budget preparation and another that facilitates their legislative activity. In deciding how much to request, agencies have a limited range. There are presidential guidelines to follow, ceilings that cannot be exceeded, and administrative costs that must be met.

Nonetheless, the agencies have some leeway when estimating their expenditures. They generally tend to request more funds than they think they will get, anticipating that the OMB will revise their requests downward as will the Congress. This expectation, in turn, contributes to their tendency to pad their estimates and the OMB's inclination to cut them. In general, the agencies that are most aggressive in requesting funds for their most popular programs that enjoy the greatest political support in Congress and from the general public. Table 12.2 outlines the major phases of the executive budgetary process.

In short, presidents have a leadership problem when it comes to the budget, a problem that has been magnified by the persistence of large deficits and the accumulation of a huge national debt. Reducing or eliminating the deficit and preventing the debt from getting out of control require tough decisions that may be unpopular with large constituencies that carry considerable electoral clout. Were presidents able to make these decisions on their own, they might have the courage and will to do so, particularly during their second term. However, because budgetary commitments made by previous legislative and executive actions limit their discretion, as does the fear that their decisions, if unpopular, could lead to their and their party's defeat in the next election, they have led cautiously, proposing only modest changes even when their party controls Congress. With limited political power to use against recalcitrant members of their own party and practically none to use against their opponents; with limited persuasive power in the absence of a consensus or a crisis; and with limited time, energy, and knowledge to devote to this perennial money problem, they remain at the mercy of a variety of political and economic forces.

Under the circumstances, for most administrations the budgetary process becomes a drag—the time and energy spent on it do not usually produce the desired outcome. It is the rare president who can use the budget to direct change. When change does occur, it is usually during the first two years in office or after decisive midterm election such as the ones in 1994, 2006, and 2010, in which budgetary and economic problems were principal issues.

To give the president more discretion and to reduce pork-barrel legislation, Congress enacted a line-item veto in 1996 that permitted the president to delete individual items in appropriation bills after approving the legislation. The law permitted Congress to disapprove of the president's actions, but if the president vetoed the disapproval, Congress had to override that veto in the usual fashion by a two-thirds vote in each house.

During the first and only year in which the line-item veto provision was in effect, President Clinton used it eighty-two times, of which thirty-eight line-item vetoes, all on military construction projects, were overridden by Congress. The president achieved savings of only $869 million with the line-item vetoes that were not overridden.

Table 12.2 The Executive Budgetary Process

Period	Actions
	Budget Policy Development
February–March	Senior government economists review the outlook for the next and future fiscal years; they predict effects of current law and proposed spending proposals on the revenues and expenditures of government and report their assumptions and findings to the president, who then sets his administration's fiscal goals.
April–June	The OMB director uses these goals as guidelines when instructing the executive departments and agencies to create their annual budgets. (Circular A-11.) If there are no guidelines, then the previous department or agency budget is used as a starting point.
	Agencies' Preparation of Proposed Budgets
July–August	Agencies then develop their proposed budgets over the summer, sending them to the OMB by the beginning of September, thirteen months before the fiscal year begins.
September	Other executive branch agencies, not subject to the OMB review process, submit their budgets later in the fall.
	OMB Review
September–October	The OMB staff analyzes proposed budgets of the departments and agencies and holds hearings with them on their requests.
October–November	Economic advisers again review the outlook for the fiscal year that begins the next October. The OMB director holds agency-by-agency reviews at which agency requests and staff recommendations are considered and recommendations are made to the president. The legislative branch and the judiciary submit their budget requests to the OMB. The OMB transmits the proposed budget and economic advisers' findings to the president by late November. The OMB gives agencies their recommended budget levels—also known as "the mark."
	Presidential Decision and Congressional Presentation
December	The president reviews OMB recommendations and decides on totals for agencies and programs. Possible appeals by agencies to the president or to a committee that he selects are made. After the appeals process is completed, the OMB prepares budget documents for transmittal to Congress.
February, 1st Monday*	The president delivers a proposed budget to Congress. The OMB sends an "allowance letter" to each agency giving its total within the president's budget and also transmitting "planning numbers" for the next two fiscal years.

*The deadline is normally extended for a month or two in the first year a new president takes office. It was also extended in 2013 for president Obama who presented his budget for FY 2014 to Congress on April 10, 2013.

SOURCE: Adapted from United States Office of Management and Budget.
http://www.whitehouse.gov/omb/budget/.

The constitutionality of the line-item veto was immediately challenged, first by a group of members of Congress who had opposed the legislation and second by those who were adversely affected by Clinton's vetoes. The Supreme Court held that the first group did not have standing but the second group did. In its decision, the Supreme Court held in the case of *Clinton v. City of New York*, 524 U.S. 417 (1998) that the law violated the veto provision of the Constitution (see Appendix C, Article I, section 7). Subsequently, Congress has tried to end earmarks in legislation which gives the executive more discretion in implementing it.

MAKING ECONOMIC POLICY

Presidents have been involved in the budget process since 1921, but not until the administration of Franklin Roosevelt in the 1930s had they been concerned on a regular basis with economic policy making. Prior to that time, presidential activities were generally limited to initiating or supporting proposals to correct specific problems that had arisen within the economy. Theodore Roosevelt's trust busting and Woodrow Wilson's labor reforms are two examples of these early forms of presidential involvement.

The depth of the 1930s Depression, the degree of public panic, and Herbert Hoover's resounding election defeat signaled the beginning of a more comprehensive presidential role in the economy. No longer could presidents enjoy the luxury of standing on the sidelines. Franklin Roosevelt's activism became the model for his Democratic successors. Even conservative Republicans, such as Ronald Reagan and George W. Bush, found that there was no turning back to the Hoover model of noninterference.

Congress expects and even requires this attention. The Employment Act of 1946 obligates the president to prime the economy to maximize employment and production and annually report on the state of the economy to Congress. The Taft-Hartley Act of 1947 gives the president the power to intervene in labor–management disputes that threatened the nation's security and well-being. Congress has not only acknowledged an expanded presidential role but has also created executive agencies to help the executive fulfill it—the Council of Economic Advisers, the National Labor Relations Board, the Securities and Exchange Commission, and the new agency established by the Wall Street Reform and Consumer Protection Act of 2010 (Dodd, Frank Act) to prevent many of the abuses that led to the 2008 financial crisis.

Every president since Roosevelt has strived to meet these expanded expectations. The job approval, reelectability, and even the legacy of contemporary presidents are thought to be closely associated with their perceived economic success. A strong economy is good news for a president; a weak economy is not.

The political implications of economic decision making have prompted an ongoing debate during administrations and into election cycles, a debate in which presidents are normally fully engaged. They are expected to use their bully pulpits to trumpet their economic gains and explain economic problems that occur and persist during their presidencies. How persuasive they can be in this debate varies with their own rhetorical skills, the amount of time they and their administrations devote to this effort, and most importantly, with economic conditions themselves.

Political scientist B. Dan Wood has found that presidents devote more attention to economic matters than to any other policy area except during periods of noneconomic crises.[11] He and other political scientists contend that presidential public relations can and do bear fruit[12] and that they can affect people's perceptions about the economy—although, as our discussion in Chapter 4 indicates, affecting those perceptions and especially changing public attitudes is a very difficult and time-consuming task. The bottom line, as far as the president is concerned, is that the economy is almost always a salient issue, and during economic downturns it is *the* issue.

The economic policies of presidents have varied. Truman, Kennedy, Reagan, and George W. Bush desired to lower taxes to stimulate economic growth. Clinton advocated increased productivity through investment tax credits to encourage business to modernize and expand and to provide tax credits to allow more people to get a higher education or more advanced job training. Obama has proposed additional aid for education, especially for improving training in science, technology, and math, expansion of preschool programs, and government grants to stimulate technological innovation, but he also advocated increasing taxes on wealthy individuals and corporations.

Differing fiscal approaches lay at the core of competing presidential policies. A fiscal strategy is a plan to manipulate government revenue and expenditures to influence economic conditions. In contrast, a monetary approach regulates the supply of money. Presidents cannot directly affect monetary policy, generally the prerogative of the Federal Reserve Board, nearly as much as they can influence fiscal policy.

Until the mid-1970s, fiscal strategies were predicated on the economic theories of John Maynard Keynes, an eminent British economist who argued that increases in government spending and reductions in government taxes stimulate demand and invigorate the economy during periods of sluggish activity, but they also produce budget deficits. Keynes was not worried about these deficits, however, because he believed that in the long run a vibrant economy would generate greater revenues, reducing or eliminating the difference between expenditures and income. With the exception of Eisenhower, presidents Truman through Nixon subscribed to Keynes's economic beliefs.

An expanding economy coupled with relatively low unemployment and inflation during most of the 1950s and 1960s seemed to confirm the merits of the Keynesian approach. But as we noted previously in this chapter, by the beginning of the 1970s, economic conditions began to deteriorate. Budget deficits increased, the rate of economic growth declined, and inflation rose dramatically. Keynesian economics did not contain satisfactory solutions to these problems, prompting other economists to propose new theories.

Professor Milton Friedman of the University of Chicago postulated one of these theories. He contended that the supply of money was the key to sound economic growth, particularly to control the ravages of inflation. Increasing interest rates would reduce the amount of money in circulation, thereby decreasing inflationary pressures and cooling the economy. Lowering interest rates, in contrast, would have the opposite effect, stimulating demand and output by making borrowing cheaper and more money available. In periods of high inflation and an overheated economy, a tight money policy made sense. But when inflation was high and the economy stagnant, it did not. It was precisely this latter condition in the late 1970s that gave credence to supply-side economics.

The supply-side philosophy combined the Keynesian approach to generating demand with the monetarist's regulation of currency. Tax cuts stimulate spending, whereas reducing the supply of money controls inflation. Ronald Reagan and George W. Bush, advocates of supply-side economics, desired to reduce corporate and personal income taxes. Barack Obama took a more Keynesian approach, supporting a large government spending program to stimulate economic growth. The clash between economic philosophies continued throughout his first term and into his second. (See Box 12.1.)

Box 12.1 The Presidency in Action: Obama Tackles the Great Recession

The great recession that began in the winter of 2007 and was accentuated by the financial crisis in the fall of 2008 helped elect Barack Obama, shaped his policy agenda, and kept the economy the principal issue throughout his first term, during the 2012 election cycle, and into his second term. It dominated news media coverage for most of this period, heightened already deep partisan divisions, and affected public evaluations of the job that the president and Congress were doing.

Even before he took office, as president-elect, Obama met with his economic advisers to assess the state of the economy. They presented data that indicated the decline was larger and quicker than previously thought and than the Bush administration had indicated. The $150 billion stimulus package that candidate Obama had proposed in the 2008 campaign would not come close to halting this downward cycle, much less reversing it. The president's economic advisers recommended nearly $900 billion in additional government spending to prevent a "catastrophic failure," although they did not believe that even this amount would be sufficient to stabilize the projected economic decline.

The economic discussions in which the president-elect participated lasted four hours. By the end, Obama had agreed to a large stimulus package, leaving his economic advisers to work out the numbers, his political aides to decide on spending priorities, and Congress to draft the bill and, in doing so, make the necessary compromises to achieve a successful legislative outcome. Speed was of the essence. The president wanted to approve the legislation on the day of his inauguration. He received it in mid-February and signed it into law on President's Day. Strong leadership, fast action, and expressions of confidence buoyed his approval ratings to 62 percent right after he signed the legislation.[13]

The $787 billion American Recovery and Reinvestment Act had three principal goals: to stimulate the economy and create jobs through government-initiated "shovel ready" projects; to give aid to states to maintain public sector employment in the light of decreasing state revenues; and to make a down payment on Obama's campaign promises to improve health care, mass transit, renewable energy, the electric grid, Internet connectivity, and scientific education.

The economy was slow to recover, however. Unemployment continued to increase, real estate values bottomed out, housing forecloses increased, and tight credit hampered businesses. Republicans who had overwhelmingly opposed the stimulus bill claimed that the money was not well spent and

that tax cuts were necessary to generate economic growth.

With the exception of the health care debate, the BP oil leak in the Gulf of Mexico, and the killing of Osama bin Laden, the economy dominated the news. And much of the coverage was negative, focusing on people who were out of work, lost their homes, and found their savings depleted. Concern about huge budget deficits and an increasing national debt added to the administration's travails, fueled partisan opposition, and contributed to the Democrats' defeat in the 2010 midterm elections. Republican control of the House of Representatives and gains in the Senate following the elections precluded other major policy initiatives within the economic sphere by the president, placed him on the political defensive, and set the stage for his reelection campaign. It took two years of constant campaigning, political brinksmanship, and modest economic recovery for Obama to improve his public standing.

President Obama's experience suggests that economic policy takes time to have an impact; the more severe the downturn, the longer it takes to reverse. Yet politics is driven by the here and now, by tangible consequences and conditions.

In recent years, presidents have devoted increasing attention to international economic issues, specifically free and fair trade. The Clinton administration concluded two free trade agreements, the North American Free Trade Agreement (NAFTA) and the General Agreement on Tariffs and Trade (GATT). The Bush and Obama administrations pursued free trade agreements with South Korea, Colombia, and Panama, and Obama proposed one with Europe.

Clinton, Bush, and Obama were not the first presidents to promote international trade. Ever since the Wilson administration, when the United States emerged as a major world power, presidents have sought to lower the barriers to international commerce for American industry. They have met with frequent opposition, however, much of it from organized labor, which fears the loss of American jobs to lower-paid foreign workers, and from small businesses that fear lower-price foreign competition. Older manufacturing industries, environmentalists, and even consumer advocates have also been critical of such agreements. Big business, in contrast, particularly firms engaged in international commerce, such as high-tech companies and service industries, and most economists and investors tend to be more supportive of a free-trading international environment.

To make and implement domestic and foreign economic policy decisions, presidents have assembled large advisory and administrative staffs. Housed in the Executive Office and the executive departments, they differ in their mission, clientele, and substantive policy expertise. Coordinating them is a major task. Figure 12.3 lists the primary economic advisory units in the executive branch.

Executive Departments	
Treasury Department	**Commerce Department**
The first department to play a major role in the financial affairs of government, the treasury oversees the revenue side of the budget: the collection of federal funds, debt financing, including the sale of government bonds, import controls, and international financial transactions.	The principal link to the business community, this department promotes economic development and technological innovation as well as enforcing international trade agreements.

Federal Reserve System
Federal Reserve Board
Created by Congress in 1913, the FED regulates the supply of money. It sets the discount rate that commercial banks must pay when they borrow money, the percentage of deposits that they must maintain, and the purchase and sale of government securities on the open market.

Executive Office of the President		
Office of Management and Budget	**Council of Economic Advisers**	**National Economic Council**
In addition to its budgetary, legislative, and regulatory review functions, the OMB provides economic information and advice to the president.	Created by Congress in 1946 to advise the president on macroeconomic policy, the council analyzes economic conditions, forecasts trends, and helps prepare the president's economic report to Congress.	Established by President Clinton to help formulate, coordinate, and oversee the implementation of the president's economic program, the council is composed of presidential appointees not subject to Senate consent; it has become the major body on which presidents depend for their ongoing economic policy decisions.

FIGURE 12.3 The President's Economic Advisers

THE POLITICS OF THE ECONOMY

Economic policy making has become more political, more pragmatic, and less stable. These changes have affected the advice that presidents receive as well as the accommodations they must make. They have also affected the time and energy that must be devoted to economic matters.

Economic policy making has always been sensitive to outside pressures from Congress, the bureaucracy, and organized interest groups, each of which has its own interests to protect and its own political axes to grind. Members of Congress must consider the economic impact on their constituencies, department and agency heads must be responsive to their clientele, and organized groups must placate their members and supporters. To the extent that economic decisions require coalition building to become public policy—and most do—presidents must take these varied interests into account.

The politics of economic decision making has made long-range planning more difficult. The election cycle must be considered when calculating the effects of policy change. Naturally, an administration will manipulate recoveries to serve its own political benefit whenever possible. And there is evidence that it helps them in the electoral arena.

Political scientists have been engaged in a debate over the relationship between presidential partisanship and economic performance. Professor Larry Bartels, in his book *Unequal Democracy*, contends that family income rose faster during Democratic administrations than Republican ones from 1948 to 2005, the time frame of his study. He also found that unemployment was lower and economic inequality less when the Democrats controlled the White House.[14] James Campbell, measuring similar economic data but in a slightly different manner, attributed the differences in income and unemployment levels to the economic conditions inherited from previous administrations. He argues that Democrats began their presidencies with healthier economies than did Republicans. Taking the previous year's economy into account, Campbell found "no significant differences in the records of Democratic and Republican presidents with respect to economic growth, unemployment, or income inequality."[15] Presidential candidates and their partisan surrogates have continued this debate.

In addition to affecting general trends, the policy decisions of presidents can reap significant benefits for specific groups. Tax proposals, government assistance programs, defense spending, even regulatory activity have consequences for individuals and groups—some benefit, some do not. These outcomes influence evaluations of the president and the party in power and manifest themselves in political contributions and voting behavior.

Even the implementation of ongoing programs, in which the executive exercises discretion, can reap political largess. Political scientists Christopher Berry, Barry Burden, and William Howell found that 4 to 5 percent more government funds go to congressional districts represented by a member of the president's party.[16] This spending helps solidify partisan support; it also helps build generic support for presidents running for reelection.[17] Others have found that presidents and their party also benefit from the distribution of disaster relief.[18]

Not only do short-run considerations such as elections tend to drive economic decision making but they also enhance the pragmatic character of the decisions themselves. Presidents are more inclined to strive for what is politically desirable than what may be theoretically optimal. Perhaps this political inclination explains why most presidents are more apt to pursue a policy of selective personal involvement in economic matters rather than become a micromanager of the economy. They wish to claim credit for economic successes and avoid blame for failures.

The impact of politics on economic policy decisions has also made those decisions less stable over time. Unanticipated events and unintended consequences have frequently forced presidents to adjust their economic programs. President Ford abandoned his Whip Inflation Now (WIN) program as economic conditions deteriorated and the country fell into a recession. President Carter had to recant on a promise to provide taxpayers with a $50 rebate as the budget deficit soared. President Reagan had to support a large revenue increase one year after getting a large tax cut through Congress. President George H. W. Bush violated his "read my lips, no new taxes" pledge in 1990 by agreeing to higher taxes; President Clinton was not able to keep his 1992 campaign promise to cut middle-class taxes; President George W. Bush had to support a massive government bailout bill to buttress major banks and other lenders after the financial crisis of 2008; and President Obama was forced to accept major cuts in government spending, including some in programs that help the poor, and a smaller revenue increase than he proposed.

Other factors also impact economic policy making. Although presidents are ritually blamed for unfavorable conditions and expected to improve them, many events and situations lie beyond their immediate control. As we have noted, existing laws establish levels of revenue and expenditures and limit the amount of money the government can borrow; interest rates dictate the cost of that borrowing; and cost-of-living adjustments (COLAs) automatically raise federal outlays. Presidents must meet these legal obligations. Over time, they can try to get Congress to change them, but change is more difficult to achieve than maintaining the status quo. Similarly, international forces and events affect the American economy in ways that they did not prior to World War II. The rise in the price of imported oil contributed to inflationary pressures and to declining economic growth. Industries, particularly in Asia, have adversely impacted American competition in steel, shipbuilding, textiles, and automobile manufacturing. The weakness or strength of the dollar affects the flow of trade and tourism, the stability of financial markets, and the ability of countries to meet their debt obligations.

The increased complexity of the economic decision-making process compounds the president's leadership tasks. There are more people inside and outside the government that are interested in economic policy, more interests that must be balanced, and more coordination that is necessary. In no other policy sphere are presidential limits more visible and harder to overcome than in the economy.

CONCLUSION

Presidential responsibility has been enlarged in budgetary and economic spheres. That enlargement has been a product of need, statute, and precedent. Acknowledging its inability to fashion comprehensive budget and economic policy, Congress has required the president to do so. This requirement, coupled with the expanded role of the federal government, has forced presidents and their staffs to devote increasing resources to budget and economic policy making.

Expectations of presidential performance have grown, but the president's capacity to affect budgetary and economic matters has not kept pace. More than half of the expenditures in the budget are dictated by existing law and previous policy decisions. Presidents can affect discretionary funding in their budget requests, but even here, political pressures and congressional opposition often undercut their efforts to reorder spending priorities in a significant way. They do have some discretion in how policies are implemented, where money is spent, and on what, although government policies on competitive bidding, federal grant applications, congressional earmarks, and criteria written into legislation provide limits here as well. Moreover, many outside factors over which they have little or no control affect the economy and the success or failure of the president's economic policies.

And they must devote considerable time and energy to explain what they are doing, defend their actions, and highlight their accomplishments. The saliency of economic issues forces presidents to engage in a continuous public debate with their political opponents. Unless times are good, presidents are often on the defensive in these debates as their partisan opponents and the news media highlight the problems.

More often than not, the reelection of incumbents turns on their economic performance. Both Jimmy Carter and George H. W. Bush lost primarily because the electorate found their economic performance unsatisfactory.

In short, presidential roles have increased within the budgetary and economic spheres, but presidential influence has declined. Leadership is more difficult to exert and maintain. Presidents have less ability to control the factors that affect their judgments. However, those judgments are increasingly expected to solve national problems and promote national prosperity.

Directing change under normal conditions is difficult. Presidents need crises as action-forcing and coalition-building mechanisms, as evident during the early years of the Franklin Roosevelt and Obama presidencies. This need raises the stakes, delays solutions, and frequently shortens the time frame in which those solutions are designed and implemented. In general, the best that presidents can do is to facilitate action. To do so effectively, they must devote more time to budgetary matters and must selectively involve themselves in economic issues. They must coordinate support within the executive branch, build coalitions within Congress, balance group interests, and maintain the confidence of the general public—a tall order, to be sure.

Discussion Questions

1. In what ways can the contemporary budget serve as an instrument of presidential influence in Congress and the executive branch departments and agencies, and in what ways can it not do so? Explain and illustrate the scope and limits of the president's budgetary power.

2. Persistently large budget deficits and the growing national debt have been contentious issues during the last three decades. Do they merit such attention? How do they impact on the economy? Why are these issues so difficult to resolve? From the perspective of your generation, how do you think the president and Congress should resolve these issues?

3. Ever since Franklin Roosevelt's administration, the president has been expected to be manager of the economy. Can the president really perform this role? What are some of the ways in which presidents can affect the economy, and what are some of their toughest limits? Illustrate with examples from the Obama administration.

 ## Web Exercises

1. Go to the OMB website, http://www.whitehouse.gov/omb, to access the budget for the current or (if available) future fiscal year. You can also access it via the Government Printing Office website, http://www.gpo .gov. Indicate how much discretionary spending has been requested by the president and how the money is to be divided between defense and nondefense expenditures. How much has the president requested for the Executive Office of the President? Compare that amount the costs of the Congress and the judiciary. Do you think the president's bureaucracy is too large and expensive?

2. Access the Congressional Budget Office (CBO) website at http://www .cbo.gov. Compare its projections for spending and revenue for the next fiscal year with those found in the president's budget of that year. Why do the projections differ?

3. Go to the Department of the Treasury's website (http://www.treasury.gov) to determine the size of the national debt, the amount of it that is owed to the public, and the percentage of that amount that is owed to non-Americans. Do you think the debt owed to non-Americans is a problem, and, if so, how should the administration deal with it? How much would every American have to contribute to retire the debt?

Selected Readings

Bartels, Larry M. *Unequal Democracy: The Political Economy of the New Gilded Age.* Princeton, NJ: Princeton University Press, 2008.

Berry, Christopher, Barry Burden, and William Howell. "The President and the Distribution of Federal Spending." *American Political Science Review* 104 (November 2010): 783–799.

Campbell, James E. "The Economic Records of the Presidents, Party Differences, and Inherited Economic Conditions." *Forum* 9, art. 7 (2011): 1–29.

Carroll, Richard J. *An Economic Record of Presidential Performance: From Truman to Bush.* Westport, CT: Praeger, 1995.

Comiskey, Michael, and Lawrence C. Marsh. "Presidents, Parties, and the Business Cycle, 1949–2009." *Presidential Studies Quarterly* 42 (March 2012): 40–59.

Eshbaugh-Soha, Matthew, and Jeffrey S. Peake. "Presidents and the Economic Agenda." *Political Research Quarterly* 58 (March 2005): 127–138.

Farrier, Jasmine. "Barack Obama and Budget Deficits: Signs of a Neo-Whig Presidency?" *Presidential Studies Quarterly* 41 (September 2011): 618–634.

Farrier, Jasmine. *Passing the Buck: Congress, the Budget and Deficits.* Lexington: University of Kentucky Press, 2004.

Fisher, Louis. "Presidential Budgetary Duties." *Presidential Studies Quarterly* 42 (December 2012): 754–790.

Ippolito, Daniel. *Why Budgets Matter: Budget Policy and American Politics.* University Park: The State University of Pennsylvania Press, 2003.

Kriner, Douglas L., and Andrew Reeves. "The Influence of Federal Spending on Federal Elections." *American Political Science Review* 106 (May 2012): 348–366.

Schick, Allen. *The Federal Budget: Politics, Policy, Process*, 3rd ed. Washington, DC: Brookings Institution, 2007.

Spiliotes, Constantine J. *Vicious Cycle: Presidential Decision Making in the American Political Economy.* College Station: Texas A&M University Press, 2002.

Tomkin, Shelley Lynne. *Inside the OMB.* New York: M. E. Sharpe, 1998.

Weatherford, M. Stephen. "The Wages of Competence: Obama, the Economy and the 2010 Midterm Elections." *Presidential Studies Quarterly* 42 (March 2012): 8–39.

Wood, B. Dan. *The Politics of Economic Leadership: The Causes and Consequences of Presidential Rhetoric.* Princeton, NJ: Princeton University Press, 2007.

Woodley, John T. "Persistent Leadership: Presidents and the Evolution of U.S. Financial Reform, 1970–2007." *Presidential Studies Quarterly* 42 (March 2012): 60–80.

Notes

1. For a discussion of the budgetary process during this early period, see Louis Fisher, *The Politics of Shared Power: Congress and the Executive* (Washington, DC: Congressional Quarterly, 1992), pp. 177–178; Louis Fisher, "Presidential Budget Duties," *Presidential Studies Quarterly* 42 (December 2012): 761.

2. The legislation, known as the Anti-Deficiency Act of 1905, has been cited as the statutory basis of the president's impoundment authority—that is, the president's power not to spend money appropriated by Congress if that expenditure would not be wise or prudent.

3. The national debt increased from about $1 billion in 1916 to over $25 billion by 1919. Fisher, "Presidential Budget Duties," p. 763.

4. In 1920, federal expenditures totaled $6.357 billion. By 1930 they had been reduced to $3.320 billion.

5. The size of the cost-of-living adjustment (COLA) is determined by the Bureau of Labor Statistics on the basis of a formula that reflects the rate of annual inflation.

6. The General Accountability Office (GAO) was originally given the responsibility to

determine the size of these cuts after receiving estimates from the Office of Management and Budget and the Congressional Budget Office. The Supreme Court, however, ruled that this arrangement violated the constitutional separation of powers by involving an agency of Congress in executive branch decisions.

7. The name referred to the Boston Tea Party in 1773 when settlers, objecting to a new tax imposed by the king, dumped tons of imported tea into the water.

8. The key to reducing spending is the amount of public and organizational support for the program. Beneficiaries of most government programs organize to protect their interests, using well-connected lobbyists to advocate on their behalf and sophisticated communication technologies to alert and mobilize their supporters.

9. Louis Fisher, *Presidential Spending Power* (Princeton, NJ: Princeton University Press, 1975), p. 35.

10. William Greider, "The Education of David Stockman," *Atlantic*, December 1981, pp. 33–34.

11. B. Dan Wood, *The Politics of Economic Leadership: The Causes and Consequences of Presidential Rhetoric* (Princeton, NJ: Princeton University Press, 2007), p. xiii.

12. Matthew Eshbaugh-Soha and Jeffrey S. Peake, "Presidents and the Economic Agenda," *Political Research Quarterly* 58 (March 2005): 127–138.

13. "Presidential Approval Ratings," *Gallup Poll*, February 16–22, 2009. http://www .gallup.com/poll/124922/Presidential-Approval-Center.aspx (accessed November 26, 2012).

14. Larry Bartels, *Unequal Democracy: Political Economy of the New Guilded Age* (Princeton, NJ: Princeton University Press, 2008), chap. 2.

15. James E. Campbell, "The Economic Records of the Presidents, Party Differences, and Inherited Economic Conditions," *Forum* 9, art. 7 (2011): 15, and "The President's Economy: Parity in Presidential Party Performance," *Presidential Studies Quarterly* 42 (December 2012): 811–818.

16. Christopher Berry, Barry Burden, and William Howell, "The President and the Distribution of Federal Spending," *American Political Science Review* 104 (November 2010): 783–799.

17. Douglas L. Kriner and Andrew Reeves, "The Influence of Federal Spending on Federal Elections," *American Political Science Review* 106 (May 2012): 348–366.

18. John T. Gasper and Andrew Reeves, "Make It Rain: Retrospection and the Attentive Electorate in the Context of Natural Disasters," *American Journal of Political Science* 55 (February 2011): 340–355; Andrew J. Healy and Neil Malhotra, "Myopic Voters and Natural Disaster Policy," *American Political Science Review* 103 (August 2009): 387–406; Andrew Reeves, "Political Disaster: Unilateral Powers, Electoral Incentives, and Presidential Disaster Declarations," *Journal of Politics* 73 (October 2011): 1142–1151.

13

FOREIGN AND DEFENSE POLICY MAKING

Few would question the obligation of presidents to preserve and protect the nation. Few would deny them the constitutional and statutory authority to do so. Still, the extent of presidents' foreign policy powers has been subject to controversy over the years.

Traditionally, executives have enjoyed a broad prerogative in foreign affairs, a prerogative that expands during crises that threaten national security. That expansion, however, is limited in scope and time. One critical aspect of presidential leadership is how those limits are defined, both in legal and political terms. Another is the willingness of other institutions of government and the American people to impose those limits.

Other components of the leadership equation in foreign affairs are the multiple roles presidents assume and the multiple pressures that affect them. The roles derive from the Constitution, statutes, and precedent. They have been more expansive in foreign affairs than in the domestic arena, but the president's leadership problem stems from the same basic root: presidents do not control the environment in which they must act; they do not exercise their responsibilities alone; and they may lack complete and accurate information on which to base their decisions. Moreover, there are additional actors in the international arena that must be considered; other nation-states, regional alliances, world organizations, multinational corporations, and nongovernment organizations operate independently and are not responsive to the internal political forces that condition policy making in the United States.

Congress is empowered to act in foreign affairs; an increasing array of interest groups plus professional lobbyists that represent foreign corporations and governments seek to influence U.S. policy decisions. The news media regularly provide coverage of conditions and events abroad in a manner that both informs the American public and often shapes their reactions to international situations and events.

Within the international arena, the United States is one player among many; with the economies of the world increasingly interrelated, with critical resources in short supply, and with national and international interests often in tension with one another, presidents have their work cut out for them. Moreover, even among their advisers, there often is disagreement.

How these factors affect a president's capacity to lead in foreign affairs and shape policy will be the subject of this chapter. We first describe the president's formal authority in theory and practice. We then turn to the expansion of the president's foreign policy-making role, identifying the principal reasons for that expansion. Our discussion focuses on changes within the international and domestic environment since the end of the cold war with the Soviet Union. The threat of terrorism, proliferation of weapons of mass destruction, and the growing interdependency of national economies all impact on presidential policy making. The final part of the chapter describes and evaluates the advisory mechanisms that have been created to help the president formulate, coordinate, articulate, and implement foreign and defense policy.

CONSTITUTIONAL AND STATUTORY AUTHORITY

The Original Design

The president's powers in foreign affairs and national defense have expanded significantly. The framers of the Constitution anticipated a foreign policy-making role for the president, but they did not want the executive to exercise that role alone. Their fear that a president might pursue interests that adversely affected the nation's welfare, as they believed European monarchs had done for centuries, led them to divide and share foreign policy-making responsibilities, just as they had done for domestic and economic matters. The president could initiate treaties with the advice of the Senate; ratification required the concurrence of two-thirds of the upper chamber. Similarly, the president could appoint ambassadors, but that too required Senate approval. The determination of war policy was to be Congress's alone. The president had discretion to act in times of emergency to repel attacks but presumably not to initiate hostilities or in any other way establish permanent war policy. The performance of the ceremonial duties of a head of state and the conduct of foreign policy were seen as executive responsibilities.

In fulfilling these functions, presidents would inevitably make decisions that had policy implications. The framers did not fear this. They anticipated that Congress, by virtue of its power to appropriate money, authorize programs, and regulate commerce, would set the contours of that policy and be able to check presidential initiatives adequately.

The Exercise of Powers

Treaty Making

Appointments and treaty making were to be jointly exercised with the Senate. From the outset, the Senate has demonstrated its independent judgment in these matters. During the first administration of George Washington, the upper house refused to confirm the president's nomination of Benjamin Fishbourn to be the naval officer of the port of Savannah, Georgia. To prevent future rejections, Washington began to consult informally with senators in whose state the nominee would serve. This practice, known as senatorial courtesy, acquired a partisan tinge with the development of the party system at the end of the eighteenth century.[1]

Nor has Senate advice and consent in treaty making been automatic. In fact, rarely have presidents sought the Senate's collective advice even though the framers envisioned that the upper house would serve as an advisory body to the president in the area of foreign affairs. An incident that occurred early in the Washington administration soured this arrangement. In August 1789, President Washington came to the Senate to request its advice on a treaty with Native Americans in western Georgia. Armed with thirteen questions prepared by his secretary of war, General Henry Knox, Washington requested the Senate's guidance in the negotiations. Instead, he was treated to a long, discursive discussion that reached no conclusion. Forced to return two days later for what turned out to be insipid advice, Washington did not go back to the Senate again for its counsel.

Washington's experience had a profound effect on future presidential–senatorial relations. It discouraged his successors from involving the Senate in the negotiation phase of treaties, although some consultation has occurred. Woodrow Wilson's refusal to consider the Senate opinion in the negotiations on the Treaty of Versailles and his proposal for a League of Nations represents one of the most flagrant and unsuccessful examples of a chief executive trying to go it alone.[2]

Historically, the Senate has approved about three-fourths of the treaties that have been submitted to it by the president since 1789. Only a small number of treaties have been rejected because presidents frequently do not even introduce them, or they withdraw them if they perceive the treaties stand little chance of passage.[3] (See Table 13.1.)

The Senate can approve treaties without modification, as it did with the Strategic Arms Reduction Treaty (START) with Russia in 2009, the Intermediate Range Nuclear Forces Treaty (INF) with the Soviet Union (1988), and the Chemical Weapons Treaty (1997), or reject them outright as it did with the Comprehensive Nuclear Test Ban Treaty (1999); it can also approve them with reservations or with amendments, thereby requiring the president to negotiate these changes with the governments involved. For example, in early 1978, the Senate consented to two treaties dealing with the Panama Canal but added a reservation to one of them stating that the United States had a right to use military force, if necessary, to keep the canal open.

Table 13.1 Treaties and Executive Agreements Approved by the United States, 1789–2010

Year	Number of Treaties	Number of Executive Agreements
1789–1839	60	27
1839–1889	215	238
1889–1929	382	763
1930–1932	49	41
1933–1944 (F. Roosevelt)	131	369
1945–1952 (Truman)	132	1,324
1953–1960 (Eisenhower)	89	1,834
1961–1963 (Kennedy)	36	813
1964–1968 (Johnson)	67	1,083
1969–1974 (Nixon)	93	1,317
1975–1976 (Ford)	26	666
1977–1980 (Carter)	79	1,476
1981–1988 (Reagan)	125	2,840
1989–1992 (G. H. W. Bush)	67	1,350
1993–2000 (Clinton)	209	2,048
2001–2008 (G. W. Bush)	136	1,998
2009–2010 (Obama)	11	422

Note: Varying definitions of what comprises an executive agreement and its entry-into-force date make the above numbers approximate.

SOURCE: Harold W. Stanley and Richard G. Niemi, *Vital Statistics on American Politics: 2011–2012* (Washington, DC: Sage/CQ Press, 2011).

Even when the Senate approves a treaty, it can limit the president's discretion in implementing it, especially if the treaty requires authorizing legislation or appropriations, as was the case with the North Atlantic Free Trade Agreement (NAFTA) and the General Agreement on Tariffs and Trade (GATT). When accompanying legislation is required, the House participates as a coequal legislative branch.[4]

Sometimes presidents also request additional legislation. To assuage his party's concerns about workers who lose their jobs because of foreign competition, President Obama asked Congress to renew the Trade Adjustment Assistance Program before he would submit free trade agreements with Colombia, South Korea, and Panama, negotiated by the Bush administration, to the Senate for ratification. Obama and congressional Democrats wanted to make sure that health and unemployment benefits would be available to workers who might be displaced by the competition stemming from these agreements.

Senate participation in treaty making can weaken the president's negotiating position if other countries believe that additional conditions may be required before ratification. To rectify this problem, Congress enacted fast-track authority in 1974. The legislation allowed the president to introduce treaties for an up or down vote, provided members of Congress participated on the negotiating team. This authority lapsed in 1994; it was renewed in 2002 but lapsed again in 2007.

Whereas Senate consent is necessary for the ratification of treaties, it has not been considered essential for their termination. When President Jimmy Carter ended a long-standing defense treaty with the Chinese Nationalists on Taiwan and George W. Bush announced the 1972 Anti-Ballistic Missile (ABM) Treaty to be obsolete, they did not request approval of the Senate. The legality of Carter's actions, challenged by Senator Barry Goldwater, were upheld by the Supreme Court.[5]

Presidents also have discretion in their interpretation and reinterpretation of treaties so long as they do not digress from the position that they or their predecessors presented to the Senate during the treaty's ratification hearings.[6] The Reagan administration conveniently contended that the ban against space-based missiles in the ABM Treaty, ratified in 1973, did not apply to the development and testing of space-based weapons but only to their deployment.

Formulating Executive Agreements
The need to obtain the Senate's consent has encouraged presidents to enter into executive agreements that do not require Senate approval although they may require congressional appropriations for their execution.[7] When President John Tyler failed to get the Senate to ratify a treaty annexing Texas, he entered into an executive agreement to do so. Recent examples include the Yalta and Potsdam agreements in 1945, the Vietnam peace agreement in 1973, and, more recently, the Status of Forces Agreement with Iraq signed in December 2008. The number of such agreements has mushroomed in recent years.

Even though Congress does not have to approve an executive agreement, legislators do have a right to know about them. In 1969 and 1970, the Senate Foreign Relations Committee discovered that Presidents Lyndon Johnson and Richard Nixon had covertly entered into a number of secret agreements with South Vietnam, South Korea, Thailand, Laos, Ethiopia, Spain, and other countries. In response to these secret pacts, Congress enacted legislation in 1972 that requires the secretary of state to transmit the text of any international agreement, other than treaties, to which the United States is a party to Congress within sixty days. If presidents feel publication of the agreement would jeopardize national security, they may transmit the text only to members of the Senate Foreign Relations and House International Relations committees under an injunction of secrecy that only they (or their successors) may remove.[8]

Treaties supersede statutes; executive agreements do not. Agreements can be terminated by the executives who negotiated them or by their successors in office.

Policy Doctrines
Short of a formal agreement or declaration, the president can also issue a doctrine, articulate a policy, or send signals about future policy changes. Doctrines are the most comprehensive of these policy pronouncements.

Not only do they contain policy positions, but they articulate the principles upon which those positions are predicated. One of the most famous American doctrines was pronounced by President James Monroe in his State of the Union address in 1823. The doctrine stipulated that United States would not permit further colonization of the Western Hemisphere. Issued at the time the Spanish Empire in the Americas was disintegrating, the doctrine was intended as a warning to other European countries not to try to take over former Spanish colonies.

Today it is customary to summarize the basic thrust of a president's foreign policy by referring to it as a doctrine. The Truman doctrine was designed to contain the spread of communism in Europe; the Eisenhower doctrine, mutually assured destruction (MAD), indicated that the United States would respond in kind to a nuclear attack; the Reagan doctrine, the necessity of military and economic dominance to end the cold war, led to the doubling of the defense budget during the president's first term and to his strategic defense initiative, known as Star Wars, in his second. After the terrorist attacks in New York and Washington in 2001, President Bush announced that the United States would aggressively pursue the perpetrators of this crime and governments that harbored them. In December 2001, the Bush administration promulgated a new strategic doctrine that claimed the right to engage in preventative wars, preempting an attack by striking first. Bush's use of military force in Iraq was justified in part by his preemption doctrine.[9]

Box 13.1 HOT BUTTON ISSUE
Does Obama Have a Doctrine?

In his campaign for the presidency, Barack Obama promised a more realistic, less ideological approach to foreign policy than his predecessor, one based primarily on multilateral diplomacy, not the use of force. Obama amplified his position on the use of force in his speech accepting the Nobel Peace Prize in 2009. Differentiating between conflicts of self-defense in which military action might be justified and other types of conflicts in which negotiations were the appropriate response, the president contended that if force was necessary, it should be exercised by a coalition of nations, not one country imposing its will on another. Obama followed these principles when he supported international efforts to prevent a humanitarian disaster in

Libya and sent U.S. military aid to the NATO coalition that sought to remove Libya's Muammar Qaddafi from power. In the absence of an international agreement on Syria, he did not involve American military forces but imposed economic sanctions, restricting trade and freezing the assets of Syrian officials in the United States.

Obama has continued the battle against al-Qaeda and other terrorist groups. The president approved a military operation to kill Osama bin Laden. He increased the use of special forces, unmanned drones, and field-based intelligence to target leaders of terrorist groups. His administration has also pursued a vigorous counterterrorism operation at home, employing surveillance techniques, stings, and other law enforcement methods similar to those used by the Bush administration.

Although Obama has taken a pragmatic approach to foreign policy and national security, does it constitute a doctrine? People that say "yes" point to several underlying principles that guide Obama's actions: multilateral collaboration and negotiations, global engagement, humanitarian intervention, and if need be, the use of economic sanctions and military force in conjunction with America's allies. Those that say "no" note the absence of a single, all-encompassing objective and framework for policy making, the unpredictability of U.S. responses to contemporary international events, shifting regional strategic goals, and continued debate among the president's principal advisers on priorities, budgets, and the exercise of power.

Although presidents can change their predecessor's policies, they have more difficulty in changing their country's national interests. The Obama administration criticized the restraints that the Bush administration placed on civil liberties in its war on terrorism but soon found that it could not easily reverse many of them and continue to wage a strong antiterrorist campaign. Early in his presidency and with considerable public fanfare, Obama revoked Bush's order to use enhanced interrogation techniques on alleged enemy combatants, stated that his administration would release CIA and Defense Department memoranda that described the previous administration's application of these techniques, banned torture and humiliating treatment of prisoners, announced his intention to close the detention facility at Guantánamo Naval Base, and approved his attorney general's proposal to use civil courts to try suspected enemy combatants. In practice, however, the administration has been unable to close Guantánamo, prosecute suspected terrorist in civilian courts, or release information deemed harmful to the national security by the CIA and Defense Department.[10] The Justice Department has invoked the state secrets doctrine to prevent the use of classified information in the trials that have been held.

Congress can, of course, modify a presidential policy or doctrine through its authorization and appropriation powers; it can monitor the execution of that policy using its oversight authority. But Congress lacks the institutional resources to compete with the president's policy initiatives. It may also lack the political incentives.[11] Not only has constitutional authority, statute, and precedent established the president's preeminence in foreign affairs, but it has shaped the American public's perceptions of the president's and the Congress's respective roles in foreign policymaking. The policy initiative clearly lies with the president in foreign affairs.

The Supreme Court has recognized the president's foreign policy prerogative. In *United States v. Curtiss-Wright*, 299 U.S. 304 (1936), the Court upheld an executive agreement that banned the sale of weapons to countries involved in armed conflict on the grounds that the president was the principal organ of the government in foreign affairs; in *United States v. Belmont*, 301 U.S. 324

(1937), the Supreme Court upheld an executive order that seized Russian assets when that country defaulted on debt payments to the United States; and in a subsequent decision, *United States v. Pink*, 315 U.S. 203 (1942), the Court ruled that an executive agreement between Roosevelt and the Soviet Union was valid and superseded state law.

Recognition and Nonrecognition

In addition to negotiating treaties, formulating executive agreements and understandings, and establishing policy doctrine, presidents can initiate or terminate relations with other countries. The right of recognition has traditionally been considered an executive responsibility. Although there is evidence to suggest that the framers intended this power to be purely ministerial, presidents have exercised their discretion when using their recognition authority.[12] George Washington was the first to do so when he officially received the representative of the new French Republic in 1789, Citizen Genet. Subsequently, he revoked Genet's credentials after the latter agitated for America to join France in its conflict with England. Washington advocated neutrality.

Presidents have gone so far as to recognize a government that has been removed from power and to acknowledge the rights of a people who lack a state. Following the signing of an agreement between Israel and the Palestine Liberation Organization (PLO) at the White House in 1993, President Clinton indicated that the United States might grant formal recognition to the PLO if it renounced terrorism and recognized Israel's right to exist. Similarly, George W. Bush and Barack Obama indicated that the United States was prepared to recognize a Palestinian state if certain conditions were met.[13] The Senate has no role in the recognition process other than to consent to the choice of an American ambassador and the establishment of an embassy.

Recognizing countries can be controversial. In 1933, Franklin D. Roosevelt recognized the government of the Soviet Union, fifteen years after it was constituted and functioning. In 1979, Jimmy Carter extended recognition to the People's Republic of China following a period of thirty years of nonrecognition. In 1984, Ronald Reagan announced the resumption of formal diplomatic relations with the Vatican. After approving a private visit to the United States by the president of Taiwan in 1995, an island over which China claims sovereignty, the Clinton administration went to great lengths to indicate to the Chinese that the visit did not imply or portend recognition.[14] Each of these actions provoked criticism about the merits of the presidents' judgments but not about their authority to make them.

Presidents can also end relations. Before war ensues, it is customary to sever diplomatic ties with adversaries. Events short of war can also result in a disruption of diplomatic activity. The revolutionary activities of Cuba and Iran led presidents Dwight Eisenhower and Jimmy Carter to cut formal ties with these countries. However, some contact was maintained by an "interests section," which operated out of the embassy of a friendly country. President Obama reversed the ban on travel to Cuba. He also withdrew the United States' recognition of Muammar Qaddafi as the legitimate head of the Libyan government and froze Libya's assets in the United States during the uprising in that country that forced Qaddafi from power. Obama subsequently made those assets available to the rebels who were opposing the Qaddafi regime.

There are other actions that presidents can take to register their disapproval of the policies of other countries. Recalling an ambassador, instituting a trade embargo, and reducing economic or military assistance are all devices that have been employed to sanction the actions of and disrupt relations with other countries. The Clinton administration labeled Sudan a terrorist country in 1993 after discovering a tie between two of its representatives at the United Nations and the terrorists who bombed the World Trade Center in New York City; in 2008, Congress identified the Iranian National Guard as a terrorist organization at the urging of the Bush administration. The Obama administration imposed economic sanctions and participated in an international campaign to pressure Iran to halt its nuclear enrichment program. Presidents can also remove sanctions if the objectionable policy is changed.

Ordering Military Actions

The Constitution gives Congress the sole power to declare war, a power it has exercised only five times (1812, 1846, 1898, 1917, and 1941). Full-scale military encounters, such as those in Korea, Vietnam, the Persian Gulf, and, more recently, Afghanistan and Iraq, were not officially declared by Congress, although legislative resolutions to authorize the president to use military force, if necessary, were enacted. George H. W. Bush and his son, George W. Bush, both claimed that they did not need a congressional resolution to act but requested it to maximize their political support and preclude later partisan opposition in Congress. When Barack Obama failed to ask Congress for authority to support NATO and its coalition partners in Libya, he was criticized by congressional Republicans and Democrats alike for not doing so.

Presidential involvement of armed forces in hostile or potentially hostile situations presents a conflict between constitutional theory and practice. As commander-in-chief, head of state, and head of government, every contemporary president from Truman through Obama has committed the nation to battle.[15] Armed with a near monopoly on first-hand information, a potential for engaging public support, and an oath to provide for the common defense, presidents have used their prerogatives to broaden their constitutional powers. Presidents have employed a more limited use of force abroad without declarations of war or statutory authority more than 130 times.

Theoretically, Congress could have resisted such actions. In practice it has been unable and unwilling to do so.[16] The House of Representatives condemned James K. Polk's order to send the army into disputed territory with Mexico, but only after the Mexican War had been concluded. Congress forced Richard Nixon to end bombing in Cambodia, but only after that action had been carried on for more than two years. During periods of crisis, Congress finds it difficult, if not impossible, to oppose the president. Despite public opposition to the U.S. military presence in Iraq and Afghanistan, Congress was unable to impose a timetable on the withdrawal of American forces. In both cases, it was the administration in consultation with defense department officials that negotiated or established the withdrawal.

To give Congress a voice in the decision to involve the U.S. military in hostile or potentially hostile situations, Congress passed the War Powers Resolution in 1973. It requires presidents to consult with Congress in writing within forty-eight hours after ordering U.S. armed forces into hostilities. Congress then has sixty days to approve the action (which is not subject to a presidential veto), or the president must withdraw the troops. At any time, Congress can end the use of American armed forces by passing a concurrent resolution.[17]

The law has aroused considerable debate about just what "consultation" means and whether the president could, in sixty days of hostilities, place the United States in a position from which Congress could not extract it. Neither the evacuations from Southeast Asia in April 1975, the rescue of the Mayaguez from Cambodia in May 1975, the attempted rescue of the hostages from Iran in 1980, the Grenada invasion of 1983, nor the use of armed forces in the Persian Gulf (1991), in Afghanistan (2001 and in Iraq (2003) was approved on the basis of the War Powers Resolution. Moreover, in practically every administration since 1973, there have been instances that could have fallen under the purview of the act but were not reported to Congress. Why? What is the problem?

The answer is institutional rivalry. Presidents believe that the War Powers Resolution unconstitutionally constricts their obligation to provide for the common defense by constraining their powers as commander-in-chief. Although they have not challenged the constitutionality of the legislation, they have narrowly interpreted its provisions, particularly its consultation and reporting requirements. They have also maintained that they do not need congressional approval to order American forces into situations that may involve combat; they claim that they have this authority as commander-in-chief. In short, the War Powers Resolution has not provided the check Congress had intended.

Is the resolution unworkable? Perhaps. Is it irrelevant? No. In theory, it reasserts congressional authority while acknowledging expanded presidential powers; in practice, it does not prevent presidential initiatives but forces the president to consider the possibility that Congress, through action or inaction, could terminate those initiatives. This consideration reinforces the public and congressional opposition that exists or can develop over time if the operation is not successful. Presidents, particularly those facing reelection, are mindful of the potential political costs of their actions that put American forces in harm's way.

Although Congress is not likely to oppose presidential involvement in emergency situations, its influence on policy in nonemergencies has increased. The power to authorize conscription or maintain an all-volunteer military, to appropriate money for defense, even to affect the sales of arms, is vested in

Congress. In 1981, President Reagan had to use all of his persuasive powers to keep Congress from preventing a sale of special reconnaissance aircraft to Saudi Arabia. Later in his presidency, he was forced to modify or abandon other arms deals because they faced certain defeat in Congress. Since the Vietnam War, presidents can no longer count on bipartisan support for all military appropriations, actions, alliances, and aid.

Commanding the Armed Forces

The constitutional framers anticipated that the president would take the initiative in times of emergency, particularly if Congress were not in session. They gave the president the authority and responsibility to summon the legislature into special session, provide it with information on the state of the union, and recommend necessary and expedient legislation. Moreover, by designating the president as commander-in-chief and head of state, the framers provided a constitutional basis for unilateral presidential actions in times of crisis. These actions, taken by presidents beginning with Washington, established precedents that have been cited, followed, and in some cases expanded by their successors. Practice has been codified into tradition.

Washington supervised his administration's campaign against Indian tribes in the Northwest Territories and exercised command over the Pennsylvania state militia to put down the Whiskey Rebellion. Thomas Jefferson ordered the navy to protect U.S. shipping from the Barbary pirates, although he was careful to differentiate his actions from war. Although James Madison was a weak and ineffectual commander-in-chief during the War of 1812, Andrew Jackson, a successful general in that war, ordered troops to the state of South Carolina as president to gain the compliance of its citizens with a new tariff law.

By far the most extensive use of presidential powers during a national emergency in the nineteenth century was Lincoln's at the onset of the Civil War. He assembled the state militias, enlarged the army and navy beyond their statutory limits, pledged the government's credit for a large loan, and instituted a naval blockade of the South. Not only did he unilaterally suspend the writ of habeas corpus, thereby enabling the government to hold, for indefinite periods and without evidence, those suspected of providing aid and comfort to the southern secessionists, but he also authorized the establishment of military courts in areas of civil insurrection. His attorney general allowed private homes to be searched without court-issued warrants. Only after this unilateral exercise of power did Lincoln convene a special session of Congress to legislate what he had decreed.

The expansive exercise of presidential powers during wars and periods of civil unrest continued into the twentieth and twenty-first centuries. Even before Congress officially involved the country in World War I, Woodrow Wilson closed a private communication station in Massachusetts after the station refused to abide by the navy's censorship regulations. He appealed to Congress for statutory authority to arm private ships. When a Senate filibuster killed his proposal, Wilson ordered their arming anyway.[18]

After Germany attacked Poland at the beginning of World War II, Franklin Roosevelt declared a limited state of emergency. He froze the assets of Axis countries in the United States. Despite the strong congressional sentiment for neutrality, the president pursued a calculated policy of helping the Allies. He negotiated an executive agreement with the United Kingdom in which he exchanged fifty overaged destroyers for leases on Britain's Caribbean bases; he also agreed to defend Greenland and Iceland, if attacked, and established a U.S. defense presence on both islands to do so.

Roosevelt's most controversial actions, however, were on the home front. He issued an order to the secretary of war and military commanders to use their discretion to maintain domestic security. Acting on the basis of his order, the general in charge of the northwest region of the country ordered a curfew in the state of Washington and subsequently set up camps to detain approximately 120,000 people of Japanese descent, more than half of whom were U.S. citizens. The president also ordered the establishment of a military tribunal to try eight German saboteurs who were captured in the United States.

During periods of war, most court decisions have validated, not overturned, the exercise of expanded presidential powers. In 1863, the Supreme Court upheld Lincoln's actions, specifically his order to seize enemy ships and take their cargo as prizes of war. In *The Prize Cases*, 67 U.S. (2 Black) 635 (1863), the Court stated that the president's authority to protect the Union extended to his orders on the high seas—even if Congress had not legislated on the matter. Similarly, in *Ex Parte Milligan*, 71 U.S. (4 Wall) 2 (1866), the Court upheld the president's authority to establish military tribunals for those accused of aiding and abetting the enemy. The Supreme Court reiterated this judgment in the case of the eight German saboteurs in *Ex Parte Quirin*, 317 U.S. 1 (1942). It also upheld Roosevelt's order that resulted in the mass detention of Japanese Americans in *Korematsu v. United States*, 323 U.S. 214 (1944). Following the war, however, the Supreme Court reversed a military court's conviction of a U.S. citizen in the case of *Duncan v. Kahanamoku*, 327 U.S. 304 (1946), on the grounds that it was not Congress's intent in authorizing martial law in Hawaii to replace civilian courts with military tribunals.

President George W. Bush was not as fortunate as Roosevelt in the Court's acceptance of his actions after 9/11. In three separate cases, the Supreme Court ruled that he had exceeded his authority in holding suspected enemy combatants indefinitely without the right to a habeas corpus appeal, that his creation of military tribunals in the absence of legislation was unlawful, and that the Geneva Convention applied to prisoners held at Guantánamo. Subsequently, Congress granted the president authority to establish military courts.

Challenges by members of Congress to presidential war powers have also been rejected by the Court on the grounds that individual members of Congress did not have standing to sue or the case involved a political question that was not a justiciable issue.[19]

FOREIGN POLICY MAKING AND PRESIDENTIAL LEADERSHIP

The increasing involvement of the United States in the international community, the public's desire for strong presidential leadership, and the political ramifications of that leadership have all contributed to expanded presidential initiatives and policy making in foreign affairs.

Political Incentives

Since the end of World War II, the United States has been a dominant economic, military, and political power. It has tried to shape international developments by aiding its allies and resisting its adversaries, building its defenses yet promoting peaceful coexistence, fostering its interests yet supporting international cooperation, and promoting its political and social values throughout the world. The industrial capacity, technological skills, and resource base of the United States were essential to the revitalization of the economies of countries in Western Europe and Asia in the aftermath of World War II. Today the economies and resources of nation states are more interdependent than ever. They cannot help but affect the domestic economy that impacts directly on presidents and their party's political fortunes.

The end of the cold war in the late 1980s initially decreased the president's incentive to focus on national security at the expense of domestic matters. One of the criticisms voiced about President George H. W. Bush in the 1992 elections was that he spent too much time on foreign affairs. Public perceptions of America's invulnerability were shattered by the 9/11 terrorist attacks. The public looked to the president for leadership in this time of crisis, and President Bush responded accordingly.[20]

In exercising this leadership, presidents have used their informational advantage to maximize their congressional and public support. In some cases, however, the information they provided proved to be incomplete and even inaccurate. In 1964, President Johnson told the American people that there had been two attacks on U.S. naval forces in the Gulf of Tonkin, attacks by North Vietnam. He requested authorization from Congress to respond. Later it was discovered that the first attack was minor and the second one never occurred. In 2002, President Bush declared that British intelligence had evidence that Iraq was rebuilding its nuclear capacity; he also claimed that Iraq possessed other weapons of mass destruction. The weapons were never found. In both cases, however, Congress, acting on this information, enacted the resolutions that each president requested to use force if necessary to protect U.S. national security.[21]

Presidents have also been accused of "saber rattling," threating America's might to initiate or reinforce the country's international policy goals. Saber rattling can be dangerous if unfriendly countries take a more militant posture in countering what they perceive as a possible American attack. Moreover, the threat of force can cause serious political and economic repercussions at home. A study by B. Dan Wood found that from 1978 to 2005, presidential saber rattling increased concern about future economic performance; more specifically it created anxieties that lowered consumer confidence, spending, and borrowing.[22]

In the short run, presidential actions during a crisis usually increase the public's approval of the president's job performance. Presidents use their "bully pulpits" to their advantage in such situations. Over time, when other information becomes available or when the military action is not successfully concluded, the president's popularity declines as it did for Truman, Johnson, and Bush in their last years in office.

In addition to the short-run support that crises can generate, foreign policy leadership contributes to the image of a strong president. This image is particularly useful during reelection campaigns, as it was for Ronald Reagan in 1984 and George W. Bush in 2004. The public wants to feel secure. They look to the president to satisfy that feeling.

Policy Influence: The Two Presidencies Thesis

Are presidents apt to be more successful in crafting foreign policy than domestic policy? According to Aaron Wildavsky, they have tended to be, particularly in the period from 1948 to 1964.[23] In examining congressional action on presidential proposals during this period, Wildavsky found that presidents had significantly more legislative success in foreign and defense policy than in domestic affairs. He gave several reasons for this institutional dominance:

1. Presidents have more constitutional and statutory authority in foreign affairs and more expertise available to them.
2. By tradition, presidents have assumed a more active role in foreign affairs.
3. Presidents can act more quickly and decisively than Congress.
4. Because there are fewer interest groups active in the foreign policy arena, presidents have more discretion to act as national leaders.

Wildavsky concluded that there were actually two presidencies, one in foreign affairs and one in the domestic arena, but he completed his analysis studied an era of bipartisanship in foreign policy that followed World War II and the onset of the cold war.[24] Since that time, the domestic impact of foreign policy has become more pronounced, blurring the old distinction between foreign and domestic affairs and creating new incentives for Congress to get involved. The old adage that "politics stops at the water's edge" is no longer applicable.

There are more organized interest groups today that are concerned with the economic, social, and political impact of foreign policy issues than there were studied the period that Wildavsky examined, and the groups are more powerful. They have greater resources and technologies to reach and mobilize their members and supporters to pressure government and affect election outcomes.

A second factor that has forced the president's hand is the 24-7 news media cycle and continuous Internet communications. The attention given to certain international events and conditions combined with the more recent flow of pictures and words from around the world on the Internet via YouTube, Twitter, and other social networks has raised public awareness and increased political costs of inaction for presidents.[25] Accounts replete with visual imagery of hunger in Somalia, ethnic cleansing in Kosovo, and repression of popular demonstrations in Libya prompted George H. W. Bush, Bill Clinton, and Barack Obama to order U.S. military forces into these parts of the world, which have very limited strategic value to the United States. In contrast, the failure of the news media to cover the massacres in Rwanda and other civil strife in Africa resulted in little public pressure to do so.[26]

In general, the more salient the issue and the stronger the public preferences for or against a particular policy outcome, the more likely that presidents will be forced to take a stand and involve the United States in the matter.[27] Although the general public may not be attentive to many of the details of an administration's policy, people do tend to be cognizant of the results, especially if those results fall short of presidential promises, public expectations, or both. Military interventions, in particular, are judged by their outcomes, regardless of whether a majority initially supported the president's decision to go to war.[28]

Increased public attention has led to greater congressional involvement in foreign policy matters. With more committees and subcommittees dealing with international issues; more staff and better information facilities at their disposal; more foreign travel by legislators and their aides; and more groups, governments, and individuals trying to affect policy judgments, members of Congress, individually and collectively, have become less disposed to acquiesce quickly and quietly to the president's foreign policy initiatives.

Greater congressional scrutiny of foreign policy making has led scholars to reexamine Wildavsky's two presidencies thesis. In general, political scientists have found that presidents are still more likely to prevail on foreign affairs than on domestic issues, but they are also more likely to have Congress debate and modify their proposals than in the past.[29] Trade agreements, which can have significant domestic impacts, represent one area in which Congress has shown continued concern and involvement over the years.

Partisanship is also a factor that affects foreign policy making.[30] Trade agreements in particular have been subject to partisan bickering.[31] The partisan composition of Congress also affects the exercise of war powers.[32] The time frame for military actions shortens when presidents face an opposition partisan majority in Congress.[33]

In short, the consensus that characterized U.S. foreign policy during World War II and the cold war has weakened and on some issues ended. Presidents can no longer take public support for granted. Nonetheless, the two presidencies thesis may still be valid. When presidents' ability to affect domestic change decreases, they devote more time to foreign affairs. Bill Clinton and Barack Obama are examples of presidents elected primarily to fix the economy who turned increasingly to foreign policy after their party suffered losses in midterm elections.

Obviously, presidents need all the help they can get to meet their multiple tasks of formulating and articulating foreign policy, building a public consensus for it, lobbying Congress to obtain the necessary approval, and overseeing the conduct of foreign affairs. It is to their advisory and administrative national security structures that we now turn.

THE ADVISORY SYSTEM

As we noted in Chapters 6 and 7, the environment for decision making, the advisers who participate, and the presidents' involvement in the process affect the timing of their decision, the assumptions on which it is based, and the resulting policy outcomes.

The Departments of State and Defense

Throughout the nineteenth century and well into the twentieth, presidents turned to their department heads for information, advice, and political support on foreign policy issues with the secretary of state the president's principal adviser on nonmilitary issues and the secretaries of the war and navy departments on military ones.

In performing these roles, these secretaries have been assisted by political appointees, civil servants, and foreign service officers in the state department and military officers and civilian personnel in the departments of war and navy. Figure 13.1 lists the principal units in the state department today, and Figure 13.2 lists those in the Department of Defense.

Other departments, including treasury, state, commerce, agriculture, transportation, and energy, supplement the flow of data from around the world and the advice the president receives.

The National Security Council and Staff

In 1947, Congress enacted the National Security Act that created a National Security Council, a combined Department of Defense, and the Central Intelligence Agency. The council initially consisted of four statutory members: the president, vice president, secretary of state, and secretary of defense. Over the years, a number of advisory members have been added: the chair of the Joint Chiefs of Staff, the head of the Arms Control and Disarmament Agency, the ambassador to the United Nations, the national intelligence director, and others whom presidents have designated from time to time.

The council's charge is primarily advisory, but its mandate is broad—to help define goals and priorities; to coordinate and integrate domestic, foreign, and military policies; and to suggest specific courses of action, all within the national security sphere. During the Truman presidency, the

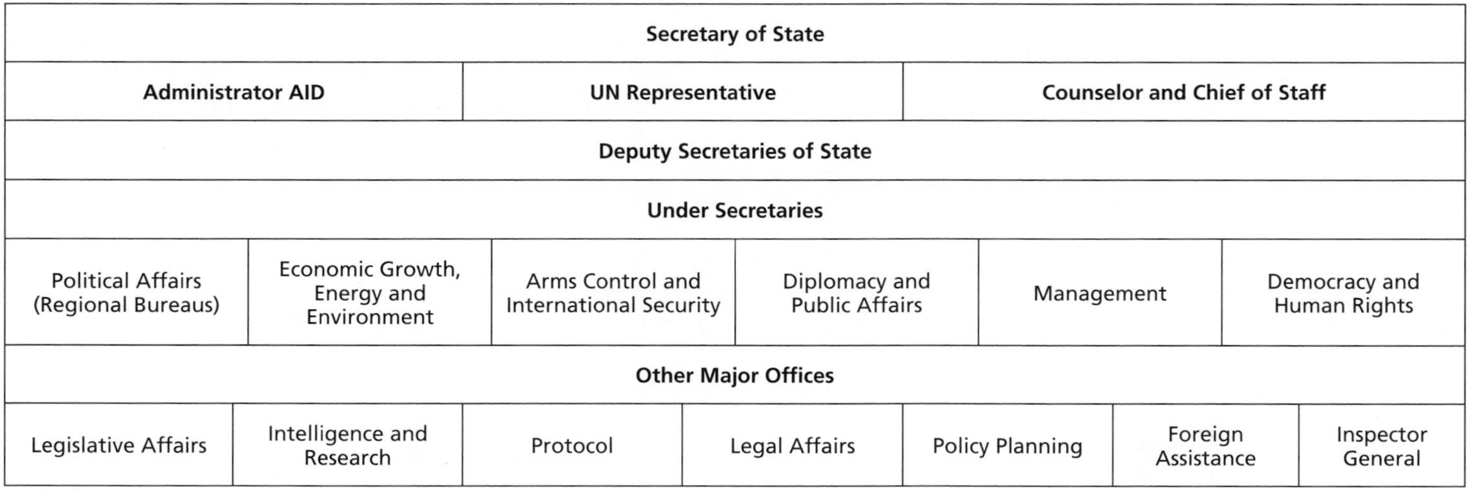

Secretary of State

Administrator AID　|　UN Representative　|　Counselor and Chief of Staff

Deputy Secretaries of State

Under Secretaries

| Political Affairs (Regional Bureaus) | Economic Growth, Energy and Environment | Arms Control and International Security | Diplomacy and Public Affairs | Management | Democracy and Human Rights |

Other Major Offices

| Legislative Affairs | Intelligence and Research | Protocol | Legal Affairs | Policy Planning | Foreign Assistance | Inspector General |

FIGURE 13.1 The Principal Divisions in the Department of State*

*There are a total of twenty-two assistant secretaries in the State Department, forty-four political appointees, and approximately 32,500 full-time employees. "Federal Civilian Employment in the Executive Branch," U.S. Budget for FY 2013, Analytical Perspectives. www.whitehouse.gov/sites/default/files/omb/budget/fy2012/assets/management.pdf

Source: State Department, http://www.state.gov; and Washington Post, http://projects.washingtonpost.com/2009/federal-appointments/agency/state-department/.

Secretary of Defense

Deputy Secretary

Undersecretaries

Comptroller	Acquisition Technology and Logistics	Intelligence	Personnel and Readiness	Policy

Assistant Secretaries*

Legislative Affairs	Information Integration	Public Affairs

Other Major Offices

Inspector General	General Counsel	Operational Test and Evaluation	Administration and Management	Net Assessment

FIGURE 13.2 The Principal Divisions in the Department of Defense

*There are a total of five undersecretaries and fifteen assistant secretaries in the Department of Defense. The department had about 50 political appointees and 757,000 civil servants, plus 1.4 million active-duty military and 1.1 million in National Guard and Reserve units during the 2013 fiscal year. "Federal Civilian Employment in the Executive Branch," U.S. Budget for FY 2013, Analytical Perspectives.

Source: Department of Defense, http://www.defense.gov/about/ (accessed August 21, 2012) and *The Washington Post*, http://projects.washingtonpost.com/2009/federal-appointments/agency /defense-department.

council functioned as a forum for discussion and had an important advisory role during the Korean War.[34] President Eisenhower converted it into a planning board for developing general policy positions. Kennedy eliminated the council's policy-making function and reduced its advisory role, turning instead to a presidential assistant for national security affairs and an informal group, which he dubbed the Executive Committee of the National Security Council (ExCom).

For the most part, the presidents who followed Kennedy have preferred a White House–based assistant and staff rather than a department-based council to inform and advise them on national security matters.[35] They have looked to their national security assistant, who functions as a senior White House aide, to coordinate input from the departments and agencies, funnel information to the president, and focus on problems that merit presidential attention.[36]

The increasing importance of the national security assistant and staff has allowed presidents to maximize their discretion, exercise more central control, act more decisively, and do so in a manner that is consistent with their basic political beliefs, partisan needs, and policy objectives. Unburdened by administrative responsibilities, the national security staff can respond more quickly and less visibly, particularly in times of emergencies. Leaks can be minimized, but as Barack Obama and almost every contemporary president has discovered, not eliminated entirely.[37]

There is a downside to vesting too much power and with it, dependency on the White House's national security staff. Presidents may not be attentive to external influences that should be considered in policy formulation and may affect its implementation and the political repercussions that follow from it. The ideological and partisan perspectives of the president's staff maybe too narrow; as a consequence, there may be greater likelihood that the information the president receives is incomplete, ill-informed, and ill-advised.

The creation of a "groupthink" mentality may be initially comforting to the president but harmful to policy decisions. The near unanimity of opinion that Presidents Johnson and Bush received from their White House advisers on the pursuit of military action in Vietnam and Iraq shielded them from other perspectives from which their policy judgments might have profited.

In addition, a strong and visible national security assistant that serves as a presidential spokesperson, negotiator, and liaison with other governments can generate internal conflict within an administration, particularly if the secretaries of state and defense believe that their roles, access, and influence are being circumvented in the process. Presidents Nixon and Carter relied primarily on their national security advisers, Henry Kissinger and Zbigniew Brzezinski, to perform multiple roles, leading to dissent within their respective state departments and ultimately to the resignations of their secretaries of state.[38] Nixon tried to remove the tension by nominating Kissinger to be secretary of state as well as national security adviser at the beginning of his second term, but when Gerald Ford became president, he disengaged the two positions, and they have remained separate ever since.

In short, the innovation, decisiveness, and policy consistency that presidents gain from having loyal, hardworking presidential aides inform and advise them on national security matters, allow them to speak with a single voice, and project a strong leadership image comes with potential costs: limited information, unexplored policy alternatives, and tenuous political support, particularly if the policy is viewed as unsuccessful down the road.

CONCLUSION

The role that the framers of the Constitution envisioned for the president in foreign and military affairs has been expanded significantly. Today, presidents are expected to take the policy-making initiative in both spheres. They are expected to oversee the conduct of war and diplomacy; they are also expected to perform the symbolic duties of chief of state and commander-in-chief.

Although presidential expectations have increased, the ability of the president to satisfy these expectations has not expanded as much, particularly since the Vietnam War. That decline is a product of several factors: the interdependence of the United States with the economies, resources, intelligence, and security of other countries; the increasing impact of foreign policy decisions on domestic affairs; the proliferation of groups and governments trying to affect U.S. foreign policy and national security decisions; and the more assertive posture that the opposition in Congress has assumed in critiquing national security and foreign policy decisions.

These potential constraints require presidents to devote more time and increasing resources to foreign policy. Their advisers have had to make greater efforts at coordination within the executive branch, at consensus building outside it, and at gaining and maintaining congressional and public support. In this sense, the needs of presidents in foreign and national security affairs are not much different than those in the domestic arena, although expectations—their own and those of the American public and foreign government leaders—seem to be greater, as is their constitutional and statutory authority, the precedent of strong executive leadership, and the public expectation that, in foreign affairs, presidents make national policy decisions.

With the increasing importance of foreign and defense policy, presidents have turned to their national security staff for help. Established in 1960 and expanded in size and specialization since then, this internal White House policy mechanism has provided a cadre of loyal experts to help presidents with the international problems they encounter. The national security staff functions primarily to inform and advise presidents and secondarily to oversee the content of their correspondence, speeches, and briefings within this policy sphere. Having such a staff within the White House has increased the information available to presidents, maximized their discretion, and improved their capacity for rapid and decisive decision making. But it also has produced tension within the executive branch, leaks by disgruntled officials, "kick and tell" books by former aides, and in some cases the persistence of a "groupthink" mentality that directs decision making.

Despite the obstacles they face, presidents continue to emphasize foreign policy matters, particularly as their administrations progress, in part because they have to do so. Any major world event is likely to have a perceived impact on U.S. interests and concerns—a consequence of the country's superpower status. In addition, there are other psychological and political incentives for presidents getting involved. As foreign policy leaders, particularly during times of crisis, presidents can act as unifying figures, overcome perceptions of partisanship, and work to achieve specific policy goals. Demonstrating leadership in this manner stands to increase their popularity, improve their chances of reelection, and enhance their place in history—provided that their actions are seen as successful.

Moreover, if their political support declines at home, they may have less motivation to focus on the domestic and more on the foreign policy arena, in which they are likely to be more influential. Finally, there is that intangible, yet real, desire to try to affect events, and particularly to promote American values, culture, and interests around the world. In international affairs, American presidents want, and expect, to be more than facilitators. They want, and expect, to be world leaders. The international community also expects them to fulfill this role even though parts of that community may resent and criticize U.S. policy if that policy conflicts with their own.

Discussion Questions

1. Presidents are expected to be chief foreign policy makers and chief diplomats. However, a number of obstacles impede their ability to initiate and conduct foreign policy. Indicate some of the obstacles they face and how they have tried to overcome them. Note situations in which they have been successful and those in which they have not. Explain the reasons for the successes and failures.

2. Is conflict or consensus among presidential advisers more desirable for presidential decision making in foreign and national security affairs? Note the benefits and the problems that each of these conditions can produce for presidents and illustrate your discussion with examples.

3. How have modern-day presidents handled the problems resulting from 24-7 news media coverage and continuous Internet reporting? What mechanisms have they established in their administrations to collect, coordinate, and evaluate information, even information overload; to make decisions; and to ensure that these decisions are carried out in a manner they desire? Illustrate with examples from recent presidencies.

Web Exercises

1. Go to the White House website (http://www.whitehouse.gov) and follow the president on a recent trip to abroad. Look at the president's public statements and activities during that trip and indicate the principal message the president wished to make and the impression he wanted to leave in the area to which he traveled and in the United States as well. Then access public opinion polls before and after the trip to assess the short-term effect of the trip on the president's job and policy approval. Is it possible to measure a long-term effect?

2. Select any national security issue that is presently commanding public attention. Look at statements issued by the president or the press secretary, a department official at the department's website, and the congressional leadership of both parties, including the chairs of the appropriate House and Senate committees. Do these statements indicate a consensus or a conflict on the issue? Explain.

Selected Readings

Bowie, Robert, ed. *Presidential Judgment: Foreign Policy Decision Making in the White House.* Hollis, NH: Hollis, 2001.

Burke, John P. "The Neutral/Honest Broker Role in Foreign Policy Decision Making: A Reassessment? The National Security Advisor and Presidential Decision Making." *Presidential Studies Quarterly* 35 (June 2005): 229–258.

Burke, John P., and Fred I. Greenstein. *How Presidents Test Reality: Decisions on Vietnam: 1954 and 1965.* New York: Russell Sage Foundation, 1991.

Caruson, Kiki, and Victoria A. Farrar-Myers, "Promoting the President's Foreign Policy Agenda: Presidential Use of Executive Agreements as Policy Vehicles." *Political Research Quarterly* 40 (December 2007): 631–644.

Clarke, Richard A. *Against All Enemies: Inside America's War on Terror.* New York: Free Press, 2004.

Edwards, George C., III, and B. Dan Wood, "Who Influences Whom? The President, Congress, and the Media?" *American Political Science Review* 93 (June 1999): 327–344.

Famham, Barbara. "Impact of Political Context on Foreign Policy Decision Making." *Political Psychology* 25 (June 2004): 441–463.

Fisher, Louis. "Judicial Review of the War Power." *Presidential Studies Quarterly* 35 (September 2005): 466–495.

Howell, William, and Jon C. Pevehouse. *When Dangers Gather: Congressional Checks on Presidential War Powers.* Princeton, NJ: Princeton University Press, 2007.

Korb, Lawrence J., and Laura Conley. "Fighting Two Wars." In *The Obama Presidency,* edited by Andrew J. Dowdle, Dirk C. Van Raemdonack, and Robert Maranto. New York: Routledge, 2011, pp. 172–183.

Kriner, Douglas L. "Presidents, Domestic Politics, and the International Arena." In *The Oxford Handbook of the American Presidency,* edited by George C. Edwards III and William G. Howell. Oxford, UK: Oxford University Press, 2009.

Krutz, Glen S., and Jeffrey S. Peake. "The Changing Nature of Presidential Policy-Making on International Agreements." *Presidential Studies Quarterly* 36 (September 2006): 391–409.

Krutz, Glen S., and Jeffrey S. Peake. *Treaty Politics and the Rise of Executive Agreements: International Commitments in a System of Shared Powers.* Ann Arbor: University of Michigan Press, 2009.

Lindsay, James M. "Deference and Defiance: The Shifting Rhythms of Executive–Legislative Relations Foreign Affairs." *Presidential Studies Quarterly* 33 (September 2002): 530–546.

Martin, Lisa L. "The President and International Commitments: Treaties as Signaling Devices." *Presidential Studies Quarterly* 35 (September 2005): 440–465.

Mitchell, David. "Does Context Matter? Advisory Systems and the Management of the Foreign Policy Decision-Making Process." *Presidential Studies Quarterly* 40 (December 2010): 631–659.

Newman, William. "Causes of Change in National Security Processes: Carter, Reagan, and Bush Decision Making on Arms Control." *Presidential Studies Quarterly* 31 (March 2001): 69–103.

Peake, Jeffrey S, Glen S. Krutz, and Tyler Hughes, "President Obama, the Senate, and the Polarized Politics of Treaty Making," *Social Science Quarterly*, 93 (October 2012): 1295–1315.

Pious, Richard M. "Inherent War and Executive Powers and Prerogative Politics." *Presidential Studies Quarterly* 37 (March 2007): 66–84.

Pious, Richard M. "Prerogative Power in the Obama Administration: Continuity and Change in the War on Terrorism." *Presidential Studies Quarterly* 41 (June 2011): 263–290.

Rodman, Peter. *Presidential Command: Power, Leadership and the Making of Foreign Policy.* New York: Knopf, 2009.

Shull, Steven A., ed. *The Two Presidencies.* Chicago: Nelson Hall, 1991.

Wood, B. Dan, and Jeffrey S. Peake. "The Dynamics of Foreign Policy Agenda Setting." *American Political Science Review* 92 (March 1988): 173–184.

Woodward, Bob. *Obama's Wars.* New York: Simon and Schuster, 2010.

Yoo, John. *The Power of War and Peace: The Constitution and Foreign Affairs after 9/11.* Chicago: University of Chicago Press, 2005.

Notes

1. Presidents try to gain prior approval for their nominees from senators of their party, in some cases even choosing candidates recommended by senators. With the in-stitutionalization of a standing committee system, prior notification of nominees has been extended to the committee chairs, responsible for calling and conducting hearings on the president's nominee.

2. For a psychological explanation of Wilson's rigidity at this critical point in his presidency, see Alexander L. George and Juliette L. George, *Woodrow Wilson and Colonel House.* New York: John Day, 1956.

3. More than 150 treaties have been with-drawn since World War II. At the end of the first term of the Obama administra-tion, there were approximately 30 treaties still awaiting ratification, several for as long as 40 years. Senate Foreign Relations Committee, 112th Congress (http://www.senate.gov/treaties). See also "Treaties Pending in the Senate," United States Department of State. (www.state.gov/s/l/treaty/pending/index.htm)

4. David Auerswald and Forrest Maltsman, "Policymaking through Advice and Consent: Treaty Consideration by the United States Senate," *Journal of Politics* 65 (November 2003): 1097–1110.

5. *Goldwater v. Carter*, 444 U.S. 996, 998 (1979).

6. When debating the Intermediate Range Nuclear Forces Treaty in 1988, the Senate declared that any digression from the "common understanding" of the treaty at the time of ratification would require joint action by Congress and the president. Louis Fisher, *The Politics of Shared Power: Congress and the Executive* (Washington, DC: Congressional Quarterly, 1993), p. 156.

7. For a discussion of how partisan polarization has increased the difficulty of treaty ratification in the U.S. Senate see Jeffrey S, Peake, Glen S. Krutz, and Tyler Hughes,"President Obama, the Senate, and the Polarized Politics of Treaty Making," *Social Science Quarterly*, 93 (October 2012): 1295–1315.

8. Presidents Richard Nixon and Gerald Ford did not fully comply with this legislation, however. Some agreements were not submitted to Congress, and others were submitted after the sixty-day period. Consequently, in 1977, Congress passed legislation requiring any department or agency of the U.S. government that enters into any international agreement on behalf of the country to transmit the text to the State Department within twenty days of its signing. Neither of these two laws actually limits the president's power to act, yet their passage indicates that Congress is increasingly unwilling to defer blindly to the president's judgment.

9. Another critical component of the Bush administration's national security doctrine was the protection of humanitarian rights and the promotion of democratic beliefs. The administration believed that failed states controlled by ruthless dictators fueled religious fanaticism, hence its justification for instituting democratic practices.

10. Richard M. Pious, "Prerogative Power in the Obama Administration: Continuity and Change in the War on Terrorism," *Presidential Studies Quarterly* 41 (June 2011): 263–290.

11. William G. Howell, *Power without Persuasion: The Politics of Direct Presidential Action* (Princeton, NJ: Princeton University Press), pp. 19–23.

12. David Gray Adler, "The President's Recognition Power: Ministerial or Discretionary?" *Presidential Studies Quarterly* 25 (Spring 1995): 267–286.

13. In 2008, Bush recognized Kosovo after it declared its independence from Serbia.

14. Similarly, when the George W. Bush administration allowed the president of Taiwan to visit the United States, it also indicated that the visit was private and did not augur a change in policy toward China.

15. Other examples include the orders of President Eisenhower to send armed forces to Lebanon in 1958; President Kennedy to blockade Cuba in 1962; President Johnson to dispatch troops to the Dominican Republic in 1965; President Nixon to bomb Cambodia in 1970; President Ford to attack Cambodia in order to rescue the crew of a seized U.S. merchant ship in 1975; President Carter to rescue the American hostages in Iran in 1980; President Reagan to send an armed force to the Caribbean island of Grenada and marines to Lebanon in 1983; President George H. W. Bush to send military forces to Panama in 1989; President Clinton to bomb Iraq, to increase the size of American forces in Somalia, and send troops to Bosnia; and President Obama to increase U.S. military presence in Afghanistan.

16. See Christopher Deering, "Foreign Affairs and War," in Paul Quirk and Sarah Binder, eds., *The Legislative Branch* (New York: Oxford University Press, 2005); Louis Fisher, *Congressional Abdication on War and Spending* (College Station: Texas A & M University Press, 2000).

17. The president may extend the use of force for thirty additional days if deemed necessary to protect departing American forces.

18. Louis Fisher, *Constitutional Conflicts between Congress and the President* (Princeton, NJ: Princeton University Press, 1985), pp. 295–296.

19. Louis Fisher, "Judicial Review of the War Power," *Presidential Studies Quarterly* 35 (September 2005): 466–495.

20. Fred I. Greenstein, "Popular Images of the President," *American Journal of Psychiatry* 22 (November 1965): 523–529.

21. Louis Fisher, "The Law: When War Begins: Misleading Statements by Presidents," *Presidential Studies Quarterly* 40 (March 2010): 171–184.

22. B. Dan Wood, "Presidential Saber Rattling and the Economy," *The American Journal of Political Science* 53 (July 2009): 695–709.

23. Aaron Wildavsky, "The Two Presidencies," in Steven A. Shull, ed., *The Two Presidencies: A Quarter-Century*

Assessment (Chicago: Nelson-Hall, 1991), pp. 11–25.

24. Ibid.

25. Douglas L. Kriner, "Presidents, Domestic Politics, and the International Arena," in George C. Edwards III and William G. Howell, eds., *The Oxford Handbook of the American Presidency* (Oxford: Oxford University Press, 2009), p. 684; Piers Robinson, *The CNN Effect: The Myth of News, Foreign Policy, and Intervention* (New York: Routledge, 2002).

26. Matthew Baum, "Going Private: Public Opinion, Presidential Rhetoric, and the Domestic Politics of Audience Costs in U.S. Foreign Policy," *Journal of Conflict Resolution* 48 (October 2004): 603–631.

27. Thomas Knecht, *Paying Attention to Foreign Affairs: How Public Opinion Affects Presidential Decision Making* (University Park, PA: The Pennsylvania State University Press, 2010), p. 205.

28. Although the presidential decisions to use American military forces in Vietnam (1965–1973), Afghanistan, (2001–2014), and Iraq (2003–2012) were initially backed by a majority of the population, over time, public opinion turned against these wars when they were not resolved successfully and Americans became more aware of their costs.

29. Ralph G. Carter, "Congressional Policy Behavior: Persistent Patterns of the Postwar Period," *Presidential Studies Quarterly* 16 (Spring 1986): 333–334.

30. Quantitative studies of presidential success on roll-call votes in Congress lend support to this proposition. When the White House and Congress were controlled by separate parties, Republican presidents have done better on "conflictual" foreign policy than domestic policy, while Democratic presidents have not, according to a quantitative study by Richard Fleisher and Jon R. Bond. Richard Fleisher and Jon R. Bond, "Are There Two Presidencies? Yes, But Only for Republicans," *Journal of Politics* 50 (August 1988): 747–767. See also Terry Sullivan, "A Matter of Fact: The Two Presidencies Thesis Revitalized," in Steven A. Shull, ed., *The Two Presidencies* (Chicago: Nelson Hall, 1991), pp. 154–155.

31. Helen Milner and B. B. Rosendorff, "Democratic Politics and International Trade Negotiations: Elections and Divided Government as Constraints on Trade Liberalization," *Journal of Conflict Resolution* 41 (February 1997): 117–146; David Karol, "Divided Government and Trade Policy: Much Ado about Nothing?" *International Organization* 54 (September 2000): 825–844.

32. William Howell and Jon C. Pevehouse, "Presidents, Congress and the Use of Force," *International Organization* 59 (January 2005): 209–232.

33. Kriner, "Presidents, Domestic Politics, and the International Arena," p. 671.

34. Political scientist John Burke reports that during this war, President Truman attended sixty-four of the seventy-one weekly meetings of the Council. John P. Burke, "The National Security Advisor and Staff: Transition Challenges," *Presidential Studies Quarterly* 39 (June 2009): 283–321.

35. Reagan was the exception. During his administration, particularly during his first term, the National Security Council operated within a cabinet council system, helping to coordinate policy among the various agencies involved with national security affairs. A White House secretariat, headed by a special assistant to the president for national security affairs, helped provide organizational support. Fred I. Greenstein and Richard H. Immerman, "Effective National Security Advising: Recovering the Eisenhower Legacy," *Political Science Quarterly* 115 (Fall 2000): 337.

36. In the words of Colin Powell, one of seven national security assistants to President Ronald Reagan:

"We must make sure that all the relevant departments and agencies play their appropriate role in policy formulation. We must make sure that all pertinent facts and viewpoints are laid before the President. We must also make sure that no Cabinet official completes an "end run" around other NSC principals in pushing a policy line on which they too have legitimate concerns."

Colin L. Powell, "The NSC System in the Last Two Years of the Reagan Administration," *Presidential Studies Quarterly* 6 (Spring 1989): 206.

37. President Obama was reported to be furious about leaks early in his administration; his anger was quickly and perhaps purposely leaked to the press. Jonathan Alter, *The Promise* (New York: Simon and Schuster, 2010), p. 5. Bob Woodward writes in his book *Obama's Wars* that the president and his top aides were also angry about the leak of the report by General Stanley McChrystal on the war in Afghanistan in September 2009. Bob Woodward, *Obama's Wars* (New York: Simon and Schuster, 2010), pp. 195, 280.

38. Henry Kissinger's personal relationship with President Nixon and his and Nixon's closed style of decision making, combined with the president's penchant to consult primarily, sometimes exclusively, with his national security adviser, reduced the influence of Secretary of State William Rogers, who was not even informed of the president's China initiative until it was underway.

APPENDIX A

METHODS OF STUDYING THE PRESIDENCY

Although political scientists have always been keenly interested in the American presidency, their progress in understanding it has been relatively slow compared to studies of other institutions of government. One reason is their reliance on methods that are either irrelevant or inappropriate to the task of examining the basic relationships in which the presidency is involved. This appendix examines some of the advantages and limitations of methods used by scholars to study the presidency. Throughout, we should remember that methods are not ends in themselves but rather techniques for examining research questions generated by the approaches discussed in Chapter 1.

TRADITIONAL METHODS

Studies of the presidency typically describe events, behaviors, and personalities. Journalists[1] or former executive-branch officials who rely on their personal experiences write many of these studies. Many are also written by scholars[2] or journalists who rely primarily on the observations of others—who may be insiders.

Unfortunately, such anecdotal material, although it may be insightful, is generally subjective, fragmentary, and impressionistic. The commentary and reflections of insiders, whether participants or participant-observers, are limited by the insiders' own perspectives. For example, the memoirs of aides to President Lyndon Johnson and President Richard Nixon reveal very different perceptions of the president and his presidency. Henry Kissinger wrote this about the Nixon White House staff:

> It is a truism that none of us really knew the inner man. More significant, each member of his entourage was acquainted with a slightly different Nixon subtly adjusted to the President's judgment of the aide or to his assessment of his interlocutor's background.[3]

Similarly, Dick Morris's account of President Bill Clinton's reelection suggests that the author called all or most of the shots—an account disputed by other White House insiders.[4]

Proximity to power may actually hinder, rather than enhance, an observer's perspective and breadth of view. The reflections of those who have served in government may be colored by the strong positions they advocated in office or a need to justify their decisions and behavior. Faulty memories further cloud such perceptions. Moreover, few insiders are trained to think in analytical terms of generalizations based on representative data and controls for alternative explanations. This is especially true of journalists.[5]

Several examples illustrate the problem. One of the crucial decision points in U.S. involvement in Vietnam occurred during July 1965, when President Johnson committed the United States to large-scale combat operations. In his memoirs, Johnson goes to considerable lengths to show he considered very carefully all the alternatives available at the time.[6] One of his aides' detailed account of the dialogue between Johnson and some of his advisers shows the president probing deeply for answers, challenging the premises and factual bases of options, and playing the devil's advocate.[7] Other participants and scholars have also concluded that Johnson kept an open mind regarding U.S. intervention in Vietnam during that period.[8] Yet other scholars and participants have concluded that this "debate" was really a charade, staged by the president to lend legitimacy to the decision he had already made.[9]

Another useful example, this one focusing on attributions of influence, is President Johnson's efforts at obtaining the support—or at least the neutrality—of the Senate Finance Committee chair, Harry Byrd of Virginia, for what became the 1964 tax cut. Byrd had resisted a tax cut because of his concern for increasing the budget deficit. Hubert Humphrey reported in his memoirs that Johnson cajoled Byrd into letting the tax bill out of committee, relying on Lady Bird's charm, liquor, and his own famous "treatment."[10] Presidential aide Jack Valenti told a different story, however. He wrote that the president obtained the senator's cooperation by promising to hold the budget under $100 billion.[11] Thus, we have as eyewitnesses two experienced political professionals who knew both Byrd and Johnson very well. Each reported on a different tactic employed by the president and each attributed Senator Byrd's response to the presidential behavior that he observed.

To confuse matters further, Henry Hall Wilson, one of the president's congressional liaison aides, indicated that both eyewitnesses were wrong. According to Wilson, when the president proudly told his chief congressional liaison aide Lawrence O'Brien about his obtaining Byrd's agreement to begin hearings on the tax cut on December 7, O'Brien replied: "You didn't get a thing. I already had a commitment for the seventh."[12] In other words, according to O'Brien, Johnson's efforts were irrelevant and both eyewitnesses were wrong in attributing influence to him.[13]

Even tape recordings of conversations in the Oval Office may be misleading. As Henry Kissinger explains with respect to the Watergate tapes:

Anyone familiar with Nixon's way of talking could have no doubt he was sitting on a time bomb. His random, elliptical, occasionally emotional manner of conversation was bound to shock, and mislead, the historian. Nixon's indirect style of operation simply could not be gauged by an outsider. There was no way of telling what Nixon had put forward to test his interlocutor and what he meant to be taken seriously; and no outsider could distinguish a command that was to be followed from an emotional outburst that one was at liberty to ignore—perhaps was even expected to ignore.[14]

Even with a less complex personality than Richard Nixon, it would be difficult years after the event to disentangle the sarcastic from the genuine, the tentative from the serious, the fleeting thought from the carefully worked out proposition.[15]

Aside from the difficulty of assessing Nixon's true intentions, the tapes also pose other challenges for the researcher. They do not provide a context for the president's remarks or information on who else said what at a different time or place. They also provided the president and his chief of staff the opportunity to arrange tableaus to enhance the historical record or to provide a basis for shifting blame if policies failed. As Kissinger put it, "Ironically, Nixon's obsession with the historical record came close to destroying the ability of historians to render an accurate account of his presidency."[16]

Problems also arise in studies employing traditional methods when authors make assertions about the behavior of the public. They often fail to look at available systematic data. For example, numerous authors premise analyses of the administration of Ronald Reagan on the president's enjoying substantial support among the public. In reality, as we saw in Chapter 4, Reagan's average approval level was a quite ordinary 52 percent.[17]

When Reagan's pollster found that the public overwhelmingly disapproved of the administration's reductions in aid to education, Michael Deaver—the president's longtime public relations guru—arranged for Reagan to make a series of speeches emphasizing quality education. Deaver later gloated to the *Wall Street Journal* that public approval of the president regarding education "flip-flopped" without any change in policy at all.[18] If public opinion did change as Deaver described, it would indeed have been an impressive performance of presidential persuasion. However, opinion did *not* change. Deaver was referring to the addresses, including national radio addresses, Reagan delivered in the spring and summer of 1983. Yet in Gallup's August poll, only 31 percent of the public approved how Reagan was handling education.[19]

Similarly, in his memoir of the Reagan years, Deaver reports that the president was distressed about the lack of public support for defense spending. According to Deaver,

Reagan pulled me aside one day; "Mike," he said, "these numbers show you're not doing your job. This is your fault; you gotta get me out of Washington more so I can talk to people about how important this policy is." I did, and he would systematically add his rationale for more military spending to nearly every speech, and eventually his message would get through to the American people.[20]

In fact, however, public opinion on defense spending did not move in the president's direction, as we saw in Chapter 4. One does not have to challenge the sincerity of the author's memory to conclude that such commentary contributes to the misunderstanding of presidential leadership.

Although insider accounts have limitations, they often contain useful insights that may guide more rigorous research. They also provide invaluable records of the perceptions of participants in the events of the presidency. As long as the researcher understands the limitations of these works and accepts them as one among many perspectives, they can be of considerable use.

QUANTITATIVE ANALYSES

For several decades, then, research on the presidency often failed to meet the standards of contemporary political science, including the careful definition and measurement of concepts, the rigorous specification and testing of propositions, and the use of empirical theory to develop hypotheses and explain findings. This presented a striking irony: The single most important and powerful institution in American politics was the one that political scientists understood the least.

Scholars needed to think theoretically to develop falsifiable propositions about presidential leadership and test these systematically with relevant data and appropriate econometric techniques. They needed to discover generalizations about behavior rather than produce discrete, ad hoc analyses, repeat colorful anecdotes from presidential press clippings, or reach facile conclusions about Lyndon Johnson's skill at swaying members of Congress or Ronald Reagan's ability to mobilize the public behind his proposals. Quantitative analysis has been an extremely useful tool in these endeavors.[21]

Overcoming Obstacles

To gain insight into the nature of presidential leadership, scholars have had to overcome several obstacles that had impeded systematic analysis. Some, but not all, of these hurdles were unique to studying the presidency.

Asking New Questions

The first and most important obstacle, however, was not presidency-centric. To move toward generalizations based on systematic analysis, scholars had to refocus their inquiries. At its core, this effort focused on posing analytical rather than descriptive questions. Discussions of powers and thus the boundaries of appropriate behavior do not explain why actions occur within those boundaries or what their consequences are. Similarly, tracing the persistence and adaptation of organizations and processes over time, such as the Executive Office of the President or central clearance of legislation in the Office of Management and Budget, does not lend itself to explanations of the impact of presidential leadership.

The view that each president (and administration) is relatively unique also impeded rigorous analysis. The personalities of individual presidents and their staffs, the particular events and circumstances of their times in office, and the specific problems and actions of their administrations led scholars to treat each presidency and the times in which it operated as if it were unique. Emphasizing the differences rather than the similarities between presidencies made the identification of patterns and relations more difficult and, in turn, made it more difficult to generalize. Description rather than analysis, and speculation rather than generalization, were the standard fare. In addition, traditional scholars' heavy reliance on case studies inevitably made the basis of their generalizations rather tenuous.

It is not that all such studies lacked rigor but rather that most of them emphasized description at the expense of explanation. We still know a great deal more about how presidents have organized their White House staffs, for example, than about how these arrangements have affected the kinds of advice they have received. In other words, we know more about the process than about its consequences. Most significantly, little of this research contributed to understanding the central presidential task of leadership.

Richard Neustadt's *Presidential Power* was the first great leap toward a more analytical focus on leadership. His central premise was that presidential leadership was problematic because the president operates in a pluralistic environment in which there are numerous actors with independent power bases and perspectives different from his. In most instances, the president cannot act alone because he shares powers with others. Thus, the president cannot rely on expanding the institution's legal authority or adjusting its support mechanisms. Instead, he must marshal resources to persuade others to do as he wishes.

Neustadt's work encouraged scholars to focus on the people within institutions and their relationships with each other rather than to focus primarily on the institutions themselves and their formalities. As Neustadt saw it, power was a function of personal politics rather than of formal authority or position. It was not the roles of the president but the performance of those roles that mattered. It was not the boundaries of behavior but the actions within those boundaries that warranted the attention of scholars.

Power is a concept that involves relationships between people. By focusing on relationships and suggesting why people respond to the president as they do, Neustadt forced us into a more analytical mode. To understand relationships, we must explain behavior. Describing it is not enough, nor is storytelling about interesting but unrepresentative incidents—a temptation that is only natural when writing about the presidency. Neustadt, however, was concerned with the strategic level of power:

> There are two ways to study "presidential power." One way is to focus on the tactics . . . of influencing certain men in given situations. . . . The other way is to step back from tactics on those "givens" and to deal with influence in more strategic terms: what is its nature and what are its sources? . . . Strategically, [for example] the question is not how he masters Congress in a peculiar instance, but what he does to boost his chance for mastery in any instance . . . [22]

Neustadt, then, was less interested in what causes something to happen in one instance than in what affects the probabilities of something happening in every instance. To think strategically about power, we must search for generalizations and calculate probabilities. Whether we are interested in explaining the consequences of efforts at persuasion or prescribing a strategy to obtain or maintain resources useful in persuasion, the critical questions are, "What is the potential of persuasion"—with Congress, the public, or others? And specifically, "What is the potential of various persuasive resources with those whose support the president needs?" Seeking answers to these questions inevitably leads to explanations and generalizations. Although he employed neither the language nor the methods of modern social science, Neustadt's emphasis on reaching generalizations about presidential power was a significant contribution to research on the presidency.

Increasing the N

The second constraint on presidency research has been the small number of presidents. Only forty-three people have served as president—one of whom survived only a few weeks, and another only a few months, in office. Moreover, the tenure of these presidents spans more than two centuries. How can you generalize from such a small universe of chief executives who have served in such different circumstances?

Scholars overcame the issue of the small universe of presidents when they began viewing the presidency as a set of relationships and asking about interactions between the president and others. Many people are involved in relationships with presidents, including the public, members of Congress, the federal bureaucracy, and world leaders. Employing measures of these interactions produced an enormous amount of data, and analysis of the data provided scholars with a solid foundation for reaching generalizations.

Finding Data

The third obstacle to more systematic and rigorous scholarship on the president was the lack of data. The relatively closed character of the institution contributed to the problem. The presidency is difficult to observe from a distance and, up close, the view may be partial and even biased. Public pronouncements and actions tell only part of what happens and why—and usually only the part that the people in power wish to convey. Inside information is difficult to obtain. Officials' busy schedules, combined with their natural reluctance to reveal information that may be embarrassing, sensitive, or in other ways controversial, often make them unwilling, unresponsive, or unreliable sources.

The key to solving the data problem was posing analytical questions, which naturally led scholars to search for data on the causes and consequences of presidential behavior. Regarding leadership, they typically ask what responses presidents desire from other actors. Among other things, chief executives want support from the public, positive coverage from the media, votes for their programs from members of Congress, sound analysis from their advisers, and faithful policy implementation from the bureaucracy. Thus, scholars employing quantitative analysis develop data on these political actors, whose behavior is usually the dependent variable in their hypotheses—that is, in what we are trying to explain. Similarly, scholars seek data on independent variables, on causes of behavior toward the president, such as the determinants of public opinion, congressional support, bureaucratic faithfulness, and judicial responsiveness.[23]

Scholars have made considerable progress in providing data for students of the presidency. For example, the White House is making a wide range of data available on its website. Lyn Ragsdale published a volume entitled *Vital Statistics on the Presidency*.[24]

Proper Use of Quantitative Analysis

The proper use of quantitative analysis, like any other type of analysis, is predicated on a close linkage between the methods scholars employ and the theoretical arguments that underlie the hypotheses they test.[25] A statement that something causes something else to happen is an assertion, not a theoretical argument. A theoretical argument requires an emphasis on explanation on why two variables are related. Quantitative analysis is not an end in itself. Instead, it is a means of rigorously analyzing the components of theoretically meaningful explanations of behavior.

Quantitative analysis is not easy to do, nor is there always consensus on appropriate methods or measures. Inevitably, some authors will employ indicators that lack validity and reliability and tests that are inappropriate. Their conclusions are likely to be controversial and may even be incorrect. In addition, findings can and should be refined as our indicators and tests are improved. In essence, quantitative analysis poses methodological problems precisely because it attempts to measure concepts and to test for relationships carefully. Studies that do not involve such concerns avoid methodological questions, but often at the expense of analytical richness.

Limits to Quantitative Analysis

Despite its utility for investigating a wide range of questions, quantitative analysis is not equally useful for studying all areas of the presidency. It is least useful where there is little change in the variables under study or the subject being examined is at a very high level of abstraction. If the focus of research is just one president and the researcher is concerned not with the president's interactions with others but with how factors such as the president's personality, ideas, values, attitudes, and ideology have influenced his decisions, then quantitative analysis will be of little help. These independent variables are unlikely to vary much during a president's term. Similarly, important elements in the president's environment, such as the federal system or the basic capitalist structure of its economy, change little over time. It is therefore difficult to employ quantitative analysis to gauge their influence on the presidency.

Quantitative analysis is also unlikely to be useful for the legal approach to studying the presidency. There are well-established techniques for interpreting the law, and scholars with this interest will continue to apply them.[26]

Normative questions and arguments have always occupied a substantial percentage of the presidency literature, and rightly so. Can quantitative analysis aid scholars in addressing these concerns? The answer is, "partially." For example, to reach conclusions about whether the presidency is too powerful or not powerful enough (the central normative concern regarding the presidency) requires a three-part analysis. The first is an estimation of just how powerful the presidency is. Quantitative analysis can be useful in measuring and explaining the power of the presidency in a wide range of relationships. For example, it can aid us in understanding the president's ability to influence Congress or the public.

The second step in answering the question of whether the presidency is too powerful or not powerful enough requires an analysis of the consequences of the power of the presidency. In other words, given the power of the presidency, what difference does it make? Are poor people likely to fare better under a weak or a powerful presidency, for example? Are civil rights and civil liberties more or less likely to be abused?

To answer rigorously these and similar questions requires that we correlate levels of power with policy consequences. This analysis does not have to be done quantitatively, of course, but such analyses are likely to be more convincing if we have valid empirical measurements of economic welfare, school integration, wiretapping, military interventions, and other possible consequences of presidential power, as well as measures of mediating variables.

Quantitative analyses will be much less useful in the third part of the analysis: Do we judge the consequences of presidential power to be good or bad? Our values, of course, will determine our evaluation of these consequences. Nevertheless, it is important to remember that quantitative analysis can be very useful in helping us to arrive at the point where our values and not questions of fact dominate our conclusions.

In short, quantitative analysis leads us to examine theoretical relationships, and it has considerable utility in testing and refining them. The question remains, however, whether quantitative analysis is useful for developing theories themselves—that is, basic conceptions of the relationships between variables.

Although quantitative studies cannot replace the sparks of creativity that lie behind conceptualizations, they may produce findings on which syntheses may be built. Conversely, quantitative analysis may also produce findings contrary to the conventional wisdom and thus prod scholars into challenging dominant viewpoints. To this extent, it may also be useful in theory building.

CASE STUDIES

One of the most widely used methods for studying the presidency is the case study of an individual president, a presidential decision, or presidential involvement in a specific area of policy. The case study method offers the researcher several advantages. It is a manageable way to present a wide range of complex information about individual and collective behavior. Because scholars have typically found it difficult to generate quantitative data regarding the presidency, the narrative form often seems to be the only available choice.

Conversely, case studies are widely criticized on several grounds. First, scholars have used them more for descriptive than for analytical purposes, a failing not inherent in the case study. A more intractable problem is the idiosyncratic nature of case studies and the failure of authors to employ common analytical frameworks. This failure makes the accumulation of knowledge difficult because scholars often, in effect, talk past each other. In the words of a close student of case studies:

> The unique features of every case—personalities, external events and conditions, and organizational arrangements—virtually ensure that studies conducted without the use of an explicit analytical framework will not produce findings that can easily be related to existing knowledge or provide a basis for future studies.[27]

Naturally, reaching generalizations about the presidency on the basis of unrelated case studies is a hazardous task.

Despite these drawbacks, case studies can be very useful in increasing our understanding of the presidency. For example, analyzing case studies can serve as the basis for identifying problems in decision making[28] or in policy implementation.[29] These in turn may serve as the basis for recommendations to improve policy making. Scholars may also use case studies to test hypotheses or disconfirm theories, such as propositions about group dynamics drawn from social psychology.[30]

Some authors employ case studies to illustrate the importance of looking at aspects of the presidency that have received little scholarly attention, such as presidential influence over interest groups.[31] On a broader scale, Richard Neustadt used several case studies to explicate his influential model of presidential power,[32] and Graham Allison and Philip Zelikow used a case study of the Cuban missile crisis to illustrate three models of policy making.[33]

Writing a case study that has strong analytical content is difficult to do.[34] It requires considerable skill, creativity, and rigor because it is very easy to slip into a descriptive rather than an analytical gear. It is especially important to have an analytical framework in mind before one begins—to provide direction to data gathering and the line of argument. Those who embark on preparing case studies are wise to remind themselves of the pitfalls.

CONCLUSION

Few topics in American politics are more interesting or more important to understand than the presidency. Researching the presidency is not a simple task, however. There are many reasons for this, including the small number of models to follow and the relative scarcity of research that has applied the approaches and methods of modern political science. But the obstacles to studying the presidency also present researchers with an opportunity. Few questions regarding the presidency are settled, and there is plenty of room for committed and creative researchers to make important contributions to our understanding. The prospects for success will be enhanced if researchers realize the implications of the approaches and methods they employ and choose those that are best suited to shed light on the questions they wish to investigate.

Useful Websites

The official White House website: www.whitehouse.gov/

Essays on White House offices and presidential transitions, and interviews with White House officials: www.whitehousetransitionproject.org/

Links to many websites relevant to the presidency: cstl-cla.semo.edu/renka/ presidencylinks.htm

Information on presidential appointments: www.presidential-appointments.org/

Executive orders, proclamations, and other presidential documents: www.archives.gov/federal-register/publications/index.html

Public papers of the presidents: www.gpoaccess.gov/pubpapers/-index.html

Information and resources regarding presidential rhetoric: www.presidentialrhetoric.com/

Information on many aspects of the presidency: www.presidency.ucsb.edu/

Selected Readings

Edwards, George C., III, John H. Kessel, and Bert A. Rockman, eds. *Researching the Presidency.* Pittsburgh, PA: University of Pittsburgh Press, 1993.

Edwards, George C., III, and Stephen J. Wayne, eds. *Studying the Presidency.* Knoxville: University of Tennessee Press, 1983.

Howell, William G. "Quantitative Approaches to the Study of the Presidency." In *Oxford Handbook of the American Presidency,* edited by George C. Edwards III and William G. Howell. Oxford: Oxford University Press, 2009.

Hult, Karen M., Charles E. Walcott, and Thomas Weko. "Qualitative Research and the Study of the U.S. Presidency." *Congress & the Presidency* 26 (Fall 1999): 133–152.

James, Scott C. "Historical Institutionalism, Political Development, and the Presidency." In *Oxford Handbook of the American Presidency,* edited by George C. Edwards III and William G. Howell. Oxford: Oxford University Press, 2009.

Skowronek, Stephen. "The Paradigm of Development in Presidential History." In *Oxford Handbook of the American Presidency,* edited by George C. Edwards III and William G. Howell. Oxford: Oxford University Press, 2009.

Notes

1. The most prominent examples are the books of Bob Woodward, including most recently, Bob Woodward, *The Price of Politics* (New York: Simon & Schuster, 2012); and *The War Within: A Secret White House History 2006–2008* (New York: Simon and Schuster, 2008).

2. An outstanding and rare example of direct observation from the inside by a scholar is Martha Kumar, *Managing the President's Message: The White House Communications Operation* (Baltimore, MD: Johns Hopkins University Press, 2007).

3. Henry Kissinger, *Years of Upheaval* (Boston: Little, Brown, 1982), p. 1182.

4. Dick Morris, *Behind the Oval Office* (New York: Random House, 1997).

5. Excellent studies of the misperceptions of participants in presidential policy making include Richard E. Neustadt, *Alliance Politics* (New York: Columbia University Press, 1970); and Fred I. Greenstein and Richard H. Immerman, "What Did Eisenhower Tell Kennedy about Indochina? The Politics of Misperception," *Journal of American History* 79 (September 1992): 568–587.

6. Lyndon B. Johnson, *The Vantage Point: Perspectives of the Presidency, 1963–1969* (New York: Popular Library, 1971), pp. 144–153.

7. Jack Valenti, *A Very Human President* (New York: Norton, 1975), pp. 317–319, 358.

8. See George W. Ball, *The Past Has Another Pattern* (New York: Norton, 1982), p. 399; and George McT. Kahin, *Intervention: How America Became Involved in Vietnam* (New York: Knopf, 1986), pp. 366–390.

9. Gordon M. Goldstein, *Lessons in Disaster: McGeorge Bundy and the Path to War in Vietnam* (New York: Holt, 2008), pp. 204–218; Larry Berman, *Planning a Tragedy: The Americanization of the War in Vietnam* (New York: Norton, 1982), pp. 105–121; Chester Cooper, *The Lost Crusade: America in Vietnam* (Greenwich, CT: Dodd, Mead, 1970), pp. 284–285; U.S. Department of Defense, *United States–Vietnam Relations, 1945–1967*, vol. 3 (Washington, DC: Government Printing Office, 1971), p. 475.

10. Hubert H. Humphrey, *The Education of a Public Man: My Life and Politics* (Garden City, NY: Doubleday, 1976), pp. 290–293.

11. Valenti, *A Very Human President,* pp. 196–197. See also Russell D. Renka, "Bargaining with Legislative Whales in the Kennedy and Johnson Administration" (paper presented at the annual meeting of the American Political Science Association, Washington, DC, August 1980), p. 20.

12. Transcript, Henry Hall Wilson Oral History Interview, April 11, 1973, by Joe B. Frantz, p. 16, Lyndon B. Johnson Library, Austin, Texas.

13. For another example of the unreliability of "eyewitness" accounts, see Robert Dallek, *An Unfinished Life: John F. Kennedy, 1917–1963* (Boston, MA: Little, Brown, 2003), pp. 318–319.

14. Kissinger, *Years of Upheaval,* pp. 111–112. Recently, transcripts of tapes from several presidents have been published. These include Ernest R. May and Philip D. Zelikow, *The Kennedy Tapes* (Cambridge, MA: Belknap Press, 1997); Michael R. Beschloss, ed., *Taking Charge: The Johnson White House Tapes, 1963–1964* (New York: Simon and Schuster, 1997); and Stanley I. Kutler, ed., *Abuse of Power: The New Nixon Tapes* (New York: Free Press, 1997).

15. Henry Kissinger, *Years of Renewal* (New York: Simon and Schuster, 1999), pp. 63–64.

16. Kissinger, *Years of Renewal,* p. 67.

17. See George C. Edwards III, *Presidential Approval* (Baltimore, MD: Johns Hopkins University Press, 1990), p. 175.

18. Quoted in Rich Jaroslovsky, "Manipulating the Media Is a Specialty for the White House's Michael Deaver," *Wall Street Journal,* January 5, 1984, p. 44.

19. Gallup poll, August 5–8, 2003. In a Gallup poll of January 28–29, 1987, only 32 percent of the public felt the Reagan administration had made progress in solving the problems of education.

20. Michael K. Deaver, *A Different Drummer: My Thirty Years with Ronald Reagan* (New York: HarperCollins, 2001), p. 154.

21. For a more extensive discussion of quantitative analysis of the presidency, see George C. Edwards III, "Quantitative Analysis," in George C. Edwards III and Stephen J. Wayne, eds., *Studying the Presidency* (Knoxville: University of Tennessee Press, 1983), pp. 99–124; Gary King, "The Methodology of Presidency Research," in George C. Edwards III, Bert A. Rockman, and John H. Kessel, eds., *Researching the Presidency* (Pittsburgh, PA: University of Pittsburgh Press, 1993), pp. 387–412; William G. Howell, "Quantitative Approaches to the Study of the Presidency," in George C. Edwards III and William G. Howell, eds., *Oxford Handbook of the American Presidency* (Oxford: Oxford University Press, 2009).

22. Richard E. Neustadt, *Presidential Power and the Modern Presidents* (New York: Free Press, 1990), p. 4.

23. Recent examples of quantitative studies of the presidency include George C. Edwards III, *Overreach: Leadership in the Obama Presidency* (Princeton, NJ: Princeton University Press, 2012); Douglas L. Kriner, *After the Rubicon: Congress, Presidents, and the Politics of Waging War* (University of Chicago Press, 2010); B. Dan Wood, *The Myth of Presidential Representation* (Cambridge: Cambridge University Press, 2009); George C. Edwards III, *The Strategic President: Persuasion and Opportunity in Presidential Leadership* (Princeton, NJ: Princeton University Press, 2009); Frances E. Lee, *Beyond Ideology: Politics, Principles and Partisanship in the U.S. Senate* (Chicago, IL: University of Chicago Press, 2009); Jeffrey E. Cohen, *The Presidency in the Ear of 24-Hour News* (Princeton University Press, 2008); David E. Lewis, *The Politics of Presidential Appointments* (Princeton, NJ: Princeton University Press, 2008); B. Dan Wood, *The Politics of Economic Leadership* (Princeton, NJ: Princeton University Press, 2007); William G. Howell and Jon C. Pevehouse, *While Dangers Gather: Congressional Checks on Presidential War Powers* (Princeton, NJ: Princeton University Press, 2007); Brandice Canes-Wrone, *Who Leads Whom?* (Princeton, NJ: Princeton University Press, 2006); Lawrence J. Grossback, David A. M. Peterson, and James A. Stimson, *Mandate*

Politics (Cambridge University Press, 2006); George C. Edwards III, *On Deaf Ears: The Limits of the Bully Pulpit* (New Haven, CT: Yale University Press, 2003); William G. Howell, *Power without Persuasion: The Politics of Direct Presidential Action* (Princeton, NJ: Princeton University Press, 2003); Andrew Rudalevige, *Managing the President's Program* (Princeton, NJ: Princeton University Press, 2002).

24. Lyn Ragsdale, *Vital Statistics on the Presidency*, 3rd ed. (Washington, DC: CQ Press, 2008).

25. See, for example, George C. Edwards III, "Presidential Approval as a Source of Influence in Congress," in George C. Edwards III and William G. Howell, eds., *Oxford Handbook of the American Presidency* (Oxford: Oxford University Press, 2009).

26. For more on legal analysis of the presidency, see Louis Fisher, "Political Scientists and the Public Law Tradition," in George C. Edwards III and William G. Howell, eds., *Oxford Handbook of the American Presidency* (Oxford: Oxford University Press, 2009); and Louis Fisher, "Making Use of Legal Sources," in Edwards and Wayne, eds., *Studying the Presidency,* pp. 182–198.

27. Norman C. Thomas, "Case Studies," in Edwards and Wayne, eds., *Studying the Presidency,* p. 52.

28. See, for example, Alexander L. George, "The Case for Multiple Advocacy in Making Foreign Policy," *American Political Science Review* 66 (September 1972): 765–781; Burke and Greenstein, *How Presidents Test Reality*; Ryan J. Barilleaux, *The President and Foreign Affairs* (New York: Praeger, 1985); and Patrick J. Haney, *Organizing for Foreign Policy Crises* (Ann Arbor: University of Michigan Press, 1997).

29. See, for example, Robert F. Durant, *The Administrative Presidency Revisited* (Albany: State University of New York Press, 1992).

30. See Irving L. Janis, *Groupthink,* 2nd ed. (Boston: Houghton Mifflin, 1982).

31. See, for example, Bruce Miroff, "Presidential Leverage over Social Movements: The Johnson White House and Civil Rights," *Journal of Politics* 43 (February 1981): 2–23.

32. Neustadt, Presidential Power.

33. Graham T. Allison and Philip Zelikow, *Essence of Decision: Explaining the Cuban Missile Crisis,* 2nd ed. (New York: Longman, 1999).

34. Examples of work focusing on a single president in an insightful and analytical fashion include Charles O. Jones, *The Trusteeship Presidency* (Baton Rouge: Louisiana State University Press, 1988); Lawrence R. Jacobs and Robert Y. Shapiro, "Issues, Candidate Image, and Priming: The Use of Private Polls in Kennedy's 1960 Presidential Campaign," *American Political Science Review* 88 (September 1994): 527–540; and Roger B. Porter, "Gerald R. Ford: A Healing Presidency," in Fred I. Greenstein, ed., *Leadership in the Modern Presidency* (Cambridge, MA: Harvard University Press, 1988), pp. 199–227.

APPENDIX B

NONELECTORAL SUCCESSION, REMOVAL, AND TENURE

T he Constitution and statutes provide for contingencies that might require the selection, removal, or replacement of a president outside the normal electoral process. In addition to the provisions of Article I ("Impeachment") and Article II ("Impeachment and Succession"), there have been three amendments (numbers 20, 22, and 25) and three laws concerning succession and term of office. This appendix will examine these contingency arrangements. It will also briefly describe the impeachment process and the three most serious attempts to remove a sitting president. The Constitution and statutes provide for methods of succession and removal.

SUCCESSION

The principal reason for creating the vice presidency was to have a position from which the presidency would automatically be filled should it become vacant. Death, resignation, and impeachment constitute clear-cut situations in which this succession mechanism would work. Eight presidents have died in office and one has resigned. In each of the nine instances, the vice president became president.

One contingency the founders did not consider was temporary or permanent disability while in office. On a number of occasions, presidents have become disabled, unable to perform their duties and responsibilities. James Garfield, shot by a disappointed job seeker, lingered for almost three months before he died. Ronald Reagan was hospitalized twice, the first time following an attempt on his life and the other for an operation for cancer of the colon. During both hospital stays, he was unconscious for several hours and incapacitated for several months. Other presidents have also been incapacitated. Woodrow Wilson suffered a stroke that disabled him for much of his last year in office, and Dwight Eisenhower's heart attack, ileitis operation, and minor stroke severely limited his presidential activities in 1955, 1956, and 1957.

During none of these periods did vice presidents officially take over. In fact, Chester Arthur and Thomas Marshall, Garfield and Wilson's vice presidents, respectively, avoided even the appearance of performing presidential duties for fear that their actions would be wrongfully construed. Vice President Richard Nixon did preside at cabinet meetings in Eisenhower's absence but did not assume the president's other responsibilities. Vice President George H. W. Bush, away from the capital at the time Reagan was shot, flew back to Washington immediately to be available if needed. However, to avoid any appearance of impropriety, he had his helicopter land at the vice president's residence even though he was scheduled to meet at the White House with senior presidential aides. By prearrangement with the vice president, President Reagan passed his powers and duties to Bush during the period when he was under the influence of anesthesia during his colon operation in 1985. He reassumed them when he declared himself able to do so several hours after his operation.

It was not until 1967 that procedures were established for the vice president to become acting president in the event of the president's disability. The Twenty-Fifth Amendment to the Constitution permits the vice president to exercise the duties and powers of the presidency if the president declares in writing that he is unable to do so or if the vice president and a majority of the principal executive department heads reach that judgment. The president may resume office when he believes that he is able to, unless the vice president and a majority of the principal executive department heads object, in which case Congress must make the final determination. The procedures, however, are weighted in the president's favor. Unless Congress concurs in the judgment that the president is disabled, the president is entitled once again to exercise the duties and powers of the office.

Another important provision of this amendment provides for filling the vice presidency should it become vacant. Prior to 1967, it had been vacant sixteen times. The procedures permit the president to nominate a new vice president, who takes office upon confirmation by a majority of both houses of Congress. Gerald Ford and Nelson Rockefeller were the only two vice presidents who came to office in this manner. Ford was nominated by President Nixon in 1973 after Spiro T. Agnew resigned. After succeeding to the presidency when Nixon resigned, Ford nominated Rockefeller.

Although the presidency and vice presidency have never been vacant at the same time, Congress has provided for such a contingency should it arise by establishing a line of succession. The most recent succession law, enacted in 1947, puts the Speaker of the House next in line, to be followed by the president pro tempore of the Senate and the department heads in chronological order of the creation of their departments, beginning with the secretary of state. The provision for appointing a new vice president, however, makes it less likely that legislative and executive officials would ever succeed to the presidency, barring a catastrophe such as a terrorist attack on the White House or a joint session of Congress, or an unlikely set of events that resulted in a president's death before a new vice presidential nomination could be made or confirmed.

REMOVAL

In addition to providing for the president's replacement, the constitutional framers also thought it necessary to provide for the president's removal. They believed that it was too dangerous to wait for the electors' judgment in the case of a president who had abused the authority of the office. Impeachment was considered an extraordinary remedy but one that could be used against executive officials, including the president and vice president, who violated their public trust.

Article II, section 4 of the Constitution spells out the terms. The president, vice president, and other executive officials can be removed from office for treason, bribery, or other high crimes and misdemeanors. Precisely what actions would be considered impeachable offenses is left for Congress to determine.

The House of Representatives considers the charges against the president. If a majority of the House votes in favor of any of them, a trial is held in the Senate with the chief justice of the Supreme Court presiding. The House presents its case against the president. The latter, who may be represented by outside counsel, defends against the charges. A two-thirds vote of the Senate is required for conviction. A convicted president, who is removed from office, may still be subject to civil or criminal prosecution.

Only two presidents, Andrew Johnson and Bill Clinton, have ever been impeached. Neither was convicted.

The incident that sparked Johnson's impeachment was his removal of Secretary of War Edwin Stanton. Congress had passed a law over Johnson's veto that required appointees to remain in office until the Senate approved their successor. Known as the Tenure of Office Act (1867), it permitted the president some discretion during a congressional recess but required the Senate's advice and consent after Congress reconvened. In the absence of senatorial approval, the office reverted to its previous occupant.

During a congressional recess, Johnson removed Stanton. The Senate refused to concur in his removal upon its return. Under the law, Stanton was entitled to his old job. However, the president once again removed him. When he was removed for a second time, the House of Representatives passed a bill of impeachment against the president. The Senate trial lasted six weeks. In its first vote, the Senate fell one vote short of the required two-thirds. A ten-day recess was called by those favoring Johnson's removal. Extensive lobbying ensued, but when the Senate reconvened, no one's vote changed. Johnson was acquitted. The Tenure of Office Act was subsequently repealed during the administration of Grover Cleveland.

A second attempt to impeach a sitting president occurred in 1973. When Richard Nixon dismissed Archibald Cox, the special prosecutor who had been investigating charges of administrative wrongdoing in the Watergate affair, members of Congress called for Nixon's removal. The Judiciary Committee of the House of Representatives began hearings on the president's impeachment. During the course of these hearings, the committee subpoenaed tapes of conversations that the president had held with aides in the White House, conversations that had been secretly recorded by the president. Claiming that these were privileged communications, Nixon refused to deliver the tapes, although he did send edited transcripts of them to the House committee. Not satisfied with this response, the House took its case to court and won. The Supreme Court ordered Nixon to release the tapes. When he did so, the recordings revealed his early knowledge of the break-in and his participation in the cover-up. This information heightened calls for the president's ouster.

The House Judiciary Committee approved three articles of impeachment against Nixon. It looked as if the full House would vote to impeach him and that the Senate would vote to convict him. Faced with the prospect of a long trial and probable conviction, Nixon resigned on August 9, 1974.

A third attempt to impeach a sitting president was begun in September 1998 when the independent counsel investigating President Clinton's relationship with a White House intern reported to the House of Representatives that the president may have committed eleven possible impeachable offenses. The House sent the report and the White House's responses to its Judiciary Committee, which conducted hearings on whether to recommend four articles of impeachment to the full House: abuse of power, obstruction of justice, and two counts of perjury before the Grand Jury investigating the matter. After a raucous debate, the Republican-controlled House of Representatives voted largely along partisan lines to impeach the president on one count of perjury and one count of obstruction of justice. Democrats were livid, and the president was defiant. The proceedings then moved to the Senate with the chief justice presiding. With forty-five Democratic senators and a two-thirds vote necessary for conviction, the result was never in doubt. After debating the matter with much pomp and eloquence, the Senate voted largely along party lines. A majority, but not the two-thirds necessary, supported the count of perjury. The Senate was evenly divided on the other, obstruction of justice. Clinton survived, more popular than he was prior to the whole ordeal, while the Republicans lost Senate seats in the 2000 election. The Republican experience was not lost on the Democratic congressional leadership that came to power in 2007. They nixed impeachment proposals to remove George W. Bush from office on the grounds that he abused executive powers, and in doing so, violated constitutionally-protects rights of American citizens.

The presidency suffered, however. Court decisions weakened the president's claim of executive privilege. Not only was Clinton forced to testify before a grand jury but his top White House aides also were compelled to testify about their conversations with the president, and Secret Service agents were required to testify about the president's movements during this period. Diaries of White House personnel were subject to judicial scrutiny as well.

TENURE

Electoral defeat and impeachment prematurely conclude a presidency—at least from the incumbent's perspective. Initially, the Constitution imposed no limit on the number of times a president could be elected. Indeed, reeligibility was seen as a motive to good behavior. Beginning with Washington, however, an un-official two-term limit was established. Franklin Roosevelt ended this precedent in 1940 when he ran for a third term and won.

Partially in reaction to Roosevelt's twelve years and one month in office, a Republican-controlled Congress passed and the states ratified the Twenty-Second Amendment to the Constitution. It prevents any person from being elected to the office more than twice. Moreover, it limits to one election a president who has succeeded to the office and has served more than two years of his predecessor's term. Eisenhower was the first president to be subject to the provisions of the amendment; others have included Nixon, Reagan, Clinton, George W. Bush, and Barack Obama.

One of the consequences of this amendment is that it seems to weaken the president in the second term, particularly during the last two years in office. Not being able to run for the presidency again reduces a president's political power and lessens the capacity to mobilize public backing for the administration's programs and policies. Conversely, it may improve the president's ability to mobilize a bipartisan coalition because political motives may be less subject to suspicion if a president cannot seek reelection.

Another consequence of a term limit is that it encourages presidents to exercise unilateral authority in their second term. Late in his tenure, Bill Clinton approved regulations that imposed more stringent environmental standards. On his last day, he issued 140 pardons and commuted the sentences of thirty-six others. George W. Bush also used his executive powers extensively but did so throughout his administration, not just at the end.

APPENDIX C

PROVISIONS OF THE CONSTITUTION OF THE UNITED STATES THAT RELATE TO THE PRESIDENCY

ARTICLE I

Section 2

(3) [Representatives and direct Taxes[1] shall be apportioned among the several States which may be included within this Union, according to their respective Numbers, which shall be determined by adding to the whole Number of free Persons, including those bound to Service for a Term of Years, and excluding Indians not taxed, three fifths of all other Persons.][2] The actual Enumeration shall be made within three Years after the first Meeting of the Congress of the United States, and within every subsequent Term of ten Years, in such Manner as they shall by Law direct. The Number of Representatives shall not exceed one for every thirty Thousand, but each State shall have at Least one Representative; and until such enumeration shall be made, the State of New Hampshire shall be entitled to choose three, Massachusetts eight, Rhode-Island and Providence Plantations one, Connecticut five, New York six, New Jersey

four, Pennsylvania eight, Delaware one, Maryland six, Virginia ten, North Carolina five, South Carolina five, and Georgia three.

(4) When vacancies happen in the Representation from any State, the Executive Authority thereof shall issue Writs of Election to fill such Vacancies.

(5) The House of Representatives shall choose their Speaker and other Officers; and shall have the sole Power of Impeachment.

Section 3

(4) The Vice President of the United States shall be President of the Senate, but shall have no Vote, unless they be equally divided.

(5) The Senate shall choose their other Officers, and also a President pro tempore, in the Absence of the Vice President, or when he shall exercise the Office of President of the United States.

(6) The Senate shall have the sole Power to try all Impeachements. When sitting for that Purpose, they shall be on Oath or Affirmation. When the President of the United States is tried, the Chief Justice shall preside: And no Person shall be convicted without the Concurrence of two thirds of the Members present.

(7) Judgment in Cases of Impeachment shall not extend further than to removal from Office, and disqualification to hold and enjoy any Office of honor, Trust or Profit under the United States: but the Party convicted shall nevertheless be liable and subject to Indictment, Trial, Judgment and Punishment according to Law.

Section 7

(2) Every Bill which shall have passed the House of Representatives and the Senate, shall, before it become a Law, be presented to the President of the United States; If he approve he shall sign it, but if not he shall return it, with his Objections to that House in which it shall have originated, who shall enter the Objections at large on their Journal, and proceed to reconsider it. If after such Reconsideration two thirds of that House shall agree to pass the Bill, it shall be sent, together with Objections, to the other House, by which it shall likewise be reconsidered, and if approved by two thirds of that House, it shall become a Law. But in all such Cases the Votes of both Houses shall be determined by Yeas and Nays, and the Names of the Persons voting for and against the Bill shall be entered on the Journal of each House respectively. If any Bill shall not be returned by the President within ten Days (Sundays excepted) after it shall have been presented to him, the Same shall be a Law, in like Manner as if he had signed it, unless the Congress by their Adjournment prevent its Return, in which Case it shall not be a Law.

(3) Every Order, Resolution, or Vote to which the Concurrence of the Senate and House of Representatives may be necessary (except on a question of Adjournment) shall be presented to the President of the United States; and before the Same shall take Effect, shall be approved by him, or being

disapproved by him, shall be repassed by two thirds of the Senate and House of Representatives, according to the Rules and Limitations prescribed in the Case of a Bill.

Section 9

(2) The Privilege of the Writ of Habeas Corpus shall not be suspended, unless when in Cases of Rebellion or Invasion the public Safety may require it.

(8) No Title of Nobility shall be granted by the United States: And no Person holding any Office of Profit or Trust under them, shall, without the Consent of the Congress, accept of any present, Emolument, Office, or Title, of any kind whatever, from any King, Prince, or foreign State.

ARTICLE II

Section 1

(1) The executive Power shall be vested in a President of the United States of America. He shall hold his Office during the Term of four Years, and, together with the Vice President, chosen for the same Term, be elected, as follows:

(2) Each State shall appoint, in such Manner as the Legislature thereof may direct, a Number of Electors, equal to the whole Number of Senators and Representatives to which the State may be entitled in the Congress, but no Senator or Representative, or Person holding an Office of Trust or Profit under the United States, shall be appointed an Elector.

[The Electors shall meet in their respective States, and vote by Ballot for two persons, of whom one at least shall not be an Inhabitant of the same State with themselves. And they shall make a List of all the Persons voted for, and of the Number of Votes for each; which List they shall sign and certify, and transmit sealed to the Seat of the Government of the United States, directed to the President of the Senate. The President of the Senate shall, in the Presence of the Senate and House of Representatives, open all the Certificates, and the Votes shall then be counted. The Person having the greatest Number of Votes shall be the President, if such Number be a Majority of the whole Number of Electors appointed; and if there be more than one who have such Majority, and have an equal Number of Votes, then the House of Representatives shall immediately choose by Ballot one of them for President; and if no Person have a Majority, then from the five highest on the List the said House shall in like Manner choose the President. But in choosing the President, the Votes shall be taken by States, the Representation from each State having one Vote; A quorum for this purpose shall consist of a Member or Members from two thirds of the States, and a Majority of all the States shall be necessary to a Choice. In every Case, after the Choice of the President, the Person having the greatest Number of Votes of the Electors shall be the Vice President. But if there should remain two or more who have equal Votes, the Senate shall choose from them by Ballot the Vice President.][3]

(3) The Congress may determine the Time of choosing the Electors, and the Day on which they shall give their Votes; which Day shall be the same throughout the United States.

(4) No person except a natural born Citizen, or a Citizen of the United States, at the time of the Adoption of this Constitution, shall be eligible to the Office of President; neither shall any Person be eligible to that Office who shall not have attained to the Age of thirty-five Years, and been fourteen Years a Resident within the United States.

(5) In case of the Removal of the President from Office, or of his Death, Resignation, or Inability to discharge the Powers and Duties of the said Office, the same shall devolve on the Vice President, and the Congress may by Law provide for the Case of Removal, Death, Resignation or Inability; both of the President and Vice President, declaring what Officer shall then act as President, and such Officer shall act accordingly, until the Disability be removed, or a President shall be elected.[4]

(6) The President shall, at stated Times, receive for his Services, a Compensation, which shall neither be increased nor diminished during the Period for which he shall have been elected, and he shall not receive within that Period any other Emolument from the United States, or any of them.

(7) Before he enter on the Execution of his Office, he shall take the following Oath or Affirmation: —"I do solemnly swear (or affirm) that I will faithfully execute the Office of President of the United States, and will to the best of my Ability, preserve, protect and defend the Constitution of the United States."

Section 2

(1) The President shall be Commander in Chief of the Army and Navy of the United States, and of the Militia of the several States, when called into the actual Service of the United States; he may require the Opinion in writing, of the principal Officer in each of the executive Departments, upon any subject relating to the Duties of their respective Offices, and he shall have Power to Grant Reprieves and Pardons for Offenses against the United States, except in Cases of Impeachment.

(2) He shall have Power, by and with the Advice and Consent of the Senate, to make Treaties, provided two thirds of the Senators present concur; and he shall nominate, and by and with the Advice and Consent of the Senate, shall appoint Ambassadors, other public Ministers and Consuls, Judges of the supreme Court, and all other Officers of the United States, whose Appointments are not herein otherwise provided for, and which shall be established by Law: but the Congress may by Law vest the Appointment of such inferior Officers, as they think proper, in the President alone, in the Court of Law, or in the Heads of Departments.

(3) The President shall have Power to fill up all Vacancies that may happen during the Recess of the Senate, by granting Commissions which shall expire at the End of their next Session.

Section 3

He shall from time to time give to the Congress Information of the State of the Union, and recommend to their Consideration such Measures as he shall judge necessary and expedient; he may, on extraordinary Occasions, convene both Houses, or either of them, and in Case of Disagreement between them, with Respect to the Time of Adjournment, he may adjourn them to such Time as he shall think proper; he shall receive Ambassadors and other public Ministers; he shall take Care that the Laws be faithfully executed, and shall Commission all the Officers of the United States.

Section 4

The President, Vice President and all civil Officers of the United States, shall be removed from Office on Impeachment for, and Conviction of, Treason, Bribery, or other high Crimes and Misdemeanors.

ARTICLE IV

Section 4

The United States shall guarantee to every State in this Union a Republican Form of Government, and shall protect each of them against Invasion; and on Application of the Legislature, or of the Executive (when the Legislature cannot be convened) against domestic Violence.

ARTICLE VI

(3) The Senators and Representatives before mentioned, and the Members of the several State Legislatures, and all executive and judicial Officers, both of the United States and of the several States, shall be bound by Oath or Affirmation, to support this Constitution; but no religious Test shall ever be required as a Qualification to any Office or public Trust under the United States.

AMENDMENT XII[5]

The Electors shall meet in their respective states and vote by ballot for President and Vice President, one of whom, at least, shall not be an inhabitant of the same state with themselves; they shall name in their ballots the person voted for as President, and in distinct ballots the person voted for as Vice President, and they shall make distinct lists of persons voted for as President, and of all persons voted for as Vice President, and of the number of votes for each, which lists they shall sign and certify, and transmit sealed to the seat of the government of the United States, directed to the President of the Senate; —The President of the Senate shall, in the presence of the Senate and House of Representatives, open all the certificates and the votes shall then be counted; —The person having the greatest Number of votes for President, shall be the President, if such number be a majority of the whole number of Electors appointed; and if no person have such majority, then from the persons having the highest numbers not exceeding three on the list of those voted for as President, the House of Representatives shall choose immediately, by ballot, the President. But in choosing the President, the votes shall be taken by states, the representation from each state having one vote; a quorum for this purpose shall consist of a member or members from two thirds of the states, and a majority of all the states shall be necessary to a choice. [And if the House of Representatives shall not choose a President whenever the right of choice shall devolve upon them, before the fourth day of March next following, then the Vice President shall act as President, as in the case of the death or other constitutional disability of the President.][6]—The person having the greatest number of votes as Vice President, shall be the Vice President, if such number be a majority of the whole number of Electors appointed, and if no person have a majority, then from the two highest numbers on the list, the Senate shall choose the Vice President; a quorum for the purpose shall consist of two thirds of the whole number of Senators, and a majority of the whole number shall be necessary to a choice. But no person constitutionally ineligible to the office of President shall be eligible to that of Vice President of the United States.

AMENDMENT XV[7]

Section 1

The right of citizens of the United States to vote shall not be denied or abridged by the United States or by any State on account of race, color, or previous condition of servitude.

Section 2

The Congress shall have power to enforce this article by appropriate legislation.

AMENDMENT XIX[8]

The right of citizens of the United States to vote shall not be denied or abridged by the United States or by any State on account of sex.

Congress shall have power to enforce this article by appropriate legislation.

AMENDMENT XX[9]

Section 1

The terms of the President and Vice President shall end at noon on the 20th day of January, and the terms of Senators and Representatives at noon on the 3rd day of January, of the years in which such terms would have ended if this article had not been ratified; and the terms of their successors shall then begin.

Section 2

The Congress shall assemble at least once in every year, and such meeting shall begin at noon on the 3rd day of January, unless they shall by law appoint a different day.

Section 3

If, at the time fixed for the beginning of the term of the President, the President elect shall have died, the Vice President elect shall become President. If a President shall not have been chosen before the time fixed for the beginning of his term, or if the President elect shall have failed to qualify, then the Vice President elect shall act as a President until a President shall have qualified; and the Congress may by law provide for the case wherein neither a President elect nor a Vice President elect shall have qualified, declaring who shall then act as President, or the manner in which one who is to act shall be selected, and such person shall act accordingly until a President or Vice President shall have qualified.

Section 4

The Congress may by law provide for the case of the death of any of the persons from whom the House of Representatives may choose a President whenever the right of choice shall have devolved upon them, and for the case of the death of any of the persons from whom the Senate may choose a Vice President whenever the right of choice shall have devolved upon them.

Section 5

Sections 1 and 2 shall take effect on the 15th day of October following the ratification of this article.

Section 6

This article shall be inoperative unless it shall have been ratified as an amendment to the Constitution by the legislatures of three fourths of the several States within seven years from the date of its submission.

AMENDMENT XXII[10]

Section 1

No person shall be elected to the office of the President more than twice, and no person who has held the office of President, or acted as President, for more than two years of a term to which some other person was elected President shall be elected to the office of the President more than once. But this Article shall not apply to any person holding the office of President when this Article was proposed by the Congress, and shall not prevent any person who may be holding the office of President, or acting as President, during the term within which this Article becomes operative from holding the office of President or acting as President during the remainder of such term.

Section 2

This article shall be inoperative unless it shall have been ratified as an amendment to the Constitution by the legislatures of three fourths of the several States within seven years from the date of its submission to the States by the Congress.

AMENDMENT XXIII[11]

Section 1

The District constituting the seat of Government of the United States shall appoint in such manner as the Congress may direct:

A number of electors of President and Vice President equal to the whole number of Senators and Representatives in Congress to which the District would be entitled if it were a State, but in no event more than the least populous State; they shall be in addition to those appointed by the States, but they shall be considered, for the purposes of the election of President and Vice President, to be electors appointed by a State; and they shall meet in the District and perform such duties as provided by the twelfth article of amendment.

Section 2

The Congress shall have power to enforce this article by appropriate legislation.

AMENDMENT XXIV[12]

Section 1

The right of citizens of the United States to vote in any primary or other election for President or Vice President, for electors for President or Vice President, or for Senator or Representative in Congress, shall not be denied or abridged by the United States or any state by reasons of failure to pay any poll tax or other tax.

Section 2

The Congress shall have power to enforce this article by appropriate legislation.

AMENDMENT XXV[13]

Section 1

In case of the removal of the President from office or of his death or resignation, the Vice President shall become President.

Section 2

Whenever there is a vacancy in the office of the Vice President, the President shall nominate a Vice President who shall take office upon confirmation by a majority vote of both Houses of Congress.

Section 3

Whenever the President transmits to the President pro tempore of the Senate and the Speaker of the House of Representatives his written declaration that he is unable to discharge the powers and duties of his office, and until he transmits to them a written declaration to the contrary, such powers and duties shall be discharged by the Vice President as Acting President.

Section 4

Whenever the Vice President and a majority of either the principal officers of the Executive departments or of such other body as Congress may by law provide, transmit to the President pro tempore of the Senate and the Speaker of the House of Representatives their written declaration that the President is unable to discharge the powers and duties of his office, the Vice President shall immediately assume the powers and duties of the office as Acting President.

Thereafter, when the President transmits to the President pro tempore of the Senate and the Speaker of the House of Representatives his written declaration that no inability exists, he shall resume the powers and duties of his office unless the Vice President and a majority of either the principal officers of the executive departments or of such other body as Congress may by law provide, transmit within four days to the President pro tempore of the Senate and the Speaker of the House of Representatives their written declaration that the President is unable to discharge the powers and duties of his office.

Thereupon Congress shall decide the issue, assembling within forty-eight hours for that purpose if not in session. If the Congress, within twenty-one days after receipt of the latter written declaration, or, if Congress is not in session, within twenty-one days after Congress is required to assemble, determines by two thirds vote of both houses that the President is unable to discharge the powers and duties of his office, the Vice President shall continue to discharge the same as Acting President; otherwise, the President shall resume the powers and duties of his office.

AMENDMENT XXVI[14]

Section 1

The right of citizens of the United States, who are 18 years of age or older, to vote shall not be denied or abridged by the United States or any state on account of age.

Section 2

The Congress shall have power to enforce this article by appropriate legislation.

Notes

1. The Sixteenth Amendment replaced this with respect to income taxes.

2. Repealed by the Fourteenth Amendment.

3. This paragraph was superseded in 1804 by the Twelfth Amendment.

4. Changed by the Twenty-Fifth Amendment.

5. Adopted in 1804.

6. Superseded by the Twentieth Amendment, section 3.

7. Adopted in 1870.

8. Adopted in 1920.

9. Adopted in 1933.

10. Adopted in 1951.

11. Adopted in 1961.

12. Adopted in 1964.

13. Adopted in 1967.

14. Adopted in 1971.

APPENDIX D

2012 ELECTORAL AND POPULAR VOTE SUMMARY

State	Popular Vote		Electoral Vote	
	Democratic Party (Obama / Biden)	Republican Party (Romney / Ryan)	Obama	Romney
AL	795696	1255925		9
AK	122640	164676		3
AZ	1025232	1233654		11
AR	394409	647744		6
CA	7854285	4839958	55	
CO	1322998	1185050	9	
CT	905083	634892	7	
DE	242584	165484	3	
DC	267070	21381	3	
FL	4237756	4163447	29	
GA	1773827	2078688		16
HI	306658	121015	4	
ID	212787	420911		4
IL	3019512	2135216	20	
IN	1152887	1420543		11
IA	822544	730617	6	
KS	440726	692634		6
KY	679370	1087190		8

| State | Popular Vote | | Electoral Vote | |
	Democratic Party (Obama / Biden)	Republican Party (Romney / Ryan)	Obama	Romney
LA	809141	1152262		8
ME	401306	292276	4	
MD	1677844	971869	10	
MA	1921290	1188314	11	
MI	2564569	2115256	16	
MN	1546167	1320225	10	
MS	562949	710746		6
MO	1223796	1482440		10
MT	201839	267928		3
NE	302081	475064		5
NV	531373	463567	6	
NH	369561	329918	4	
NJ	2122786	1478088	14	
NM	415335	335788	5	
NY	4018385	2145628	29	
NC	2178391	2270395		15
ND	124966	188320		3
OH	2827621	2661407	18	
OK	443547	891325		7
OR	970488	754175	7	
PA	2990274	2680434	20	
RI	279677	157204	4	
SC	865941	1071645		9
SD	145039	210610		3
TN	960709	1462330		11
TX	3308124	4569843		38
UT	251813	740600		6
VT	199239	92698	3	
VA	1971820	1822522	13	
WA	1755396	1290670	12	
WV	238230	417584		5
WI	1620985	1407966	10	
WY	69286	170962		3
Totals	65446032	60589084	332	206

Total Electoral Votes: 538. Total Electoral Vote Needed to Elect: 270.

SOURCE: "2012 Presidential Election, Popular Vote," National Archives. http://www.archives.gov/federal-register
/electoral-college/2012/popular-vote.html (Accessed March 31, 2013).

INDEX

Note: Page numbers followed by f and t indicate Figures and Tables